FINDING COMMON GROUND

Creating the Library of the Future Without Diminishing the Library of the Past

EDITED BY
CHERYL LAGUARDIA AND BARBARA A. MITCHELL

THE NEW LIBRARY SERIES

NEAL-SCHUMAN PUBLISHERS, INC.
NEW YORK   LONDON

Published by Neal-Schuman Publishers, Inc.
100 Varick Street
New York, NY 10013

Copyright © 1998 by Cheryl LaGuardia and Barbara A. Mitchell

All rights reserved. Reproduction of this book, in whole or in part, without written permission of the publisher, is prohibited.
Printed and bound in the United States of America.

Library of Congress Cataloging-in-Publication Data

Finding common ground : creating the library of the future without diminishing the library of the past / Cheryl LaGuardia and Barbara A. Mitchell, editors.
      p. cm. — (The new library series)
  Includes bibliographical references.
  ISBN 1-55570-290-2
  1. Libraries—Data processing—Congresses. 2. Libraries—Special collections—Electronic information resources—Congresses.
3. Digital libraries—Congresses. 4. Libraries—United States—Data processing—Congresses. 5. Libraries—United States—Special collections—Electronic information resources—Congresses.
6. Digital libraries—United States—Congresses. I. LaGuardia. Cheryl. II. Mitchell, Barbara A. III. Series.
Z679.9.A1F56 1998
025'.00285—dc21   97-51663
                                                                                            CIP

THE FUTURE OF INTELLECTUAL ORGANIZATION

Ahronheim, Judith R., Kevin L. Butterfield, and Lynn F. Marko, University Of Michigan. "Reducing Complicity in Bibliographic Systems: An Exercise in Collaboration." — 333

Ciuffetti, Peter, SilverPlatter Information, Inc. "Cataloging for a Worldwide Digital Library: A Proposal for Organizing Ephemeral Metadata Information." — 337

Davis, Christopher and Cheryl J. Burley, Consortium for International Earth Science Information Network (CIESIN). "Lessons Learned from the Development of a Global Information System." — 345

Lasher, Rebecca, Stanford University. "Unique Permanent Identifiers for Management and Retrieval of Distributed Digital Documents." — 353

McCue, Janet, Matthew Beacom, William J. Kara, Gillian McCombs, Cornell University / Yale University / Cornell University / SUNY Albany. "Providing 'Services' to the Electronic Library: The Role of Technical Services." — 357

McManus, Jean C., Tufts University. "Archiving the Content of Print and Electronic Reference Works in the Digital Age: An Analysis and a Proposal." — 375

Pollard, Russell Owen, Harvard University. "A Picture Is Worth a Thousand Words of Bibliographic Description." — 381

Shieh, Jackie, University of Virginia. "Common Good: Cataloging Operations and Electronic Text Processing." — 388

Silipigni Connaway, Lynn and Danny P. Wallace, University of Denver / Kent State University. "Organized Access to Engineering Internet Resources Using Indexing Principles." — 392

Wool, Gregory James, Iowa State University. "Bibliographical Metadata; or, We Need a Client-Server Cataloging Code!" — 398

OUR INDIVIDUAL AND COLLECTIVE FUTURES: THE LIBRARY AS AN ORGANIZATION

Bobay, Julie, Indiana University. "An Organizational Model for Library Faculty and Staff Involvement in the Development of New Electronic Services." — 405

Diaz, Bob and Shelley Phipps, University of Arizona. "The Evolution of the Roles of Staff and Team Development in a Changing Organization: The University of Arizona Library Experience." — 408

Gibson, Craig and Allan Bosch, George Mason University Libraries / Consultant. "Critical Thinking in Future Libraries: Re-Inventing Staff Development Programs." — 424

Jurow, Susan, Association of Research Libraries. "Rethinking Organizational Structure: Academic Library as Network Organization." — 429

Lippincott, Joan K., Avra Michelson, and Kathleen Flynn, Coalition for Networked Information / MITRE Corporation / MITRE Corporation. "Team-Building, Collaboration, and the Reengineering of Library Services." — 434

Mendina, G. T., University of Memphis. "The Human Side of Organizational Effectiveness: On Delegation in Libraries." — 447

Lester, Linda, and Karen Kates Marshall, University of Virginia. "Traditional Library Services and the Research Process: Are Social Sciences and Humanities Faculty Getting What They Need?" 211

Libutti, Patricia O'Brien, Eleanor Langstaff, Lois Cherepon, Karen Svenningsen, and Ree DeDonato, Fordham University / Baruch College / St. John's University College of Staten Island / City University of New York / Columbia University. "Twenty-first Century Scholarship: Expertise, Energies, and Expenses." 219

Max, Patrick, Castleton State College. "'No Bar-Rooms or Theatres or Idle Vicious Companions': Criteria for the 21st Century." 245

McKinzie, Steve, Dickinson College. "Research across the Curriculum: Integrating Our Teaching with Our Institution's Academic Goals." 250

Palmer, Carole, University of Illinois. "Ways of Working and Knowing across Boundaries: Research Practices of Interdisciplinary Scientists." 253

Reddick, Mary J., University of Utah. "The Changing Face of Social Science Research: Building and Protecting Gateways between the Past and the Future." 262

Schenck, William Z., Library of Congress. "Librarians Are from Venus, Scholars Are from Mars." 269

CHANGING MATERIALS, CHANGING ECONOMIES

Barnum, George D., Margaret S. Powell, and Mary Webb Prophet, Case Western Reserve University / The College of Wooster / Denison University. "Elsewhere in the Forest: The Place of U.S. Government Information in Libraries of the Future." 275

Bentley, Stella, Auburn University. "Wave of the Future: Supporting Interdisciplinary Collaborations." 294

Coccaro, Cynthia, and Joseph Straw, University of Akron. "Reference and Electronic Document Delivery: A Marriage Made in Heaven or Hell?" 298

Malamud, Judie and Florence Schreibstein, Albert Einstein College of Medicine. "Just in Time vs. Just in Case: An Alternative to Traditional Collection Development and Interlibrary Loan." 306

Pintozzi, Chestalene, University of Arizona. "Having It All: Strategies for Providing Monographic, Serial, and Electronic Information Resources in Tight Budget Times." 309

Summerfield, Mary C., Columbia University. "Online Books: What Role Will They Fill for Users of the Academic Library?" 313

Webb, Kerry Adrian, National Library of Australia. "Working Together on the Global Electronic Library." 326

SATISFYING OUR USERS

Baker, Betsy, Natalie Pelster, and William McHugh, Northwestern University. "Refinding Reference: Carrying the Reference Mission into the Libraries of the 21st Century." — 99

Basile, Abbie J., Rensselaer Polytechnic Institute. "Extending a Virtual Hand: Promises and Problems of Electronic Instruction." — 111

Bristow, Ann, Paul J. Constantine, Jane G. Bryan, and Alan Solomon, Indiana University / Cornell University / University of Pennsylvania / Yale University. "Reference Services in Research Libraries: Some Definitions, Questions, and Answers Concerning the Integration of the Print and Network Service Environments." — 116

Crist, Margo, University of Massachusetts Amherst. "In Their Own Words: Building a Data Base of User Views." — 131

Grassian, Esther, UCLA. "alt.help.I.can't.keep.up! Support for the 'Electronically-Challenged.'" — 136

Gutierrez, Carolyn and Mary Ann Trail, Richard Stockton College of New Jersey. "Research Strategies Conference Course: Using a Computer Conference System for Bibliographic Instruction." — 140

Hoffmann, Gretchen McCord, University of Houston. "Library Instruction In Transition: Questioning Current Views." — 144

Kirk, Elizabeth, Johns Hopkins University. "Exploiting Technology to Teach New and Old Skills: Novice Researchers and Milton's Web." — 152

Marcum, James W., Centenary College of Louisiana. "Core Competencies and 'Learning for Change' in Academic Libraries." — 161

Rettig, James, College of William and Mary. "Users and Bibliographic Resources: Blind Dating by OPAC." — 168

Tyckoson, David A. and Trudi E. Jacobson, University at Albany—SUNY. "What Are Users Doing in the Electronic Library?" — 182

THE CHANGING FACE OF RESEARCH

Down, Nancy, Bowling Green State University. "Literary Texts and the Internet." — 193

Elliott, Clark, Massachusetts Institute of Technology. "Scholars as Bibliographic Specialists: A Probe Pointing to a Partnership." — 196

Hazen, Dan C., Harvard University. "Understanding Research Agendas: Explanations for Change and the Library Response." — 201

Table of Contents

ACKNOWLEDGMENTS ... ix
FOREWORD BY CHERYL LAGUARDIA ... xi
INTRODUCTION BY RICHARD DEGENNARO ... xiii

KEYNOTE ADDRESS
FINDING COMMON GROUND
By Clifford A. Lynch, Coalition for Networked Information ... 1

ALL-CONFERENCE SPEECH
UNCOMMON KNOWLEDGE: MYTHBREAKING FOR THE FUTURE
By Walt Crawford, Research Libraries Group ... 16

CONTRIBUTED PAPERS

TECHNOLOGY AND THE NETWORK: DAIMONS OR DEMONS?

Begg, Amy A. and Martin R. Kalfatovic, Smithsonian Institution. "Project Access: Providing Internet Access to the Smithsonian Institution Research Community." ... 27

Brookes, Kim, Jean Boise Cargill, Mary F. Daniels, Michael Fitzgerald, Leslie A. Morris, David De Lorenzo, Mackenzie Smith, and Susan Von Salis, Harvard University and Radcliffe College. "From Leaves to Bytes: The Harvard Digital Finding Aids Project." ... 37

Campbell, James, University of Virginia. "Digital Library = Holistic Library: Collection Decisionmaking in the Electronic Environment." ... 42

Fark, Ronald, Anne Cerstvik Nolan, and Tovah Reis, Brown University. "Technology and the Network: Redesigning an Academic Library Reference Department." ... 47

Kupersmith, John, Washoe County Library. "You Are Here, But Where Is That?: Architectural Design Metaphors in the Electronic Library." ... 58

Roecker, Fred, and Virginia Tiefel, Ohio State University. "Migrating a Successful Information System to the Web: The WWW Gateway to Information." ... 68

Treadwell, Jane B., Emory University. "Traveling Through the Wilderness: The Long Transition to the Digital Library." ... 74

Whyte, Susan Barnes and Loretta Rielly, Linfield College and Oregon State University. "A Computer Is Like...: Imagination, Learning, and Computers." ... 80

Zald, Anne, Oren Sreebny, Theresa Mudrock, Bernice Laden, and Andrea Bartelstein, University of Washington. "UWired: A Collaborative Model for Integrating Technology and Information Skills across the Curriculum." ... 86

Menna, Elizabeth Bentley and William D. Hollands, New York Public Library. "Staff Training and Development in an Era of Rapid Change: A Model Program." 459

Schwartz, Charles, University of Massachusetts Boston. "Restructuring Academic Libraries: Organizational Development in the Wake of Technological Change." 463

APPENDIX: DEMONSTRATED PAPERS **467**
INDEX **469**

Acknowledgments

We would like to take this opportunity to thank the many people who worked so hard to make *Finding Common Ground* a great success. They include:

the Executive Conference Steering Committee: Richard DeGennaro (Chair), Larry Dowler, Laura Farwell, Carrie Kent, Cheryl LaGuardia, Susan Lee, and Ed Tallent;

the Conference Implementation Committee: Carrie Kent and Cheryl LaGuardia (Co-Chairs), Michael Blake, Joe Bourneuf, Barbara Burg, Ellen Cohen, Laura Farwell, Michael Fitzgerald, Deb Garson, Lee Anne George, Jeff Horrell, Amy Kautzman, Dennis Marnon, Barbara Mitchell, Jane Ouderkirk, Hazel Stamps, and Ed Tallent;

the Paper Jury [who "blind-jury" winnowed hundreds of paper submissions down to what you see here]: Cheryl LaGuardia (Chair), Stella Bentley, Laura Farwell, Rod Goins, Dan Hazen, Michael Hopper, Barbara Mitchell, Ilene Rockman, and Ed Tallent;

the Demonstrated Paper Jury: Amy Kautzman (Chair), Kwasi Sarcodie-Mensah and Steve McKinzie;

the Registration Table and Room Monitor Volunteers: Gillian Bartoo, Barbara Burg, Ken Carpenter, Ellen Cohen, Lee Anne George, Barbara Halporn, Michael Hopper, Maryellen McCarthy, Christine Oka, Ilene Rockman, Kwasi Sarkodie-Mensah, Mary Sears, Julian Stam, John Vasi, and Cliff Wunderlich;

and the all-conference speakers and the contributed paper authors (whose work you are about to read).

We also wish to recognize the efforts of a number of conference participants whose work could not be included in these proceedings because the "spontaneous," interactive, or alternative formats of their presentations did not allow publication. Our thanks are extended to:

the faculty and publishing panelists and moderators: Tyrone Cannon, David Ferriero, Heather Cameron, Sonja Gustafson, Ann Hartman, Patricia Glass Schuman, Gary Anderson, Suzanne Blier, and Stuart Shieber;

the Creativity Workshop team (Marybeth Clack, Team Leader): Sarah Becker, Laura Farwell, Roberta Schwartz, and Heidi Simon;

Maureen Sullivan and Shelley E. Phipps for their interactive workshop, "The Library as a Learning Organization";

and the demonstrated paper authors. A complete list of demonstrated paper titles and authors is included in the Appendix.

We would also like to express our sincere thanks to Jan Weiner, Staff Assistant for Public Services in Widener Library, for her considerable assistance in the preparation of this manuscript;

our personal thanks to Carrie Kent, Chris Oka, Michael Hopper and Ken Carpenter for advice and moral support, to Ed Tallent for handling so many "challenges" daily, and to Dennis Marnon for the distinctive conference logo and designs;

and a special THANK YOU to Charles Harmon, our wonderfully keen and accomplished editor at Neal-Schuman Publishers.

Cheryl LaGuardia and Barbara A. Mitchell
Cambridge, Massachusetts, February 1998

Foreword

By Cheryl LaGuardia
Harvard University

The idea for the Finding Common Ground conference came from some idle conversations Carrie Kent and I had about virtual libraries shortly after I got to Harvard, about the time the frenzy concerning digital cum virtual cum non-physical libraries was reaching its peak (in its first manifestation, at least). To illustrate candidly my feelings about the concept of "virtual libraries," my initial suggestion for a conference title was, "Virtual, Schmirtual: There Ain't NO Sech Animal." This was voted down roundly by the Conference Steering Committee at our first meeting, along with a few other gems. . . .

Our talks about the likelihood of all things library-like (libraries, books, readers, researchers, librarians), eventually being exterminated were fueled by the reactionary backlash to computerization that was then germinating in print (about the time The Gutenberg Elegies was published and just before Silicon Snake Oil hit the streets). "Local" discussion escalated in both frequency and fervor until we realized we needed a larger dialogue about these issues with colleagues nationwide. We did not see the particular theme of "Finding Common Ground" (as we defined it) addressed in the schedules for existing library conferences in the foreseeable future.

It was a tiny step from that point to the idea of a conference at Harvard, and once we decided on the (slightly expurgated) title, several variations on our theme emerged concerning user needs, changing research models, increased materials' availability in reduced budget times, changes in the ways we are organizing information and our institutions to handle that information, and about the nature of technology itself. The paper tracks were laid out as if decreed by the fates. The rest of the conference planning process was blood, sweat, and tears—of frustration and joy—on the parts of a great many people: to see just how many please take a good close look at this publication's acknowledgments' page, as well as the Table of Contents.

It wasn't until we took our discussion public with the call for conference papers that we found we'd touched a nerve in the global library consciousness: the prospect of talking about library realities (as opposed to speculation and fantasy) appealed to a wide audience. Whereas we thought we were stating the obvious—something along the lines of "Let's not throw the baby out with the bath water"—fellow librarians convinced us by phone and in countless e-mails the conference theme was welcome, and overdue, relief from the contrasting omnipresent dire predictions about the death and destruction of libraries. Paper proposals poured in from as close as Boston and as far away as Estonia. Many folks had something in mind about just what constitutes the library common ground, and how to go about finding it. Some veered towards the Library of the Future end of the spectrum, others towards the Library of the Past; most were located somewhere in-between on the vast continuum that separates the Technocrats from the Luddites in the daily workings of libraries.

The Henny-Penny-like phrase, "it's the end of libraries as we know them," has always struck me as fatuous: just at the point I think I "know" any library (no matter how long I may have used it or worked there) I discover some new resource that makes me aware libraries have, like Cleopatra, infinite variety. And just as age did not wither nor custom stale that famous ruler, so, too, do libraries flourish with age and familiarity—our collections typically grow as time passes, and as use increases we count our successes greater. It has ever been the case that we are bringing about "the end of libraries as we know them." We are actively in the process of working towards an ideal of "libraries as we—and our users—want them."

From the perspective of 1998, it seems the hysteria about the end of libraries has abated somewhat, and we believe the thoughtful conversations among librarians and other information industry professionals such as those that took place at this conference helped clarify the reality of our future. It's been especially interesting to note the large number of conferences worldwide that have incorporated the idea of "finding common ground" across a multitude of disciplines just since 1996—we are not alone in striving to define and achieve common goals!

We're very pleased to have provided this forum for finding common ground. By building on the library of the past, adding improvements and refinements via computerized access and storage, we are in the process of creating the library of the future. These proceedings reveal that ongoing process.

Introduction

By Richard DeGennaro
Former Roy E. Larsen Librarian of Harvard College (Retired)

This conference was a first for the Harvard Library, and we were gratified by the interest it generated and the wonderful turnout: registration closed within a few days of being opened. The program was rich and varied, with an enthusiastic attendance from all over the U.S. and from abroad as well. Attendees came from as far away as Australia and Ireland, as well as from Canada and 37 of the United States.

The title of this conference was carefully chosen by the Conference Steering Committee: myself, Carrie Kent, Cheryl LaGuardia, Larry Dowler, Susan Lee, Ed Tallent, and Laura Farwell. I note "carefully chosen" because we rejected a number of possible other titles, ranging from: "Beyond the Electronic Epiphany" to "Surviving the Hype," and "Resistible Forces and Movable Objects." We finally knew we had gone too far when we found ourselves considering "The Ashless Phoenix," and that's when "Finding Common Ground" sounded very good.

But you can recognize the common thread running through all those titles. The conference title upon which we finally decided, "Finding Common Ground: Creating the Library of the Future Without Diminishing the Library of the Past" seemed to describe the best aspects of the world in which librarians operate as we approach the year 2000. It implies that there IS common ground to be found between print and digital resources, that they complement each other, and that we can build the new digital library while continuing to build and preserve our indispensable legacy collections.

Harold Billings (who attended the conference) summed up the challenge we face very simply in a recent paper. He said, "A major task for libraries in the coming years will be the addition of appropriate books and journals in paper-based format, the management of an increasing proportion of information that will become available in digital form, and the melding of these information streams into a common pool for the fishing of information."

We have entered a period of transforming change in the world of libraries and information, but I continue to be optimistic about our ability to cope with that change and the theme of this conference reflected that optimism. I read somewhere once that when the aging Prince Talleyrand was asked what he did during the tumultuous years of the French Revolution, the Terror, and the Napoleonic Wars, he replied simply that he had survived.

When I look back on all the technological wars and revolutions that I have lived through since I became a librarian forty years ago, I'm thankful that, like Talleyrand, I survived. Not only did I survive, but all the libraries that I worked in also survived, despite the many predictions of their imminent demise. When I think about the many waves of technology that have already washed over us and those that are coming at an ever-accelerating pace, I am still confident that libraries and librarians are going to survive. And I think they will continue to bear their traditional names and carry out their traditional mission. That mission is to select, organize, preserve, and provide access to the records of human knowledge in whatever form they take. And increasingly, the form will be digital as will the means for performing library functions. This transition to networked digital information is going to change libraries profoundly—much more profoundly in the coming decade than in the last three decades combined. The years of the autonomous library are clearly numbered.

The library of the future will play its role and fulfill its mission not as an autonomous unit as it did in the past, but as a node in a worldwide network of libraries and a variety of other information suppliers. We can see the beginnings of this at

Harvard with the campus network and HOLLIS, melding Harvard's once autonomous libraries into a coordinated system that is in turn part of an emerging national and international library system.

As we said in our original invitation, this conference was a forum for exploring reasonable, cost-effective ways of developing working libraries amidst a climate of continual transformation, invention, and hype. Thanks to the many participants for joining us in Cambridge to share your ideas and your solutions to the problems that face us all. And thanks to all—participants and readers—for accepting our invitation to take part in this commonsense conversation.

Keynote Address— Finding Common Ground

By Clifford A. Lynch
Coalition for Networked Information

This is an edited version of a transcript from a keynote address given at the "Finding Common Ground" conference. My thanks to Cheryl LaGuardia and Janice Weiner for undertaking the painful process of transcribing this talk. My thanks also to Dick DeGennaro for an excessively lavish introduction at this meeting, which fortunately wasn't transcribed. C.A. Lynch

INTRODUCTION

The theme and title of this conference address— "finding common ground"—is compelling and timely. When we talk about libraries and their transition into a world of networks and digital information, it is important to establish common ground among the diverse communities that have both stakes in and expectations of this transition. Today, I will try to map out and define—and perhaps even defend—some common ground of understanding, goals, and values for libraries as they face this transition. I'll talk about the environment and how it's changing. And I'll also share some of the opinions held by groups outside of the traditional community of librarians and heavy users of existing print-based libraries about both the capabilities and limitations of libraries. In this context, I'll range widely in discussing some of the social, legal, and even political issues arising from digital information and computer-communications technology.

I spend a lot of time in the computer networking community, a community that has matured a great deal in the last five years in terms of its understanding of the uses of networks rather than just the enabling technologies. Now that we've gotten the wires connected and the bits flowing over these wires, the computer networking community is facing some hard questions about what to do with this ever more ubiquitous, capable, and robust worldwide Internet. The computer networking community and the information technology evangelists have promoted the promise of this network, often with rather vague assertions (the network will revolutionize teaching and learning, shopping, commerce, political discourse, . . .) interspersed with compelling and explicit scenarios (Vice President Gore's Tennessee schoolchild browsing dinosaur pictures from the Library of Congress over the Internet, for example), first to the research and education community and more recently to the public at large. These consumers, now that the network is coming into place, are starting to ask questions about what they are receiving: Where is the content, the promised wealth of information? How do we find anything? How do we understand and evaluate the things that we do find? What are the ground rules for using information in this new environment? How much will information access cost? Who will know what information I'm using?

And now a lot of people in the networking community are turning to libraries, expecting them to have ready answers to these questions. After all, they say, isn't that what libraries do? I think that there are some peculiar, unrealistic or perhaps inappropriate expectations abroad about what libraries do or don't do, should or shouldn't do, and can and cannot do.

We are in a time of great change; there are lots of cross-currents and opposing trends and forces surfacing as information technology begins to permeate our society and our institutions at all levels. A lot of diverse institutions have a great deal—in some cases, even their continued existence—at stake. It's not at all clear how some of these conflicting trends are going to be resolved. Not everyone recognizes that libraries are, ultimately, extraordinarily complex social constructs on many different levels. At the most basic level, a library is an organization with missions to acquire, organize, provide access to, and preserve information for a user community. It may operate out of a building, perhaps even a very large and attractive architectural monument; but the library is not equivalent to the building that has housed it. A library may hold and provide access to a massive, rich collection which includes all manner of treasures. But a library isn't just the owner and manager of a collection; it's also an organization that relates to and lives inside a social (and often organizational) context. We cannot talk about the future of libraries without talking about how this context is changing.

For special libraries, this is often a corporate or similar organizational context. In a sense, special libraries probably have the most direct relationship to their parent organizations. Organizational and corporate cultures are changing, and many special libraries are either vanishing (replaced with other methods of information access and delivery) or have been reconceptualized and re-integrated, particularly in knowledge-intensive corporations, in new ways that are often more intimately connected with the activities of their parent corporation.

Research libraries are typically imbedded in a higher education context. In fact, for convenience, when I discuss research libraries I'll focus on university research libraries, recognizing that there are some unique research libraries standing outside of the higher education context which will have special (and fascinating) opportunities to define new directions for their future. These non-university research libraries are special situations which I cannot discuss in detail here. But the typical university research library is an essential part of its parent educational institution. These universities are beginning to understand that their missions are shifting and that they're going to have to make major changes in the way they operate if they are to survive and prosper in the future. And, as the missions and response strategies of the universities evolve, the future agendas of their research libraries will be shaped by this evolution. Research libraries no longer have the luxury of considering (at length and at leisure) the question of how information technology will interact with the research library mission, heritage, and tradition while the parent institution remains static and awaits the answer from its research library. Increasingly, research libraries will be responding to changing demands from their parent institutions.

Public libraries are in some ways the most interesting because they connect most directly with the public, with society as a whole. Public libraries, at least in the United States, serve a number of very specific and intricate functions, such as providing access to government documents. Public libraries are rooted in their communities and reflect those communities; they are funded primarily by the local tax base rather than by federal programs. All the assumptions that guided public libraries are changing with the introduction of networking. Most notably, they no longer have simple answers about what public they serve. Public libraries face some of the most vexing questions about their future roles, and indeed even their future survival.

INFORMATION TECHNOLOGY AND THE DECLINE OF THE GEOGRAPHIC ORDER

Information technology is proliferating everywhere. It's creeping into every corner of our existence and changing in a gradual but very steady way almost everything we do and almost everything about our society. We underestimate the magnitude of this proliferation. It's not just about how many households and businesses have computers and Internet connections; it's also measured by everything from the deployment of networked sensors that form intelligent roadways, the flow of financial telemetry between businesses, consumers, and nations, the pervasive recording of public and private events and activities, and the remaking of the entertainment industries. Information technology is generating all kinds of subtle and unsubtle economic disruption and increasingly, I would suggest, social and political disruptions and discontinuities as well.

If you look at the history of libraries and information technology since the 1950s or 1960s, we were basically concerned with introducing information technology in the form of automation into libraries, very much as we automated other kinds of commercial and consumer functions. The result of this automation was really a direct extrapolation of traditional roles and activities. What we are dealing with now is different. As information technology has become truly pervasive in society, it has begun to change the ways in which we communicate. So the whole nature of the content and the discourse that libraries are trying to capture and organize and preserve for their collections has altered. The channels through which this content is acquired and accessed are changing. This is a very different issue than how to automate, and reaches towards much more fundamental questions.

One of the most profound themes we're seeing emerge from the deployment of information technology and networking, on a really broad basis is a fading of geography as an organizing principle. This is social and political dynamite. I have been speaking for some years about the Internet as an instrument of the decline of geography and national boundaries (as have others, such as Walter Wriston in his book, The Twilight of Sovereignty: How the Information Revolution Is Transforming Our World (NY: Scribners; 1992)). Until a year or two ago, I could discuss this (sometimes comfortably, sometimes with unease) as a trend that traditional institutions such as governments had not yet recognized. This is no longer true; the traditional, geography-based institutions are beginning to recognize the threat, and starting to fight back out of self-preservation. We are entering a very dangerous time, full of reactionary proposals which may well constrain and circumscribe the new information access and communication technologies to such a degree that many of their most promising payoffs are in doubt.

Communities have been recognized historically as groups of people perhaps united by some common interests and values, but ultimately unified by geographic proximity. Communities form a context for discourse; they manage commons and common goods. Institutions are typically designed and managed to serve communities. But communities on the Internet spring up anywhere, and they're not geographically based. Indeed, they are often worldwide, connected only by a common interest. Participation in a community comes without costs and without any responsibility for supporting services to that community, other than through a general spirit of participation and mutual support. Everything is voluntary. Our traditional management, governance, consensus-creation, and funding mechanisms simply don't work in this new environment. Yet these mechanisms are the underpinnings of libraries.

For example, public libraries are funded on a very geographical basis—property taxes or local income tax assessments. All of a sudden they're serving constituencies that can be worldwide; no place is very far from another on the Internet. Public schools may face the same issue as more and more instructional technology comes online to permit the support of distant learners.

Community standards have always been a touchy issue for libraries, particularly public libraries. But it's no longer clear what community standards are important. Someone operating an "adult" bulletin board in California was recently tried, judged, and convicted in Tennessee, based on Tennessee's community standards of decency. A nasty border dispute erupted a couple of years ago between the US and Canada over a Canadian court's gag order on the press covering a sensational trial. Tomorrow an information provider in the US might face a court that is part of a fundamentalist regime. The recent introduction of the communications decency act language into the telecommunication reform bill that was recently passed in Congress, brings this issue of community standards—and, thereby, the issue of what and who really make a community—to the center stage. While the CDA will likely, in my view, be found to be unconstitutional, the issues motivating the legislation will, I fear, continue to reappear at both the national and international levels. All of a sudden communities and governments at all levels want to exercise control over what are really global information flows. Societies that do not share the tradition of fairly diverse and free-wheeling discourse traditional in the US are deeply threatened by the Internet. We are already seeing nations like China and Singapore attempting to place extensive controls on information flows to their people, and we may see entire nations firewalling themselves from the Internet at various levels in the next few years.

Not only have our local and state geographical boundaries weakened, but international boundaries have faded as well. Different cultures in different countries are getting face to face with unfamiliar viewpoints. The impact of the English language flooding the world over the Internet and in broadcast media via satellite and cable is causing concern in other countries. Local cultural content controls are another form of community standards coming under pressure. France has issued government regulations requiring a fair amount of radio airtime dedicated to French language programs because their radio stations are full of American rock music. Other nations have implemented various forms of "local content" legislation. While it's relatively easy to apply such protections to broadcast media, where content is emitted only from a limited number of sources which mostly fall under the regulatory control of specific nations, and characteristics of that content can be measured, nobody knows how to define and enforce similar effective restrictions on networked information and communication.

In this connection it is worth nothing that English is the de facto language of the Internet. In fact, it is only recently that serious attempts (such as Unicode) have been made to support non-roman languages on an equal footing with English and, to a lesser extent, the other romance languages. Some nations and cultures understandably find this a disturbing situation, and we may yet see a backlash from it.

Other unexpected issues are surfacing. Governments are starting to recognize that they have increasingly lost control of their own currencies, first through private foreign exchange trading enabled by computer-communications networks, and now even through the creation of new private electronic currencies. Airline frequent-flyer miles are troublesome enough, behaving as a form of specialized limited-use shadow currency (which the airlines have tried hard to prevent from becoming truly fungible). But now, various enterprises are forming to support electronic commerce on the Internet. This goes beyond traditional credit cards, which simply represented one more step in a progression of more efficient and convenient ways to conduct commerce denominated in government-issued currencies. Approaches to electronic commerce on the Internet are splitting into two categories. One simply pushes credit-card models a step further; one transacts in government-issued currency that is cleared through the credit-card systems. Other, more revolutionary-minded players, such as Digicash BV, propose to offer digital "cash" which can be exchanged with traditional currencies, but which behaves like currency in that it can be independently issued and exchanged anonymously.

Governments are also becoming very concerned about their ability to track financial transactions (they typically frame this question as maintaining their ability to detect criminal activities such as money laundering). The use of cryptography by businesses and private citizens both to protect communications and to secure financial transactions—and particularly the ability of governments to monitor communications within their own borders, across international boundaries, and in foreign countries—has become a major policy flashpoint. A very complex debate has emerged about the appropriate balance between the interests of national security and law enforcement to monitor, the national interest in building secure and robust systems of all types (financial, control, etc.) in the networked environment, and rights to privacy. Interestingly, and ironically, the use of cryptographic technology is central to any number of network-based applications such as managing authentication, integrity, and minting digital cash. Its importance goes far beyond simply protecting the privacy of communications. Governments would like to permit and even encourage certain of these applications while discouraging or banning others. Time does not permit a more detailed exploration of these issues today, however; I mention them only to give a sense of how pervasive, profound, and potentially threatening the effects of the networked information age are likely to be on traditional geographically based institutions, and how complex and wide-ranging the policy debates are becoming. And I invite you to follow developments in the emerging area at the intersection of policy and technology called "information warfare."

The melting away of geographic and physical constraints has a potentially huge impact on the economics of publishing companies. The "creative industries," which include various types of print publishing, film, television, music, etc., are a major multi-national economic power. The industries' interests are now fully focused on the potential threat that the networked information environment represents, and are using all means at their disposal to protect themselves. Indeed, they are taking the opportunity, at a time when many of the basic rules and compacts are being reassessed, to try to roll back what they view as incursions on their markets carved by older technologies such as the photocopier and the VCR, and the legal decisions that have supported them. And they are arguing, as Carol Richer wrote in a recent position paper for the American Association of Publishers, that "digital is different." Libraries and their patrons—once promised to be the greatest beneficiaries of the shift from physical information artifacts to disembodied networked information content—are relatively minor players in this high-stakes battle to determine the legal and economic framework for electronic information. And it's now becoming clear that libraries' ability to provide information to their patrons may be severely compromised rather than enhanced in the shift to digital content.

A public library serves a fairly modest geographical community. Circulation of a physical book is limited by the number of copies purchased by the library and mechanics of loaning the copies; patrons must physically go to the library to borrow and return books, and they generally keep them for relatively long periods of time. Each copy can only go to one patron at a time. Thus, the impact of a library purchase on individual sales of the work by the publisher is real, but limited. Publishers have a nightmare about the networked environment: One copy of a work is sold to a library; the library makes it available for reading on the Internet; and everyone in the world can read that one copy, simultaneously and conveniently! With the network as amplifier, a single local action can have instantaneous and massive worldwide ramifications which have historically been damped by geography and the properties of physical artifacts.

"Unpublished" materials available on the Internet have infinitely more visibility than special library collections that are inaccessible (and possibly unknown) to all but a fortunate few. Suddenly, anyone's statements—accurate or inaccurate—can be shared worldwide and cause all kinds of fuss in a matter of minutes or hours. Purloined documents or forgeries can be instantly placed into the public arena from any source, without the need to interest a major mass media provider (which will usually do at least some verification and exercise some level of responsibility in content dissemination). The Internet has vastly raised the stakes, giving anyone capabilities previously reserved to the major national and international mass media.

Access to the competition for the public's attention is now open to everyone through the Internet. There is little gatekeeping; publishers and reviewers are less important; there's a lot less vetting and fewer damping mechanisms for misinformation. To my knowledge, we've not yet seen any large-scale misinformation campaigns (except perhaps for some now under investigation in the stock markets, and certain urban legends that periodically resurface on the Internet as fact). But if there's ever been an environment that's ripe for deliberate misinformation and disinformation campaigns, it is the Internet. Part of the problem is that while the public has at least some experience in assessing the credibility of mass media, they have relatively little training or experience in making similar assessments of information available over the Internet; and this is complicated both by the difficulties of establishing the actual sources of information and by the way in which the digital medium is infinitely plastic in its ability to permit content (including sound and images) to be manipulated.

Information technology is producing massive disintermediation in a range of professions and industries. There's an important cautionary tale here for librarians and libraries. Agents, brokers, intermediaries of all types are losing their jobs on a large scale as their clientele perceives their roles as unnecessary overhead—bank tellers, stock brokers, travel agents, order takers. Newspapers—intermediaries for access both to news and advertising—find their economic basis in doubt. The public now has direct access to automated systems—ATMs, Web pages (for catalog ordering, reservations, stock trades, etc.)—that perform the same functions, but are available 24 hours a day, are never rude, don't have waiting lines, and charge less. Here the breakdown is not one of geography so much as it is of gatekeeping.

In terms of information access, there's a tremendous amount of information, particularly in electronic form, that is increasingly and easily accessible to everyone. Twenty years ago, one would need professional help in a library to find and use information such as government documents. At that time, the average person could get information from three sources: bookstores, the mass media (newspapers and broadcast), and libraries. Today it's more and more all out there on the Internet, direct from the information sources. As just one case in point, consider the impact of the SEC EDGAR database on investors. Until a couple of years ago, this information was rather arcane and mostly available to financial professions (though individual investors could get it if they knew what it was, how it was structured, where to order it, and were prepared to pay a good deal of money for it—and a library could help them with this research effort if they thought to ask). Now it is available to the public (with no cost for the content of SEC filings, only a charge for Internet access perhaps) for a few clicks through any Web browser. (Though, to be fair, most individual investors still don't understand this information resource and how it's structured; and libraries still have a significant role in explicating this.)

So how will libraries maintain the value of their services in the face of all of this directly accessible information? They certainly are not going to be gatekeepers, in this electronic world without boundaries. What will their role be? I'll return to this question shortly.

Before leaving the discussion of the decline of geography, let me make a few comments about universities. Consider the historical importance of geography to the university: Similar courses are delivered in thousands of colleges and universities every year, accessible only to those students enrolled in and living near the particular university, and in a position physically to attend lectures. The reliance on face-to-face instruction requires this massively redundant teaching effort. Now, there are clearly some people who teach first year calculus, for example, better than others. And we are waking up to the fact that in the next ten years we might move into an environment where some classes can be delivered without regard to geography, at a distance, where some of the courses can be content embedded in instructional technology. Rather than teaching calculus locally, one can just license one of the few "master teacher" calculus classes. Classes will find constituencies who are no longer limited by physical presence. Of course, questions must be raised about the role and importance of face-to-face human interaction (both among students and between student and teacher) in learning in order to assess the real potentials here. And much of education—particularly higher education—goes beyond simply covering the material in a given course and really deals with the formation of intellectual and social communities and the integration of students into these communities. But it seems clear that at least to some extent the changing character of teaching and learning will not only affect the structure and definition of universities—with one result being a great reduction in the redundant generation of instruction due to geographical constraints—but will have profound ramifications for research libraries as well. Research libraries need to look at the much broader role of managing the instructional content generated by their parent universities, and of obtaining access to instructional content generated by other (competing) universities, and should not limit themselves as passive storehouses of knowledge for research. Public and special libraries may also become portals to this instructional content.

VISIONS OF LIBRARIES FOR A NEW CENTURY: EVOLUTION AND DIVERGENCE

I don't think we can begin to have a complete picture of what the 21st century library, transfigured by electronic content, worldwide computer-communications networks, and ubiquitous information technology will be. I think there will exist a much broader diversity of organizations declaring themselves libraries. I think we can agree that if an organization acquires, organizes, preserves, and provides access to information, then it is indeed a library. But in the minds of information consumers, "library" is getting to be a fairly broad term, particularly in the electronic world that includes many different kinds of information providers. Some people see the only difference between a library and a bookstore as free or purchased information. Others, who realize that libraries aren't really free but are simply paid for through less-direct mechanisms than bookstores, are becoming more and more comfortable viewing any comprehensive information provider as a "library."

Let's look at a few possible views of libraries of the future. There is the classical ("traditional"?) library: a library that's still dealing primarily with paper (although it probably has an online catalog), and that spends a lot of time celebrating history in various forms—that has, increasingly, a bit of a museum air to it. This is certainly a legitimate, though niche, future. Some people think that this is the future for many existing public and even research libraries. They have been left behind by the electronic information transition, and have stayed with print (which is not going to vanish anytime soon). Indeed, they cherish, maintain, and celebrate the printed work. I have to stress that this is, in my view, a legitimate evolutionary path for libraries, though perhaps not an inspiring one.

Consider another extreme. Most of you have probably had some encounter with the NASA/ARPA/NSF-funded digital libraries projects. Every time I hear the results of these research efforts described as digital libraries, I get a little more uncomfortable. I don't mean to belittle these projects in terms of the importance of the technology research they are doing, which I believe will be quite valuable. But most libraries, at least as I conceive of them, do not operate under these sorts of four-year sundown clauses. I think a better way of describing these collections is as certain kinds of information access systems—as information management systems. Obviously, perspectives of librarianship and information science can inform the development of the systems that are being produced under this program; but that doesn't make the results of these programs libraries.

There is yet another vision. Someone coined the phrase, "the Network is the library." It's a very regrettable phrase. People are unfortunately identifying the WorldWide Web as a worldwide digital library. And that view, I believe, is incorrect. The information on the Web looks much more like the collected output of the printing (not publishing) industry. If everything that was printed went to one place in paper form, I suppose you could call that place a library. But I don't think that's what it really is. It's a repository, but not a library. On the Web you'll find old dinner menus and wedding pictures along with scholarly papers along with invitations to seminars that met last year. Certainly there is information on the Web that appropriately becomes part of library collections; but equating the content available on the Web with the collection of the future global library misses the point.

As a result of so much information existing electronically, we are seeing a dangerous trend. People are beginning to believe that if information doesn't exist electronically, it doesn't exist at all. Even worse: if it's not available for free on the Internet, it doesn't exist or isn't relevant.

To some extent, in research libraries the introduction of abstracting and indexing databases supplemented with access to full electronic text presaged this trend. The A&I databases go back in electronic form only to the 1970s or at best mid-1960s. All of a sudden the print that predates the coverage of those A&I databases becomes a little more invisible to each year's new students. The material that is in the A&I databases but not immediately available online as full text is increasingly considered less significant and less interesting. Once critical mass is achieved, the evidence is that what's immediately available online effectively defines the literature.

And now we're beginning to see enough content on the Internet, or accessible from it, that people are starting to assume that everything is on the Internet, or at least that what is on the Internet defines the literature. I'm sure many of you have enjoyed the spectacle of some dedicated Internet surfer proudly diving in and spending four hours to find some bit of factual information that could have been located out of a desk reference book in 30 seconds. Some people are moving away from a view that information is accessible from a diversity of sources, both print and electronic, and that part of the art of research is selecting the right source. Instead, they are letting what is accessible through the Internet serve as a definition of the "published" literature.

The Web search engines—Lycos, Alta Vista, and the like—have been identified by many as the future of information organization. These systems build their databases by indexing all of the material that they can find on the Internet. Aside from the fact that these systems lack high-quality retrieval capabilities for many applications (when contrasted to systems designed around retrieval from intellectual cataloging, abstracting and indexing by human beings, such as online library cataloging or good A&I database implementations), it is important to recognize the fact that there is not a selection process underlying them in the sense of collection development as practiced by libraries. They are as likely to capture a restaurant menu from last year as they are a scholarly essay in their incessant scanning of information on the Web. If we accept that the Web is not the library of the future, then the Web search engines are not tomorrow's online catalogs.

Further, the whole idea that the Web is the library of the future and that Web search engines are the online catalogs and A&I databases of tomorrow is running on a collision course with the notion that there will be information that's sold as well as information that's given away on the Internet. I don't believe that major publishers, major information providers in the network environment will declare open house to any program that wanders around the Web extracting items from their content and moving it elsewhere. I believe that the Webcrawler technology will eventually become more of a niche interest and a far less dominant mode than it is now. The interface between Web indexing services and content providers is going to become very complex and highly negotiated, as content providers try to balance their desire to make their wares visible to potential purchasers with their need to protect their content so that it can be sold.

None of these future pictures I've sketched of libraries in the network environment reflect a very comfortable extrapolation of what libraries are about today. Some are too limiting, too rooted in current print traditions. Others miss the essence of what libraries are about. We face the challenge of charting a course from current libraries to a future concept which somehow captures the essence of libraries as organizations and institutions, in contrast to these ideas of digital libraries. Libraries will be involved with both print and digital information, and I find the use of the adjective "digital" troubling and possibly misleading.

Many people are starting to complain about the quality of material on the Web. They are looking to libraries and librarians to solve this problem—or at least the system developers who have built the Web and the Web search engines are referring them to the library community for solutions. There may be a real misunderstanding here (in the sense that these people haven't realized that the Web isn't the worldwide digital library, and that in fact a "digital" library is an oxymoron, and liable to remain one for the foreseeable future). But for libraries concerned with their future roles there's an opportunity as well. When I think about library collections, I think of efforts to provide both coherence and comprehensiveness, about the attempt to reflect a range and diversity of viewpoints. Building and managing collections involves tracing authenticity, integrity, and provenance of materials in the collections and helping users understand these attributes. There is a commitment to preservation and continuity of access over time. These qualities characterize library collection development and indeed underpin the mission of libraries. The issue is how to extend them to encompass the new digital forms of content.

THE CHANGING NATURE OF CONTENT CONTROL IN THE DIGITAL ENVIRONMENT

Print information is passive. It contains the seeds of its own preservation, and it exists as an artifact that can be kept. Films, videotapes and audio recordings are also passive and exist as artifacts today. Broadcast media transmissions can be recorded and saved; there is nothing technical to prevent this (although there are substantial legal issues); even broadcast transmissions are passive in this sense, waiting to be recorded and preserved. But the digital environment is different: All of the rules and assumptions may change, and with them the ability of libraries to collect, offer access to, and preserve information. There is a frightening perception developing of information as commercial culture—something that we never need preserve. Information today just screams at us, primarily in broadcast TV and now on the Internet in the form of chunks of entertainment or facts that we can obtain and that are endlessly repackaged just for us. As a culture we are beginning to view content as entertainment or as business information rather than as a record of intellectual discourse and interchange of dialogue, as a history of society. And I believe that this view is embodied in some of the proposals we are hearing these days about the change in copyright laws and about the introduction of rights management technologies.

I think many of you have seen the Lehman report and noted the changes to the intellectual property laws that it proposes. I know that many of us have some concerns about the proposed changes to the law. What we haven't yet recognized is that technology may render moot many of the debates about the changes to the laws governing intellectual property. There's a whole set of new technologies surfacing now called, variously, envelopes or secure containers; IBM calls its offering in this area "Cryptolopes." These products are basically software containers that control access to the information wrapped within them. Regardless of the legal situation with regard to copyright, no one can use information transmitted within one of these containers except through the mediation of the enveloping software, which controls what uses are permitted and has the capability of reporting on, and charging for, these uses.

Remember that fair use is a defense against copyright infringement. At least as I understand the history and doctrine of fair use, there is no affirmative obligation on the part of the rights holders to make information available so that people can make fair use of it. Rather, the doctrine protects people who want to make certain uses of copyrighted information under the assumption that they have been able to make this use in the first place.

The container technologies create an environment in which technology defined by the information provider determines use, not legal processes.

And in the proposed revisions to the copyright laws, tools and apparatus to circumvent rights management technologies such as secure containers are made illegal. Perhaps this is the obvious next step down the path that began when license agreements for electronic information supplanted traditional purchase of physical artifacts, which is governed by copyright law and the doctrine of first sale, and where the capability to use material is clear, thus allowing purchasers to invoke the fair use defense when necessary.

These envelopes can communicate over the Internet with their creators or with other clearinghouses. As you download this envelope containing information you want to use, it is calling home to billing central, logging the time you spent reading pages and printing selections. And it can potentially ask billing central to debit your credit card for the bill. You used to be able to borrow a book from the library, or purchase it from a local bookstore, and use it as you wished in the privacy of your own home. If you wanted to copy a page for your future use and convenience, no one would know, much less care. If you lingered over a particular passage or returned to it frequently, or reread a work in its entirety periodically, it was nobody's business but your own. But as Pam Samuelson has so eloquently argued, our private space in this new digital environment is profoundly threatened.

In the 21st century, it may well be that one of the increasingly important roles of libraries will be to offer anonymous access to content that is more and more capable of reporting on how it is used, assuming that libraries can negotiate appropriate arrangements with content providers. Libraries have always offered relatively anonymous access to information (as have bookstores, if you paid cash); in the future they may be the last refuge of anonymity.

The container approach to managing information access not only breaks down the boundaries of our private space, but profoundly threatens the tradition of archiving. I think that all of us who have been looking at the growth of digital content share a nagging concern about the long-term preservation of all this electronic material. I'm convinced that we can migrate the bits indefinitely as long as there's funding to do so. We know how to copy information from one storage medium to another. Being able to interpret those bits 20 or 30 years from now gets us into a nightmare of formats and standards and software that intertwines with data. And that's an area in which we are profoundly uneasy. We don't have enough experience and there are some financial tradeoffs that we don't really understand.

For example, I've convinced myself that an image in almost any storage format is probably going to be understandable, assuming that the format is documented, 20 years out, because images are simple things. The degree of interpretation and mediation that software provides in viewing an image is fairly minimal. The human perceptual system and the human brain does most of the interpretive work. You can port the software that displays an image to any computer in a reasonable amount of time. The situation for more structured and complex information, where the computer plays a much broader role in interpreting and presenting the data, is more problematic. When considering a database, for example, which plays an integral part in and reflects decision-making within an organization, the notion of trying to make it usable 30 years later is mindboggling—and probably hopeless in most cases.

In the face of this envelope technology, we no longer merely face the challenge of interpreting a relic format; but we have to worry about whether the billing and usage monitoring service, upon which the envelope technology is based and dependent, will survive 20 or 30 or 50 years from now. Will the company go broke? Will it change its identity through mergers and acquisitions? Will it change its protocols? Do we need to break into these packages to preserve the information within, just in case? These issues move us into a whole new level of concerns about preservation.

Envelope technology is about removing information distribution and access from its broader cultural context. It diminishes information access to a relatively transient (and invasive) pact directly between provider and consumer, with no room for libraries either as access providers or as preservers of information. As such, it is an excellent illustration of the way in which cultural assumptions about the common ground that libraries represent—in terms of the public good of preservation—is in doubt.

PERSONALIZATION AND THE DEVELOPMENT OF INTELLIGENT INFORMATION ACCESS SYSTEMS

People are facing a new challenge which is sometimes referred to as "information overload." The problem is no longer finding relevant information; rather it's that there's simply too much relevant information. Another, perhaps more insightful way to view the problem is that human time and human attention are becoming scarce resources.

Many of our existing information access tools only serve to highlight this problem. Our online catalogs can easily provide users with comprehensive lists of hundreds or even thousands of works on a given subject. But they cannot answer a query that says "I need to learn about this and I have two hours to spend on it—how can I most usefully spend those two hours?" Many of the demands for filtering information on the Internet, for quality control and selection, are really about something quite different: They are not requests for high-quality collections of works, but rather for small, highly selective (rather than comprehensive) personalized "collections" that can be prepared for individuals in response to specific needs. Often the user's need is not to develop comprehensive expertise, but simply to become conversant. There are tools that help users construct such answers today—book reviews, social "filtering" systems (ask an expert you respect), readers' guides to literatures—but these are not integrated with retrieval and access systems, and most are not personalized. The most personalized systems are based on social interaction—ask a friend, a colleague, an expert, a reference librarian—and this personalized and interactive character may explain why they have been so persistently successful, and why they continue to be used despite the availability of all sorts of abstracting, indexing, and current awareness services, for example.

Both technological infrastructure and actual services are being created that can help users to meet these needs, and which can supplement (but not supplant) social interaction as a means of locating information. A central question for me in trying to understand the potential roles of libraries in the new information technology environment is how library systems and content will fit into these new information services. What will be the boundary lines in the future that define library service offerings? What functions will be built into services provided directly by content providers, into services offered by content aggregators and organizers (including, but not limited to, libraries), and what will be the functions of independent systems that work directly on behalf of information seekers and users? Another way to frame the question is to ask what the balance will be between highly personalized information offerings from suppliers and highly selective filtering and retrieval by personal mediation systems that interact with these supplier-provided services.

One key to these new services is the development and deployment of large numbers of truly personal machines—machines that learn about you and your behavior and adapt to your preferences and needs. This is the antithesis of a centralized, anonymous-use system like an online catalog. Personal computers will, I believe, soon host highly personalized information access and management systems that mediate between the user and the huge external world of digital (and even to some extent print) information resources, including library collections.

This is actually happening. Personal computers are really becoming personal. Not too many years ago we frequently saw the horrible phenomenon of numbers of users sharing a "personal computer" in an office. Today, a growing number of people have two or three computers at work and at home that are truly personal and are not shared. More and more, these personal computers will be the tools of mediation in a universe of content and service providers. We need to understand and to some extent define what functions will be inside of these personal machines and what will be external to them. There are many factors, not all of them technical, which will come into play: privacy, economic control, ability to collect information and context comprehensively, and competition and overlap among information services. The user will always need tools that span and integrate the offerings of a range of service providers.

It's helpful to keep in mind here as well that the personal computer per se is in some sense only a symbol of this evolution: The key attributes are absolute control over some computational resource, and the ability to personalize this computing environment. Technically, this environment could be provided on a networked timesharing machine, for example, or through a distributed computing environment with very limited local computational resource.

There are many fertile areas here for research and product development. Most computer systems and application software today have only the most limited tools for personalization and don't learn actively or remember very much. If anything, they undergo a continued process of tuning and customization by their owners during their life spans. And remember, these personal machines have definite, limited, and often rather short life spans. So we also need to learn how to manage continuity of function and context across generations of hardware and software. Many of us are now on our second or third generation of personal machine, perhaps our second or third word processor, possibly on our second or third database manager. Moving to yet another new computer takes a lot of time, and represents one step forward and two steps back in the sense that one has to invest energy over a substantial period of time to re-customize the new machine. While we talk about long-term preservation of digital content in large institutions like libraries, we are constantly enduring a series of personal information discontinuities with files less than a decade old that are on media or in formats that we can no longer easily read.

As these personal systems come into wide use and grow smarter, they can maintain context and history about their use and their users. They can, at least potentially, fuse and correlate incoming information from multiple sources. As they become more sophisticated, however, the problems of continuity become very severe. Imagine trying to migrate from one system to another a very complex knowledge representation structure of what someone's been researching, reading, citing, listening to, viewing, or purchasing for the last three years—what they've seen and what information is new, what they have found useful, what information sources have been found to be cost-effective. . . . Imagine trying to export this from one software system and import it to another.

If the prospects for personal systems that select, retrieve, filter, rank, organize and manage information seem promising (despite some of the problematic issues I've just discussed), what are the prospects for information delivery services becoming more intelligent and personalized? At least for now, information access systems keep to a very shallow context; an online catalog, for example, doesn't even know who you are, much less track the citations you've seen or the materials you've borrowed. Such a system makes no use of context and history. There are a lot of reasons for this. The context and history that any one system can gather will not be comprehensive; people use many such systems and also get information through other channels. Historically, it's been expensive to collect history and context, and many systems have not been updated to do so, even as the economics have become more tractable. It's not clear how to use such context and history effectively. There are concerns about privacy; perhaps the best context and history databases with which we have experience are credit card and point of sale databases (from the increasingly ubiquitous cash register scanners), and the public is growing increasingly wary of the exploitation of such databases by advertisers, marketers, and snoops. And finally, until recently most information retrieval systems have offered only citations, rather than primary content, making it very difficult for the system to capture much data about the use to which the citations were put. Some of these parameters are changing; others remain constant.

Perhaps the answers will ultimately come down to convenience and cost, and to characteristics of user behavior. We can be certain that many service providers will continue to attempt to "own" their users to the maximum extent possible, and try to keep them within the information service to the extent possible. They will make it difficult, technically, for software that works on behalf of the user and spans and integrates multiple services to function effectively, for example, by not providing programmatic interfaces but only screens designed to support human navigation (and which change frequently in small ways designed to cause problems for programs). Think about news services for example. Most people read one or two newspapers, or view one or two broadcasts as sources of news. Technology is well along to permit the construction of personalized news services (the so-called "daily me") based on profiles supplied by users and perhaps refined through ongoing feedback mechanisms. This could simply be delivered as an enhancement to services to which people are already accustomed to subscribing: a personalized newspaper derived from a published newspaper. The other scenario, based on personalized retrieval software, involves the user selecting a wide range of news services and licensing access to them (or contracting to acquire articles from them transactionally), and then setting up his or her software to work with this range of suppliers; this is a more complex and probably substantially more expensive proposition. We don't fully understand how much more a user gets from this broader array of sources or when the extra coverage will be worth the trouble and expense to the user.

THE NEW DIGITAL GENRES AND THE AVALANCHE OF NEW CONTENT

We have, in the digital world, items that we call documents. Someone (I think Stuart Weibel of OCLC) coined the awful neologism "document-like objects," which actually communicated remarkably well with many people—digital objects that exist in the tradition of documents, possessing such traditional traits as authorship and genre. We understand document-like objects fairly well; we know, at least to a first approximation, how to describe them for retrieval.

There are many other classes of digital content appearing that we do not understand as well, such as multimedia hypertextual databases. In some ways these are document-like objects in that they have author and genre; but you cannot tell when you have exhausted their contents as you can when you read a book serially from beginning to end. When these databases are updated on a continuing basis, new intellectual problems appear having to do with editions, citation, and fixation. Print editions of an encyclopedia are important snapshots of knowledge and culture at points of time; a continually updated digital encyclopedia has the advantage of offering more timely information, but makes it very difficult to take a historical view of the evolution of knowledge or social views.

But perhaps the strangest and at the same time largest class of new digital information (at least in volume) is what you call telemetry in its broadest sense—remote sensing data, whatever's being recorded in every security video camera in every convenience market in the country, satellite imagery, and every securities transaction in every financial market. There's a wonderful story in Neal Stephenson's book *Snow Crash* (NY: Bantam Books, 1993, c1992), in which the Library of Congress and the CIA have privatized and merged; they operate an enormous commercial digital library and information marketplace. There are, in this future, people who basically roam around with video cameras, just filming random events, such as all the people who enter or leave a particular office building. The information is uploaded; perhaps nobody every looks at it, and the uploader doesn't get any royalties. But perhaps, and with the help of some face recognition software, someone will get really lucky and glean some valuable information; or perhaps someone knows that there's a law office in the building being filmed that specializes in mergers and acquisitions, and a record of who is coming and going suddenly becomes valuable.

This scenario is actually happening in the sense that we are starting to accumulate enormous amounts of sensor data. The smart highway systems now being tested record every license plate that drives by its camera. All that data is going somewhere—I'm not sure where—but somewhere. Probably to the same place that all the video surveillance information goes. I am told, for example, that it is becoming commonplace in some locales for the police to pull video captured by cameras in the bank automatic teller machines in neighborhoods where there has been a street crime; often one of the cameras has picked up some information. And some communities are beginning to hang surveillance cameras in public areas, even on the street. We need to think about what all this information gathering means: Where does it go? How is it organized? How long is it kept? Who has access to it? What does it mean about our definitions of public spaces? Vast numbers of public and semi-public events are being systematically recorded: city council meetings, congressional hearings, symposia, lectures, seminars, and trials. It's important to recognize the characteristics of these recordings as telemetry rather than creative endeavors: These are fixed cameras that just record what happens in a room with little or no regard to specific content.

And it's not just images that are being collected. Numeric imagery, from temperature readings at thousands of weather stations all the way through financial telemetry from various kinds of markets, is becoming part of our record. How much of this is kept for the long term and how does it fit with our concepts of the roles and purposes of libraries? How much of this is really part of the published record accessible to all (though perhaps not for free), and how much remains in private hands, accessible to the public only according to the whims and business plans of the private owners, and perhaps only in edited forms?

A central problem around all this information is how to organize it. All I'll say about this issue is that we don't do very well organizing information in formats other than print. The traditional approach of libraries has been to rely on intellectual description—cataloging and indexing—rather than technologies such as full-text searching for printed material, even as it migrates into electronic formats. This has been possible, barely. Libraries have been largely overwhelmed by the output of the existing broadcast media, which will be dwarfed by the avalanche of telemetry coming online. There are a range of interesting new technologies coming into use: various forms of speech recognition and transcription, image recognition and classification systems, and video summarization methods. None of these systems work perfectly, but some are starting to work well enough at least to offer some help. But their employment represents a significant cultural and intellectual shift for libraries.

I spoke earlier of how changes to copyright law may constrain libraries, and also of how rights management technologies may allow publishers more control over their materials, rendering irrelevant some legal authorizations that libraries possess. My belief is that we will see a whole second front open up in the intellectual property debates around this kind of telemetry. This debate will be about rights of publicity; rights to images and trademarks; who has the right to take your picture, or a picture of a building, or of a painting; who owns satellite passes at the earth; who can resell them. It will, ultimately, lead to new forms of definition of the limits of the "public domain" in the sense of the common, shared, public societal and cultural heritage. For example, we know that copyright expires, although the durations of copyrights have been steadily increasing. After enough time has passed we all collectively "own" what was once a copyrighted work. There is a body of law now that suggests that performers have some rights to characters that they create. How long do these rights last after the death of the performer?

To the extent that libraries become involved in managing, organizing, and preserving these telemetry information resources they will be at the center of these controversies. In the intellectual property arena, libraries have been focused on the extent to which owners of copyrights can dictate the uses of their copyrighted materials by libraries and their users. At least here there's usually general agreement about who holds the rights. Publishers have eliminated that ambiguity as part of the process of producing their goods for sale or licensing. The new world of digital telemetry will be much more complex, perhaps taking on some of the character of legal difficulties that can sometimes surround special collections today, but on a much larger scale.

COMMON GROUND: LIBRARIES AS SOCIAL CONSTRUCTS

Why do people think they want libraries as a networked information environment? Some want them for free access to information resources, or for a sort of safety net to insure some level of information access for everybody. We haven't figured out the legal and economic models in a world without geography to enable these goals. As we've talked about telecommunication reform and national information infrastructure in the US over the past few years, the notion of universal service as an objective has been extensively discussed. Universal service has long been a public policy interest. With voice telephony, universal service basically means everyone should be able to have a phone, and phones should be everywhere. Phone service should be sufficiently inexpensive that everyone can have it. Another issue that is sometimes raised as part of universal service is that people shouldn't be penalized economically because of where they live (for example, in rural areas), even though it is much more expensive to wire these rural areas for telephone service than it is to wire a densely populated urban area. Earlier, universal electrification was a public goal, and universal access to electricity raised many of the same issues.

When you hear public policy people talking about universal service for the Internet, they are still thinking about wires—if we can get the wire that terminates the Internet into everyone's home, then we've achieved universal service. When we really talk about universal service, and what it means, and whether it should be an objective, and what kind of objective it should be, what we're really going to end up discussing is access to content. This issue really hasn't emerged in a useful way in our public debate about the national information infrastructure. It is still too much involved in incentives for wiring. But libraries have framed and highlighted this public policy issue about the public's need to have access to information, to our historical and cultural discourse, and to our scientific knowledge for a long time, independent of the specifics of digital information. More recently, the library community has tried to focus policy attention on some of the specific issues around public access to networked information, but very much from the perspective that libraries are the solution for digital information just as they have been for other forms of information, and that they need certain new subsidies and legal accommodations to serve as a solution in the digital age.

I've already reviewed the demands for libraries to provide quality control and filtering and selection in the networked information environment. Clearly many people look to libraries to provide these services. As I indicated, I believe that there are actually multiple needs being conflated in this area, some of which deal with the need for library collections, and some of which look towards new forms of information access and management systems that may or may not be provided by libraries.

There is yet another role for libraries as the conservators of our intellectual and cultural heritage, our history, our discourse. I believe that this is a critically important role for libraries. It's not articulated often or clearly as a role for libraries by the public at large, perhaps because libraries have done it so well that everybody just assumes it. It is not widely recognized how fragile is the ability of libraries to continue to function in this role. It depends on the legal framework surrounding copyright. Libraries have done well with printed materials, which is linked intimately to our notions of copyright and of publishing—the concept of publishing as a dissemination of copies to autonomous control by a variety of different geographically and organizationally dispersed institutions. The first sale notion in copyright—the idea that once those copies are published, they belong to the publishing institution—leaves the preservation and access responsibilities to those institutions. This framework has facilitated libraries' success in managing print. But many of the assumptions on which print preservation and collection management are based don't extend well to all the broadcast media that have been created in the last century. Perhaps even more importantly, they are profoundly in question in the new digital regime.

It is generally assumed that libraries will continue to maintain their archival role in the electronic environment. But the changing legal framework combined with the difficulties of preserving digital content leaves libraries' success in this realm open to serious doubt. I worry that people will be very disappointed 20 years from now when they discover how much may be missing from libraries' archives from the early days of digital content, simply because we hadn't set up the social and legal permissions to allow libraries to accomplish that task. I hope that eventually everyone will recognize that it is such an important and compelling social benefit that this issue will be resolved. At least there have been some glimmers of recognition of the importance of this issue—for instance, in some of the proposed copyright law changes.

So what, then, constitutes the common ground, the common values, that can help us chart a course for libraries in the digital environment, in an age no longer structured by the geographic order? I believe that several directions are clear.

We have looked at the role of libraries in the preservation and long-term access to the entire record of our society's discourse and actions. Libraries must serve as a counterweight to the growing private control of this record. They must create and protect an environment for people who want to continue their scholarly and cultural discourse under the umbrella of fair use. The elimination of the act of publication, of abdication of control to many autonomous entities, for digital information is a significant issue: It allows the subsequent "withdrawal" of content that is embarrassing, awkward, counterintuitive, and incorrect. It makes our history too mutable. Once materials went in and out of "print"; in the digital environment they will go totally in and out of public consciousness.

I believe that the record of our history, our discourse, and our culture is critically important. And it must have integrity; it must be preserved; and it must be accessible. Libraries will ensure this.

We have also considered the issue of quality filtering in all its ambiguity. Clearly, libraries have a role to play here, and clearly people are also going to want something more than the filtering and selection that libraries have traditionally provided. We need to clarify what description and organization of materials really mean in the electronic context and how to integrate those issues with the apparatus of content review and evaluation that traditionally takes place outside the library. Meeting these new needs may be a less critical role for libraries, but their role in maintaining collections that are comprehensive, coherent, and diverse is clearly central. If nothing else, these collections will provide essential raw materials in meeting the need for good information sources that can be filtered in an economy of attention.

I believe that collection development as historically practiced by libraries, will continue to be important. We will need these collections. The network is not the library.

And then there's a final role, with which I want to close, for libraries in the digital age: education, training, and information literacy. I haven't spent much time on this. Outside the library, you don't hear this topic discussed. But when we think of libraries as organizations in social contexts rather than as buildings or as passive heaps of books or papers, it's very clear that a lot of what libraries do is train— they provide value-added education, working one on one with people seeking information and helping people with information literacy issues. They play a whole set of service and educational roles. These roles have been underestimated and undervalued over the past 20 years. Consider, for example, that the online catalog was the first computer system that many people encountered, aside from automatic teller machines. I think that these roles will be terrifically important as we move into the digital universe. The literacy aspect may be the most important role, at least for the next 20 or 30 years, because we have a lot of people who don't yet understand the issues of integrity and quality evaluation as applied to digital information. As we grew up with print, and even with the broadcast mass media, those considerations were part of our general, if not explicit, education. Hopefully, future generations will absorb similar knowledge about the digital environment. But adults need to catch up, and who are better than the libraries to educate them?

The roles of preservation, access, collection development, and education are areas for libraries to fill as new social constructs as we move into the digital age. They are my candidates for directions towards common ground and common understanding.

All-Conference Speech—
Uncommon Knowledge: Mythbreaking for the Future

By Walt Crawford
Research Libraries Group, Inc.

INTRODUCTION

If we are to make sensible futures, we must first deal with nonsensical futures. That's what got me started speaking out about the future of libraries and print: because I saw and heard so many assertions and projections that made no sense to me, based on what appeared to be "common knowledge" about the future. A little straight thinking and casual investigation demonstrated that the common knowledge, while widely assumed and asserted, did not appear to be based on much of anything. Neither history, nor the marketplace, nor any explicit investigation of people's preferences supported this common knowledge—and yet these unfortunate, dystopian futures were being treated as inevitable.

I proposed the title for this talk when the call for papers first went out: "Uncommon Knowledge: Mythbreaking for the Future." The apparent common knowledge of inevitable trends is, in fact, a projective mythology: a set of future myths. What we need at this point is uncommon knowledge—which you might also call common sense. We need to break away from the myths of the past, present, and future that lead us astray.

Michael Gorman and I took one big step toward refuting future myths when we wrote *Future Libraries: Dreams, Madness & Reality* [ALA Editions, 1995]. I hope today to point out a diverse handful of myths and suggest some bases for mythbreaking.

THE ONE-MILLIMETER ROLLS AND DOUBLING COMPUTER POWER

I'd like to remind you of the old saw about automobiles and personal computers. You know how it goes. If cars had improved the way that computers have in the past 50 years, a Rolls-Royce would now cost $2.50 and get 1,000 miles to the gallon. Here's the reality: that Rolls-Royce would be one millimeter long.

Still, computers really *have* improved that much, haven't they? Moore's Law, proposed many years ago by Gordon Moore, founder of Intel, says that the number of transistors that can be formed on a given surface area of silicon doubles every 18 months. You've probably heard it as "computers double in power every 18 months" or "the computing power available for a given price doubles every 18 months." The law has been true at the CPU level, although that 18-month cycle will run up against serious physical barriers in another few years. But what does that mean for real-world use? Let's take a ten-year example.

In January 1986, Dell Computers (then called PC's Limited) introduced its first AT-compatible computer. It sold for $2,852. That got you an Intel 80286 CPU running at 6MHz, 256K of RAM, one diskette drive, a 20MB hard disk (probably around 65ms.), and a 12-inch monochrome monitor. No software was included, not even DOS. It probably had a 90-day warranty. Ten years later, in January 1996, Gateway 2000 sold a decent computer for $2,829—almost exactly the same amount. For the same money, you get an Intel Pentium 16MB CPU running at 120MHz; 256K of RAM—but that's synchronous pipelined burst cache, not DRAM; one diskette drive, a one-gigabyte 10ms hard disk, and a 17-inch Trinitron-based color monitor. And a quad-speed CD-ROM drive, a 64-bit graphics accelerator with 2MB of display RAM, a wavetable sound card and Altec-Lansing speakers, Microsoft Windows 95 and

Office Professional 95, and a three-year warranty with one-year on-site support and lifetime around-the-clock telephone technical support.

What's changed in a decade? The CPU runs at 20 times the clock speed, but is probably six times as fast running at the same clock rate; in other words, 120 times the processing power. 64 times as much memory (plus another 5 times as much for cache and display), albeit considerably faster memory. Fifty times the hard disk space, operating six times as fast. An incomparably better monitor. A very substantial amount of software. And a CD-ROM drive four times as fast as was available in 1986 (when a single-speed drive probably cost $1,000 or so). Now that's change: perhaps fifty times the system for the same price, in a decade.

No wonder we get carried away with the rate of change. This is amazing stuff. It doesn't follow Moore's Law, however, except for the CPU itself. That's almost precisely on target, as Moore's Law projects 128–times improvement from January 1986 to July 1996. The system as a whole has improved less than half that much, but still by an impressive amount.

SIGNIFICANT CHANGE REQUIRES ATTITUDE CHANGE

But look again. Does anyone get 50 times as much work done on that brand-new Pentium as they did on that awful old 286? Not really. Can you write 50 times as fast? Well, I don't know about you, but I can only type about 80 words a minute and can rarely create more than a thousand words an hour, or 16 a minute. For anyone who's just using a PC as a typewriter or a terminal, the 1995 computer offers little or no speed improvement. The same goes for those doing basic spreadsheet work, except on relatively large spreadsheets.

I get enormous advantages from the power of my 486 at home, and really want a Pentium. I can do desktop publishing far more rapidly and effectively, and I use a range of world-class typefaces never available to a typical print shop. My CD-ROM drive makes possible an incredible range of entertainment, information, and pure storage capabilities unheard of in the PC of 1986. Windows 95 provides robust, easy-to-use multitasking and fine graphics. I wouldn't go back to an AT under any plausible circumstances.

But that significant change in my computer-using abilities only comes about because I've changed my attitude. The fastest PC in the world won't improve your productivity or make you a different person unless you've decided to change. Technological capabilities don't matter, by and large, until people decide to use them—and people's abilities and needs don't double every 18 months, even if computing power at a given price does.

Here we have one myth: technological improvement automatically equals societal revolution. It doesn't, not as a rule, not as long as people are involved.

SOME MYTHS OF "COMMON KNOWLEDGE"

Let's look briefly at some other examples of common knowledge gone wrong. First, some current myths of ascendant technology.

"One Big Wire": The Myth of the All-Digital Future

We are told, and told, and told again that any day now we'll get all our information and entertainment and do most of our shopping and communicating over that one big wire, our personal connection to the all-digital future. Convergence is upon us, and there's no resistance. We'll all be wired, and anything that isn't digital will be irrelevant. The myth of the all-digital future supported by the one big wire is the most pervasive technological myth, and the one that drives too many print- and library-related myths.

This is, of course, impure nonsense. I would say that it mistakes technological feasibility for societal inevitability, but that supposes simple error. The prophets of convergence and the all-digital future aren't simply mistaken; they are pushing their own agendas, making their personal fortunes and reputations by promulgating these simplistic, nonsensical futures. Realistic market analysts now recognize that online and digital marketplaces are not taking over everything and that the one universal wire seems increasingly unlikely.

"Essentially Free": The Myth of Unending Technological Improvement

The all-digital prophets tell us that bandwidth is becoming essentially free, that computing power is becoming essentially free, that telecommunications speed is becoming essentially infinite, and that these "facts" make an all-digital future inevitable. This is the myth of unending technological improvement: everything keeps getting faster and faster, cheaper and cheaper, until it's all essentially immediate, free, and unlimited.

Variations on this myth are particularly pernicious. A whole generation of college students and faculty apparently believes that the Internet is free, because it is institutionally subsidized. People urge others to use more Internet bandwidth, so that "they" add more bandwidth—which, of course, won't cost anybody anything.

Here's the truth. "Essentially free" is another way of saying "phenomenally expensive, but the incremental cost becomes small." Remember that the 50–times-as-powerful January 1996 computer does *not* mean you can buy a workable computer for $56 (one-fiftieth of the 1986 price). Technology does *not* work that way. Technological improvement is neither consistent, nor unending, nor free. Nothing is free.

"Build It and They Will Come": The Myth of Universal Technological Acceptance

Build it, and they will come. That's the myth of universal technological acceptance, and it's amazing that this myth manages to persist. If you believe the market analysts of years past, we all use personal digital assistants, we all carry flip phones, we're all spending $50 a month on interactive television, and we're all just waiting for our set-top boxes and network computers.

The reality is far more unnerving: *Most innovations fail.* Sometimes before really penetrating the market; sometimes after a short blaze of glory. There's no sure way to predict which will fail and which will succeed. For that matter, the quotation's even wrong. The line in *Field of Dreams* is "Build it, and *he* will come"—one ballplayer, not 200 million customers.

"We All Use Risc Computers and Flat Screens Now": The Myth of Uniform Technological Replacement

A slightly different but related myth is the myth of uniform technological replacement: when something new comes along, it sweeps away its predecessors. Thus, the train doomed river freight, trucks doomed freight trains, the printing press eliminated the oral tradition, radio destroyed newspapers, television wiped out radio *and* motion pictures—well, you get the idea. It's inevitable.

Notice anything about that list? Every statement on it is false. Even the first one, the one you probably accepted. If any of you live along the Mississippi, you probably know the truth about river freight: there's a *lot* more of it now than in the golden age of riverboats, even if the glamour has declined substantially.

And yet this ongoing myth keeps cropping up. This time it's different. This time, everybody will adopt the new within a very few years—and everyone will abandon what they use now. History is for chumps. We know better now.

"Information Wants to be Free": The Myth of Zero-Cost Organization and Distribution

Here's the great killer economic argument of the future: information wants to be free. Take away the cost of distribution—and, as already mentioned, that's "essentially free"—and information becomes so cheap as to be, well, free.

Call it zero-cost organization and distribution of facts, information, and knowledge, and you begin to see the problem. Quite apart from the absurdity of essentially free distribution, there's a huge difference between data, facts, information, knowledge, and wisdom. Data costs money to gather, but that's nothing compared to the effort of turning data into useful information.

I'm always amazed by librarians, writers, and faculty members who assert that information wants to be free. Do they feel they should organize, filter, and gather that information for nothing? Or are all those salaries really provided as institutional welfare, with any actual work being so much lagniappe?

Digital distribution isn't free, or close to it—and if it was, so what? I've used the estimate that 14 percent of the price of a typical book can be accounted for by its being a physical item: that is, typesetting, printing, paper, binding, and distribution don't make up more than one-seventh of the price. In a capitalist economy, the other 86 percent has nothing to do with means of distribution; organized information simply does not "want to be free."

"Being Digital": The Myth of the Information Age

Consider the "Third Age" we're now in. The first age was the Agricultural Age. Then came the Industrial Age. We've now left the Industrial Age and are squarely in the Information Age. Thus, we get Nicholas Negroponte's judgment on codex books, bound collections of ink on paper. He has explained that they are inevitably doomed, because they are industrial products, and after all the industrial age is over. End of discussion.

My first reaction is to wonder how Negroponte and his ilk get along on their digital diet—since food must long ago have become obsolete, being the product of the long-lost agricultural age. I grew up in the heart of California's Central Valley, one of the richest agricultural areas on earth—but of course it's long since vanished, since we all eat electrons nowadays.

Silly? Consider further. Other profound thinkers told us more than a decade ago that mass production was dead, that everything would be custom-made in the information age—that is, what few objects would be created at all. Oh really? Is there anyone out there who believes that today's powerful, inexpensive personal computers got that way because mass production is dead? I guarantee you that if this year's one gigabyte hard disk costs as little as 25 cents a megabyte, or less than the ten megabyte disk of eleven years ago, it's not because the industrial age has ended and those disks are custom-built to order or somehow magically created out of information. Hogwash! They are cheaper because there is more demand and because industrial processes, vastly improved, make it possible to produce them less expensively. And, to be sure, because there are several hotly competitive companies building hard disks—not just the one anointed producer that can do the most efficient job.

Whatever the age of information may be, it neither spells an end to industry nor suggests that people will achieve some wonderful new simplification, a digital convergence doing what harmonic convergence failed to accomplish. Life isn't like that. Agriculture still matters. Industry continues to be vital. The Age of Information is a metaphor, an organizing principle, an image. Things go astray when people seize on that image and reshape their views of reality to fit it. This cluster of technological myths works together to make the inevitable futures we hear so much about. Don't believe them; they range from pure nonsense to seriously misleading. When someone says "well, it may take longer, but . . . " the proper answer is "or it may not happen at all." Let's move on to some myths of print and reading, before getting to those myths dealing directly with libraries.

"Ink on Paper Can't Compete": The Myth of the Death of Print

We've heard about the death of print for years now, too often from within our own field. While print has been busily dying, the publishing industry has been growing; more books are being published and purchased, more magazines circulate more copies, more revenue makes a substantial industry even larger. But we're well into a period when, by all projections, print should be fading away. We're now four years into a five-year period in which, according to one library expert, "the market for information printed on paper can be anticipated to shrink by 50 percent." Well, since it's a good deal larger now than it was in 1992, 1996 should be one astonishing year—the print market will have to shrink by some 60 percent in a single year.

Publishers don't spend much time talking about the death of print any more; that was last decade's news. Sure, they want to be in the new markets that complement print, but they know print isn't going away.

"Nobody Reads Anymore": The Myth of the Death of Textual Literacy

One remarkable myth, sometimes coming from within the library field, is that nobody reads anymore—that libraries need to move on to multimedia and virtual reality, because the era of universal book reading is dead. This myth combines false nostalgia with bad information. Remember those wonderful decades when every adult read books as a primary means of leisure—and when they all had the leisure to read books. Can anyone place those decades in history? Back before book and magazine publishing began their dramatic decline? Back when every adult took the daily newspaper? Just when were those decades, and why did they end?

The decades I'm describing don't exist, as far as I can tell—just as book and magazine publishing keeps growing, not declining. Surveys indicate that two-thirds of adult Americans do use their public libraries—and most studies show that public library use is increasing, in some cases dramatically. These people are reading. Book stores are flourishing. Book sales have increased 27% in the last ten years. The Department of Commerce expects the book publishing industry to continue to grow through the rest of the decade—and publishers don't print books if they don't sell.

"Just the Facts": The Myth of Books as Fact Delivery Systems

Here's one of the stranger myths about books and print—one that makes me wonder about some futurists and commentators. I call this one "just the facts"—the myth that books and magazines are nothing more than fact delivery systems. A book, magazine, or newspaper, in this view, is nothing more than sets of paragraphs bound together because of old-fashioned delivery methods. Hypertext and digital networks can deliver the individual paragraphs more precisely and link them together in interesting ways.

But most books, most magazines, and indeed most newspapers aren't simply sets of facts. Where they are—some reference works, for example—they are indeed prime candidates for digital replacement. Online services and CD-ROMs make fine replacements for *Reader's Guide* and huge collections of phone directories—but most publications represent much more than collections of unrelated facts in bindings.

"The End of the Golden Age": The Myth of Declining Support for Public Libraries

Here's a library-specific myth that I've only seen from library schools and academic librarians. It's the end of the golden age; public libraries are in a state of decline, and there's no support for funding them. Thus, we must replace old-fashioned physical public libraries with the Internet Public Library and other wonders of the digital age.

You don't see this myth from public librarians who know what they're doing, because they know better. The golden age of public library use is right now; the statistics are quite clear on that matter. And when it comes to support, the record is also clear. When public libraries are locally funded and make their cases, they gain support; 77 percent of library funding elections succeed, even faced with such awful rules as California's two-thirds majority.

"Everything, Anywhere, Anytime": The Myth of the Universal Scholar's Workstation

Then there's the piece of common knowledge that's caused so many academic librarians and support organizations to go so far astray, one that's been around for some two decades. This is the myth of the universal scholar's workstation as a realistic and desirable goal. Desirable, perhaps, if resources were infinite. But if undertaken at the expense of browsable collections, at the expense of sensible monographic acquisitions, at the expense of reference—well, the universal scholar's workstation is as undesirable as it is impossible. "Everything, anywhere, anytime" isn't going to happen, and it's a dangerous myth when it undermines real-world library services. We go into considerable detail about this in *Future Libraries*—none of which I've seen challenged or refuted—and I'll say no more today.

I'll also refer you to the book for discussion of three more library-related myths: the myth that academic libraries are big expensive buildings full of dead trees that nobody wants; the myth that academic libraries are eating up ever larger shares of their institutions' budgets; and disintermediation, the myth that in the future everyone will and should be his or her own reference librarian.

COUNTER-MYTHS AND NOSTALGIC MYTHS

I've already mentioned a couple of nostalgic myths—for example, the idea that there was a golden age in America, an age in which everybody read books. Let's look at a couple of other counter-myths and nostalgic myths.

"Bring Back the Card Catalog": The Myth of Automation as the Destroyer of Acquisition Budgets

This myth is courtesy of Cliff Stoll, repeated by him on PACS-L: the death of the card catalog is a major step backwards and dehumanizes libraries—and skyrocketing automation expenditures have gutted acquisitions budgets, to the expense of us all. I haven't seen any facts offered to back up the latter claim, probably for the simple reason that no such facts exist. Everyone here probably knows the real culprits in gutting acquisition budgets for monographs and humanities serials: to wit, the Black Hole of STM journals and the increased stinginess of campus funding for libraries. While I recognize that card catalogs do certain things better than online catalogs in general, and certainly work better than bad online catalogs, this general nostalgic myth is pure nonsense. Quite apart from the pure economic necessity of abandoning the card catalog, good online catalogs with union-catalog extensions offer faster, better, and even more humanistic support for library operations. But then, I'm biased; I make my living from library automation, and know how important automation is to effective libraries of all stripes.

"When Everyone Got All Their Current Information at the Library": The Myth of Libraries as the Information Place

Here's another golden-age myth, the idea that libraries are losing their role as the place everyone gets their current information. If libraries don't change drastically, people will go elsewhere for current sources. The related myth, unfortunately spread by the American Library Association among others, is that the library is The Information Place, capital T, I, P.

Here's a tip: libraries can't lose their role as The Information Place, because it's a role libraries have never really had. There's two aspects to that statement, and both deserve a little amplification.

Most people don't rely on the public library for the most current facts: That's what newspapers, television and radio are for. Most middle-class and upper-class people don't get their primary information in their key areas of interest from the public libraries: That's what personal magazine subscriptions, bookstores and online services are for. But most people do use their public libraries for pleasure reading, adventures in new areas and many other aspects of life. Libraries also serve as safety nets for the displaced and primary places where young people learn to love reading and knowledge.

The other problem with "The Information Place" is that it substantially reduces the scope of academic libraries and impoverishes the real scope of public libraries. Public libraries are not just places that people go to get up-to-the-minute facts. That is not even the predominant role of public libraries. Good public libraries serve a range of functions, many of them purely physical, all of them important. Don't devalue the free circulation of romance novels and mysteries to lower-income patrons, and don't devalue story-telling hours and community programs. Those are valuable services, helping to make the community stronger and improve the overall mental and social health of its people.

A good library is not an InfoKiosk. It's a vital part of the community, one that electronics won't and can't replace.

NEW MYTHS FOR STRANGE TIMES

Before moving beyond myths, let's look at three peculiar ones that have arisen in the last year or two. I call them new myths for strange times.

"Everyone's Online": The Myth of the Web as Sole Solution

People are always looking for the magic bullet, the single solution that will handle all our problems. This year's magic bullet is the World Wide Web and the inevitable fact that everyone in the world will be on the Internet and using the Web by, oh, the end of 1997. Shazam: universal literacy, universal access, universal information, the sole solution to information and entertainment—and shopping as well.

There are no magic bullets, and the Web is about as unlikely a solution as I've seen. Everyone is *not* going to be online. It's fairly well recognized that the huge estimates of Internet users are grossly exaggerated, and there's strong suspicion that supposed commercial online service usage is far less than optimistically estimated. Yes, millions of people have signed up for an online service—and millions have canceled their accounts.

For that matter, few prophets have faced up to the real-world costs of using the Web. Most Internet service providers are losing money. Twenty dollars a month for all the Internet time you can use seems unlikely to survive as a business model. If you want a truly silly idea, it's Oracle and Sun's Network Computer, a $500 box that means all your word processing and other computing must be done hooked up to the Internet—and that all your files are sitting on someone else's server somewhere. Your Internet services provider goes under, as many are doing? Tough: your work is gone, gone, gone. Now there's a magic bullet for you.

Of course I find the Web useful, when I can get through to the small number of high-quality sites that I actually use. *Condé Nast Traveler*'s Web site complements the print magazine nicely, and was quite useful when our favorite cruise line went bankrupt last fall—but I'd never consider that Web site as a plausible replacement for the monthly magazine or my other print resources.

"We're All Publishers": The Myth of Universal Self-Publishing as a Grand Solution

There's another Web-related myth. With the Web and the Internet, we're all publishers—and this is a good thing. The Web is, in essence, the world's largest experiment in self-publishing. At last, authors can be free of all that stifling editorial interference and gatekeeping from editors and publishers. Isn't it wonderful?

My hope is that a couple more years of Web activity will show people the virtues of editors and publishers. Gatekeepers are there for a reason, and that reason isn't that books and magazines cost so much to publish. Actually, that's happening already; apart from library sites, nearly all the Web sites I use are commercial sites, many run by print publishers. I trust them to exercise some editorial control and insight—and I'd probably pay for that control.

If there really does prove to be a substantial Web-using population willing to pay for good quality, which is a possibility, then I think there will be real markets for Web editors: people who make livings by selecting sites or rewriting material for coherence and clarity. I might find such a job interesting—but for now, I won't quit my day job.

"If Journals Are Too Expensive, Then All Print Is Dying": The Myth of Scholarly Journals as the Tip of the Iceberg

As a last myth, let's look at another one that's rarely stated explicitly but surely sits behind some of the arguments for the death of print. Observers within the academic library community *correctly* observe that STM journals—that is, scientific, technical, and medical journals—are out of control, getting too expensive and raising real questions for their future. True enough, and for many very small circulation journals, the cost of physical distribution may be a significant factor—and, more importantly, the ratio of published pages to reader interest is absurdly high.

The myth, however, is that this problem means that print publishing *in general* is economically unsound and must be put to death: that STM journals represent the tip of the iceberg. That just isn't so, and almost any publisher can tell you as much.

If all STM journals were published by American publishers, and if all those journals went out of business in 1996, the net effect on American periodical publishing revenues as a whole would be *slower growth*. American newspaper and magazine revenues typically grow at an annual rate considerably higher than the *entirety* of worldwide STM publishing. STM journals represent less than one percent of worldwide publishing.

More significantly, the economics of STM journals bear no relationship to the economics of normal book, magazine, and newspaper publishing. There is no serials crisis—for typical public library serial collections, the increase in subscription costs is roughly that of inflation. There is an STM journals crisis—but where else do publishers sell their wares to someone other than the buyers, and where else do academic libraries represent the *principal* market for publications? Well, yes, maybe some specialized academic monographs, but that's about it.

Academic libraries and their institutions need to work out many partial solutions to the STM journals crisis, but don't mythologize it: it simply has nothing to do with print publishing as a whole.

MYTHBREAKING: COMMON SENSE AND UNCOMMON KNOWLEDGE

Why do we get such myths, and the many others I haven't mentioned? There could be many reasons, including technolust, the urge for simplification, library school faculty out of touch with real libraries and publishing, and people with vested interests attempting to create self-fulfilling prophecies. Maybe it doesn't matter why myths arise. What matters is that we need to use common sense to gain uncommon knowledge. We need to break down myths to get to sensible futures.

One common aspect of myths is that people don't matter, or at least people's preferences don't matter. So, for example, the prophets of convergence and an all-digital future argue that because it is *possible* to communicate most information in digital form, therefore it is *inevitable* that all information will be communicated online.

That is sheer nonsense, and leaves out the most important element of any projection: people. People have preferences, and the history of technological innovation shows clearly that people's preferences matter. People don't all have the same preferences, and many of us take some pride in maintaining individuality.

Just as people differ, so do libraries. Different kinds of libraries have different missions. Public libraries are not *primarily* scholarly research institutions—but research does take place there. University libraries do not *primarily* serve entertainment needs—but every good university library has a fiction collection.

Many libraries must take special care to preserve the record of the culture. No other institution does this as well. But that's not the mission of every library, although it is one of the missions of the field. Librarians should value complexity and diversity. There's nothing new about diversity within the library. What public library collection in 1996 contains nothing other than printed hardcover books? Not that books lack diversity, by any means, but almost every library has gone beyond sole adherence to that medium for many years.

Diversity is *inherently* a good thing, which makes it curious that the fevered futurists seem to disdain it so. Any thoughtful observer will say that electronic distribution of information will be used more in the future than it was in the past, but that does not suggest that books will or should cease to be published or read. For that matter, diverse electronic distribution makes more sense than the idea that you always fetch things over one big network whenever you want them. CD-ROM and other digital publications make useful additions to the diverse ways that libraries serve their patrons. So do microfiche and microfilm (with their abundant limitations); so do videocassettes, videodiscs, compact discs, print magazines, and books. So do online searches—of the national bibliographic database, of commercial databases and of Internet resources.

BUILDING DESIRABLE FUTURES

I look forward to hearing other speakers set forth paths toward desirable futures. We need many such paths, many small solutions to make libraries more effective and better supported. As we grow to understand that digital collections enrich libraries but don't make them digital libraries, as we understand that grand solutions simply don't work, we can find the common ground toward even better libraries.

Supporting Your Supporters

Libraries and librarians need to support their supporters. You need to build strong support organizations within academia, just as public libraries build Friends groups that (among other things) lobby for sound funding.

One specific aspect of supporting your supporters is protecting adequate monograph and humanities acquisitions budgets. The humanities have not been wracked by the excess cost increases of STM journals, but too often these areas—where academics rely on library collections and typically appreciate libraries—have been hurt by the unending demand for STM funding. It's heartening to see a growing number of academic libraries that explicitly protect book and humanities serials budgets. If you must move toward just-in-time services in some areas—and most libraries must—those areas should be the ones where there's the biggest payoff and the least case for strong retrospective collections. The humanities still work largely through books, and these fields work through a long accretion of knowledge and theory, well served by strong established collections. These are your strongest supporters; don't abandon them.

Making Common Cause: Working with Public Libraries

Academic libraries should make common cause with public libraries, and academic librarians should be aware that they aren't the only ones with good ideas or innovative techniques. My own public library has integrated other media in with the book stacks, to very good effect, and with the particular result of making vertical-file materials far more evident as part of the collection. Would that work for every academic library or for any academic library? Perhaps not—but it's not clear that the isolation of medium-specific rooms or collections serves users very well.

That's just one example; there could be many others. I sometimes get the sense that some academic librarians, and some library school faculty, regard academic libraries as the only *real* libraries, with public libraries and librarians being somehow sullied by their vast popularity and near-universal use. Such snobbery ill-serves academia, and can cut you off from valuable partners. In my experience, most communities with exceptional academic libraries also have exceptional public libraries; the two should complement one another and should explicitly work together.

Journals: Isolating the Problems

Finally, when dealing with real problems of collection funding and maintenance, try to identify those problems clearly. For most academic libraries, the most difficult funding problem is not just-in-case collecting in general. It is not print materials in general. It is not even serials in general. It is scientific, technical, and medical journals, more specifically those published by the international oligopoly and publishers that emulate their techniques.

No, I don't have a single solution for the STM journal problem, and I don't believe any single solution will either be legal or workable. But an important step along the road to many small solutions is to isolate the problem. *Which* fields pose the greatest problems? Is it possible to identify the areas where collecting print journals is not only untenable but pointless? Can you work with scholars to limit the proliferation of ever-narrower, ever more expensive new journals in those areas?

Isolate, specify, define. Saying that print must die because STM journals are too expensive is not only nonsensical but self-defeating. Saying that all serials are too expensive is simply ignorant. You know better.

CREDO: AND, NOT OR

Some of you have no doubt heard or read this ending before, but it's still a useful way to break away from specific myths and summarize my convictions about the future of print and libraries. I believe that electronic publishing and dissemination will continue to grow in importance, displacing print where electronic does it better. I also believe that printed books, magazines and newspapers will survive as vital media for the indefinite future. I believe in a future of print *and* electronic distribution.

I believe many future users will get most of their information without the mediation of librarians. That's true now; how would it be otherwise in the future? I also believe librarians will organize, collect, interpret and mediate for the many cases where professional understanding is needed. I hope that funding will improve for libraries, and particularly for strong support of the true expert systems in libraries: the wetware, the stuff between the ears of good librarians. I believe in a future of librarians as intermediaries *and* direct access.

I believe that libraries will *and must* rely more heavily on access to materials (and non-material information) that they don't own, and that they will find ways to share the risks, costs and benefits of such access. I also believe that most libraries, except for some in specialized areas, will *and must* continue to maintain and build strong collections of print and other media, to serve the essential needs of their users. I hope that librarians won't accept monolithic solutions to access problems; therein lies disaster. I believe in a future of collection development *and* access.

I believe librarians will reach beyond the walls of the library, providing many services electronically and gaining much information in that manner—and, for that matter, continuing to make use of physical delivery systems. I also believe that the library will stand, in the future as in the past, as the heart of every good academic institution and the soul of every city. I believe in the library beyond walls, but not the library without walls. I believe in future libraries as edifice *and* interface.

And, not or: that's what I believe, and what I hope for. It is also, I firmly believe, both the only realistic and the only worthwhile future for libraries and their users.

Technology and the Network: Daimons or Demons?

Project Access: Providing Internet Access to the Smithsonian Institution Research Community

By Amy A. Begg and Martin R. Kalfatovic
Smithsonian Institution

INTRODUCTION

Internet access for library users is quickly becoming a standard service for all types of libraries, from academic, to public, and even special libraries. No single method of providing Internet access to library users is applicable across the range of libraries or even within the larger groups of academic, public, or special. The Smithsonian Institution Libraries (SIL) has been described by Assistant Director Nancy E. Gwinn as being "a foot in three camps," those of museums, research libraries, and special libraries (Gwinn 1989, 210). To address the unusual nature of the Smithsonian and Smithsonian Institution Libraries, a special plan for access to electronic resources and the Internet in particular was devised: Project Access.

THE SMITHSONIAN ENVIRONMENT.

The Smithsonian Institution is a trust instrumentality of the Federal government devoted to public education and research. The world's largest museum complex, the Smithsonian attracts more than 26 million visitors annually and employs over 6,700 staff members working in 13 museums, four research centers, and in field research worldwide.

The Smithsonian Institution Libraries (SIL) is an integral part of the Smithsonian research operations and provides access to information in all forms for Smithsonian researchers and staff. SIL serves the Smithsonian Institution's varied programs with collections of approximately 1,200,000 volumes, including over 15,000 journal titles, 40,000 rare books, and 1,800 manuscript groups, through a system of eighteen branch libraries.

The varied user community of SIL includes: permanent staff members (curators, museum technicians, exhibition designers); post- and pre-doctoral fellows using the Smithsonian's collections for academic research; interns working with either permanent staff members or fellows on research; and volunteers conducting bibliographic or other research for permanent staff. The distributed natures of the Smithsonian Institution and of Smithsonian researchers, however, make traditional library service challenging.

The Networked Environment.

The advent of a networked environment, client-server applications and end-user research tools have provided SIL with the opportunity to maintain and even expand service in a time of constricting finances. To this end, like many research libraries, SIL has worked to find ways to utilize resources available on the Internet to supplement the traditional print and electronic reference materials provided in branch libraries.

At the Smithsonian, as on many campuses, the key element to bringing electronic resources to users was creating the basic data network. In the research and education environment, interconnectivity of students, researchers, data centers, and information centers has resulted in major efforts to bring "fiber to the door," or desktop and dorm room.[1] The Smithsonian began construction of SINET (Smithsonian Institution NETwork) in the 1980s. This Wide Area Network (WAN), which connected the various buildings on the National Mall and in the greater Washington area, was plugged into the Internet via SURANet in 1992. The Smithsonian Internet initiative, the allocation of funds, and the

Institutional drive were directed by the Institution's Office of Information Resource Management (OIRM, now Office of Information Technology, OIT), the Museum Support Center (MSC), and SIL's Director of Libraries, Barbara J. Smith.

Even after SINET had linked most of the buildings on the National Mall, the Institution lacked a central or Campus Wide Information System (CWIS) as recently as 1993. Staff had to rely instead on a variety of systems including two VAX machines, two WANG Office systems, an IBM 4381, and a GEAC 9000 system. The electronic mail system was even more complex with different parts of the Smithsonian using variously IBM PROFS/Office Vision, Wang Office, the VAX MailMan, GEAC Electronic Mail, plus a number of other mail programs such as Eudora.

PROJECT ACCESS

To deal with the current and forthcoming forms of electronic access to information, SIL outlined a plan of action termed Project Access.

History of Project Access.

Under the initiative of Bonita Perry, SIL's Assistant Director, Research Services, Project Access was begun in 1991. The focus of Project Access at that time was primarily the implementation of SIL's planned CD-ROM network and the coordination of emerging electronic resources. In 1992, the position of Information Access Coordinator was created to implement and expand Project Access.

Soon, the offerings of Project Access were expanded to include the following:

- Smithsonian Institution Research Information System (SIRIS);
- CD-ROMs, a varied collection of subject specific CD-ROMs that were mounted in stand-alone units in the appropriate branch libraries;
- BORROW, an electronic mail-based interlibrary loan request system;
- SILIBS-L, a listserv for the internal dissemination of SIL information.

The initial public outreach for Project Access consisted of promotion by branch staff and distribution of a Project Access information sheet by our branch librarians. The transition of SIRIS from a terminal to a PC environment occasioned by the move from the GEAC system to NOTIS (effective in late 1993) allowed Project Access to take an important next step by providing branch libraries with an increased number of multi-functional computers.

Text-Based Project Access.

The move from dumb terminals to a PC-based online public catalog (OPAC) allowed for increased flexibility in information delivery. At the same time, networking of the Institution under the SINET initiative continued, bringing most Smithsonian buildings, but not individual offices or departments, access to the Internet. The Libraries, through Project Access, took this opportunity to provide full Internet access to staff through its branch libraries.

In SIL, DOS was (and is) still the dominant operating platform in the branch libraries. Thus, both DOS and Windows Project Access stations were developed concurrently. For DOS platforms, the Novell local area network that ran the SIL CD-ROM Network (MAGSRV1) was selected to host Project Access. This allowed the SIL LAN, devoted to library staff operations, to remain secure. Project Access PCs attached to the MAGSRV1 LAN and using the Direct Access Network menu system (v.5.1.8), present a menu of the following services:

- SIRIS (including the SIL OPAC)
- Anthropological Literature (CitaDel)
- UnCover (CARL)
- History of Science and Technology (CitaDel)
- FirstSearch (OCLC)
- Library of Congress (LOCIS)
- SIL CD-ROM Network
- Local CD-ROM Databases
- FTP
- Telnet
- Office Vision (one of the Smithsonian's electronic mail systems)
- Staff Functions (Dialog, OCLC, etc.—password protected)

All these services, with the exceptions of CD-ROM products and SIRIS, are accessed via the Internet, using the basic NCSA Internet clients.

Graphical Project Access.

For Windows platforms, PCs were phased in slowly as resources, both economic and staff, could be allocated. Hyper Text Mark-up Language (HTML) was the chosen delivery mechanism and the NCSA Mosaic browser was used.

As a pilot project, graphical Project Access stations were placed in three SIL branches, the National Museum of American History Branch (NMAH), Anthropology Branch, and the Museum Support Center Branch (MSC) in early 1995. These branches were selected for a number of reasons: library staff proficiency with GUI (graphic) interfaces and the Internet, site connectivity, and user traffic and information needs.

The text-based Project Access platform was limited in the number and type of resources that could be easily accommodated. With HTML and a graphical Web browser, however, the full power of the Internet could be used.[2]

In addition to presenting the "basic" services available on the text-based Project Access stations, librarians in the selected branches were to cull subject appropriate resources from the Internet, roughly categorize them, and provide brief annotations. The point was not to "catalog" the Internet, but, using the analogy of traditional collections' development, select and provide access to information resources.

The selection of resources was delegated to the subject specialist branch librarians. To insure a common "look and feel," a standard format or template was created by the Information Access Coordinator (Martin R. Kalfatovic) with the assistance of the SIL Publications Officer (Nancy L. Matthews). In the initial phase of the project, those developing the documents worked under general SIL publishing policies and procedures with the guidance of Smithsonian Institution Libraries' Director Barbara J. Smith. As the creation of branch home pages began to expand from the initial pilot group, as is the case at many libraries,[3] policies and procedures to meet the demands of World Wide Web are being developed.

Electronic Resources from Project Access: Examples from the National Museum of American History Branch

The National Museum of American History Branch serves the staff, interns, post- and pre-doctoral fellows, and research volunteers of the Museum of American History. While outside researchers have access to the collections, the resources available through Project Access are limited for the use of registered library patrons. The most consistent users of Project Access resources are the interns, primarily college students, conducting research under the direction of curatorial staff, and pre- or post-doctoral fellows conducting research.

There are four public access terminals in the NMAH Branch: A Pentium is an example of the Windows (graphical based) Project Access system. This computer runs Windows and offers patrons access to MOSAIC, America Online, SIRIS, and LOCIS (via a Windows based 3270 program), and FirstSearch (using UWTerm, a freeware Telnet software package). The second and third terminals run the DOS based Project Access menu, featuring batch files which link patrons to SIRIS, LOCIS, FirstSearch, CARL UnCover, Office Vision (the Smithsonian's primary e-mail system) and a basic Telnet package. The fourth public terminal, an IBM PS/2, features a direct link to SIRIS.

SIRIS

SIRIS (Smithsonian Institution Research Information Service) includes the Smithsonian Institution Libraries OPAC, with the holdings for all 18 branch libraries; the Archives and Manuscripts Catalog (which includes many archival units of the Smithsonian as well as the Archives of American Art); the Art Inventories Catalog (an extensive database that catalogs American paintings executed before 1914 and American sculpture); and the Research / Bibliographies Catalog (including the Museum Studies Database, the Cephalopod Bibliography, and others to come). SIRIS, a NOTIS system, is fairly simple for patrons to use, following an initial orientation. New patrons receive a cursory overview of search techniques, focusing on the difference between a keyword search, which searches for terms in several fields, and a subject search, which requires use of Library of Congress Subject Headings. The addition of PACLINK (a Z39.50 interface) in January 1996, allows a seamless interface to a number of other OPACs, including the Library of Congress (LOCIS) and the ALADIN (Access to Library and Database Information Network) system of the Washington Research Library Consortium (WRLC). SIRIS's library OPAC is the most heavily used resource in the NMAH Branch. Patrons search SIL's holdings of monographs and serial titles. NOTIS screens are easily read, and patrons are able to determine independently the circulation status and location of an item.

Firstsearch (OCLC).

OCLC's FirstSearch, available via Telnet,[4] is the most frequently used Project Access resource at the NMAH Branch. Most patrons use the periodical indexes, rather than WorldCat (the OCLC Online Union Catalog). It has proved to be a good resource for researchers because of the diverse databases available, including Periodical Abstracts, Newspaper Abstracts, and a few of the psychological indexes. Due to the relatively low total volume of use, Smithsonian Institution Libraries provides access to FirstSearch in the form of FirstSearch cards (with unique authorization codes/passwords), each with ten searches. Cards are distributed by branch librarians or from SIL's Central Reference and Loan Service Branch.

Typically, a patron comes into the library, wanting to conduct a survey of literature on a broad topic, such as "working class communities and culture." It is easy to imagine the wide range of periodicals which might include articles on working class culture! Prior to the inclusion of FirstSearch in the library, a mediated search would be on DIALOG or EPIC. But now, patrons are shown to one of the three terminals offering access to FirstSearch, assigned a search card with an authorization code and password, and provided a basic orientation to the service. The patron can search numerous databases, using search terms of their own choosing, at their convenience, either at their desk or in the library, or at a remote terminal, using Smithsonian's Telnet software, available through the Institution's Office of Information Technology.

Orientation to FirstSearch involves a brief overview of the system. OCLC's instruction sheets on FirstSearch (requested via their home page, http://www.oclc.org) are next to each terminal. These sheets describe each FirstSearch database, including the general content and subject and date coverage of the system.

CitaDel (Research Libraries Group).

The Smithsonian Institution Libraries subscribes to selected Research Library Group's CitaDel collection of databases. These selected databases are: History of Science and Technology and Anthropology Literature. Access to the Avery Architectural Index is planned for mid-1996. Smithsonian researchers connect to CitaDel through Telnet; access to the databases is controlled via an account/password system. Use of the Zephyr Z39.50 interface to CitaDel will be tested sometime in 1996.

Library of Congress Information System (LOCIS).

The Library of Congress's online information system, LOCIS, is also used frequently by NMAH Branch patrons. The Museum's close proximity to the Library of Congress makes it a convenient resource for researchers, who often need resources outside the scope of NMAH Branch's collection. Patrons consult LOCIS prior to going to the Library of Congress, get call numbers for books they want to consult, and arrive at Library of Congress with the numbers in hand. Others use LOCIS to identify a title not in the SIL collection, and request it via interlibrary loan.

Other options for searching Library of Congress's collection off-site include searching FirstSearch's WorldCat (which although it has an easier search engine, means searching catalogs in addition to that of the Library of Congress), or having a librarian search OCLC, removing the patron from the direct search.

Searching LOCIS is a challenge for the most skilled patrons. Printed copies of LOCIS searches are placed next to each terminal, to provide some guidance. Patrons are advised to use only the basic LOCIS commands, B (browse) and F (find). The recent addition of the Z39.50 interface to SIL's own SIRIS system will significantly ease LOCIS searching for SIL patrons.

UnCover (CARL).

Use of the UnCover table of contents database is increasing throughout the Smithsonian, though it has not received much use in the NMAH Branch. Additional training and publicity may increase its use.

AMERICA ONLINE.

An additional service offered to Smithsonian staff in selected branches is access to America Online (AOL). SIL has been provided with a courtesy account by Smithsonian Online (a group of offices and museums that provide information content to the America Online service) for use on-site.

AOL is used for basic reference inquiries, primarily news related events. AOL is an excellent starting point for patrons who are unfamiliar with a Windows environment because of its user friendly screens. AOL requires little training.

This winter, NMAH curators were considering accepting a gift of the cellular phones used at the Dayton conference on Bosnia. NMAH Branch staff assisted a patron search AOL for news stories on the conference, which we printed full text for his review. The other option would have been a DIALOG search, which would have been costly, and would have removed the patron slightly from the search.

WORLD WIDE WEB RESOURCES: NMAH BRANCH HOME PAGE[5]

The World Wide Web is another frequently consulted resource. Patrons have used the WWW for a variety of purposes, including tracking legislation (most notably the status of relevant appropriation bills), reviewing museum exhibitions on the Web, and searching library catalogs.

The WWW starting point for most patrons is the NMAH Branch Home Page. This page features links to WWW resources related to the research done at NMAH. Yale's American Studies Home Page, The Charles Babbage Center Home Page, and the American Civil War: WWW Information Archives are a few of the commonly consulted sites on the NMAH Branch Home Page. In addition, the NMAH Branch Home Page features links to SIL's Project Access resources, including SIRIS, FirstSearch, LOCIS, and CARL UnCover.

On occasion, a reference inquiry has been answered using the WWW. One patron, interested in the history of keyboard development, ran a YAHOO search on the keyword "keyboard" and found several sites dealing with the development of keyboards, for musical instruments, typewriters, and computers. One of the sites featured downloadable images.

TECHNICAL, TRAINING AND PUBLICITY ISSUES

Technical Issues.

The SIL Systems Office maintains over 130 PCs in a variety of settings. Unlike most universities, there is no single, centralized library location. Many SIL branch library locations have only two PCs, and the largest concentrations are of only four or five PCs. Each of the 18 branches has its own particular networking setup (e.g. twisted pair cabling versus fiber optic cabling) which makes each installation different.

The first Project Access GUI stations were installed at the pilot locations in early 1995. The basic PC used in these installations is described in Appendix I.

Initially lacking a Hyper Text Transfer Protocol (HTTP or World Wide Web) server, the Libraries mounted the Project Access HTML pages on the individual PCs, which made synchronizing changes in the individual pages a time consuming task.

Training.

Training issues of both Libraries' staff and users were a primary concern. Most SIL staff had no exposure to GUI interfaces. Thus, an early priority was to give SIL staff instruction in Windows as the PCs were moved to their branches.

With a fairly stable population of library users, instruction for users was primarily done on a one-to-one basis. In some instances, for example in the NMAH Branch which has large influxes of summer interns and research fellows, specific instructional sessions were organized by the branch library staff. Additionally, targeted groups of users, such as Smithsonian Magazine staff and departments within the NMAH were given special instruction sessions.

As with other library users, SIL patrons have a wide range of comfort levels on computer systems. Some patrons are computer literate, and readily adapt to new search engines and services. Other patrons have never used a mouse before and are in need of simple, basic instruction. We resisted requests from the second group of users for specific and numerous help sheets and guides.

Publicity.

To announce the availability of Internet access in SIL, the numerous print and electronic outlets available at the Smithsonian were used. In addition to the Libraries' own listserv, SILIBS-L, an announcement was sent to SICHAT-L, a listserv with a focus on IT issues. Announcements appeared in Smithsonian print publications (primarily in-house) including News to SIL, Information (the Libraries' newsletter with a circulation of 2,500) and The SI Blue Bulletin. Also, branch librarians introduced the stations to staff on a one-on-one basis, conducting impromptu demonstrations of the system when a reference question could be answered using it.

PROVIDING INFORMATION AT SIL

To take full advantage of the Internet, both as an information access point and as an information provider, SIL needed an HTTP-based platform. SIL applied for and received a grant from the Institution's Atherton Seidell Endowment for a pilot project to electronically re-publish selected Smithsonian Institution publications. A portion of the funds from this grant went towards a HTTP server, which serves as the platform for the re-publishing project. The server, a Silicon Graphics Indy Web Force machine with Irix 5.3 Operating System running Netsite Communications Server software, went live on October 25, 1995.

Current offerings on the SIL server include:

Project Access collection of databases and services;
"Science and the Artist's Book," an online version of the SIL exhibition of the same title;
HTML versions of selected SIL publications including the SIL User Guide and users' guides for selected branches.

Nearing completion is an electronic republication of "Hair Pipes in Plains Indian Adornment" by John C. Ewers (in Bureau of American Ethnology Bulletin no.164, 29–85 and plates 13–37, Washington: General Printing Office, 1957), a report in the Smithsonian's Bureau of American Ethnology's (now Anthropology Department) publication series.

Two factors, the implementation of the SIL server and expanded access to the Internet by Smithsonian staff (Charlotte, a text-based Web browser was implemented on the IBM mainframe in April 1995; earlier, in January 1994, VMGopher was mounted on the IBM mainframe), allow not only the presentation of this type of information, but also the expansion of Project Access from a service available only in branch libraries now extended to the desktop of any staff person with Internet access.

EVALUATION

Users of Project Access

Interns and Fellows.

Interns and fellows are the heaviest users of Project Access. They conduct broad searches in SIRIS, LOCIS, and all the indexes available. Most of the hits they receive are printed off and used in bibliographies for proposals, requested via normal circulation procedures, or are later requested via interlibrary loan (assuming the item is not in our collection).

One of Project Access's goals was to create an atmosphere where patrons could directly access databases of interest, without relying on an intermediary searcher. This atmosphere predominates the system, and interns and fellows benefit from it. They each gain search skills from their exhaustive use of the databases. It is hoped that these interns and fellows will be more aware of the vast array of resources potentially available in a library setting and will become more skilled, more knowledgeable library users in the future.

Smithsonian Institution staff.

Smithsonian staff use Project Access primarily for SIRIS and LOCIS. These patrons conduct very few searches of periodical indexes, relying on their own surveying of relevant professional literature to locate articles of interest.

A significant portion of Smithsonian staff have access to some Project Access resources from their desk tops. Many have WWW access, and interact with Project Access via SIL's Home Pages. These patrons provide a reference challenge, because they come to the library with search questions after the fact, and often the details of the search are fuzzy. More and more, library staff are stopping by patrons' offices, and providing reference assistance over their shoulders. In addition, technical and search questions are e-mailed to reference staff, which are answered online—a virtual house call.

Usage Statistics.

Usage statistics for the SIL CD-ROM Network show extensive use of the life science databases (Biological Abstracts, Zoological Record, etc.). The other databases also receive enough use to warrant continued subscription. Because of the relatively small user populations for each title, simultaneous use of any of the databases is negligible. For FirstSearch, OCLC-provided statistics show that WorldCat remains the overall most popular database, with ArticleFirst, Periodical Abstracts, and Readers Guide also being heavily used. Of SIL's two CitaDel databases, Anthropological Literature has received consistent and heavy usage. History of Science and Technology, has, as of yet, not been as heavily used.

Statistics on the SIL Web server show that since December 6, 1995 (when the statistics program began operation) the server had 67,019 hits (through January 31, 1996). "Hits," of course, are a dubious and debatable standard for WWW usage. Of more interest to SIL was the statistic that (for the same period above) there were 5,842 unique hosts visiting the site, and that of these 5,842, over 100 had visited the site more than 50 times. The most popular content page was that listing SIL exhibitions (with 1,904 accesses), followed by the branch listings page (1,611 access). The NMAH Branch Page was the most popular, with 618 accesses.

CONCLUSIONS

More Independent Patrons

Patrons are able to conduct a variety of searches—at their own pace, and frequently at their own desks. Since many of our patrons are subject specialists in their areas, the library staff's ability to help them construct useful successful searches is limited to explaining the technical end of searching.

These independent patrons need more direct assistance than might be initially assumed. In addition to general reference questions, which involve assistance with database selection and keywords for searching selection, questions concerning the technical end of searching often arise. Regrettably, we are at the mercy of the technology this project embraces. Occasionally connections fail to go through, and curious error messages are received. Often, the only answer for a patron who is in this situation is "Come back later" or "Try again in an hour—maybe the remote host is overloaded."

Users Want More Paper Documentation.

Patrons have often asked for paper documentation, explaining key features of each system. We have placed a one page sheet, describing some of the basic procedures for each system, next to the computers, but providing specific, detailed explanations of each system was not feasible because of the rapid changes in many of the systems.

Need for Powerful, High Memory PCs.

WWW resources which include images or utilized new technologies, like JAVA, require substantial memory on the users computer—prior to placing a Pentium in the public area, the WWW access was excruciatingly slow—and resulted in the computer locking up. Patrons often left the terminal without the desired information.

Success.

Overall, Project Access has been a success in delivering the increasing amount of electronic information to our users. As developments in network technology advance and as an even wider variety of information is made available over world-wide networks, Project Access will continue to be the foundation of SIL's service to its users.

ACKNOWLEDGMENTS

We would like to acknowledge the assistance of Nancy L. Matthews in the proofreading of this paper. Also, the work of Anne Gifford (Systems Librarian) for compiling the technical specifications listed in Appendix I.

ENDNOTES

1. For an interesting discussion of campus networking issues, see Robert L. Jacobson, "Study Finds Colleges Are Ignorant of How Their Computers Are Used," The Chronicle of Higher Education 42.19 (January 19, 1996): A22.
2. See Beverly K. Duval and Linda Main, "Building Home Pages," Library Software Review 14.4 (Winter 1995): 218–27.
3. See Nancy McClements and Cheryl Becker, "Writing Web Page Standards," College and Research Library News 57.1 (January 1996): 16–19.
4. FirstSearch is expected to become available through a World Wide Web interface in February 1996.
5. For URLs of sites mentioned below, please consult the Smithsonian Institution Libraries' National Museum of American History Branch Page at: URL: http://www.sil.si.edu/nmahhp.htm.

REFERENCES

Balas, Janet. "The Internet and Reference Services." Computers in Libraries 15.6 (June 1995): 39–41.

Doran, Kirk. "The Internot: Helping Library Patrons Understand What the Internet Is Not (Yet)." Computers in Libraries 15.6 (June 1995): 22–26

Duval, Beverly K., and Linda Main. "Building Home Pages." Library Software Review 14.4 (Winter 1995): 218–27

Gwinn, Nancy E. "Smithsonian Institution Libraries: Afoot in Three Camps." College & Research Libraries (March 1989): 206–14.

Jacobson, Robert L. "Study Finds Colleges Are Ignorant of How Their Computers Are Used." The Chronicle of Higher Education 42.19 (January 19, 1996): A22.

Kalfatovic, Martin R. "Planning Basics for a Library FTP Site: The 'Increase and Diffusion of Knowledge' at Smithsonian Institution Libraries." In The Internet Library: Case Studies of Library Internet Management and Use, ed. Julie Still, 37–44. Westport, CT: Mecklermedia, 1994.

———. "Project Access." Information 76 (Spring/Summer 1994): 1, 5.

McClements, Nancy, and Cheryl Becker. "Writing Web Page Standards." College and Research Libraries News 57.1 (January 1996): 16–19.

McLeod, Jennifer, and Michael White. "Building the Virtual Campus Bit by Bit: World Wide Web Development at the University of Maine." Computers in Libraries 15.10 (November/December 1995): 45–49.

Neff, Paul. "Virtual Librarianship: Expanding Adult Services with the World Wide Web." RQ 35.2 (Winter 1995):160–72.

Tenopir, Carol, and Ralf Neufang. "Electronic Reference Options: Tracking the Changes." Online 19.4 (July-August 1995): 67–73.

Tenopir, Carol. "Integrating Electronic Reference." Library Journal 120.6 (April 1, 1995): 39–40.

———. "Internet Issues in Reference." Library Journal 120.16 (October 1, 1995): 28–30.

APPENDIX I:

Technical Specifications For WWW Stations

DOS/Windows based workstation accessing the World Wide Web

Hardware:
- 90 MHZ Pentium Personal Computer
- 16 MB Random Access Memory (RAM)
- 420 MB Hard drive
- 15 inch .28 Non-interlaced 1280 X 1024 Monitor
- Video Card with 1 MB of Memory
- Dual Speed CD-ROM (not necessary for Web access)
- 1.2 MB and 1.44 MB Floppy Disk Drives
- 16 Bit Sound Card with Speakers
- Mouse
- Windows 3.11 and DOS
- A network interface card installed in the PC and configured to support the TCP/IP protocol. An IP (Internet Protocol) address assigned to the workstation.

Communications:
- A communications infrastructure that supports access to the Internet (in the case of the Smithsonian Institution, this "backbone" is termed SINET—The Smithsonian Institution Network) through a Novell LAN configured to support the TCP/IP protocol.

Software:
- TCP/IP networking software for Windows (available commercially or as shareware).
- Windows based Internet service clients such as FTP (File Transfer Protocol), Telnet and TN3270 (available commercially or shareware). NOTE: These first two are often combined in a commercial package.
- WWW client software. A number of these are available commercially, or as free- or shareware. Among the more well-known are NCSA Mosaic and Netscape.
- Software referred to as viewers for various types of file formats (MIME type) that exist on the WWW. For example, MPEG video viewers, JPEG image viewers, audio wave format "viewers." Many of these viewers are available as shareware. This viewer software enables the PC to display the particular file type for which it is designed. For example Mpegplay (shareware) enables the PC to display MPEG type video.

APPENDIX II:

Smithsonian Institution Information Servers

Smithsonian Institution Web Site (The Electronic Smithsonian)
URL: http://www.si.edu

The Electronic Smithsonian provides access to a wide range of information for visitors and researchers about the Smithsonian and Smithsonian programs. The Electronic Smithsonian provides a gateway for those museums and research centers that maintain their own information servers (see below) as well as a platform.

Smithsonian Institution Research Information System (SIRIS)
URL: Telnet//siris.si.edu

SIRIS is the platform for SIL's OPAC as well as the online catalog for several archival collections of the Institution (including the Smithsonian Institution Archives, Archives of American Art, National Anthropological Archives, and others), the Inventories of American Painting and Sculpture (a program of the Smithsonian's National Museum of American Art), and the Research Bibliographies database (currently includes the Cephalopods Bibliography and the Museum Studies Database).

Smithsonian Institution Libraries
URL: http://www.sil.si.edu

See text for a discussion of the SIL web site.

Museum Support Center Web Site
URL: http://www.simsc.si.edu

The Museum Support Center, located in Suitland, Maryland, is a specialized research, conservation, and collections storage facility. It is dedicated to the mission of providing the optimum environment for both the preservation and the study of Smithsonian collections. The Museum Support Center's Home Page provides information about the work done at MSC, links to other conservation and preservation resources on the web, and a virtual tour of the facility.

National Museum of American Art Web Site
URL: http://www.nmaa.si.edu

The National Museum of American Art's Home Page allows guests to view over 500 pieces of art, and reports upcoming events. In addition, virtual tours of the permanent collection, and recent exhibitions are featured, as is a visit to the Director's office, and online interactions with museum staff and featured artists.

National Museum of American Art Gopher
URL: gopher://nmaa-ryder.si.edu

NMAA-Ryder is the Internet server maintained by the National Museum of American Art, Smithsonian Institution, to provide public access to text-based museum research and educational materials.

National Museum of Natural History Web Site
URL: http://www.nmnh.si.edu

The Smithsonian Institution's Natural History Web offers information about Museum research and the national collections, which comprise more than 120 million scientific specimens and cultural artifacts. Information about upcoming events and exhibitions is also provided at this Web site.

National Museum of Natural History Gopher
URL: gopher://nmnhgoph.si.edu

The Smithsonian Institution's Natural History Gopher contains information and resources compiled by Natural History staff, including newsletters, project documents, and pointers to other information of interest to researchers in natural history.

Office of Printing and Photographic Services FTP Site
URL: ftp://photo1.si.edu

The Smithsonian Institution's Office of Printing and Photographic Services runs an FTP (File Transfer Protocol) site. Images files are available in DOS or Macintosh formats for transfer. These images can be used for educational purposes only; any commercial reproduction must be cleared through the Office of Printing and Photographic Services.

Office of Printing and Photographic Services Web Site
URL: http://photo2.si.edu

The Smithsonian Institution's Office of Printing and Photographic Services makes countless images available via their World Wide Web site. Guests can download pictures of recent events in DC, including the Million Man March, and Clinton's Inaugural. Images of exhibits in the Smithsonian collections are also available for downloading. These images can be used for educational purposes only; any commercial reproduction must be cleared through the Office of Printing and Photographic Services.

National Museum of Air and Space Web Site
URL: http://www.nasm.edu

The Smithsonian Institution's National Air and Space Museum's Web Site includes virtual tours of the Museum's exhibition galleries, a calendar of events for the Museum, information about Museum departments and resources, and links to other aeronautical resources on the Web.

Center for Earth and Planetary Studies Web Site
URL: http://ceps.nasm.edu:2020

The Center for Earth and Planetary Studies is one of the scientific research departments of the Smithsonian Institution's National Air and Space Museum. The Center plays a role in research related to planetary and terrestrial geology using remote sensing data from Earth-orbiting satellites and manned and unmanned space missions. The Web site includes Space Shuttle Photographs and imagery of the planets.

Office of Elementary and Secondary Education Web Site
URL: http://educate.si.edu

The Office of Elementary and Secondary Education serves teachers and students across the country—as well as others interested in museum-related education. The office's programs, publications, and online networks inform teachers about Smithsonian educational resources and provide instructional approaches in art, language arts, science, and social studies.

From Leaves to Bytes: The Harvard Digital Finding Aids Project

By Kim Brookes, Jean Boise Cargill, Mary F. Daniels, Michael Fitzgerald,
Leslie A. Morris, David De Lorenzo, Mackenzie Smith, and Susan Von Salis
Harvard University and Radcliffe College

Librarians have labored to automate their catalogs because they have realized the benefits to themselves and their patrons of making their records more readily available. No longer is access to bibliographic information bound to a physical card catalog. Both librarians and researchers can, increasingly, directly access this information from anywhere, whether within the library building itself or from a computer on the other side of the globe.

Harvard, with the largest university library in the world, will maximize these benefits when it completes its retrospective conversion project for roman alphabet monograph and serial cataloging records, creating an electronic database of some eight million records in its on-line catalog, HOLLIS. This is an impressive figure. However, it is misleading to think that this immense database represents all, or even most, of the research materials available within the Harvard system. "Non-book" collections at Harvard—archives, manuscripts, photographs, drawings, and more—number in the hundreds of millions of items. How can Harvard make the descriptive information for these important and unique research collections more widely available as well?

To begin to answer this question, the Harvard University Library Automation Planning Committee appointed a Special Collections Task Force in the spring of 1994, charged to discuss the automation needs of repositories that acquire, preserve, and make accessible such material, and to examine the descriptive practices for Harvard's special collections, as distinguished from unitary items such as books and serials. The report of that Task Force, issued in November 1994, covered many issues, but focused on significant differences between electronic bibliographic records describing single items such as monographs, and those that describe collections. It pointed out that the records for collections now in on-line library catalogs, that is, "collection-level" records, are derived from and only briefly summarize detailed listings that more comprehensively describe, control, and provide access to the collection. These listings are often referred to as "finding aids" because they help locate items or small groups of items within larger collections; they may also be called container listings or inventories.

FINDING AIDS: KEYS TO THE COLLECTIONS

The importance of creating a finding aid for a collection becomes clearer if we consider the physical nature of archival collections. These collections are often quite large (sometimes hundreds of boxes), generally consisting of loose sheets of paper that are exposed to repeated handling. It is understandably difficult for a researcher looking for material from a particular year or a particular correspondent to rummage through the collection box by box. Accordingly, the archivist creates information-rich descriptions of collections to let scholars know what materials are available, how they are arranged, and what information they contain. This descriptive finding aid helps researchers locate the box and the folder likely to contain the information they seek. Finding aids are the keys to intellectual control over these valuable and unique research materials.

Finding aids are not a new invention. Today, repositories use finding aids created over generations on handwritten cards, in ledger volumes, and as typewritten leaves stored in three-ring binders. These are unique documents (except for occasional photocopies), produced locally, and varying in length from a single sheet to hundreds of pages. Composed on paper sheets, these documents are usually difficult to edit and to update to reflect new research and acquisitions. And generally, funding has been scarce to publish and distribute finding aids by traditional means.

While in the last ten years archivists and curators have been able to create electronic collection-level descriptions in on-line catalogs using the USMARC Archives and Manuscript Control format, these descriptions cannot replace finding aids in providing access to archival collections. These records can point researchers to specific collections by providing selected name and subject headings but such records are only brief summaries, reflecting the content of hundreds of pages on only a few screens of video display. It is in the finding aid that repositories provide the most detailed information about what they have, and it is this detailed information that is of most interest to researchers. Because the collection's finding aid is equal in importance to the collection-level bibliographic record, the Special Collections Task Force felt strongly that the information in finding aids must be as readily available to scholars in electronic form as is the collection-level record.

For many years, archivists and curators have been searching for an appropriate computer-based environment where these detailed descriptions can reside. While most repositories have been using computers to create finding aids in electronic form in the last two decades, electronic access has been rudimentary. A survey of computer usage in Harvard's archive and manuscript repositories in 1993 showed that more than half used a local word-processing or database system to automate archival functions. But as the large majority of repositories reported no public access to their computer systems, it is evident that these were designed primarily with in-house technical operations, not direct access, in mind.

The Harvard University archive and manuscript community concurred that the wealth of information provided in their collection finding aids should be available in electronic form and searchable in a common database. We did not want researchers to be compelled to contact each of the forty-nine repositories at Harvard individually. With no common software standard in use (and no desire to mandate one), the only way to combine all this information into a Harvard-wide electronic database was to convert the data to plain text (ASCII), the "lowest common denominator," and mount it on a gopher server. The Archives and Manuscripts at Harvard and Radcliffe Gopher was established, but it soon became obvious that such unstructured text offered only clumsy and frustrating searching, particularly with large files.

The Special Collections Task Force further came to realize that in order to make all finding aids at Harvard accessible as if in a single database, a common structure was necessary, and it found such a structure in Standard Generalized Markup Language (SGML). The Task Force concluded that SGML would be a powerful but flexible tool that would address the varying needs of the large community of archivists for production and output of finding aids; make the electronic files available remotely; and meet the growing expectations of our research clientele. SGML offered the ideal, indeed the only, way to turn typewritten leaves into electronic bytes.

SGML: KEY TO THE FUTURE

What is SGML? In the Guidelines for Electronic Text Encoding and Interchange, SGML is defined as "an international standard for the definition of device-independent, system-independent methods of representing texts in electronic form." That is, one could add SGML coding with any kind of editor on any kind of computer. Further, it is "a set of markup conventions used together for encoding texts." (Sperberg-McQueen and Burnard 1994, 1:13) What is markup? Traditionally a copy editor would add to an author's text instructions for the typesetter and others responsible for producing the printed copy. Those instructions are called markup. Using a word-processing program, an author now routinely adds markup to the electronic text with a mouse or keyboard. "A markup language [like SGML] must specify what markup is allowed, what markup is required, [and] how markup is to be distinguished from text. . . ." (ibid.) An SGML-conformant document specifies the markup language in its SGML declaration and its Document Type Definition (DTD). The DTD may include elements that describe or distinguish, for example, personal and corporate names, titles, or quotations as well as structural units like paragraphs, chapters, and lists.

As Eric van Herwijnen explains in Practical SGML, "[a]n SGML document by itself only has structure (in addition to its contents), since it was dissociated from any machine or process-specific information. Once an SGML document has been verified by a parser, it has to be processed. The structure has to be translated into, for example, word processor-, formatter- or database loader-commands. The processing of SGML documents is not under the control of the SGML standard." (van Herwijnen 1994, p. 29).

Among the primary benefits to the scholarly community of using SGML to encode finding aids is the capacity to enhance access to this wealth of information as well as make it available from a remote location. The detailed indexing enabled by SGML allows researchers to develop more sophisticated and immensely more useful searches both within and between collections. For example, it is useful to know (as one can now learn from HOLLIS) that there are World War II materials in 630 collections in 12 Harvard repositories in subject libraries as diverse as law, theology, botany, theater, medicine, and business. A database of SGML-marked-up finding aids, however, will go further to tell the researcher the precise location, quantity and provenance of World War II material within each collection, whether it is the original plans for the courtroom in Nuremburg held by the Design School Library, or the transcripts of the Nuremburg trials in the Law School Library, the photographs depicting women's work with European refugees in the Schlesinger Library, or the war propaganda speeches written for Franklin Roosevelt in Houghton. All this can be done with greater thoroughness and without the demands of corresponding with staff at every different Harvard repository.

Further, scholars often want to look at everything available by and about the particular author or subject area they are studying, and the only way this information can be found is through the finding aids. For example, there are three T. S. Eliot collections at Houghton, but there are also letters by him in the E. E. Cummings Papers, the James Family Papers, the Rothenstein Papers, and more. Because these may be only one or two letters in a particular collection, however, Eliot is not an added entry in the HOLLIS records, but he is listed in the finding aids. A scholar who has traveled across the continent to investigate resources for a book on Eliot wants to know about every single letter in a Houghton collection and wants to see it.

SGML also offers opportunities for improvements over the current paper-based presentation of finding aids. Navigating a lengthy paper finding aid can be baffling even for the most experienced researcher. Materials can nest deeply within a hierarchical arrangement with the headings that clarify the hierarchy spread over many pages. Taking advantage of the structure of SGML, visual displays of such hierarchies can be rendered more understandable, for example, by displaying headings in outline form in a window to the side of the text, the outline changing as one scrolls through the different sections and subsections of the hierarchy. When looking at a folder description within a collection it is crucial that one understand the specific heading under which the folder is described; it is often difficult to provide this kind of information in a paper format, especially for lengthy series and other groupings.

Another problem currently posed by lengthy finding aids is the time it takes to find pertinent information. Because SGML is able to define context and meaning as precisely as one wants, researchers can perform more complex and exact searches. For example, scanning inventories that are hundreds of pages long looking for containers in different collections that hold materials relating to Amelia Earhart is an annoyingly cumbersome and time-consuming task for a researcher. Provenance usually directs the location of items within a repository, so that documents by or about Amelia Earhart will not necessarily be put together in one place. However, navigating through the SGML-marked-up finding aids for "Amelia Earhart" (personal name as a subject) and "job application" (form and genre), cuts an hours-long task to under a minute. This type of search refinement is particularly important in an era where the number of hits using broad subject headings has become unwieldy (see Tibbo 1994).

Finding aids marked up in SGML and made available via Internet provide detailed information directly to researchers. Not only will scholars from Cambridge to Karachi be happier and their research improved, but local library staff will be freed of the repetitive, time-consuming tasks needed to get this information to researchers. Use of SGML markup will allow better access to our collections, and also allow archivists unprecedented levels of administrative control over our collections. It will make it possible for archivists to create an environment in which specifics about the number of collections processed in a given period, the number of individual collections, the size of various parts of our holdings (by collection, genre, container size, etc.), the level of control we have over our collections, documentation on who performed the various kinds of work on individual collections, etc., will be readily and quickly available.

TURNING THE LEAVES

The immediate impetus for the Harvard archival community to apply SGML to its finding aids came from the University of California, Berkeley, where an SGML Document Type Definition (DTD) for finding aids was developed. The Berkeley DTD, now known as the Encoded Archival Description (EAD), specifies SGML markup to be used in encoding finding aids and has been eagerly embraced by leaders within the archival community as finally providing a standard flexible enough to accommodate its diverse needs while identifying its commonalities. Further, the Berkeley Finding Aid Project, after its initial development phase, is working with the entire professional community, developing standards through the Society of American Archivists. People advocating the use of SGML for finding aids recognize that success is more likely when efforts are coordinated and based on standards. This approach gives high priority to ease of interchange with and portability to other database systems and has as its long-term goal the creation of an international union database of finding aids. SGML, as a standard independent of software and hardware, assures that continual reformatting and rekeying of data to fit into changing local systems will be unnecessary.

This independence from devices and systems was particularly appealing to us at Harvard, given that forty-nine independent repositories each had to be accommodated. Further, the EAD allows each repository to decide how detailed the markup of its finding aids should be. A curator could use either the full range of tags or minimal markup, and yet still make all finding aids available within the shared database.

To experiment with the EAD, the Automation Planning Committee established the Digital Finding Aids Project (DFAP) in February 1995. The DFAP's first task was to review available options for the production of SGML-encoded texts. The choices ranged from free, simple SGML tools that work with existing document editors to expensive SGML-based publishing systems, and accordingly, costs ranged from zero to thousands of dollars. The Project tried to recommend software that could be used by all repositories, regardless of hardware platform, so that Harvard archivists could develop and share a common experience and knowledge. The software also had to be affordable, since many repositories are single-person operations with minimal financial support. Also, software capability to import existing ASCII and word-processed files was a factor. DFAP concluded that in most cases an off-the-shelf "SGML-aware" word processor would be both economical and effective.

The second step was to decide on a way to "publish," that is, make available to everyone, the SGML-encoded finding aids on-line. Concurrently, the Search Engine Evaluation Committee, also appointed by the Automation Planning Committee, investigated available SGML-aware publishing/searching software, and recommended that the University Library's Office for Information Systems acquire OCLC's SiteSearch, which supports the inclusion of SGML documents in a database, allows for sophisticated Z39.50–based searching of them, and renders the search results as World Wide Web documents that can be viewed by any Web browser (such as Mosaic or Netscape). Using the World Wide Web as the DFAP's publishing medium will allow a wide range of users to access these documents, any accompanying images, and any appropriate links to other documents available on the Web. DFAP is also working with the Office for Information Systems to design the user interface for the finding aids database, and to select the appropriate indexes to access them usefully. Because the finding aids are in SGML, Harvard can easily switch to another publishing medium (including paper, because SGML also allows flexible formatting of printed documents) in the future if that seems to be better for our researchers.

The third step was to mark up some Harvard finding aids using SGML. This work continues, and the task of converting all existing handwritten and typed finding aids will be faced as well. Finally, and most importantly, the Digital Finding Aids Project will be the first step towards establishing a strong administrative structure for the creation and technical support of SGML-encoded archives and manuscripts finding aids at Harvard. The Harvard DFAP is not the result of a single, technically-inclined person working in an isolated unit. Rather it is a collaborative effort drawing upon the expertise of curators, archivists, catalogers, electronic text specialists, and systems librarians, and engaging participants from across the decentralized complex of faculties, colleges and institutions known as Harvard University. The Project is designed for the long term as it integrates the efforts of archivists with those of books and serials catalogers, reference, and collection development staff at all levels, whose common goal is to make the materials we are charged to preserve available to all.

Looking to the future, the Project plans to take advantage of emerging standards such as HyTime, a hypermedia extension of SGML, to link digital finding aids to corresponding collection-level records in the University's on-line catalog. Eventually, the catalog can provide links to the finding aids using the new MARC 856 field for Electronic Location and Access. And standards like HyTime will make it possible to link images of the manuscripts from the collection, to, say, related photographs and artwork, as well as to the finding aids which document them. Overall, SGML promises future flexibility as such standards are adopted by the scholarly community and the computer systems that support us.

The Digital Finding Aids Project is developing the personnel and computer resources to transform our paper leaves to electronic bytes, providing a superior tool for managing our collections and making them available to the international community of scholars. The vitality of our project begins with, but does not depend solely on, local initiatives. We recognize the importance of working in concert with colleagues in sister repositories around the world to guarantee the overall success of this project to improve and facilitate access to Harvard's wealth of archival materials.

REFERENCES

van Herwijnen, Eric. 1994. Practical SGML. 2d ed. Boston: Kluwer, 1994.

Sperberg-McQueen, C. M. and Lou Burnard, eds. Guidelines for Electronic Text Encoding and Interchange. 2 vols. Chicago and Oxford: TEI P3, Text Encoding Initiative, 1994.

Tibbo, Helen R. The Epic Struggle: Subject Retrieval from Large Bibliographic Databases. American Archivist 57 (Spring 1994): 310–326.

Digital Library = Holistic Library: Collection Decisionmaking in the Electronic Environment

By James Campbell
University of Virginia

Libraries today are confronted by a dual challenge: serving their customers' continuing need for traditional media while also meeting new types of information needs; and reshaping staff to continue providing quality services in a constantly changing information environment. Meeting the challenge will require a new support structure for users and staff and a new concept of the division of library work. Since each library will make basic decisions in a local context, this paper focuses on identifying questions and a range of answers rather than seeking a "one size fits all" solution.

THE SELECTION ENVIRONMENT

For paper materials we have a relatively stable process for acquiring and organizing new titles, disseminating information about them, and circulating them to users. Cataloging utilities, approval plans, and shelf preparation programs have changed where things are done but have not substantially changed the process. For special formats such as audiovisual materials, libraries have devised routines that may differ from those followed for print materials but are analogous and relatively stable. Users too are supported by a familiar system that shelves books and journals in an established sequence and has policies and procedures for access to them. Selectors then assume an environment that will support their decisions and make materials available to users. Decisions are based on need and available funds, and different formats are seen as complementary, not competitive. The decision to buy the video of *Sense and Sensibility* is made independently of the decision about a new critical edition on paper.

For most digital materials there is no such stable environment for selector or user. Instead of buying a book at a list price though a vendor, putting it on a shelf and waiting for someone to take it out, the selector may have to negotiate a price and a license with the publisher, predicting how many people are likely to want to use this item at any one time. Even the most common digital medium in libraries, the CD-ROM, requires for each acquisition a cost and feasibility decision about networking (which may require a knowledge not just of the library's facilities), a knowledge of supported platforms, and, for networked items, of user preferences for platform. Not only is each decision a complex decision, but commercial factors, data formats, delivery systems, and user acceptance change constantly. While we strive to mainstream the selection of electronic information[1], we're handicapped by the truth of Heraclitus' dictum that you can't step into the same stream twice.

Eventually mainstreaming will happen. Until then libraries must strive to educate their selectors about the technical, commercial, and social issues, but they must also begin to create the support environment that exists for decision making about other types of information. What is needed at this stage is not policy that specifies always buying CD-ROMs for the chemistry department, a mix of paper and Internet databases for English, and so on. These things will change hourly and too much specificity can inhibit response to changing customer perceptions and new trends in digital publishing. Instead, support should focus on the decisions above and below that level and on help with individual decisions by providing:

1. Broad policies based on emerging standards to help selectors choose among available options.
2. Specific procedures, frequently revised, for handling orders and received materials to reduce the frustration encountered whenever we deal with non-standard situations.
3. A personal support infrastructure that identifies experts to be called on when questions arise.
4. Continuing education of selectors in the library's digital information environment and encouragement that they become aware of digital opportunities in their areas and of attitudes and facilities in the departments they serve.

STANDARDS FOR USER INTERFACES AND FOR LONGEVITY

Probably only those librarians who deal with binding contracts think much about standards in connection with the currently dominant information format, yet we take for granted that information will be on paper between covers and will usually fall within a certain size range, that there will be standard-sized shelves and trained shelvers ready to receive it, and that rebinding or reformatting will be available if the physical medium deteriorates from wear or age.

Standards for digital information are a key element in establishing the support infrastructure that enables collection decisions. Standardizing on a small number of information delivery systems allows users to focus on information rather than on how to get it and reduces library investment in staff and equipment required to set up new databases and educate readers about them. Implementation can be a special problem with Internet databases, each with a different method of user authentication and different access requirements, and those problems may be compounded by a consortial environment. Fortunately some standards are beginning to have an effect. Newer OPACs provide Z39.50 connectivity to bibliographic databases and links to URLs and the World Wide Web. The Web in turn allows multiple platform access, handles database queries through at least superficially familiar forms, and serves as a front end for various types of text and image viewers.

Standardization is important not only for interfaces but also for data format. It is impossible to predict what data formats will be in use in ten or twenty years, much less in one hundred, but one can choose current standard formats that will likely be convertible into future standard formats. In text databases this suggests use of Standard Generalized Markup Language (SGML) or its subset, HTML, the basis for the Web. Other formats can be converted into SGML, but usually tagging in the text will have been limited to the possibilities of that format, while SGML offers enough flexibility to be adapted to the needs of the particular text. Data stored in a standard form may be displayed in that form, as when SGML is viewed with Panorama, or in some other format, as when SGML tagged text is converted to HTML or images archived in the TIFF format are made available for active use in the compressed GIF or JPEG formats.

Decisions about storage media have less importance for collection decisions. No electronic medium is truly permanent, so any format may be chosen, as long as provision is made for backup copies, preferably stored at a different site, and for refreshing the data regularly. Format choice can lengthen the period before refreshing is necessary (e.g., CD-ROMs have a longer life than tape), but if a longer period elapses it may be difficult to find machines that can read the older data. What selectors do need to understand is that data can be converted from one physical format to another. Data purchased on one medium may not seem to fit the library's delivery systems, but, if the license allows, data shipped in one format can be provided to users in another, as when it is loaded from a CD-ROM onto a hard disk, or it can be recopied to a more permanent medium, as when data on a diskette is moved to a hard disk or written to a CD-ROM. Economic factors can also affect data life. If a database is provided from a remote server, the library can decide to ignore the possibility that the company may go out of business (for basic bibliographic data, it's likely that some other provider will be available), or the selector can try to negotiate some provision to transfer the data if necessary.

POLICIES IN THE TRANSITIONAL LIBRARY

The first step in adding a digital title is still the assessment of customer need, but then factors unique to each title and local situation come into play: licenses that place limits on use; technical issues, such as data format, status of networks in the library and around the university, available hardware and software, and the ability to provide reliable connectivity to remote sources; access issues, including catalog records and links from Web pages or directly from the OPAC; public service issues involving data interfaces and user instruction for new and complex search systems. Further, since the digital information may be equivalent to a paper document, the selector must decide whether to acquire it instead of or in addition to the paper version, a decision based on the added features (e.g., ability to search) or deficiencies (e.g., current limits on display of color images) of the digital version, but also on the readiness, both in attitude and in equipment, of users to deal with the digital format. In such an environment, collection development policies[2] and detailed procedures are of limited use, and the need for constant revision could become a hindrance to actually acquiring and making available information.

If mainstreaming decision-making about electronic information is a desirable mid-term goal, it can be dangerous in the short term. Far too many of our decisions have been made by analogy with print information. The CD-ROM of a bibliography is purchased because the library already had the print version. The bound volumes sat on a shelf in the reference room, so the CD sits on a shelf next to the computer or on its jukebox. It may be that this is a conscious decision, based on finances or a reasonable suspicion about investing in CD-ROM technology, but it's easy to drift into a decision without making a policy determination. The increased availability of information over the Internet, often the same information that we had in print and then on CD-ROM, is forcing more systematic consideration of the digital library, where information is delivered directly to the user's desktop and may come from anywhere in the world. The ubiquity of the Web means that our users are moving toward the digital library whether we like it or not, so that, while a very few libraries are still ignoring this phenomenon, most have accepted it to at least some degree.

The first decision a library makes is whether to adopt a relatively passive or a relatively active approach to digital information. The passive approach takes prepackaged information, usually on CD-ROM or from remote servers via the Internet, and makes it available to users in the library, often with some effort to publicize and interpret it to users. Usually this information is bibliographic or encyclopedic in nature, and access is through reference interview or some sort of electronic menu rather than through the OPAC. The most active approach is an aggressive effort to acquire and digitize information of all kinds, organize it, and get it out to the user's desktop. Either approach or anything in between can be a valid decision for a particular situation. If there's no wiring in the English department's building, providing networked access to the *MLA Bibliography* or the *English Poetry Database* can probably wait until another year, while purchasing access to the prepackaged ARTFL database is currently the most useful way to extend digital service to a French department.

If a more active approach is taken, the next decision is how much of a local infrastructure to create. This may require a significant investment in servers and programming, as is true at the University of Virginia and some other libraries that have undertaken to provide SGML-encoded text over university networks, or it may mean simply buying CD-ROM networking software. Infrastructure also includes access to data, such as building Web pages to lead users to data or cataloging electronic resources with hot links from the OPAC.

Once basic decisions about support of electronic acquisitions are made and communicated to both staff and users, other decisions begin to fall into place. Acquisitions that fit the structure (or like ARTFL do not require a local structure) receive a higher priority, and it's possible to draw up a decision tree to help selectors through the process. Of course, there will always be a need for items that don't fit the system. Sometimes vendors will negotiate and allow a library to adapt the data, but more often the vendor's mind or the technical problems can't be changed, the user need has to be met, and the data is taken as is.

The specific structure will change over time. At Virginia, we've been using a Web page to provide links to electronic journals. With a new OPAC, we'll be able to link from the catalog record, and with the coming of 1500 full-text journals from IAC through a recent acquisition by the VIVA consortium, it seems likely that we will give up adding titles to the Web page and move to the OPAC for all our access to e-journals. But even if we change the method, the basic decision to provide easy access to electronic journals remains.

PROCEDURES IN THE TRANSITIONAL LIBRARY

Decisions about electronic information are more complex and take more time than selecting a new book, but interviewing people, gathering information, and making decisions is the normal work of a selector. In all our work, those things that we do regularly we know how to do. Those things that we do occasionally can become time-consuming and frustrating when we are unsure of procedures. In the traditional environment an order follows a standard format, but new types of information require new types of information for ordering. Where does a URL go? What is the location for networked information? These are small matters, but when so many decisions must be made for each acquisition, clearly stated processes, preferably with print or electronic forms setting out the information required can do much to relieve frustration and make subject librarians active participants in building the digital library.

Order information is an example of adapting existing procedures to the new situation, but digital decisions may also require new types of documentation. A decision between paper and microform is a complex decision, but the tradeoffs are well known and knowledge of them has probably been internalized by the experienced selector, so that decisions are made with little conscious weighing of alternatives. In the transitional library, the tradeoffs among various forms of digital information will not be so clearly understood and it may be helpful to make a decision tree, ranking choices according to characteristics such as ease of implementation by library and by user and number of users that the delivery system can reach. This does not relieve the selector of the burden of ensuring that information can be used by a particular user community or of making a cost benefit decision about additional charges for particular formats or adding users, but it gives a framework for decision-making and reminds the selector of the options.

A MATRIX OF PEOPLE

Having clear procedures makes a difference, but inevitably issues arise that haven't been thought of or that require additional input. Can we network this Mac disk? Will the telnet program on our workstations support printing from this database? How many simultaneous users do we typically have for this sort of database? Has that building been wired yet? It's crucial to identify people who can provide answers to these types of questions. In a large organization, it's also crucial to have people nearby when questions arise and to ensure that questions are asked at the right level, that someone fields the simple ones and refers the tough ones so that staff time is well used. Issues that might be considered in compiling such a resource directory include negotiating contracts and the university's contract review process, copyright and license enforcement questions, networking, reformatting data, and user interfaces and training.

For subject areas where digital information is particularly important, either on an ongoing basis or for a special project, and for large decisions, such as a full-text journal database, it may be useful to form a specific team, whose work should not end with the decision to acquire. At Virginia we have set up electronic centers for major data types. Their coordinators work closely with faculty and students to make digital information available and collaborate with selectors to identify new needs and new materials. User-educators participate in the design and delivery of instructional programs on new materials. When we acquired a CD-ROM with a 120–page manual, we put a technical and a subject specialist together to prepare a 3–page digest which became the basis for a class.

BEYOND THE LIBRARY

Training in the new library environment must be a key element in any support structure, but any training program should also take note of the changes in distribution of information, both in the commercial sector and in the broad range of non-commercial information distributed over the Internet. The latter presents few technical difficulties, since it is usually available through the Web, but it does present problems of assessment. In areas such as government information and news of all kinds, the Web already has great importance; in most other areas the proportion of useless and even misleading information is still quite high. The selector does not have the traditional authorities to help with decisions and must be supported in developing new criteria. Experience with the print media is certainly transferable, but it's not enough to recognize a bad Web site. The selector must also be helped to understand that the speed, ease, and availability of Web information have created new types of information needs. Classes and, in some cases, pairing a selector with a more experienced Web user can bring this about.

Selectors must also develop new relationships with their customers. As has been noted, it does little good to network information if the department for which it is intended has no network access. It does little good to buy the Mac version of *Perseus* if the classics faculty all use IBM clones or to provide telnet access to the *MLA Bibliography* if the telnet program the English Department uses can't connect to that type of address. Librarians have to get out of the library and go learn the work environment of faculty and students if they are to make good choices about resources. They also have to learn the mental environment, the willingness to use digital information. In both cases the librarian should be not only a learner but also a potential agent of change. At Virginia the library's liaisons to English got the department to use a different telnet program, and people who hadn't cared if there was any difference between a modem and IBM now routinely use bibliographic and other databases from office and home.

THE HOLISTIC LIBRARIAN

Assembling the digital collection in the transitional library requires a holistic approach, considering not only user need for information, but presentation, bibliographical and physical access, the user's willingness or ability to take advantage of the format, and what instruction or helps may be needed to make effective use of the item possible. That there are no problems, only opportunities, is a canard, as anyone who has had to deal with CD-ROM networks or Windows telnet programs can testify, but the process of rethinking how we make all these decisions comes at the same time as libraries are confronting shrinking budgets and major changes in higher education and research. Developing a holistic approach to digital information can be the focus for an effort to reengineer and reshape routines and structure into an interdependent, customer-oriented system.

ENDNOTES

1. For a recent example, see Samuel Demas, Peter McDonald and Gregory Lawrence, "The Internet and Collection Development: Mainstreaming Selection of Internet Resources," *Library Resources and Technical Services* 39, no. 3 (1995): 275–287.
2. Dan. C. Hazen, "Collection Development Policies in the Information Age," *College and Research Libraries* 56 (January 1995), 29–31 is good on the limitations of collection development policies.

Technology and the Network: Redesigning an Academic Library Reference Department

By Ronald Fark, Anne Cerstvik Nolan, and Tovah Reis
Brown University Library

BACKGROUND:

The John D. Rockefeller Jr. Library at Brown University houses the main collections in the social sciences and humanities. During Summer 1994, the reference area of the Rockefeller Library underwent a dramatic transformation. There had been a desire to renovate the area for several years, because the layout of the room had presented a number of problems and challenges. For example, the card catalog, which had not been updated since Josiah, our OPAC, was brought up in 1988, occupied prime real estate in the center of the principal service area, forming a barrier that effectively pushed the Reference desk into the background. The limited number of electrical and networked outlets dictated the location of computer workstations, which resulted in their being hidden from view. Fortunately, through the generous support of the Champlain Foundation, a $150,000 grant was made available to the Library to accomplish an extensive renovation of the area. The Champlain Foundation is located in Rhode Island and its primary recipients are Rhode Island institutions of higher education and libraries. It also provides support for cultural, scientific and technological activities. The grant covered 75% of the cost of the project.

An Electronic Reference Desk Task Force (ERDTF) was formed in January of 1994 to begin planning a service point for the next century with a new Reference and Information Center as its hub. The Task Force members from the Library included the Assistant Head of Reference; the Medical Library Coordinator; a representative from the Systems Office; the Head of Circulation; the Government Documents Coordinator; the Head of Serials; and the Head of Reference as chair. Members from outside the Library included a Senior Consultant/Analyst from Computing and Information Services and a consultant from Physical Planning and Construction. The Task Force was specifically charged with creating a new library environment that would feature a merge of the reference and government document service points; relocation of the card catalog; a new layout for the service area; appropriate workstations; integration of electronic services for users; and sufficient staffing levels. This area would incorporate both electronic and printed reference sources in an environment that provided for quality consultative services. It was hoped by all that the main floor would become the principal service point for the Library and the Task Force membership reflects this philosophy. An incentive for timely completion was provided by the fact that the money from the Champlain grant had to be encumbered by June of 1994. The renovated area was to be ready by the beginning of the Fall semester, 1994.

Members of the Task Force were chosen for their ability to bring a wide variety of skills and perspectives to the challenging job at hand. From the Computing and Information Services representative, the Task Force gained information about networking capabilities, security, workstations, printers, and router hubs. The Systems representative was vital in keeping the Task Force aware of Systems capabilities and concerns. From Plant Operations, the Task Force received information on companies to approach for workstation tables, chairs and carpeting. The Plant Operations representative also made sure that the plan was completely in compliance with the Americans with Disabilities Act. Because Government Documents was to be merged with Reference, the presence of the Government Documents Coordinator was invaluable. The input from Circulation and Serials was also vital as both of those departments have a different perspective on reference and share primary public service space on the main floor of the Rockefeller Library. The Medical Library Coordinator attended in anticipation of chairing a similar project at the Sciences Library in the future.

Each member of the Task Force was responsible for a different section of the project. For example, the Assistant Head of Reference was responsible for the furniture, including the Reference desk. The Head of Serials and the Head of Circulation were responsible for the move of the card catalog, and the Medical Library Coordinator was responsible for keeping track of the budget which went through many revisions from initial estimates to final figures (see Appendix 1). The Head of Reference served as liaison to the Administration and attended the weekly meetings with the contractors to ascertain that all was going as planned. As a group the Task Force determined what information was needed and the representatives were able to bring to the committee various options for their respective sections, which were then discussed. It gave everyone a stake in the success of the project and made it possible to accomplish what was needed in the short time given. This team approach proved very successful. The Task Force met weekly for two to three hours over a nine month period. All issues were thoroughly discussed, and the Task Force was able to come to consensus on every issue, although not without a certain amount of lively debate. Members of the Task Force rotated taking minutes, which were distributed on email. This was a way of keeping a record of decisions, and for informing anyone unable to attend a meeting. It was also an excellent method for forwarding and sharing information with others in the Library. Open sessions for all Library staff were held to inform and solicit feedback on such items as moving the card catalog, the goals of the plan, the construction phase, and temporary location of services. The Head of Reference also gave presentations to the Brown University Corporation's Library Committee.

To bring about significant changes, the Task Force knew they needed the cooperation and assistance of a broad representation within the Library. For example, the area for the new Reference and Information Center was where the card catalog had stood for 30 years, so its disposition was of major concern to many people inside and outside the Library for three main reasons. The move would affect the work flow of those still working with the card catalog on the retrospective conversion project, and any space the card catalog occupied in the future was most likely already being evaluated by others for expansion of their department or services. The Task Force also took this discussion to the Faculty Library Committee. It was necessary to move rather than discard the card catalog with approximately ten percent of the catalog not in machine readable format. Based on its historical relevance, the decision was made to "enshrine" the catalog in the former smoking reading room one floor below. Ironically, the decision was made during the same time as Nicholson Baker's now infamous article on discarding library catalogs was published in the New Yorker.[1]

THE PROCESS:

As the design and planning for the new Reference and Information Center and surrounding area proceeded, the services to be provided were outlined and the shape of the new environment was defined. Both entailed making a variety of decisions, large and small. The new desk was to accommodate increased staffing levels and multiple-use workstations were to be installed. A central location for the desk, visible to all users of public workstations and the surrounding resources, was desired. The desk was required to serve as the initial point for user interactions, as well as an area for individual consultations. Space was also needed to accommodate a small collection of heavily used reference books within the desk. Consideration had to be given to the carpeting and the finish of the desk, so that they would blend in with the existing decor and feel of the room. The Head of Circulation attended a conference on library design and shared information with the other members of the Task Force.

The immediate area on both sides of the new desk would house clusters of public workstations. A main focus of the project was readying the room for these workstations. Networking (Ethernet and electrical) had been added during the last several years, but only around the exterior walls of the room. The Task Force attempted to determine what services the Library would want to offer users for the next several years. For example, to accommodate future expansion, networking for a possible 50 workstations was installed. The Reference desk was moved to the Periodicals Reading Room while work was being done and a wall of heavy-duty plastic protected the Reference collection. A bulletin board was created and placed at the main entrance to the Library. The board reflected what services were available throughout the construction period and featured photographs of various stages of the renovations. Announcements were made regularly on the University's electronic bulletin board. The enthusiasm and flexibility of the Reference staff and other Library staff at this time are to be commended.

The Task Force's desire to open the room up would result in the relocation of some stack ranges. This would provide a view to downtown Providence and relieve the congested area along the outside edge of the room, turning it into a quality study space, a "living edge."[2] A "living edge" in the room would encourage users to study and work in an inviting atmosphere endowed with natural light and spaciousness. Several dumb terminals solely for access to Josiah, the Brown Library OPAC, were retained; others were relocated to the lobby from the entrance area to the Reference Room. This was done to provide a higher visibility of the Reference desk.

Adjacent to the workstation area, a space was allocated for the government documents shelflist. A plan was designed for moving the Social Science Data Services (SSDS) from its isolated location on an upper floor to an area adjacent to the new Reference desk. SSDS is a sub-unit of the Government Documents department working with geographic imaging systems (GIS), specialized software and data tapes.

The Task Force recognized the need to have as many public services staff as possible located near this new service hub. A recommendation was made to move Documents staff to the same area as the SSDS staff. The current Documents office is the only adjacent office space that provides a clear view of the new Reference desk. The space made available by that move could then be occupied by the Reference staff, who are currently housed one floor below the Reference and Information Center. It is crucial for the Reference staff to be accessible to users for referrals from the Reference desk, to be available for one-on-one consultation with users, and for a greater awareness of the level of activity in the new area. This move is planned to occur during the current academic year.

Lengthy consideration was given on how best to integrate print resources with the newer electronic resources. Prior to the renovation, there were several locations for Reference materials throughout the area which were not noted in the OPAC. In a move designed to make the area easier to navigate, all index tables were removed and the entire reference collection was placed in call number order in a physically logical formation. Counter-height tables were placed at the ends of the stacks for ease of use of large index sets. A new location was added into the OPAC for materials housed in the Reference desk.

A design for a new Reference desk was drafted after it was determined that the available ready-made furniture would not fit in either style or lay out of the area of the Reference and Information Center. The design was based on Task Force decisions that the desk should serve as a center for both reference and information queries and be highly visible to those entering. The desk would provide librarians with the ability to see users at the workstations clearly, include space for one-on-one consultation, and would allow librarians to leave the desk easily and to rove the area assisting users. To accommodate these varied functions, a bi-level design was created. The front counter-height unit would allow users to interact with staff at eye-level. The back unit would be desk-height and conducive for individual consultation. The choice of wood for the desk was important as the Reference area has existing wood paneling. The traditional appearance of the area combined with the more high-tech look of the new workstations and furniture creates an image of the Library of the past blended with the technology of the future.

Workstation tables were chosen for their sturdiness and excellent cable management. In addition, these workstation tables were selected for their clean lines. The Task Force believed that using tables rather than carrels would enhance the ability of the Reference staff to see the users at work, enabling staff to determine more quickly when assistance was needed. The chairs were chosen because of their ergonomic design combined with a sled base and the absence of movable parts. The chairs selected were already known to be comfortable and durable since their purchase and use at the Orwig Music Library at Brown.

Determining the type of computer workstations to install was based on an assessment of the various electronic services the Library wanted to provide. The goal was to have as many databases and Internet functions available as possible from one single workstation. At the time, Microsoft Windows™ was the only interface which would accomplish our goal in a menu environment. Consideration was given to subject and alphabetic groupings for the menu, as well as division by system and software types. Access was needed to the original CBIS CD-ROM network (ELibrary) already in place, and for a new network based on client/server architecture (SilverPlatter's ERL). Additional items for consideration included the ability of applications to work within Windows™, the hard drive security, the ramifications of Web access, and maintenance of software and hardware. In addition, Government Documents needed to provide access to its growing collection of non-networked CD-ROM products. All workstations would need internal CD-ROM drives and a separate menu for these resources using Saber™ software. The Task Force also wanted to provide access to the Internet, which had not been available previously from any public Library workstation. This would include access to World Wide Web and Gopher resources, and to databases available on the Internet such as FirstSearch and UnCover. The resources which were made available are listed in Appendix 2. The final menu design was laid out to incorporate Brown-held databases first and then access to remote databases and services. The Electronic Resources and Services Committee is charged with reviewing and recommending new databases and services for the Library and proposing changes to the menu. Chart 1 represents the current Electronic Reference Desk (ERD) workstation menu.

Initially, there were to be sixteen public workstations consisting of IBM Value Point 486s with individual CD-ROM drives and several Gateway 2000s. These were arranged in groups of four on either side of the desk. An additional sixteen tables were acquired and interspersed in preparation for future growth; they currently serve as study tables. Three workstations were placed at the desk (Mac Quadra, IBM 486, and Gateway) for staff use. Printing was to be provided in a networked environment by two HP LaserJet 4siMX printers for fast, quality printing. While the Task Force discussed charging for printing, the lack of appropriate technology at Brown for charging in a networked environment influenced the decision to continue the current policy of free printing. However, early in the process it became apparent that duplex printing should be added to reduce paper waste. A policy was enacted requiring all full-text materials to be downloaded as opposed to printed. To ensure the security of the equipment, a fiber optic system was selected. The decision was based in part on the success of a similar system at the University's Computing and Information Services public computing clusters. Other factors influencing the choice of fiber optics included the flexibility of adding and removing workstations at any time and that fiber optic systems do not require attachment of the workstation to the table surface. The security system is linked to the Brown University Police Department.

The Reference and Information Center was

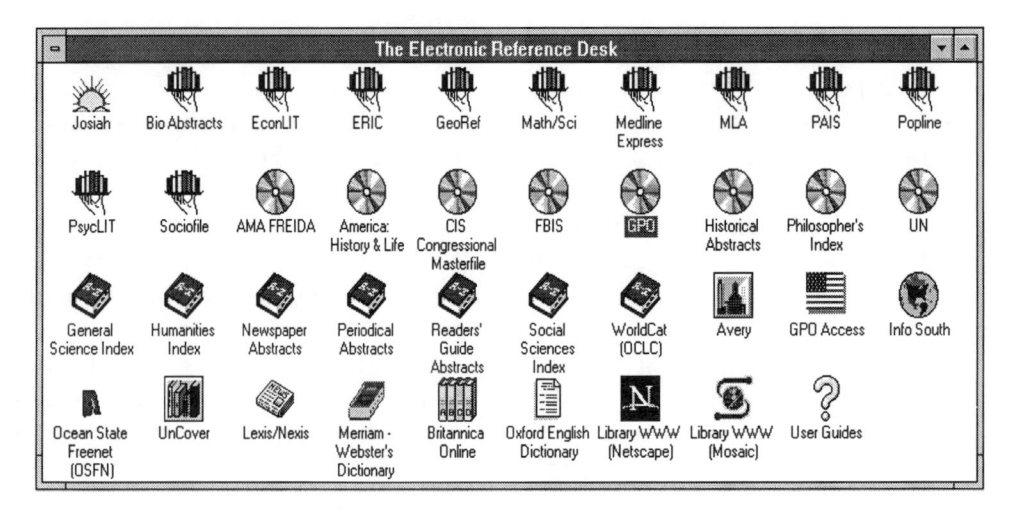

Chart 1

opened to the Brown University community in late September 1994, and users quickly embraced the new area. They were excited about the ability to use multiple resources from one workstation including Internet access. One outcome of their enthusiasm has been substantial growth in the use of the Reference area, and an increase in the use of both print and electronic resources. More library instruction sessions have been requested, the Library has instituted classes on database searching and using Web resources, and the volume of interactions increased dramatically, 42% during the first year. The Task Force had anticipated this growth, and planned for additional staffing. The growth in total workstations, combined with the number of different databases and Internet access, would undoubtedly prove the need for greater numbers of staff at the desk, particularly during peak times. The goal was to provide basic information to all entering or telephoning at the desk. General services include informational services, interlibrary loan verifications and in-depth reference with more sophisticated service being offered throughout the Reference and Information Center by librarians who would rove the area.

It should be noted that three years ago the interlibrary loan process was reorganized to provide better and more timely service to our users. It was felt the intervention of Reference desk staff was essential in ensuring that users took full advantage of the Library's own collections before requesting interlibrary loan. Reference desk staff took over the accepting of all interlibrary loan requests, and verifying them on bibliographic databases such as OCLC and RLIN. This process enabled the requests to be sent out more quickly by the Interlibrary Loan Department (ILL). The relationship between ILL and Reference has resulted in quicker, better service, but greatly increased ILL interactions at the Desk.

Once the services to be provided were established, the Task Force began to consider how best to staff the area. The Reference Department of the Rockefeller Library at the time consisted of three full-time reference/collection development librarians, one part-time librarian, a full-time paraprofessional, and the Head and Assistant Head, who are present on the desk on a limited basis. Graduate students and volunteers had also been used minimally. This would not be sufficient to provide the level of service the Task Force envisioned for this new area.

Given the knowledge that funding for additional permanent Reference staff was not available, the Task Force considered how best to implement services in the new Reference and Information Center, and what levels of staffing would be required. Based on an initial list of duties, the Task Force identified three basic types of reference interactions, which were designated as "A" (informational and directional), "B" (general reference), and "C" (consultation and instruction) and indicated which staff were designated to respond to each type. These types of reference interactions are described more fully in Chart 2.

The times of days, and days of the week during which there is high, medium, and low demand for reference/information services were also identified. High periods would ideally be staffed by three individuals, one C, one B and one A. Medium periods would be staffed by two individuals (one C and one B or A). Low periods would be staffed by one individual, ideally a C or B. An outline of a week-long schedule showing these periods is shown as Chart 3.

Using Chart 3 as a basis for staffing the Reference desk, the Task Force needed to creatively find solutions for additional staffing. This was facilitated by holding a meeting with all librarians to discuss the new service paradigm, and by offering one and one-half hour sessions for the entire Library staff on the new Reference and Information Center. As a result of staff response to the sessions, the Reference desk now features a wide variety of people serving the Brown community of users. Volunteers include staff from Cataloging, Circulation, Interlibrary Loan, Preservation, Serials, and the John Carter Brown Library, an independent research library on campus. In addition, graduate students in the humanities and social sciences serve on the Reference Desk. The volunteers bring to Reference their own expertise and take back with them better research skills and greater insight as to the information needs of the Brown community.

Training has become a major issue due to the large numbers of non-Reference staff and students that need to be trained in anticipation of working in Reference. The Assistant Head of Reference is responsible for coordinating all training at the desk, and many of the Reference staff are asked to participate in the process. In preparation for the new area, weekly sessions were held with Reference and Documents staff where staff also discussed the elec-

TYPES OF REFERENCE SERVICE

Type A: Informational and Directional

Typical Functions:
- provide directional assistance
- answer call number and location questions
- answer telephone (includes answering ready reference questions and making appropriate referrals)
- perform ILL verifications
- assist with basic equipment/workstation functionality questions
- experienced individuals may also provide basic ready reference service

Who:
student assistants
staff volunteers
library school interns

Type B: General Reference

Typical Functions in addition to type A functions:
- provide ready reference services - using tools in the Reference desk collection and core list of electronic tools available at the Reference desk (including JOSIAH, RLIN, ERL, ELibrary, FirstSearch, and the Web Campus Information Service) to answer reference questions, typically spending no more than five minutes on any question, and referring to librarians, subject specialists or other units when appropriate
- provide general reference services - using print and electronic tools in the Reference collection to answer reference questions, referring to librarians, subject specialists, or other units when appropriate.

Who:
Reference and Documents Senior Library Associate Specialists
Librarian volunteers
Manager volunteers

Type C: Consultation and Instruction

Typical Functions, in addition to type A and B functions:
- serve as field consultants (rovers), providing point-of-use instruction at workstations
- provide advanced reference services, including subject specialization
- provide "off desk" services, including training for electronic services, provide Reference workshops, library instruction sessions, developing guide and handouts to assist users

Who:
Reference and Documents Librarians

Chart 2

ACADEMIC YEAR

	MON	TUES	WED	THURS	FRI	SAT	SUN
8:30	Low: B	Low: B	Low: B	Low: B	Low: B		
9:00	Low: B	Low: B	Low: B	Low: B	Low: B	Low: B	
10:00	Med: C A	Med: C A	Med: C A	Med: C A	Med: C A	Low: B	
11:00	Med: C A	Med: C A	Med: C A	Med: C A	Med: C A	Low: B	
12:00	Med: C A	Med: C A	Med: C A	Med: C A	Med: C A	Low: B	Med: C
1:00	High: C B A	High: C B A	High: C B A	High: C B A	High: C B A	Med: C A	Med: C
2:00	High: C B A	High: C B A	High: C B A	High: C B A	High: C B A	Med: C A	High: C C
3:00	High: C B A	High: C B A	High: C B A	High: C B A	High: C B A	Med: C A	High: C C
4:00	High: C B A	High: C B A	High: C B A	High: C B A	High: C B A	Med: C A	High: C A
5:00	Med: C A	Med: C A	Med: C A	Med: C A	Low: C	Med: C A	High: C A
6:00	Med: C A	Med: C A	Med: C A	Med: C A			High: C A
7:00	Med: C A	Med: C A	Med: C A	Med: C A			High: C A
8:00	Med: C A	Med: C A	Med: C A	Med: C A			High: C
9:00	Med: C A	Med: C A	Med: C A	Med: C A			Med: C

Chart 3: Sample Rockefeller Desk Schedule

tronic resources being made available and received in-depth training in their utilization. In addition, staff worked on creating the necessary one-page user guides for the individual databases; these user guides are now on the Library Home Page via the World Wide Web (http://www.brown.edu/Facilities/University_Library/library.html) for the benefit of remote users. Similarly, as new issues arose, user guides had to be quickly generated. For example, a user guide on how to print and download from the most common interfaces was drawn up when the problems inherent in printing and downloading from multiple software packages created unforeseen complications.

The initial instruction period before serving on the desk is approximately 12 hours. An outline of the training is shown as Chart 4. There is some variation in the training, depending on experience and what level of reference knowledge the trainee has. For example, a graduate student in History will have very different needs than those of the Head of Preservation. In addition, refresher training is handled in the bi-weekly meetings of the Reference staff and in unstructured help sessions run by the Assistant Head of Reference. At those sessions, many topics are covered at the request of the staff. For those volunteers and student assistants who are unable to attend Reference meetings, detailed minutes are sent via email. In addition regular announcements affecting services at Reference, are sent via email to everyone who staffs the Reference desk.

The most important benefit of the creation of the new staffing pattern was the opportunity for librarians to provide more flexible reference service. Because there are one or two others at the desk handling duties such as phone calls, OPAC searches and ILL verification (types A and/or B), the librarians (type C) are free to rove around the area and to spend time with individual users. By providing point-of-use instruction at the workstations, we provide a quality service to our users. This is particularly important since there is no formal library instruction required at Brown. It has been noted that many more questions are generated at the workstations than in the old configuration, due to the variety of services offered. Users are often not comfortable coming to the desk for assistance, but will ask for help if staff is near to their workstation.

Beyond the staffing of the new Reference and Information Center, the Task Force needed to study support issues for the area, particularly system support, including trouble-shooting and workstation software and hardware maintenance. As a result of this study, a position was transferred into the Sys-

> **TRAINING OUTLINE**
>
> 1. Overview of the goals of the Reference Department in providing various levels of service and each trainee's role in the process.
> 2. Philosophy of reference service at Brown and basics of the reference interview. Emphasis on the importance of referral to other desk staff, particularly for non-informational or non-technical workstation questions. Include mention of providing librarian business cards for extended referral.
> 3. Desk procedures for telephone, using the desk computer workstations, making Lexis-Nexis appointments, and signing users on to Lexis-Nexis, and the use of JOSIAH in staff mode.
> 4. Review of verification of interlibrary loans & philosophy behind ILL service at Brown.
> 5. Overview and specifics on every book in the small Reference desk collection and when to use.
> 6. Two overview sessions of the entire Reference collection including where particularly useful tools are located.
> 7. A session with the Government Documents Coordinator on documents reference, including when to refer to the Documents Department. Includes a brief discussion of Social Sciences Data Services and its role.
> 8. Overview of Windows software & ERD workstation functionality. Includes how to trouble-shoot problems on the Electronic Reference desk workstations, printers & JOSIAH terminals.
> 9. Overview of the concepts behind the creation of the Electronic Reference Desk interface and discussion of each group icon and its purpose.
> 10. Workshop on using FirstSearch databases, including how to print in our environment.
> 11. Workshop on all Silver Platter ERL databases; emphasizing use of the ERL WinSpirs client.
> 12. Workshop on all ELibrary databases including an overview of the 5 software interfaces.
> 13. Workshop on using Web resources offered by the Library such as Britannica, the Oxford English Dictionary, general information on using Netscape and Mosaic, including search services.
> 14. Brief discussion of use of other communication software on the workstations.
> 15. Overview of the User Guides and when to refer to them.

Chart 4

tems Department to address the needs generated by the new area as well as other Library system needs. The position was made available as a result of technological changes in the Circulation Department. Software upgrades and updates are routinely handled by this person. A trouble-shooting guide, developed by Systems with input from Reference has been developed to assist staff in diagnosing hardware/software problems.

CONCLUSIONS:

The success of the Reference and Information Center can be attributed to the following factors:

- The Task Force had a high level of decision-making power.
- Library Administration provided strong support.
- The cross-departmental composition of the Task Force and the team-building approach were essential.
- The ability to integrate all electronic resources into one menu was accomplished.
- Tri-level staffing is beneficial to both the volunteers and users.
- There is a strong commitment to training.
- A continuing review of electronic resources and services has been instituted.

The new Rockefeller Reference and Information Center represents the direction of Library services at Brown. Faculty and students can now easily access bibliographic databases, catalogs of libraries from around the world, full-text information services, statistical data, full-color graphic images, and audio/video files. Equally important, many of these services are available campus-wide over the University computer network. These resources help to enhance, but not replace, the already rich print collections in the Brown Library. The new area provides the physical environment where all of the intellectual resources conveniently come together, along with the professional assistance necessary to guide users through an increasingly complex world of information. Technology has become a force for change not only in the resources that the Library provides, but in how they are serviced. The Rockefeller Library Reference renovation project is just one example of how the technology has shaped the Library collections and services it provides.

REFERENCES

1. Baker, Nicholson. 1994. Annals of Scholarship: Discards. New Yorker, 70(7):64–86.
2. Designing Library Interiors as Information Gateways. ALA Workshop given by Aaron Cohen Associates at the American Library Association Midwinter Meeting, February 1994.

APPENDIX 1

Budget for the Rockefeller Reference Department Renovation

Description	Qty	Total
Move card catalog (including carpet and other work on Level A)		$6,926
Carpet & Wiring ($77,617) Networking ($4,230)		$81,847
Network Devices		
"Mother" Ethernet Hub	1	$1,240
"Baby" Ethernet Hub	1	$681
Subnet Router	1	$400
Workstations		
IBM @ $2,477	20	$49,540
Printers		
Laser printers @ $4,242	2	$8,484
Laser-Jet Cards @ $340	2	$680
Duplex printing upgrade @ 551	2	$1,022
Security		$2,600
Network cables		$365
Mouse pads @ $4	20	$80
ADA Software for Visually Impaired	1	$595
Furniture		
Chairs @ $221	36	$7,956
Tables for workstations @ $305	30	$9,150
Table with Adjustable legs (ADA) @ $463	2	$926
Wheeled chairs @ $375	2	$750
Stools @ $550	2	$1,100
Re-Upholster	9	$409
Reference desk	1	$22,300
	TOTAL	$197,051

APPENDIX 2

Networked Electronic Resources in the Brown University Library

America: History and Life. 1982–present; article abstracts and citations of reviews and dissertations on the history and culture of the United States and Canada. (Elibrary)

Avery Index to Architectural Periodicals. 1979–present; treats architecture and related subjects such as city planning, historic preservation, and interior design. (WWW)

Bio Abstracts. Current year; international coverage of research in the life sciences. For other years back to 1991, ask at the Sciences Reference Desk. (ERL)

Britannica Online. Latest edition supplemented by material not yet in the printed version. Includes the 10th edition of Merriam-Webster's College Dictionary. (WWW)

CIS Masterfile. 1789–1969; index to U.S. Congressional reports, documents, hearings, and other publications. (Elibrary)

ClariNet e.News. Current; the largest electronic news service on the Internet, offering general, international, sports, technology, entertainment and financial news, special features and columns. (WWW)

EconLIT. 1969–present; literature in the field of economics and allied disciplines. (ERL)

ERIC. 1982–present; source for information on all aspects of education including counseling, tests, and measurement. (ERL)

FREIDA. Current; provides information on graduate medical education programs in the United States. (Elibrary)

General Science Index. May 1984–present; more than 100 journals and magazines from the U.S. and Great Britain, covering such subjects as anthropology, astronomy, biology, computers, medicine and health. (WWW)

GeoRef. 1988–present; international source for literature of geology and geophysics. Coverage for North America from 1785; from 1933 for other regions. For coverage prior to 1988, ask at the Sciences Library Reference Desk. (ERL)

GPO Access. Current; online access to the Federal Register, Congressional Record, U.S. Code, and other federal government sources. (WWW)

Historical Abstracts. 1982–present; article abstracts and citations of books and dissertations on the history of the world from 1450 to the present. Excludes the U. S. and Canada. (ELibrary)

Humanities Index. February 1984–present; more than 300 periodicals in archaeology, art, classics, film, folklore, journalism, linguistics, music, the performing arts, philosophy, religion, world history, and world literature. (WWW)

Index to Foreign Broadcast Information Service (FBIS) Reports. 1991–present; covers English translations by the CIA of foreign broadcast and media reports. (ELibrary)

Index to United Nations Documents. 1990–present; indexes U.N. official documents and sales publications. Also includes full-text of selected documents. (ELibrary)

InfoSouth. 1988–present; bibliographic citations and abstracts on Latin America and the Caribbean. Includes social, political, economic, and business news. (In Library Only)

LEXIS/NEXIS®. Said to be one of the world's largest full-text online databases, containing more than 60 million full-text articles, citation abstracts, and documents. Emphasis is on current news, legal and business information.

MathSci. 1940–present; world's literature on mathematics and its applications in a wide range of disciplines. (ERL)

MEDLINE Express. 1966–present; major source for biomedical literature. (ERL)

MLA Bibliography. 1963–present; multilingual index to books and journals in the fields of modern literature, languages, linguistics, and folklore. (ERL)

Monthly Catalog of U.S. Government Publications. 1976–present; index to United States government publications cataloged by the Government Printing Office. (ELibrary)

Newspaper Abstracts. 1989–present; coverage of over 25 national and regional newspapers, including the Boston Globe. (WWW)

Oxford English Dictionary (OED). The complete, full-text of the second edition (1989) of the OED, an authoritative work on the usage and meaning of English words and phrases from 1150 to the present. (WWW)

Pais International. 1972–present; information on political science, government, international relations, law, economics, business, finance, and other social sciences, on the local, regional, national and international level. (ERL)

Periodical Abstracts. 1986–present; 1,500+ general and academic journals, covering business, current affairs, economics, literature, religion, psychology, and women's studies. (WWW)

Perseus. 1992; a multimedia interactive library, published on CD-ROM for the study of ancient Greek literature, history, art, and archaeology. (CIS Cluster Services)

Philosopher's Index. 1940–present; abstracts for books and journal articles on epistemology, ethics, logic, metaphysics, and the philosophy of various disciplines. (ELibrary)

Popline. 1991–present; information on topics relating to population such as demography, vital statistics, family planning, and related health, law, and policy issues. (ERL)

PsycLit. 1974–present; international source for information in psychology and related disciplines such as sociology, linguistics, law, business, and anthropology. (ERL)

Readers Guide Abstracts. 1983–present; popular periodicals published in the U.S. and Canada. Includes current events and news, fine arts, fashion, education, business, sports, health and nutrition, and consumer affairs. (ERL)

Social Sciences Index. February 1983–present; more than 350 international, English-language periodicals in sociology, anthropology, geography, economics, political science, and law. (ERL)

Sociofile. 1974–present; information in sociology and related disciplines. (ERL)

UnCover. UnCover is a table of contents service. Over 14,000 journals are covered and 4000 current citations are added daily. UnCover offers you the opportunity to order fax copies of articles. (WWW)

WorldCat. Books, journals, sound recordings, videos and manuscripts collected and catalogued by your library and libraries around the world. Includes manuscripts written as early as the 11th century. WorldCat does not include individual articles, stories in journals, magazines, newspapers, or book chapters. (WWW)

You Are Here, But Where Is That?: Architectural Design Metaphors in the Electronic Library[1]

By John Kupersmith
Washoe County Library

The relationship between architecture and computer system design is rich and complex. Virtual-reality computer simulations are used to design buildings, and architectural techniques are used in designing computer systems.[2] We speak of computer hardware and software as having or embodying architectures. This paper deals with another aspect of the relationship: the use of conventional architecture as a structuring metaphor or a design element in electronic library systems.

One of the key issues in planning any computer system is the choice and presentation of an overall design metaphor that will enable the user to form a useful mental model of the system and facilitate the process known as "sensemaking." As Karl Weick points out, raw presentation of data does not by itself convey context or meaning: "The electronic world makes sense only when people are able to reach outside that world for qualitatively different images that can flesh out cryptic representations."[3]

In the past, design metaphors were the province of system vendors, and the options available for displaying information on a computer were generally limited to 24 lines of 80-character text—the electronic version of what Edward Tufte calls "flatland."[4] Recent developments in Internet-based presentation systems and authoring tools have given librarians the power to create World Wide Web sites, Gopher menus, Z39.50 clients, and other "front-ends"—along with the responsibility for making the essential design decisions.

The concepts of space and place are basic to human life, and permeate the way we think about computers. Serena Lin describes how "In interacting with our environment, we are enveloped by a desire to make what is abstract into something discrete, what is imagined into something palpable."[5] Thus, files on a disk are said to be "moved" when in fact what is done is to change their directory path names. Although the Internet has annihilated traditional constraints of distance, we still perceive it in spatial terms, as an information highway. It is common to speak of navigating, jumping, tunneling, or surfing through cyberspace, gopherspace, or webspace to distant sites which are often under construction.

Although cyberspace is not real space, it is nonetheless a "built environment" in which some of the same phenomena occur and some of the same principles apply. An architect's analysis of spatial orientation and wayfinding involves the way people perceive themselves and other elements in a given space, read and interpret cues in the environment, develop a "cognitive map" of the space, identify and locate potential destinations, and form and execute plans to reach a chosen destination.[6] A building or town in which these processes are easily performed is said to have "environmental legibility," with clearly defined paths, landmarks, nodes, edges, and districts.[7] Similarly, a computer system can be laid out and presented so as to facilitate orientation and wayfinding. Cyberspace architect Michael Benedikt thus refers to the need to provide users with both navigation data and destination data.[8]

Wayfinding is a process with emotional as well as rational aspects. Finding and exploring a destination provides satisfaction. On the other hand, as Romedi Passini describes, "the state of being disoriented, of being confused about one's position in a surrounding space and the actions necessary to get out of it, is a deeply felt experience."[9] Similarly, the distressful feeling of being lost in cyberspace—whether in an online catalog, a web site, or one's own hard disk—is one form of technostress.[10]

VIRTUAL SPACES

The metaphor of a virtual building or other "information space," in which users navigate and operate by analogies to the known physical world, abounds in current end-user systems. In some cases, the architectural model is presented verbally, as when users are offered a menu of several "rooms." In others, the presentation is explicitly spatial, as when users navigate through floorplans or graphics representing real or imagined structures. In both kinds of systems, architectural devices such as arrows also serve as wayfinding aids and cues, just as they do in physical buildings.

The most familiar example of a spatial metaphor in everyday computer use is the virtual desktop embodied—with varying degrees of virtuality—in the Macintosh, Windows, Windows 95, and other operating systems. The success of this computing environment is based on the ease with which users can manipulate document icons, folders, a trash can, and other representations of real-world objects. Moving out from the desktop, various programs use the metaphor of a virtual room, office, or home; perhaps the most notable recent example is Microsoft's "Bob" interface, which allows the user to redecorate his/her "home" and populates it with software agents in the form of cartoon characters. Although neither the virtual desktop nor the virtual home are exact duplicates of their real-world counterparts, they are enough like them to provide a sense of familiarity and useful cues for how to proceed.

On a larger scale, online systems offer the capability of linking multiple resources and arranging them according to some organizing structure. Developers of the FreePort software for the original Cleveland Free-Net system used the metaphor of a virtual town—including a public square, post office, business park, and library—to reinforce the concept of community.[11] This interface arguably helped to make the system understandable and encouraged its adoption in numerous locations, but later web-based community networks tend to use other organizing schemes.[12] A similar pattern is evident with the "InfoSlug" system at the University of California, Santa Cruz. The initial gopher system was organized as a virtual campus, whose sections included The Classroom, The Computer Center, and The Library. The subsequently developed web site uses a more topical and less architectural scheme.[13] [Figure 1]

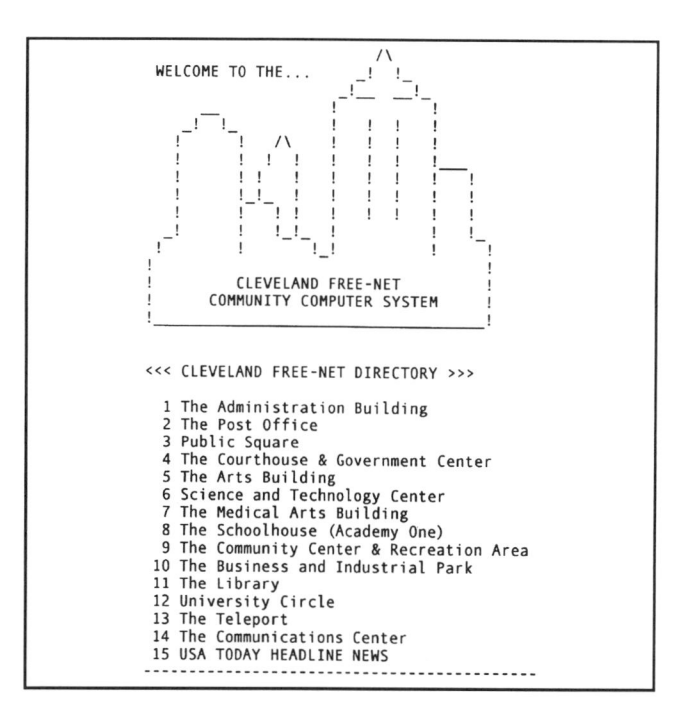

```
               WELCOME TO THE...
                          /\
                        _!  !_
                       !      !
                       ! /\   !
                     _!_!  !_ !_
                    !  !    !  !
                    !  !    !  !
                  _!_!_!    !_!_!_
                 !  !         !  !
                 !  !_       _!  !
                 !    !     !    !
                 !    !_   _!    !
        _____!_____!_!_____!_____
        !        CLEVELAND FREE-NET       !
        !       COMMUNITY COMPUTER SYSTEM !
        !_____!

        <<< CLEVELAND FREE-NET DIRECTORY >>>

         1  The Administration Building
         2  The Post Office
         3  Public Square
         4  The Courthouse & Government Center
         5  The Arts Building
         6  Science and Technology Center
         7  The Medical Arts Building
         8  The Schoolhouse (Academy One)
         9  The Community Center & Recreation Area
        10  The Business and Industrial Park
        11  The Library
        12  University Circle
        13  The Teleport
        14  The Communications Center
        15  USA TODAY HEADLINE NEWS
```

Figure 1. The Cleveland Free-Net, one of the first virtual towns

Virtual places of all kinds are flourishing on the World Wide Web. As William Mitchell points out, we are in the process of constructing a disembodied "city of bits" in which "computer-generated graphic displays are replacing built facades as the public faces of institutions."[14] With graphical browser software, it is possible to tour a multimedia design firm's office or an advertising firm's "Idea Factory,"[15] visit many campuses, explore several different virtual towns (including at least one with a working library),[16] and navigate through a community's virtual archipelago.[17] Architects and artists have created a number of interesting computer-generated spaces.[18]

Evolving technologies offer the capability of going beyond text and static graphics into three-dimensional virtual reality environments through which the user can navigate. For example, by means of specialized client software, Internet users can visit several Virtual Reality Modeling Language sites,[19] or build their own structures in the color-and-sound environment known as AlphaWorld.[20] [Figure 2]

These environments are at least somewhat modeled on ordinary physical structures, but others are attempting to transcend these limitations. In developing a "cyberspace domain" for a slide library at the University of Texas at Austin, Michael Benedikt and his associates deliberately avoided a representational approach:

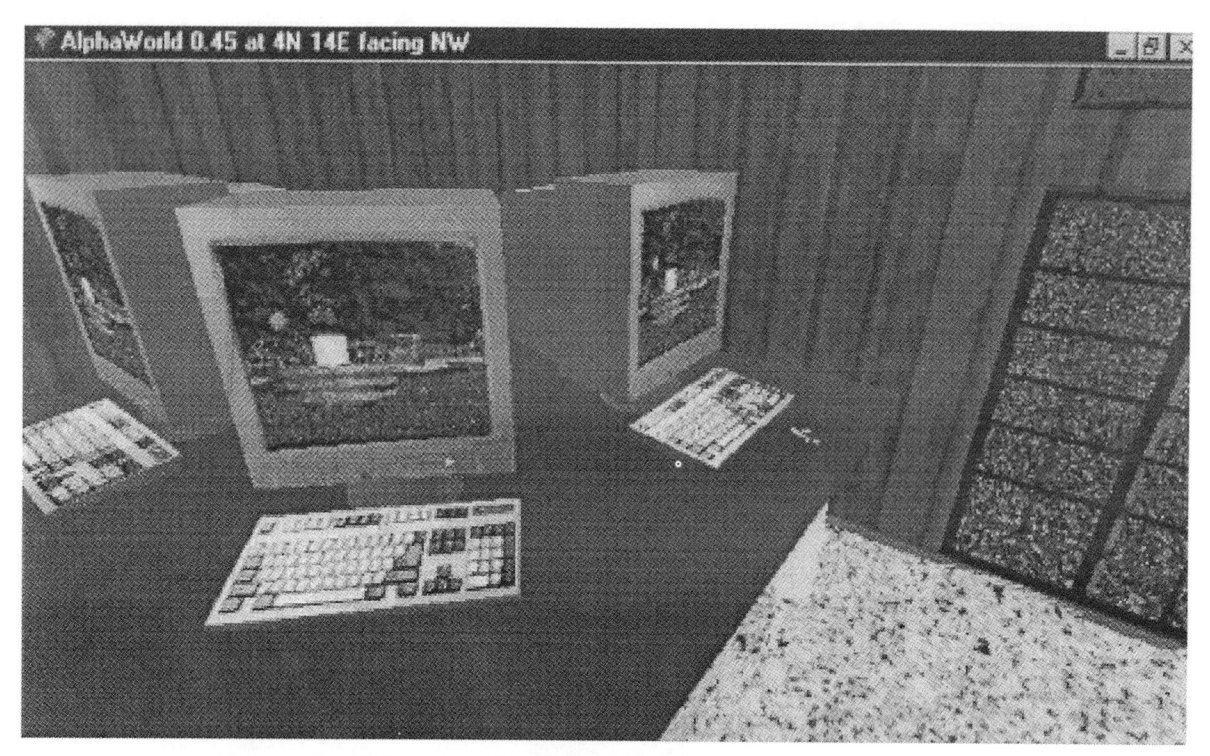

Figure 2. Objects in AlphaWorld, such as these terminals, can be linked to other Internet resources.

It was quickly evident that creating a virtual building of sorts, like a museum . . . that transcribed the hierarchical categor[ies] into assemblages of rooms with doors, passages, etc., would not be efficient. Easy enough to do, coherent movement through such a model would offer none of the advantages of a database. Instead, we would be as locked into a pre-established scheme, and as locked away experientially from other rooms and the overall form of the collection, as we are presently in the real space of the slide library.[21]

Instead, they created a three-dimensional virtual space in which the user flies a "pod" among data cells arranged and sized to represent their contents. It remains to be seen how well this approach will scale to the kind of data universe represented in a large research library, or how easily untutored users will be able to operate in such an environment; but given the imperfection of existing systems, the effort is certainly worth pursuing.

VIRTUAL LIBRARIES

Since spatial and architectural metaphors have evident appeal for both designers and users in a number of different settings, it is no surprise that they have been widely used in information systems. In his prophetic 1945 article proposing the "memex," Vannevar Bush used the terminology of space and movement: "Wholly new forms of encyclopedias will appear, ready-made with a mesh of associative trails running through them, ready to be dropped into the memex and there amplified. . . . There is a new profession of trail blazers, those who find delight in establishing useful trails through the enormous mass of the common record."[22]

In the most literal sense, several "virtual library" systems provide such trails by using analogies to traditional library buildings. As in the InfoSlug and FreeNet systems, such a metaphor can be presented through simple textual cues, in the naming of parts. For example, the Washoe County Library (Reno, NV) operates an "Internet Branch" web site, whose sections include a Reference Desk, Bookstacks, Children's Room, Map Room, and Government Documents Room. [Figure 3][23] This system has been well-received by users and the basic structure will probably be maintained, with some changes and adjustments for resources that do not fit into the traditional print-based structure. Similar verbal presentations are used in the Boulder Public Virtual Library,

Figure 3. This virtual branch library is organized along traditional lines.

the University of Kansas "Carrie" system, and the Virtual Library of Hampton Roads, which incorporates some playful elements including a snack bar, soda machines, and restrooms.[24]

Moving beyond text presentations, some library web designers have adopted elements of traditional library architecture—such as a marble background, a bookcase, or the image of an actual library building—to present a familiar appearance to users, even if the underlying organizational scheme is not explicitly architectural. [Figure 4][25] Other systems are partly or wholly organized around a floorplan—whether of a real library, such as the University of Texas at Austin Undergraduate Library or the Saarlaendische Universitaets- und Landesbibliothek, or of an imaginary one, such as the Planet Earth Virtual Library.[26]

Perspective drawings can also enhance the realism of such a site. For example, the JEFFLINE system at Thomas Jefferson University presents itself as a virtual medical office, whose several clickable components include links from a bookshelf to the institution's library catalog and the MEDLINE database.[27] [Figure 5]

Perhaps the most thoroughly implemented graphics-intensive virtual library is the Internet Public Library developed at the University of Michigan. This site's "lobby" takes the form of a traditional building directory. A user selecting the "Reference Center" sees an image-map showing a perspective drawing of a reference room, containing 16 embedded links that lead to specific subject areas or functions. [Figure 6] This innovative system also capitalizes on another Internet technology to offer a MOO (Multi-user Object Oriented environment) staffed by actual librarians—in effect, a functioning virtual-reality reference room.[28] [Figure 7]

How far can this metaphor be taken? Reflecting on technological advances in computer games, W. David Penniman has developed a vivid sketch of a fully realized synthetic library which "would have the illusion of physical space, shelves with books arranged in a classification scheme, an area to display recent acquisitions, an on-line catalog, a circulation desk, and a reference or help facility." A user would navigate through this library with a mouse, configuring its appearance to suit his/her taste, going to a virtual terminal which would display an OPAC session, then calling up known items on the screen or going to the virtual stacks to browse through representations of related items. The system would also feature extensive hyperlinks among texts, document delivery and remote printing, and real-time human help.[29]

Much of this design could be accomplished with technology already in place. For example, a virtual terminal in AlphaWorld can in fact "morph" into another Internet resource, such as an OPAC. Several catalog systems feature related-item browsing, and some are beginning to offer links to the actual information content of items. E-mail, fax-on-demand, and remote printing are established means of document delivery. Chat functions and MOOs offer the ability to interact in real time with expert guides.

Penniman's essay prompts an interesting question: if we could somehow, given enough bandwidth, totally recreate a physical library—right down to the spine labels—should we do it? Perhaps the most useful implementation would be one which takes maximum advantage of the presentation possibilities described here, but also minimizes the amount of virtual navigation required.

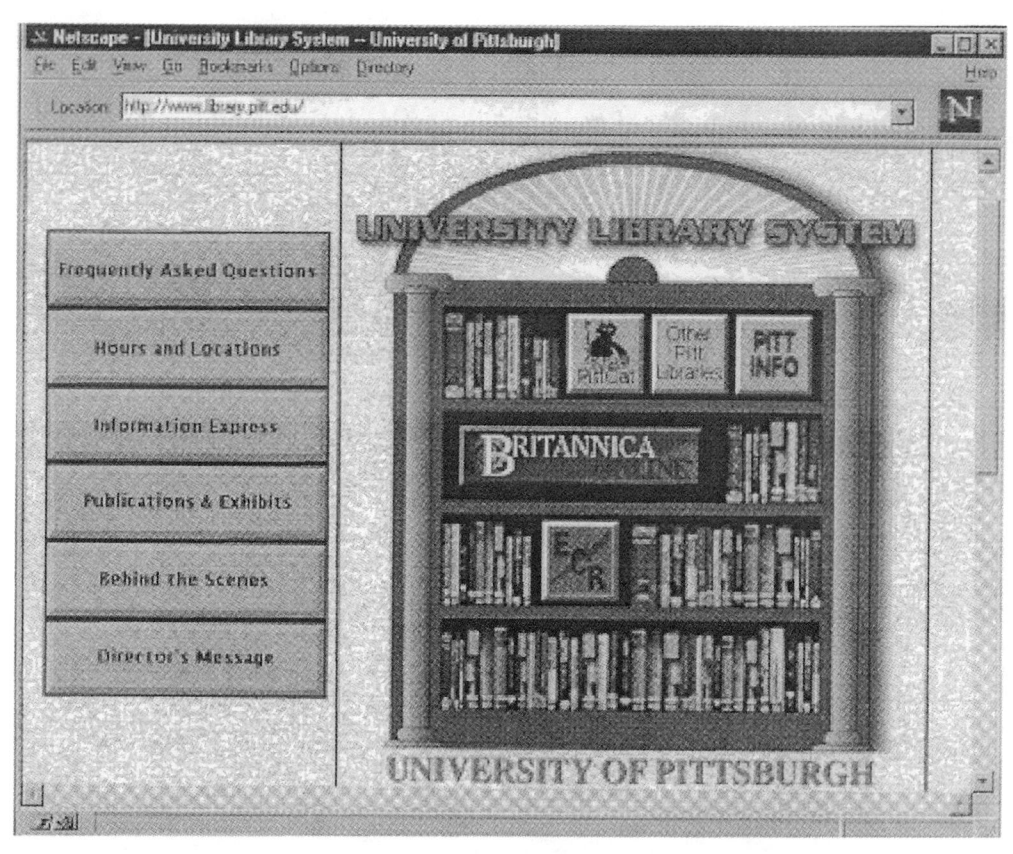

Figure 4. An architecturally styled facade/entranceway.

LIMITATIONS

Despite the examples cited above, the fact remains that relatively few systems use the traditional brick-and-mortar library as an organizing metaphor. More common are schemes derived from topical organization or publication design. There are at least four reasons for this:

First, beyond the simplest level of presentation, it takes a good deal of time—always a scarce resource—to design and implement a system that mimics library architecture. Graphics-intensive systems require computing power and bandwidth that may make them impractical for some libraries and some users.

Second, the layout of the physical library—based as it has been on traditional divisions among books, periodicals, and other print formats—does not necessarily map well to the abstract concepts used in defining subject matter. Items on a given subject tend to fall into several format groups, or outside any traditional format, necessitating cross-references, double-linking, or ignoring possible access points. Of course, topical organization also has its shortcomings, especially when subject matter defies classification or changes rapidly.

Third, the architectural model does not handle the arrangement of individual items, especially in large collections. Some additional level of organization is needed. It may be, as more and more resources become available in the virtual library, that designers will turn to (or re-invent!) the classification schemes used for print materials. With a more limited number of items, however, many designers have opted for topical hierarchies which also serve as a top-level organizing structure.

Fourth, while the traditional library may be the fruit of many centuries of human effort and development, users do not necessarily perceive it as such. Library anxiety, as expressed by students, is often directed at the monumental building itself: "Big, expansive, vast, majestic, awesome.... It was like a big maze to me.... The library seems like a huge monster that gulps you up after you enter it.... I'm still frightened every time I push

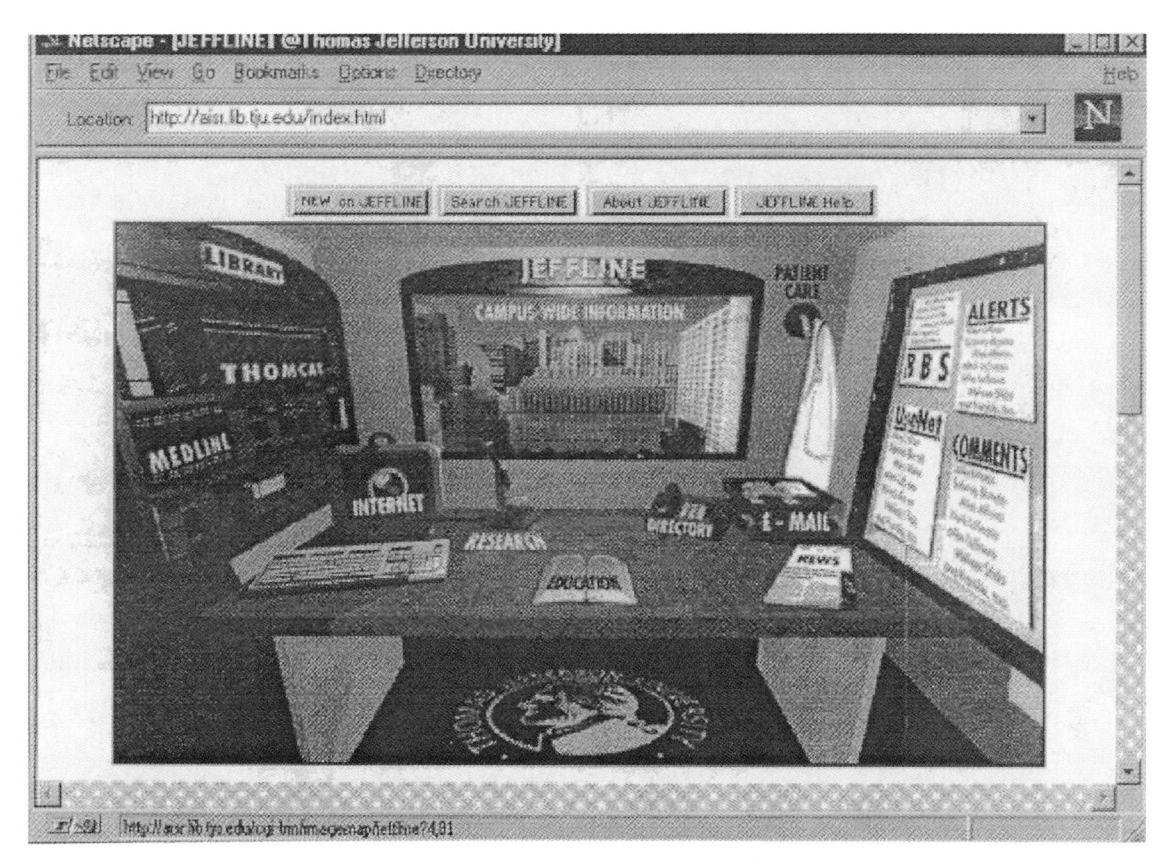

Figure 5. This virtual office at Thomas Jefferson University includes links to the library.

those wide glass doors apart!"[30] It may not be surprising that some designers have looked for other structures to emulate.

Given these limitations, does the virtual library as a design metaphor have a future? Donald Norman, in his critique of cyberspace navigation, poses the question "Why have any organization?", suggesting instead "retrieval by description." However, the vagaries of keyword searching are such that it is best used as an adjunct. Also, a visible organizing structure, besides giving a sense of institutional identity and community, can provide quick access to groups of known resources and serendipitously reveal previously unknown resources. Nonetheless, Norman's skepticism and his call for understandable and flexible structures are certainly worth noting.[31]

Serena Lin frames the development of virtual architecture in the context of an evolutionary cycle: "Following Marshall McLuhan's assertion that the beginning stages of any new media replicate those that preceded it, the development of cyberspace closely mimics that of physical architecture before careening off in its own directions, propelled by vastly different cultural influences."[32] Marcos Novak portrays cyberspace as embodying "liquid architectures," as much akin to music as to the traditional forms of buildings.[33] Thus, the virtual library modeled on the physical one may be a transitional phase—simultaneously a historical artifact, a useful device in the present, and a bridge to new patterns of organization.

IMPLICATIONS FOR DESIGNERS

What are the implications for those designing catalogs, web sites, and similar systems for libraries? Here are some suggestions:

> If you do use a virtual-building metaphor, design and implement it appropriately for your user community. As architect Eliel Saarinen advised, "Always design a thing by considering it in its next larger context." Just as with physical features, what works well in a public library may not fit a large research institution, and vice versa.

Figure 6. A comfortable-looking virtual reference room.

Pay special attention to what user experiences in the first few seconds of contact. Kristina Hooper points out that the initial screen of a system, often compared to a facade, actually serves the more important function of an entranceway, where users receive their initial cues about what the structure contains and how to proceed. "In the architectural domain, entrances have been traditionally finely crafted to control the presentation of a place to a visitor.... The viewpoint of a visitor is carefully planned to reveal the whole of a place in a very systematic way."[34]

Take into account the dynamic nature of computer usage. People moving through your system will continue to learn about it as they exchange information with it, inputting commands and viewing displays. Architect Richard Saul Wurman stated his design goal for urban architecture in terms that apply very well to computer systems: "The goal of all the ways of displaying and communicating information is an informative and attractive environment interacting with informed, self-informing citizens."[35]

Heed the famous dictum of another architect, Mies Van der Rohe: "God is in the details." For example, just as you would in a building, label web pages with clear titles, the name of the institution, and verbal or graphic navigation aids.[36] In cyberspace, the signs are the structure.

Most fundamentally, think like an architect when you design your system, paying careful attention to the user's experience and the wayfinding/sensemaking process. This is relevant no matter what metaphors or devices you use. The following, written sixteen years ago, seems as applicable to the virtual library as it is to the physical one: "Every user receives cues from the environment; this is true whether these cues are planned or unplanned, consistent or random, helpful or confusing. Whether the environment will be an aid or an obstacle to the user depends upon the extent to which the library acts to shape its environment as an instructional tool."[37]

64 *Finding Common Ground*

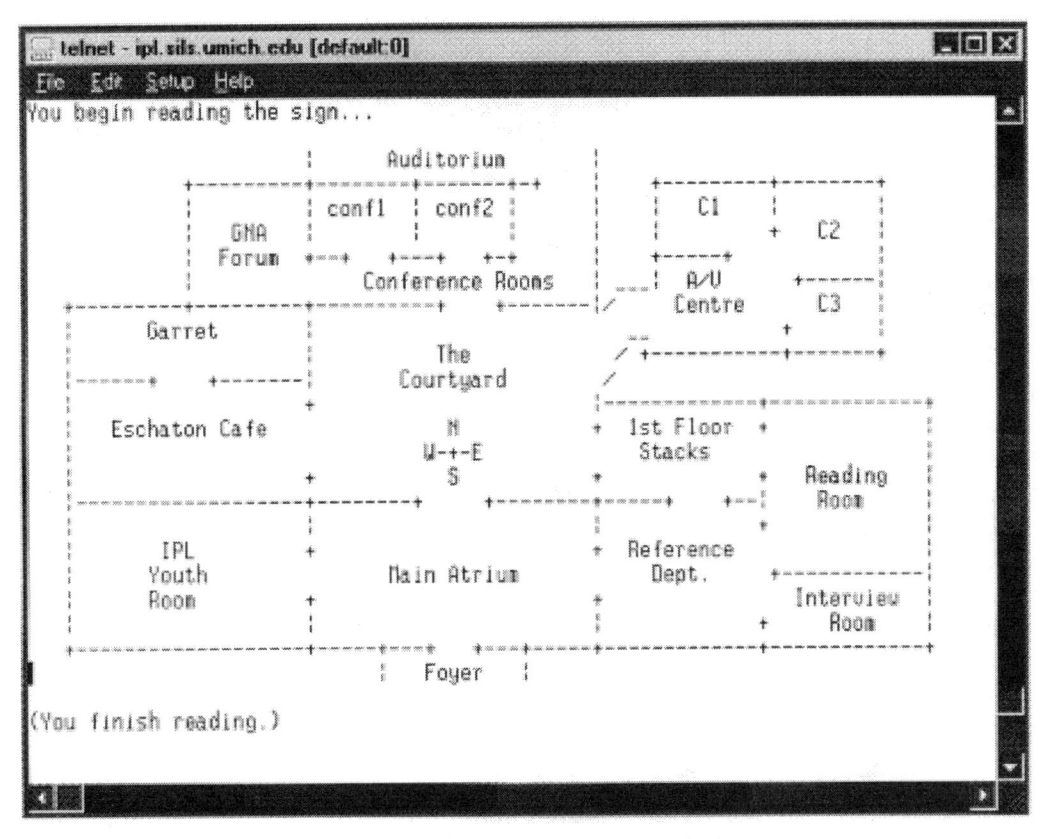

Figure 7. This map guides users in the Internet Public Library's MOO environment.

ENDNOTES

1. For links to the Internet sites mentioned in this paper, and others, see the author's home page <http://www.greatbasin.net/~jkup>.
2. Kristina Hooper, "Architectural Design: An Analogy," in User Centered System Design, ed. Donald A. Norman and Stephen W. Draper (Hillsdale, NJ and London: Lawrence Erlbaum Associates, 1986), pp. 9–23; Robert Jacobson, "Designing with Forms and Forces in Virtual Environments," paper presented at Fifth World Congress on Tall Buildings and Urban Habitat, Amsterdam, May 14–19, 1995 (text received electronically); Jennifer Cram and Myrl Allison, "Homesteading on the Web: The Queensland Department of Education Virtual Library," IRSQ: Internet Reference Services Quarterly v.1 no.2 (forthcoming in 1996).
3. Karl E. Weick, "Cosmos vs. Chaos: Sense and Nonsense in Electronic Contexts," Organizational Dynamics 14 (1985): 50–64.
4. Edward Tufte, Envisioning Information (Cheshire, CT: Graphics Press, 1990), 12.
5. Serena Lin, "Metaphors, Architectures, and Cyberspaces—An Introduction," course paper, University of Maryland-Baltimore County, 1995 < http://imda.umbc.edu/imda/people/serena/paper/page1.html >.
6. Roger M. Downs, "Mazes, Minds, and Maps," in Dorothy Pollet and Peter C. Haskell, ed., Sign Systems for Libraries: Solving the Wayfinding Problem (New York: Bowker, 1979), 17–32; Romedi Passini, Wayfinding in Architecture (New York: Van Nostrand Reinhold, 1984). See also Ben Shneiderman, Designing the User Interface: Strategies for Effective Human-Computer Interaction (Reading, MA: Addison-Wesley, 1992), pp. 403–418.
7. Passini, pp. 109–115; cf. Kevin Lynch, The Image of the City (Cambridge, MA: MIT Press, 1960).
8. Michael Benedikt, "Cyberspace: Some Proposals," in Cyberspace: First Steps, ed. Michael Benedikt (Cambridge, MA: MIT Press, 1991), pp. 173–177.
9. Passini, p. 2.
10. John Kupersmith, "Technostress in the Bionic

Library," in Recreating the Academic Library, ed. Cheryl LaGuardia (New York: Neal-Schuman, forthcoming in 1998).

11. Cleveland Free-Net < telnet://freenet-in-a.cwru.edu >.

12. David Mattison, Community Computer Networks & Free-Net{R} Web Sites < http://www.freenet.victoria.bc.ca/freenets.html >. Anne Beamish, Communities On-Line: A Study of Community-Based Community Networks (Thesis, Department of Urban Studies and Planning, MIT, 1995): < http://alberti.mit.edu/arch/4.207/anneb/thesis/toc.html >.

13. University of California, Santa Cruz "InfoSlug" < gopher://scilibx.ucsc.edu/ >; Web site < http://www.ucsc.edu/ >.

14. William J. Mitchell, City of Bits: Space, Place, and the Infobahn (Cambridge, MA: MIT Press, 1995) <http://www.mitpress.mit.edu:80/City_of_Bits/Recombinant_Architecture/Facade Interface.html>.

15. Presentix Multimedia virtual office < http://www.qbc.clic.net:80/~presentx/plane.html >; Chiat/Day "Idea Factory" < http://www.chiatday.com/cd.www/evolu/virtual/virtual.html >.

16. Anachron City < http://www.euro.net/markspace/AnachronCity.html > features a library, museum, and other public spaces. Virtual City of Freeside < http://www.ecafe.org/freeside/ > includes a virtual monorail line. See also FreePort City (no known relation to Free-Nets) < http://www.freeport.de/Welcome.e.html > and Silica < http://www.intersphere.com/silica/ >.

17. PAN Islands (Smart Velley's Public Access Network) < http://www.svi.org/pan.html >.

18. See, for example, the Bar Code Hotel <http://www.portola.com/People/Perry/BarCodeHotel/index.html>; the virtual spaces of Daniela Bertol < http://www.echonyc.com/~danb/ >; and the Collective Memory Palace developed by Serena Lin < http://imda.umbc.edu/imda/people/serena/map.html >.

19. VRML requires special viewer software <http://www.construct.net/tools/vrml/browsers.html>. For background information, see VRML*Tech < http://vrml.wired.com/vrml.tech/ > and the VRML page at UCLA's Department of Architecture and Urban Design < http://www.gsaup.ucla.edu:80/vrml/ >. Planet 9's Virtual SOMA site < http://www.hyperion.com/planet9/vrsoma.htm > models a San Francisco neighborhood and provides examples viewable with standard browsers. Lightscape Virtual Walkthrough Library < http://www.lightscape.com/models.html > includes a variety of interior spaces (though not a library per se).

20. AlphaWorld < http://www.worlds.net/alphaworld/ >.

21. Benedikt, pp. 192–202.

22. Vannevar Bush, "As We May Think," Atlantic Monthly 76 (July 1945), 101–108; quoted in Shneiderman, p. 404.

23. Washoe County Library "Internet Branch" < http://www.washoe.lib.nv.us/ >.

24. Boulder Public Virtual Library < http://bcn.boulder.co.us/library/bpl/home.html >; University of Kansas "Carrie" < http://ukanaix.cc.ukans.edu/carrie/carrie_main.html >; Virtual Library of Hampton Roads < http://wwwp.exis.net/~cwt/ >.

25. See, for example, the library entrance pages at the University of Pittsburgh library site <http://www.library.pitt.edu/ > and the University of California at Berkeley <http://www.lib.berkeley.edu/ >.

26. UT Austin Undergraduate Library < http://www.lib.utexas.edu/Libs/UGL/Tour/ >; Saarlaendische Universitaets- und Landesbibliothek < http://www.uni-sb.de/z-einr/ub/wir/rundgang.html >; Planet Earth Virtual Library <http://www.nosc.mil/planet_earth/library.html >.

27. Thomas Jefferson University JEFFLINE < http://aisr.lib.tju.edu/ >.

28. Internet Public Library < http://ipl.sils.umich.edu/ >.

29. W. David Penniman, private e-mail message, October 30, 1995. A substantially similar text was published as "From the President: Virtual Reality and Information Discovery in the Library" CLR Reports, N.S. 5 (September 1994), 1.

30. Composite of student quotes from Constance A. Mellon, "Library Anxiety: A Grounded Theory and Its Development," College & Research Libraries 47 (March 1986): 160–165.

31. Donald A. Norman, Things That Make Us Smart: Defending Human Attributes in the Age of the Machine (Reading, MA: Addison-Wesley, 1993), pp. 175–180.

32. Lin, "Metaphors, Architectures, and Cyber-

spaces" <http://imda.umbc.edu/imda/people/serena/paper/page4.html >.
33. Marcos Novak, "Liquid Architectures in Cyberspace," in Cyberspace: First Steps, pp. 225–254.
34. Hooper, p. 15.
35. Richard Saul Wurman and Joel Katz, "Beyond Graphics: The Architecture of Information," AIA Journal 63 (October 1975), 40,56.
36. An excellent introduction is the Web Style Manual produced by Patrick J. Lynch at the Yale Center for Advanced Instructional Media <http://info.med.yale.edu/caim/StyleManual_Top.HTML >.
37. John Kupersmith, "Informational Graphics and Sign Systems as Library Instruction Media," Drexel Library Quarterly 16 (1980), 54–68.

Migrating a Successful Information System to the Web: The WWW Gateway to Information

By Fred Roecker and Virginia Tiefel
Ohio State University

BACKGROUND

In the late 1980s, users of The Ohio State University Libraries faced a confusing array of research materials. They entered a library system of over 4.5 million print materials, 2 million microforms, and 30,000 periodical titles. The online catalog and CD-ROM databases appeared in standalone workstations throughout the 21 University Libraries. It was an information-rich, yet seemingly hostile environment for many students.

Novice users flocked to the Reference Desk and instructional brochures for assistance. They were confused about whether print or electronic resources better met their information needs, which computer workstation contained information useful to them, how to successfully search the resources, and finally how to evaluate the results of their search. Without help with these information-seeking skills, users could not begin, much less succeed in their research.

Virginia Tiefel, Director of The Office of Library User Education, realized research in the University Libraries would soon become even more complex. If the Libraries personnel in both Reference and User Education were overwhelmed trying to keep up with user demands for help, the situation would only get worse as more resources appeared in electronic format.

Tiefel looked at the traditional approaches to increasing user information-seeking skills: adding additional staff, workshops and brochures. But with the shrinking budget of the Libraries, she saw there was little chance for the addition of library positions to offer users assistance at the Reference Desk or at the computers. Increasing the number of workshops offered also was not feasible as workshops could never reach our student population of 50,000 nor the 20,000 staff members, even if there were enough library personnel to teach these sessions. More instructional brochures could be produced, but these again may not reach every user, nor could they address all the instruction for finding information in the Libraries. Something new would have to be created.

In 1988, Tiefel envisioned The Gateway to Information, a computer information system to help people become independent, successful information users. With an emphasis on the search strategy and user-friendly pathways to hundreds of relevant materials, The Gateway would be designed so even novice users could identify, locate, and evaluate relevant resources in print or electronic format without brochures, workshops or staff assistance.

Working with Susan Logan, the Coordinator for Automated Library Systems, Tiefel successfully obtained four grants to finance the development of the first Gateway. A programmer was hired and new computer hardware obtained to network CD-ROMs, front end the online catalog and other electronic databases, and provide Gateway Macintosh workstations in public areas. Consultants from both outside and on campus contributed their ideas, as did committees, staff and user test groups. Nancy O'Hanlon, head of Undergraduate Library Reference, pulled all the resources and ideas together into one prototype for pilot testing. In January 1990, The Gateway to Information was made available in the Main Library and later expanded to workstations in the Undergraduate Library.

The Gateway provided pathways to hundreds of relevant resources, both electronic and print, through 90 broad subjects (e.g., astronomy, zoology, etc.) and also by resource type (e.g., encyclopedias, periodical indexes, etc.). Each recommended title had a "source card" screen complete with description of the item, call number, location in the Libraries along with campus map and floorplan. Electronic resources could be accessed from this source card and, with custom programming, searched using a common interface.

In 1992 the Macintosh computers which housed The Gateway became the primary access point for users in all University Libraries. Over 50 workstations were available in all locations. The University College Library Instruction Program used The Gateway for both its library assignments required of all 10,000 freshmen and transfer sophomores yearly. Librarians contributed advanced information sections on Women's Studies, Communication, and Business to meet the needs of more experienced users. The project received national and international acclaim through articles, conference presentations, and visits from librarians and researchers from around the world.

The project was continuously evaluated to gauge user response. Evaluation forms were left by all workstations and collected by User Education staff to enter onto a database for examination and dissemination to administrators. Modifications were made to The Gateway whenever users noted any confusion about screen displays, pathways, or search capabilities, making The Gateway truly a user-driven information system. These evaluations from users showed how much library researchers appreciated The Gateway. From 7,000 evaluation forms recorded, over 87% of users said they were completely or mostly satisfied with their Gateway search results. Over 90% said they would use The Gateway again for research.

NEED TO MIGRATE THE GATEWAY

As successful as The Gateway was, by 1992 the Office of User Education already was considering a complete revision of the system. The Gateway in its Macintosh format had reached its potential. The HyperCard software used to display The Gateway information seemed more and more limited in its capabilities. In the late 1980s HyperCard was considered an innovative software capable of the user-friendly graphics, point-and-click navigation, and simple programming for quick modifications. By 1992, however, HyperCard seemed an old-fashioned software without color, limited to a single screen of information at a time, and relatively slow.

Also, The Gateway was a programming nightmare. It translated DOS databases and the online catalog into Macintosh-readable files, and then placed a custom front-end on top of the screens. This special programming had to be constantly maintained by programmers to adapt to CD-ROM enhancements. Additional software used for this custom front-end programming began to show signs of stress with the heavy usage of The Gateway and eventually caused the computers to freeze periodically throughout the day.

The Macintosh Gateway also could not be made available remotely to University offices, dorms, and home due to a variety of reasons. Costly, complex software was necessary to mount on each individual computer to front-end the databases. Remote users were restricted to Macintosh computers only. Licensing agreements for networked CD-ROMs also restricted access locations. A VT100 version of The Gateway was developed to address remote access, but its look was primitive, in black and white, and did not allow front-ending of databases. Programming and maintenance on the VT100 was very difficult and, without grant funding to develop simplified programming templates, the VT100 Gateway never was launched to the public.

The Library Automation Office was using its Gateway resources to keep the system stabilized. Without grants, the Libraries could not hire a programmer exclusively assigned to The Gateway. Maintenance was done by student workers under the direction of the Automation Office. User Education was unable to update resources or modify screens to meet users needs during the year while the support technology and hardware were being upgraded. The Gateway was being driven by its technology rather than by the needs of users.

NEW DESIGN CONSIDERATIONS

A new version of The Gateway which incorporated better technology had to be created. This version had to utilize software which was robust and would not freeze up under intensive use as did HyperCard and other software. The software needed to incorporate high-level speed, color, and even multi-media features. Finally, the cost of purchasing, programming and maintaining this software had to be relatively low.

To make this new Gateway useful to upper division undergraduates, graduates, and even faculty as it was originally conceived, this new Gateway also needed to expand its titles available to include advanced information resources on all subjects, including those from the Internet. The design also needed to be upgraded to focus more on the search strategy, facilitate links between related topics and titles, and display information in a layout more clear and extensive than was possible with HyperCard. Finally, it should run as a client-server format to minimize software needs for each public computer and permit remote access.

Of course, this new Gateway had to maintain the original goals of the project: to guide users to relevant resources; not require brochures, workshops or staff intervention to use; and represent the cutting edge of user assistance in display and usability.

THE WWW GATEWAY PROTOTYPE

In 1993 The World Wide Web (WWW) gathered attention in the world of computing. To the User Education Office, this format seemed to meet many of the requirements of the new Gateway. The software was fast, inexpensive (free!), robust, and multi-faceted. HTML (Hypertext Markup Language) programming could create innovative screen displays and links to related information. HTML was also simple to program. It would not require special computer experts to maintain as the original software did. It seemed ideal.

The first step to a new version was to examine and revise the Macintosh Gateway. A simpler, more consistent screen design and text would improve the current Gateway as well as facilitate migration to the Web. From 1993–94, The Gateway Function/Narrative Advisory Team, one of The Gateway's on-campus consulting groups composed of Libraries personnel and classroom faculty, took on the challenge of updating the layout and pathways of the Macintosh Gateway. They reviewed the entire Gateway program and redesigned the pathways, text, and screen display in HyperCard format. With a consistent layout design to each screen and improved links to related information, the new screen designs would migrate much more easily to the WWW format.

But it was still undecided who would do this programming of The Macintosh Gateway for Web access. In 1993, no one in the OSU Libraries knew much about HTML programming. Those in the Office of Library Automation who were familiar with this programming did not have the resources to undertake this project, nor did they have the time to consult or instruct anyone else on HTML programming, design, or functionality. If any migration was to take place, User Education would have to do it.

Fred Roecker, User Education Librarian and chair of this Advisory Team, began to work on this re-programming. He knew nothing about the Web, programming of any sort beyond basic HyperCard design and had never accessed the Internet. He sought advice and direction from The Ohio State University Academic Computing Services Office. Although they were only just beginning to experiment with this new medium, they offered an enthusiastic go-ahead for the project. They said The Gateway looked like an exciting project for the Web, one of the best systems at The Ohio State University at that time. Following their instructions Roecker downloaded NCSA Mosaic, the only browser available at that time, and began his search for online documents and tutorials about HTML programming.

From November 1994 through February 1995, Roecker worked on re-programming the Macintosh Gateway HyperCard screens into HTML format. He created a template screen for each hierarchy of the old Gateway, then added the text created by the Advisory Team. User Education student workers re-entered data information screens for hundreds of titles onto these templates. After a lot of false starts and odd-looking screen displays (due to Roecker's learning curve on HTML programming), The WWW Gateway began to resemble the screens created by the Functions/Narrative Advisory Team. A prototype was completed in early 1994.

This prototype satisfied many of the goals of the new system. It used advanced, cheap, stable software. It was faster than the HyperCard version. It displayed more information on screens and in color. It showed improvements in layout, text, and links to related information. And best of all, it could be accessed remotely.

The WWW Gateway, however, lost the ability to front-end catalogs and databases when the project discarded HyperCard and other software. Fortunately, the Libraries recently had joined OhioLINK, the consortium of 25 major academic libraries in

Ohio. Ohio State changed its catalog to the same user-friendly system as was shared by all OhioLINK libraries. OhioLINK also provided access to many online databases, all with the same menu-driven front-end as the catalog. Users now had little difficulty searching these catalogs and databases. Gateway developers were thereby freed from the costly, time-consuming programming task of front-ending electronic resources, knowing users could access and search these items without assistance.

WWW GATEWAY SUBJECT VERSION PROTOTYPE

But as Tiefel and Roecker examined this prototype, they noticed some weaknesses of the Macintosh Gateway remained. Previous evaluations of the Macintosh Gateway showed users had not been using all the Gateway resources available for their topic. The WWW Gateway did little to encourage users to follow the search strategy of moving from broad background information resources to more focused materials. Also, the Web version still required users to examine many levels of screens to retrieve all relevant titles. Finally, this version did not take advantage of HTML programming features such as scrolling screens of information, jumping to specific sections of long screens, forms, and other user-friendly features. The new WWW Gateway was merely a HyperCard design re-programmed into another format.

Roecker began work on an alternate WWW Gateway prototype to address these concerns. The goals of this new version were to improve user awareness of the search strategy and simplify access to a wider variety of resources. The new version also had to incorporate more HTML features that would speed users to information. Finally, it had to expand to meet the needs of upper level undergraduates, graduates, and faculty.

Relevant titles were identified in this new version via broad subjects rather than by resource type (e.g., encyclopedia, periodical index, etc.) as in the Macintosh version. Users now selected a topic to view the titles on that subject recommended by subject specialists. These titles were organized on a single screen in a search strategy layout by resource type, beginning with "Broad Background Information" (encyclopedias) and "Current Information" (periodical indexes) to more specific categories of "Opinions" (reviews), "People" (biographies), etc. Users could scroll through the entire list of resources or jump to a specific resource type to view those titles only.

Titles now contained brief annotations on this same screen to facilitate user evaluation. A title was then linked to a screen which contained further descriptive information, location, call number and links to the electronic version of the item when available. In addition, users could access a glossary of library terms, help tips, and links to the online catalog and other networked databases from these screens.

This Subject WWW Gateway accomplished three major tasks. It encouraged users to do a complete search by arranging titles in the search strategy format for each subject. Users could view a large number of titles, yet understand how to select the most useful for their information needs. Second, it reduced the number of levels users had to search to find information. The Subject WWW Gateway has an opening screen, a list of subjects, the relevant titles for that topic arranged in the search strategy, and a "resource information screen" for each title. Finally, all resource types were combined on the same screen. Users could find titles for different resource types in one place rather than having to select "Encyclopedias," to identify encyclopedia titles, then back out to the main menu and select "Statistical Resources," or other resource types for additional titles. This version seemed to answer the research needs of users as well as to fulfill the search strategy goals of The Gateway.

DEVELOPMENT AND REFINEMENT

The Libraries Automation Office mounted the HyperCard-based WWW Gateway prototype on the Libraries server. The URL for The WWW Gateway was not publicized, even in the OSU Libraries, as developers felt the project was to undergo significant changes in the coming months. Automation also took over the conversion of source cards to resource information screens in HTML format, added graphics and a new opening screen display, and made The WWW Gateway a menu choice from the new WWW Libraries Home Page.

The User Education Office now needed suggestions and moral support from those working with undergraduate students and Libraries administrators. Both early prototypes were demonstrated to members of the Advisory Team, representatives from the Undergraduate Library, the Library Director, the Coordinator of Automation, and even the President of the University.

It was also important to gather suggestions from other personnel regarding how the development should progress. The inability to revise the Macintosh version in a timely fashion had prevented the involvement of most Libraries' personnel. User Education wanted to make sure The WWW Gateway was considered by Libraries personnel and administration as a "Libraries system," not just a User Education or Automation project.

To achieve this, more Libraries personnel had to have a voice in its development. The Gateway Functions/Narrative Advisory Team, renamed The Gateway Development Committee, expanded to include a more-representative membership, a new charge, and permanent status in the Libraries. Brown bag lunches were offered to Libraries personnel and presentations were made for department library heads and subject specialists to talk about The WWW Gateway and gather ideas about how to improve the project.

The results from this information campaign were encouraging. Collection development staff agreed to update all resource information screens in their subject areas. This was a huge job as there were over 800 resource information screens which needed to have call numbers, library locations and descriptions checked. They could also suggest new titles for their subjects, including Internet resources. Most specialists voiced their appreciation at being consulted for this development and vowed to contribute new titles and maintain the content in the future as well.

Other results from these information sessions confirmed the original goals of Tiefel and Roecker. Library personnel wanted the new version to be fast and stable above all. Next they wanted direct access and full functionality without front-ends to all networked electronic resources in the Libraries. They believed it important to guide users to resources available in the University Libraries first, not just send users to the Internet.

HIRING A CONSULTANT

To aid in the evaluation and refinement of the WWW Gateway versions, the Libraries hired Nancy O'Hanlon as a design consultant. O'Hanlon had been one of the original designers of The Macintosh Gateway and, since leaving the Libraries, has had extensive experience with the Internet and information systems such as the Eisenhower Clearinghouse Project, a federally funded science computer system. Currently working as a independent consultant for FoolProof Solutions Digital Publishing, she was eager to contribute to The WWW Gateway.

Working with User Education and the Gateway Development Committee, O'Hanlon examined the comments from the information sessions held with Libraries personnel, reviewed evaluations from the Macintosh Gateway, met with library administrators, the Automation personnel, and subject specialists. With their ideas, she created a series of prototypes and graphics which were incorporated for review by the Development Committee.

FINAL PROTOTYPE

O'Hanlon redesigned the screen listing relevant titles for each subject. A graphical map of the search strategy was designed for the top of each page of titles. A table display replaced the original scrolling list of 90 subjects and included related subjects and descriptions of contents of these subjects. Now, "Substance Abuse" clearly showed it covered topics of "Drugs," "Alcoholism," etc. as well as linked users for further research to related subjects such as "Law" and "Social Welfare." Areas were also created for titles of Internet resources and bibliographies to attract more advanced researchers.

This new version addressed the concerns by Libraries' personnel for the limited number of subject areas, expanded the available titles, emphasized the search strategy, incorporated HTML features of scrolling screens and links to related information, and provided simple direct access to the online catalog and other networked databases. Coupled with the clean graphics and tables used to enhance the displays, O'Hanlon's prototype presented an innovative information system useful to novice and advanced researchers as well as a foundation for Libraries' subject specialists to promote core resources in their collections.

The new version of the WWW Gateway is being tested now with users and Libraries' personnel. Plans are being made to have the WWW Gateway available for use by 6,000 freshmen and sophomores for their two library assignments in Fall 1996. Testing will begin on these students during Spring and

Summer Quarters 1996 to allow time for modifications and test stability.

SUMMARY

We learned many lessons during the months of migrating the system to a new environment. We learned to keep the original goals of project in mind and refer to them whenever design, content, or other decisions are made. A flexible attitude will help you incorporate changes in functionality and layout, as well as address any setbacks encountered.

The project needs to be continuously re-examined through ongoing evaluation, and revised whenever possible to incorporate suggestions from users. As many people as possible need to be involved in the creative process, but a core team of developers must be relied on to keep the project on track and moving forward. Consultants outside the library can provide a fresh perspective. Critical to any development project is the full support of the library administration. Ask for their suggestions often and provide them with frequent updates on the progress.

Publicity for the project gives it credibility. Conference presentation, publications, and demonstrations are valuable tools to spread the word about your design and gain ideas and suggestions from off campus users and professionals.

CONCLUSION

We have migrated a successful information system from an old technology to a new technology while maintaining its original concept of providing users with guidance to identifying, locating and evaluating relevant information. In this migration we have been able to update, enhance and improve the content and display incorporating the advantages available from the new technology.

The WWW version is now capable of reaching The Gateway's original design objective of assisting not only undergraduate users, but all library researchers on and off campus using any type of computer and a limitless number of access locations. With this migration, The WWW Gateway is now available to the world.

Traveling Through the Wilderness: The Long Transition to the Digital Library

By Jane B. Treadwell
Emory University

"Farewell my friends, I'm bound for Canaan, I'm travelling through the wilderness..."

These are the opening lines to one of my favorite hymns[1] from that great American collection of shape-note songs called the *Sacred Harp*. The words are an allusion both to the wilderness experience of the Israelites after they left Egypt, on the way to the Promised Land, as well as to the experience of the Christian on the way to heaven. We in libraries are making our own journey these days, to the promised land of the digital library. But this journey is not without its perils, and as we make the transition from the traditional to the digital library we are going through our own wilderness experience. We are aware of the tremendous changes going on in libraries as we struggle to reach our promised land. However, we haven't fully grasped the enormity of the psychological consequences of this process. This is the subject of my paper today.

Last spring either by accident, or by the happy serendipity that can occur in academe, I stumbled across an article that illuminated for me the situation in which we now find ourselves. Someone from the Business School had posted via e-mail a call for volunteers for a focus group on "organizational disidentification," a feeling on the part of employees that their company had changed so much that they could no longer identify with it, or that they themselves had changed, so that their values and the company's were no longer in sync. (I believe that the example given was of a person who worked for a logging company, but might identify with the Wilderness Society or some other environmental group.) "Hmm, this is interesting," I thought, because some of the people who work in libraries, or certainly some of our patrons, just don't identify with the direction libraries are taking these days, away from print and toward the electronic library. They started working in libraries because they liked books, or they liked helping people, or they liked the wonderful orderliness of cataloging... and now they're expected to know how to cruise cyberspace. "The library of the future," the "virtual library" that library leaders talk about—some people just can't identify with it.

Being intrigued with this concept of "organizational disidentification," I left my e-mail and went to the "Information Gateway" of our local system, where I searched on this term in both ABI-Inform and PsycInfo. To my surprise, I pulled up only one citation, to a 1986 article in the journal *Organizational Dynamics* by an author named William Bridges. In his article, "Managing Organizational Transitions,"[2] and in a 1991 book[3] that expanded on the concepts presented in 1986, I found a model which I believe perfectly describes the situation in which we, both individually and collectively, find ourselves as we journey toward the digital age of libraries. I would like to share that model with you, tell you why I think it's so applicable, and encourage you to use it as you plan for and manage change in your libraries.

Change—that's the watchword in libraries today, isn't it? Change as the only constant has become a fact of life. Why is it, then, that there are always some people on our staffs or among our faculty who are so resistant to change? We bring in consultants, we send people to workshops on change; they seem to get it, but when we introduce the new system, or reorganize a department, or change the set-up of the reference desk, some people still seem unprepared for the event. We label these people as "resistant to change."

We have introduced a change, but *they*—our staff, or students, or faculty—still need to go through a transition. We're all familiar with the dictionary definition of "transition" as "a passing from one form, stage, activity, place, etc. to another." But we usually don't think about "transition" as a psychological process. Bridges says that transition is the process which people go through to absorb change. "Change" and "transition" are two words which are often used interchangeably; however, Bridges suggests that we should regard them as two distinct concepts. According to his model,[4] change is external and therefore situational; it's something to which you can attach a date—on July 25 we brought up the new system, on May 1 the reorganization went into effect. Transition, on the other hand, is an internal process which allows us to process the effects of change, and may take longer for some individuals and organizations than for others.

Transition has three phases, and paradoxically enough, it starts with an ending. Then it goes on to a neutral zone, or wilderness phase, and finally it reaches the end, which is a new beginning.

Transition starts with an ending because the old reality has to end before the new reality can take its place. If you get married, you end your life as a single person. If you buy a new house, you have to give up your old house. Most likely you're excited about your new house: it's bigger, it's more convenient, it has a modern kitchen. But it's hard saying good-bye to your old house: perhaps this is where your children were young, or you've worked hard on the landscaping, and there are special plants that you'll leave behind. Nevertheless, you've made the decision that a change to a new house is for the best, and now you have to leave the old house.

In libraries, too, we have our endings. To bring up that new system we had to turn off the old one. In bringing up the first system, we at some point closed the card catalog. And right now, as we introduce more and more of what we call the digital library, the library as we have known it for over one hundred years (some would say two thousand) is ending.

This ending is a time of great excitement, but it is also a time to grieve for the past. "The failure to identify and be ready for the endings and losses that change produces is the largest single problem that organizations in transition encounter."[5] Sometimes, because we ourselves have not acknowledged endings adequately, our patrons have done it for us. A case in point that may resonate so much at Harvard that I hesitate to bring it up, is the famous Nicholson Baker *New Yorker* article[6] in which Baker lamented the passing of the cherished card catalog files. Many of my colleagues dismissed this article as hysterical romanticism, and some even pointed out its logical inconsistencies, like the failure to recognize that there had been problems with the card catalog, too. But this was not a logical piece of writing. It was an expression of loss, and we were stung because we realized that we as a profession perhaps had not acknowledged this major ending as well as we could have. In embracing the future, we had not done enough to honor the past.

Bridges identifies three aspects of the ending phase:[7]

1. Disengagement—the actual breaking away from the past: the point where people have to let go of the familiar.
2. Disidentification—the loss of one's old identity, or the psychological pulling away from the new identity of the organization. For instance, we used to know what it meant to say that a person was a cataloger, or a reference librarian. But as we see job announcements for things like "metadata organizer," we realize that these old identities are breaking down. And it's been even swifter and in some cases more difficult for our colleagues in formation technology. Some of these people spent twenty years becoming experts on the IBM mainframe, and now they see UNIX and client-server applications taking over. Their old identity is becoming passé, and they either cannot, or are not asked to, assume the new identity.
3. Disenchantment—the feeling that you've been had; that you invested all those years in something, and for what? Not everyone will experience this most extreme and bitter reaction to an ending, but you shouldn't be surprised if in the course of organizational change you encounter this emotion.

They may not express it quite this eloquently, but there are probably people in your organizations right now feeling the way essayist Sven Birkerts felt when he wrote: "I worry that the world will become increasingly alien and inhospitable to me, but also that I may be gradually coerced into living against my natural grain, forced to adapt to a pace and a level of technological complexity that does not suit me, and driven to interact with others in certain prescribed ways."[8]

As you deal with people in the ending phase of transition, it is appropriate to remember (or if you never knew, to find out), about the stages that people go through in times of grief. It is a time to acknowledge losses directly and straightforwardly. Talk to individuals and find out what problems they are having with the change being introduced.

Better yet, before you introduce a change, figure out who stands to gain and who stands to lose something as the innovation is introduced. For instance, in the information technology example above, it is obvious that as client-server architecture replaces the mainframe the people who would stand to lose are the old IBM hands. In the transition to the digital library, in the simplest possible terms, "printies" (as I've heard them called) stand to lose, while "techies" stand to gain. If we are prepared to compensate for the losses, as we should be, then we are looking at a huge investment in training and continuing education.

One strategy for minimizing disidentification and disenchantment is to make the reason for the change clear. What is the problem that the change will address? And is there widespread agreement that the problem is real? Often organizations, libraries included, begin promoting a solution without having convinced staff that there is a problem. We've started organizing people in teams and sending them off to workshops without a common understanding of the problem we hope to address. Quality improvement efforts are especially prone to founder if there is not widespread understanding of the customer-service goals that the many changes in organizational structure are supposed to further. An example comes to mind from a facilitation workshop I participated in on campus a couple of years ago. In a brainstorming exercise a young woman from a unit on campus which had been involved in extensive TQM, threw out, "every idea is a good idea." Incredulous, I couldn't help but reply, "Surely you don't mean that. Some ideas are bad ideas." "Well, that's what they've taught us to say," was her response. I was aware that this unit had been trying to "empower" its staff, but instead this person, at least, had only picked up a new dogma.

In addition to making clear why change is required, it's important during the ending phase, and throughout the transition process, to give people information, to give it to them more than once, and to give it to them in more than one manner. When we were migrating from our first to our second-generation integrated library system, in addition to periodic announcements in the library newsletter, we set up an e-mail list with the clever (we thought) name of NETMA-L (for "Nobody Ever Tells Me Anything"). Announcements were posted to NETMA-L on almost a daily basis, but we noticed that there were very few queries and virtually no discussion. Then one day the president of the support staff organization within the library approached me with a request for a meeting on the subject of the migration. It turned out that people wanted to hear directly from those of us most intimately involved with the project. We had been giving them information, but not in the way in which they wanted to receive it. The meeting was a success, and there were several subsequent "town hall meetings" at critical intervals.

Finally, mark the endings. You may feel foolish and sentimental, but do it anyway. Again, in the example of systems migration, we had a "wake" for the old system. This event was especially important for individuals who had been very involved in the implementation of the first system. It recognized that their efforts had not been forgotten, and had, in fact, served as building blocks.

Even if you've done everything you can to acknowledge an ending, there's still a stage to go through before you get to a new beginning, what Bridges calls the "neutral zone" or the wilderness time. The ship has left the harbor, but you're definitely "at sea." The Israelites have escaped from Egypt, bound for the Promised Land, but they are still travelling through the wilderness.

This, I submit to you, is precisely the circumstance in which we in libraries collectively find ourselves today. We have begun the series of endings that are taking us away from the traditional library, but despite what some would have us believe, we are still a long way from the promised land of the digital library. Listen to what Jay Lucker says about the situation in the introduction to MIT's annual report for 1994: "It is clear that academic research libraries are continuing to exist in the bimodal world of information technology and works on paper. While the range, depth, and variety of services that are available through electronic access is growing at an exponential rate, we still maintain extensive collections of books, journals, theses, microforms, audio and visual materials, manuscripts and archives. Circulation, principally of books, is 20% higher than five years ago and has increased significantly every year since 1988/89."[9]

This is our neutral zone: one where we're adding technology faster than our budgets or our staffs can keep up, but where we're still doing everything else that we did in the past. And it's a time that some of our best forecasters say could last just as long as the wilderness experience of the Israelites. Many of you are familiar with the chart, prepared by the AAU/ARL Task Force on Scientific and Technological Information, which shows the timeline from the traditional to the electronic library.[10] The period of emergent technologies is predicted to last for 40 or 50 years. By the same token, remember that what happened with the Israelites, was that the old leadership died off, and the people who entered the Promised Land hadn't been formed by the Egyptian experience. It's true that most of us will retire, and like Moses, not make it into the Promised Land. But what can we do to help our staff and users through the wilderness? And what are some of the typical behaviors that we are likely to encounter there?

As they say, it's not a pretty picture. Anxiety will very likely rise and productivity may fall. There will be conflict between those who want to move forward quickly and those who want to return to the past. Here's how my fellow South Carolinian, John C. Calhoun, expressed it: "The interval between the decay of the old and the formation and establishment of the new constitutes a period of transition which must always necessarily be one of uncertainty, confusion, error and wild and fierce fanaticism."[11]

This sounds grim, but there is a silver lining. In addition to the disorientation and disintegration that may be experienced in the wilderness, there is also the possibility of discovery.[12] Innovation is more likely to emerge in a time when the old ways have broken down and a new order has not yet risen. We can see this happening on a fairly large scale right now. The various digital library projects that many of our libraries are engaged in, the full-text centers that we are establishing, the Web pages we are creating, the collaboration or outright merger with academic computing, the outsourcing of previously sacrosanct activities such as cataloging—these are all examples of the creative kinds of activities that are emerging out of the wilderness experience.

What we have to be very careful about is the temptation to rush to closure. There is a natural tendency in times of anxiety and confusion to want to get things settled. We say to ourselves, "there, we've set up our home page, now things can calm down for awhile." Or, "there, we've set up some teams, that ought to hold us as far as organizational change goes for a while." But not only are we kidding ourselves if we think we can stop change, we are also limiting the opportunities for further innovation.

Also, we walk a fine line between building a sense of solidarity and stifling dissent. There will be people who don't like the direction you or your organization has taken and they need to be allowed to have their say. What is important is to allow people the time to make the change from the old way to the new. How to do this without things coming to a grinding halt? One way would be to create a group specifically charged with facilitating communication between the leadership of the organization and those most affected by the change.[13]

If transition is a psychological process that begins with an ending, then it makes sense that it ends with a new beginning. At some point, to the question, "are we there yet?" you can answer, "yes". Beginnings occur when a psychological commitment has been made to the change, so they won't happen at the same time for everyone. They can't be forced, but Bridges suggests several things that you can do to encourage them, and he helpfully begins each suggestion with a "p" so that we can remember them better: [14]

1. Purpose—explain what the purpose is of the outcome you seek. People need to know there's a logical reason for what you want them to do.
2. Picture—describe (or get the participants to describe) how the outcome will look and feel.
3. Plan—develop a method for phasing in the outcome.
4. Part—give everyone in the organization a part to play.

For those of you who just can't get enough of Meyers-Briggs, Bridges also relates these four aspects of encouraging new beginnings to the four main Meyers-Briggs types.[15] The purpose, or the main idea behind the change, should have great appeal for *thinking* types, who want to know what the logical reason is for the change. The picture (or as we often call it today, the vision statement) could well be favored by *intuitive* types. These are the people who have no problem imagining how a new service, for example, will look and feel on opening day. Some people need things a bit more concrete than the two types above. For these *sensing* types, a detailed plan, explaining what will happen when in terms of training, etc. will be immensely helpful. Finally, *feeling* types will want to know that everyone's included, that everyone has a part to play. For instance, in planning for a new building at my library, we have established almost a dozen working groups or task forces to deal with various aspects of the project, and we called for volunteers to insure widespread involvement—so that just about everyone who wanted to, could have a part to play.

I wish there were more time to spend on each of these aspects, but I would like to emphasize one point: try to be sure that you have a readily discernible purpose for any changes that you're implementing. This seems like common sense, but often change efforts fail either because there was not a real purpose, or because the purpose was never made sufficiently clear to people.[16] Also, the purpose needs to grow out of an organization's own circumstances: a change effort should not be launched merely because it's fashionable. So before you outsource all your cataloging or flatten your organization, ask yourself if this is something that is really called for by your circumstances.

As with any model, this model of transition is not as discrete as it sounds. In the larger transition to the digital library, there will be smaller transitions going on all the time. One transition may be in its wilderness phase as another one is just beginning. You could think of transition as a process akin to the change of seasons. When does spring start, for instance? On the calendar date of March 21 or 22? When you see the first crocus or daffodil? Or when everything is in full bloom? At some point, there can be no denying—it's spring! But this new beginning, signaled by the end of winter, was accomplished by many individual transitions, some of which took longer than others.

To be consistent I should finish this talk with another Biblical reference. But given that I'm writing this paper at the end of December, I thought I should pay homage to a transition many of us are going through now: life without *Calvin and Hobbes*.

Bill Watterson fortuitously supplied me with two Sunday strips in December which make good illustrations of transition.

In the first, Calvin and Hobbes are sledding.[17] Calvin seems excited; Hobbes seems a little apprehensive. Calvin says, "Let's try this path over here!" Hobbes: "I don't see a path." Calvin: "We'll *make* a path!" Hobbes: "Huh boy." Hobbes is obviously reluctant to proceed, but Calvin, instead of helping Hobbes to see the path, or helping him to want to make the path, merely offers a recitation of the glories of change, with the implication, "Hobbes, you old fuddy-duddy, why can't you get with it?" All the while they are hurtling downhill.

Did Calvin have a clear purpose for going down that hill? No, he was engaging in change for change's sake. And even if they hadn't gone over the edge, Calvin did not have Hobbes with him psychologically. Hobbes, as always, comes up with a bit of wisdom for us as he lies half-buried in the snow: "The problem with new experiences is that they're so rarely the ones you choose." The transition to the digital library is not something that most people working in libraries or using libraries have chosen. Like the other great upheavals in our history—the introduction of the printing press, the industrial revolution—forces of economics, invention, and culture have combined to bring us the Information Age. It is our responsibility to facilitate the transition to it, and not simply to take off downhill as Calvin did.

But let's conclude on a happier note. In the final *Calvin and Hobbes* strip,[18] we find our heroes once again out in the snow with a sled. This time, however, both Calvin *and* Hobbes look happy and excited. This time, they give voice to the positive side of the wilderness experience: the opportunity for creative activity, for discovery. Listen to what Hobbes says this time: "Everything familiar has disappeared! The world looks brand-new!" Calvin concurs: "A day full of possibilities!" And in the end, we see them gleefully heading downhill, with Calvin exclaiming, "It's a magical world, Hobbes, ol' buddy . . . let's go exploring."

There will be times as all of us go through the psychological transition to the digital library, when we will crash and find ourselves face down in the snow. The important thing is to be able to pick ourselves up and continue on the journey to a new beginning. Let's go exploring!

ENDNOTES

1. "Parting Friends" in *The Sacred Harp*, 1991 Revision (Bremen, Ga.: Sacred Harp Publishing Co., 1991), 267.
2. William Bridges, "Managing Organizational Transitions," *Organizational Dynamics* 15 (Summer 1986): 24–33.
3. William Bridges, *Managing Transitions: Making the Most of Change* (Reading, Mass.: Addison-Wesley, 1991).
4. Ibid., 3
5. Ibid., 5
6. Nicholson Baker, "Annals of Scholarship: Discards," *New Yorker* 70, no. 7 (April 4, 1994).
7. Bridges, "Managing Organizational Transitions," 27–28.
8. Sven Birkerts, *The Gutenberg Elegies: the Fate of Reading in an Electronic Age* (Boston: Faber and Faber, 1994), 28.
9. "From the Director," *MIT Libraries' Year, 1994* (Boston: Massachusetts Institute of Technology Libraries, 1994).
10. *Reports of the AAU Task Forces: on Acquisition and Distribution of Foreign Language and Area Study Materials: a National Strategy for Managing Scientific and Technological Information: Intellectual Property Rights in an Electronic Environment* (Washington, D.C.: Association of Research Libraries, 1994), 63.
11. John C. Calhoun, as quoted in Bridges, *Managing Transitions*, 36.
12. Bridges, "Managing Organizational Transitions," 29.
13. Bridges, *Managing Transitions*, 42.
14. Ibid., 52,
15. Ibid., 66.
16. Ibid., 53.
17. Bill Watterson, "Calvin and Hobbes," *Atlanta-Journal Constitution*, 17 December 1995, Comics section.
18. Watterson, "Calvin and Hobbes," *Atlanta-Journal Constitution*, 31 December 1995, Comics section.

A Computer Is Like . . . :
Imagination, Learning and Computers

By Susan Barnes Whyte and Loretta Rielly
Linfield College and Oregon State University

In a recent essay, Peter Lyman challenges instruction librarians to rethink tool-based instruction methods by posing the question: "Is using a computer like driving a car, reading a book, or solving a problem?"[1] How can librarians design effective instruction for students but still engage in the exploration of ideas? In our zeal to master the machines ourselves and our predilection towards organizing knowledge and combating ambiguity, we do a disservice to our users, particularly undergraduate students, who need a conceptual understanding of machine-based retrieval systems rather than an approach which emphasizes the importance of the right key for the right answer. There is no longer one correct, linear way to do library research. Indeed, we question whether there ever has been one, though many of us have certainly tried to pretend otherwise in our instruction.[2]

Frequently our library systems demand that we train students to use the machine at the cost of developing the critical thinking/problem solving skills needed in the online environment. Skills to use systems should be "embodied" or "tacit" so that we do not need to ask: "How do I make this machine work?" but rather "What does this information mean to me and my search?" We need to progress from teaching computer commands to teaching about another medium for ideas. Moreover, we need to emphasize flexibility and ambiguity as people switch from system to system, be it bibliographically-based or web-based. The more that learning is focused upon a discrete task rather than upon learning by discovery, the less transferable the skills.

Our challenge as teachers when working with systems is to always keep in mind and communicate to our audience:

1. Computers "know" nothing;
2. Language is of paramount importance in a computerized information environment, more so than in a card catalog or print index where there is a visible, immediate context for the words;
3. Computerized library databases, and even web-based home pages, require the same critical thinking, problem solving skills that understanding a print index does.

Computers can—and should—be objects to think with. We need to get beyond the tool to the text within.

What *do* we teach students about library research? For years, the model has been a process: define your topic using encyclopedias, identify books and articles on your topic using the library catalog and periodical indexes, locate the articles and books and evaluate their usefulness. Beginning early and following the process assures success in library land. Is this realistic, however, especially in the interactive world of hypermedia?

In preparing for this paper, we found ourselves bemused by our own process. The kernel of this proposal sprang from a note on a list-serv.[3] We began a search of the literature, which we quickly, and independently of each other, abandoned because we did not have a clear enough picture of our topic and, therefore, did not have the words to use. We certainly never considered looking at an encyclopedia article; had we thought about it, we would have dismissed the idea, again because we were not really certain what we wanted to find and, thus, did not have the words to use. Instead, we began tracking down citations in Lyman's essay, more or less serendipitously leaping from source to source. We also browsed in the books and journals stacks and talked with colleagues and with each other. Our research process reflected that of academic faculty as described by Virginia Chappell and others: "The scholarly research that professors do . . . is complex, idiosyncratic, and even messy, quite different from the ordered linear procedure presented by traditional library instruction."[4] As we plunged further on in this reckless fashion, we better understood why the linear model of bibliographic instruction just does not work anymore. Focusing upon the process at the expense of the content is like looking at the sentence and ignoring the words.

Libraries and their organization depend upon words used well. Language makes the computers "work": the correct string of characters typed on a screen yields the proper match in any retrieval system, be it an electronic periodical index or an Internet search engine. The catch, of course, is finding the *correct* string of characters. We know that a facility for thinking of different ways of stating a research problem is the key to finding information. Undergraduate students often do not have this flexibility with language nor do they understand the computer's mindless mirroring of language. Often, too, they cannot conceive that there is any other way to state an idea. Imaginative research seems to be an oxymoron! Donna Rubens writes that, "Each person has a unique semantic network of associations."[5] Our facility with language is based on our experiences. The language used in our computer systems is language devised by us. Too frequently, it is a language not understood by our students. We need to both draw on and broaden our students' networks of associations if we are to help them use our systems with success.

Several articles have been published which carefully consider search success on online catalogs (OPACs). Not too surprisingly, users generally do not understand the capability of keyword searches nor the implicit imperative of using synonymous terms. Playing with language is a concept which eludes many undergraduates. Patricia Wallace underscores this important point in discussing the transaction log of her university library's OPAC. She not only notes the problem of thinking of "alternative search terms or strategies," she reminds the reader of "Monster" words such as "History, Government, and Political" that disable many library systems, leaving the user with no results.[6] Wallace underscores the problem when she tracks the history of OPAC development: "Early online systems, containing elaborate search protocols and screens cluttered with extraneous data, were developed on the assumption that the majority of online searching would be done by trained professionals or by end users who had received sufficient training."[7] The stakes have now changed; most libraries have OPACs and students generally are accustomed to that face-to-screen encounter in every library's lobby. Ironically, the physical act of using computers is more familiar to our students than to us. We, not they, are the ones who still fear "breaking" something, or who worry about pushing the right key.

For students aged 18–24, computers are objects that they have grown up with in school and often at home. Jim Rettig points out that "1993–94 college freshmen were in first grade when the Atari craze captured the nation and Pac-Man achieved enough recognition in the popular culture to be enshrined on t-shirts."[8] 1995–96 freshmen entered the first grade in the fall of 1984; the Macintosh entered our world in January 1984. Many students today are used to pointing and clicking, to figuring out how things work on a computer screen, to writing on a computer. In *The Second Self: Computers and the Human Spirit* (published in 1984!), Sherry Turkle points out that even then " [children] take [computers] for granted. To them it is not a new technology but a fact of life."[9] The "children" she speaks of are now in college, and if they are arguably the first group to use computers in their educational and daily lives, consider those who are now in middle school and high school. Steven Gilbert, the Director of Technology Projects for the American Association for Higher Education, noted recently that "the percentage of entering freshmen who already had some academic computing experience moved above 50% in 1995."[10]

Again, as Turkle indicates, in 1984 children were accustomed to this kind of learning, i.e., figuring out how to make the machines work. This "tinkering" does not recede as one ages; rather, like bicycle riding or playing an instrument, a certain residual intrinsic skill level, a level of comfort in working with keyboards and screens, remains. Consider this description of playing Pac-Man: "you always have to think faster than the monsters move, and this means that in order for you to play successfully, the general principles, like the patterns, have to be more than memorized. It's more than thinking—in a way it is beyond thinking. The hand learns what to do and does it automatically, just as the hand 'knows' after playing chord X on the piano to go directly and inexorably to chord Y."[11] Many students *do* have this intrinsic notion of how to play a computer game. It is highly visual, interactive and they can win! Losing is a challenge to try another approach. A mistake is information to be used in the next game. How can we translate this same sense of tinkering with computer games to working with library systems? Turkle could be describing how librarians search online systems. The sense of discovery and the facility with problem solving (both of which flourish in computer games) should exist with online computer library systems.

If we continue to teach a linear process and keyboarding skills, we do our students a great disservice. What has not changed in education is the quest, for truth, for ideas, a concept which extrapolates easily to library research. Mona McCormick suggests that we have gone astray in our persistence in teaching keyboard skills, a predilection which no doubt stems partially from our own struggle to make these machines work for us: "Somehow in our preoccupation with library procedures, we have ignored the reason for searching—to learn, to make informed decision, to evaluate applications of knowledge, to find truth."[12] Barbara Fister underscores this concern that library instruction fits into the greater framework of researching and writing texts: "This emphasis on retrieval systems and their manipulation tends to suggest to students—whether we mean to or not—that research consists of the ordered use of tools to locate pieces of information from which research projects can be assembled. There are two major problems with this concept: first, students should not be engaged in assembling parts but in creating texts; second, most of our systems don't retrieve information, they retrieve texts."[13]

Too often we, as librarians, perpetuate this technonirvana by concentrating on the machine and forgetting our audience, the students. The key issue is connecting students and the ideas embedded in a text, whether they reside upon a library's shelf or somewhere on the Internet. How do we get beyond the screen to the ideas embedded in the text? Taylor Hubbard writes about "look[ing] consciously 'at' the media as well as 'through' it." He sees computers as "rhetorical machines that invite students to manipulate text, images, and sounds, thereby participating in the creation of knowledge."[14] This idea of "looking through" implies the need for students to connect with the ideas within a text, to compare and contrast them to other ideas in other texts, to create, and build their own ideas. Jacobson and Jacobson use the metaphor of a scaffold to describe providing support for students learning this research process.[15] The scaffold directs students but does not constrain their imagination. How can we help build the scaffolding so that students can go on to more independent research and be able to reflect upon the process and the texts that they encounter?

Although our students are increasingly comfortable with computers, their encounters with library machines can be overwhelming and not fun, and certainly not conducive to a learning experience. For one, as James Rettig points out, they are "drab."[16] Most are monotone, consisting only of words, which in and of themselves are dull. OPACs, in particular, are also monochrome, without color or visual interest. Second, students are often perplexed because the computers do different functions: some access books, some journals, some Internet resources. But then, some computers perform all these functions, creating another kind of confusion. Finally, any given search can spew out a dizzying amount of information. As Ellul indicates, the normal reaction to information overload is to reject all of it: "They throw it all out, including the data that might be of interest, which they miss because the information received is neither knowledge nor organization. . . . Or else it constitutes a kind of confused mush. . . ."[17]

For many students, library computers represent "an endless, undifferentiated information system."[18] They often have little concept of where the information came from and cannot connect with it. They have no way of knowing whether the information is good or bad, but the assumption seems to be that if it's "in there" it's good. In their context of fast food, automated cash machines, and one-stop shopping, it is perhaps a logical assumption that library computers can perform the same function of producing fast and good information.

So, what's a librarian to do? Caught between machines and their linear way of reacting to "strings of characters" entered into them, how do we engage students in thinking *with* their machines? How do we capitalize on their sense of discovery and yet also connect them with the ideas in the texts, be they print or electronic?

There is no way to wave the wand and have magical understanding appear. Yet there are a few simple, easily implemented ideas which can work. Tie the library instruction to the class's particular content, involve the classroom instructor before and during the library class, teach from the students' topics, treat the class like a reference encounter and "interview" the students, pay attention to language, use stories to convey concepts, teach from mistakes, and, finally, use humor throughout. Keeping a sense of play alive in the classroom, and at the reference desk, will ease their and our anxiety about the process.

The most important part of the scaffold we can provide for our students is to connect our instruction with what matters most to them—getting a good grade. The more closely library instruction addresses their immediate need, the more the students will respond to it. The relativist approach advocated by John Carroll works: "teach people what they need to learn in order to do what they wish to do."[19] Talk with the classroom instructor before the class. Determine her objectives. Find out everything you can about the topics and the students. Working with faculty before the class presentation also engages the person who gives the grades and who has much more influence on students' attitudes with the process than we, the librarians, ever will. If the process of researching a topic is important to the instructor, and especially if it's reflected in the grade, the students will be more receptive. Have the teacher participate in the class as well. Not only does it reinforce the importance of the instruction, it provides a model of a "real" researcher and links the bibliographic and the subject content. The instructor knows the language of the particular discipline and can contribute to a five minute brainstorming session on words to describe a topic. She can frequently contribute the name of an expert in the discipline, reinforcing the idea that library research is about connecting with people's ideas and discovering a bibliographic trail to follow.

Work with the students' topics, not one prepared in advance because it demonstrates concepts nicely and neatly. We know that library research is rarely a tidy process. Teach from the real not the ideal. Problematic topics are especially good. If a student wants to write a five page paper about global warming, let the other students help her discover it's unrealistic. The goal is to provide students with a learning experience that replicates what they will really encounter as researchers. Treat the class like a reference desk encounter and "interview" the students. Involve them in the learning process. Have a student do the keyboarding so you can join the class and participate in the brainstorming. Don't teach—coach.

Pay attention to language. Words matter immensely in working with any library computer or text-based system. Spend at least five minutes thinking of synonymous terms and phrases. Do it as a large group or in small groups. Not only have the students identified words to use, they have spent time actively thinking about their topic.

Then, bring the words to the computer. Prepare the students for the tricks of searching electronic systems. Use very vivid examples. We all have false drop stories which always entertain students. How many different ways can the word "environment" be used? What happens when you type the word "cherokee" into any given database? What about "sports bars"? Try "tubby tubers." How about oxymorons? Military intelligence? Or, how about LCSH? There are abundant ways to demonstrate language and its limitations. This activity prepares them for the computer database and it also humanizes library research, and frankly, us. Talking of our past mistakes is a way of telling them that we all learn and remember from mistakes.

Emphasizing the ambiguity and the absurdity of systems can elucidate that playing with them is a good way to make them work. Marvin Minsky speaks of this becoming used to a new way of doing something, and his theory works well for librarians and students: "In the early stages of acquiring any really new skill, a person must adopt at least a partly antipleasure attitude: 'Good, this is a chance to experience awkwardness and to discover new kinds of mistakes.' It is the same for doing mathematics, climbing freezing mountain peaks, or playing pipe organs with one's feet. Some parts of the mind find it horrible, while other parts enjoy forcing those first parts to work for them."[20] Teaching from mistakes is a recognized method of learning with computers. Of course for us to convince students that this is part of learning, we need to be at ease with this uncomfortable process ourselves and drop any pretense of being the sage on the stage. John Carroll emphasizes that the "essence of the minimalist approach is to obstruct as little as possible the learner's self-initiated efforts to find meaning in the activities of learning.... The minimalist model tries to capitalize on what learners do spontaneously instead of being embarrassed by it.[21]

To work further on building a scaffold for students, we need to encourage logical interaction with the machines. Have the students ask "Where am I?" when they sit down at a computer.[22] This simple question reminds students that computers do different things. Even if the color of the screen stays the same, the information inside does not. This question also helps them focus on the task at hand. Display a screen from the library's online catalog and ask what they see, instead of *telling* them what to see. This reinforces the importance of their paying attention to the screen. Ask "What is important to you, as researchers, on this screen?" This positions them in their role as researchers not simply students being told what to do and how to think; it turns the authority over to them. There are several important things on any bibliographic screen. Asking them to point out several and explain why can make for lively discussion and engagement. Why is it important to see where or when a book is published? Who is this publisher? Would you view this book differently if it were published by Harvard University Press? Why? Why is it important that there is an index? A bibliography? We see and understand the bibliographic information on the screen. It is not at all apparent to the student. To them, this is entirely new unexplored terrain.

Rubens argues that end users "have no model of information flow, no knowledge of the bibliographic chain, no knowledge of subject relationships or of knowledge creation."[23] She suggests that a brief introduction to the writers or producers of these texts and how they are funneled into library systems helps to connect students with the information terrain. For example, to a student *Private Forest Investment* is a title on a screen, an example that Oberman calls "disembodied information."[24] But, the producer, the Forest Service, is something with which they *can* connect. It is no longer "disembodied information" when it is linked to a familiar creator, whether it's a person or an institution.

Remind students of their daily connection with information decisions. How do they decide which shampoo to purchase? Which candidate to vote for? Lex Runciman and Chris Anderson, English professors at Linfield College and Oregon State University, make a compelling case for our frequent use of information to solve a problem, answer a question, or make a decision:

> Research isn't just something a college-writing assignment forces you into. You gather and use information from the moment you get up in the morning. Often the information comes directly from your own experience: You look out the window, see that it's raining, and decide this isn't a good day to wear shorts. Your own experience—the rain you saw—has told you what to do.... When you rely on what your own senses and thinking tell you, you're using experience as a form of evidence or support. When you make plans based on the weather forecast in the newspaper or on television, you're using someone else's information: You're doing research.[25]

This takes some of the mystique out of the research process. To make the unfamiliar familiar, compare the known with the unknown. Compare an article about communication between men and women in *Glamour* with one in *The Journal of Social Psychology*. Talk about audience, authority, and reasons for producing information. Once you have established this difference, you can naturally move to the indexes: *InfoTrac* and the *Social Sciences Index*. Comparison and analogy work well as part of the scaffolding.

The point is to keep the instruction simple and to engage the students. Teaching like this is very much improvisational—but it works. It engages the students. It can help them problem solve with the computer. They can easily perceive that if some word does not work, then another will. Learning from trying is part of the process. This makes the process more like discovery, especially when delivered with an attitude from the teacher/coach which is encouraging and humorous.

ENDNOTES

1. Peter Lyman, "Is Using a Computer Like Driving a Car, Reading a Book, or Solving a Problem? The Computer as Machine, Text, and Culture," in *Work and Technology in Higher Education: The Social Construction of Academic Computing*, ed. Mark A. Shields (Hillsdale, NJ: Lawrence Erlbaum, 1995), 19.

2. We're suggesting that we, practicing instruction librarians, tend to take a tool-based or process approach because that's what we've always done. We want to acknowledge the many librarians who have written and spoken so well about concept-based instruction and critical thinking. Those who have most influenced our thinking are Deborah Fink, Craig Gibson, Frances F. and Michael J. Jacobson, Barbara MacAdam, Mona McCormick, Cerise Oberman, and Mary Reichel.
3. Ellen Hoffmann (1995, February 17), Tools and Play [Discussion] LIBrary Women and Technology [Online]. Available e-mail LIBWAT-L@UBVM.cc.buffalo.edu
4. Virginia A. Chappell, Randall Hensley, and Elizabeth Simmons-O'Neill, "Beyond Information Retrieval: Transforming Research Assignments into Genuine Inquiry," *Journal of Teaching Writing* 13 (1994): 212.
5. Donna Rubens, "Formulation Rules for Posing Good Subject Questions: Empowerment for the End-User," *Library Trends* 39 (Winter 1991): 289.
6. Patricia Wallace, "How Do Patrons Search the Online Catalog When No One's Looking? Transaction Log Analysis and Implications for Bibliographic Instruction and System Design," *RQ* 33 (Winter 1993): 247.
7. Wallace, 249.
8. James Rettig, "The Convergence of the Twain or Titanic Collision? BI and Reference in the 1990's Sea of Change," *Reference Services Review* 23 (Spring 1995): 10.
9. Sherry Turkle, *The Second Self: Computers and the Human Spirit* (New York: Simon and Schuster, 1984), 66.
10. Steven Gilbert (1996, January 12), AAHESGIT [Discussion] AAHESGIT [Online]. Available e-mail AAHESGIT@list.cren.net
11. Turkle, 68.
12. Mona McCormick, "Critical Thinking and Library Instruction," *RQ* 22 (Summer 1983), 339.
13. Barbara Fister, "The Research Processes of Undergraduate Students," *The Journal of Academic Librarianship* 28 (July 1992): 212.
14. Taylor E. Hubbard, "Bibliographic Instruction and Postmodern Pedagogy," *Library Trends* 42 (Fall 1995): 449–50.
15. Frances F. Jacobson and Michael J. Jacobson, "Representative Cognitive Learning Theories and BI: A Case Study of End User Searching," *Research Strategies* 11 (Summer 1993): 128.
16. Rettig, 10.
17. Jacques Ellul, *The Technological Bluff* (Grand Rapids, MI: Eerdmans, 1990), 330.
18. Cerise Oberman, "Unmasking Technology: A Prelude to Teaching," *Research Strategies* 13 (Winter 1995): 37.
19. John Carroll, *The Nurnberg Funnel: Designing Minimalist Instruction for Practical Computer Skill* (Cambridge, Mass.: The MIT Press, 1990): 3.
20. Carroll, xvii-xviii.
21. Marvin Minsky, *The Society of Mind*, quoted in Richard Saul Wurman, *Information Anxiety* (New York: Doubleday, 1989): 154.
22. Abigail Loomis and Deborah Fink, "Instruction: Gateway to the Virtual Library," in *The Virtual Library: Visions and Realities,* ed. Laverna M. Saunders (Westport, Conn.: Meckler, 1993): 49–50.
23. Rubens, 272.
24. Oberman, 37.
25. Chris Anderson and Lex Runciman, *A Forest of Voices: Reading and Writing the Environment* (Mountain View, CA: Mayfield, 1995): 56.

UWired: A Collaborative Model for Integrating Technology and Information Skills across the Curriculum

By Anne Zald, Oren Sreebny, Theresa Mudrock, Bernice Laden, and Andrea Bartelstein
University of Washington

INTRODUCTION

The UWired project began as an outgrowth of the Provost's initiative on teaching and technology. The primary goal of UWired is to use technology and information resources to foster the formation of new learning communities of students, librarians, faculty, and computing professionals. The focus of the project is not just technology; more importantly, it is collaboration. We see technology as a catalyst for collaboration that will lead to curricular change, and a tool that can strengthen a sense of community by allowing community members to communicate and exchange ideas without being time or place bound.

Computer technology also provides access to information resources on the Internet. Teaching students to use information resources is a major part of our project. We feel that if students have the opportunity to use information and technology resources early in their education, that they will perform better in upper division courses and will graduate with life-long learning strategies as well as a level of technical skill useful in all, and expected in most, careers.

Our focus in this paper is on collaboration and the integration of information literacy skills across the curriculum. As we tell our story, you will see that collaboration has occurred on many levels throughout the planning and implementation phases as well as in day-to-day instructional activities. From UWired's outset, major campus units have worked together: University Libraries, Computing & Communications, Undergraduate Education, and University Extension. At a major university large units can develop their own culture in terms of how they operate, the jargon they use, and the unwritten standards of behavior and interaction. These differences can often be a barrier to collaboration, and we sometimes wonder among ourselves why we have been able to work together. However, the University Libraries have had a history of collaboration with Computing & Communications, and this may have helped to stabilize the larger collaboration. Another conjecture for our successful collaboration is that once the top level administrators decided the UWired project was a good idea, they gave us the charge of implementing it and stood out of our way. Without micromanagement or overly detailed program goals set by an elaborate planning process, the program participants were free to take risks and move the program forward. Further, the talents of each partner in our collaboration are complementary and we have a common goal: We want to improve undergraduate education. We respect each other's cultures and operating limits; we try to be inclusive and to communicate; we try to be flexible; and we believe we can make a difference.

COLLABORATIVE RELATIONSHIPS AMONG CAMPUS UNITS: BEFORE UWIRED

Librarians at the University of Washington provided a range of orientation and instruction activities to students for many years before the UWired program came into being. In particular, the Undergraduate Library has provided formal course-related and course-integrated library and information skills instruction for the past sixteen years. In order to infuse library skills into core courses across the curriculum librarians have had to spend a great deal of energy marketing the instruction program and cultivating individual faculty members to see the importance of course-integrated instruction. This is due primarily to the fact there is no common course that all UW students must take that would allow librarians to develop course-integrated library instruction around that curriculum. Further, information literacy is not a formal university requirement. It is assumed that students will graduate with information literacy skills, but no formal steps have been taken to assure this. The UWired project is a first step in the development of a university-wide information literacy component in the curriculum.

The University of Washington Libraries and Computing & Communications had established a successful working relationship as a result of the joint development in 1992 of the campus-wide information system known as UWIN, or the University of Washington Information Navigator. At the same time, the Libraries were moving from a proprietary automated system to one that could be integrated into the campus network. Together, Libraries and Computing & Communications staff developed graphical and character-based interfaces to the online catalog and locally mounted indexing and abstracting databases.

THE UWIRED PROJECT

The UWired project began to take shape in the spring of 1994, with a group of about fourteen people meeting on a weekly basis to hash out everything from policy issues to equipment and furniture specifications for a new computer lab. This group even adopted its own jargon that includes words such as "collaboratory," which is a computer lab conducive to collaboration, and "podular," which describes the modular pod-shaped furniture used in the Collaboratory. This initial group included the Associate Vice Provost of Undergraduate Education, the Computing & Communications Director of Planning and Facilities Infrastructure, the Associate Director of Libraries for Public Services, the Director of the Undergraduate Library, the Manager of Classroom Support Services, the Computing & Communications Assistant Director for Client Services, several consultants from Computing & Communications, three librarians representing various specialties, an undergraduate student, the Director of New Student Programs, and the Director of Curriculum and Planning. The group met weekly, and in any given week the group could have grown or shrunk from this core. Those who were able to attend discussed possibilities, made decisions, and divided the work. Thus the first year's administrative style was a loosely organized collective effort best described as a well-functioning anarchy.

The first phase of the UWired project targeted entering freshmen with the well-established UW Freshman Interest Group (FIG) program providing the framework. A FIG is a group of twenty to twenty-four students who share a cluster of two or three courses organized around a common theme, such as anthropology and composition, literature and imagination, or health sciences. In all cases there is at least one class—usually English composition—in which members of the group are the only members of the class. In addition to sharing the same classes, students in each UWired FIG attend a weekly information and technology seminar. By building on the established model of learning communities that the FIGs offered, we have been better able to work with faculty and teaching assistants in a given FIG and build information retrieval and evaluation skills into the course objectives. In this sense networked technology has been the catalyst for curriculum transformation.

We felt it was important for students to have good access to computing in order for them to use information and technology resources in their studies. Thus for the first year, with assistance from Apple Computer, we lent each of the 65 UWired FIG students a Macintosh 540c PowerBook laptop computer. We built a Collaboratory with the capability to network the laptops and used it as the classroom for the information and technology seminar. Students had network access not only in this facility, but through dial-IP service from home.

THE INFORMATION & TECHNOLOGY SEMINAR—YEAR 1

In the first year of the project, librarians taught the information and technology seminar with assistance from a student staff member from Computing & Communications who provided technical support, and to whom we refer as the "UWired Technical Lead." Concurrently with this seminar, students attended a weekly meeting with a FIG peer advisor who oriented them to campus academic and social resources and conducted class sessions on topics such as career choice, course registration, and time management.

The information and technology seminar had four goals: to introduce electronic communication skills; to develop information navigation and evaluation skills; to emphasize skills which would enable students to identify the best information for a project regardless of format, whether that be print, CD-ROM, microfiche, video, the Internet, or another resource; and to the extent possible, to relate these skills to the content and assignments of the students' other courses. While the FIG program runs only during autumn quarter, during the pilot year the information and technology seminar continued for three quarters, the students' entire freshman year.

Individuals brought varying levels of computer knowledge to the class. Many had some experience with word processing but few had ventured onto the Internet or dallied with e-mail. The goal of autumn quarter therefore was to ensure that all students reached an elementary level of understanding and expertise in basic computer, communication and information navigation skills. The Technical Lead provided needed expertise to lead the students through the ins and outs of the PowerBook, the intricacies involved in connecting to the campus computer network, and the nuances of Fetch (a Macintosh FTP client).

Once students gained some familiarity with the computer itself, they learned various communication applications. E-mail quickly became integral to students both as an academic tool (e.g., contact with faculty or turning in assignments) and as a social tool. Each FIG had its own electronic discussion list that included the FIG students as well as faculty, teaching assistants, librarians and the Technical Lead. These discussion lists became class forums in which to disseminate and discuss assignments, policy and reading material. The discussion lists also served a social function for the students.

Newsgroups and e-mail served as a segue into issues concerning netiquette and responsible use of the Internet. For first-year students the FIG experience helps to establish a sense of being a member of their class, their university and the larger academic community. Both the class discussion list and participation in the wider community of Usenet reinforced this understanding of their role in the academic world as well as in the virtual electronic community.

Librarians introduced information navigation skills in three sections: The UW campus information system (UWIN), library-related databases (UW Libraries catalog and networked periodical databases), and the WWW. In this manner students were introduced to information in an ever widening circle from local information (campus information system and library catalog) to the wider range of sources offered by commercial online databases and the expanse of the Internet.

The WWW was naturally a great hit with students. As they had when introduced to Usenet newsgroups and bibliographic databases, students were required to evaluate the information they found. Each student selected a WWW site (some class-related, others recreational) and evaluated the content, identified information about the author and determined the potential use of a site. Students then shared this information as they presented the site to the class. It slowly became clear to students that not all information published on the Internet or even in a journal or book was necessarily authoritative, reliable, or useful—in this ever increasing world of information, evaluation becomes more and more critical.

By the end of autumn quarter students were active users of e-mail, many were frequent participants in Usenet newsgroups, most were exploring the Web, and all had a basic ability to find a book or article on a topic.

The subject focus during winter quarter became the Internet itself—an exploration of the social, political and economic issues related to the Internet and information technology. Students reviewed and reinforced the skills learned during autumn as they began working on group projects focused on some socio-economic aspect of the Internet; e.g., censorship, commercialization, interpersonal relations, cyberculture, and privacy. The group project consisted of finding secondary information on the topic (articles and books), monitoring newsgroups related to the topic, and finding and evaluating related WWW sites. Students then presented their findings to the class using some of the technological tools they had learned (*PowerPoint* or Web pages) and prepared a final annotated bibliography of sources consulted.

Students became creators of information as they began work on personal home pages. Some students used the WWW to provide personal information about themselves, their family and friends while others provided links to favorite sites. It became increasingly evident to the students in their first experience publishing that anyone, even a freshman at the UW, could put information on the Internet—both a daunting and exhilarating notion. This experience subtly reinforced the importance of evaluation of information; after all, if I can do it, can't anyone?

Synthesis and creation were the mainstays of spring quarter's seminar. Students in all three UWired FIGs collaborated in creating a WWW Freshman Survival Guide, an introduction to the ins and outs of UW college life from a student's perspective. The Survival Guide included tips on registering for classes, where to find the best coffee (this is Seattle, after all), what to do on the weekends, life in the dorms, and life off-campus. A student editorial board and student reporters were responsible for content (including adding links to other relevant WWW sites and adding a bibliography of related printed materials), layout and design of these Web pages. This final UWired project attempted to synthesize and consolidate students' skills and completed the circle begun with searching, locating and evaluating information and culminating in producing and publishing information for others to use. The UW Freshman Survival Guide can be viewed at the following URL:

http://weber.u.washington.edu/ ~uwired/

EVALUATION OF THE UWIRED FIGS—YEAR 1

From the outset, the project has been committed to ongoing evaluation. The long range goals of the program will require tracking students over time in order to judge the efficacy of the program. However, in the short term, the planning group has used a variety of evaluative strategies to compare the effectiveness of UWired activities to non-UWired activities, to look at students' perceptions of this approach, and to look at the acquisition of knowledge and skills relevant to information literacy.

During autumn 1994, four evaluation instruments were used: (1) Information & Technology Survey, (2) E-mail Survey, (3) FIG Participant Survey, and (4) UWired FIG Survey. The Office of Educational Assessment (OEA) monitored e-mail traffic on FIG discussion lists, interviewed autumn quarter UWired instructors, and conducted focus groups during spring quarter with volunteers from each of the UWired FIGs. Some of the surveys were given to FIGs that were not part of the UWired program in order to help identify which outcomes might be attributed to the information and technology component and which might be attributed to the sense of community created by the FIG alone. Results of the four evaluation instruments are summarized below. Comments from focus groups and instructor interviews are not discussed here because of space limitations.

The Information & Technology Survey consists of 10 items (many with multiple parts) to test students' knowledge of computer terms, library terms, and their ability to apply this knowledge to information retrieval situations. One item addressed students' perceptions of their computer and technical expertise, while another addressed comfort with academic skills (e.g., writing, using the library, working in teams). This survey was administered to UWired FIG students as well as a set of non-UWired FIG students for comparison between the two.

On knowledge-based items, at the start of the quarter, scores between UWired and non-UWired students were similar, indicating that despite self-selection into the FIGs, students were starting at the same baseline. At the end of the quarter, all students (UWired and non-UWired) showed increases in some items. However, UWired students showed substantially greater increases over their peers in non-UWired FIGs, indicative of the content of the information and technology seminar they completed. Specifically, UWired students were better able to distinguish between an index and an online catalog, and they grasped the concept of Boolean operators in searches with a gain greater than their peers. When presented with an information need (e.g., to find the latest research report on passive smoking), UWired students showed a marked advantage over their peers in their ability to identify correctly the information source that was most appropriate.

On self-assessment items, both UWired and non-UWired FIG students rated themselves similarly on comfort with academic skills. Further, at the end of the quarter none of the students rated themselves higher. However, there were differences in students' perceptions of their expertise with various software and online tools such as the library catalog, electronic discussion groups, and word processing. At the end of the quarter, ratings showed that UWired students perceived themselves as having an intermediate skill level, while non-UWired students perceived themselves more as novices. It is interesting that although UWired students perceived themselves as more expert at the end of the quarter, they did not rate themselves higher on comfort with academic skills that are supported by this technology. It is likely that maturation is a more important factor in students' comfort level than acquisition of skills.

The E-mail Survey, sent to students while the quarter was under way and used as a mid-term evaluation, posed four questions concerning the students' perception of the UWired program. Its purpose was to provide instructors with mid-term feedback. The students who responded (27%) indicated positive experiences. They felt they were learning useful skills as well as building friendships with other students, gaining rapport with faculty, and applying technology in their lives. It is not clear why the response rate was low, but the fact that the survey was not a requirement of the course, combined with the students' course load (many students felt they had a lot of homework to do) were likely contributing factors to the response rate. E-mail monitoring showed the students were engaged in sending large volumes of e-mail to each other and to the FIG instructors, and the survey may have been perceived as too time consuming to complete.

The FIG Participant Survey was developed several years ago for the FIG program, and consists of 26 multiple-choice items. Six relate to the student's reasons for participating in the FIG program, five questions relate to academic goals, ten are concerned with the contribution of the FIG program to the student's college experience, and five relate to the contribution of the peer advisor. This survey was administered to non-UWired FIGs as well as UWired FIGs to allow a comparison of the two types of FIG experiences.

For the most part, both sets of students rated their reasons for joining a FIG similarly, except that the UWired students gave a significantly higher rating to the reason that the UWired section was recommended in a new student orientation session, and the students were more motivated to meet others with similar interests. The greater response to new student orientation on the part of UWired students can be attributed in part to the more extensive conversations interested students had with staff who were recruiting UWired involvement. Both groups rated statements concerning academic goals similarly while UWired students rated statements regarding the contribution of the FIG program to their education significantly higher.

The UWired FIG Survey was administered to UWired FIG students at the end of autumn quarter and consists of 26 items. The items were designed to elicit students' opinions about the UWired FIG activities, their reasons for joining a UWired FIG, the structure of the class, and the Collaboratory facilities used for the FIG seminar.

Students were overwhelmingly positive toward all UWired FIG activities except two assignments: Keeping a journal and attending lectures given by computer science faculty. In the first case, students did not think that keeping a journal was helpful to their studies. In the second case, students did not find the lectures interesting, and this may be due to the level of the lecture—students simply did not have enough background to understand fully the lectures. However, students did report that use of electronic mail, file transfer programs (such as Fetch), library resources, UWIN and the Internet (the World Wide Web in particular) were useful. In addition, they were extremely positive about the Collaboratory facility, and felt this allowed them to work on team projects as well as provided a good environment for working alone. They felt the Collaboratory contributed to their sense of belonging and helped the University to seem more "personable."

Thus, in the short time of one quarter the UWired project demonstrated that UWired FIGs provided a more positive experience to students than the non-UWired FIG program. By the end of the year, the students in each FIG group had a remarkable rapport with each other as well as with their instructors. This sense of community was due to a combination of factors, an important one being shared course schedules. This meant more face-to-face contact with other members of the FIG. However, a number of online activities helped to create, sustain, and strengthen this sense of community among the students. How their participation in the UWired project will affect long term goals, grades and other factors such as retention is yet to be determined, but it is clear that the students are off to a positive start toward becoming information literate.

INFORMATION AND TECHNOLOGY SEMINAR—CHANGES FOR YEAR 2

What we learned from the evaluation of the program, combined with our goal to scale the project to include more students, motivated a number of changes for the 1995–1996 academic year. The UWired FIG program was expanded from three FIGs involving about sixty students to eight FIGs with more than two hundred students. This more-than-double expansion necessitated both quantitative and qualitative changes in the operations of the UWired program, the two most notable being the addition of more staff and a new Collaboratory to allow more students access to computing facilities.

Enough additional librarians were recruited during the spring and summer of 1995 to assign one librarian to each FIG. One student was assigned to provide computing support for two FIGs (compared with one student for three during the first year), for a total of four students. As mentioned earlier, during the first year the FIG students met weekly with a peer advisor—an activity separate from the information and technology seminar. For the second year, the information and technology seminar was combined with the peer advisor/student weekly meeting, making peer advisors and librarians jointly responsible for the newly christened course, "University Resources, Information & Technology," with changes made in the curriculum to reflect this collaboration.

To try and create tighter connections between the UWired seminar and the other classes which were part of the FIGs, we involved the faculty members teaching those classes as much as possible. In addition, faculty members who are knowledgeable in the uses of information technology in those disciplines participated as faculty consultants to the FIGs. Thus, while our collaborations during the first year were primarily among campus units for the purpose of planning and implementing UWired, our second year collaborations expanded to include collaboration in the instructional process. FIG instructional teams for autumn 1995 had from 3 to 5 members. Core members were a librarian, a peer advisor, and a student for technical support. Auxiliary members were faculty who teach FIG classes and/or faculty consultants.

The first year's experiment with laptop computers, while very successful, could not be scaled for the second year. The cost of fully configured laptop computers for two hundred students, peer advisors, librarians, computing advisors, and faculty was far too high for the University to fund centrally, and it was not realistic to require all of the students to acquire the high-end laptops that are appropriate for this venture. Therefore all but one of the second year FIGs used a workstation equipped computer classroom built in time for autumn 1995. One FIG was outfitted with Apple PowerBooks in order to continue the exploration of the use of a portable computing environment in the curriculum.

The new UWired Collaboratory was located immediately adjacent to the original Collaboratory. To encourage collaborative activities the twenty-eight workstations were arranged in roughly circular pods with four workstations at each table. Workstations were equipped with high quality 17-inch monitors, and all workstations were outfitted with a set of software including productivity applications (*Word, Excel, PowerPoint, Photoshop*) and Internet software (*Netscape* and FTP and telnet clients).

Due to the stationary equipment installed in the new Collaboratory we decided to keep the lab staffed during all open hours. Users were required both to present identification and to log in to the workstations. Only UWired students could use the facility, so although students may not have had a laptop to use, they had a space they could consider their own, and that was accessible to them without waiting lines.

In addition to the eight FIGs, UWired undertook a completely new program in the second year focused on the men's and women's varsity basketball teams. This is part of an effort to try to integrate more closely the student athletes on campus with the academic mission of the University. Both basketball teams were outfitted with Apple PowerBooks in order to give these students access to computing during their extensive travel schedule during the school year. These students attended an information and technology seminar similar to the one for the FIGs, but with emphasis on the use of information resources to help them complete assignments while traveling, and the use of file transfer and e-mail tools for submitting assignments while out of town.

UWIRED: EXPANSION BEYOND THE FIGS

In addition to the expansion of the UWired FIG program this year, UWired has become an umbrella for campus efforts to incorporate technology into the curriculum. Other recent efforts have included workshops for faculty and teaching assistants, a lecture/demonstration series on integrating technology into the curriculum, a faculty lab, the construction of a third Collaboratory (sixty seats) and distance education courses which combine televised lectures with course web pages and e-mail. Some of these activities will be described in more detail.

We recognized from the outset that it would not be enough to train students in the use of electronic information tools. In order for true curriculum transformation to occur, the faculty needed to have opportunities to learn not only the technological skills involved, but to develop innovative and meaningful ways of integrating these tools into their courses. We knew that once students completed the courses in their FIGs during autumn quarter and began choosing courses in departments across campus, they would serve as "emissaries" and would not only expect integration of technology across the curriculum, but ideally would transfer their own newly acquired skills to their work in these subsequent courses. With the confidence gained as a result of their participation in UWired and as a result of having participated in a learning community model of instruction, it wasn't unthinkable that some students would feel comfortable enough to step outside the usual teacher-student hierarchy and suggest or instruct faculty and teaching assistants in ways to use such tools as e-mail, discussion lists, and the World Wide Web in their courses. Indeed this happened in a number of cases.

However, to have a more widespread effect on the integration of technology into the curriculum, a crucial element of the program has been the marketing and development of teaching and technology workshops for faculty and TAs across the campus. For many years, Computing & Communications offered workshops open to all faculty and staff that cover topics ranging from an introduction to Pine, the e-mail program developed at the University of Washington, to Macintosh and PC basics, to use of file transfer tools. Recently, courses on HTML (Hypertext Markup Language) and advanced HTML were added. However, not all faculty were on the catalog mailing list, and few of those who were took the time to read through the catalog of offerings. To encourage faculty to take these courses, we created sections of these workshops open only to faculty and teaching assistants and created several new workshops also targeted specifically at faculty (e.g., Introduction to Educational Resources on the Web; Presentation Software for Lectures; Effective Use of the Web for Education: Design Principles and Pedagogy). We advertised these to all faculty with a flyer titled "Teaching and Technology Workshops for Faculty and Teaching Assistants."

We have also sponsored a lecture/demonstration series to showcase use of technology and information resources in classes taught at the UW. Speakers have discussed such topics as using e-mail tools to facilitate teaching large lecture classes; sociopolitical aspects of information technology; incorporating the Internet into instruction, and the challenge of changing the campus culture by training faculty in educational technology.

We are currently planning a lab for faculty and teaching assistants to develop instructional materials that is scheduled to open during spring quarter 1996. This facility will have eight workstations, peripheral equipment such as a scanner and a color printer, and a collection of resources on instructional technology. Besides accommodating individual faculty projects, the lab will be used for workshops and demonstrations. We plan to staff the facility with consultants who have specialties in various areas of instructional technology, including librarians, computing professionals, and faculty who are leaders in the use of information resources and technology.

ADMINISTRATIVE CHANGES DURING YEAR 2

The first year's loosely organized administrative style was not likely to scale into the second year. The numerous new activities necessitated hiring a coordinator for the UWired project whose job is to help manage day to day operations. We continued the meetings of the "Wednesday group," which incorporated anyone from the team of librarians and staff from computing support and Undergraduate Education who could make the meeting times. This group's responsibility evolved into managing the ongoing operations of the program, from details about furnishing the Collaboratories to planning UWired events.

A number of committees were formed to take care of the details of various tasks such as curriculum development, faculty development, program evaluation, equipment and facilities. Committee members are largely members of the "Wednesday group," and are responsible for hashing out and implementing the details of all the projects, or bringing to the attention of the Wednesday group details that need to be decided upon.

In addition to the operational group we created a UWired Steering Committee that includes chairs of all UWired committees. This group has had the primary responsibility for shaping policies and fleshing out new UWired initiatives as the possibilities are identified. Finally, large scale policy and budget issues are guided by a team of three people—the Associate Vice Provost, the Computing & Communications Director of Facilities and Infrastructure Planning, and the Associate Director of Libraries for Public Services. On paper, this additional structure makes UWired appear to have grown into a bureaucracy, but the growth is really a reflection of the expanding scope. The people involved still have an informal, cooperative style and a "can do" attitude.

CONCLUSION: WHAT FOSTERS COLLABORATION

In closing, we would like to summarize what has seemed to work as well as what doesn't. Rosabeth Moss Kanter, in an article published in 1994, outlined "Eight 'I's That Create Successful 'We's." It is useful to analyze our experiences within this framework.

Individual Excellence

All of the participants in the UWired program are very talented and committed individuals, who are regarded in their own units as being very high achievers. These individual abilities were a very important factor in establishing a shared atmosphere of trust between the partners in the collaboration.

Importance

The UWired project has been given a very high priority by all of the partners in the collaboration. Resources which were sorely needed within the individual units were dedicated wholly or in part to the UWired project. A great deal of work has been accomplished in a very compressed time frame due to this high level of commitment. The willingness to put the needs of the collaborative activity ahead of the needs of the participating organizations has helped contribute to the atmosphere of trust and reliance that we enjoy.

Interdependence

The linking of responsibilities within the UWired project has created a truly collaborative environment—no one unit has responsibility for the parts of the project, and it takes parts of all of the units to continue to make progress. A key component to creating this interdependence has been the willingness of the participants to cede control of pieces of their traditional turf. Undergraduate Education has ceded parts of their curricular control, the Libraries have given over control of a good bit of space and staff, and Computing & Communications has relinquished quite a lot of the decision-making power about the computer labs for UWired. The willingness of the partners to transcend the traditional boundaries has helped make possible the free-flowing and fast-paced development and operation of this effort.

Investment

Each of the UWired partners has made a substantial contribution of staff time, space resources, and money to the project. This contribution has deepened the commitment to the project.

Information

Sharing information freely among staff at all levels through e-mail, the web and frequent meetings has fostered the development of new ideas, helped us share our varying cultures, and made all the participants feel ownership of the venture. One of the problems that was frequently mentioned with the second year FIG program was that the teams leading the FIGs felt a lack of information, which at least partly stemmed from our inability to scale our freewheeling, anarchic communication style from the limited number of participants in the first year to the much larger cast of the second year.

Integration

The integration of the disparate cultures of the units involved in this collaboration has had profound ongoing effects that extend well beyond the bounds of the UWired FIG project. Undergraduate Education, the UW Libraries, Computing & Communications, and University Extension are now in constant contact on many projects and working together on a level which is quite unusual.

Institutionalization

The commitment of top level management in all of the participating units is absolutely crucial to an effort of this sort. This commitment has resulted in a good deal of visibility for the project throughout the University, and will hopefully result in permanent budgeting for the future.

Integrity

From the first day of this project it has been a given that all of the partners had a true interest in helping undergraduate students successfully use information technology to advance their intellectual growth, and that this was the primary concern of all of the partners. While individual partners have differing perspectives and approaches to problems, there have been no hidden agendas, and none of the types of animosities that can sometimes arise when partners are perceived as being out for individual gain.

To make collaboration succeed at the rank and file level, that is, with the people who really get the work done, it helps to understand campus cultures, to respect others' cultures and operating limits, to communicate, and to be flexible. There are many ways to accomplish the same goal, and when people with varying perspectives put their heads together, innovative solutions often arise.

In addition to Kanter's eight "I"s, we would like to posit an additional two "I"s.

Inclusiveness

Success of the project rests on including people from all areas of the university: Students, faculty, librarians, and computing professionals. Each individual brings his or her own strengths and perspectives to a collaborative project. We recommend that any institution planning a similar venture include students in the planning process; they bring many new ideas and unique perspectives that are essential in designing a program for students.

Independence

The support of administration is essential in bringing a project such as UWired to life, but equally important is freedom from the constraints inherent in the academic bureaucracy. We were given a broad mandate without preset tasks or objectives. In short, we were not micromanaged. Furthermore, individuals were able to act on their own initiative without prior approval from the group or administrators if the need arose. For example, librarians had broad latitude to design the information and technology seminar.

Our final piece of advice for those of you who decide to take up the challenge: Remember our motto—Nil Simplex.

REFERENCES

Fox, Louis, and Kathryn Sharpe. "UWired: Driver's Ed for the Information Highway." Educators' Tech Exchange 3 (1995): 18–24.

Kanter, Rosabeth Moss. "Collaborative Advantage." Harvard Business Review (July-August 1994): 96–108.

Peters, Paul Evan. "Collaborative Advantage: Tough Love in the Transforming Academy." Paper presented at the annual Seminars in Academic Computing, Snowmass, CO, August 1995.

Tinto, Vincent, and Anne Goodsell. "Freshman Interest Groups and the First-Year Experience: Constructing Student Communities in a Large University." Journal of the Freshman Year Experience 6 (1994): 7–28.

University of Washington UWired Program [Online]. Available HTTP: http://www.washington.edu/uwired/

UWired: Beyond Technology. Produced by UWTV. Directed by Ann Coppel. 10:17 min. University of Washington, 1995. Videocassette.

APPENDIX

Student Voices from UWired: Quotes from student journals and evaluation forms

I also set up the computer to my phone line and that is working fine. I even wrote e-mail to my dad!! That is so incredible. Just think, in only seconds he received my message and could just as quickly reply. This all still blows my mind.

I did more with the e-mail today, trying to e-mail some of my TAs and professors telling them my e-mail address and asking them questions. Another thing in which this computer has helped is that I don't have to personally go to a professor or TA to talk to them because I can easily do it at home and get it over with, also ask all the questions I need to immediately instead of having to wait for office hours, and it makes it convenient for the teachers to answer questions.

Back to e-mail; I have been using it in both my personal life and in my academic life. First my personal life—I have a lot of friends attending the U and don't always have time to stop and see them at their dorm rooms or even talk on the phone for that matter; with the pine program it's so easy just leave a message and then they can write back anytime they want (it's a great way to keep in touch). Next my academic life—it's not exactly easy trying to talk to professors or even TAs for that matter, so when you e-mail them it's so much easier to ask questions and also get to know each one better.

I really enjoyed having the collaboratory—I have used it so much all quarter long for studying. It was a great place to do group studying, work with students in my FIG. It is a great room.

Today I am at WSU [Washington State University] for the three day weekend and have been using my computer to write my art extra credit. Anyway, I've been typing a paper and everyone over here looks at my computer and I have to show them all of the things it will do. Hopefully a program like ours will be integrated over here—the students would really get involved. Just one more reason they should have gone to the UW.

I probably wouldn't have a clue as to how to use E-mail right now were it not for this Fig, and any knowledge about the Internet would probably be years down the road for me. I have the tendency to leave technology alone unless I'm pushed a little to use it, so the little nudges we're getting right now are great. The benefits we're getting right now totally outweigh the minor inconvenience of having to wait a little while every now and again for a piece of information to come through. This is an amazing opportunity and I think we're all getting a little too spoiled, but I don't want to be the one to try to tell my Fig that.

And I don't feel so intimidated by this little machine anymore. I love to sit down, log in, and have an inbox full of mail. Friends from all across the country and relatives abroad, and the people that I meet when I am on the net. This is such a tool of unmeasurable need, for everyone. And if possession is not possible, then the skills are just as, if not more, important.

It's pretty scary as a freshman to approach a professor. UWired gave us an initial excuse, and then it was easy and even fun, to meet and talk with our professors.

Satisfying Our Users

Refinding Reference: Carrying the Reference Mission into the Libraries of the 21st Century

By Betsy Baker, Natalie Pelster, and William McHugh
Northwestern University

We are very happy to be here today and to have the opportunity to talk about the future of reference services in academic libraries. We are all members of the reference department of an institution that, like many others, is in the process of looking at the question of how to shape the library of the twenty-first century. This question has come home very strongly at Northwestern over the past couple of years, spurred forward by the retrospective conversion of our card catalog and the prospect of now removing those rows upon rows of cabinets from their very prominent position in the library. Library-wide discussions and planning are taking place. How do we want the library to look? What can we now do with that space? How will we use technology to extend services in new and exciting ways? What messages do we want to send out to our users about what the library is?

All of this discussion in the library has brought up for us, more pointedly than ever before, questions about reference itself. We have been working at articulating the views we hold about reference and at trying to give concrete expression to some of our more abstract ideals. In the midst of thinking about how we view reference services in our library, we saw and were drawn to the announcement of this conference. Its title, "Finding Common Ground: Creating a Library of the Future Without Diminishing the Library of the Past," with its emphasis on finding our way to the future while preserving what we have already done and worked to accomplish, spoke to us. In the reference literature there has been much talk about the urgent need to "redefine," "reshape," "reconfigure," and "rethink" reference. In all of this talk, however, it seems that the past is being forgotten and is seen as becoming increasingly irrelevant to today's and tomorrow's environments. When we read things like "'Reference' is the wrong name; its meaning is outmoded; its connotations are obsolete" or "We can agree without argument that 'bibliography' is an obsolete term," it is easy to feel a whole new urgency—an urgency prompted by the feeling that something important is, indeed, being overlooked and is consequently in danger of being lost. And there is added urgency in knowing that this loss is being precipitated, not from outside, but from within the library profession itself.[1] How good it is to take a moment, as this conference is doing, to look, not only at the answers we are finding about the future of the library, but also to look at the questions we are asking ourselves, for we can find the right answers only if we begin with the right questions.

Neil Postman writes in his new book, *The End of Education*, that there are two kinds of questions that can be asked. One deals with the mechanics, the engineering, really the "how" of an institution. The other kind of question is metaphysical, dealing with the purpose, with the "why." (3) The question that is most urgent for reference services today is not "how"—How will we be incorporating the Internet into our services?—How will we instruct remote users?—How will we use technology in the library?—How will we organize reference?—but rather, "why." The urgent question we need to pose and answer is "Why reference?" We need to answer this question so that we can better articulate what it is that is valuable about reference. We need to answer this question in order to find a context for and give direction to all the "hows" that naturally follow from it. We believe that the answer to the question "why reference?" does not break with the past, but builds upon it. The future role of reference has more to do with our long-standing mission than it does with carving out a totally new purpose for our existence. New technologies and new avenues of information retrieval do not negate or eclipse this mission, but instead give us new ways of fulfilling and strengthening it. We need to find the reason, the meaning, and the energy in reference librarianship and let that propel us forward. In a 1980 article, Joseph Rosenblum, a reference librarian at Guilford College, wrote that "what reference librarianship needs . . . is a rebirth of faith in itself. It needs to believe what its founders knew . . ." (153). In our quest to answer "Why reference?", we decided to go back and to look ourselves for what the founders knew. We decided to "refind" reference.

THE FOUNDATIONS OF REFERENCE

As we explored the theory and history of reference, we found that, in the literature, discussion and thinking of reference as a service is most often traced back to 1876—the year that the first article about reference was published, in the first volume of *Library Journal*. Since this is the first article on reference, it is not surprising that many subsequent articles relate back to it. In this article, Samuel Swett Green, librarian at the Worcester Free Public Library, called for what he termed "personal relations" between librarians and readers. Green showed through example after example how reference assistance, even though that is not what he calls it, is of use to library patrons, is beneficial to the library, and is invigorating for the librarian. "There are few pleasures comparable to that of associating continually with curious and vigorous young minds, and of aiding them in realizing their ideals" (81).

In his examples, he talks of providing information on styles of ornamentation directly to a painter; of teaching a school boy how to use encyclopedias to find information on the Suez Canal, as well as on other topics that will come up in his studies; of handing a homeowner a book, opened to the appropriate pages, with information on the scientific principles of lightning rods; of telling a young girl seeking the name of the king whose arm determined the length of the yard that "there are many stories and traditions which it will not do to accept as facts without careful examination of the evidence adduced in their corroboration" (75). He further says that "scholars, as well as unlearned persons, receive much aid in pursuing their studies from an accomplished librarian" (78). Through his examples, Green shows that the librarian can offer this aid by directly providing information, by instructing readers in the use of resources, or even by what he calls "extending to readers the hospitality of his institution" (78).

Green's article, which could be read as a personal account of one librarian's reference experiences, really does illuminate the spectrum of what is involved in reference librarianship. In a 1995 article in *Reference Services Review*, James Rettig wrote that when a library science student had asked on LIBREF-L what the "hot" library reference issues of the week were, he was tempted to answer that they had all been summed up by Green back in 1876. Rettig says,

> Green touched on issues such as the librarian's obligation to provide information without injecting personal values, the inability of any librarian to know everything, the need sometimes to refer a patron to another agency, SDI services, the value of proactive rather than passive service, the challenges of the reference interview, and, of course, what has come to be called the "information versus instruction debate" ("Convergence of the Twain," 7).

Green himself, however, did not present "information versus instruction" as a debate. He offered up examples of reference service—sometimes providing information, sometimes offering instruction—but did not postulate that this constituted or even foreshadowed any great philosophical rift.

But rift indeed there came to be. It was noted by many writers, including John Cotton Dana, James I. Wyer, Samuel Rothstein, and Robert Wagers.[2] Early practitioners naturally talked about the amount and nature of the service they were giving and the educational role of that service, but these concerns were not codified into a general theory until Wyer published the first textbook on reference work in 1930. Wyer's formulation is probably familiar to all of us. It posits three basic theories of reference work. First, there is the conservative, which stresses the need of users to learn to use the library for themselves and the librarian's role in assisting them and teaching them to do this. Secondly, there is the liberal (which Wyer called the "liberal, progressive, and enlightened theory of reference work") that stresses the "wish to find or to create ways and means to satisfy every questioner" (9).

This choice between liberal and conservative service has often been summarized as the choice between "providing the answer" and "teaching the user to find the answer," though that precise language belongs more to later commentators such as Rothstein than to Wyer. Finally, there is the moderate theory, which is pretty much like the conservative, but requires the librarian to actually supply information at times, particularly to simpler enquiries. It is the adherents of the moderate theory that Rothstein said are "in the middle and, I fear, in a muddle." In this "middling" service, he said, "expediency vies with principle," expediency being the provision of information, principle being the belief in the "pedagogical superiority of instruction." He said that "the result is a pattern of wonderful inconsistency" (40–41). There is no clearly defined reason for choosing one method over another, and the kind of service offered is dependent less on policy or program than on any number of variables in particular situations.

In his article, "Shaking the Conceptual Foundations of Reference," Jerry Campbell, now University Librarian at USC and keynote speaker at the "Rethinking Reference" institutes held at Duke, Berkeley, and Iowa in 1993–1994, says that when he started to look in a focused way at reference services, what he found was "conceptual disarray" (29). Indeed, in the literature of reference, we find many outcries about the need for theory and for a true definition of what reference service is. We believe that the lack of theory and the conceptual disarray can be traced directly back to the information versus instruction debate. This debate has been with us for a long time and never seems to really go away. It was being argued in 1915, in 1955 and in 1995. It has dominated the literature of reference and, with its view of conflicting services supported by people holding conflicting theories, has, in fact, been a major stumbling block in constructing a unified theory of reference. Information provision and instruction have been viewed, not as Green had presented them—complementary forms of reference services—but as "antithetical," "opposing courses," "divergent strains of librarianship," and "inconsistency in adhering to philosophy."

Campbell also says that in his explorations of reference he encountered many "sacred cows," in fact, a "whole herd" of them (29). Reference, we are certain, does have many sacred cows. Today, however, we are most interested in addressing its two very sacred "hows"—the how of information and the how of instruction. These hows have distorted the view of what reference service is by trying to be more than they are—by trying, each independently, to supply the over-arching why of reference and to argue against the other's importance or even existence. To answer our question, "why reference?", we have to "debunk" these impostors, finding how each falls short as a "why" for reference. It is only then that we can move on and find a true theory of reference.

DEBUNKING THE IMPOSTORS

The Myth of the Answer

The first impostor is sometimes called information and sometimes the answering of questions. "What is reference service? At its most fundamental it may be defined as answering questions" (Katz, v.1, 3). So begins William Katz's *Introduction to Reference Work*, read by countless beginning library science students each year. It is easy to see the pervasiveness of the question answering view of reference services just by sampling slogans from some of the American Library Association's recent public relations campaigns. "Don't settle for half an answer." "Ask a professional. Ask your librarian." "Your right to know." "Get answers to all your little questions, too." The "provide the answer" explanation of reference has built into it a focus on information as the raison d'être of reference services. Charles McClure wrote back in 1974 that the true theory of reference is the theory of specific information. He said, "If reference librarians cannot accept the proposal that the major theoretical basis of the library is the dissemination of specific information, the entire usefulness and need for the reference librarian—and more importantly the library—cannot be justified" (208). This theory, he says, offers a clear direction for the provision of reference services. We provide specific information in response to specific queries. In this view of reference, instruction completely falls out.

However, information in response to questions is really a very narrow definition of what reference is about, and, given that reference is in many ways the face of the library, it is a very narrow definition of what the library itself is. It is, in fact, too narrow to be true. Thelma Freides wrote the following to show that questions at the reference desk are not always straight-forward information requests.

"Why is democracy better than communism?" "Does urban renewal reduce crime?" "What is Margaret Mead's major contributions to anthropology?" "Are political attitudes changed by education?" Questions such as these—and they, or analogous ones, are asked constantly in libraries of all kinds—require a much higher order of skill and an entirely different set of concepts than is ever called into play by "Who was Catherine the Great's maternal grandmother?" or "What was the per capita consumption of peat as fuel in Finland in 1844?" It is, of course, much easier to come up with a list of references under the headings democracy, communism, urban renewal and so forth, than it is to produce a precise figure for peat consumption, but the former is not at all the same thing as answering the question, unless by this we mean simply processing people past a reference desk and chalking up statistics (2008).

Information connotes discrete facts, statistics, verifications. It does not connote the kind of mental involvement and grappling with ideas and theories entailed in Freides' questions.

In the desire to be full-service information providers, some librarians have suggested that information provision should be carried to its logical, or maybe illogical, end. One wrote,

> How much better if the patron can leave a request and come back to find a neatly organized file of material, compiled just for his or her search. . . . No fuss, no muss, no explanations. Just results (Mood, 29, 28).

The problem here is that, once again, the view is too narrow. How can someone take over another person's research when we are talking about questions like the ones Freides mentioned above? Freides called it "the broad, open-ended inquiry which is often not capable of precise definition except as an integral part of the process of finding the answer" (2008). And even in the area where what is being sought really is "information" in the more restricted sense of the word, there can be much fuss, much muss, and many explanations and goings back and forth among the librarian, the patron, the patron's research partners, the database vendors' resource specialists, and so on.

The biggest flaw with the "answer" impostor is that it first assumes that users have questions, and then further assumes that these questions are answerable. This view over-simplifies the uses to which a library can be put. Sometimes, what users have are interests, or beginnings of ideas, or gnawing little pieces of questions. The whole investigative process, the whole process of inquiry, is much broader than a quest for information. If you ask people why they go to the library, it's probably not only to locate information—not simply to find answers to questions. Much of what takes place in libraries involves the discovery of what information, if any, is needed.

Oscar Handlin, historian and professor at Harvard University, states most eloquently the problem of viewing the library as a bastion of information at the expense of its other offerings.

> Information must be correct, current, concise, clear and unambiguous . . . and a certain kind of teaching aims to coach its students to return, on demand, answers that are correct, current, concise, clear and unambiguous. However, another kind of teaching aims to raise questions rather than to answer them. Correct, current, concise, clear and unambiguous are not the only values in learning—perhaps not even the highest values; and they are certainly not the attributes associated with browsing among books. Browsing may indeed wrap ideas in qualifications and conditions that challenge the imagination but do not yield precise answers (211).

As Handlin states, finding information is definitely a part of education and is definitely a part of the use of libraries. However, the library is often important long before specific questions are posed. For this reason, we need a theory of reference that includes discovery, inquiry, and curiosity more completely than the answer or information provision theory does.

The Myth of the Independent Library User

The other side of the information versus instruction debate has been ruled by the second impostor, the creation of the independent library user. If we look back to Green, we find that he wrote that librarians should give users "as much assistance as they need, but try at the same time to teach them to rely upon themselves and become independent" (80). Many proponents of library instruction have seen this, the creation of independent library users, to be the overall objective of instruction and, in fact, of reference. With this as their objective, they are completely at odds with the view that the library should provide information on demand. John Cotton Dana posited that the real work of finding the answer should be left to the patron or they would never learn to use the library—fostering a dependency on librarians (108). Willard Austen went so far as to recommend that bibliographies given as handouts to students not contain call numbers, so that students would learn to use the card catalog. He said that "it is often more worth while that a student get practice in bibliographical self-help than to acquire the facts after he gets the books" (275). It is easy to see how views like these conflicted with those of the information provision proponents, who insisted that readers wanted their questions answered, not to be put through their paces, so to speak, learning something they really do not need or want to learn.

In the early years, instruction took place as part of the interaction in the reference room and the debate centered around whether these interactions should be answer-driven or instruction-driven. It was when the bibliographic instruction movement took off in the 1970s and early 1980s, however, that the debate really heated up. Instruction left the reference desk and went into the classroom, thereby widening the gap between the instruction and information provision proponents. What had been a personal style issue now seriously threatened to—and often did—take resources away from what many viewed to be the real service of reference—the reference desk. To make matters worse, in the zeal required to successfully launch a new and different kind of service, many administrators, inadvertently or otherwise, sent out the message that the most valued thing a reference librarian could do was bibliographic instruction. Hence, other ways of engaging with the user, including the reference desk, seemed to be devalued and to take on a secondary kind of status. There was a tension between the librarians who worked at the reference desk and those who did instruction. Librarians who were resistant to the instruction movement were seen as stodgy, old-fashioned, passive, and dull. On the other hand, instruction and outreach were criticized as being fluffy, "will-o-the-wisp activities" with instruction librarians acting like "traveling salesmen" or mendicant preachers instead of tending to the work of being reference librarians—namely, answering questions and providing information at the reference desk (Rosenblum).

The view of instruction as a competitive service with "traditional" reference led to its being discussed in terms of how well it fulfilled "traditional" reference needs. Even though it was separate from reference desk services, it was seen by many as having a direct link to that service, and its success, or lack thereof, was measured in large part by its effect, or lack of effect, on the reference desk. Did, for instance, desk statistics go down? If not, then how could instruction be justified? If direct questions did not decrease in response to the indirect answers offered through instruction, then instruction must be failing at its purpose of creating independent library users. Many articles have argued just this point; instruction is not meeting its obligations, and the time, energy, and resources being expended on it could be better used in other ways of offering service.

In our discussion of the information or answer provision side of reference services, we said that the main problem with it as a "why" for reference was that it is too narrow in its view of what reference service is. The main problem with instruction as a "why" for reference, however, is that the real purpose of instruction has rarely been understood. The oft-cited purpose of making library users independent, if by that we mean that users will be so self-sufficient in their use of the library and its resources that they never have to ask a question, is faulty. It suggests that asking for assistance is a sign of dependence on the librarian, and using the library without this kind of personal interaction is a sign of independence. However, Evan Farber, librarian emeritus at Earlham College, makes an interesting point by showing that librarians are not the only things upon which users can become dependent. He believes that users can become dependent on the catalog, as they can on other tools, using it at times that are inappropriate and when it would, indeed, be better to ask a librarian. Farber even says that instruction can, in a way, add to this kind of dependency: "We may be teaching just enough about using a library to make students think they don't need to know any more" (326). Therefore, users who have what Green called the ability "to rely on themselves" are not users who never ask questions. Rather, they are users who have a sense of what to turn to when, including when to turn to a librarian. They are users who have some control over how profitable and efficient their visits to the library are.

The emergence of electronic information sources seemed to many to greatly further the goal of creating independent library users because of the belief that online systems could be created that would be so self-apparent in their use that users would require no reference assistance at all, either instructional or informational. But, if we look back, we will see that there have been other times in library history when a tool was thought to be all that a user would need. Many librarians in the late nineteenth century met the idea of reference services with resistance and skepticism; they felt that the newly developed card catalog represented the ideal tool for accessing information in the library, and that library users would need no additional assistance. This may seem to us today quite unrealistic, and was soon recognized to be so, but it reflected the natural confidence of a generation of early librarians who put their energy into developing a better and more satisfactory tool than had ever before been available to library users. We, of course, want tools to be as user-friendly as possible; however, we do not want to overlook the fact that the need for personal assistance often goes beyond assistance in the use of particular tools. We are fooling ourselves if we think that our users will become independent, either through our instructional efforts or through tools themselves, however sophisticated.

In a 1978 article, James Rettig summed up the information/instruction debate, saying that looking at levels of service, such as conservative, liberal, or moderate, does not constitute a reference theory.

> No matter how noble and useful providing library users with information is and no matter how noble and useful teaching them how to find information in libraries is, these are merely levels of service, not theories of reference. A valid theory of reference must explain and accommodate both of these types of service and the hybrid moderate or middling service. ("Theoretical Model," 20).

Information and instruction are both part of reference services, but the information/instruction debate represents an ideological conflict rather than a reference theory. To get to a real theory of reference, we have to set this debate aside and ask ourselves once again, "Why reference?"

WHY REFERENCE?

So we have seen that neither information provision nor instruction offers a working theory of reference. Theory, however, is necessary for a profession. In a 1965 article, Barbara Petrof, assistant to the dean of the School of Library Service at Atlanta University, wrote, "Librarianship needs a theory to provide clarity of conception and to enable librarians to venture into the realm of supposition" (317). Theorists, she says, are the "tool-makers" who are involved in "the discovery of new regularities and their elucidation" (317). Theory is needed because it is on this "discovery" and "elucidation" that good practice hinges. Theory is the tool that provides the framework that lets us know what we should and should not be doing in practice.

S.R. Ranganathan, whom we hold to be a true theorist of librarianship, remarked that it was the search for such a framework that led him on his quest for a theory of librarianship, resulting in his Five Laws of Library Science.

> Prior experience in scientific study and pursuit induced a sense of revolt against having to hold in memory and deal with myriads of unrelated pieces of information and independent types of practices. Cannot all these empirical aggregates of information and practices be reduced to a handful of basic principles? Cannot the process of induction be applied in this case? Cannot all the known practices be got by the process of deduction out of the basic principles? Do not the basic principles contain, as necessary implications, many other practices not current or known at present? Such questions began to simmer in the mind from the first half of 1925. (20)

Ranganathan says that this went on for three years as he was working on setting up the Madras University Library and engaging in all of the work that that entailed. He reached a point late in 1928 when the fully formulated "laws" emerged, and he had his theory of librarianship, a theory that could be induced from the work he was doing and from which current and future practices could be deduced. It is theory that lets us see, as Ranganathan said, "practices not yet current or known." It is theory that gives us the framework for seeing, as Neil Postman writes, "what we must note and what we can ignore" ("Learning by Story," 122). It is very necessary, at this time of change and redefinition that we have the "clarity of conception" which Petrof talked about and that we move forward to the call of, as we might say, "a certain trumpet." This is what theory can give us.

Sociologist Murray S. Davis once wrote,

> It has long been thought that a theorist is considered great because his theories are true, but this is false. A theorist is considered great, not because his theories are true, but because they are interesting (309).

This is what we need for reference: an interesting theory, a theory that captures the imagination and gives us useful insights; a theory that offers us a framework, or what Postman calls "a story," to show us where we should be going. In *The End of Education*, Postman looks at the school crisis and says that it is caused by a lack of theory, not a lack of "method" and the theories that underlie various methods, but rather the lack of an underlying theory, or story, of why we have schools in the first place. Without the sense of purpose or understanding of "why" that comes from such a theory, Postman says there will be a crisis, regardless of how many "hows" you have. The theory of reference, we would hazard to say, need not adhere to some strict, scientific definition of theory, but rather needs to give us something in which we can believe and find a sense of purpose. That purpose should be broad enough to encompass the spectrum of reference librarianship and narrow enough to define a distinct mission in the world.

As we went back into library history to find for ourselves what the founders knew, we were impressed because, contrary to what complaints about a lack of theory would lead us to expect, we found a true richness of thinking about what reference is and about what libraries are. We found much that can be the basis of a theory, or story, that can inspire and that can lead forward into the future. We found that there were reference librarians with clarity of purpose and with belief in themselves and in what they were doing.

Let's begin with Eleanor Woodruff, reference librarian at the Pratt Institute Free Library, who, in 1897 wrote,

> The aim of the reference department is, as you all know, to afford to readers the simplest, easiest, and quickest access to the resources of the library on any subject in which they may be interested or desire information. This may be accomplished by either introducing the inquirer directly to the books where his questions will be answered, or helping him to an understanding of the mysteries of the catalog, or explaining the use of indexes, bibliographies, and other library tools, or compiling lists for him—in short, by doing anything and everything which will conduce to getting him the right book at the right moment (65).

What is interesting to us about this is, first of all, the word "conduce." Woodruff says the librarian does "anything and everything which will conduce to getting [the user] the right book at the right moment." This leaves a lot of room for the librarian to choose the how—direct information provision, instruction, exhibits, publicity, talks, "lists" as she calls them. There is no concern here that these things are in conflict or that taking one of a variety of approaches represents "inconsistency in adhering to philosophy." Information provision and instruction are in their proper places; they are not whys, but hows. They are complementary forms of reference service.

Woodruff's view of the reference librarian as one who conduces the reader's getting the right literature or resources meshes very well with Ranganathan's Five Laws of Library Science and his summary of their implications for reference services. We found what he says about reference and the Third Law to be particularly interesting because it expands reference more broadly than most of the literature we encounter. The Third Law, "Every book its user," Ranganathan says, means this for reference:

> Books are mute. They are inert. They cannot make a journey into the world of readers to find out their respective readers. This entire journey will have to be done on their behalf by the reference librarian all by himself. In fact, the Third Law expects the reference librarian to act as the canvassing agent for every book and every document in the library. . . . In the hands of the reference librarian the library should be like a kaleidoscope. He should keep turning its facets in order to win over suitable readers to each one of its facets. This is the wish of the Third Law (*Reference Service*, 56)

Instruction clearly is implied by this law. Indeed, the criticism of the librarian as salesman or preacher that we talked about earlier contradicts what Ranganathan saw as a real role for reference librarians. Louis Shores also very clearly stated this role for the reference librarian.

> Almost any conscientious librarian must blame himself, as I have so often blamed myself, for not evangelizing more with these good books, for not having succeeding in carrying the good news into the classrooms and into the very circulatory system of formal learning (91).

These perspectives open up a very rich paradigm for libraries and for reference services. The library has in the past been labeled "the heart of the university," "the storehouse of knowledge," "the gateway to the human record." It is now also being talked about by some as a "switching station" or "node" on the information highway. But more interesting than any of these to us is a paradigm that places libraries in the center of the creation and sharing of human knowledge. Joan Bechtel, a librarian from Dickinson College, proposed "conversation" as a true paradigm for libraries. As she describes it:

> Libraries, if they are true to their original and intrinsic being, seek primarily to collect people and ideas rather than books and to facilitate conversation among people rather than merely organize, store, and deliver information. The primary task, then, of the academic library is to introduce students to the world of scholarly dialogue that spans both space and time and to provide students with the knowledge and skills they need to tap into conversations on an infinite variety of topics and to participate in the critical inquiry and debate on those issues (221).

This sentiment was also very eloquently and succinctly stated by W.C. Berwirk Sayers in his introductory remarks to Ranganathan's *Five Laws of Library Science*.

> [The library is] a living and growing organism prolonging the life of the past and renewing it for this generation, but giving also to this generation the best that its own workers, thinkers, and dreamers have to offer (17).

The message in all of these voices is that reference has a proactive mission—and proactive does not necessarily mean standing up and talking instead of sitting down and listening. It means that we are in the business of creating demand for the intellectual wares of the library and, as an extension of that, we are ultimately working in the business of knowledge creation. When we look at reference in the context of Woodruff, Ranganathan, Bechtel, and so on, we see that reference is a link—a link between people and the object of their intellectual pursuits or interests. To talk in the language of the day, reference can be thought of as an interface—a smart interface designed to link unknowns, an interface that can assess a situation and provide personalized, customized solutions. Further, it is an interface that is not content to sit idly by and wait to be queried to draw up information. To push the computer metaphor suggested by reference as interface, we could say that reference is an interface that consciously tries to bring as much of what is on its "hard disks" into the "RAM" of human consciousness.

Viewed as an interface, reference lies between the user and the resources. Bernard Vavrek wrote in 1968 that everything that falls in this in-between area is reference. With this view, reference includes all parts of the library, the publishers of reference resources, online database vendors, etc. Vavrek stated,

> To suggest that reference is all of the variables between the information and the reader may prove too much to swallow. If this idea is untenable it may at least provide a basis for further refinement. The central theme, however, is sound. No workable reference theory can be developed if the context is a unidimensional continuum. The referral process is infinitely more complicated than we care to believe ("Theory of Reference Service," 510).

In a later article, he says that this theory had some weaknesses but did have "one merit":

> It attempted to lay to rest the notion that the basis of reference librarianship was singly a collection of books or a place or answering questions. Whatever it was it was a combination of these things and many more—all existing in the same continuum. ("Nature of Reference Librarianship," 213)

The quality of lying in-between has provoked some criticism of reference. Campbell has said that "reference as we know it places a person between the public and the information," implying that service would be better if users and resources could be directly together without intermediaries. ("Shaking the Conceptual Foundations," 32). However, there is always something between a user and a resource—it may be unfamiliar surroundings, lack of time, lack of facility, a complex system, an unfamiliar search engine, unknown possibilities, the complexity of the literature itself, and so forth. Reference came about in the first place to mitigate these obstacles and to link people to ideas and data in resources and ideas and data in resources to people. This is the why of reference.

It is interesting to note that "reference" is an exceptionally apropos term for what we are describing and is not in the least bit "obsolete." "Reference" describes what lies at the heart of the idea of library as gateway—to refer to things beyond. It also describes precisely what users need to successfully navigate the resources and channels of information distribution available to them—a point of reference. Finally, in its etymology, reference goes back to relationships—and reference librarians, services, and resources specialize in finding relationships and bringing people and resources together. The term reference does not have to be something we "drag behind us"—an artifact of the past with obsolete connotations. Rather, it can be a beacon, with its multifarious meanings showing us a multi-pathed direction for the future.

HOW TO CARRY THE REFERENCE MISSION INTO THE TWENTY-FIRST CENTURY

The hows of reference, we think, are wide open, both in terms of the kinds of services we provide and how we choose to provide them. Technology is a definite forerunner in current discussion of how to offer reference services. As we have mentioned earlier, there have been predictions that technology will, at some point, replace the personal services offered by reference librarians. Although we do not believe this will happen, the prediction is certainly not unfounded. There is a process that sociologists of the professions call the commodification of knowledge, or the reduction of some form of professional knowledge into a commodity or product. (Abbott, *System of Professions*, 146–148). Examples of commodification abound in the professions, from legal forms to the commercial medications that rendered the skillful formularies of pharmacists obsolete, to commercial computer programs that allowed organizations to enjoy the benefits of computerization without hiring a programmer to do original programming, to shared catalog records. The danger of commodification to professions is that it may render some form of professional knowledge obsolete; so Poole's index perhaps rendered obsolete the knowledge of some nineteenth-century librarian who could remember the location of important articles. And the development of the large bibliographic utilities in our own era has marginalized the importance of the traditional bibliographer's intricate knowledge of national and enumerative bibliographies.

Sociologist of the professions Andrew Abbott has noted, however, that reference librarianship has been remarkably resistant to threats of commodification (*System of Professions*, 223). Both the development of print and online reference sources have tended to extend what reference librarians can do rather than to marginalize them. Ranganathan saw the same thing.

> The mechanical organisation of a library—however desirable—can never be carried to the point of dispensing with personal service. The requirement of the Third Law defies and transcends machinery.... It is doubtful whether the card catalogue, by itself, will ever become the guide, philosopher and friend of the ordinary reader of a library. (*Five Laws*, 269, 268)

Despite all of the technological breakthroughs, there is and will continue to be a need for personal service. Before we start talking about "robots at the reference desk" and "nodes on the network," we need to think about what reference really is. In 1993, Neil Postman told an Educom audience the same sentiment that he expressed in *Technopoly*—in our applications of technology we need to think not only about what we will gain, but also about what we might lose. He says that this is not an argument against technological progress, but rather a call for forethought. We need to use technology in ways that support what we need to be doing rather than undermine it. Just because what we have said reference is cannot be commodified does not mean that it cannot be lost.

To be an effective interface, there are certain things that reference requires. First, for reference to really "conduce" users to get to the right materials at the right times—or the other way around, to get the right materials to the right users at the right times—it has to be an integral whole. Resources, people, and services must converge at reference. We need to integrate the full range of resources, whether electronic or print, general or specialized, full-text or bibliographic, in-house or remote, into the reference program. If we organize resources in such a way that users can readily move from one related source to another, we will be helping them make the links between and among sources that are so necessary when doing research. To distance related sources from one another would actually diminish the quality, the level, and the relevance of our role and would also, ultimately, sacrifice our mission. Second, to "conduce" users to use resources, we need to be able to do more than produce the right resource at the right time. We need to have a broad view of what reference entails and how reference is offered. The ideals of reference encompass much more than the offering of discrete services at designated service points. They extend to how and where users encounter the library and what the library communicates to them, both purposefully and incidentally. Third, we need to keep the hows in perspective, and not let them turn into whys, especially that most forward-looking how of the time, technology. There have, in recent years, been many discussions about reshaping the mission of reference to fit the needs of the new technological environment. We believe, however, that the question we should be asking in regard to these developments is "How can we use the technologies and resources now available to further the true mission of reference?"

CONCLUSION

All the "change, change, change" talk of recent years has made many think that a break with the past is necessary to be progressive. It has been said, "You can't go to sea without leaving sight of the shore." True, but before we set sail we want to know at least where the north star is; we want to know where we are trying to go and to be able to see if we get there or not. If we break with the interesting and inspiring groundwork of our profession's history, we certainly will be aimlessly drifting. What is solid, really, in reference librarianship is the why. It is the hows that are changing. That solid why, however, has been neglected, almost lost. By "refinding" and reaffirming the true mission of reference, we will be able to continue our time-honored tradition of opening the world of knowledge to our users. We will move into the future, not diminishing the past, but building upon it.

ENDNOTES

1. These quotes from Jerry Campbell ("Shaking the Conceptual Foundations of Reference," 32) and Janice Simmons-Welburn (65), were chosen as representative of the discussion we have seen and heard in recent years around the theme of "rethinking reference." This discussion has centered around restructuring reference services in the light of changes, technological and otherwise. While it is of course important to critically examine practice, particularly in a time of rapid change, we are concerned about statements that ask us simply to abandon what we have been or to move into the future without understanding how we arrived at the present.

2. Though further work needs to be done to clarify the origin and relationships between these two traditional notions of reference work, it seems to us that they originate in two different concepts of the utility of the library. One concept, of great importance early in the library movement (as it remains today), stresses the library as a cultural institution, an institution devoted to the education and betterment of its patrons. Obviously this ideal is strongest in academic libraries, where the notion of reference having a significant instructional component has also been the strongest. The more extreme forms taken by this sense of educating patrons (as having them look up catalog numbers that could easily be provided on handouts) relate probably to older notions of "mental discipline" as central to education, notions that were never entirely abandoned as education moved from a strictly classical curriculum to a broader curriculum in which the library played a greater role. The second concept of the utility of the library stems from notions of efficacy and expertise common in the Progressive Era, the formative era for the library movement. Here librarians claim legitimacy because of their

efficiency in finding and supplying information, efficiency stemming from their expertise. These concepts obviously influenced the special library movement and can imply that the library function essentially is an information bureau, a model that is suggested in reference literature from at least the time of Wyer. This conflict of "cultural" and "modernist" values is noted in Neil Harris, "Cultural Institutions and American Modernization," *Journal of Library History* 16 (Winter 1981) 28–47 (especially 39–40).

REFERENCES

Abbott, Andrew. "The Future of the Professions: Occupation and Expertise in the Age of Organization." *Research in the Sociology of Organizations* 8 (1991): 17–42.

Abbott, Andrew. *The System of Professions: An Essay on the Division of Expert Labor*. Chicago & London: The University of Chicago Press, 1988.

Bishop, William Warner. *The Backs of Books and Other Essays in Librarianship*. Baltimore: Williams and Wilkins Company, 1926.

Brough, Kenneth J. *Scholar's Workshop: Evolving Concepts of Library Service*. Illinois Contributions to Librarianship, No. 5. Urbana: University of Illinois Press, 1953.

Campbell, Jerry D. "Shaking the Conceptual Foundations of Reference: A Perspective." *Reference Services Review* 20.4 (Winter 1992): 29–35.

Campbell, Jerry D. "It's a Tough Job Looking Ahead When You've Seen What's Dragging Behind." *Journal of Academic Librarianship* 17.3 (July 1991): 148–151.

Chappell, Marcia H. "The Place of Reference Service in Ranganathan's Theory of Librarianship." *Library Quarterly*, 46.4 (1976): 378–396.

Clement, Richard W. "Renaissance Libraries." *Encyclopedia of Library History*. Wayne Weigand, Donald G. Davis, Jr., eds. New York: Garland, 1994.

Davis, Murray S. "That's Interesting! Towards a Phenomenology of Sociology and a Sociology of Phenomenology." *Philosophy of the Social Sciences* 1 (1971): 309–344.

Farber, Evan Ira. "Catalog Dependency." *Library Journal* 109 (1984): 325–328.

Freides, Thelma. "Will the Real Reference Problem Please Stand Up." *Library Journal* 91 (1966): 2008–2012.

Galvin, Thomas J. "Reference Service and Libraries." *Encyclopedia of Library and Information Science*. Allen Kent, Harold Lancour, eds. Vol. 25. New York: Marcel Dekker, 1978.

Green, Samuel Swett. "Personal Relations Between Librarians and Readers." *Library Journal* 1 (1876): 74–81.

Handlin, Oscar. "Libraries and Learning." *American Scholar* 56 (1987): 205–218.

Kaplan, Louis. *The Growth of Reference Service in the United States from 1876 to 1893*. ACRL Monographs, no. 2. Chicago: Association of College and Research Libraries, 1952.

Lipow, Anne Grodzins. *Rethinking Reference in Academic Libraries: The Proceedings and Process of Library Solutions Institute Number 2*. Berkeley, California: Library Solutions Press, 1993.

Mood, Terry Ann. "Of Sundials and Digital Watches: A Further Step toward the New Paradigm of Reference." *Reference Services Review* (Fall 1994) 27–32+.

Petrof, Barbara G. "Theory: the X Factor in Librarianship." *College and Research Libraries* 26 (1965): 316–317.

Postman, Neil. *The End of Education: Redefining the Value of School*. New York: Alfred A. Knopf, 1995.

Postman, Neil. "Learning by Story" *Atlantic* (December 1989): 119–124.

Postman, Neil. *Technopoly: The Surrender of Culture to Technology*. New York: Knopf, 1992.

Ranganathan, S. R. *Reference Service*. Bombay: Asia Publishing House, 1961.

Ranganathan, S. R. *The Five Laws of Library Science*. Bombay: Asia Publishing House, 1963.

Rettig, James. "The Convergence of the Twain or Titanic Collision? BI and Reference in the 1990s' Sea of Change." 23.1 *Reference Services Review* (Spring 1995): 7–20.

Rettig, James. "A Theoretical Model and Definition of the Reference Process." *RQ* (Fall 1978): 19–29.

Rosenblum, Joseph. "Reference Service in Academia—*Quo Vadis*?" *Journal of Academic Librarianship* 6.3 (July 1980): 151–153

Rothstein, Samuel. "The Development of the Concept of Reference Service in American Libraries, 1850–1900." *The Library Quarterly* 23 (1953): 1–15.

Rothstein, Samuel. *The Development of Reference Service Through Academic Traditions, Public Library Practice, and Special Librarianship.* ACRL Monographs, no. 14. Chicago: Association of College and Reference Libraries, 1955.

Rothstein, Samuel. "Reference Service: The New Dimension in Librarianship." *Reference Services.* Contributions to Library Literature, no. 5. Hamden, CT: Shoe String Press, 1964.

Schiller, Anita R. "Reference Service: Instruction or Information." *Library Quarterly* 35 (January 1965): 52–60.

Shera, J.H. *Sociological Foundations of Librarianship.* London: Asia Publishing House, 1970.

Shiflett, Orvin Lee. *Origins of American Academic Librarianship.* Norwood, NJ: Ablex Publishing Corp., 1981.

Shores, Louis. *Reference as the Promotion of Free Inquiry.* Littleton, CO: Libraries Unlimited, 1976.

Simmons-Welburn, Janice. "From Vision to Reality: Change at the University of Iowa." *Rethinking Reference in Academic Libraries: The Proceedings and Process of Library Solutions Institute Number 2.* Anne Grodzins Lipow, ed. Berkeley, California: Library Solutions Press, 1993.

Vavrek, Bernard F. "The Nature of Reference Librarianship." *RQ* (Fall 1969): 33–34.

Vavrek, Bernard F. "A Theory of Reference Service." *College and Research Libraries* 29 (November 1968): 508–510.

Viet, Fritz. "Library Service to College Students." 25 *Library Trends* (1976): 361–378.

Wagers, Robert. "American Reference Theory and the Information Dogma." *Journal of Library History* 13 (Summer 1978): 265–281.

Woodruff, Eleanor B. "Reference Work." 22 *Library Journal* (1897): 65–67.

Wyer, James I. *Reference Work: A Textbook for Students of Library Work and Librarians.* Chicago: American Library Association, 1930.

Extending a Virtual Hand: Promises and Problems of Electronic Instruction

By Abbie J. Basile
Rensselaer Polytechnic Institute

I'd like to talk about providing instruction to remote users. What I'd like to be able to do is stand here and announce the end of our instruction worries and troubles. No more need for concern about remote users wandering through the electronic forest without the aid of marked trails or breadcrumbs to help them find their way. The dark days are behind us and the glory days are ahead—just sunshine and light from here on in. New technologies have come to the rescue, helping us maintain a presence even when we are not able to be there in person.

But I'm here to take a more realistic approach to information technologies and their impact on our instructional goals and services. I'm going to raise some questions about electronic instruction, to which I do not necessarily have the answers. The library instruction community is energetic and active and I think, through dialogue, we will identify some possible answers. As in other areas of librarianship, there are many issues facing instruction librarians: changing user populations, as stated in Gretchen McCord Hoffmann's paper; continual developments in information delivery; an overabundance of search interfaces; increases in our remote user population; downsizing of organizations; the need for users to gain overarching information gathering skills . . . The list goes on, but I don't want to depress everyone this early in my paper.

Our libraries, and our positions within them, exist in a world where information is increasingly electronically-based. Our services and our organizations are undergoing a metamorphosis. Reference staff and patrons are not as often faced with whether a query can be answered using a print or an online resource, as they are involved in reference transaction decisions regarding whether to use a CD-ROM, Web site or online database. Libraries spend a good portion of their budgets providing remote access to our electronic resources. How much do we spend to provide instruction to the people using those resources?

The multitude of online library resources, and their different interfaces, requires our instructional skills more than ever. But, many users no longer come into the library. Our metamorphosis has quite naturally affected them as well. It is becoming increasingly likely that our patrons are not in, or even near, the library when they need instruction. They are at home, in their offices or in a campus lab. They may not have time to attend in-person group instruction sessions. We need to be there for these people as well. We need to strengthen our outreach, via electronic means, to these users.

I want to focus on the extent to which we can exploit technology to help us meet this challenge and the limits that same technology places upon our effectiveness as instructors. I will concentrate on the following types of computer-based instruction: system-integrated online instruction or, to be more plain, online help; electronically-delivered courses; and library Web systems.

BENEFITS TO LIBRARIES

Let's talk about the good news first—the benefits of online instruction and the library's role in developing that service. Our libraries provide multi-faceted services. We are not simply access providers to electronic resources and we should not want to be viewed as such. By providing instruction for our remote services, we present ourselves as the full service organizations that we are. The library organization as a whole profits from the increase in positive patron relations that new outreach programs engender.

Discussions in the past few years regarding the rethinking of how reference services are provided, have not been conclusive about the role of formal library instruction in a restructured environment. However, it is clear that the new model, in order to accommodate pervasive changes in our information-based environment, involves reducing the number of repetitive and basic "how-to" questions handled by librarians at the reference desk. One way to facilitate this is to provide assistance in a different way, at a different time, and in a different place. The different way is via online rather than in-person means; the time is whenever the user needs the help; and the place is out there in the ether.

Computer-assisted instruction's ability to deliver the same instruction many times to large numbers of users has positive ramifications for instructional staff issues such as burnout and overloaded instruction calendars. Staff involvement in designing and providing such services would serve to increase their skills and make them more conversant with and effective in their use of information and instructional technologies. The organization as a whole benefits by helping our users, which, in turn, has a positive effect on user attitudes toward the library and the services it provides.

BENEFITS TO OUR USERS

Let us not forget why we're doing all of this. Do we have any doubt that our users would be very well served by such outreach? Just as they have been helped by the bibliographies and print guides we create, users of electronic library services can greatly benefit from in-house development of online help, electronically-delivered courses, and, the grand prize, Web systems. There they sit, in their homes, their offices, their favorite computer labs, using our electronic resources, many of them learning from that indifferent, but ever present teacher, trial and error. Conventional library wisdom tells us that it is the rare patrons who will sift through help screens for answers or assistance.

So, are the majority of folks out there tying up their phone line or clogging the network just to sit staring helplessly at the database screen? Not at all. Many online products are not terribly difficult to use to perform a rudimentary search. But, we all know that this is not the optimum result we are looking for from these costly products. On their own, users "tend to learn the newer electronic tools as they have learned manual tools in the past: superficially, inadequately, from peers . . . "[1] Although it is not necessary to turn our users into mini-librarians, we are right to have expectations, on behalf of our users, for a more rigorous use of these products.

Electronically-based instruction offers many of the same benefits as technology-based information: expanded hours of access; user-controlled pace; interactivity; multiple simultaneous users.[2] It is an efficient way to deliver teaching to the masses, many of whom may never be motivated to attend an in-person instruction session. Computer-assisted instruction allows the learner to not only progress and review material at their own speed, but to also participate in their learning when it is most convenient, desirable, or needed. Room and staff scheduling conflicts are not a problem. Imagine: instruction delivered at time of need, not just during a time convenient to room and staff schedules.

ONLINE HELP

It is true that many of our products have vendor-produced online help, but it is often minimal, not context-sensitive, and most importantly, it is too easily avoided altogether. These help screens are commonly accessed by starting up a separate help program where the user's search screen or search results are visually replaced with the online help information. It is not common for the online help text to be displayed on the same screen where your command prompt is still active. So, you often must leave the help information behind when you return to the part of the system where you were having difficulty to begin with. The user must choose between assistance and performing a search. This separation of help and active search screens means that if you never make a conscious effort to ask for help in these systems, you're very unlikely to receive any. [3]

ELECTRONICALLY-DELIVERED COURSES

More comprehensive instruction, such as a course, can be delivered electronically, as demonstrated by the University of Illinois at Chicago Library's E-Train course. The entire content of this Internet course was delivered through a listserv subscribed to by interested UIC parties. The course was offered twice during the 1994–1995 academic year and was subscribed to by over 650 people. Two lessons, delivered via e-mail, were sent out once a week for eight weeks. The lessons are archived on the Library's Gopher, Web and FTP site for ease of access for those who missed the course or were not affiliated with UIC. A four-person Internet Training Class Task Force spent two semesters planning and designing the course and preparing the course materials. Having identified a need to address additional Internet topics and issues, and having seen a positive response and increased Internet use from the first two offerings, the UIC task force prepared an advanced class called E-train II. The instruction for the advanced class was delivered via a World-Wide Web page, instead of a listserv.[4]

CHALLENGES: DIVERSE USERS

So, our organization benefits, as do our staff and our users, by our provision of online help to remote users. Sounds like sunshine and light all the way, right? Well, as usual, things are not as easy or simple as they seem. The users we're focusing on are without in-person assistance. But that may be all they have in common. Their library skill levels may vary greatly. Being individuals from different age groups, academic and socioeconomic backgrounds, it is almost certain that these patrons come to our electronic library environments with very different computer literacy skills. As Gretchen McCord Hoffmann notes in her paper for this conference, differences among our users equate to differences in their needs.[5] One of the outcomes of these dissimilarities is our need to accommodate various learning styles.

CHALLENGES: TEACHING & LEARNING STYLES

Any online instruction, be it help screens that are integrated into our OPAC, electronic courses, or Web pages, would ideally be able to deliver the necessary information, despite the various needs and differences stated above. "Good teaching takes into account diversity in learning styles and adjusts instructional goals and methodologies in view of individual student differences."[6] One of the advantages attributed to online instruction is the ability to deliver instruction to the masses easily and consistently. But, the masses are not of one mind, background, skill level, or learning style. "Students enter learning situations with established learning styles. Most teaching methods, however, appeal only to a certain learning style and handicap those who would prefer to learn in another way."[7] Therefore, is it really a benefit to users to have the information delivered in a format designed one way but offered to many? Sound advice appears in *Learning to Teach*, "Make sure your instruction offers a wide variety of opportunities for learning. Increase your chances of reaching everyone by varying presentation styles, formats and methods."[8]

And what about teaching styles and their ability to speak to different learners? Lana Dixon's article in the Fall 1995 issue of *Research Strategies* points out the advantages of computer-assisted instruction. She states, "Each student could receive the same information in identical lessons. There would be none of the disparity that came with differing teaching styles, levels of enthusiasm, or class lengths."[9] I wonder if removing the disparity in our teaching styles is really a good thing, and whether the lack of opportunity for the enthusiastic instructor to express herself is truly advantageous.

I know one could argue that taking the human presence out of the classroom eliminates the possibility for negative instructor body language and flat, unenthusiastic delivery of material. But, I think we would all agree that the primary goal of computer-based instruction is not to remove poor instructors from the classroom. That issue is best dealt with by other means. Students also benefit from positive instructor body language. The importance of visual cues during a class session should not be underestimated. A few student brows start to furrow and an alert instructor knows it's time to shift gears, use some humor, or offer an illustration, verbally or visually, to make the point clearer. The majority of current electronic communication lacks the important face-to-face communication between teacher and learner.

CHALLENGES: EFFECT ON STAFF

Another challenge presented to us is the cost of online instruction on our staff. In most libraries, there will be a definite need for staff training and skill building in such areas as online screen design and software manipulation. Remote instruction has

Reference Services in Research Libraries: Some Definitions, Questions, and Answers Concerning the Integration of the Print and Network Service Environments: A Four-Part Discussion

Part 1:
Traditions: Research and Reference Services

By Ann Bristow
Indiana University

In a recent issue of the Journal of Academic Librarianship, David Lewis declared that "Traditional Reference is Dead, Now Let's Move on to Important Questions." One reaction to this proclamation is a sense of welcome release from pain. Who are these recently departed?: teachers who are burnt out. Those surviving the fire were then told to make themselves scarce, require appointments, get some respect. If you are still called a "reference librarian" the respect may not be forthcoming, perhaps if you are an "access engineer"?

A BRIEF SYNOPSIS OF THE REFERENCE LITERATURE OVER THE PAST TWO DECADES

Earlier in the literature, however, there are definitions of reference service, its history and its purpose which I find more helpful and will use as a framework for these remarks. Samuel Rothstein dates reference services in university libraries in the United States from about 1900 and defines "reference" as the organized provision by libraries of personal assistance to individual users—not instruction to a group of users, not one individual librarian responding when possible to one individual's inquiry but an organized service provided by libraries.

The setting and the clientele I want to address must also be defined. The settings are those general, principal research libraries attached to research universities. And "research" throughout my remarks I hope will be understood as something like "a critical and exhaustive inquiry directed toward the extension or modification of knowledge," not "research" as a description of any search for any information bits. Within this setting, the primary clientele will be research workers, largely faculty and graduate students by the nature of their work and its requirements, not status (alone).

I offer these definitions because I believe they are essential to any clear-thinking on this topic. To the assertion that such a service is no longer needed or relevant, there may be several appropriate responses, not one right answer for all libraries. Arguably, there are library settings in which the answer is yes, such a service is obsolete—these might include even some which call themselves "research libraries" but are not likely to include great, historical collections. The universities of which such libraries are a part most probably identify research in their mission statements but their actual practice would not support the purpose fully. These are not the settings I want to discuss today.

My focus is on universities still declaring research as central to their mission and supporting that declaration in their choices among competing priorities. The libraries I discuss support that research mission and fill that "common ground" which I take to be the focus of this conference. They are concerned about "creating the library of the future without diminishing the library of the past" not because that is a cultural or a political preference but because those engaged in research still use and require the entire scope of our great collections, printed and digital.

In this institutional setting, the service under discussion is a centralized, "general" (meaning concentration in humanities and social sciences in most places) reader assistance service, one which offers guidance on the use of tools and services and answers to particular inquiries. More broadly it is a service which attempts to address the research need presented; one available dependably and regularly (i.e. not depending on one librarian alone but a staffed service point with a central location in the principal library building and staffing multiple service points in the library's electronic "home"). I want to sketch a model of such a Research Reference Services unit (not, how we do it at Indiana or Yale or Penn or Cornell, necessarily) and suggest why it might be useful and desirable. Also, before sketching this service, I must place it in a context of other necessary services. The model I am going to argue for probably cannot exist in isolation where the potential to overwhelm it with numbers would be real though perhaps might be exaggerated. Such a service is probably viable only where it is complemented by a separate undergraduate library and/or separate "information" desks. The targeting of user groups in the design of services is not without its difficulties but is almost certainly necessary if such services are to be useful to their clientele.

WHAT DO "RESEARCH WORKERS" NEED FROM THE RESEARCH LIBRARY?

In the past many faculty believed themselves (and some were) masters, quite literally, of the research library environment. They are no longer masters of the changing library. I make this assertion with confidence and further assert that any librarian who challenges it is not listening to those scholars (older and younger), not hearing their needs. They need "individual personal assistance."

Some years ago, a faculty member wrote the following dedicatory in his book on Saint Paul: "To the Reference Librarians of Indiana University, humanists, and my true colleagues." When I thanked him and protested that he had been too generous he said "no, no, I meant it; years ago I used to get occasional support from my colleagues but now, no matter what my question it elicits only one response: 'I have no idea, that's not my area.' More recently I work with faculty every day who are pleased with many individual changes—the ability to get to the library's catalog from home and office and for many the ability to use their principal index remotely (MLA, PsycInfo). Some are very skilled users of these two or three resources but beyond these, most all faculty are befuddled about the electronic environment and its relation (if any) to the print environment. Without much further development I will just offer two points: 1) that the changing nature of research (narrowing to very fine points in some respects and opening broadly, blurring the traditional discipline lines, in others) when 2) coupled with the changing nature of research tools and libraries, present research libraries with a possibly unique opportunity to assert our present value to our institutions—if we wish to seize the opportunity.

In the constant barrage of confident predictions about the shape of the future only one rings true to my ear: the next period of years (twenty, twenty-five, more) will be one of unremitting change and instability. The range of scholarly tools and resources will grow steadily, building on a relatively unchanging and very complex base. The scholar will be offered more tools—and more complexity. The investment in time to use these tools effectively (effectively as a scholar, not an individual hunting for a film review) will be considerable. The choices to be made will be daunting. The background needed to sort out the hype from the real, considerable.

I admit that these words—daunting, complex, unremitting—reflect not only what I hear from others but my own experience. Among my principal tasks are responsibilities to contribute to guiding these changes locally (as an 'access engineer'), to select and evaluate tools and approaches, to resist being inappropriately drawn to one format or another and identify the most appropriate approach—drawing on the holdings of the research collections built and described over many generations and on the powerful new tools being redesigned each day. If you have not tried this lately,—it's a challenge! Not a challenge many faculty are eager to take on, for very good reasons. The complexity and, even more, the instability of our present environment leads many faculty to be willing to accept (to wish for) a reliable guide, an experienced explorer—who knows the entire terrain of the changing research library, not just particular corners of it. If we could agree that such a service might be needed then other questions might follow. I will try to sketch those questions but should acknowledge first that clearly we cannot agree.

Rothstein, throughout his study, speaks of opposing "conservative" and "liberal" views. These roughly correspond to the 'teachers' and 'spoon-feeders' of some time back and seem possibly reversed in their contemporary connotations. Rothstein gives wonderful examples of the adherents of the "conservative" view in university libraries. To one policy statement which read "personal resourcefulness and independence on the part of the student and of the faculty are to be desired and encouraged at all times," Rothstein observed "just what educational purposes were being served by denying faculty more than minimal assistance was seldom made clear. Tacitly, however, the policy was undoubtedly based on the old assumption that the mature scholar did not need help—or at any rate ought not to need it." With a different tone and intention but in the same tradition, Brian Nielsen wrote in 1982 "If librarians truly wish to work towards the best interests of their users, it is absurd to continue to advocate the old classic professionalism, which places users in a dependency relationship with librarians. Such a relationship does a disservice to users and ultimately retards the development of library services, of librarians, and of much library technology."

Half a century after Rothstein and fifteen years after Nielsen the mere suggestion that skilled assistance is required stands in indignant opposition to the dominant rhetoric about the desk-top; that rhetoric celebrates, even sanctifies, the person engaged in "research" seated at his desk where he has access to all he needs and all he needs to know; he is pictured as enjoying and valuing the experience of learning and relearning how to surf, explore, and hunt. We all know such people. I know not one among those faculty in their thirties, very at-ease with computers, and fully engaged in the task of writing a book, having it published and reviewed before the beginning of the sixth year of their appointment; nor more than a few of any age who have active research programs. Faced with this dissonance between my own experience and the claims of the information marketplace, I choose to describe the conclusions to which my experience points.

HOW IS SUCH A SERVICE PROVIDED?

Not best, I would suggest, as it is too often done: by hiring those with least experience and asking them to function usefully as independent agents taking on whatever comes, in whatever language, whatever subject, whatever knowledge or ignorance of technology for three to six hours a day. (In some settings, Indiana as an example, we compound the problem by adding graduate students to the confusing mix of skills and lack of skills available at the "Desk.") Looking at this model critically, it is difficult to argue in its defense and it is an appropriate target for criticism. But it is the way the service is offered that is vulnerable, not the service itself.

WHAT DOES THE COLLECTIVE STAFF OF A GREAT RESEARCH LIBRARY OFFER?

Considerable subject expertise, extraordinary language expertise, remarkable (and relevant, sympathetic) technological expertise—exactly the combination of skills and abilities needed to assist those whose work occasionally leads them beyond their own areas of expertise and who need to find the answer, the direction, the tool, to further that work—and need to find it immediately.

HOW COULD SUCH A SERVICE BE PROVIDED?

By asking our best and most senior librarians whether titled reference librarian, or bibliographer or instruction librarian or other. The titles and the best configurations would differ slightly in different research libraries. Each librarian would most likely have a tie or ties to specific faculties, managing common resources for that faculty and the library but also working as part of a truly cooperative group, able and expected to call on one another, to call on anyone in the library with the necessary expertise to find the answer to the question, the solution to the problem. They must work in a library that views such work as important work, demanding immediate, timely attention. Their services should be available from one common location inside the physical library, both by appointment and without appointment, during the hours that their assistance is most regularly sought whether that conforms to the "regular" work week or does not. Such a group of experts can sort out those questions which require specialized knowledge and those which require a generalist, re-directing inquiries when necessary with confidence and authority.

It is important to add that the idea of assigning librarians with primary responsibilities of a completely other nature to two hours a week at the reference desk is utterly unacceptable. It may be an administrator's answer to a personnel problem, a staff development officer's idea of job enrichment—but it is no way to run a credible service. The challenge of learning and relearning required to offer a service which would earn and retain a researcher's confidence is very great. It requires constant engagement with the shape of the developing electronic library and its relationship to the printed scholarly record. The responsibilities of these research reference librarians may vary but each position must have coherence and have the provision of individual assistance to researchers as a core responsibility.

This same group of library research experts must have a presence in the electronic face of the library—intruding themselves with repeated offers of assistance, designing and redesigning the best ways to do that. The electronic library is, in fact, an ideal setting for the delivery of many instances of this expert assistance, allowing the targeting and forwarding of the inquiry to the right point, aiding the joint participation in the provision of the answer or the needed assistance. Allowing one to review the answer given, to offer additional information, from another angle.

WHAT ARE THE SERVICES WHICH MIGHT BE PROVIDED?

This topic deserves a fuller treatment; I will assume (perhaps I should not) that most of us interested in this discussion know enough to imagine the usefulness of a service which provides an address (street, fax, phone, e-mail, URL, however the 'address' might be defined) close to the moment one needs it and have some sense of the great number of languages and tools, printed and digital, which one must know to do that reliably and accurately in a research library environment. I will offer just one example of another sort.

Those libraries which had a fee-based search service which earned the respect of faculty and graduate students (who were overwhelmingly its clientele) may have noticed that it is sometimes missed. When a faculty member, at the beginning of a new effort perhaps or perhaps looking for the treatment of a question from a completely different angle from her own, is given the "good news" that there is little available in Dialog pertinent to that area of inquiry which is not now subsidized by the library and available for her own use without cost, that good news is not always viewed as good. The cost which we now describe as free or subsidized can be measured by the user in several ways: money, distraction, time.

One task such a research reference unit might take on is redesigning such a service. How should we respond to such inquiries? Is a fee-based model the only limit to volume we can imagine? Is it the only model which can inspire confidence? What was it that made the service valuable? Did confidence in the skill of the librarian add any value?

Among the several tests we might put to ourselves about our confidence in this "good news" approach as our only present option might be to ask: how do we respond to the dean or the provost? Do we give them the good news or the answer? A usual response to this observation is that there is one provost and there are too many others. There are many others; if we understand their needs and design our services effectively it is possible that there are not "too" many.

BENEFITS TO THE LIBRARY?

Such a service is honestly user-centered and would bring much of our rhetoric into some alignment with practice. It will be seen by the faculty as such and seen as among highest priorities of the library—not a common courtesy, not a favor they are able to extract from a willing or unwilling staff member. They could be offered a service representing the total skills, talents and willingness of the entire staff of the libraries—not just one person who having whatever level of competence and willingness can only do so much. (Or, in worst but occasionally real cases, present himself and be viewed, as "our" person in the library, the only one protecting us from the incompetence and unwillingness of the library as an organization.) Nor, on the other hand, help from an ill-defined, uneven service point staffed by—it's not clear exactly whom: a woman with a Ph.D. and twenty years of experience and another who started graduate library school last month (and came to town the day before).

The library has invested in a large range of tools which aid the librarian in identifying and delivering expert assistance. Tasks which were once unthinkably time consuming and expensive are now feasible. The librarian who spends many hours learning and relearning new tools (and stubbornly refusing to forget old ones) now has an adequate infrastructure at hand to support the identification and delivery of extended assistance. In providing such assistance, the library can demonstrate the purpose and potential of these investments.

BENEFITS TO THE LIBRARIAN?

Beyond the benefit I have just described which extends to the individual professional, this is not the most important question, I would again assert but with more trepidation than earlier assertions. All the articles in our literature which suggest that a change in title, a requirement that the user wait a respectful period of time and move to a setting in which the reference librarian's status and control is more secure—all these approaches are wrong, and embarrassing. So many seem modeled on the professional ideal of the physician, ironically at the moment that ideal is itself under considerable challenge.

I do believe, however, that there are enormous benefits to the librarian—both the "generalist" librarian and the "specialist" librarian. The specialist becomes part of a larger environment, responsible for having an enlarged view of the possibilities but not responsible for 'knowing everything and therefore nothing' because they are supported by a group of people all working towards a common purpose: each with strengths (and weaknesses), each expected to assist the other and together to assist the individual student and faculty member. The "generalist" too becomes part of a larger environment, expected to call on colleagues not forced to admit failure, rescued from occasional naiveté and substitution of a guess for an answer, allowed to demonstrate the usefulness of the enlarged perspective. In this setting respect can be earned, not contrived, and imagined by working together to present a service which deserves respect and is needed more than ever in the period of profound and unremitting change awaiting us all in at least the next quarter century.

Research libraries exist to serve research and researchers, those already holding credentials, the faculty, and those earning credentials, their students. It is my experience that librarians are not always comfortable with this identification with research; and they are not alone. The universities of which we are a part are themselves undergoing profound scrutiny and self-scrutiny. Challenges come from parents, legislators, trustees, benefactors, the popular press—all questioning the priorities of higher education. Internally, university administrators are searching for new sources of revenue and challenging the older assumptions about the ownership of intellectual property, whether such property is an invention or an article or a class syllabus. The threat to the "traditional" classroom and to the role and status of the faculty are very serious.

Libraries of many descriptions, sizes and missions can play interesting new roles in service to new instructional models. I think most libraries will be comfortable and competent in doing that even if the outlines are not yet clear. If we guess that along with instruction some respect and support for research will survive the current questioning we might ask ourselves: how comfortable are we in asserting our own respect and support for research? How willing and competent to offer individual assistance to those engaged in critical and exhaustive inquiry?

There is, of course, not much new in the model I sketch here. That is part of its attraction. I should probably add, however, that I do not view the tradition of such reference service in university libraries (that "liberal service philosophy" Rothstein himself clearly held) as a strong tradition. I have no confidence that many libraries will maintain commitment to such a service. I do believe, however, that research libraries have the ability to work with those engaged in research more helpfully and collegially and that we should do it. The need for such assistance has not disappeared in this challenging historical moment, it has intensified. We are presented with an opportunity we should seize. We can serve those engaged in research and serve the argument for continued support of the great research libraries whose interests are allied with those of the faculty in profound and (so-to-speak) unchanging ways.

Part 2:
Reference Service in a Large Research Library: Finding Common Ground in a Time of Change

By Paul J. Constantine
Cornell University

Finding common ground is an interesting theme for this conference. The common ground I want to touch on is the common ground we must find between the new and the old, the innovative and the traditional in this time of transition for large research libraries. Large research libraries today often deal with tensions. One tension arises as we provide access to the world of print and the world of the electronic. Another arises as we try to provide service within the walls of our buildings while also developing services for users no matter their location. Still another arises as we pride ourselves on the high quality of service rendered to faculty and graduate students while—like most areas of the university—we are re-emphasizing our services to undergraduates. We must now tailor our reference programs and services for two different ages—the age of the book (which may also be characterized, perhaps, as the age of the library with walls and the age of the scholar) and the age of the computer (characterized, perhaps, as the age of the library without walls and the age of the undergraduate) if we are to maximize our historic and continuing intellectual and capital investment in "the library" and serve the best interests of our users. In other words, we must find a common ground between the old and the new in order that our users may seamlessly navigate our libraries. What are we as Reference Librarians faced with in creating this common ground? What are we doing to achieve it?

In beginning, let me briefly describe the situation in the Olin•Kroch•Uris Libraries {O-K-U} at Cornell. In 1994, after much discussion and planning, Cornell's Uris Undergraduate Library was administratively merged with Olin, the research library, and Kroch, the new library on campus housing the Asian and Rare and Manuscript Divisions. In the merger, Uris lost its designation as the undergraduate library.

The Reference staffs of Olin and Uris were merged into one division. I left Yale to become head of this new division in August of 1995. The division consists of 11 Reference Librarians, the Map Librarian, 7 Information Assistants (paraprofessionals), 2 Map Assistants, and 2 Support Staff members. We staff three service desks—one in Olin, one in Uris, and one in the Map Collection. We also serve as the US and UN Documents Repository. In addition, we coordinate User Education for O•K•U, do a bit of collection development, and have played a major role in the introduction of various new technologies to the Cornell University Library. We are able to accomplish as much as we do, I think, largely because of our staff model—professional Reference Librarians and paraprofessional Information Assistants. These Information Assistants go through a rigorous training program which probably includes much more practical information than most library school reference courses. It is only after several months of training that they are scheduled on the desk and even more months of desk-work before they are scheduled by themselves.

While we regard our desk staffing pattern as somewhat fluid and subject to change as needs (and statistics) change, we strive to balance a high level of top-notch service at the desk with an eye toward cost-effectiveness and a recognition that, seemingly more than ever, Reference Librarians are being asked to make contributions to public service—indeed to provide service—away from the desk. We currently schedule Information Assistants alone during statistically slow times such as early morning, the dinner hour, late evening, and some weekend hours. The Reference Librarians' offices are in fairly close proximity to the desk and the Info Assistants are encouraged—and do—seek help whenever needed. At other times, the desk is staffed with a combination of Reference Librarians and Information Assistants. At these times, too, the referral process seems to work quite smoothly. There are certain types of "subject" or extended reference questions which are automatically referred to the librarians. In other cases, the Information Assistant takes the question as far as he or she can and then passes it on. As demands for instruction, development of new electronic services, and so forth increase, we frequently look at our statistics in order to come up with the optimum blend of staff which will enable us to continue to provide a high level of service while allowing us to meet the other demands on our time. While Reference Librarians continue to provide reference desk service, other service models—the discussion of which abounds in the literature—are being explored. Soon, perhaps, we'll provide live interactive electronic reference and instruction via MOOs, chat programs, or interactive video.

A fact noticed at several large research libraries, but not often discussed, is a drop in the number of reference questions asked at our desks. It seems that as increasing numbers of students and faculty spend more and more of their research time utilizing networked electronic resources, it is less necessary for them to come into the library to do research. With a network connection and an easy-to-use gateway, a scholar need not leave his office nor a student leave her room. If Reference Librarians are to continue to play a major service role in this environment, we need to think of ways of reaching our users outside the library. One way would be to take reference and instruction on the road. At Yale, each of the residential colleges (dorms) has a writing tutor and a math/science tutor available to students with an office in the college. This could be an exciting model for Reference Librarians to follow. Reference staff members could have office hours in dorms and departmental offices where, equipped with network-connected laptops and small ready-reference collections, we could provide on-site reference services to our users on their turf. Similar things can be done with instruction; at the University of Pennsylvania, reference staff is providing Lexis/Nexis training in dorms. The reference staff at Cornell has also begun a similar program on a very small scale; we plan to continue and enlarge the program in future.

While providing first-rate reference service to our in-building users, we can't neglect training and support issues related to remote users of our resources. These remote users may be one of our students or faculty members dialing in from home, connecting from the office, or telnetting in from the site of a sabbatical. It may be a student or scholar at another institution trying to tap into the riches of our online catalog. To what degree should we provide support to these users? Who should provide it? How? How do we utilize our electronic services to create a positive, exciting image of our library and university? While we may not provide a high level of service to non-affiliated users, we must certainly support our remote students and faculty. Creating and mounting well-designed documentation online for our electronic resources would be one fairly easy-to-provide form of support. A more difficult, and more useful, form of support, is the provision of online instruction. At Cornell, we use the World Wide Web to provide some basic undergraduate library instruction. We have also assisted faculty members in the creation of Web pages for their classes.

As we begin at Cornell to cross-deploy Reference staff at our two reference desks (in different buildings), we are putting a new emphasis on training. We have begun a series of workshops presented by Reference Librarians to Information Assistants and other Reference Librarians. These training/refresher sessions have had several purposes. One has been to familiarize and train staff from one library with the resources of the other library. Another has been to introduce new resources such as Dyabola or L'annee philologique on CD-ROM. Still another has been to update and remind staff of printed sources in the collections which—while certainly still important, if not indispensable—are less often used today than they were even a few years ago. Over Winter break this year, in-depth sessions open to all Reference Staff were presented on our departmentally-produced Cornell Clipfile; our public access Macintoshes; both reference collections; the card catalogs; multi-media, statistical, social science, and humanities CD-ROMs; microform collections; UN documents; US documents; census material; and the Map Collection. The Division's Reference Librarians meet weekly, the Information Assistants meet together on a regular basis, and the entire division meets together monthly. We try to fit some shorter training/refresher sessions into these meetings as well. Currently planned are presentations on Genealogical Sources, Statistical Sources, and British Parliamentary Papers.

We are also coming to grips with the World Wide Web and changing modes of access to electronic information; after all, reference staffs are expected to be as at home on the net as they are on the desk. Yet, the intelligent utilization of the Web is not intuitive to many librarians who began their careers before the 1980s. In many cases, especially in places with large numbers of senior staff members, it is up to us to help our colleagues reach a comfortable level of understanding. Just as staff have presented sessions to other members of the division on printed tools, so, too, have they presented sessions on electronic tools ranging from the CETEDOC Library of Early Christian Texts on CD-ROM to the latest Web search engine. Clearly, it is necessary for Reference Librarians today to find the common ground in dealing with print and electronic sources if we are to meet the needs of our clientele; continuous training and refresher sessions are one way accomplishing this.

Defining our clientele can be difficult. At universities with both research libraries and undergraduate libraries, this definition may be simpler. Large research collections have traditionally served the needs of faculty and graduate students. At most universities, however, there is a renewed emphasis on undergraduate education and the experience of the undergraduate within the university. We ignore undergraduates at our peril. At Yale, we did not have a separate undergraduate library nor do we any longer at Cornell. Undergraduates are encouraged to make use of all of our research treasures. This can pose a problem for reference staff. Meeting the needs of undergraduates—which can obviously differ greatly from those of an advanced doctoral student or faculty member—is quite different than meeting the needs of our traditional clientele. The merger of the undergraduate and research libraries at Cornell resulted in a reference division which has staff who have excellent understanding of and skills in meeting the needs of faculty and graduate students as well as staff who have spent their careers working with undergraduates. We hope that as we cross-deploy and work together some of those skills will transfer and that many staff members will provide equally capable service to the user—no matter what his or her academic standing may be.

There is another problem facing us in meeting the needs of our users. Large research libraries are the natural habitat of many scholars yet many scholars are not quite as at home in our libraries as they should be in this era of change. We need discreetly to provide them with training and support and to work with them to develop new services and programs for their colleagues and students. Faculty members generally do not like to reveal their ignorance. They especially do not like to do it in public. In helping them develop new skills, the skills necessary for scholarship in today's hybrid world of print and electronic, two ways seem to be most successful. The first is, in a way, indirect. By insisting as much as possible that faculty members accompany their classes to user education sessions, librarians can insure that the instructor receives the same training as the students. Another way which also seems to work is to offer one-on-one instruction to faculty members either in the privacy of their offices or in a private spot within the library. Faculty appreciate the time spent with them, develop new skills, and do so away from the eyes of their students and colleagues.

In meeting the needs of faculty, it is important to offer to meet their information needs—however defined—wherever they arise. At Yale, reference staff members often met with individual scholars—sometimes in the library, sometimes in the faculty members' office—to discuss appropriate research strategies, assist in connecting to the online catalog, or help in connecting to the e-mail server. These faculty members, in most cases, became staunch friends of the reference department and the library, as well as more highly skilled. When I arrived at Cornell—replacing someone who had been head of reference for more than twenty-five years—I was very pleased by the number of faculty members who stopped me to tell me their views of the division. Most often they were favorable views and they usually reflected on specific librarians who had taken the time to work individually with the faculty member. I have to believe that much of our ability effectively to meet the needs of this clientele—needs which must often be met away from the desk—is largely due to our staffing model which combines high-quality desk-coverage with time away from the desk for librarians to provide other user services.

Given our staffing model, our user programs, our emphasis on training, and our heightened attempts to meet the needs of our users, have we found the common ground? Probably not yet. What we are doing works for us, though, and we are well on our way to finding the common ground whereby all our users will comfortably mine our riches—both new and old.

Part 3:
Where Is the Reference Desk Now?

By Jane G. Bryan
University of Pennsylvania

Over the last decade, academic libraries have worked diligently and successfully to "empower the user." By making electronic information easily accessible from just about anywhere, we have laid the foundation and built the first floor of our virtual libraries. Our faculty, students, and staff can consult on-line catalogs, indexes and abstracts, electronic encyclopedias and dictionaries, and full-text versions of an increasingly important set of journals and newspapers without leaving their offices or residences.

This is progress. Our libraries' successes in providing access to electronic resources, in offering library services by utilizing electronic forms, and in organizing cyberspace through thoughtfully designed web pages are all rightfully praised and promoted. Students e-mail their thanks for on-line electronic interlibrary loan forms; faculty lobby for additional full-text resources.

However, as the range of networked electronic resources grows, and as libraries shift materials dollars from paper to electronic versions of sources, the use of library facilities and services—including reference services—changes. Since information and services that were once available in a single location are now available from virtually anywhere, and since it is certainly more convenient to search the catalog from an office than to make a trip across campus, many large academic libraries have seen a decline in the number of researchers coming in to the library and using library space and library equipment. At Penn's Van Pelt Library, for example, we have seen a drop in the number of queries at our central reference desk. Just two years ago we staffed the reference desk with four librarians during peak afternoon hours; now three are often more than enough.

All this could be nothing but good news. It could mean that students and faculty working outside the library are finding the information they need on-line, efficiently and effectively. It could mean that faculty and students are now able to find materials in our collections and elsewhere without help. Our experience, however, tells us that this is only partly true. Some folks are empowered and some are floundering. Cyberspace is one more place to look, the array of choices can be overwhelming, and messages saying all this is EASY may actually discourage some users from asking how or where. And for those who do want to ask, it is now often more convenient to ask whoever is closest—be that a colleague in the next office, a classmate at an adjacent computer, or a friendly newsgroup—rather than a librarian.

From my perspective as a working reference librarian who believes in the value of the service Ann Bristow has described, the challenge is this: How can we position reference service in this new electronic environment so that we remain as obvious a resource for assistance and consultation as we have been traditionally? How can we make reference service as useful from outside the library as it has been inside the building? How can we best serve those who are foundering in cyberspace, and foundering for many of the same reasons people have been frustrated over the years by vast collections of information on paper?

I believe we will have to develop a whole array of new approaches to taking our service beyond the library building, all the while maintaining a home-base reference desk. These will likely include both "virtual" services and new practices. As we continue to try out and develop these new approaches, a rosy future for reference services will depend on our energy, creativity, flexibility, and perseverance.

Let me offer some suggestions on approaches for your consideration. You will see that some of these are what might be called promotional and others are "content-rich." The former aim at raising awareness of reference service, placing it prominently in the virtual environment, and actively promoting its use. (One might ask why we need to promote reference service still, or yet again, after it has proven its value through the years. I would answer that our reference services do not have sufficient visibility or prominence in the virtual environment, which even tends to hide them, and that we must work hard to gain recognition, in that environment. Our users have discovered worlds of help beyond our domains. New sites such as the Engineering Village offer subject-specialist expert help, 24 hours a day, presumably as conveniently as ATMs offer cash. Frankly, we are competing for our local clientele, and if we believe our service is valuable and unique, we need to promote it.) The latter involve new ways of presenting information to our clientele. Here they are:

1. *Become ubiquitous on the web*. An electronic environment offers us the opportunity to highlight reference service in every virtual space that we help develop. "Ask your librarian!" can appear on any library web page. Just as the reference desk offers experts at a specific physical location, an icon or distinctive phrase can point to that same high level of service from virtually anywhere on the network. We can lobby with academic departments that have their own web pages to include the reference icon or phrase prominently; faculty members who appreciate our work may become sponsors of the reference icon in their home domains or even link to it from their personal homepages. Create FAQs collecting commonly asked or especially interesting questions, and be sure that these answers are indexed by our web's search engine.

2. *Intrude gently*. Reference questions are being posted to campus-wide newsgroups, and reference librarians can and should answer them. Ready reference questions give us the opportunity to demonstrate a "best practices" model by providing full and accurate answers and by citing a source. In responding to technical questions relating to library resources, we can direct users to help pages and documentation we have already prepared. Being "live" in the newsgroup environment puts us in touch with an even broader campus community than we would encounter at the reference desk and introduces us as individuals that can be called upon for help.

3. *Set up satellites*. If our users are not coming to us as often, then we need to go to them. Ask to place staff in departmental or residential computer labs at specific times and publicize these hours widely. Make clear what services would be available (for example, consultation on connecting to library resources, navigating the internet, or searching databases). Work with faculty or lab managers to choose the most useful times for this service, even if they fall outside usual staff schedules. Take along technical support staff if the network environment is unfamiliar.

4. *Make house calls*. Offer to visit faculty offices (or even faculty homes) to demonstrate a resource. Do it on their home ground and with their equipment. Work with computer support staff from the library or from a school or department to help faculty acquire and configure all the hardware and software needed for easy access to library resources. Make a follow-up visit or call to be sure everything is working well. Keep faculty aware of changes and new developments through e-mail or special library-tips pages on their departmental webs.

5. *Experiment with a MOO*. Create a multi-user text-based virtual reference desk and assign staff to be on MOO duty during certain periods. Consider staffing the MOO when the reference desk is not staffed (late evenings, for example). Create special rooms in your MOO—virtual offices or seminars—for subject bibliographers or other staff with particular expertise. If other departments on campus sponsor MOOs, encourage reference staff to become active participants.

6. *Publish on-line*. Experiment with various kinds of helper documents, bibliographies and guides to the discipline or the literature. Develop these publications graphically and make them accessible from a number of appropriate web pages. Create annotated on-line pathfinders and teaching guides that incorporate web sites, databases, and gopher servers and highlight important

graduate student whose research did not progress beyond the electronic version of America: History and Life or Historical Abstracts. Similarly, we have encountered faculty members who neglect both print and electronic sources because the former takes too much time and the latter is either cumbersome to use or covers too limited a period. Most troubling, I suppose, are those faculty for whom early scholarship has no relevance; who are content with only the most recent bibliographic information.

If a group from this audience were charged to design the ideal electronic American history citation database, it would be a vast improvement over what we currently have. Our designers would undoubtedly begin with the whole of America: History and Life, a portion of Writings on American History, parts of Poole's Index to Periodical Literature, and, perhaps, sections of my favorite, Readex's Microprint edition of Early American Periodicals Index to 1850. The group might elect to include in its database important monographic bibliographies like the Harvard Guide to American History or the Library of Congress's A Guide to the Study of the United States of America. The list could easily go on and on.

Another group, charged with planning the ideal English literature database in electronic form, would surely not limit their choices to the post-1963 version of the MLA Bibliography. They might choose to include Abstracts of English Studies, the Annual Bibliography of English Language and Literature and appropriate parts of the Wellesley Index to Victorian Periodicals as well as Poole's Index. As with the American history librarians, the designers of an English literature database could easily contribute an endless stream of candidates for conversion to digital form.

I offer these hypothetical teams to support three contentions. First, public service librarians who occupy the "common ground" have a special obligation to preserve intellectually the scholarly bibliographic record. Second, we have an obligation to oversee the transfer of our printed bibliographic tools into electronic form in the same way that our colleagues in technical services and systems have managed the conversion of card catalogs. Finally, we bear responsibility for planning the content of improved, discipline-based bibliographic systems. This responsibility includes a commitment to the design of better and easier-to-use retrieval systems, as Cheryl LaGuardia argued in her contribution to the previously-mentioned issue of the Journal of Academic Librarianship.[3]

Our commitment to preserve and convert important printed indexing and abstracting services and bibliographies can benefit from the lessons learned by preservationists using digital imaging technology. Their success in transforming paper-based works and microform editions into digitized images and then linking those imaged works to online catalog records has been remarkable. A 1994 symposium on digital imaging at Cornell[4] reminded us that while there have been improvements in the delivery of digital images, similar improvements in access to them have been elusive. Too much emphasis has been placed on indexing the existing structure of the imaged monograph or serial rather than linking those images to machine-readable versions of existing bibliographies. One can assert that the conversions of printed bibliographic sources, especially older ones, should serve as guideposts for deciding what works should be reformatted. Under this model, bibliographic citations would be linked to a digitally imaged edition of the work whether it be a journal article, book chapter, book, report, etc. In effect, we would take advantage of existing access tools to retrieve the products of digital imaging preservation initiatives.

I suppose this model represents every librarian's pipedream: massive, subject-oriented online bibliographic databases linked to digital images of the actual documents. It would embody our highest aspirations for bibliographic control and for the far-reaching distribution of electronic text. As with many of our dreams, we are handicapped by both the restrictions of copyright law and a paucity of resources, both fiscal and human. While I have no specific recommendations for realizing the dream, I would like to describe a recent, promising development and offer a modest suggestion for advancing the dream.

Public service librarians have long relied on the Handbook of Latin American Studies as a definitive source of bibliographic information on Latin America. Starting in 1991 with volume 51, this work has been available as a CD-ROM product, the Latin American Database, and as one of RLG's selection of Citadel files. More recently, the editorial staff of the Handbook spearheaded a project to retrospectively convert volumes 1 through 50. This initiative[5] involved a three-part process of scanning, optical character recognition, and clean-up of text to produce a simple ASCII database on CD-ROM. In the future, the Handbook staff plans to convert the post-volume 50 MARC database into ASCII text so it can be merged with the retrospective database and distributed as a complete database over the Internet.

This project has obvious advantages for students of Latin America, whose premier bibliographic tool will be available in its entirety in a highly distributable electronic form. The complete electronic Handbook will also serve, I hope, as a corpus of electronic records which will guide preservationists and provide them with bibliographic records to which imaged text might be linked. By linking imaged text to the electronic records found in important bibliographic works, we, along with our colleagues in preservation, would truly realize the goal of improved access.

Of course, it's easy to extrapolate from one success and draw, as I have, rather far-fetched conclusions. There are significant economic hurdles as well as some nagging copyright issues facing any organization seeking to convert older printed bibliographies to electronic form. In preparation for this talk, I posed several questions to the Reference Editor of the Yale University Press, Fred Kameny, about the economic viability and practicality of large-scale conversion projects and the subsequent marketing of the products. His replies contained several hopeful elements.

First, he believed that academic presses offered the best hope for marketing the electronic edition of important older bibliographies. Mr. Kameny preferred the CD-ROM format, even if the production process differed greatly from the print equivalent, because they could be marketed like books. Second, he argued that few, if any, individual academic presses would possess adequate resources to undertake such a technically complicated publication project. Instead, he envisioned a consortial arrangement in which several large research libraries would join forces with several equally large academic presses to plan, produce, and sell retrospectively converted bibliographies and indexing and abstracting publications. Third, Mr. Kameny did not regard copyright issues as a serious problem. Most copyright holders of older, out-of-print bibliographies would permit reformatting and republication with only minimal compensation, since the works under question were no longer income-producing. Finally, we were both intrigued with the possibility of "selling" access to full-text databases in which electronic bibliographic records are linked to imaged versions of the actual works. However, this concept struck my publisher friend as somewhat beyond the current scope of academic publishing.

I would assert that the union of academic presses (with their considerable marketing and sales experience) and large academic research libraries (with their subject and technical skills) might offer a unique and affordable way to realize the retrospective conversion of older bibliographies, their connection to digital images, and their eventual distribution to the wider academic community. It might also be fruitful to engage organizations like RLG in such ventures.

The proliferation of laudable conversion projects like the Handbook of Latin American Studies is not without risks for those of us who seek to shift the "common ground" into an increasingly electronic twenty-first century. If academic libraries cede responsibility for creating and maintaining the scholarly bibliographic record to commercial vendors, as we have done, we cannot exercise absolute control over the quality of the record or the permanence of the storage medium. Has this been a serious problem? In general, I think that there has been no evidence to suggest failure on the part of database producers. As a profession, however, we must exercise vigilance in our dealings with commercial delivery services like OCLC FirstSearch and SilverPlatter. Search interfaces, updating schedules, database completeness, record quality, and—particularly—pricing structures demand our constant attention. One need only compare the cost of receiving the MLA Bibliography online via the Internet from FirstSearch as opposed to SilverPlatter to appreciate the severity of that problem.

The efforts of public service librarians to shape the future of the historic bibliographic record will depend upon collaboration with preservationists, academic publishers, and library organizations. The conversion of important printed bibliographies to electronic form and their subsequent linking to the products of digital preservation will give real meaning to our dual concern for preservation and access. We will certainly continue to rely on commercial database producers and delivery services, but we should not depend on them to give us the best retrieval systems, farsighted retrospective conversion projects, or imaginative and affordable schemes for linking and delivering digital images of historic materials. That responsibility falls upon those of us who understand the importance of the printed scholarly bibliographic record and wish to maintain its vitality and scholarly utility in the next century.

ENDNOTES

1. Lewis, David. "Traditional Reference Service is Dead, Now Let's Move on to Important Questions" Journal of Academic Librarianship. Vol. 21, No. 1, January 1995. p. 10.
2. Campbell, Jerry. "Shaking the Conceptual Foundations of Reference: A Perspective" Reference Services Review. Vol. 20, No. 4, Winter 1992. pp. 29–35.
3. LaGuardia, Cheryl. "Desk Set Revisited: Reference Librarians, Reality, & Research Systems' Design" Journal of Academic Librarianship. Vol. 21, No. 1, January 1995. p. 9.
4. Digital Imaging Technology for Preservation. Proceedings from an RLG symposium held March 17–18, 1994 at Cornell University, Ithaca, New York. Mountain View, CA: Research Libraries Group, 1994.
5. Mundell, Sue. "The Retrospective Conversion of the Handbook of Latin American Studies, Volumes 1–49." Paper presented at the Latin America and the Caribbean Section, IFLA General Conference and Council Meeting, 60th, Havana, 1994.

In Their Own Words: Building a Data Base of User Views

By Margo Crist
University of Massachusetts Amherst (formerly at the University of Michigan)

The University of Michigan Library has undertaken a variety of types of assessment of user needs and user opinion. In 1990–91 a major user study was undertaken including use of focus groups which then identified issues for a broad random telephone survey. Since then, library units have also undertaken focus groups and surveys and we know that staff have extensive anecdotal information about user needs. These efforts have been useful and have provided valuable background information for service and budget decisions. However, it also has become clear that there is need for a more systematic and continuous way both to capture user opinion.

In a time of such radical and rapid change, it seems essential to have a means to have users tell us about the trends they see and the ways they are moving through this transitional time of paper/electronic/multi-media/networked sources of information and knowledge. We have identified our own need to allow the users individually to describe their own research or study methods and their use of library services so that we can understand them better. Interviews with individual users seem the best means to this end.

The Library has tested and is now engaged in a systematic approach to interviewing and then coding the content of the interviews into a data base of user views. This type of research is intended to give more form to previously anecdotal sources of data, to provide direct input for managerial decision making, and to provide a recognized research method of data collection and analysis. The results are to be shared with the campus community to inform its ongoing assessment of the library resources and services it wishes to support. Reports from this data base will also inform the Library staff as we seek to develop and support the "library" elements and build appropriate collections and resources for the new emerging information environment.

A PROTOTYPE STUDY—DEVELOPING A METHODOLOGY

How Did We Begin?

Little was known about qualitative research by the initial members of the study team when this project began. A small group of staff were asked to create a "prototype" to test how interviews might be conducted and results captured. The staff involved did a review of the literature to find out more about how individual interviews of library users could be the basis for a quantified presentation of user needs. One of the sources discovered connected the project to qualitative research techniques and offered this point of commonality for our efforts. "Qualitative research aims at understanding people from their own point of view. Its purpose is to describe how people behave and to understand why they behave the way they do . . ." This description matched our intentions directly and the approaches discovered helped shape our methodology.[1]

Based on their review, the team began developing a plan for faculty interviews and drafted a set of 25 open ended questions. In an iterative process, those questions were reviewed, critiqued and improved among the study team, our User Literacy Committee, and the Study Director. During this exploratory phase the team began to tap as a resource Lynn Westbrook who became a significant review "expert" as the study proceeded. Her doctoral work was based on just such qualitative research methods and her involvement became more important in later phases as the study needed refinement and improvement.[2]

How Were the Interviews Handled?

Three social science departments (Social Work, Economics, and Anthropology) were chosen on the basis of their responsiveness and support of library staff in those areas. The Study Team fully recognized that the choices represented neither the social sciences in full not the faculty at large. The initial invitations to participate were sent by the Assistant Director for Public Services to explain the background of the study. The interviewers personally made appointments with the individuals who were identified by their program chairs as useful subjects. Our short time line for the test was due to the fact that almost all of the subjects were at the full professor rank. Thirteen audio-taped interviews were then conducted in-person by librarians on the Study Team. Interviews were limited to one hour to encourage participation. A service was then hired to transcribe the interviews in full.

How Was the Coding Created?

After reading the transcriptions and reviewing the questions, the team created a list of basic codes. These were defined and applied to all of the interviews. For example, the interview excerpt "I use the Internet. I think not a lot but I think that, as I get more facile with it, I probably will do more" was coded as "computers" because that was its primary topic.

While useful as an exploratory tool, this basic coding failed to provide the specific information needed to make real use of the interviews. for example, in coding the above excerpt as "computers" there was no way to tell what aspect of technology use was under discussion.

Therefore a new and far more complete set of 118 codes was created using the initial basic codes as broad categories or themes. These codes were drawn from the ongoing doctoral research of Lynn Westbrook which involved similar interviews with faculty on a similar topic. This allowed a more meaningful and detailed analysis to be made. For example, the basic category of "computers" now included the specific codes: "using the Internet," "email is useful to me," "problem with my software," and several more.

After this further refinement of the coding definitions, all of the new codes were applied as needed to all of the interviews. The team used HyperResearch, a software program designed just for this task, to keep track of the coding decisions. Reports were generated from HyperResearch to identify all of the interview segments listed under each of the codes as well as patterns amongst codes. For example, it was not only possible to list out the interview excerpts coded under "Computers: I use a laptop or multiple PC's" but also to list the interviews in which both that and "Computers: I use the Internet or gophers" had appeared. The whole point and focus of the coding is to reveal patterns across the interviews. Clearly, thirteen interviews across 3 disciplines is not a basis for conclusions. However, the results are helpful in shaping and refining the future interviews. And, they offer food for thought and a "flavor" of what such a process can show! You will note there are more questions than answers so far, although there are clear cases where responses are consistent with other studies.[3] Some full quotes are offered to give an enriched sense of what we heard beyond the segments coded.

SELECTED FINDINGS

Browsing

Browsing journals at the library is fairly common, mentioned by 7 of 13 scholars. This implies that these senior faculty actually come into the buildings more often than is generally indicated by user needs research.

> Quote from one faculty member: "Often, I browse journals for reviews and ads rather than articles."

Is the attraction found in the currency of the journals, the chance to examine them on a full-text basis, the chance to serendipitously "discover" journals, articles, reviews, or ads, or some other factor? How will his activity translate into or be changed by the digital environment as the Library offers journals in full text on-line?

Computer Use

Email is generally considered useful, mentioned at least once by 10 of the 13 scholars. This implies that senior faculty have a basic familiarity with electronic communication despite the commonly held belief that they are least likely to do so.

> Quote from one faculty member: "E-mail offers a revolutionary way to stay in touch with co-writers in Holland or Denmark."

Is this finding at Michigan true on other campuses or special to our highly technological environment? Could existing services be expanded to make fuller use of this pattern? How might the library use but not abuse email contact for reference or collection development purposes?

Information Resources Used by Scholars

These scholars indicated that they find information through colleagues, paper bibliographies, Internet/listservs, conferences, and electronic data bases. These five resources were more commonly cited than any others. This implies that a mixture of print, electronic, and interpersonal resources are used.

What is the mix among these channels and is it changing? How does it differ from other social science areas? In the humanities? In the sciences?

Keeping Current

Journals and people are the two primary means of keeping current, being used by at least 9 of the 13 scholars. This implies that keeping current is both a solitary and a social activity. Could public service librarians become a more extensive part of that "social" pattern in some way?

Library Successes

Most of the scholars (10 of 13) mentioned at least once that the library is quite successful in collecting materials they need. Several (7 of 13) mentioned that librarians have been useful in teaching or reference services. On the other hand, seven of the scholars mentioned that the library failed to have an item they wanted. Interestingly, the common expectation was the library could not really be expected to have it.

> Quote: "I just walk through the stacks of a library and Xerox like mad."

This implies that the general level of satisfaction within the library is quite high. Yet, the responses also raise intriguing questions for further exploration.

Do faculty understand the staff role in creating the availability of and access to the collections? Why is the library not expected to have certain types of materials? How were those expectations formed? How can these expectations regarding both staff and collections be influenced?

Systematic Searching

Most of the scholars (12 of 13) described various methods of systematically searching the literature of their fields as part of class preparation or research. This implies that senior scholars actively gather information rather than relying just on their own personal network of colleagues or their own expertise.

What are those systematic searching methods? How can libraries fit into them? How can librarians help graduate students learn to use them?

Finding Connections

All of the scholars mentioned making connections between superficially disparate theories, concepts, disciplines, and other factors in their research. This implies an interest in materials and information formats beyond those commonly used.

> Quote from one interviewee: "... Find myself rummaging through tables of contents including those outside my primary discipline."

Are there patterns to the ways in which information gathering supports these connections? Could, for example, the library homepage further support scholars' efforts to conduct analysis across disciplines?

Working with Collaborators

Twelve of the scholars mentioned that they work with collaborators. This implies that information is exchanged and shared. How can we learn more about how this is done? Could the library's expertise in information management further facilitate that effort?

People as Information Resources

Colleagues and graduate students are far more commonly mentioned than librarians as information resources. What types of questions are not answered by these people? Could librarians answer those questions? If so, what interpersonal communication method (voice mail, email, in-person) would best facilitate that need?

Information Is Overwhelming

Only three people mentioned finding some aspect of information overwhelming although most mentioned feeling pressed for time. This implies that these scholars have some means of controlling the "information explosion" as it impacts their own research. What are those methods? Could they be incorporated into the library web page, instruction, or other services? Would junior faculty have the same perception?

CHANGES IN THE RESEARCH METHOD— WHAT HAVE WE LEARNED?

Subjects: While faculty of various ranks are still to be interviewed within these three programs, future efforts should include all ranks of faculty equally. In addition, as time permits, graduate students, undergraduates, and research staff will be interviewed.

Interview Questions: New interview questions have been written based on the information and resulting unresolved questions gained in this initial study. The revised list of questions is attached.

Interview Techniques: the use of follow-up and probe questions might be more fully developed. We believe that the actual questions can be asked with more consistency and persistence, given some modest training.

PLANS FOR THE FUTURE

The intended result of the current effort to broaden this prototype is to create a database of user needs and user opinions based on these types of individual interviews. The intention is to create and maintain codes of sufficient commonality to be able to draw reliable and valid reports indicating user needs both for internal decision making and to inform the campus community. The objective is to systematically build this database over a period of years so that a broad array of user groups and disciplines/departments served are fully represented.

It will be essential that the database that is built has sufficient tags and codes to allow both for the themes that run across units and user groups but also to allow for more customized approaches to be taken within particular disciplines and units. Reports should be possible both for the broad results and for more targeted data as well.

There are some fundamental questions to be answered as we broaden this approach and build a more extensive patron opinion database. Namely, how do the very preliminary findings from three social science disciplines apply in the humanities or the sciences? How are they different? Will such preliminary findings hold up across families of users, i.e., more junior faculty, graduate students, and undergraduates?

CONCLUSION

Moving the prototypes approach to a library-wide endeavor is under way at this time. Interviews have begun or are beginning in the disciplines of art and architecture, basic sciences, and education. The goal is to develop a broad landscape of user views—how they work and study, their use and reliance on new technology, the trends that they are seeing, their expectations of the future. This will not give a scientific representation of user needs, but it will allow us to develop a database of patterns, opinions, and experience that can be utilized in shaping an enriched concept of user needs and of needed shifts in collection development and service profiles. It is envisioned that this will continue to be used in concert with other user needs assessment tools rather than being the only source that will advise our decisions and services.

Acknowledgment: Significant contributions were made to this project and these results by the Study Team: Yaw Agyeman, Ginger Feary, Fred Gilmore, Patricia Welch, Lynn Westbrook.

APPENDIX

Based on what was learned in this initial study, these revised questions were created to be used in future interviews.

1. Please tell me a little bit about the research projects you are currently working on.
2. What are your most successful or productive means of getting information? Thinking about some of these research projects you're working on, where and how did you get what you need for them?
3. Consider the information gathering you do for teaching and for research. How does it differ for one or the other? How do teaching and research relate to each other in terms of your information gathering?
4. What roles do computers play in the information searching you do? We're interested in your use of email, MIRLYN, the Internet—any time

a computer helps you identify, locate, or store information.
5. What roles do people play in the information searching you do? Again, we're interested in anybody who helps in any way—graduate students, colleagues, friends, editors.
6. Are there any frustrations that you must deal with in finding or handling information? Is anything just more difficult than it should be?
7. Is there anything else about the way you find information which we haven't covered?

ENDNOTES

1. Raya Fidel, "Qualitative Research Methods in Information Retrieval Research." *Library and Information Science Research* 15 (1993): 222.
2. Lynn Westbrook, "Qualitative Research Methods: A Review of Major Stages, Data Analysis Techniques, and Quality Controls." *Library and Information Science Research* 16 (1994): 241–54.
3. Stephen Stoan, "Research and Information Retrieval among Academic Researchers: Implications for Library Instruction." *Library Trends* 39, no. 3 (Winter 1991): 243; Peter Hernon, "Information Needs and Gathering Patterns of Academic Social Scientists, with Special Emphasis Given to Historians and Their Use of U.S. Government Publications." *Government Information Quarterly* 1, no. 4 (1984): 409.

alt.help.I.can't.keep.up!
Support for the "Electronically-Challenged"

By Esther Grassian
UCLA

Java, VRML, cool sites, spam, RealAudio, Open Text. All of these words appeared on the front cover of a recent issue of *Internet World*. How many of them are meaningful to you today? How many did you know last year or even six months ago?

Librarians used to be the first to know about upcoming information tools and resources. We were horrified at the thought of letting the public get to information tools and resources before we had a chance to learn their use ourselves. Today many of us frantically struggle first to get to new technology, then to learn it, and almost immediately to turn around and teach it to our colleagues, who are depending on us, so we can all teach our users. All of this is occurring as the time lag between releases of new software or new versions of existing software keeps shortening. Hardware upgrades at home and at work are also an ongoing necessity if we are to make any sort of attempt at least to keep pace with the demand.

Gopher and Web browser release, quick adoption and use, provide graphic examples of the intense, speeded-up world in which we now live. Gopher appeared on the Internet scene in 1991. In that same year, CERN released the World-Wide Web, developed by Tim Berners-Lee, and NSFNET traffic was over 10 billion packets per month.[1] In 1992, the number of Internet hosts went over the million mark.[2]

In January 1993, about two years after Gopher was released, there were 50 HTTP servers in the world.[3] The first alpha version of NCSA's "Mosaic" was released in February 1993. In October 1993, there were over 200 known HTTP servers.[4] That year, the Web grew at an annual rate of 341,634%, while Gopher grew at a rate of 997%.[5] In March 1994, Marc Andreesen and others left NCSA and started a company later known as the Netscape Corporation.[6] The Netscape browser, which went from version 1.1 to 2.0 beta in about six months, now dominates the Web.

Intelligent filtering agents loom large as one of the next big developments in the online universe. According to a recent *Infoworld* article, U.S. Online is now shipping a tool called "Internet Made Easy."[7] The author describes this package as "a search tool that automatically retrieves information from hundreds of different World Wide Web sites based on criteria set up by individual users. Users can change their individual profiles at any time and can have more than one profile. The tool also advises users about which on-line service might best suit their needs."[8] In a prior article, *Infoworld* reported that vendors are placing high priority on developing and improving help desk software.[9] One vendor has developed an expert system called PNMS or "Service Center," which functions as a "neural network."[10] "As problems are reported and solved, a stronger and stronger basis for the resolution will be built. It doesn't require ongoing maintenance. It saves time, resources, staff, and money."[11]

"Online communities" like "AlphaWorld"[12] and "Worlds Chat"[13] are another potentially huge development area. These communities bring the cyberpunk novel *Snow Crash*[14] to life, by "combining 3–D graphics, virtual reality, Internet chat and multi-user avatar technology."[15] So, theoretically, you could enter one of these online communities, pick an avatar to represent yourself, say as a librarian, and wander around asking others in this community if they need help doing research. At some point it may even be possible to build truly virtual libraries within these communities.

Is it any wonder that even the trailblazers are beginning to feel they can't keep up, much less the rest of the library staff who depend on them to keep hanging on by their fingernails? In spite of the rapid development of subject trees, search engines and meta-search engines like "Savvy Search"[16] we all feel like we are smothering in information. Bob Metcalfe, a well-known columnist for *Infoworld*, believes that the entire Internet may soon come to a great grinding halt due to its own weight,[17] and some probably hope he is right! But assuming the Internet continues to grow at the current rate, or even expands, how can we possibly manage to keep on top of all of this, and support our "electronically challenged" colleagues and users at the same time?

Will online communities, intelligent filtering software and help desk software like these, and even the Internet itself, undermine the librarian's function or should we embrace new technology and try to influence its development? And in a practical sense, just how does one find the time, the energy, the talent, the training, and the support to "embrace" new technology continually?

How many of you take the lead by pouncing on new software, new releases of existing software, and other new developments in the high-pressure online world? How many of you rely on one or two other people in your library to keep on top of all of this, and educate colleagues, and/or serve as computer gurus for all library staff? My guess is that the guru paradigm is quite widespread, and that the vast majority of librarians and other staff gingerly trail along behind.

The computer guru has a thrilling role to play. One can truly get addicted to the rush of always being first to know about new software and hardware, but it is a junkie's life, and it can be tough. It can easily lead to exhaustion and burnout, and leave the institution or organization leaderless and floundering in a technological tidal wave, not knowing what to learn next, where to focus, and where to put limited dollars.

What about library information systems departments? you may ask. What is their role in all of this? Library systems departments have generally been established to handle all sorts of technology-related problems and concerns. But if your institution is anything like mine, your library systems staff is overwhelmed just with the task of keeping up with hardware and software installation and troubleshooting, not to mention training staff or users on new software. Technological growth and development has expanded at such a geometric rate that I would venture to say that most systems departments can no longer manage to do it all.

When I began this paper, I had intended to recommend that institutions establish "first strike" teams to handle these new developments in technology, similar to the Internet Training Group (ITG) which we established at UCLA in 1993. On second thought, though, I am not so sure that this approach will work with all types of situations.

ITG is a voluntary, loose knit group of librarians who have been courageous enough to volunteer to learn Internet resources and then teach them to users. ITG has developed and modeled various Internet classes, and set up a support model for internal training. Though it started with a push from our Biomedical Library, which was drowning in demand for its rather comprehensive Internet class in early 1993, it just took one person to take a risk and develop a general class "for the rest of us."

This model and these people now have an energy of their own, as each of us has moved from terrified "newbie" to optimistic and confident Internet instructor, learner and even training leader. This is largely due to positive moral support from colleagues, and a lot of hard work in developing and sharing support aids—e.g., scripts, overheads, PPT shows and handouts.

ITG has turned out to be a successful experiment in developing training and support first for library staff, and then for library users. It has worked well for a variety of reasons. For one, ITG volunteers come from all sorts of UCLA libraries—the undergraduate library, the cataloging department, the Map & Government Information Library, the University Research Library, and others. ITG members have learned and taught Gopher classes, Web classes, and an FTP/Telnet class. Some have gone on to develop and teach subject-specialized Internet classes. In addition, librarians have shared their technological expertise openly and generously, and have even tried out "raw" classes in friendly, supportive demos with other library staff.

This is all to the good. I am concerned, though, that we be cautious in extending this model to all developing technology problem areas. I am particularly concerned because at UCLA we are now working on replacing our tried and true, text-only OPAC

(ORION) with something very different. Our library has embarked on an extremely thorough investigation of alternatives to ORION, yet may be leaning toward an informal ITG-like group to develop and carry out the massive retraining[18] which will be necessary for successful migration to a new system. I like the idea of trying new approaches, but hope that we do not all assume that success in one arena automatically transfers to success in all arenas.

In other words, I am hoping that we can learn positive lessons from the ITG-team experience, and apply them to all sorts of problems, utilizing a variety of approaches, rather than blindly jumping on the informal, grassroots "team-approach" bandwagon to solve all of our major problems. Instead, I would suggest an eclectic approach, where informal teams are applied to specific problems, yet are under the general direction of an established group or department. I would like to see the established group follow the three main principles I learned from chairing ITG from 1993 to mid-1995, and co-chairing it since then. The three main lessons I learned from chairing ITG for two years are:

1. Give some direction to whatever sort of rapid response group you set up, whether it be a voluntary team or an appointed committee, and establish some form of rotating leadership.
2. Provide an encouraging, somewhat laissez-faire environment, where it is all right to stumble once in a while on the risk-taking road.
3. Provide continuous and consistently positive support, and incentives in the form of clerical help, recognition, and rewards.

With these three principles in mind, I believe we can all move from being "electronically stiff and challenged," to being "electronically limber and empowered." The author of a recent letter to the editor of *Infoworld* quite eloquently wrote that "... the Internet is a force that will not be denied. It's low-cost, general purpose, multimedia, interpersonal, fun, incomprehensibly broad and deep.... What more could any 21st century citizen want?"[19] Personally, I couldn't agree more.

ENDNOTES

1. Zakon, Robert Hobbes. "Hobbes' Internet Timeline v2.3" Updated: 10 January 1996; cited: 28 January 1996. Available World Wide Web site: http://info.isoc.org/guest/zakon/Internet/History/HIT.html
2. Ibid.
3. CERN. "A Little History." Webmaster: Robert Cailliau; updated: 03 October 1995; cited: 28 January 1996. Available World Wide Web site: http://www.w3.org/pub/WWW/History.html
4. Ibid.
5. Zakon, op. cit.
6. Ibid.
7. Scannell, Ed. "U.S. Online releases Internet search tool." Infoworld, December 18, 1995, p. 50.
8. Ibid.
9. Fine, Doug. "Help desk's new hat." Infoworld, October 23, 1995, pp. 66–67ff
10. Peregrine Systems Inc., Carlsbad, CA. Fine, op. cit., p. 70.
11. Answer Systems' Apriori Hands Free. Fine, loc. cit.
12. "AlphaWorld 'online community' beta free for the downloading." Updated: 30 November 1995; cited: 27 January 1996. Available World Wide Web site: http://infoweb.infoworld.com/archives/html/15world.htm
13. "Worlds Chat." Updated: 1995; cited: 29 January 1996. Available World Wide Web site: http://www.worlds.net/products/wchat/
14. Stephenson, Neal. Snow Crash. New York: Bantam, 1992.
15. Gardner, Dana. "AlphaWorld 'online community' beta free for the downloading." Infoworld, November 30, 1995. Cited: 27 January 1996. Available World Wide Web site: http://infoweb.infoworld.com/archives/html/15world.htm
16. According to the Savvy Search Home Page, this is a meta-search engine—"... an experimental search system designed to query multiple internet search engines simultaneously ... When you submit your query, a Search Plan is created wherein the nineteen search engines are ranked and divided into groups. Ranking factors include: The text of your query; estimated Internet traffic; anticipated response time of remote

search engines; and the load on our computer." Cited: 27 January 1996. Available World Wide Web site: http://guaraldi.cs.colostate.edu:2000/

17. Metcalfe, Bob. "From the Ether Predicting the Internet's catastrophic collapse and ghost sites galore in 1996." Infoworld, December 4, 1995. Cited: 27 January 1996. Available World Wide Web site: http://infoweb.infoworld.com/archives/html/dt_IWE49–95_23.htm

18. There are 18,000 undergraduates alone, at this campus of 32,000 students, not to mention the large numbers of faculty and staff who regularly use our OPAC.

19. Folk, Roy. Letter to the Editor of Infoworld, December 25, 1995/January 1, 1996. Cited: 28 January 1996. Available World Wide Web site: http://infoweb.infoworld.com/archives/html/dt_IWE52–95_25.htm

Research Strategies Conference Course: Using a Computer Conference System for Bibliographic Instruction

By Carolyn Gutierrez and Mary Ann Trail
Richard Stockton College of New Jersey

Research Strategies is a four credit interdisciplinary library research course designed to develop in-depth research skills in electronic and print media. We designed and taught the course for the first time in the fall of 1994. It replaced a previous Library Research Methods course which used the traditional lecture method. Our new course utilizes an electronic conferencing system.

An electronic conference is topically arranged electronic mail. Stockton's Conferencing System, called CoSy, was introduced about eight years ago as a system support for the curriculum by Ken Tompkins, a Stockton literature professor with a strong interest in educational technology. The software was developed in Guelph, Ontario. The CoSy system is used for electronic mail, discussion groups or electronic classes. The conferences can be open to everyone or only to a registered group of users, such as class members. There are many conferences in a wide variety of topics offered currently at Stockton.

Our course conference was conceived in response to a challenge grant extended by our President calling for the development of new courses incorporating emerging technology. This represented a unique opportunity for us to apply a new style of teaching to Bibliographic Instruction. We felt that our previous BI course, in which we lectured on reference tools, had grown a little stale and, since we are always on the lookout for ways to infuse new life into our program, we leapt at the opportunity.

OBJECTIVES AND GOALS OF THE COURSE

We had several objectives in mind when we offered the course on CoSy: First, that students would be introduced to the universe of resources open to them, electronic as well as print, and become adept at exploring it. For students who have not been exposed to a wider world through travel or reading, this step is especially critical. Secondly, that students would develop an awareness that a variety of research methods can be employed. It has been our experience that many students have no conception that there may be more than one avenue of inquiry to pursue. They also have pre-conceived notions about the validity of the information they find on electronic media. Finally, we expected that students would take a more active role in the learning process by taking responsibility for their research. In our other classes students tended to assume a passive role as the instructor imparted and, the students, hopefully, absorbed the material. The realization that they had the capability to design their own research strategy came only at the end of the course.

Our specific goals included the development of basic competency and confidence in using computers. This involved the ability to use E-mail and Internet resources, such as the Stockton Gopher and the World Wide Web, CD ROMS and a grasp of the fundamentals of on-line database searching. Secondly, the students would understand the specific strengths and weaknesses of print and electronic resources and various search strategies. Lastly, students should be able to apply established criteria for evaluating information.

COURSE DESCRIPTION

In this course students are expected to prepare research strategies, evaluate information and explore print and electronic resources. We meet with the class physically once a week for 2–hour sessions each. The remaining two hours of this four-credit course is to be spent in the computer lab researching the assignments. The assignments are posted on the CoSy conference. One particular assignment, the case study, we found worked particularly well. In these case studies, students would be given a real life situation and be asked to research it from various perspectives, i.e., legal, medical, psychological, etc. This kind of assignment forces students to use a wide spectrum of sources. In addition to the assignments, we also post issue questions in which students debate controversial topics and cite sources that support their position. The major project is an annotated bibliography on a topic approved by the instructors and student presentations of their research.

ADVANTAGES OF TEACHING A BI CONFERENCE COURSE

A conference course reduces the restrictions imposed by time and location on instruction. If you, as the instructor, wish to impart some "pearls of wisdom" to your students, you can do so at any time of day and from any location by posting them on a conference. Students can not use absence from class as an excuse for not getting the assignments in. Using a conference course helps in times of staff shortage (and what library does not suffer from staff shortage?) to spread your resources further since classroom time is only two hours per week.

Another advantage is that a conference encourages peer instruction. The faculty member becomes a moderator rather than the dominant figure in the classroom. Students are encouraged to teach themselves and each other. Struggling to master the conference system technology engenders bonding. The sense that the students are all involved in something new decreases overweening competitiveness.

Conference classes take place in a democratic environment that permits shy students an opportunity to express themselves out of the spotlight of classroom attention. All students seem to articulate their ideas more freely in the relative privacy of the conference.

One final advantage of great importance to us as librarians is that a conference bridges the gap between print and electronic media. So much hype has been given to the wonders of electronic media and, especially, the Internet that students lose sight of the fact that content is more important than the medium used to transport the information.

PREPARATION AND ADJUSTMENTS IN TEACHING

Before embarking on teaching a conference course, the instructors should be aware that it requires a significant amount of advance preparation. The instructors have to establish a conference and register the students. Lectures, assignments, directions, etc. have to be tailored to the medium. You can not usually lift whole lectures verbatim and post them on a conference nor would you want to do this.

The instructor gives up a lot of control in this method. The environment is less structured than the classroom situation. Students may wander off on tangents. Technical problems may sabotage the best laid plans. The system may go down. You have to be prepared with back-up plans.

Some students find using an electronic conference a frustrating experience. These are the students who are more comfortable in a traditionally structured class.

COURSE EVALUATION

We attempted to measure the course in several ways. We devised a pre/post test to attempt to measure quantitatively the effectiveness of this type of instruction, we examined the standard Student Evaluation Test (S.E.T.) conducted by the college, and we compared student projects with other projects from traditional BI classes.

In doing so, we had to take into account our sample or class composition. The most notable characteristic of the class membership was its heterogeneity. Although all the students were juniors or seniors, the age spread ranged from the late teens to middle-age. All the students but one were matriculated. The students' majors surprised us. In the past, humanities majors predominated in our classes but this class included a number of science majors. The breakdown of majors was: 1 business, 2 psychology, 1 literature, 1 economics, 1 pre-physical therapy, 1 criminal justice, 3 biology and 2 environmental studies students.

Students exhibited even more diversity in their levels of academic preparation. In general, they all believed themselves to be good students, however, a few admitted that they had never used the library. Some were comfortable using computers while others described themselves as "computer phobic." Their writing skills, as exhibited in their assignments, varied widely also. Three students had good-to-excellent proficiency while others found writing even short paragraphs difficult.

Motivation was another factor to consider. When asked why they took the course, a few said that they wanted to be able to find material for their papers but several mentioned that they took it because the course was free and did not involve as much in-class time as other courses. (It did not take long for them to find that our homework assignments which took the place of class lectures took lots of time to complete!)

When compared with the pre-test, post-test scores of students showed considerable improvement. We suspect, but have no evidence since the test was anonymous, that the improvement came from those students who scored at the lower end in the pre-test. The major areas of improvement were in comprehension of primary and secondary sources, indexes and abstracts and reference materials.

We believe the bibliography project, case studies, and topical discussions on CoSy, because they were graded, provided better measures of the students' competencies. Some of these assignments were in the form of case studies requiring them to use different types of sources. We also used topical issues in which some of the students participated in the debates with great gusto and learned to back up their opinions with sources. All came out of the class realizing that there is a source for nearly everything. They learned that no matter where they found their answers, whether in a book or on a CD ROM or on the Internet, they had to "cite their sources." This refrain became a litany.

This class also drew in students who, otherwise, probably would have never set foot in the library. Several had never used the library before and were amazed to find there was so much information in it! All the students became comfortable using computers in general and in exploring the Internet.

Close scrutiny of the final project, the annotated bibliography, did not reveal any major differences between this class and BI classes taught in the traditional way. In fact, despite the number of electronic sources we had the students examine, the bibliographies relied heavily on print sources. This class just did not react the way we expected.

S.E.T.

The Student Evaluation Test (S.E.T.) is given each semester, in every class, to every student. It allows the students to express their opinion of the faculty, the effectiveness of the course, and specific course materials. In the past, our S.E.T. scores had consistently ranged from good to exceptionally good. This class rated us as average, and they complained bitterly about the amount of work. At first we were greatly dismayed by these results. We believe, though, that factors such as technical difficulties which resulted in CoSy going down frequently that semester and the expectations of the students that this would be an easy class influenced the outcome to a great extent. Happily, in the next two classes our S.E.T. scores returned to normal.

NEGATIVE ASPECTS

One of the negative aspects of the course was the extraordinary amount of time it took to teach a largely computer-illiterate class to perform basic functions such as logging on and off, connecting to CoSy, connecting to the Stockton gopher, etc. and, rearranging the syllabus and schedule around technical difficulties. Originally we had expected to have most of the course work involve using the conferencing system. Due to the aforesaid technical problems, CoSy was used only about 60% of the time for assignments. Students complained bitterly about the editor on CoSy and preferred turning in their answers on paper. Given that some of the students had slight grasp of grammar and punctuation, which was further exacerbated by problems when using the CoSy editor, reading a lengthy answer to an assignment on CoSy could be a tortuous and mystifying experience for the instructors.

We are ambivalent as to whether we met the goal of teaching students to select and evaluate sources wisely. Some students had difficulty comprehending that we were not interested in their personal opinions, but wanted sources supporting their position, and not just any source but a reputable, preferably scholarly, one. This proved to be a topic that required several old fashioned lectures on how to evaluate a source and a few good old fashioned quizzes to make sure the information stuck.

NEXT STEPS

Would we teach the course this way again? Yes, and, in fact, we taught it in the Spring of 1995 and are teaching it again in the Spring of 1997. First of all, we believe in experimentation as a way of infusing new life into, what is often a deadly subject, library instruction. Second, we know that electronic databases will be a major component of research. We have, however, made some modifications in the class.

Composition of such a class is critical to its success. The course has since been turned into a GIS course which at Stockton is a course for upper level students where the subject matter crosses disciplines and allows students to look at an issue from various perspectives. This promises to attract a more motivated and academically-prepared student.

This Fall, we incorporated some of the components in a class designed for entering freshman. We used the conferencing ability but much more infrequently. We have not yet decided what the critical mass is for conferencing but a class size of 25–30 is possibly too large.

And finally, there is no doubt in our minds that the Internet and World Wide Web will exert a profound change on education and research. We believe, however, that the traditional role of librarians as guides or pathfinders through the informational maze will not change, though the paths themselves will change. This is why we insist that librarians must be active participants in this transformation and bibliographic instruction using a computer conferencing system is one way.

Library Instruction in Transition: Questioning Current Views

By Gretchen McCord Hoffmann
University of Houston

In this exciting period of transition from reliance on locally accessible printed information to instantaneously accessible and transmittable electronic information, the amount of information created increases exponentially; unfortunately, the misconceptions and unrealistic expectations of library patrons seem to grow at a corresponding rate.

The term information literacy refers to the skills and knowledge required to thrive in a rapidly evolving information environment. We can expect that information literacy will become as essential in the twenty-first century as is reading literacy in the twentieth. Indeed, as an almost unlimited amount of information becomes available, the ability to effectively access, evaluate, and apply information becomes imperative.

At the same time that librarians are struggling to help patrons acquire these skills, demographic changes in higher education are reflected in a far greater diversity among academic library patrons than ever before. In this context, the role of instruction librarians takes on an entirely new dimension. This paper will call attention to the need for instruction librarians to (1) examine some of our traditional assumptions about our patrons and their needs, and (2) develop new ways of working with our patrons in the context of an expanded conception of information literacy.

LIBRARY INSTRUCTION TODAY

Our current conception of information literacy is based on the assumption that we can teach our patrons to function most of the time in the upper levels of Bloom's taxonomy (analysis, synthesis, and evaluation). This model objectifies these skills in an effort to simplify the goal of information literacy. It envisions information literacy as a set of definable, obtainable skills, and the process of attaining information literacy as a fixed path to a distinct endpoint. However, the level of instruction that is needed to reach this point requires a great deal of time, and thus is an unrealistic goal for many library instruction programs. As a result, we as instructors find ourselves racing against the clock, knowing that we will not reach the finish line, but, nonetheless, striving to get as close as possible. Rather than recognizing the accomplishments we do achieve, we measure them against an unrealistic standard. The practical consequence is that what should be a feeling of achievement is instead a feeling of partial failure. We thus hinder ourselves from helping our patrons most effectively.

We must critically examine our fundamental assumptions and the models we create from them and consider more appropriate alternatives. Instead of defining information literacy as a final state to be reached via a linear procedure, we should regard it as a lifelong process in which library instruction is only one step. We need to think of ourselves as a part of the process of information literacy, as facilitators, rather than as deliverers of a goal. Although we can help our patrons become more information literate, we cannot control the process for them. Our role is to help them to develop the process for themselves, in terms of their own needs and goals, rather than in terms of our needs and goals for them.

We might follow the example of health professionals helping their patients move toward health—a lifelong, continual process, in which health professionals are only one of many elements. Few people achieve perfect health, partly because health professionals do not have the resources to ensure health for everyone, but also because patients vary in their physical and emotional states, their needs, interests, desires, and the choices they make. But ideally, the professionals listen to what their patients say they need at a particular time, what they wish to achieve, and what works for them—and patient and professional select and work together toward more immediate goals which they both know will contribute to the long-term goal of health.

We continually question how changes in the world of information will affect us as professionals. But we often neglect to ask: How do these changes affect our patrons? How do our patrons perceive the library now? How do they approach the process of library research? How do they perceive interactions with us? What do they, themselves, think they need to know? If we are to help our patrons become more information literate, we must guide them in developing critical thinking skills that give them the ability and freedom to make their own choices in meeting their needs, and we must admit that our patrons may be able to judge their own needs better than we think. We tend to make our patrons' choices for them, by pushing so-called "standard" sources on them, for example. Instead, we need, first, to work to empower them to make their own choices; second, recognizing the diversity among our students, to give them alternatives; and, finally, to allow them the freedom to choose their own sources, methods, and models.

Rettig (1995) distinguishes between the values of independence and freedom. Although both involve helping users attain higher level skills in judgment, evaluation, and synthesis, the two are fundamentally different. When we successfully train patrons to use our models, they are independent users who can use the library without our assistance but who must fit their needs into models we have chosen for them. In contrast, we educate patrons to exercise freedom when we teach them the skills necessary to develop and apply their own models and make their own choices. If we wish to empower patrons to exercise freedom, we must examine our assumptions about our patrons and their library needs, as well as our patrons' assumptions about libraries; how these assumptions shape what we do in library instruction; and, consequently, whether we need to change what we are doing.

WHO ARE OUR PATRONS?

The profile of the typical college student has changed dramatically in the past few decades, and these changes are expected to continue. In the past twenty-five years, the numbers of older adults, women, and minorities enrolled in colleges have increased rapidly (see tables 1–3). There are more first-generation college students than ever before (Dillard 1989, 149), and the number of students from middle-class and lower-class families continues to increase (U.S. Department of Education 1995, 42). A significant and growing number of college students are over the age of twenty-four, and the majority of these students are enrolled part-time, consider themselves "workers" rather than "students," and are married or supporting dependents (see table 4).

How do these statistically non-traditional students fit into the picture academically and intellectually? Davis and Schroeder (1983, 147) lament that "they seem economically motivated, uncommitted to the inherent worth of liberal learning" (see table 5). Another study reports that ninety percent of college-bound high school seniors plan to attend college for the purpose of increasing their chances of securing a better job and maintaining a more satisfying career (Dillard 1989, 8). Davis and Schroeder (1983, 150) note a connection between such extrinsic motivation and a "lack of confidence in . . . intellectual abilities and . . . abstract ideas"—exactly, as it happens, the abilities and concepts essential to information literacy.

These trends create the students we see who have no interest in learning how to use the library or library resources and are only interested in fulfilling the minimal requirements of an assignment ("no choices, please"); who expect to do very little work and spend very little time in the library yet still achieve good results; who have difficulty applying concepts to new situations; and who may resent library assignments and classes.

Finally, the National Center for Education Statistics (Washington, D.C. 1992) reports that less than half of seventeen-year-olds "can find, understand, summarize, and explain relatively complicated information in a text"; one-quarter of high school seniors do not achieve even a basic level of reading; and only thirty-seven percent had reached the reading level of "solid academic performance and demonstrated competence" (ibid.) that the National Assessment

Governing Board says all students should meet (1993, 6–7). No more than 4% reached the level of "superior performance" (ibid.).

Yet 42% of all high school graduates now attend college. Perhaps most revealing of all, research also tells us that the ability to reason abstractly is not common among today's college students and, indeed, may not even be attained by graduation (Collins, Mellon, and Young 1987, 73).

The growing diversity in age, race, ethnicity, socioeconomic status, and level of preparation for college implies differences in learning styles, skills, values, and expectations—and thus needs. Kuhlthau (1991, 362) affirms the significance of these differences when she reports that "criteria for making . . . choices [in using library resources and information in general] are influenced as much by . . . prior experience, knowledge, and interests . . . as by the relevancy of the . . . information . . . The information search is a process of construction which involves the whole experience of the person, feelings as well as thoughts and actions."

WHAT DO OUR PATRONS ASSUME ABOUT LIBRARIES?

Misconceptions about computerized information are as varied as are the students themselves. Oberman (1995, 37) reports on "numerous documented studies demonstrating that students, regardless of needs, express high levels of satisfaction with searches performed on computers . . . [despite] dismal abilities to match their subject needs with appropriate computer retrieval systems." This is only one example of the computer-as-God malady, whose afflictions also include the belief that computers have no limits; the conviction that any information obtained from a computer is by definition reliable; and feelings of total powerlessness at the mercy of a computer. These misconceptions reflect patrons' tendency to define needs and judge material by format rather than by content. Significantly, they are directly related to the inability to think and evaluate critically.

Students who have never been taught to think for themselves have no reason to suspect that thinking will be expected of them in college—thus many manage to find ways around it, completing their college careers without ever applying higher level thinking skills. Using student focus groups, Valentine (1993, 302) found that undergraduates look for the "easiest, least painful" method of doing research; that the "desire for knowledge seemed to have little influence" on students' research process; that students used "methods they thought would get them in and out of the library as quickly as possible;" and that "none of the students [studied] used the kind of organized strategy" taught in library instruction.

This study is one of many (Astin 1990; Barbett 1995; Choy and Premo 1995; Dillard 1989; Oberman 1995; U.S. Department of Education 1992, 1993) confirming that our patrons' needs are changing; that different patrons will have needs that differ in more than information content; and that the disparity of patron needs is increasing.

WHAT DO WE ASSUME ABOUT OUR PATRONS?

While we disparage the assumptions and misconceptions upon which our patrons base their library experiences, we often base our interactions with patrons on equally skewed assumptions. We adjust our programs based on an equation that says "PATRON'S NEEDS (based on my assumptions) + CHANGES IN LIBRARIES/INFORMATION (as I perceive them to be) = NEW NEEDS AND NEW METHODS." The entire model is based on our own assumptions. We assume that we know our patrons' needs better than they do. When we base our interactions with our patrons on our own assumptions, we add more obstacles to the communication between us. Ironically, some of our assumptions cause us to unintentionally reinforce our patrons' misconceptions and unrealistic expectations.

We frequently assume that we should attempt to ease the anxiety of the novice by simplifying various aspects of the information retrieval process. If simplification is indeed superficialization (Eadie 1990), are we doing library users a favor by trying to simplify what is in reality a complex process? Any novice library user will run into problems, and if we lead patrons to believe that they will not, or should not, they will feel incompetent and frustrated when they do. Instead, we need to acknowledge that library research is hard work, and that there will be problems.

Probably the worst assumption we make about our patrons is that they are like us. I recently attended a meeting of an English Department committee at which most of us agreed that we had learned as undergraduates to use the library by trial and error and with minimal assistance from library staff. But what worked for those present at that meeting—English faculty, graduate students, and a librarian—will not necessarily work for everyone. As the demographics presented above clearly show, our patrons are not younger versions of ourselves. We are academics; we are intellectually curious; but many of our patrons are not. When LaGuardia (1992, 51) says "I really didn't want to make minilibrarians [of them]," she is pointing out that patrons use the library differently than we do and, in all likelihood, differently than we did when we were in their shoes.

THE CHALLENGE TO LIBRARY INSTRUCTION

If library users in the Information Age are different from those of previous decades; if the need for information literacy is imperative; and if library instruction based upon traditional assumptions is inadequate; then we need to rethink our goals and redesign our programs. But how do we provide effective library instruction to our patrons, if this means that we must teach critical-thinking, analytical, and evaluative skills to students who "are eager to learn but limited to the needs of the moment," (Surprenant 1993, 3)?

Instruction librarians attempt to meet this challenge in a variety of ways, ranging from one-shot classes to semester-long courses. Classes may arise from faculty requests or be initiated by the library and open to all, required or voluntary, credit or non-credit, designed for a specific assignment or not. We generally assume that the amount of time we spend with our students determines our degree of success. All too often, we find ourselves trying to compensate for time restrictions. Perhaps we try to cram as much as possible into our limited time; or we figure we cannot teach higher level skills in the limited time, so we put them aside for more logistical information; or we sigh and say "Well, if only one student learned something today . . . " or "If the only thing they learned was to come to the reference desk . . . " " . . . then it was worth while."

THE UNIVERSITY OF HOUSTON AS AN EXAMPLE

The University of Houston typifies the leading edge of the national trends in both student body composition and in electronic library resources and is the perfect example of an institution in the transitional period of the Information Age. UH is, in every sense, an urban university. Our student body of over 30,000 is older, more ethnically diverse, and contains more part-time students than the average institution (see tables 6–8).

The main library at UH has over one hundred public workstations that access a network of over seventy different databases, including indexes and abstracts, full-text articles, full-data resources, and Internet access via the World-Wide Web. Many of the databases are available remotely to our students, faculty, and staff. On entering the library, a new user finds herself facing a sea of computers—an experience which can be thrilling, overwhelming, or both. In such an environment, we encounter every conceivable attitude, expectation, knowledge and skill level, fear, and myth.

THE UH LIBRARY INSTRUCTION PROGRAM

Our instruction program is administered by a Coordinator of Library Instruction who supervises two full-time staff members and one half-time student worker. The Libraries have approximately twenty-five "subject librarians," or bibliographers, each of whom is responsible for teaching classes within her or his subject areas. We offer instructional classes, brief guided tours, printed guides of varying types, and most recently, web-based guides and instruction. In addition to classes requested by faculty and University programs, we offer pre-scheduled classes open to all faculty, staff, and students. We also receive many requests from groups not associated with the University. We work in conjunction with the English Department to provide a self-paced library orientation workbook for all freshmen English students.

One of our major challenges is finding of a means of equitably distributing teaching duties in the face of a dramatically increasing number of classes. In the last two years, the number of classes we provide has increased by forty-six percent. For some time, the program has recruited librarians and staff from throughout the library to lead guided walking tours. We have recently begun to include in our pool of instructors a few qualified and interested paraprofessionals who work at the reference desk. We are specifically focusing on balancing out teaching loads by assigning general, introductory classes to instructors outside of their subject specializations. We give instructors an estimate in advance of how many classes they may be asked to teach each semester.

We expect the number of classes we teach to continue to increase, and the responses that we are currently investigating include how to take advantage of computer aided instruction, specifically using the World-Wide Web.

HOW ARE WE IDENTIFYING OUR PATRONS' NEEDS?

Identifying patron needs is something we are paying much more attention to now than in the past. Until recently, we based our work on our own assumptions about and experiences with patrons using the library. Now we are beginning to be more proactive in seeking direct input from patrons regarding their library and instructional needs.

The most direct method of determining our patrons' needs is to hold a discussion with them. Instructors do this in various ways, but generally ask at the beginning of each class what the class as individuals or as a group hopes to get from the session. They keep track of the responses and review the objectives in order to see that as many as possible are addressed. This information is collected and used to shape changes in the program. Our plans for the future include holding focus groups to solicit the input of both students and faculty.

The issue of determining what our patrons really need most from us continues to be one of the greatest challenges for instruction librarians. We will be experimenting with various methods of doing this in the near future.

HOW DO WE TEACH CRITICAL THINKING SKILLS?

Our efforts to incorporate higher level thinking skills into our classes are still in their formative stages. We are actively seeking effective ways to teach transferable concepts and critical thinking skills and are experimenting with "hands-on" experiences and active learning in our classes.

We stress the need to understand transferable concepts, often by pointing out to our patrons that we can never teach them about every source in one class. We emphasize the importance of understanding how things work over remembering every detail they hear in the class, and we let them know that our goal is to teach them how to teach themselves. We emphasize the importance of knowing what to do with information once it has been found. We provoke students to question the information they have found by asking them to evaluate resources in class.

We provide hands-on instruction whenever possible, which is conducive to active learning, by allowing students to do their own work, as well as cooperative learning, where students work in groups at each workstation.

Although we are striving to find effective techniques of incorporating these concepts into our instruction, it is too early to determine the effectiveness of our efforts and to make changes based on those results.

HOW ARE WE ADDRESSING INSTRUCTOR TRAINING?

We are just beginning to actively examine the methods used in class by our diverse body of instructors and to explore ways of strengthening our effectiveness. Typically, library schools provide little or no training in how to teach. Ironically, the very nature of the teaching we do—mostly brief, one-shot sessions—allows very little feedback on how well we have done and therefore little opportunity to improve our skills.

At the University of Houston, we hold regular monthly training sessions for library instructors. These sessions address relevant topics, including teaching methods, and give us the opportunity to learn from one another's experiences. We also encourage library instructors to observe each other in the classroom.

A major challenge in our training sessions is to take into account the wide variety of teaching styles among our instructors so as to take advantage of their rich pool of experience. It is only recently that we have begun to devote a great deal of attention to the training of instructors, and much of what we are doing is of such a nature that results may not be immediately obvious.

HOW DO WE KNOW HOW EFFECTIVE WE ARE?

Conducting valid, reliable evaluations is a science in itself, and one in which, again, few librarians receive training. Whenever possible, librarians should work closely with other professionals with appropriate training in evaluating their programs.

Even so, it is legitimate to ask "will we ever really know how much, if anything, our patrons have gained?" If our goal is to be part of a process rather than to deliver a final state, measuring our success becomes even more difficult. If we base our goals on empowering individual patrons to choose their own paths toward meeting individual needs, what can we measure? Are we measuring the success of meeting our goals or theirs?

CONCLUSION

Although the need for information literacy continues to increase, most academic libraries do not have the resources to meet this need according to the current definition of information literacy. We need to rethink our definition of information literacy—is world view on which that definition is based realistic when, with increasing frequency, our patrons will be locating, accessing, and using information outside of libraries? We must also rethink our current beliefs and assumptions about how we are best able to help our patrons become successful information users.

The key to meeting these challenges is in listening to our patrons. We alone cannot provide them with all of the skills they need. Nor can we always predict what will be their best strategies for information seeking and management. Options in the Information Age continue to increase, as does the variety of patron needs. Knowing that there is no single correct or best way to find, access, and use information, we can embrace that variety.

When we are flexible and adaptive, we can help our patrons find their own paths by facilitating their understanding and expression of their own needs and thus giving them the freedom (Rettig 1995) of making their own choices. By establishing a truly open dialogue between ourselves and our patrons, we can work together to make the most of the exhilarating opportunities of the Information Age.

TABLE 1
NATIONAL ENROLLMENT BY AGE (%)

	1972	1980	1992
18–24 years	68.8	63.5	59.4
25–34 years	19.3	23.7	22.2
35 + years	8.6	10.6	16.8

Source: Data from U.S. Department of Commerce. 1994. Bureau of the Census. Statistical Abstract of the United States. Washington, D.C. 179.

TABLE 2
NATIONAL ENROLLMENT BY GENDER (%)

	1970	1980	1992
Male	59	47	44
Female	41	53	56

Source: Data from U.S. Department of Commerce. 1994. Bureau of the Census. Statistical Abstract of the United States. Washington, D.C. 156.

TABLE 3
NATIONAL ENROLLMENT BY ETHNICITY (%)

	1970	1980	1992
Caucasian	89.5	81.4	75.0
African-American	6.9	9.2	9.6
Hispanic	2.0	3.9	6.6
Asian-American	1.1	2.4	4.8
Other	0.5	3.1	4.0

Source: Data from U.S. Department of Commerce. 1994. Bureau of the Census. Statistical Abstract of the United States. Washington, D.C. 178.

TABLE 4
SELECTED COMPARISONS OF OLDER AND YOUNGER UNDERGRADUATES (%)

	Older (24 years +)	Younger (< 24 years)
full-time enrollment	31	73
full-time employment	46.3	23.0
first-generation college student	54.7	33.4
"worker" rather than "student"	75.8	16.7
married	55.7	6.5
dependents (other than spouse)	18.9	2.9

Source: Data from Choy, Susan P. and Mark K. Premo. 1995. Profile of Older Undergraduates: 1989–90. Statistical Analysis Report. ED382122. Washington, D.C.: National Center for Education Statistics. 8,9,16,41.

TABLE 5
OBJECTIVES CONSIDERED TO BE ESSENTIAL OR VERY IMPORTANT (%)

	1970	1980	1990
Be very well off financially	39.1	63.3	73.7
Develop a philosophy of life	75.6	50.4	43.2
Have administrative responsibility	21.7	38.7	42.9
Succeed in my own business	43.9	49.3	43.3
Be an authority in my field	66.8	73.1	65.4
Obtain recognition from my peers	39.9	54.4	54.9

Source: Data from Astin, Alexander W. et al. 1993. The American Freshman: National Norms for Fall 1993. ED Los Angeles: Higher Education Research Institute, Graduate School of Education, University of California-Los Angeles. 56.

Astin, Alexander W. et al. 1981. The American Freshman: National Norms for Fall 1983. ED Los Angeles: Lab for Research on Higher Education, Graduate School of Education, University of California-Los Angeles. 57.

American Council on Education. Office of Research. National Norms for Entering College Freshmen - Fall 1970. 1970. Washington, D.C. 42.

TABLE 6
ENROLLMENT BY AGE FOR 1993–94 (%)

	U.H.	National
18–24 years	55.0	58.9
25–35 years	31.3	22.3
36 + years	13.7	13.7

Source: Data from University of Houston. Office of Planning and Policy Analysis. 1994. Fact Book. Houston. 10.

U.S. Department of Commerce. 1995. Bureau of the Census. Statistical Abstract of the United States. Washington, D.C.

TABLE 7
ENROLLMENT BY ETHNICITY FOR 1993–94 (%)

	U.H.	U.H Freshmen	National (1992)
Caucasian	60.3	53.9	75.0
African-American	8.4	8.9	9.6
Hispanic	11.8	12.6	6.6
Asian-American	12.0	12.5	4.8
Other	7.5	12.2	4.0

Source: Data from University of Houston. Office of Planning and Policy Analysis. 1994. Fact Book. Houston. 33, 41.

U.S. Department of Commerce. 1995. Bureau of the Census. Statistical Abstract of the United States. Washington, D.C.

REFERENCES

American Council on Education. Office of Research. 1970. National Norms for Entering College Freshmen - Fall 1970. ED0463342. Washington, D.C.

Astin, Alexander W. et al. 1981. The American Freshman: National Norms for Fall 1983. ED207404. Los Angeles: Lab for Research on Higher Education, Graduate School of Education, University of California-Los Angeles.

Astin, Alexander W. et al. 1993. The American Freshman: National Norms for Fall 1993. ED351908. Los Angeles: Higher Education Research Institute. Graduate School of Education. University of California-Los Angeles.

Barbett, Samuel F. et al. 1995. Enrollment in Higher Education: Fall 1984 through Fall 1993. Washington D.C.: U.S. Department of Education, Office of Educational Research and Improvement, National Center for Education Statistics.

Choy, Susan P. and Mark K. Premo. 1995. Profile of Older Undergraduates: 1989-90. Statistical Analysis Report. ED382122. Washington, D.C.: National Center for Education Statistics.

Collins, Bobbie L., Constance A. Mellon, and Sally B. Young. 1987. The needs and feelings of beginning researchers. In Bibliographic Instruction: The Second Generation, edited by Constance A. Mellon.

Davis, Marjorie T. and Charles C. Schroeder. 1983. New students in liberal arts colleges: Threat or challenge? In Perspectives on Liberal Education: Pioneers and Pallbearers, edited by JoAnna M. Watson and Rex P. Stevens.

Dillard, John M. 1989. Today's new college students and their implications for the 1990s. The College Student Affairs Journal 9(1):4-13.

Eadie, Tom. 1990. Immodest proposals: User instruction for students does not work. Library Journal 115(17):45.

Kuhlthau, Carol C. 1991. Inside the search process: Information seeking from the user's perspective. Journal of the American Society for Information Science 42(5):361-371.

LaGuardia, Cheryl. 1992. Renegade library instruction. Library Journal 117(16):51-53.

Oberman, Cerise. 1995. Unmasking technology: A prelude to teaching. Research Strategies 13(1): 34-39.

Rettig, James. 1995. The convergence of the twain or titanic collision? BI and reference in the 1990s' sea of change. Reference Services Review 23(1):7-20.

Surprenant, Thomas T. 1993. Welcome to obsolescence: What is good instruction now? In What is Good Instruction Now? Library Instruction for the 90s, edited by Linda Shirato. Ann Arbor: Pierian Press.

University of Houston. Office of Planning and Policy Analysis. 1994. Fact Book. Houston.

U.S. Department of Commerce. 1995. Bureau of the Census. Statistical Abstract of the United States. Washington, D.C.

U.S. Department of Education. Office of Educational Research and Improvement. 1992. Meeting Goal 3: How Well Are We Doing? ED352397. Washington, D.C.

U.S. Department of Education. Office of Educational Research and Improvement. National Center for Education Statistics. 1993. NAEP 1992 Reading Report Card for the Nation and States. Washington, D.C.

U.S. Department of Education. Office of Educational Research and Improvement. National Center for Education Statistics. 1995. The Condition of Education. Washington, D.C.: Government Printing Office.

Valentine, Barbara. 1993. Undergraduate research behavior: Using focus groups to generate theory. The Journal of Academic Librarianship 19(5): 300-304.

Exploiting Technology to Teach New and Old Skills: Novice Researchers and Milton's Web

By Elizabeth Kirk
Johns Hopkins University

The advent of networked information has provided a means for scholars and researchers to view and use extraordinary resources independent of time and place. At the same time, the technologies used to access networked information are complex and often difficult to use; the opportunity to mine these resources is often lost or diminished, especially for new students. To further complicate the issue, the inexperienced are the group least likely to understand the currently limited nature of "The Virtual Library" and assume that all the resources necessary for producing scholarly work are online. This lack of understanding is compounded in diverse ways when these novices are adult learners who return to the academic world to find libraries vastly changed from the days of card catalogs and who spend the majority of their time in distance learning centers away from the central library. How these students will receive adequate instruction in the acquisition, use and evaluation of all types of information is a pressing question for instruction librarians as distance education assumes a stronger profile in higher education. One project that attempts to meet this challenge in part is Milton's Web, a World Wide Web server created by Resource Services Librarians at Milton S. Eisenhower Library at The Johns Hopkins University. This paper discusses how Milton's Web responds to the instructional needs of adult learners in distance education settings, specifically students in the programs of the School of Continuing Studies.

Milton's Web (http://milton.mse.jhu.edu:8001/milton.html) was created in response to a document written by the Education Committee of the Resource Services Department at Eisenhower. This department is made up of subject specialist public service librarians who are responsible for research services, collection development, departmental liaison and instruction. The intensive nature of the assignment, coupled with a concern that staff burnout might become a real possibility, prompted the Education Committee to write a draft proposal for a library education program. The proposal consisted of two parts: one centered on supporting the discipline-bound instructional activities of individual librarians and the other on the creation of an electronic instruction system that would function as part of the department's general instructional activities. The goal for the creation of this electronic system was ambitious: "In the teaching library, many basic informational questions common to the majority of users ought to be anticipated, defined and responded to in ways that will seem transparent to them, being integrated as much as possible into successful and straightforward use of the library in pursuit of their scholarly activities."[1] The type of electronic system was defined as well: "... create a hypermedia access-instruction system that combines access to the networked electronic resources of the library and information about their use and the use of the library itself."[2] The architecture of the World Wide Web, combined with the relative ease with which a Web server could be constructed, was judged to be well suited to fit the outlined needs.

The server was created over the 1994–1995 academic year. Resource Services Librarians wrote instructional modules on the online catalog and related databases, provided extensive discipline-specific home pages and other resources, such as access to interdisciplinary electronic journals and tutorials on writing papers. Members of all library departments supplied information on their departments' services. A small cadre of Resource Services Librarians learned hypertext markup language (HTML, the language used in the writing of Web documents) and tutored the other members of the department. Departmental representatives took the opportunity to be tutored in HTML and produced their own Web pages. The server, which had been called A2II (Access to Information and Instruction) was named Milton's Web and officially unveiled in October 1995.[3]

WHY THE WEB?

What made hypermedia and the World Wide Web attractive as a medium for this endeavor, and how does this system respond to the needs of adult students in distance learning classrooms? The answers to these questions are entwined.

The Johns Hopkins University School of Continuing Studies (SCS), which offers part-time degree and certificate programs through the doctorate, has been involved in distance education as it is currently understood since 1974. At this writing, the majority of SCS students take classes at four off-campus centers in the Baltimore-Washington area. At least one important school entity, the Career and Life Planning Center, is based at an off-campus center. The library charged with supporting the programs of the school remains the Eisenhower Library, located on the main campus in Baltimore. Off-campus centers all maintain electronic access to Eisenhower, document delivery services, small current journal collections, and the most basic reference titles. One center houses a small library which is shared by four different Hopkins schools. It is made clear that students and faculty are to rely on Eisenhower for their library needs.

Delivery of instruction at off-campus centers is largely traditional, with faculty appearing in person to students in a classroom setting. Teleconferencing, while expected to expand, is the exception rather than the rule. Real student-instructor contact is maintained. The contrast between this and contact with Eisenhower is stark: Eisenhower is most often experienced via computer workstations. Although limited library instruction and reference services are available in some form at all off-campus centers, the collections and subject expertise needed by students remain at Eisenhower.

The need for lively human contact on a regular basis is noted throughout the literature on distance education. It is easy to see how a sense of alienation or disenfranchisement can be created when distance education students have little or no contact with faculty, administration, or other students, especially in an institution whose campus-based programs have long enjoyed international reputations. The same must be held true when the lack of contact with institutional wealth comes not from the standpoint of faculty-student contact, but contact with the informational resources of the institution. Students may rightly assert that the school is creating an academic caste system unless strong measures are taken to provide efficient and effective library services. Further, students studying at SCS off-campus centers are by and large adult learners. They have, generally, been out of academic life for over a decade, and they return to their education to find that libraries are no longer exclusively a print universe, but are now highly automated. They are insecure about their abilities to master the new information environment, sure that their present skills are inadequate, and short of time as they attempt to balance school, job, family life, and the other demands made on most adults. They may not ask questions until they are very frustrated. They are likely to put off work on projects until close to deadline. And they have little time for any kind of library instruction—formal or informal—until they have a pressing specific need to be met.

One saving grace in providing instruction for these students is their high degree of motivation. Few people would choose mid-life, with all its responsibilities, as a time to begin or complete an academic degree unless the choice is extremely goal driven: change of career, advancement, or need to prove graduate competence for continued employment or certification.[4] SCS students are generally definite about their academic choices, which are tied to their present or desired employment. The idea of real reward is clear. A recent article by Blandy is particularly on target in regard to this population: "Our students know more than we think they do... They know what they have decided is relevant for their own lives."[5] This truth provides fertile ground for active learning: students, especially those who are goal centered, will look for instruction at their point of need. This is what Dusenbury and Pease define as the "teachable moment... the optimal time when a learner is ready to learn and is the best, perhaps the only, opportunity to teach."[6] For these students,

Satisfying Our Users 153

the teachable moment is likely to take place at an off-campus center at a time when no staff is on duty, or at home at eleven o'clock at night when the children are asleep at last. It becomes necessary to create moments of instruction that are as non-traditional as the learner. When the one common denominator in all these settings (the library, the center, and the home) is a computer, then it becomes necessary to create effective and non-traditional electronic instruction.

Constructing an electronic system or platform that can meet the needs of this population, while simultaneously meeting the information and instructional needs of the other populations in a diverse research environment, is then a task that should be approached with caution. As noted at the beginning of this article, emphasis was placed on creating a system that would provide access to both online information and computer-assisted instruction. Further, the system's goal was to make the transition from information resources to instruction on the information resources as transparent or seamless as possible. Readers should not need to exit the system and call up another system, or go to another workstation, in order to get answers to common questions or help with the basic use of the most widely used electronic resources (such as the online catalog). Nor should they be required to use flip charts or other printed materials which, as well written as they may be, will not be available to readers connecting across the University network or dialing in from home. Further, they should be able to contact a librarian without leaving the system.

Currently, the World Wide Web is the electronic environment best suited to answer these needs. Graphical browsers such as Netscape and Mosaic permit (with the addition of application software) the manipulation of a wide variety of digital data coming from a variety of electronic sources (gophers, hypertext transfer protocol, FTP, and Telnet-accessible information). The browsers and the application software could be loaded on workstations at all distance learning centers as well as at Eisenhower Library and all other networked sites. The Web provided a unified platform that would allow readers to jump off or link to various types of resources.

The ability of the Web to provide a system that can deal with various data types and sources was, however, only the first positive step in choosing this environment for the goal product. Ease of use and contextuality were also non-negotiable factors. Here again the hypertext/hypermedia capabilities of the Web provided attractive possibilities. Gophers had revealed the obvious: menus are easier for casual users to understand than command-driven systems. Hypertext took the lesson learned and elevated it to new possibilities: now "menus" could become embedded within text. The menu items become the hypertext links.

"An alternative to explicit menus is to embed the menu choices within the information being displayed. With this approach, the user is less likely to be confused by menu labels because contextuality is not lost. The user is able to make an informed choice about whether she wishes to pursue a particular path. Embedded menus naturally lead to a kind of layered approach, where detail is hidden unless specifically requested."[7] The user links to another file, image or location from the location to which it is directly related. In Milton's Web, the module taking readers to the library online catalog has links to a variety of informational resources on the catalog, including a tutorial.

Within the tutorial, there are links to images illustrating various types of catalog screens that readers historically have had problems understanding. The combination of text and menu that hypertext creates, allows readers to view and read as little or as much of the tutorial as they choose. It is available yet hidden; consistent yet not insistent. It is constructed to meet the reader's point of need; it can do so differently each time he accesses it, thereby remaining a new experience each time the tutorial is viewed. Repetition is reduced even though the reader is utilizing (virtually) the same information.

In such a setting, familiarity with part of the tutorial breeds trust, not contempt. It is worth going back. This familiarity comes from the nature and presentation of embedded menus: because some information is visible, readers can remember the context. In this way, the structure of the tutorial mimics the structure of the library as a whole: "The use of technology to support the libraries [sic] traditional function of linkage and coherence confirms that knowledge is both deep and must be presented in context. Knowledge is not linear and sequential. The promise of multimedia is that it can emulate the society of the library's relationships by enabling the use of a wide range of information by people who are using it in different ways."[8]

This is not true of gopher, which relies on a strict menu-file, forward-backward structure. In this case, information, the components of knowledge, must be presented in sequential, linear manner. The Web encourages this kind of nonlinear use; gopher cannot. This also underlines a superiority over online help files. While help files included in electronic resources may certainly be well written, often they can only be accessed while using the specific resource. It is not possible to create other intelligent or logical links to them. A page explaining the differences between catalogs, electronic databases and print indices links to tutorials on three different resources. It could not link to the help files mounted on the resources themselves. It is also important to notice that online files, being title-specific, will not compare one resource to another. The hypertext files can do that.

Hypertext encourages multiple linking; it needs to be done with an eye to logic, remembering that readers may get lost if it is done indiscriminately. Further, hypertext allows something between the all-or-nothing polarization of gophers menus on the one hand and printed guides on the other. Printed guides, even when kept as lean as possible, present all their information in a single visual block. Typically, readers do not look at help documents (whether on paper or on a screen) until they are at a loss; at that point of frustration, it is easy to fall into "information overload." Hypertext provides the opportunity to show that it is, in reality, too much information at once that causes this reaction. "Multimedia technologies can progressively disclose layers of separated information and reduce the noise and clutter of the perception of 'information overload.'"[9] Careful segmentation of text and images and their display may defuse frustration. Presentation of information in Milton's Web exploits these features of hypertext architecture.

The example of the OPAC tutorial indicates one type of information provided in Milton's Web: instruction in the use of specific resources, whether electronic or in print. While this type of instructional information is an essential element in creating a "full-service" electronic platform, it is not enough to justify calling it an instructional service. In addition to resource use instruction, Milton's Web provides process-oriented and conceptual instruction. This is particularly evident in three areas: the module on writing papers, the SCS Library Lounge, and the discipline home pages.

The paper-writing module, entitled "Using library resources for scholarly writing" (http://milton.mse.jhu.edu:8001/research/papers/process.html), offers instruction on a number of topics related to the process of using the library in the preparation of a written project. The initial page emphasizes the fact that different disciplines have developed different routines for this process and that those routines must be learned over the course of one's academic career, and that this module is intended for new students to learn some basic elements that are common to all. From this page there are links to pages that describe the use of a wide variety of reference resources, as well as descriptions of catalogs, databases and print indices, and their specific values and appropriate use.

This information has been written to provide a conceptual framework for readers; while links to information on how to use specific resources are provided, the emphasis here is clearly on the why. The same is true for a link to resources on style sheets. The "JHU School of Continuing Studies Library Lounge" (http://milton.mse.jhu.edu:8001/scs/home.html) provides more unobtrusive conceptual instruction. Along with links to information on off-campus centers and instructions on getting to Milton's Web at home via a variety of connections, there is a link entitled "What to expect when you get to Eisenhower." This document purports to help students develop a "shopping list" of things to think about before they come into Baltimore; they may see it as a way to manage a "quick and dirty" trip.

In reality, it is a conceptual tour of the library and how it may be most effectively used for a variety of purposes. Embedded in the document are links to the module on writing papers and to the home pages of Resource Services Librarians (so that students can use the mail forms to send them messages for more extensive help).

Home pages are provided for each discipline taught by the Homewood (main campus-based) schools, including SCS. Each home page was written by the Resource Services Librarian (RSL) who handles that discipline. Here, all the functions of the RSL come together: the unique insight of the RSL into a particular department results in the design of a home page that responds to the emphases of that department. RSLs realize the parallels between collection development selection work and their own creation of resources, especially resources that include links to outside information sources (which are to be made with the same attention with which one selects a print resource). These pages give students an insight into the structure of information in their particular field, the scope and formats of the information, how it is accessed or held at Eisenhower, and what is available beyond Eisenhower via the Internet.

The pages define the special routines of scholarly communication and information adopted by the disciplines. They are a form of conceptual instruction on the most macrocosmic scale: what is information in one field, how is it created, how is it communicated. The most extensive of these home pages is Business (http://milton.mse.jhu.edu:8001/research/business/business.html). Links to separate documents for distinctive programs in the Division of Business, such as Finance and Marketing, continue the home page model on a more specialized level.

HOMEGROWING RATHER THAN OFF-THE-RACK

The advantages of a "homegrown" system over commercially available or "canned" computer-assisted instruction are clear in the light of the information provided by Milton's Web. The Web documents were written for the Hopkins community; even though they are freely available to anyone using the Internet and will benefit outside users, they respond to the cultures of the Hopkins departments and divisions and their particular needs, and they describe and explain the use of a particular library and its resources. Every title mentioned will be found in the Eisenhower's collections or be accessible from the library. Enormous attention to detail and tailoring are possible; this is not possible with purchased instruction products or programs. Eisenhower's mission, to support the programs at Hopkins, is not the mission of the most conscientious commercial entity.

While the process and conceptual instruction benefit all readers, they have a particular significance for adult learners in distance education settings. First, students using the Web server at off-campus centers cannot be engaged in a reference interview with a librarian at Eisenhower in the same way that walk-in students are. If they call in, the steps of telephone reference are not the same as an on-site interview, which typically includes informal instruction on the process of finding the information requested. Further, nonverbal cues often spur the librarian to ask the student if he feels at ease with the information or the process or resource used to find it; this may lead to further point-of-need instruction.

This is not a feature of telephone reference. If the student at an off-campus center receives on-site help, the resources he needs probably are not available at the center and once again the opportunity for point-of-need instruction is lost. Being remote from the collections and its finders, especially when they are in print, has its consequences. If the student investigates the conceptual instruction pages in Milton's Web, he has an idea where to begin when he gets to Eisenhower and what sort of resources he will need to look for. Since many students working at off-campus centers come to Eisenhower on the weekends, this is doubly important, as there is reduced staffing on those days.

Second, adult learners, with their focus on goal-oriented, practical, point-of-need help, are more likely to invest time in conceptual instruction when it is unobtrusive. A student with very little interest in the difference between a catalog and an index and the appropriate use of each, becomes markedly more interested when trying to write a paper and not finding any articles in the online catalog. This is one of the best opportunities for active learning to take place. Third, the conceptual area is one where adult learners may be less willing to admit ignorance; it is one thing to ask for assistance in the use of a complicated electronic information source, but there is much more at stake in admitting to not understanding the process of looking for information.

CONTEXT AND CONCEPT

There are two reasons for this in regard to adult learners: sociocultural context and self-concept. While SCS students come from a variety of sociocultural settings in the wider sense, it is possible to define certain specific contexts more narrowly, especially those of career life. Students in the business programs are generally already engaged in business pursuits; they might be employed by banks, accounting firms, stock brokerage firms, or advertising agencies. Their academic work speaks to their daily work. It is easy for these students to bring the ethos of their daily work to school with them; when that ethos teaches that knowledge is power, that admission of ignorance is political suicide, and that your colleague is your competitor, there is great pressure not to ask for help.

The sociocultural microcosm of the business world militates against the concept of "There are no dumb questions." Self-concept comes into play when adult learners walk into a library full of confident looking traditional undergraduates. Adult learners already feel at a disadvantage, as the literature tells us repeatedly. Will an adult ask for extensive help when there are blasé looking eighteen year olds lounging around the reference area? Probably not. Providing this information via Milton's Web is the electronic equivalent of having it delivered to one's home in a plain brown wrapper. Anonymity is safety.

An overarching goal of library instruction, especially that of conceptual instruction, is to enable readers to think critically about information: not just how it is to be found, but what kind is appropriate in a specific instance, how is it used, and how reliable that information is. Further, readers who achieve this kind of information literacy are aware of their options in the information environment. While this goal is extremely ambitious, reaching it is even more necessary in the electronic world than in the world of print. Electronic "information" may come from any number of sources with varying degrees of reliability. The library, which is not fully digitized, will not be first choice for readers who want everything delivered via modem.

There is real danger that the old saw "If it's in the newspaper it must be true" is being replaced with "If it's on my computer it must be true." This is why Milton's Web consists of more than an electronic bulletin board of library hours and an attractive looking gopher pointing readers to the wealth (and junk) of the Internet. This is its most important task: "In addition to the more active social relationships built with researchers, libraries must also build more creative relationships with the knowledge they collect. The context and linkages must become format independent, and we must be able to control and manage this electronic world more effectively. More information that is better managed and more flexible [is] needed to provide a better sphere for the reader.

The ability to create these new relationships is enabled by technology and organization. The results of this new environment is a new set of services which are valuable because they free the researcher in the pursuit of knowledge."[10] One of the strengths of Milton's Web is its absolute insistence that all is not electronic: that the "virtual library" is, today, much the same as "virtual reality." Documents like "Using the library for scholarly writing", "What to expect when you get to Eisenhower" and the discipline home pages take great pains to underline the scope of the universe of information. They explain the breadth, advantages, and appropriate use of the print world, the electronic world, and other media, such as video. Even though Milton's Web itself is an electronic creature, it points to worlds beyond the computer. Without this understanding, there is no freedom, as Anderson describes it; readers will believe that they are limited to what is online. There is no sense of options. Rather than enlarging the world of information, it is greatly diminished.

Teaching readers the appropriate use of the whole universe of information is an important component of critical use of the library. It is vital when adult students are working at off-campus centers, and will do most anything to avoid taking time out of a busy, crowded schedule to come to Eisenhower. This group has the greatest need in regard to these distinctions: there are more formats of information available now than there were when they completed their prior education. Further, document delivery as a service seduces many into thinking that choosing a few titles blindly from the online catalog or a database obviates the need to think about the scope of information available on a given subject. Milton's Web offers librarians the opportunity to teach adult students to expand their thinking critically: "Once we start thinking of electronic text as a web of knowledge—rather than a collection of bits and bytes—all kinds of symbiotic relationships between words and reader(s) are possible. As a much softer, more tractable form of knowledge representation, hypertext can expand intelligent tutoring systems (ITS) technology by making new, more flexible paradigms. Specifically, mediated, intelligent hypertext provides an exploratory world where the learner is helped to discover the empowering strategies of a domain expert... In a traditional classroom, the teacher performs as a 'knowledge guide': one who is familiar with the terrain of the discipline and encourages students—through guided-inductive teaching methodology—to explore the many paths of the knowledge space. Well-designed hyper-environments, because they mediate exploration, can 'virtualize' this role of the teacher."[11] The discipline home pages are a worthy beginning for this project. They outline the resources and routines of each discipline and, as such, serve as knowledge guides to its novice practitioners.

INFORMATION ASSESSMENT IS NEEDED

One issue of real importance that needs to be addressed more fully by the documents in Milton's Web is instruction on the evaluation of information. Issues that deal with assessing whether information suits a particular need or answers a specific question are dealt with. Issues dealing with the quality and provenance of information are less well dealt with, and this is not merely a statement on the content of Milton's Web but also a recognition of a more widespread problem in higher education. Yet academic libraries exercise "quality control" over traditional collections through the selection process, and provenance is a major criterion. This is not true of the Internet. While the resources to which Milton's Web links have been selected by librarians exercising the same skills with which they select other resources, there are few guides to help readers assess information that they might find on their own. The quality control factor in selection is usually invisible to readers, and it is not made explicit in documents in Milton's Web. How to address this issue will spark a lively debate, and it does need to be discussed.

INCENTIVES AND REWARDS

Adult learners at off-campus centers have the most to gain from Milton's Web, and in some ways they recognize that they have the greatest incentives to use it. As noted earlier in this discussion, the extraordinary goal orientation of this population will provide its "teachable moments." Constructing a system that will allow these readers to get help in using information without having to leave the system that provides the information is the first step. Information access and instruction need to come through the same screen; if it does not, it is likely that instruction will not be sought and information will not be found. Further, the system must be as easy to use as possible: "Everyone seems to agree that a tool enabling a user to navigate the Internet rather than just mucking around will be a breakthrough in the use of electronic information. Until then, consumers will certainly vote with their feet using the costly ignorance principle. Whatever I can get using a system I can understand is infinitely preferable to having better sources in a system that is impenetrable."[12]

Adult learners, with their outside commitments and their sense of ill-preparedness to navigate the electronic world, will be the first to walk away. Milton's Web was built on the World Wide Web because its most common browsers look and act like computer programs that people are most familiar with (the point and click worlds of Macintoshes and Windows); its documents were linked together with attention to helping readers retain a sense of where they are and how to get back to where they came from. To employ Carlson's metaphor, Milton's Web attempts to create a virtual instruction librarian, and this is of capital importance when readers are accessing the system from a small electronic library when part-time staff are not on duty.

The incentives for adult learners to use Milton's Web are multiple, but they all derive from the same goal: reward. There are important immediate and long-term rewards associated with using the Web. Among the immediate rewards are the obvious, which is response at point of need ("I got what I needed even though the paper was due the next day."). There are other, less obvious immediate rewards that create incentives to use the system: it is eminently cool to know how to use the technology that appears on the evening news on a regular basis (and self-concept is important to adult learners) and it is the path of least resistance for the increasingly large number of people whose families subscribe to America On Line, Prodigy, or many of the other commercial providers whose current software includes Web browsers (if you already have it, you will most likely use it).

Long-term rewards are both scholarly and professional. Information management skills and the development of a discipline-oriented optic are high-end scholarly rewards to students who have been outside of academia long enough to feel alienated from it. The Education and Business students who make up over ninety per cent of the off-campus adult student population see definite long-term professional rewards in becoming familiar with the World Wide Web: business sees infinite new markets to be accessed through this glamorous segment of the Internet; education sees new teaching tools and new opportunities for communication in its use.[13] Librarians have more than occasionally found the adage "If you build it, they will come" to be a lie; however, it is fairly likely that "If it has any rewards attached to it, they will come" will work. Finding oneself on the cutting edge of a profession as one enters that profession is a very powerful reward.

CONCLUSION

Is Milton's Web a limited success? As of yet, no hard statistics on its use are available; anecdotal evidence shows that it is being used consistently, especially by SCS students in Education and Business. In addition, the Resource Services Librarians for these programs include Milton's Web in their discipline-bound instructional activities. Most gratifyingly, staff at the off-campus center libraries promote its use and use it themselves. Eisenhower staff will begin to receive statistical data soon, and assessment instruments will need to be developed. One development that points to ever growing use of the server is the design of electronic courses at Hopkins. Two courses have been designed and mounted on the World Wide Web by faculty members in consultation with library staff (notably the Librarian for Electronic Initiatives). As more members of the community use the Web for purposes such as this, it will become more second nature to use Milton's Web as well. Eisenhower librarians are approached by faculty to participate in designing these courses in large part because Milton's Web is perceived as proof of expertise.

More than a limited success, Milton's Web is a success of limitations. It provides readers with much more instructional information than they have ever been given on an electronic basis, and it responds to its lofty goal of anticipating and answering common questions. It goes well beyond that goal to answer questions that are common to smaller constituencies: departments and divisions. It gives readers, most notably students remote from Eisenhower, more options when they choose to work independently. Options and choices are fundamental to information literacy: not just knowing what resources are available, but being able to choose whether or not one wants the aid of a librarian: "To the extent that students are information-literate, they will know when they can rely on information systems and when they need to seek individual consultations. In either environment, the need to think critically and to evaluate will be reinforced continually."[14] Milton's Web is not configured to replace librarians, nor has that ever been its goal; on the contrary, its documents explicitly reinforce the value and availability of librarians. This works: librarians receive messages from readers using their personal Web mail forms, and reference questions increasingly begin with the phrase: "I was using Milton's Web and . . . " This is, again, noticeable in adult students visiting Eisenhower from the off-campus centers. Librarians will need to track how reference/research questions and interviews change as more people begin to use this resource.

Milton's Web has proved to be an ambitious undertaking for the staff at Eisenhower, especially for the Resource Services Librarians. Constructing the web has been an opportunity to think about the components of instruction, how it can be more effective, and more creative. It has been the best opportunity to provide more equitable services for students in distance learning situations, who now receive the same information as readers at Eisenhower. It has added advantages for students in distance learning, because they stand to gain the most from its instructional modules on using a research library. Milton's Web offers adult students the extra coaching that they believe they need. Because of its discipline-rich environment, it has the potential to offer each constituency of the Hopkins community the instruction and information that they need. The staff knows very well that this is not a finished product, but a beginning. As needs and programs change, the information and the modules will change as well. It will always be a dynamic, protean resource. The librarians talk of creating interactive instructional modules as well as an interactive communication mode to link readers and librarians. The web will change, or become something else entirely, with the advance of technology. Eisenhower librarians are eager to meet the challenges of these advances and exploit them. Having begun so well, there can be no doubt that they will.

ENDNOTES

1. Education Committee. *Draft proposed for a library education program.* Proposal presented to the Resource Services Department, Milton S. Eisenhower Library, The Johns Hopkins University, Baltimore, Maryland, June 1994. Members of the committee at the time that the proposal was developed were Todd D. Kelley (former chair and former Resource Services Librarian for Education), Maureen Beck (Resource Services Librarian for Business), Karla Pearce (Resource

Services Librarian for Engineering, another school involved in distance education and part-time programs), and Elizabeth Kirk (current Resource Services Librarian for Education).
2. Ibid.
3. It must be remarked that Resource Services Librarians, who are responsible for the majority of the documents, the hierarchy in which they are presented, and the "look" of the server, accomplished this work while carrying out all their other duties. It was very much a labor of love.
4. See Brian H. Nordstrom's paper "Non-Traditional Students: Adults in Transition" (Bethesda, Maryland: ERIC Document Reproduction Service No. ED310686, 1989 for a discussion of the role of career and other changes as motivation in adult education.
5. Susan Griswold Blandy, "Keeping Library Instruction Alive," *Reference Librarian* 51/52 (1995): 433.
6. Carolyn Dusenbury and Barbara G. Pease, "The Future of Instruction," *Journal of Library Administration* XX, 3–4 (1995): 101.
7. Patricia Ann Carlson, "Hypertext and Intelligent Interfaces for Text Retrieval," in *The Society of Text: Hypertext, Hypermedia, and the Social Construction of Information*, edited by Edward Barrett (Cambridge, Massachusetts: MIT Press, 1992), 112. In the realm of linking and nonlinearity, this statement is more true of the structure of hypertext or hypermedia than of multimedia.
8. Gregory T. Anderson. "Dimensions, Context, and Freedom: The Library in the Social Creation of Knowledge" in *Sociomedia: Multimedia, Hypermedia, and the Social Construction of Knowledge*, edited by Edward Barrett (Cambridge, MA: MIT Press, 1992), 112. In the realm of linking and nonlinearity, this statement is more true of the structure of hypertext or hypermedia than of multimedia.
9. Ibid., 118.
10. Ibid., 119.
11. Patricia Ann Carlson, "Varieties of Virtual: Expanded Metaphors for Computer-mediated Learning," Barrett (1992), 64–65.
12. Dusenbury and Pease, 108.
13. Both the Business and the Education librarians are regularly asked how to write home pages.
14. James Rettig, "The Convergence of the Twain or Titanic Collusion? BI and Reference in the 1990s' Sea of Change," *Reference Services Review* (Spring 1995): 16.

Core Competencies and "Learning for Change" in Academic Libraries

By James W. Marcum
Centenary College of Louisiana

Like all organizations today, academic libraries are having to reassess who we are, what we do best, and what purpose we can stake out that will, hopefully, guarantee our healthy survival into the future. Determining the strategy is difficult enough. However, the most challenging task in building libraries for the future will be adapting the organization, the staff, and the culture to the new realities. Continuing education in librarianship has not succeeded in luring librarians out of the traditional mind-sets and attitudes learned in an earlier era. Clearer vision and purposeful organizational learning are required. A strategy based on core competencies and strategic value streams offers a basis for clear vision as well as direction for that learning.

CORE COMPETENCE: GATEWAY TO THE FUTURE

The idea of core competencies articulated by Gary Hamel and C. K. Prahalad is influential today as a leading approach to organizational strategy for change.[1] They define a core competency as a collectively learned, interdisciplinary bundle of skills and technologies applied to work that

1) adds significantly to the perceived value of the product or service,
2) is competitively unique,
3) is extendible to additional products or services,
4) requires communication and commitment across functional boundaries, and
5) will grow and mature with investment, use, and practice.

Sony's "pocketability" or Federal Express' "on-time delivery" are examples of major strategies based on a core competence. An organization, which normally will have no more than five core competencies, can grow this competitive edge by: a) consciously and deliberately identifying and inventorying core competencies (a task that might take a year); b) synthesizing and developing the core competencies through organizational learning; and c) leveraging the competencies through imagination and expeditionary marketing into a competitive advantage in the competition for market opportunity.[2]

Organizations must develop a unique competitive strategy for future survival. As the authors remark succinctly, "In this race to the future there are drivers, passengers, and road kill."[3] They advocate a commitment to driving since drivers alone will control their own destiny. By "driving" they mean that the successful organization of the future will shape its own industry and create its own markets for the future. To follow along behind the trailblazers, even through benchmarking, is to leave control of our destiny in the hands of others.

TECHNOLOGY AND STRATEGY

Technology is the central determining component requiring and facilitating organizational change. Recognition of this critical role is making its way slowly through the literature of management and organizational development.[4] Most management gurus remain poorly grounded in the technical side of enterprise; like senior managers they leave such matters to the "techies." Information technology is the key to such transformations as can be achieved through business process reengineering and innovation. Senior management, not the information services department, must lead the technology-informed transformation process.[5]

Dorothy Leonard-Barton achieves the linkage of technology with core competencies in her exploration of "core technological capabilities." A technological capability is a system of activities, physical systems, staff skills and knowledge bases, managerial systems of education and reward, and a system of values and norms that create advantage for an organization. These core technological capabilities can be nurtured and developed through organizational learning processes that promote:

1) shared problem-solving,
2) the integration of new technologies and capabilities,
3) constant experimentation, and
4) the importation of expertise from outside the organization.[6]

The problem is that core competencies frequently become core rigidities. There are many forces sustaining the inertia of organizational resistance to change: economics and the problems of cash flow and balanced budgets; the power relationships of organizational structure (which are always affected by change); and the ingrained habits and behaviors of people. Leonard-Barton distributes the levels of difficulty along a continuum: The physical system is the easiest to change, followed by the managerial system. Skills and knowledge take longer to transform. Changing values and behaviors are the most difficult. Core rigidities are the mirror-image of the competency-building exercise. Limited capacity and commitment to engage in group problem solving, inability to innovate, restricted experimentation, and ignoring or screening out new knowledge are all culprits.[7]

A broader perspective is brought to the issue with James Martin's concept of "strategic value streams," defined as a capability that may encompass one or more core competencies, that creates results for the customer, and which enables the development of a diversity of products or services. Both core competencies and core technologies can serve as the basis for building a diversity of products and services. A strategic value stream enables an organization to move faster with better focus and greater effect than its competition. Core competencies and strategic value streams have a number of characteristics in common: They require significant time and substantial investment to develop (since a powerful knowledge infrastructure is required). High performance teams are another requirement because of the cross-functional collaboration and high-level inspiration demanded by the process. Finally, the value of the competence/value stream is directly related to the quality and quantity of learning that occurs in the process of its development and deployment.[8]

Martin brings to the problem the perspective of the technologist. He stresses the inescapability of technology life-cycles and the importance of knowing where a process resides on the S-curve of that life-cycle. Technological discontinuities are a leading organization killer. IBM's commitment to the mainframe in face of the explosive diffusion of the personal computer reminds us of that reality. Linking new technology to a developing value stream is a powerful source for organizational strategy. Toward that end the strategist should:

1) analyze the organization's core competencies and strategic capabilities,
2) examine the core competencies and strategic capabilities of the competition,
3) develop, through the use of scenarios, what technological discontinuities might change the situation,
4) select core competencies for development and investment and study what might make them a unique, strategic resource, and
5) target value streams for reengineering and project—or develop scenarios—of what might leverage the process into a unique strategic resource.[9]

Now that the task is outlined, what are the obstacles?

OBSTACLES TO ORGANIZATIONAL LEARNING

Martin elaborates on the obstacles to organizational learning described as core rigidities by Leonard-Barton. As a consultant in organizational reengineering, he understands the many ways that organizations avoid innovation by discouraging risk-taking, hindering experimentation with excessive controls, by discouraging reflection with entrenched mental models and corporate cultures, by failing to iterate what learning does occur, and by declining to disseminate information vital to all parties.[10]

A more serious critique of the deep-seated resistance to learning and change typifying organizations comes from Richard Tabor Greene, who explores the "culture of professionalism" with its narrowness, abstraction, exclusivity, and lack of relevance as a primary cause for the loss of American competitiveness in the global marketplace. This trend in turn he attributes to the "culture of academia," an industry likely to be the last to overhaul itself and adapt to the new learning, technologies, and realities.[11] Indeed, the corporate world has begun to build an alternate system for higher education because of the inadequacies of the product of the traditional university. Many of the skills required by today's workplace, such as cooperation and working in groups, peer training, planning, and corporate citizenship are inadequately taught on our mainstream campuses. Motorola University, GE's Management Development Institute, and dozens of similar enterprises are addressing those shortcomings. Business is also investing heavily in individualized instruction programs to develop needed skills.[12] Academe's response to these challenges is, to date, inadequate.

OVERCOMING THE OBSTACLES

Leonard-Barton stresses that behavioral resistance to change is more difficult to overcome than are technological shortcomings. Organizations that successfully renew themselves on an ongoing basis show the common characteristics of enthusiasm for knowledge, the ability to learn, a tight coupling of complementary skills, and they have leaders who listen and learn.[13] Greene lists sixteen methods of implementing organization change, from parallel organization models to quality methods to an educative workplace model.[14] Martin's approach to organizational change is comprehensive, developed in his "enterprise engineering" model which encompasses continuous quality improvement, reengineering, and redesigning value streams, organizational purpose, and information management systems.[15] The tools are available; the work generally remains ahead.

ACADEMIC LIBRARIES: HOW ARE WE DOING?

Obviously, it is assumed here that academic organizations have enough in common with corporate organizations for us to learn from their experience. While it is impossible to accurately generalize about the "state" of more than two thousand disparate academic libraries, certain impressions can be drawn from the literature and from monitoring the tone of relevant e-mail discussion groups. Our condition might be described as "guarded."

Core Competencies: Librarians responded to this idea quickly. However, it appears we lost sight of the main road in pursuit of peripheral issues. While the mainstream core competency discussion developed into a strategy emphasizing interdisciplinary and cross-functional approaches, academic librarians described and debated lists of professional competencies and how they could be better taught in library schools.[16] The conscious exploration and development of group-based core competencies and value stream expertise needs further attention.

Reengineering: The core competencies, value-stream approach is closely related to the strategy of process reengineering. Shapiro and Long discussed the linkage of library and computer services at Rice University. A similar process has occurred at the University of Maryland at Baltimore.[17] The level of academic library adoption of the reengineering strategy is unclear. Reengineering provides a useful tool for substantive organizational redesign. There is, however, no broad consensus on the need for such restructuring.

TQM and Organizational Learning: The total quality management movement has had significant impact on libraries, causing renewed emphasis on satisfying the customer, continuous improvement, team development, and benchmarking. Significant accomplishments and serious remaining obstacles are widely noted.[18] Likewise, academic librarians have been quick to apply the concept of the learning organization to our organizations. Expectations, however, are muted. Worrell acknowledges the difficulties in implementing the required cultural change. Marcum proposes that a more organic approach (as opposed to a management-directed intervention model) is necessary to achieve the required change in organizational culture.[19]

Building Core Technological Capabilities and Strategic Value Streams: This is not virgin territory today, but accomplishment is concentrated to a few areas. Library organizations could doubtless do more to utilize problem-solving teams, expand experimentation, and deliberately import expertise. The construction of powerful knowledge infrastructures is another task awaiting the profession. It is suggested here that a more challenging vision is required if resistance to change is to be overcome. Two basic strategies that might inspire such visions are suggested in the hope of contributing to the dialogue.

MANAGING INTELLECTUAL CAPITAL IN THE INFORMED ORGANIZATION

Several complementary trends in knowledge management might be coordinated into a strategy for academic libraries. Zuboff's vision of the informated organization (that is, one that progresses beyond automation to utilizing what is learned to improve performance) provides a starting point.[20] Itami's conceptualization of invisible assets (from consumer trust to "brand" identity to management skills) broadened our understanding of the information-based resources of an organization as a second step.[21] Nonaka explains how an organization can become "knowledge creating" by making tacit knowledge explicit through articulation, collaboration, and internalization.[22] Tom Peters envisioned "knowledge management structures" by which networks of volunteers and experts could be developed and linked to assure customers of access to their expertise.[23] Tom Stewart popularized the vision of intellectual capital, along with a series of steps to manage it successfully. These steps include achieving clear definitions, assessing the competition, self-evaluation, and investment in knowledge development.[24] Perhaps the most useful approach is Roger Bohn's outlining ways to measure and manage knowledge (not information) processes, skills, and systems. Knowledge comes in stages. First comes awareness, then measurement, control, and finally internalization and understanding "why."[25]

The field of knowledge management systems or knowledge engineering is a branch of artificial intelligence and a fast developing discipline. To be precise, it is a field where "the train has left the station," rendering it exceeding difficult to board. The discipline is dominated by computer-information specialists and engineers. Knowledge-based systems improve human and human-technology collaboration and contribute to organizational flexibility. They have proven their value in industry and have spread throughout the public and private sectors.[26] In the limited field of expert systems, librarians appear to be "aboard the train." The worldwide web and hypertext markup language are tools quickly mastered by librarians to improve information search and retrieval and begin developing expert systems.[27] But in the broader arena of knowledge engineering it appears that American librarians need to think in terms of partnering, or importing appropriate expertise. A comprehensive report on the role of AI and knowledge systems in future libraries included only one American librarian among 25 contributors. Australians and Brits represented the library-information science field.[28] The artificial intelligence train is well under way.

A compatible approach more accessible to non-technologists is the concept of "inquiry systems" and consideration of the organization as an idea system. Inquiry systems use a methodology of inputs, outputs, operators, and guarantors to analyze the condition and prospects of a system. The approach is utilized by Ian Mitroff to propose that the "idea" inputs and products of the organization are ultimately more important than tangible, physical products.[29] Mitroff and Mason develop a vastly more comprehensive vision of the information needs of corporations seeking to maximize their systems perspective. In their view an extended knowledge infrastructure will be required to support an extended group of services scanning:

1) Issues management; scanning is needed regarding trends in the external environment that might require internal change,
2) Crisis management, tracking internal and external threats,
3) Environmentalism, tracking the impact of the organization on the environment,
4) Globalism, to seek to stay attuned to the global political-economy, and
5) Ethics, an awareness of the consequences of all organizational behaviors.[30]

Could the academic library provide such a complex of infrastructures for the university?

LOOKING BEYOND THE CAMPUS: STRATEGY NO. 2:

The second strategy suggested here is reengineering the basic role and purpose of the academic library. Librarians are prolific inquirers and reporters; library literature is extensive. However, we talk mainly to ourselves. We should be emphasizing our role as central, inter-active partners in the learning process rather than accepting an identity as responders to inquiries and disciplinary constraints. Academic libraries are enmeshed in a series of assumptions and mental models that restrict our flexibility and keep us moored to the ship of academe. This ship could run aground, restricted as it is by tunnel-visioned departments and comfortable, aging, tenured lecturers. There are new blips on those sonar screens pointed to the future, such as the corporation-sponsored learning mentioned earlier, or home-study programs like mainstream training for banking and financial planning, or television-formatted delivery such as that offered by Mind-Extension University or compressed video learning networks. Any extensive inquiry into the future of the college or university will turn up predictions such as the following major shifts:

FROM	TO
- faculty oriented teaching emphasis	- student-oriented learning emphasis
- campus-bound	- anywhere
- subject content emphasis	- competencies
- content	- learning how to learn
- profession/discipline bounded	- multi/cross-disciplinary
- time block-dedicated	- lifelong learning learning
- individual learning	- team or group learning
- theoretical emphasis	- applied, practical emphasis
- idyllic	- technology-based
- rigid schedule of classes	- just-in-time learning.[31]

Combinations of these trends could disrupt the university scene as we have known it. Librarians should determine to create our future and carve out our markets, not just go along for the ride offered by traditional faculty and established programs.

LEARNING FOR CHANGE: TEN QUESTIONS FOR ACADEMIC LIBRARIANS

To this point large dangers have gone unnamed. Are we prepared for the challenges ahead? Do we have strategies in place for the eventuality of sharply reduced resources? For the possibility of dramatic downsizing? Are we dealing with the threat of the scholars' workstation, particularly in its more visionary "virtual information center" configuration? Have we overcome the charge that the academic library has been failing for 50 years?[32] To assess our condition we might ask ourselves the following questions:

1) What is it that adds significant and unique value to our services in the eyes of our patrons? (These will be team-based skills that are extendible to other services.)

2) Are we guiding the development of library technological systems or merely responding to the offerings of vendors? (There are encouraging signs of control and fresh directions where librarians are key players; the MIT distributed library initiative is one such example.)[33]

3) Are we developing needed core technological capabilities by facilitating shared problem solving, experimentation, and the importation of expertise?

4) Should the multiple processes of selecting, acquiring, cataloging, processing, and delivering information to influence knowledge on an as-needed basis be considered a single strategic value stream? (If so, then envisioning it as such should guide our organizational redesign.)

5) Are we assessing and working to enhance the pace and direction of organizational learning, and the hindrances to learning, practiced in our libraries?

6) Should we attempt to "partner" with knowledge management specialists or seek to build our own unique road to the goal of becoming the knowledge management arm of our umbrella institutions?

7) Will the important tasks of balancing the demands of the paper and the electronic library, or mastering of the technology to serve traditional functions, enable us to develop strategies that will assure our future?[34]

8) Is the university "too big and too important" to suffer the fate of IBM and GM, or should we challenge all our assumptions and mental models in quest of new ways of thinking?[35]

9) Is the environment, the support, the guidance we offer through library services mere window dressing for the teaching process, or something

closer to the "heart of the enterprise"? (Perhaps it is time to revive the forgotten "library-college" vision of the 1960s?[36] It was unachievable then, but may offer useful guidance given the capabilities of current technology.)

10) Finally, are we driving toward our chosen future, going along for the ride, or standing startled with eyes gleaming in the headlights of approaching forces?

The answers we provide to these questions should set our agenda.

ENDNOTES

1. C.K. Prahalad and Gary Hamel, "The Core Competence of the Corporation," *Harvard Business Review*, 68:3 (May-June 1990), 79–91; and Hamel and Prahalad, *Competing for the Future*, Boston: Harvard Business School, 1994.
2. Hamel and Prahalad. *Competing for the Future*, and "Corporate Imagination and Expeditionary Marketing," *Harvard Business Review*, 69:4 (July-August, 1991), 81–92.
3. Hamel and Prahalad. *Competing for the Future*, p. 28.
4. For example, a recent compilation of "leading edge" thinking in organizational development implicitly treats technology as a peripheral, rather than central, phenomenon. See George P. Huber and William H. Glick. *Organizational Change and Redesign: Ideas and Insights for Improving Performance*. New York: Oxford University Press.
5. Thomas H. Davenport. *Process Innovation: Reengineering Work Through Information Technology*. Boston: Harvard Business School, 1993.
6. Dorothy Leonard-Barton. *Wellsprings of Knowledge: Building and Sustaining the Sources of Innovation*. Boston: Harvard Business School, 1995, pp. 3–28, 59–176.
7. Leonard-Barton. *Wellsprings of Knowledge*, pp. 34–56.
8. James Martin. *The Great Transition: Using the Seven Disciplines of Enterprising Engineering to Align People, Technology, and Strategy*. New York: AMACOM, 1995, pp. 305–323.
9. Martin, *The Great Transition*, pp. 323–357.
10. Martin, *The Great Transition*, pp. 420–425.
11. Richard Tabor Greene. *Global Quality: A Synthesis of the World's Best Management Methods*. Milwaukee: ASQC/Business One Irwin, 1993, pp. 640–694, 748–780.
12. Jeanne C. Meister. *Corporate Quality Universities: Lessons in Building a World-Class Work Force*. Burr Ridge, Ill.: American Society for Training and Development/Irwin, 1994; Edward E. Gordon, et. al. *FutureWork: The Revolution Reshaping American Business*. Westport, Conn.: Praeger, 1994, pp. 29–74.
13. Leonard-Barton. *Wellsprings of Knowledge*, pp. 259–267.
14. Greene, *Global Quality*, pp. 608–622.
15. Martin, *The Great Transition*.
16. Lois Buttlar and Rosemary Ruhig Du Mont, "Assessing Library Science Competencies," *Journal of Education for Library and Information Science*, 30 (Summer 1989), 3–18; John Corbbin, "Competencies for Electronic Information Services," *The Public Access Computer Systems Review*, 4:6 (1993), 160–175; Bernard S. Schlessinger, et al., "Information Science/Library Science Education Programs in the 1990s: A Not-so-modest Proposal," *Library Administration and Management*, 5:1 (Winter 1991), 16–19; Anne Wordsworth and June Lester, "Educational Imperatives of the Future Research Library: A Symposium," *Journal of Academic Librarianship*, 17:4 (September 1991), 204–215.
17. Beth J. Shapiro and Kevin Brook Long, "Just Say Yes: Reeingineering Library User Services for the 21st Century," *Journal of Academic Librarianship*, 20: 5/6 (November 1994), 285–290; Jacquelyn McCoy "Re-engineering Academic Libraries and Research Libraries," *College and Research Library News*, 54:6 (June 1993), 333–335. And see the multi-authored discussion of the integrated information management system at UMAB, in *Journal of the American Society for Information Science*, 45:5 (June 1994).
18. A useful resource on this issue is *Total Quality Management in Academic Libraries: Initial Implementation Efforts. Proceedings of the 1st International Conference on TQM and Academic Libraries*. Washington: Association of Research Libraries/OMB, 1995.
19. Diane Worrell, "The Learning Organization: Management Theory for the Information Age or New Fad," *Journal of Academic Librarianship*, 21:5 (September 1995), 351–357; James W.

Marcum, "Can the College Library Become a Learning Organization?," *Advances in Library Administration and Organization*, 1996.

20. Soshana Zuboff. *In the Age of the Smart Machine: The Future of Work and Power.* New York: Basic Books, 1984.
21. Hiroyuki Irami. *Mobilizing Invisible Assets*, Cambridge Mass.: Harvard University Press, 1987.
22. Ikujiro Nonaka, "The Knowledge-Creating Company," *Harvard Business Review*, 69:6 (November-December 1991), 96–104.
23. Tom Peters. *Liberation Management: Necessary Disorganization for the Nanosecond Nineties.* New York: Knopf, 1992, p. 368.
24. Thomas A. Stewart, "Intellectual Capital: Your Company's Most Valuable Asset," *Fortune*, 130:7 (October 3, 1994), 68–72; also see William J. Hudson. *Intellectual Capital*. New York: Wiley, 1993.
25. Roger E. Bohn, "Measuring and Managing Technological Knowledge," *Sloan Management Review*, 36:1 (Fall 1994), 61–73.
26. Frederick Hayes-Roth and Neil Jacobstein, "The State of Knowledge-Based Systems," *Communications of the ACM*, 37:3 (March 1994), 87–99; Bruce Abramson and Ng Keung-Chi, "towards an Art and Science of Knowledge Engineering," *IEEE Transactions on Knowledge and Data Engineering*, 5:4 (August 1993), 705–712.
27. David Stern, "Expert Systems: HTML, the WWW, and the Librarian," *Computers in Libraries* 15:4 (April 1995), 56–58; Ralph Alberico and Mary Micco. *Expert Systems for Reference and Information Retrieval*. Westport, Conn.: Meckler, 1990; F.W. Lancaster, "Artificial Intelligence and Expert Systems: How Will They Contribute?" in Lancaster, ed. *Libraries and the Future: Essays on the Library in the Twenty-First Century*. New York: Haworth, 1993, pp. 147–156.
28. John Weckert and Craig McDonald, eds., "Artificial Intelligence, Knowledge Systems, and the Future Library," Special Issue, *Library Hi-Tech*, 10: 1–2 (1992).
29. Ian I. Mitroff, "The Idea of the Corporation as an Idea System," *Technological Forecasting and Social Change*, 38:1 (August 1990), 1–14; and C.W. Churchman. *The Design of Inquiring Systems*. New York: Basic Books, 1971.
30. Ian I. Mitroff, Richard O. Mason, and Christine M. Pearson. *Framebreak: The Radical Redesign of American Business*. San Francisco: Jossey-Bass, 1994, pp. 19–52.
31. Robert H. Barr and John Tagg, "From Teaching to Learning: A New Paradigm for Undergraduate Education," *Change* (November-December, 1995), 13–25; Samuel L. Dunn, "The Challenge of the Nineties in US Higher Education: From Camelot to the 21st Century," *Futures Research Quarterly*, 10:3 (Fall 1994), 35–55; Ernest A. Lynton and Sandra E. Elman. *New Priorities for the University: Meeting Society's Needs for Applied Knowledge and Competent Individuals*. San Francisco: Jossey-Bass, 1987; David Breneman. *Liberal Arts Colleges: Thriving, Surviving or Endangered?* Washington: Brookings, 1994.
32. See the articles by Seiler and Supranant, and by Line in Lancaster, ed. *Libraries and the Future*, pp. 73–83, 157–180.
33. Greg Anderson, "Mens et Manus at Work: The Distributed Library Initiative at MIT," *Library Hi-Tech*, 11:1 (1993), 83–94.
34. Michael Buckland. *Redesigning Library Services: A Manifesto*. Chicago: ALA, 1992; Walt Crawford and Michael Gorman. *Future Libraries: Dreams, Madness, and Reality*. Chicago: ALA, 1995.
35. Ian I. Mitroff and Harold A. Linstone. *The Unbounded Mind: Breaking the Chains of Traditional Business Thinking*. New York: Oxford University Press, 1993, pp. 85–150.
36. *The Library-College*. Ed. Louis Shores, et al. Philadelphia: Drexel Press, 1966.

Users and Bibliographic Resources: Blind Dating by OPAC

By James Rettig
College of William and Mary

The creators of the second edition of the Anglo-American Cataloging Rules[1] (AACR2) were thoroughly versed in cataloging principles and practices reaching back at least as far as Panizzi. They also knew that new rules would have to function in a future in which automation would change both the way catalogers would catalog materials and the way that users would interact with catalogs. Since AACR2's debut in 1978, the profession has carried on a vigorous debate about the code's suitability to the online environment in which catalogs and catalog users have come to operate. In his literature survey Fattahi concludes that the profession has supported AACR2's accommodations of automation.[2]

However he also notes that librarians have been increasingly frustrated by limitations. These have become evident as technological change has accelerated in response to the compound need to catalog new media, new forms of electronic materials, and new modes of access to information while at the same time honoring the unique nature of each. These needs have created stress on both the cataloging code and the MARC format. Although Fattahi discerns threads of agreement that technology has outpaced the code's implicit vision, there does not appear to be a consensus on whether AACR2's 1988 revision (AACR2R)[3] can bend enough to accommodate future automation-driven and user-driven needs or whether those needs will break an increasingly brittle instrument.

Meanwhile, MARC and AACR2R are the tools available for informing catalog users what materials are available in (or, increasingly, through) a given library. Two projects give credence to the argument that these tools are up to the task. OCLC's InterCat catalog "is an experimental, proof-of-concept database created through the OCLC Internet Cataloging project"[4] to test the ability of the MARC record and AACR2R to deal with a new and very important type of information resource. One project participant has succinctly captured the essence of the challenge, saying "The Internet is a non-static space that is host to a variety of information objects. Cataloging rules were not drafted with these objects in mind, and it is difficult to apply them."[5] That difficulty was eased in March, 1995, when the Library of Congress's Network Development and MARC Standards Office issued "Guidelines for the use of Field 856," designating that field for use "for Electronic Location and Access and . . . information needed to locate an electronic resource. It contains enough information to both locate the item and retrieve it or [to] connect to a service" through which a user can connect to it.[6] A sample record in MARC format clearly shows use of this field:

The Uniform Resource Locator (URL) in the 856 field is highlighted as a hot link; since the InterCat database is accessible through the World Wide Web, this link can be activated. Librarians may be comfortable with a MARC display of a record representing an information source; however the typical catalog user prefers something more processed. The InterCat database accommodates both:

Another recent project has demonstrated that both MARC and Standard Generalized Markup Language (SGML) (including its Hypertext Markup Language [HTML] subset) can work together to make a complex bibliographic entity readily accessible through an OPAC. This project, a collaboration between the Pierian Press and the University of Illinois at Urbana-Champaign, assumed that a classified, analytical, annotated bibliography "presented

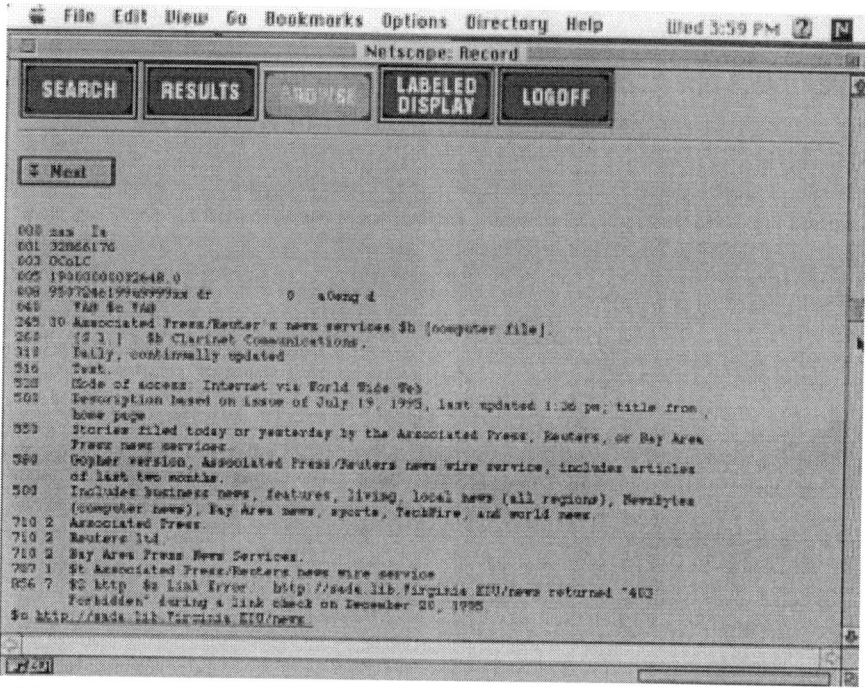

Figure 1. MARC Format Record from OCLC InterCat Database

a 'worst case scenario' for either Standard Generalized Markup Language or MARC."[7] The experiment has been founded on the premise that

> If library systems would facilitate parsing such [knowledge] constructs—portions into MARC records, and portions into text files containing hyperlinks—library systems would (could) mitigate the weaknesses of each standard by drawing upon the strengths of the other. Specifically, such enhancements would facilitate the mounting of knowledge constructs on library systems, which can function as dynamic maps and links to both internally held and external resources, and can directly draw upon the strengths of the MARC record for indexing, sorting, and searching purposes. If library vendors would enhance their systems to load MARCup resources, this in turn, would encourage other publishers of traditional knowledge constructs to parse appropriate print resources into MARCup—and greatly contribute to the evolution of our information retrieval systems into knowledge systems.[8]

Library vendors are moving in this direction. Several offer a fully operational WWW interface that takes full advantage of their native systems' capabilities, including lateral searching on headings through hyperlinks, as well as the Web's capabilities to link to external resources.

The Pierian Press bibliography merits further examination since it demonstrates the way the MARCup item allows a user to move deeper and deeper into its contents—from "title page" (Figure 3) to table of contents (Figure 4) to selected text (Figure 5) to the bibliography associated with that text (Figure 6) to the annotation for a particular item in the bibliography (Figure 7).

This experiment demonstrates the validity and the viability of combining MARC records and hypertext linkages among parts of a "knowledge construct" to provide varying levels of access to the contents of that complex construct. Assuming all licensing arrangements have been made and paid for, a library could easily download an OCLC InterCat record for this item into its OPAC and, through a WWW interface for that OPAC, users would be able to move seamlessly from the MARC record, a faint image of the item itself, to any level of information within the item.

As technology and, subsequently, library information systems have changed, catalog users' behavior has changed. Librarians must reconceptualize the roles of their libraries' users and library catalogs. At present the typical user accesses the catalog from within a library building. This has had implications

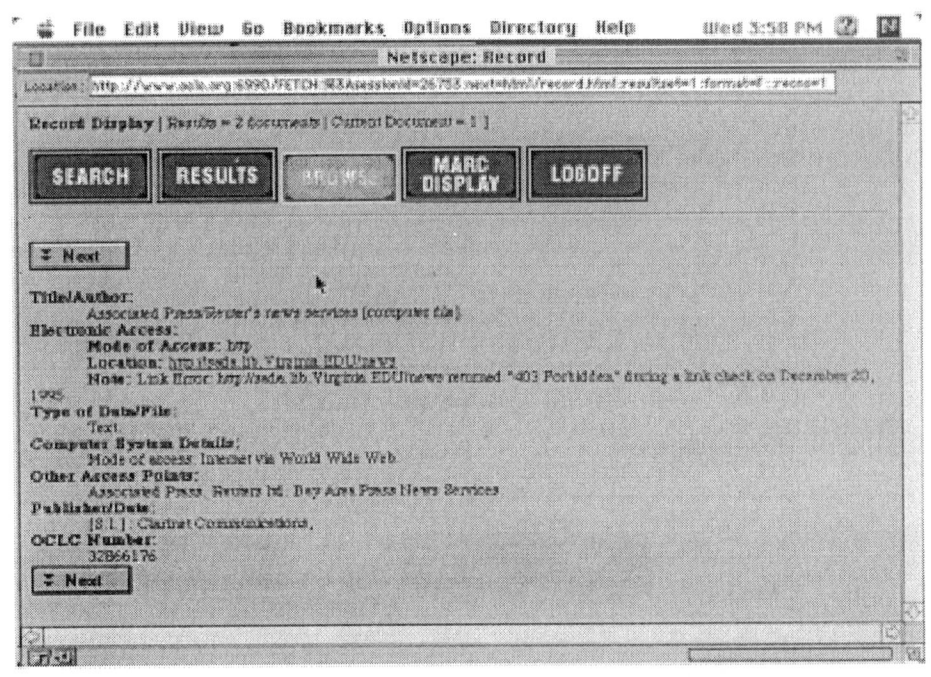

Figure 2. WWW Display of OCLC InterCat Record

for the structure, contents, and use of the catalog. The records in the catalog have traditionally represented items held locally, usually in that very same building. It required only a modicum of effort on the part of the user to go from the surrogate record in the catalog to the item itself to judge the value and relevance of the item based on examination of the item's contents. That is changing.

Remote access to OPACs, whether from the building next to the library or from another continent, is becoming the preferred option of many users. For example, the OPAC of the College of William and Mary Libraries was available on the local campus network and for dial-in users (but not on the Internet) from 1990 through 1995. (Since September of 1995 it has also been available via the WWW.) Annually the percentage of searches made on that OPAC from outside a campus library facility has risen while the percentage of searches made from within a campus library facility has declined.[9]

Eventually the converging lines will, presumably, cross and the majority of uses of the OPAC will originate from outside a campus library facility.

This trend has significant implications for the functionality and design of OPACs. For one, OPACs must do more than describe materials held locally. They must evolve, as Wall and his co-authors have noted, into "knowledge systems." The successes of the OCLC InterCat project and the Pierian Press-University of Illinois collaboration indicate that this is an attainable goal. A "knowledge system" should allow its users, regardless of their location:

- to learn what information tools are available at or through a given library
- to link (within the provision of licensing agreements) to remote resources
- to follow links from representations of items to the items themselves
- to examine enough information about an item to allow an informed judgment of its relevance to their work.

This last criterion is growing in importance. For economic and ergonomic reasons, libraries will continue to collect information in the media which they collect today even as they "collect" or provide access to information sources in new media which have no local physical presence. Users, who because they are interacting with the OPAC from a remote location, will not have access to locally held materials in the building from which they learn of the availability of those materials. They will want to know as much as possible about an item before expending their own time and energy to retrieve it from the library or before going to the trouble, no matter how

170 *Finding Common Ground*

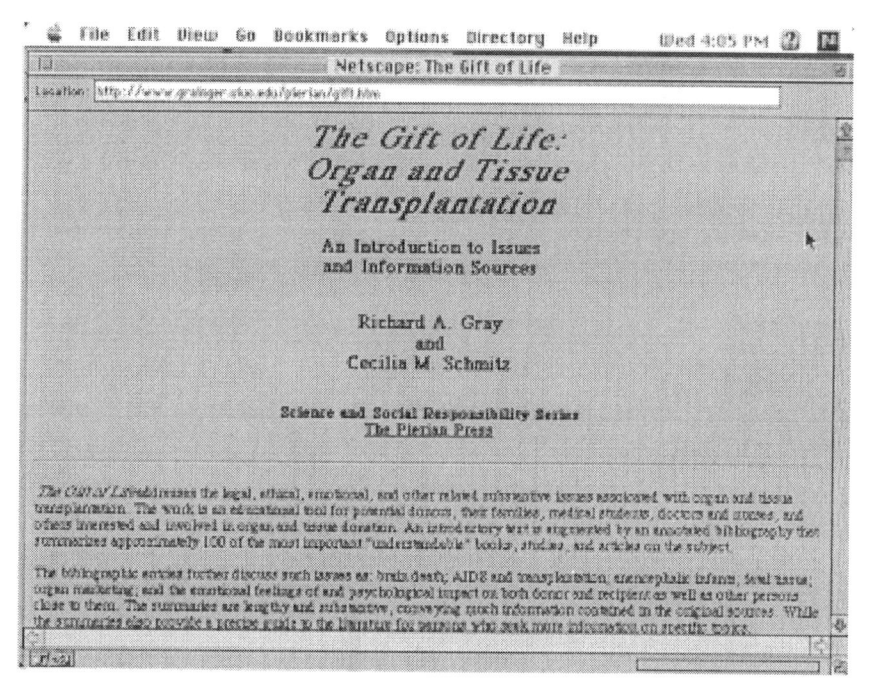

Figure 3. Pierian Press's The Gift of Life "Title Page" and Introduction

minor, of filling in an online request form to have an item retrieved from a remote storage facility or to be delivered to them.

Furthermore, some electronic resources that users identify and link to through the OPAC will carry charges based on number of transactions or number of items retrieved. If users cannot make sound judgments about such items, precious resources will be squandered obtaining information sources that are of little or no use to the individuals for whom they are obtained. Anyone who has ever worked in an interlibrary loan office has had the too-frequent experience of handing a patron a book that the patron has expectantly waited for only to have the patron examine it and return it within minutes with the explanation that it is not relevant. The patron has often based the request on nothing more than a bibliographic citation or a MARC record. Users will need more to make well informed decisions to avoid squandering resources on irrelevant information.

The traditions of the catalog may be a drag on meeting this critical need. As Ellen Waite has noted,

Although the bibliographic catalog record provides an adequate description of the physical book, it provides an inadequate description of the content of a book. If we want to provide access to the substance of a book, the least we could do is include a contents note that library patrons could use through keyword searches. Very few libraries do this on a regular basis.[11]

Thomas Mann has recognized the value of the classified arrangement of a collection of books, allowing one to examine their contents. It provides what he calls "depth of access," noting that "a retrieval system that offers both a catalog of surrogates for full texts and an array of subject-grouped full texts themselves provides much greater depth of access than one that allows only the brief surrogates to be searched. No catalog record—even with an abstract—can ever match the extent of information in the full text it represents.[12] However one must be on-site to examine the texts. Since users are increasingly seeking access to those texts (and other information constructs) from remote locations, libraries need to provide greater depth through their OPACs, both about materials held locally and about information sources accessible elsewhere through licensing or pay-per-use arrangements.

Since catalog records are crafted to describe a physical entity which contains information far better than they are designed to describe that entity's information contents, users arrange blind dates between themselves and information resources. However, whereas in the case of blind dates between

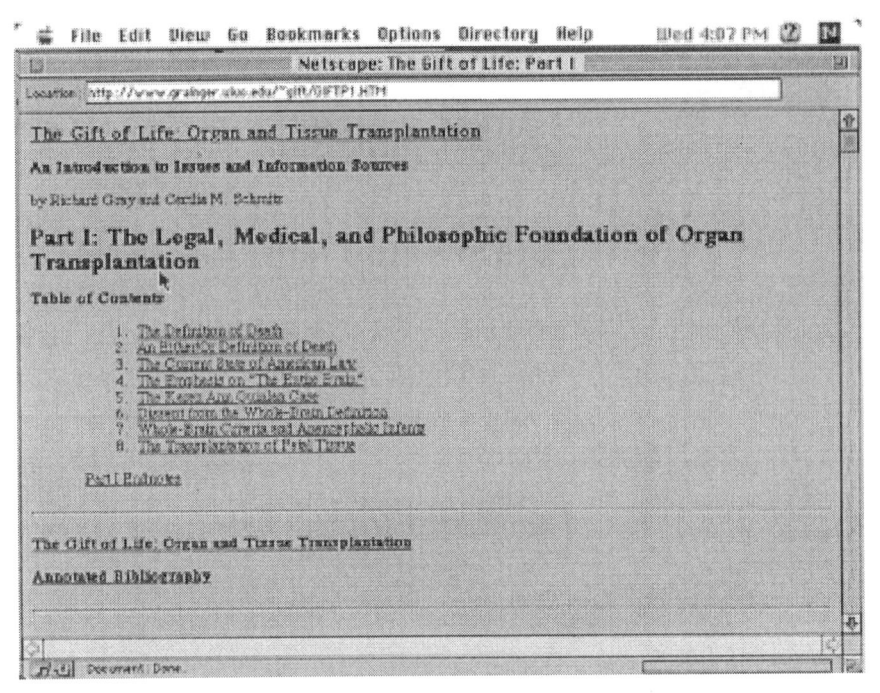

Figure 4. Table of Contents to Part I of The Gift of Life

people the go-between generally emphasizes the parties' inner qualities rather then their physical characteristics, the catalog record go-between emphasizes the physical over the internal.

Experience, brought into relief by the frequent need to help their users navigate through self-serve CD-ROM databases, has shown librarians that abstract help users judge the relevance and importance of journal articles. A database with both journal citations and abstracts is a much richer resource than one offering only bibliographic citations. Yet cataloging practice has rarely concerned itself with conveying information about the contents of the items catalog records describe.

Today's OPAC offers much greater power and many more avenues of approach than any card catalog, a truth that even sentimentalists about the card catalog of yore must acknowledge. Mann has summarized it thus:

> In an electronic catalog, each work can be represented by only one record; but that one record can have as many points of access as there are different words, numbers, or codes on it. In such a situation, presumably, catalogers can add many subject headings beyond the traditional two or three, as well as tables of contents or descriptive notes; and they can make each of these extra elements a directly searchable point of access while at the same time circumventing the prohibitive cost of creating, filing, and storing separate records for each one.[13]

Indeed, as Web interfaces for OPACs, as the Pierian Press-University of Illinois collaboration, and as the OCLC InterCat—each and every one a success—demonstrate, today's OPACs can accommodate all of this and more. The technology that today is typified by the World Wide Web and enriched records of the sort created by these demonstration projects can coalesce to form far more useful tools for OPAC users, tools that provide them with the depth that Mann finds thus far only in full texts arrayed in classified order on a shelf.

One of the goals of academic librarians in recent years has been to develop users' "information literacy" skills. Various definitions of this term are available in the published literature; suffice it to say that at its best and most meaningful the concept means that users of information recognize the need to make critical judgments about the information sources they identify through OPACs and other tools and that they are able to make those judgments on their own behalf. These judgments require more information than the typical catalog record provides.

The World Wide Web, despite its chaotic

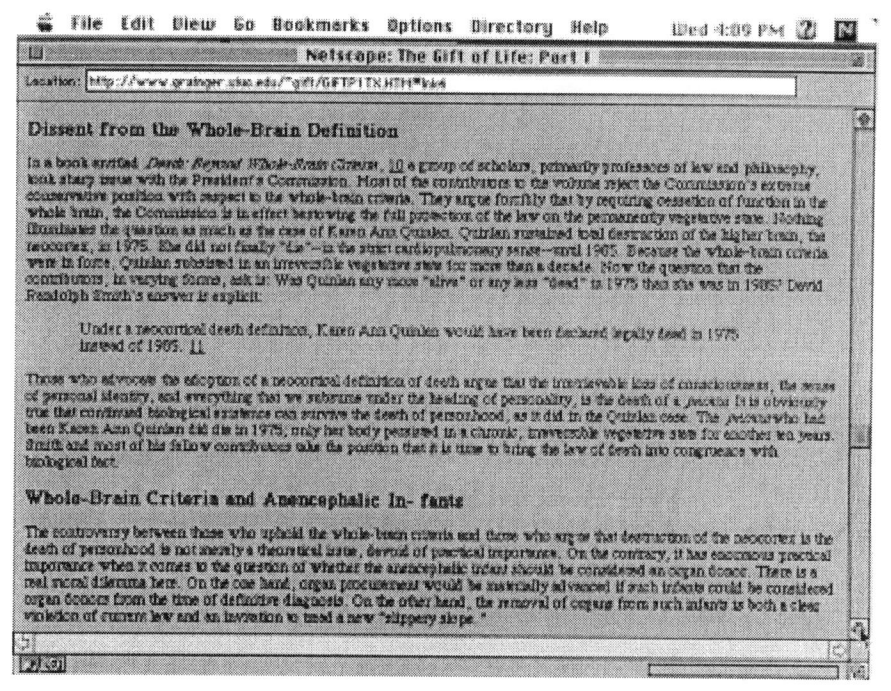

Figure 5. Selected Text from Part I of The Gift of Life

rambunctiousness, already offers some of the additional information users need to make these critical judgments. Some Web information is familiar from the international scholarly apparatus in print. Some is unique to the Web. It is becoming available because information providers long familiar with the dynamics of the marketplace and distribution channels for printed information products are seeking ways to serve and expand their market through electronic channels.

A familiar element ported over from the print world is the book review. Presumably many years of opportunity lie ahead for book review sources (as well as review sources for other media) to flourish on the Web. At present sources disseminating substantive book reviews on the Web are few and far between. Some, such as Air Chronicles Book Reviews,[14] are very specialized and others, such as the venerable Atlantic Monthly,[15] are very general in nature. In the print world too few new books are reviewed; on the Internet, even fewer reviews are available today. Presumably this will change both as existing print publications replicate themselves on the Web and as new sources such as History Reviews On-Line[16] come into being.

Reviews can be very helpful in judging the value and relevance of a particular book. However they are woefully underutilized, both because of library users' ignorance of their existence and of the process for identifying and retrieving them and because that process is labor intensive and time-consuming. If, however, reviews were made available from within the record describing the item reviewed, users would be alerted to their existence and would have access to them with the click of a mouse.

Herein lies an entrepreneurial opportunity for an organization with a proven track record in electronic information harvesting, book review indexing, or both. OCLC has a proven record in the first. Its NetFirst database makes identification and selection of Internet resources an easier, more reliable process than more typical "surfing" methods. It identifies and describes resources, selecting them based on quality.[17] A brief annotation in each NetFirst record describes the content of its resource:

In its Web manifestation a hot link from the URL in the "Location" field takes the user to that resource. Since, unlike the InterCat database, NetFirst records are not in MARC format and do not use Library of Congress Subject Headings, they are not suitable for integration into OPAC databases. Nevertheless, they demonstrate OCLC's ability to create a database of Internet resources and to automate much of the identification and link-verification processes. This forms a firm foundation for creating a ReviewsFirst database of book reviews (and reviews

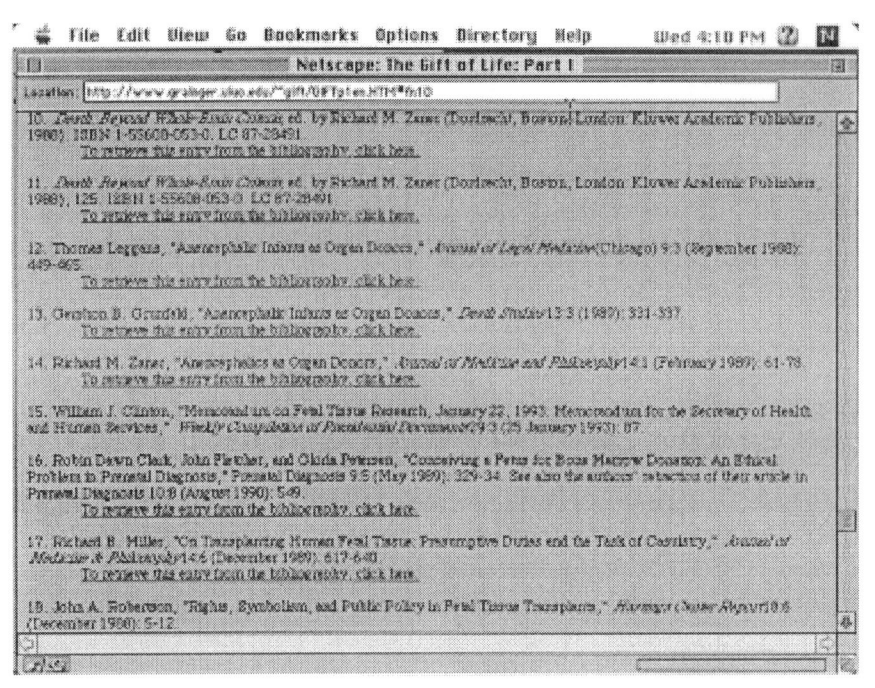

Figure 6. Bibliography Accompanying Text Shown in Figure 5

of other items, including Internet resources) available on the Internet.

By matching information in these review records to the records in the OCLC online union catalog (OLUC) database representing the items reviewed, OCLC could create a product licensed to libraries. This product would consist of enhanced MARC records for items reviewed; each of these records would include a hot link to each and every review identified on the Internet and for which OCLC has matched to a record in the OLUC. Subscriber libraries would receive a collection of records (selected because of the presence of the library's location symbol attached to that record in the OLUC) and load these into its OPAC database, bumping the older records. It would enable an OPAC user working through a Web interface to identify an item and move directly to its reviews. Authentication of a user before permitting access to the ReviewsFirst links could be determined by the user's IP address.

Gale Research and the H.W. Wilson Co. have proven records in indexing book reviews published in print sources. If OCLC does not produce a service such as ReviewsFirst, perhaps Gale, Wilson, or some other company will develop a service that can be linked by automated means to OPAC records of items reviewed.

The Internet today offers additional information about the materials represented in OPACs. Increasingly publishers make tables of contents, information about authors' qualifications, and even sample chapters of books available at their Internet sites. This information can help users judge these items' relevance and value. Whereas links to reviews must be made post-publication, links from the bibliographic record to these resources can be made pre-publication through information submitted by the publisher to the Cataloging in Publication (CIP) program. Each link embedded in the bibliographic record should specify the type of information it leads to: table of contents, sample chapter, author biography, publisher's blurb, etc. The elements needed to provide these sorts of links exist.

Take, for example, Herbert Hirsch's book Genocide and the Politics of Memory.[18] In a WWW OPAC interface its record looks like this:

Hyperlinks for lateral searches on various fields are evident in this record. Expansion of the capabilities of the MARC record as has been done with the 856 field could accommodate additional links to the Internet. In the case of Hirsch's book, a link to its entry in the University of North Carolina Press's catalog provides a description and the table of contents:

Furthermore, a substantial review is available from the History Reviews On-Line service:

A second example differs slightly in the array of

174 *Finding Common Ground*

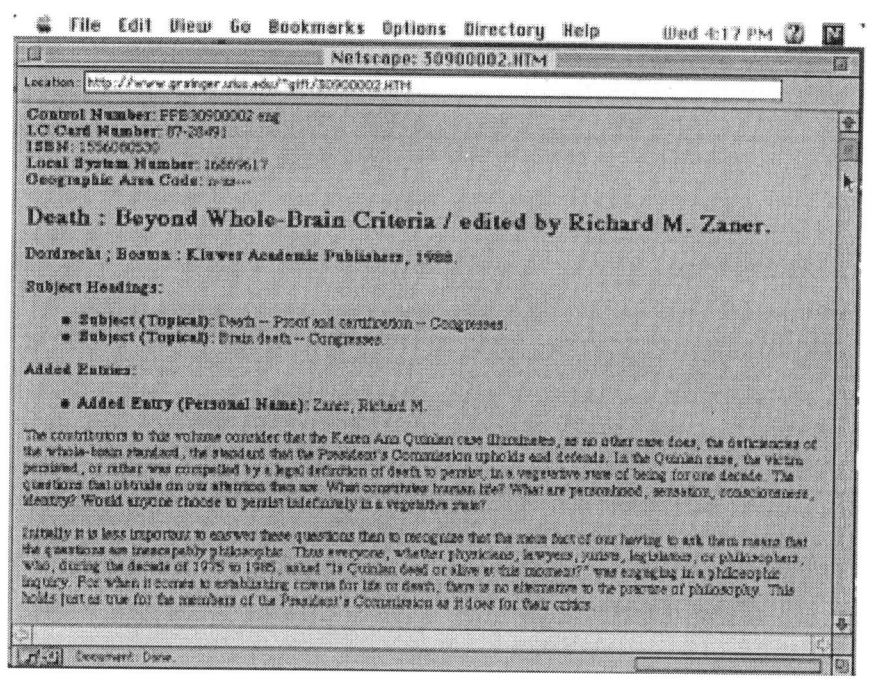

Figure 7. Annotation for Item #10 Shown in Figure 6

information elements available. Daniel Seymour's *Once Upon a Campus*[19] has, of course, a MARC record:

Its publisher makes its table of contents and preface available on the Web:

The publisher also makes a sample chapter available:

These examples demonstrate that information about the information resources libraries collect is becoming available on the Internet. If dynamically linked to their records, much of this information can help OPAC users make informed judgments about the items represented in an OPAC. Until the item is in a user's possession, "the value of information about information can be greater than the value of the information itself."[20] Existing or potential sources of such meta-information include tables of contents databases for journals, publisher's item-specific information, reviews, and full-text databases.

Tables of contents and current awareness services for journals may require special consideration. It is not difficult to imagine an OPAC user who retrieves the record for a journal, decides to examine its linked table of contents information, and then browses endlessly in a dogged search for articles on a particular topic. Such a user would, of course, be better served by an index to the pertinent subject field. This, of course, points to the value of links from serials' records to the records of the sources that index them or, if the index itself is available online to users of a given library, to the index itself. Furthermore, publishers of indexes will increasingly offer an optional package which links citations or abstracts to the full text of articles.

The examples shown relate to the print resources that continue to form the foundation of libraries' collections. The Internet also supplies supplemental information on information resources in other media. For example, the Boston Review of Books online offers reviews of audio books.[21] Motion picture studios offer unabashed hype about their films. Nevertheless well after these films have completed their big screen runs and video rentals have dwindled to a trickle of a film's revenue stream, the information at these sites, including stills and video trailers, can have value.

Permanence of information on the Internet and continuity of access to it are abiding concerns. The Internet is gaining strength as a venue for commerce. If publishers and other information providers see a commercial and competitive advantage to maintaining information about their wares on the Internet, they will maintain it. Assuming that this will happen is an act of faith, but not, in light of the 'Net's commercial growth, foolish faith. As for continuity, the replacement of URLs by Universal Resource

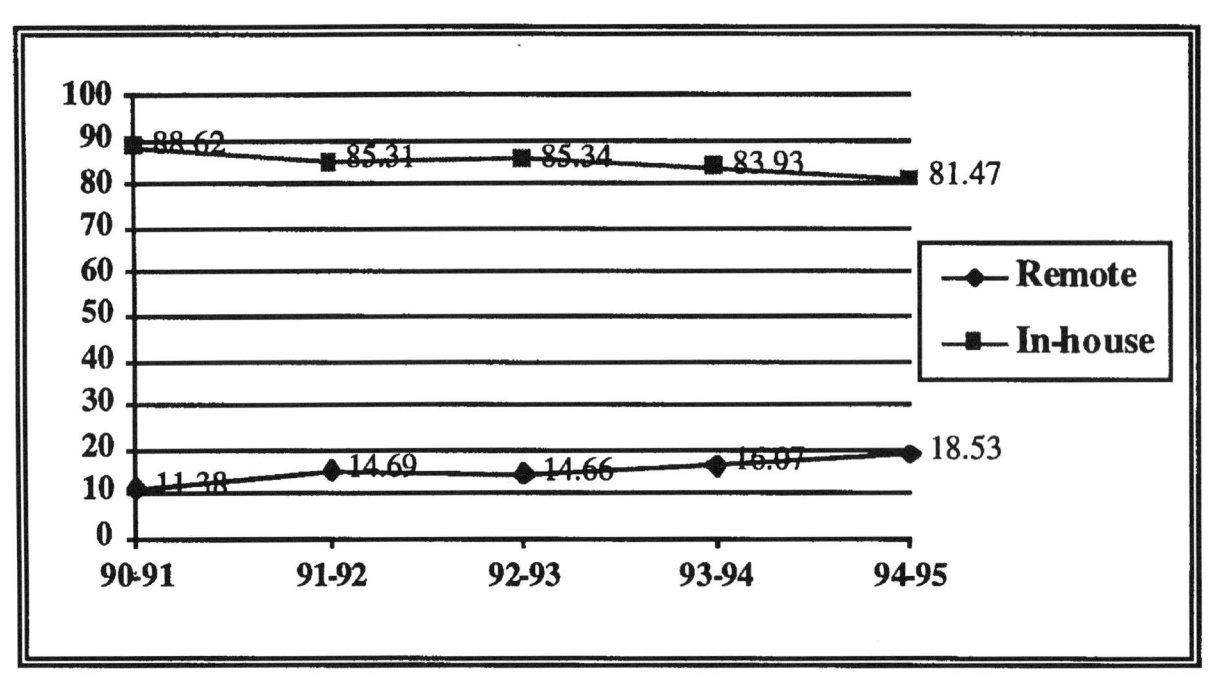

Figure 8. Percentage of OPAC Searches by Remote and In-house Access, College of William and Mary Libraries, FY1990–95 [10]

Names (URNs) which are distinct from the physical locations signified by URLs, as well as software that automatically verifies and updates links, will minimize this problem.

The elements needed to convert OPACs into knowledge systems are coalescing. In concert those elements can help users make informed decisions about the items represented in OPACs rather than rely on "blind dates" based on physical descriptions. Through additional demonstration projects, through inter-institutional cooperation, through leadership by organizations such as OCLC and the Library of Congress, and by applying pressure to integrated system vendors through user groups, academic libraries can bring about this transformation.

ENDNOTES

1. Michael Gorman and Paul W. Winkler, eds. Anglo-American Cataloguing Rules. 2d ed. Chicago: American Library Association, 1978.
2. Rahmatollah Fattahi, "Anglo-American Cataloguing Rules in the Online Environment: A Literature Review," Cataloging & Classification Quarterly 20 (1995): 25–50.
3. Michael Gorman and Paul W. Winkler, eds. Anglo-American Cataloguing Rules. 2d ed. rev. Chicago: American Library Association, 1988.
4. "Internet Cataloging Project Database Now Available," OCLC Newsletter no. 216 (July/August 1995): 10. See also Molly Brennan and Eric Childress, "Virginia Libraries Join the OCLC Internet Cataloging Project," Virginia Librarian 41 (October-December): 11–13.
5. Judith M. Brugger, "conclusion" section to "Cataloging the Internet," ftp://ftp.lib.ncsu.edu/pub/stacks/mcj/mcj-vln02–brugger.
6. "Guidelines for the Use of Field 856," gopher://marvel.loc.gov:70/00/.listarch/usmarc/856_guidelines.
7. C. Edward Wall, Timothy W. Cole, and Michele M. Kazmer, "HyperText MARCup: A Conceptualization for Encoding, De-Constructing, Searching, Retrieving, and Using Traditional Knowledge Tools," Reference Services Review 23 (Winter 1995): 13.
8. Ibid., p. 15.
9. On 12 December 1995, the author posted to the PACS-L listserv a request for similar OPAC use data from other academic libraries; it did not yield any usable responses.
10. The same data can be represented thus: OPAC Access, College of William and Mary Libraries, FY1990–95
11. Ellen J. Waite, "Reinvent Catalogers!" Library Journal 120 (November 1, 1995): 36.

12. Thomas Mann, Library Research Models (New York: Oxford University Press, 1993), 128–29. Italics in original.
13. Ibid., 107.
14. URL: http://www.cdsar.af.mil/bookmain.html.
15. URL: http://www2.theAtlantic.com/atlantic/.
16. URL: http://www.uc.edu/www/history/reviews.html.
17. "OCLC NetFirst to Improve End-user Access to Internet Resources," OCLC Newsletter no. 215 (May/June 1995): 4–5.
18. Herbert Hirsch. Genocide and the Politics of Memory: Studying Death to Preserve Life. Chapel Hill: University of North Carolina Press, 1995.
19. Daniel Seymour. Once Upon a Campus. Phoenix: Oryx Press, 1995.
20. Nicholas Negroponte. Being Digital. New York: Alfred A. Knopf, 1995, p. 154.
21. URL: http://www.bookwire.com/bbr/technology/audiobooks.html.

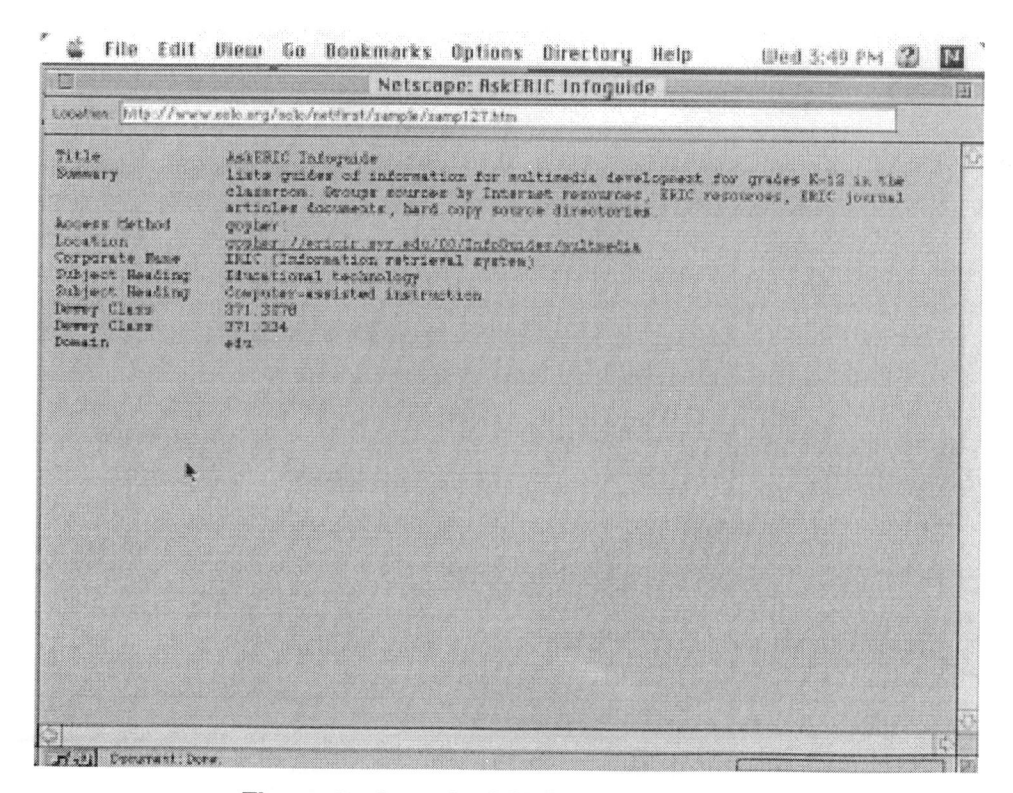

Figure 9. Sample OCLC NetFirst Record

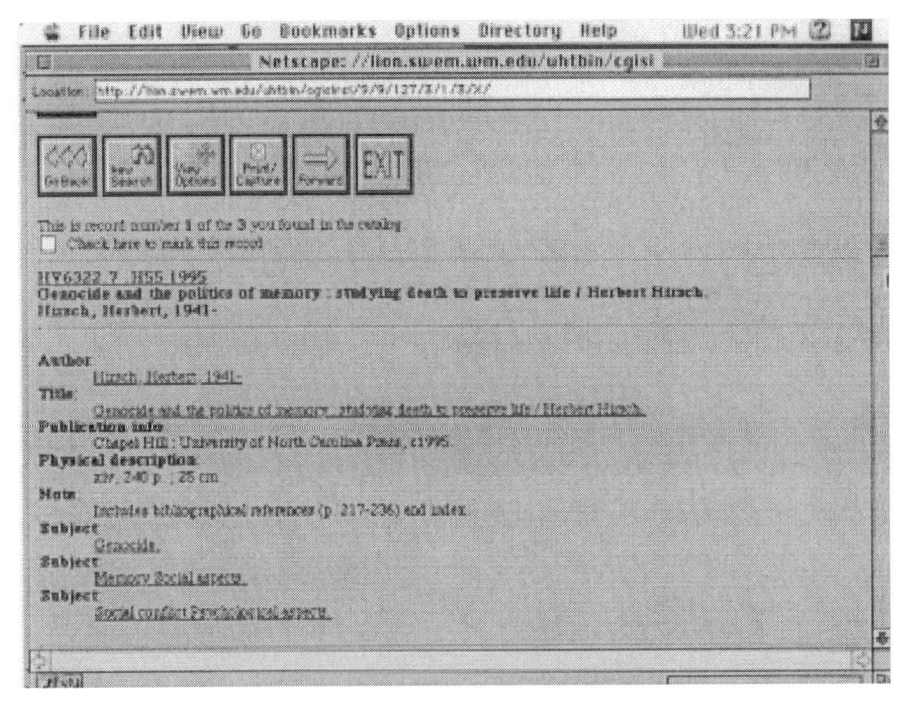

Figure 10. Web Interface OPAC Record for Genocide and the Politics of Memory

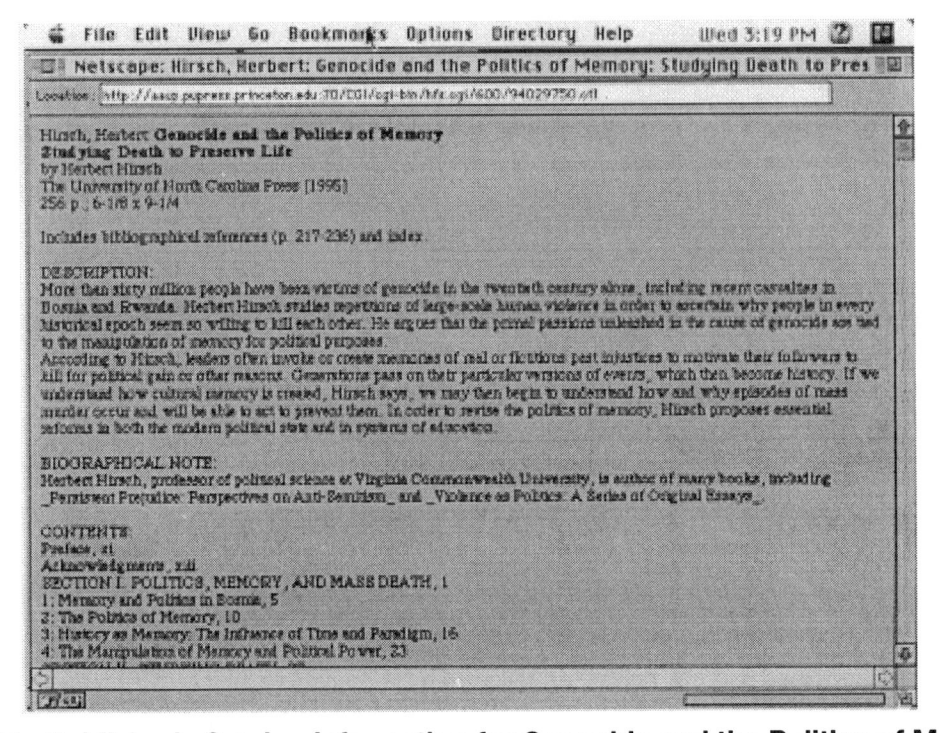

Figure 11. Publisher's Catalog Information for Genocide and the Politics of Memory

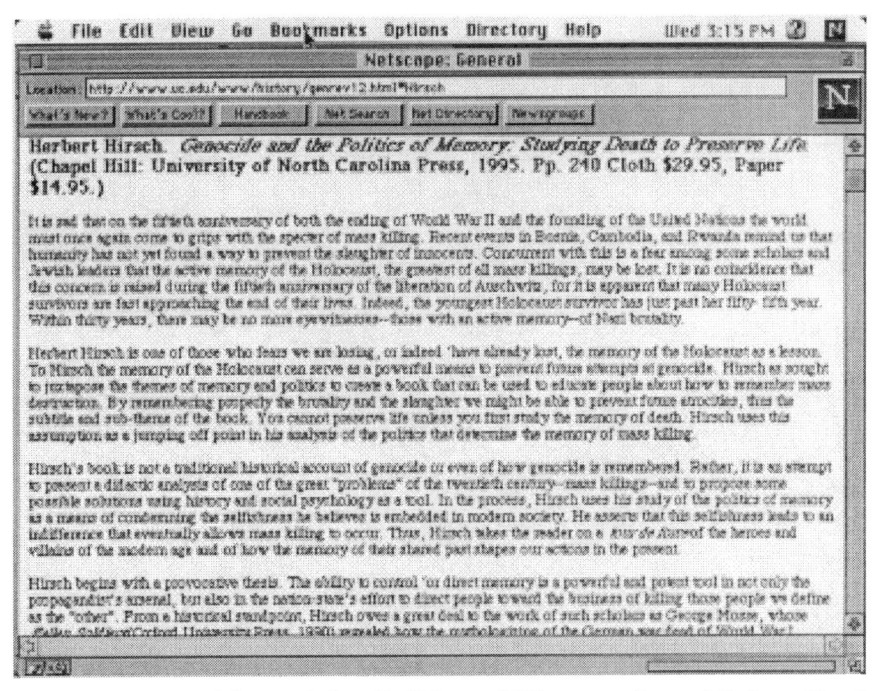

Figure 12. Review of Genocide and the Politics of Memory from History Reviews On-Line

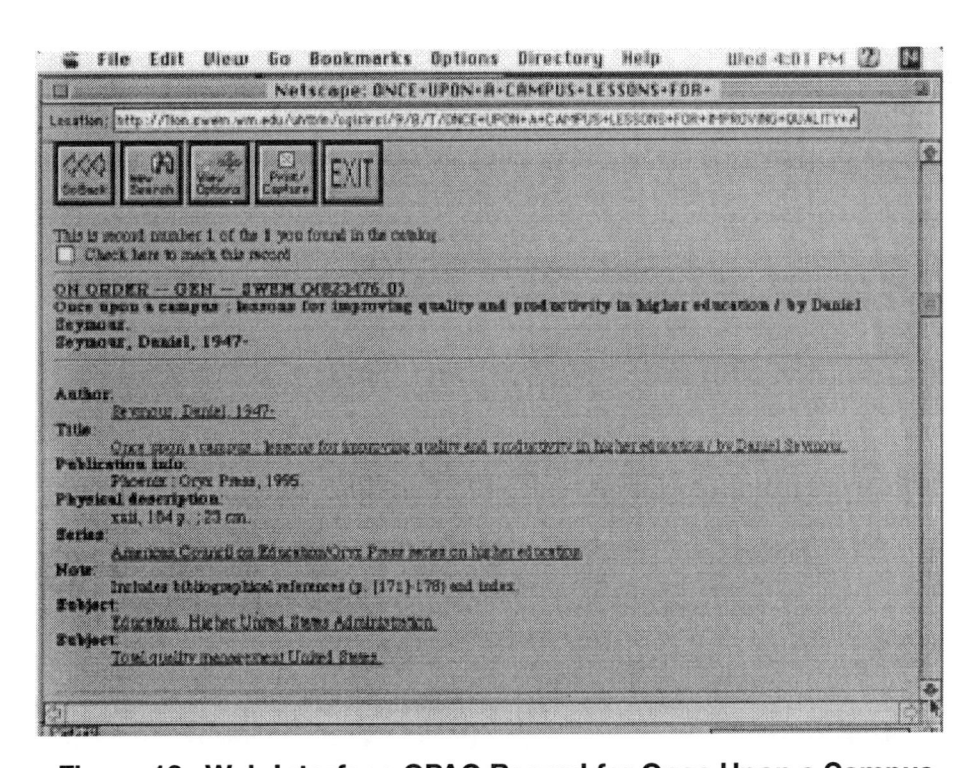

Figure 13. Web Interface OPAC Record for Once Upon a Campus

Satisfying Our Users   179

Figure 14. Publisher's WWW Information about Once Upon a Campus

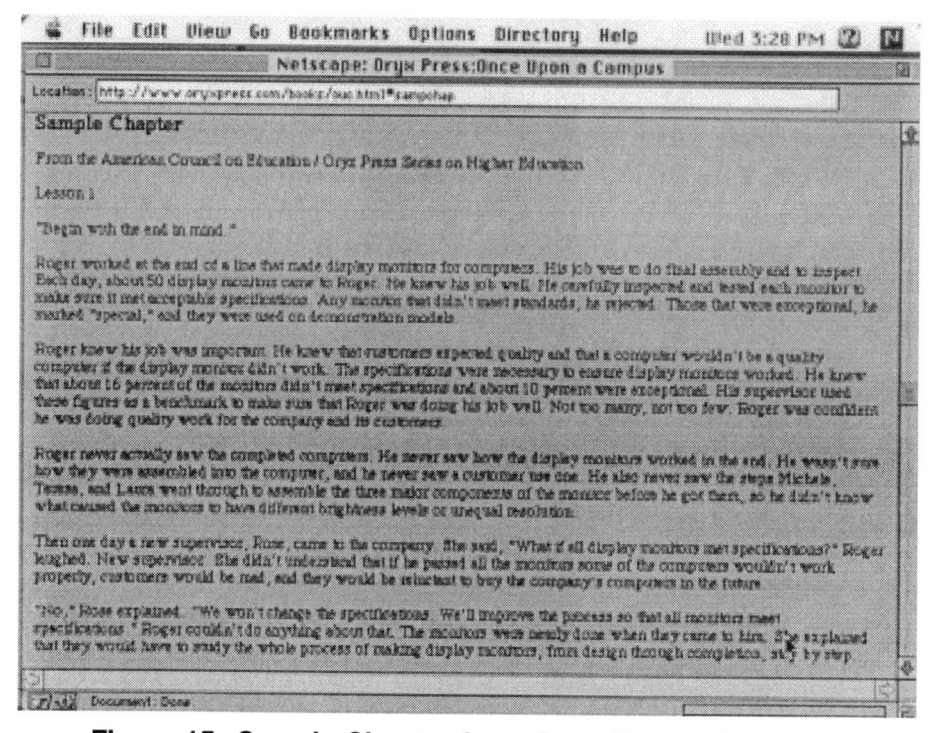

Figure 15. Sample Chapter from Once Upon a Campus

180   *Finding Common Ground*

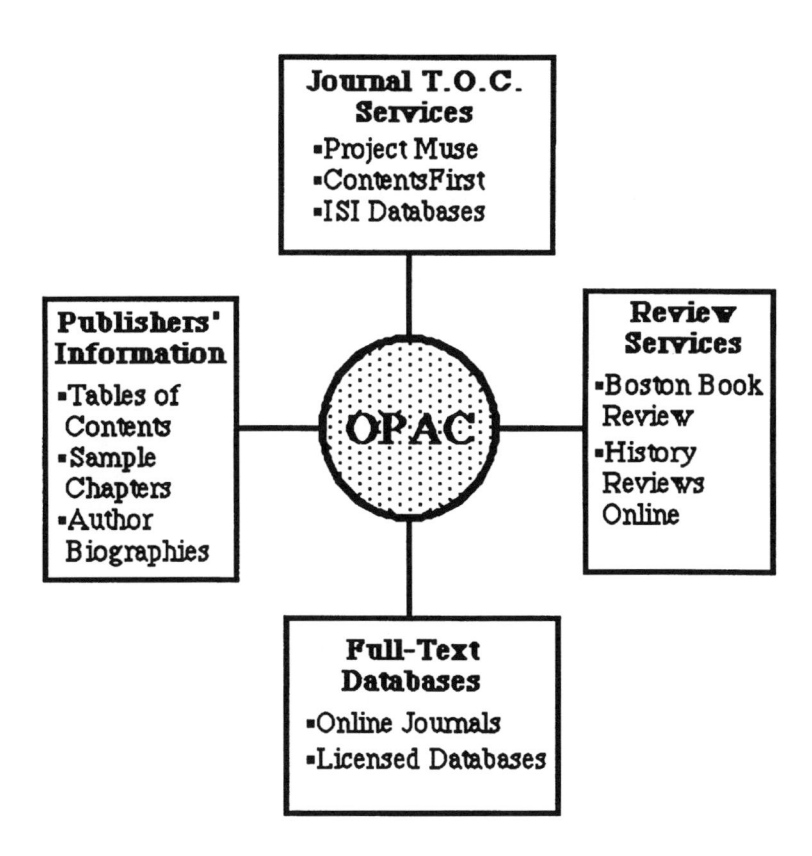

Figure 16. Existing and Potential Sources of Enriching, Linkable Information

What Are Users Doing in the Electronic Library?

By David A. Tyckoson and Trudi E. Jacobson
University at Albany, State University of New York

WHAT ARE USERS DOING IN THE ELECTRONIC LIBRARY?

The image of the electronic library has been well established in both the library and popular media. Fully networked, the electronic library contains a wide variety of databases, including bibliographic files, full text, graphics, sound, and video. Access is available from any workstation on campus and through modem and Internet connections. The electronic library is open for business 24 hours per day to anyone anywhere in the world with the proper login and password. Users do their own searching, downloading, and printing, and ask for assistance through email or interactive multimedia. The popular image of the electronic library is of a massive room full of spinning disk drives, flashing computers, and lots of wires. The librarians serve as database managers, hardware and software specialists, document delivery experts, multimedia Internet developers, and help desk gurus. The electronic library is totally designed to support the remote user. So who are all these people and what are they doing here?

For many of us, the electronic library is not some vague image of the future, but the reality of today. Online catalogs, research databases, full text files, Web pages, and interactive multimedia are already available as standard features of library services. Cornell University's Mann Library Gateway, Carnegie Mellon University's Project Mercury, and others have existed for many years. At the University at Albany, we have been making the transition from a print-based library to an electronic library for over a decade. Remote access has been available since 1978, when dial-up access was first provided to the old LCS circulation system.

Full catalog access has been provided since 1984. In 1994, remote access was expanded to the first research database (Expanded Academic Index) and as of spring 1996 there are 25 research databases available remotely through the catalog. In addition, faculty have had remote access to RLIN since 1987 and both students and faculty can search FirstSearch databases through Telnet or the online catalog. To reach Internet resources, Gopher was begun in 1994 (and eliminated in 1995) and World Wide Web access was instituted in 1995. And, of course, everyone is able to search other library catalogs around the world and a number of "free" services such as CARL UnCover.

In theory, this remote access allows users to perform many research functions without being required to come to the physical site of the library. One of the expectations of this type of access to the electronic library is that fewer users will physically enter the library building. As the University at Albany has evolved from the print to the electronic library, in-person use has indeed decreased. Table 1 demonstrates the on-site entrance count for the University Library during the months of September, October, and November for the past ten years. These months were selected because they represent the majority of the fall semester. August and December were excluded due to the varying dates of the beginning and ending of the semester over the years. In order to account for changes in enrollment, entrance counts have been normalized to an average use/hour based upon a standard enrollment of 16,000 students. According to this measure, since remote access was initially introduced the number of persons physically entering the library building has decreased by over 25%.

Table 1
University Library
On-Site Use Per Hour Based on Entrance Count
Fall Semester (September - November)

Year	Use/Hour	Enrollment	Adjusted Use/Hour
1995	267	16,053	266
1994	289	16,622	278
1993	302	16,759	288
1992	323	19,005	272
1991	332	18,807	282
1990	328	17,405	302
1989	321	16,628	309
1988	n/a	16,651	n/a
1987	358	16,219	353
1986	381	16,112	378

1988 use data is unavailable

Interviews with reference librarians who have served throughout this time period bear out this fact. When the library relied only upon a card catalog, users took much longer to find out about materials in the library collections. This often required several trips, as users accumulated their research information in a series of stages. With the electronic library, users can identify the majority of their information in a single search session and do not need to enter the library building as frequently.

The rise in remote access is also well documented in the rapid increase in dial-in access to the online catalog. Table 2 indicates catalog use over time. While total use of the catalog remains relatively stable, dial-up access has risen dramatically. Dial-up use began to take off during the 1990/1991 academic year. By 1992/1993, remote access was approaching 10% of all catalog use and the average user was searching the catalog remotely twelve times per year. Unfortunately, due to a migration to another online catalog, we do not have identical measures of catalog use since that time. Use data before 1994 is based on the number of system commands and use after 1994 is based on the number of login sessions. Using the number of search sessions logged on the catalog, remote use accounted for 15.3% of total use in the fall of 1994 and 18.1% of the total in the fall of 1995. Users are clearly migrating from on-site to remote use of the online catalog.

However, the fact that there are fewer individuals coming into the library does not mean that the value of the library as a campus resource has decreased. Other usage measures of the electronic library continue to rise, even with fewer persons on-site. Although not as many users are coming into the library, the circulation rate of library materials is higher than ever. Table 3 demonstrates University Library circulation trends over the past ten years. Since the borrowing of library materials is something that must still be done on-site (the University at Albany has no remote request and delivery services), the rapid growth in per capita circulation figures is a direct reflection of the success or failure of on-site use of the library. Most users do not borrow materials that they do not need for their research or study.

Based on that assumption, the increase in circulation per capita is directly related to an increased ability to find materials of interest in the library collections. An examination of the use of the University Library periodicals collection reveals similar re-

Table 2
University at Albany
Online Catalog Use
System Commands Executed

Year	Total Catalog Use	Dial-Up Use	% Dial-Up	Total Use per Capita	Dial-Up Use per Capita
92/93	2,949,250	228,496	7.7	155	12.0
91/92	2,987,947	178,631	6.0	159	9.5
90/91	2,932,269	140,335	4.8	168	8.1
89/90	3,008,338	18,148	0.6	181	1.1
88/89	2,847,079	12,394	0.4	172	0.75

Due to a change in online catalog systems, equivalent data is not available for more recent years. Based upon a sample of the sessions logged on the catalog, remote use accounted for 15.3% of all sessions during fall 1994 and 18.1% in fall 1995.

sults. On a per capita basis, usage has increased from a steady rate of approximately 14 uses per year (based on reshelving statistics) during the late 1980s to 27 uses per year in 1994/1995. Whether using books or journals, use per capita has more than doubled as we have moved from the print to the electronic library. Coupled with the fact that fewer trips are made to the library (as measured by the per hour on-site use figures), we can document that our users are much more efficient in their use of the electronic library than they were of the print-based library.

When users do come into the library, they are increasingly taking advantage of the ever-growing array of electronic resources available to them. Table 4 illustrates the growth in usage of electronic research databases (other than the online catalog) over time. On a per capita basis, users at the University at Albany currently average six CD-ROM sessions per year. The rapid increase in the use of these resources reflects several factors. While electronic resources continue to be extremely popular with our patrons, the University Library has also added workstations and databases over time to accommodate the growing user demands. This creates a circular cycle of demand in which additional workstations generate additional demand. The current configuration consists of seventeen workstations, nine of which are dedicated to the CD-ROM network, five of which are capable of connecting to the network as well as running as stand-alone machines, two of which are dedicated for stand-alone use, and one of which is reserved for staff. During peak use periods, in-house workstations are at capacity throughout the day, with users lining up to get onto a workstation. Users frequently will wait in line (or come back at another time) to use an electronic database rather than walk across the room to search its printed equivalent.

Since fall 1991, the Expanded Academic Index has been the general periodicals database of choice for the University Libraries. This single database replaced a number of Wilson files and is the database to which we refer users seeking information on popular topics or those who only desire a few citations for a research topic. It was originally available on CD-ROM and is now loaded as a file on the online catalog. By its second year, it was firmly established as our most popular electronic database. Academic Index consistently accounts for 20%-25% of total research database usage (see Table 4). Throughout its change in formats, the Academic Index has remained the favorite database of our users.

Table 4 also shows changes in the use of the ERIC and PsycLIT databases over time. These databases were selected for study because they have been available since the inception of electronic reference services in 1989. Surprisingly, usage per capita dropped initially. This is due to the fact that in the

Table 3
University Library
University at Albany
Circulation of Library Materials

Year	Circulation per Total Circulation	Circulation per Capita	Capita per Users per Hour (x 100)
94/95	367,130	22.1	7.9
93/94	240,277	14.3	5.0
92/93	235,865	12.4	4.6
91/92	240,819	12.8	4.5
90/91	228,609	13.1	4.3
89/90	227,565	13.7	4.4
88/89	221,417	13.4	n/a
87/88	210,280	13.0	3.7
86/87	206,842	12.8	3.3

Circulation per capita per hour represents the number of items borrowed per library user per hour that they physically spend in the building. Data for 1988/89 are not available.

early years of electronic research services, patrons were searching these databases for subjects for which no other electronic databases were currently available. As the University Libraries purchased a wider array of electronic databases, this auxiliary usage shifted to more appropriate sources. The recent increase in usage is reflective of the general increase in the use of CD-ROM databases.

The shift in user behavior from the print library to the electronic library is most clearly documented in the changing use patterns of research databases. As the use of electronic databases has increased, there has been a simultaneous drop in the use of the printed equivalent. Usage of printed indexes and abstracts is only 20% of its level before the advent of electronic databases. Most interestingly, the total usage of research databases (in both print and electronic format) is higher now than at any time in the past (see Table 5). Users today are three times as likely to search a journal indexing or abstracting service in any format than they were six years ago. Once again, users are making greater and more efficient use of the library in the electronic era than they were in the print-only era.

The University Libraries began offering remote access to research databases in the fall of 1994 with the addition of the Expanded Academic Index to the online catalog. True to the spirit of the electronic library, authorized users may search this file at any time of the day from any location in the world. Both dial-up and Internet access are provided. During the fall of 1995, use of the Expanded Academic Index accounted for 9% of all online catalog sessions. Unfortunately, it is impossible to determine the number of sessions that are currently done by remote users. In the fall of 1994, remote users accounted for 35% of all Academic Index searching. However, this number will have decreased significantly since April 1995 when we linked the CD-ROM network to this version of the Academic Index database. Because in-house users connect to Academic Index through the CD-ROM server, all in-house users are considered to be remote users by the online catalog server.

Beginning with the summer of 1995, the University Libraries have also provided remote access to all SilverPlatter databases installed on the ERL server. This allows authorized users outside the library to search 15 of the most popular research databases.

Table 4
University Library
On-Site CD-ROM Usage—Number of CD-ROM Sessions

Year	Total CD-ROM Usage / Per Capita Usage	ERIC Usage / Per Capita ERIC	PsycLIT Usage / Per Capita PsycLIT	Academic Index Usage / Per Capita Academic Index Usage
94/95	99,732	8,587	9,167	23,411
	6.0	0.52	0.55	1.4
93/94	90,050	7,333	8,233	22,307
	5.4	0.44	0.49	1.3
92/93	79,968	6,541	7,526	20,184
	4.2	0.34	0.40	1.1
91/92	62,517	9,147	7,837	5,436(*)
	3.3	0.49	0.42	0.29
90/91	45,272	9,255	8,052	n/a
	2.6	0.53	0.46	
89/90	11,183	n/a	n/a	n/a
	0.7			

(*) Academic Index was purchased in mid-year. 1991/1992 data is extrapolated from partial year data. n/a data not collected by database during 1989/1990.

Access is provided through menu selections from the online catalog, but the search software used is the standard SilverPlatter interface. This combination provides users with ease of access through the catalog, while retaining the power of the SilverPlatter search engine. Similar links are provided for the basic FirstSearch package of databases. In all, affiliated users may access 25 distinct databases through the online catalog. Unfortunately, usage data for this system is not available, since the statistical package included on the server is unable at this time to distinguish remote users. It is expected that as users become more aware of these options that remote use of these materials will rise in patterns similar to that demonstrated by the online catalog and Academic Index.

As the University Libraries have moved from the print to the electronic library, our users have adapted their research habits accordingly. Users make fewer trips to the library and are more productive during those trips. They search a larger number of research databases and they find more of the materials that they need. Some users search the library databases remotely, although the vast majority continue to do so on-site. Regardless of where the searching takes place, users still need to come into the library to find the original documents. At this stage in our evolution, we have expedited the searching for citations. Making the original books and articles available remotely will need to be the next step in our progress if we want to achieve the popular vision of the electronic library. What users are doing in the electronic library is finding what they need—faster and more efficiently than ever before.

Table 5
Electronic vs. Print Index Usage

Year	Print Index Usage (volumes reshelved)	CD-ROM Usage (sessions)	Total Research Database Usage	Total per Capita Research Database Usage
94/95	6,059	99,732	105,791	6.4
93/94	10,102	90,050	100,152	6.0
92/93	15,618	79,968	95,586	5.0
90/91	19,919	45,272	65,191	3.7
89/90	26,915	11,183	38,098	2.3

WHAT ARE USERS DOING IN THE ELECTRONIC LIBRARY?

It is clear from our data that users are accepting the concept of the electronic library and are migrating towards its use, whether on-site or remotely. But are they successful users of these electronic resources? To measure patron reaction to electronic resources, librarians at the University at Albany have been involved in two user studies, one focusing on CD-ROM searching and one on Internet use. They both present an interesting snapshot of user behaviors. Some of the results will confirm what many suspect, other results may dismay, and some might be labeled intriguing.

The first research study, funded by the Spencer Foundation, examined the effect of instruction and assistance on the search strategies of CD-ROM users. The study of 675 patrons during the spring of 1994 was designed to find out what type of impact classes and one-on-one assistance from librarians had on end-user search proficiency. We hypothesized that the sophisticated searchers would be patrons who had attended searching classes or who had previously been directly assisted by librarians. We expected that they would use more Boolean operators, field searches, and referrals to previous search terms than end-users who had no assistance or instruction. Along with collecting the surveys, we also collected 675 search printouts from SilverPlatter databases, giving us considerable insight into how patrons construct searches.

While more detailed information is available in the January 1996 issue of College & Research Libraries, we present here some highlights of the results from that study. Faculty do the highest percentage of searches using incorrect or no search operators (the term search operators is defined as encompassing Boolean operators, field searches, and referrals to previous search terms). University staff and graduate students performed the most searches that were of high or of moderate skill level. Undergraduate percentages were fairly consistent: about 30% fell into the three lower categories of no or incorrect operator use, low and moderate level, but only 13% performed searches at the highest level of skill. (See Table 6) Despite the small sample size in some categories, these results are revealing.

Neither age nor sex showed a relationship with search skill. Nor did experience in online catalog searching, use of interactive learning software, online database searching, and electronic mail. Previous search experience also did not indicate higher skill level: 31% of brand new CD-ROM users either used no operators or used them incorrectly, compared to 26% of those who had searched 6 times or more. And 19% of new users showed the highest skill level, compared to 20% of the most experienced searchers.

How did previous instruction or one-on-one assistance affect search skill? While 27% of uninstructed searchers showed a low skill level, so did 21% of those who had received instruction. But a quarter of those receiving instruction or assistance performed searches using a high skill level, contrast-

Table 6
User Groups by CD-ROM Search Skill Level

	None or Incorrect Use	Low Skill Level	Moderate Skill Level	High Skill Level	Total
Faculty	10 45.5%	2 9.0%	6 27.3%	4 18.2%	22 100%
Staff	4 26.7%	2 13.3%	5 33.3%	4 26.7%	15 100%
Graduate	77 21.6%	77 21.6%	121 34.0%	81 22.8%	356 100%
Undergraduate	77 28.3%	84 30.9%	76 27.9%	35 12.9%	272 100%

ing with just 14% who had no instruction. We found a significant but weak relationship between search skill level and instruction. (See Table 7)

The second study, undertaken during January and February 1995, surveyed 96 Internet users in the library to determine the effects of demographic characteristics and prior Internet experience on the use of Internet resources and its perceived usefulness. An article is in press that contains more detailed information than what we will present here. Just over half the respondents were undergraduates, followed by graduate students (36%) and faculty (6%). The highest percentage, 60%, were affiliated with the social sciences. These figures mirror our student population. The figure that did not reflect our user population was gender-related. Seventy percent of those surveyed were male, while just 30% were female.

A full 97% of respondents found the Internet useful, although only 45% agreed or strongly agreed that they can find most of their research/assignment needs on the Internet. Only 4% agreed or strongly agreed that the Internet is totally useless. However, we were surveying those who had made a point of accessing the Internet; this result would be different if we were surveying our students at large. We inquired about browsing versus searching (using search tools) behaviors. Just under half used tools such as Veronica, Jughead or Web search engines, compared to 20% who felt browsing was an effective way to identify resources. However, many people responded neutrally to the questions about searching vs. browsing, indicating they were unclear about how they were finding information (or about the question!) or that different methods of finding resources work at different times.

A majority of those surveyed did not use Usenet groups, listservs, in-house distribution lists or e-mail to experts to advance their research. But 57% found Internet search tools a useful way to find book and article citations. Since we specifically were not surveying those searching any bibliographic databases, we wonder whether the results of this query indicate users were knowledgeable about other Internet-based tools or whether they were uncertain about the question.

Our respondents were using the Internet to find a variety of types of resources. Seventy-six percent were after full-text documents, 58% retrieved graphics, 56% abstracts/citations, and 47% software. Faculty did not deem the Internet as important to their research as did undergraduate and graduate students, but of the three groups they felt most strongly that Internet search tools were a useful way to find bibliographic citations.

Since this study was undertaken, Internet use has exploded, as have the resources available. We would be interested in comparing results of a new study to the results of the 1995 study, and may undertake such a project. We also encourage other institutions to do the same.

Table 7
Cross-tabulation of Training by Skill Level

	None or Incorrect Use	Low Skill Level	Moderate Skill Level	High Skill Level	Total
Ever-trained	56 19.5%	60 20.9%	98 34.1%	73 25.4%	287 99.9%
Never-trained	116 29.9%	106 27.3%	111 28.6%	55 14.2%	388 100%
Total	172 25.5%	166 24.6%	209 31.0%	128 19.0%	675

Chi-Square 22.4
df=3, p<.05

CONCLUSIONS

What users are doing in the library is making faster and more efficient use of information resources. They make fewer trips to the physical building and are slowly but surely increasing their remote usage. Since the advent of electronic databases, patrons are making greater use of databases than at any time in the past. The total usage of print and electronic resources is far greater than it had been for print alone. Based on circulation and reshelving statistics, users are also finding more original documents than in the past. Despite the fact that they make fewer trips to the library, they are reading twice as many journals and checking out more than twice as many books as they did before.

Unfortunately, while users are certainly searching our electronic information systems, they are not taking full advantage of the capabilities of those systems. The majority of users still perform simple and/or inappropriate searches and do not realize or understand that there are more sophisticated search tools available. For our users to become fully involved in the electronic library, we need to:

promote awareness of electronic resources. Users are highly satisfied with the databases that they have searched, yet there are many other databases that remain underutilized. We need to ensure that users in all subject fields are aware of the sources in the electronic library that will best meet their needs.

provide more instruction on the use of the electronic library. Our users are aware that the electronic library exists, now we need to teach them how to use it productively.

develop more effective instructional methods. Traditional teaching methods are not always appropriate for electronic databases, especially when the user is accessing these databases from a remote site. We need to provide a variety of instructional programs that will match the learning styles of our users.

work with faculty to increase understanding. Unfortunately, faculty are often the last ones to adapt to the electronic library. By involving the faculty in the electronic library, we not only will improve their ability to conduct their own research but will improve the chance that they will pass that information on to their students.

continue our measurement of and research on user behaviors. We are going through a time of great change in how we provide information to our users, which is in turn significantly changing how they find it. We need to continually monitor trends in usage patterns in order to keep ourselves on track through this period in our evolution. We need to study not only how often users search electronic databases, but how they go about the search process. Monitoring user behavior will be the key to assessing the success or failure of the electronic library.

The electronic library is here and our users are definitely in it. What they are doing with it is the key for future development.

The Changing Face of Research

Literary Texts and the Internet

By Nancy Down
Bowling Green State University

During the past twenty years a number of primary literary texts have become available through the Internet. Due to the efforts of various individuals and institutions, such well known works as Shakespeare's plays, Jane Austen's novels, Emily Dickinson's poems, and a variety of other literary creations (which are in the public domain) can be found on various gophers and Web sites. These electronic literary texts are often the results of specific projects, usually connected with a particular individual and/or institution. These projects vary in their philosophies and purposes, their conceptions of the audiences they hope to reach, their principles of selection, the degree to which they mark up the texts, and their documentation of these texts. While it is impossible to examine every project at this time, I would like to look at some examples to give some idea of the similarities and variations among them.

On one end of the spectrum is Project Gutenberg. Project Gutenberg, which was started in 1971 by Michael Hart, takes as its mission "to make information, books and other materials available to the general public in forms a vast majority of the computers, programs, and people can easily read, use, quote, and search." Texts are added every month and by the year 2001 Project Gutenberg hopes to offer 10,000 books in its electronic library. Texts are chosen to fit into three categories: "heavy Literature," "light literature," and reference. Thus Project Gutenberg offers everything from almanacs and dictionaries to Shakespeare and the Bible to *Peter Pan* and *Alice In Wonderland*.

These electronic texts are made available in the simplest, easiest electronic forms to use. Therefore, the texts are created and distributed in "Plain Vanilla ASCII" (i.e. the same kind of characters you read on a printed page). This form of ASCII was specifically chosen because "99% of the hardware and software a person is likely to run into can read and search these files." For the same reason, no markup or tagging system is used with these texts. Project Gutenberg does not create "authoritative editions" and, therefore, seldom documents its texts. The philosophy of the Project has been that "once an electronic text is created in Plain Vanilla ASCII, it is the foundation for as many editions as anyone could hope to do in the future."[1]

Project Gutenberg's selection and presentation of texts is guided by its conception of its audience: 99% of the general public. It seeks to appeal to both the low and high end of this audience, to both the individual using a computer for the first time and to the scholar at his or her workstation. And, likewise, texts are chosen that will appeal to a general reading public.

Another project which seeks to be as all encompassing as Gutenberg, but for a different audience, is the Oxford Text Archive. The Archive "exists to serve the interests of the academic community by providing low-cost archival and dissemination facilities for electronic texts." Since 1976, it has managed non-commercial distribution of electronic texts and information about them on behalf of hundreds of users world-wide. In its catalog of over 1500 titles, the Archive contains electronic versions of the literary works of major authors in Greek, Latin, English, and a dozen or more other languages. The texts come from a variety of sources and vary greatly in their accuracy and the features which have been encoded. Some texts have been extensively tagged and others simply designed to mimic the appearance of the printed source. However, all texts which are publicly available from the Archive's FTP server are first converted to a standard format which conforms to the recommendations of the Text Encoding Initiative.[2]

The Oxford Text Archive, like Project Gutenberg, bases its selection and presentation of texts on its concept of the Archive's audience; in this case, a worldwide academic community. Scholars want to know what version of a text they are using and the Archive seeks to provide adequate documentation. The Archive will also select multiple editions or versions of a work for inclusion in its electronic repository.

Another project that provides electronic literary texts is Project Bartleby, begun in January 1993 by Columbia University. The audience Project Bartleby creates texts for is, as with Project Gutenberg, the general public. For, as the Bartlebian Principles of Electronic Publishing state, "allowing freedom of choice to great literature and reference materials is the foundation of any public library—supporting research, building literacy, and abetting democracy." Texts are chosen based on a variety of criteria including their use in educational settings, availability of extant authoritative editions that will not be superseded in print, regard for the author's place in intellectual history, fairness to alternative authors, and, above all, a fundamental love for the literary value of the work. Thus, Project Bartleby includes among its texts such works as George Chapman's translation of *The Odysseys of Homer*, W. E. B. Du Bois' *The Souls of Black Folk*, and William Strunk's *The Elements of Style* (1918 ed.). Each text is accompanied by a bibliographic record clearly identifying the edition of the work. For instance, we can tell that the electronic version of Emily Dickinson's *Poems* is the 1896 text edited by Mabel Loomis Todd and that Walt Whitman's *Leaves of Grass* is the 1900 version.[3]

Other electronic text projects focus on a particular genre or literary period or on an individual author. One example of a project of this kind is the Victorian Women Writers Project at Indiana University. The focus of this project is to produce "highly accurate, SGML-encoded transcriptions of literary works by British women writers in the late Victorian period." Included with each text is a header describing fully the source text, editorial decisions, and the resulting computer files. One of the great values of this Project is that many of these works, such as Mathilde Blind's *The Heather On Fire* and Helen Taylor's *The Claim of Englishwomen to the Suffrage Constitutionally Considered*, cannot readily be found elsewhere.[4]

Another category of electronic literary text projects are the increasing number of Web sites created by and/or for literature courses at individual institutions. An example of this project is the site developed as part of an American Literature class held during the Spring of 1995 at the University of Texas at Austin.[5] Such sites include electronic versions of the texts, student comments and analysis of them, student papers, class assignments and reading lists, and links to other useful sites. These course-related sites are challenging and changing our traditional modes of scholarly communication.

As we have seen in this survey of electronic text projects, literary works on the Internet vary a great deal in the extent bibliographic information is provided for them. In the past, many scholars held the notion that for any one work there must be just one text, an "ideal" text that the editor felt was closest to the author's intentions. Textual critics today more often hold the view that there is not just one text but many texts produced by the author in the process of composition and many texts produced by printers and others in the process of publication.[6] Therefore, bibliographic identification of any one text becomes increasingly important.

The case of Emily Dickinson's *Poems* provides us with a good example of multiple texts. Dickinson did not publish a volume of poems during her lifetime, though she did publish a few individual poems in newspapers and magazines and included copies of certain poems in letters to friends. She collected her handwritten manuscripts together in fascicles or booklets and often included variant words or phrases to individual lines in the margins of these manuscripts.

The first published editions of Dickinson's poetry, edited by her friend Mabel Loomis Todd in the 1890s, were full of editorial interference. For example, it was not until Thomas H. Johnson's 1955 edition that the poet's dashes, capitals and misspellings were restored in place of the earlier editions' decorous Victorian publication. Then, in 1981 R. W. Franklin published facsimiles of Dickinson's own manuscript "books," showing in footnotes her variants or alternative readings for her poems.

Depending upon which edition of the *Poems* you are reading, individual poems may vary. One example is the poem "Safe in their Alabaster Chambers." In manuscript this poem consists of four stanzas, three of which are alternative second stanzas to go with the first verse. Dickinson published two versions of this poem during her lifetime, each with a different second stanza. The version that Mabel Loomis Todd included in the 1890 *Poems*, the version that has become canonical, contains three stanzas. This poem is one, then, that Dickinson herself never contemplated even as a variant of her original poem.[7] As this example illustrates, identifying the version of the poem or of any text is often critical to our analysis and understanding of that text.

Every day more and more literary texts are being added to the Internet. As we have seen, these texts vary from project to project in their presentation and documentation. To make these texts usable for both a general reading public and a worldwide community of scholars some standards must exist. We need to know what edition or version of a text we are copying or reading. The value of electronic literary texts is not so much that we can sit and read them at our computer, but that we can manipulate the data they contain in various ways. We can link them to other intellectual endeavors like a course syllabus or student papers. We can give access to texts that are normally kept in archives or special collections. Electronic texts on the Internet may potentially change our ideas about and ways of doing literary scholarship.

ENDNOTES

1. Project Gutenberg. http:jg.cso.uiuo.edu/PG/welcome.html (25 January 1996).
2. Oxford Text Archive. ftp://black.ox.ac.uk/pub/ata (25 January 1996).
3. Project Bartleby. http://www.cc.columbia.edu/acis/bartleby (25 January 1996).
4. Victorian Women Writers. http://www.indiana.edu/~letrs/vwwp/ (25 January 1996).
5. American Literature Spring 1995. http://auden.fac.utexas.edu/~daniel/amlt/amlit.html (25 January 1996).
6. Peter M.W. Robinson, "Redefining Critical Editions," in *The Digital Word: Text-Based Computing in the Humanities*, edited by George E. Landow and Paul Delaney (Cambridge, MA: MIT Press, 1993), pp. 272–273.
7. Timothy Morris, "'My thought is undressed': Some Theoretical Implications of the Texts of Dickinson's Poems," *Resources for American Literary Study* 20, no. 2 (1994): pp. 210–211.

Scholars as Bibliographic Specialists: A Probe Pointing to a Partnership

By Clark Elliott
Massachusetts Institute of Technology (formerly at Harvard University)

BACKGROUND

Archivists and historians in the early 1990s came to recognize their increasing alienation and consequently created a study group to address the problem. From the researchers' side came the assertion that "the kind of history that historians now do would be enriched by renewing the partnership that once existed between historians and archivists. And... that the work of archivists would be strengthened by a serious reengagement with the historical community...." Similar sentiments were expressed by the archivists involved.

A disjunctive relationship between librarians and historians also is apparent. A recent summation and assessment of these relations in regard to research methods pointed to the reliance of researchers on footnote references, knowledgeable colleagues, and the like, following "a kind of informed serendipity that has its own logic," often not using the abstracts, indexes, and bibliographies that are the first line of reference for librarians. Descriptions of the information-seeking activities of historians and librarians reveal the contextual orientation of the researcher's inquiry compared to the isolated item of inquiry that characterizes the approach of the reference librarian.

This paper poses the question of how librarians and archivists can find common ground with the scholars for whom services and collections are intended. More specifically, this larger question is explored by searching for means by which to understand and maintain the linkages between the context of subject matter and resource information that are provided by historians in their work, so that it carries into the tools of scholarly access and informs the collection building and appraisal activities of librarians and archivists. There are no royal roads to this goal, but the rock bed will be built on an understanding of the ways of researchers.

CASE STUDY

In order to address the range of concerns outlined above, I have examined fifty monographs published during the last quarter century that relate to the broad area of history of science, religion, and the environment in the United States. I observed no chronological restrictions but excluded biographies, volumes of collected essays by multiple authors, theses; I included not more than one work by any author. Not all works included all three aspects of the broad area of concern, but overall the focus was intellectual history, the interplay of values, perceptions, and concepts in relation to the physical environment through American history.

A brief characterization of representative titles (and therefore the topical range of the study) will help to set the background for what follows. Roderick Nash, *The Rights of Nature: A History of Environmental Ethics* (1989) and Jon Roberts, *Darwinism and the Divine in America: Protestant Intellectuals and Organic Evolution, 1859–1900* (1988) are works representing secular and religious dimensions of human relations to nature and to science. David Miller, *Dark Eden: The Swamp in Nineteenth-Century American Culture* (1989) is an approach to attitudes through literature and to some degree through art. The conceptually difficult area of the historic correlations of human attitudes to, relations with, and effects on nature are seen in Carolyn Merchant, *Ecological Revolutions: Nature, Gender, and Science in New England* (1989). Gregg Mitman, *The*

State of Nature: Ecology, Community, and American Social Thought, 1900–1950 (1992) is a work on history of science that shows the inter-relations of the study of nature and social attitudes. J. Ronald Engel, *Sacred Sands: The Struggle for Community in the Indiana Dunes* (1983) envelops public values, politics, and the environment as played out in a regional context. Herbert Leventhal, *In the Shadow of the Enlightenment: Occultism and Renaissance Science in Eighteenth Century America* (1976) was chosen to represent the uncertain historic boundaries between science and other ways of knowing the world, while Robert Fuller, *Ecology of Care: An Interdisciplinary Analysis of the Self and Moral Obligation* (1992), though not so specifically historical, is a work that draws on science, philosophy, and religion to plot an ethic for relating both to the physical and human environments.

What I have sought in examining these works are two things: 1) the character and structure of the bibliographic platforms on which each of the works rests, and 2) self-conscious and deliberate commentary by the authors on their experiences in the research and writing of their books. To do this, I have looked specifically at the preface, acknowledgment, introduction, and bibliography of each work where they were present. For a very small sample of ten works, I have examined twenty-five footnotes from each, where I was interested chiefly in the overall character of the sources used.

From this study, what picture emerges of the research experience and its bibliographic product? Two-thirds of the works included separate bibliographies, most often containing some type of subdivisions or presented in the form of an essay (the latter characterizing ten works). In some cases, the essay or bibliographic listing, by its organization, gave what one author called a "conceptual framework" for the book's topic. In another case, the author characterized the bibliography as "the fullest available inventory of literature dealing with science and religion in the later nineteenth century...." Sometimes the bibliographies referred to other published bibliographies as sources for further study. In at least one case the author pointed to the bibliographies in other monographic works, which "lead the reader to an abundant selection of thoughtfully chosen primary and secondary sources," an observation that endorses the approach I am pursuing in this paper.

The examination of authors' bibliographies supports the contention that they are among the most carefully crafted means available for the comprehension and further exploration of a topic, often a very substantial one. Though conceived in the embrace of a research experience, and born in the final process of writing, they often represent the most informed guide to resources on a topic and have value whether or not one reads the work within which the bibliography is embedded. It is important, nonetheless, that one knows the parentage, the context of creation, even if one does not know it intimately as a reader of the book, and these concerns are addressed briefly below in considering the question of access.

I turn now to the second part of the purpose for examining these fifty works—to uncover clues that authors give that help to understand their research experience and particularly how that experience relates to the characteristics of resources. This necessarily must be rather episodic, based as it is on ferreting out statements lodged in a preface, acknowledgment, bibliographic essay, or an introductory note to a bibliographic listing. First, however, there is the less self-consciously presented evidence that authors leave, as disclosed in their footnote references. I examined a small sample of 250 footnotes (in which there were 441 references) as a window on the overall character of the documentation. As historical research, the main categories for citations were primary and secondary. In my sample, approximately fifty-eight percent of all the items referenced were classifiable as primary sources, defining "primary" very broadly as contemporary with, or composed by an observer or participant in, the events. About twenty percent of those primary items were unpublished, while more than half were books (including reprints) or articles. Of the secondary works referenced, more than half were books and about one third were scholarly or scientific articles. The smallness of this citation study precludes any generalizations likely to hold. What I have discovered, in fact, is a variety of citation patterns, from one work to another, but no great surprises insofar as the sources themselves are concerned. This group of scholars used a wide range of items but almost all were categorically familiar to librarians and archivists.

The bibliographic expertise that scholars bring to the enterprise of access and collection development is more than advice on the value of individual items or specified bodies of sources. Though not as common as hoped, the boundary regions of texts—the front and back matter, where programmatic or retrospective statements can be made—do give an author an opportunity to reflect on the research experience and thus give guidance to other scholars, librarians, and archivists. In the wake of publication of his *Beauty, Health, and Permanence: Environmental Politics in the United States, 1955–1985* (1987), historian Samuel P. Hays wrote a notable article for the *Journal of American History* that gave a first-hand account of his research experience in relation to the source materials and aimed to plot means by which that material could be identified and brought into the domain of libraries and archival repositories. This deliberate awareness of the relations between sources and scholarship, and the potential for partnership, appears less conspicuously in the monographic literature on a routine if not systematic basis.

Every librarian and archivist who feels professionally unappreciated should regularly scan the acknowledgments in scholarly monographs. They are, as one author praises, "behind the scenes of every book . . . those great organizers of information and text." Heartening as such recognition is, however, as often as not librarians have to settle for relative invisibility in the research enterprise, to take pride in the process through an awareness of the product.

To read authors' reflective statements on their research is to understand, as well, that libraries and archives are only a part and not the whole of the universe of resources. In the fifty monographs examined, there is fairly frequent reference to, and acknowledgment of, the loan or gift of books and provision of information by friends, colleagues, and other individuals, that aided in research. One scholar thanks a librarian, who "allowed me full access to his bibliography and notes . . . , saving me additional months of searching," an instance of recognition of a librarian-scholar who was fully acculturated to the service function at the heart of the academic information professions.

Access to private files, including those of participants in historical events, as well as references to interviews are not uncommon acknowledgments by scholars. It is in these circumstances that a two-way relation between scholars and librarians comes fully into view. Scholars' contacts can and do lead to the deposit of papers and of oral history recordings in repositories, where they become part of publicly available resources for further study.

Historical scholarship means immersion both in a topic and in its sources. I propose that the research phase features the sources, while the ethos of scholarly writing submerges the source as the story rises to the surface of consciousness and objectivity becomes the dominant value. Historian J. H. Hexter has set forth the idea of "the second record, which is everything that historians bring to their confrontation with the record of the past." This "second record" is both a benefit to research and a problem, to be used but also kept within restricted bounds. The nature of some of the historical studies encountered in this project were such that they necessitated certain types of sources more in the way of personal development of the historian than as direct documentary underpinning. They were part of the deliberately sought experience by the researcher that gave insight and sympathy a role.

Environmental historians express this in terms of developing a sense of the land and the environment, sometimes quite deliberately. For example, William Cronon, in his ecological study of colonial New England asserted that "The best way for a modern historian to bring . . . [an ecological] perspective to the documents is to get out and walk the landscape: no amount of library work can replace the field experience. . . . " Historians dealing with group movements or what are counter-cultural activities make similar claims. For example, David Harrell, in studying post-World War II healing and charismatic activities, was present at one hundred or more revival meetings, even though he was not sympathetic with their underlying premises. In this context, he argued the difficulty of judging "the quality of a charismatic ministry without witnessing the evangelist at work," but he also pointed to periodical literature as the "most important single source of information." What Harrell seems to suggest is the value of oral sources for an understanding of the nature and quality of a phenomenon, while the print literature best divulges what happened.

The contribution of different media to historical study is an important question but also characterized by subtlety and nuance. It may be best not to look for certainty here, but only for instances. Art historian Barbara Novak, in her book *Nature and Culture: American Landscape and Painting, 1825–1875*, addresses some of the issues involved in using both visual and written sources, expressing a concern that the art be given the "primary reading," to avoid impressing on the art perspectives from other cultural sources. There is here a certain self-protective stance but it suggests as well that, while visual sources are documentation, they take special care to insulate them from the prior experiences of the interpreter.

John Canup's comments on his study of nature and civilization in colonial New England suggests another perspective on the relations of written text to other cultural manifestations. By a close reading of a category of literature, he found that "the language that New England's intellectuals used to express their ambivalent impressions of their own Americanization" contradicts the more positive view of historians who emphasize "material culture," and economic and political practices and organization.

Despite their revelatory value in understanding the research experience, one has to bring a certain caution or hesitancy to the reading of prefatory and other such book matter. Some of the most interesting commentary on sources are found in areas outside the traditional collecting by research libraries. Samuel Hays' article in the *Journal of American History* is significant, in part, because it points to the need to collect aggressively in new ways in order to understand modern political movements. Among the works examined for this project, Ronald Numbers' study of creation scientists uncovered a vast body of resources, much in private hands. But the small citation study reported here, and an impression from considering the entire group of fifty monographs, is a reminder that much of what scholars use, especially in established areas of study, is taken for granted, is reported bibliographically, but does not so often lead to a discussion of the nature of the sources. My point is that, in considering the state and direction of a research area, we have to look at the body of work produced and not only at those that are eccentric to the general direction or overall state of the field.

Before concluding this section of the paper, I want to point to another type of particularly interesting insight, on the relations of historical study and its sources, that one can find in authors' reflections on their work. Lee Mitchell's *Witnesses to a Vanishing America* is a study of developing concern in the nineteenth century for the loss of the original land and culture. To find this sentiment, so contrary to the usual view of an American manifest destiny, Mitchell had to look at a great variety of sources. But the particularly striking conclusion is that writing, painting, photography, and other activities both revealed the preservation sentiment and were themselves attempts to preserve for the future what the authors, artists, and other creators sensed was to be lost. In this and other places the historians whose works I have studied show an awareness of the need not only to tap a source but also to incorporate into their research a sense and knowledge of the circumstances of that source's creation. Scholars are creators of historical context, as they reveal and reconstruct the past. But in a somewhat different though related sense, this also is the work of archivists and librarians, who organize and describe sources by the identities of their creators and the circumstances of their production.

CONCLUSIONS

Where, then, does this excursion through a body of scholarly literature lead? First of all, librarians, researchers, and publishers—the players in the field of scholarly communication—need to work toward taking more seriously the bibliographical insights and products that appear in the monographic literature. Cataloging practice, including the MARC record, makes the presence of a bibliography part of the cataloging product but, so far as I have observed, this is for descriptive purposes only. It is listed along with the book's index in a content note. The motivation is not to relate the availability of the bibliography to its subject or to promote access to it as means to a larger informational end. The recent trend in cataloging practice is to make no distinction between foot- or end-notes and the bibliography or bibliographic essay. As of 1989, Library of Congress practice was changed to refer to notes and bibliographies by the generic and sometimes misleading term of "bibliographical references." This regrettable retrogression should be reconsidered in light of the great value that the bibliographies in monographs could have as a means of access to the literature of a field. If anything, the description of such bibliographies should be expanded to include not only their given titles but, as appropriate, to indicate their subdivisions, which will often indicate, for example, the types of materials listed, or will give a more detailed subject breakdown. Furthermore, it would be of benefit to scholarship if technical services librarians would work with publishers and with the editors of reference tools such as *The Chicago*

Manual of Style to standardize the form and titles of book bibliographies. Such a procedure would recognize that reference to the bibliography in a cataloging record is a contribution to access to the sources for a subject of study and not for purposes of describing the host monograph alone.

The H. W. Wilson Company's *Bibliographic Index*, with coverage since 1937, includes references to book bibliographies, and a number of the works in this study are accessible through that means. There is, however, the inherent problem of consulting multiple volumes in a serially released reference work. The concerns addressed here are related as well to issues of citation indexing. *Arts & Humanities Citation Index* and *Social Sciences Citation Index*, however, analyze citations and bibliographies chiefly in articles rather than in monographs. Furthermore, the concept of the citation index has the implication of retrieving items, generally those that are tied to specific points in a text. What is proposed in this paper is developing access to bodies of inter-related sources rather than to specific works.

The electronic and online environment suggest new possibilities. One, of course, is to assure that the bibliography note field in a MARC record, augmented and standardized to reveal the true character of the bibliography, is a searchable field in conjunction with the descriptive cataloging and subject analysis of the book. Matthew Gilmore and Donald Case recognized in 1992 that the increasing dependence of publishers on authors' manuscripts received in electronic form would allow not only more efficient but different forms of publication. They suggested that "citations and abstracts may be stripped out of the full text" for supplemental use. I would endorse this idea though suggesting a more genteel and deliberate approach. Working cooperatively, publishers, scholars, and librarians could acquire from authors summaries of their works, and the projected electronic resource would be limited to bibliographic essays or separately listed bibliographies rather than foot- or end-note references. Such separation and replication of part of a book in conjunction with an author-prepared abstract, tied to the work's cataloging record, would open a previously hidden scholarly treasure to the kind of directive or mediating role in subsequent scholarship that it so much deserves. Whether this would reside in an online public catalog or in a separate database is open to discussion.

Finally, what can be said from the examination of the front matter and other reports on the research experience that appear in the monographic literature? Hopefully, this paper has succeeded in indicating something of the richness, and occasional wisdom, that resides there. Authors might be encouraged more often to combine some of the insights revealed in a preface with the bibliographies that conclude their works, thus making them accessible as a component of the distribution process outlined above. Book reviewers (generally other scholars) should be encouraged to look more carefully at these parts and to report more critically on the research base and the resources used in writing, in addition to their expected attention to what might seem the more substantive aspects of the work. As for librarians and archivists, they need to become activist readers of authors' commentaries and reports on their research experiences, tapping them for insights on how to improve access to and the development of research collections. In reading, they also should note resources not used and consider whether they are absent because access systems failed to bring them to the attention of the scholar.

Jane Rosenberg, assistant director for the Reference Materials Program at the National Endowment for the Humanities, among others, has promoted the need for librarians to know "the specialist's research habits," while recognizing "that research is both a complex and an extremely individualized process." Whatever their motivation, and however narrowly it sometimes seems, researchers open many windows on the house of scholarship as they sit to write the words that are their books' ends. For the activist librarian and archivist, they are doors as well, a way to enter and to wander through the ever-growing and constantly reconfigured edifice of scholarship. The more one wanders, the more there is a feeling of belonging, a common home for both academic information specialists and the scholars they serve.

Understanding Research Agendas: Explanations for Change and the Library Response

By Dan C. Hazen
Harvard University

Academic libraries, whose possibilities and priorities are in many ways determined by factors beyond their control, are dependent institutions. This, however, is not the whole story. Libraries also have specific responsibilities to fulfill, placing them in a constant tension between mandate and means, expectation and possibility. The process is all too familiar in the individual repositories where we do our work. But academic libraries also play a collective or corporate role in the process of scholarly communication. Here, too, they balance between dependence and autonomy.

The interplay between authority, accountability, and resources shapes how libraries function in the present and how they prepare for the future. We librarians need to understand as fully as possible the nature of our institutions' freedom and dependence, the actors and agents upon whom we rely and who rely on us, and the dynamics that affect all of these players. This essay first probes the academic library's situation at the levels of both specific institutions and the more general structure of scholarly communication. It then addresses the changes—within and also outside of scholarship—that are altering and perhaps transforming these frameworks. The concluding section, which builds from our analytical backdrop, suggests how we might most effectively assess information needs in a few broad fields. It also contrasts that hypothetical process with the motives and rhetoric behind some of our current efforts to reshape the library world.

Our goal is to understand better the spheres within which we operate. Awareness should help us to gauge the library's responsibilities, roles, and room for initiative. It may also suggest the consequences of decisions that have not been properly framed. In other words, this paper focuses on the political and ideological aspects of our enterprise. The discussion, more theoretical than empirical, should help to elucidate decisions already made and also prepare us for those yet to come.

I. BOSSES AND BOUNDARIES: THE DETERMINANTS OF LIBRARY LIFE

Many forces shape the possibilities of each academic library. The impacts vary in their focus and intensity. Perhaps most obviously, every library is sited within a college or university that exercises administrative and fiscal control. Physical plants, staffing levels, and overall funding all reflect decisions made by the parent institution. Institutional priorities for curricula and research determine the library's subject specializations and strengths. Academic communities tend to be more collegial than this stark outline might suggest: advisory groups and broadly consultative processes commonly inform their policies and allocations. Nonetheless, the library's destiny is in a fundamental sense controlled from without.

Forces external to the university also have an effect. Libraries consume research resources and scholarly information. As the so-called "serials crisis" reveals, they may have as little say as any other kind of consumer when it comes to packaging and price. They similarly more often follow than lead in developing new information technologies. Many library operations involve products originating somewhere else.

The library's dependence on scholarship is apparent in more central ways, too. Libraries acquire, organize, project, and preserve the recorded knowledge deemed necessary by scholars. Deciding what to provide in turn reflects how studies are pursued within each academic field, as well as the particular concerns of local clienteles. The library can help shape academic inquiry through its patterns of support. The disciplines themselves establish the basic priorities.

Voluntary commitments may also limit the library. Even such straightforward endeavors as cataloging through an online bibliographic utility require conformity to preordained and sometimes complicated procedures. Emerging structures for cooperative collection development and shared resources may likewise inject extramural obligations.

Finally, such less tangible considerations as image and psychology play a role. Most libraries have developed their own sense of history and strengths, a sense which informs the institutional mood and mission. Identities can have an enduring impact. On the most homely level, librarians are as susceptible as anyone else to fashion and fad. Conformity is often the rule, and opinion all too easily overpowers objectivity.

All these broad forces shape each and every academic library, its collections and its services. Three of them are particularly pertinent to the current inquiry. The library's basic mission of supporting local research and teaching connects it to the academic disciplines represented within the parent institution. This mandate also requires close contact with flesh-and-blood users. Available resources are a third critical piece. The interplay of these elements, all external to the library, establishes the sphere within which each one can act.

Libraries can also be analyzed in the aggregate, as a collective presence within the structure of scholarly communication. The system as a whole matches a number of functions with players. To oversimplify, scholars conduct research and prepare texts. Publishers select, edit, and mass produce these materials. Publishers, but even more booksellers, market the products. Libraries buy the publications, organize them, make them available to users, and preserve them. Other researchers consult these works as they prepare their own texts and thereby continue the cycle.

The library's role within this structure, while bounded, is nonetheless critical. The dynamic is familiar: the library, on one hand, is charged with operations that occur after research has been conducted and publications produced. It thus responds to scholarship rather than driving the process. On the other hand, its functions of organizing, providing, and preserving recorded knowledge are indispensable. Dependence and autonomy are again entwined.

Whether as single institutions or as a collective actor in the system of scholarly communication, libraries are both conditioned by external forces and endowed with some room for independent action. The resulting, at times exasperating tension has supported inquiry of immense scope and success. But continuing change within institutions, within scholarship, and within scholarly communication leaves the system's future very much in doubt. We now turn to this unsettling panorama.

II. THINGS COMING APART: SCHOLARSHIP, LIBRARIES, AND CHANGE

Change is affecting both local expectations for the library and libraries' broader, collective role in scholarly communication. Locally, librarians must adjust their collections and services to reflect shifts in information, technology, curricula and research, and the resources at their command. Academic libraries in the aggregate are scrambling for position as the traditional structure of scholarly communication begins to crumble. Libraries, as specific institutions entrusted with local missions and also as necessary players in the system of scholarly communication, must recognize and anticipate these shifts. It is at this point that a variety of overlapping, sometimes competing, sometimes incompatible analyses—often with very different implications for policy and strategy—come into play.

Changes in scholarly information, academic libraries, scholarship, and universities have generated a host of explanations and predictions. Unfortunately, the most popular analyses tend to be deterministic and incomplete. Some observers focus on the computer alone, arguing that information technology compels researchers, libraries, and academic inquiry to shift their behavior. Others emphasize the "crisis in scholarly communication": the traditional structure has broken down as too many scholars write too many texts that publishers cannot economically produce, libraries cannot afford or organize, and other researchers cannot digest. Still others look to distinct though related aspects of the scholarly enterprise. Some stress academic demographics as they analyze Ph.D. production, student and faculty cohorts, teaching vacancies, and tenure requirements. The spiraling output of academic publications and the associated pressures on scholarly communication are only reflections of these more fundamental trends. Others explain academic change in terms of scholarly sensitivity to broad social and political trends, as well as institutional bureaucratization and commercialization. Finally, there are still those who presume that research agendas are driven by internal dynamics unique to each scholarly field.

Each of these arguments has surface validity. All five also phrase their case in terms of only a few analytical and rhetorical tracks. Costs and benefits predominate in many discussions. Economic analyses are appealing by virtue of our readily apparent, almost ubiquitous, and seemingly fundamental struggle for funds. But these analyses can oversimplify complex realities. They may also too readily allow for—to the point of actually encouraging—the commodification of information and inquiry.

A second approach focuses on the sociology of innovation, of scholarship, and of scholarly communication. Individuals, groups, and institutions determine events. All these actors are capable of rational decision as well as less happy choices. Power relationships and ideology are often close to the surface. This sort of analysis underscores the role of conscious choice in our future, as opposed to the inexorable action of impersonal agents. On the other hand, these discussions can cross from characterization to caricature, or confuse actors with essences.

A third stream of argument, finally, is phrased in terms of ideals: scholarship itself, or some associated process, is advancing toward its fullest possible realization. The specifics of context and conditions are only incidental. These analyses are compelling for their simplicity and sweep. They can also suggest an optimistic—or perhaps simply ingenuous?—innocence.

Most discussions of change draw in varying degree from all three of these streams. Having briefly sketched five common explanations for change in scholarship and in scholarly communication, and also the three sets of terms through which these explanations are most frequently cast, we can now more fully explore each approach. Once the arguments are clear we can turn to their strategic implications.

A. Deus ex Machina: Cybernetic Creationism

Computer technology is often thought to be revolutionary in and of itself. Computers have transformed the economy and the workplace. Their capacity to store and manipulate information foretells similar effects upon scholarship and libraries. Digital technology's still-emerging capabilities to store, transmit, and manipulate images, sound, moving pictures, and real-time interactions—as well as text—are seen as necessarily, inexorably, and irreversibly transforming academic life.

Computers, by the nature of how they capture and store information, favor those sorts of inquiry that rely on the manipulation of data. Quantitative textual analysis, for instance, is simpler when machines do the work. Scholarly valuations have shifted apace: simple concordances no longer excite academic applause. Other research that requires number crunching or data analysis has been facilitated as well. The would-be corollary, that data-rich studies do or should predominate, is by no means so clear.

Arguments of technological determinism date back at least to the "Memex" vision espoused by Vannevar Bush some fifty years ago.[1] All recorded knowledge can and therefore will be miniaturized and organized so that it is immediately accessible. An era of unprecedented command over information is thus at hand. The details of how we achieve this end are trivial by comparison to the compelling appeal of the possibility.

Those asserting the computer's inevitable predominance are idealists who perceive a technological imperative that is at once immanent and transcendent. The machine, apart and aloof from either financial constraints or the hurly-burly of politics and personalities, is destined to prevail: computers will capture, store, enhance, and allow access to all recorded information.

Analyses built around technological determinism underscore dependence as a basic fact of life for libraries and for scholarship itself. Research, the dissemination of research results, and the entire scholarly process will—must—adapt to the machine. Digital dominance becomes all the more appealing in some proponents' controversial expectations that technology will foster a golden age of egalitarian knowledge and communication. Even more grandiose visions suggest that computers will transform the very nature of human discourse and thought. Dissenting predictions of information oligopolies and the commodification of knowledge are for the most part simply dismissed by those who perceive technology as protean and benign.

In the face of so strong a technological imperative, libraries and scholars would best serve society, knowledge, and themselves by moving swiftly and energetically into the electronic arena. The only alternative is obsolescent irrelevance; the only reservations are reactionary. Darker expectations of metered information will also be most effectively forestalled if libraries and kindred "open" institutions preempt the electronic market. Either way, change must be rapid and complete.

B. Transformation through Collapse: The Crisis of Scholarly Communication

A contrasting line of analysis suggests that academic inquiry and research libraries are being challenged by a "crisis in scholarly communication." While cybernetic enthusiasts associate change with expanding functions and emerging possibility, many observers instead perceive an environment driven by decline. Librarians lament that books and serials are becoming ever more numerous and expensive while our purchasing power withers away. Others take a broader view: the entire structure of scholarship is in jeopardy as academic publishers produce fewer titles at ever-higher prices, expensive journals (concentrated in science and technology) command library resources once directed toward more balanced acquisitions, information once available without charge or at minimal cost is marketed for substantial fees, and libraries and their users scrape by with less and less. The discussions easily slip into facile denunciation and self-interested moralization.

Structural crisis induces would-be panaceas as well as polemics. Some proposed solutions embody the rather plaintive hope that a single actor can transform the structure of scholarly communication, or at least neutralize the impact of crisis. Librarians thus speak of "access versus ownership," while publishers dream of pay-per-use electronic files. Yet we delude ourselves when we conclude that the materials we don't ourselves acquire will magically be collected somewhere else, described in a manner that guarantees bibliographic access, and then be available quickly and upon demand. We more fundamentally miss the point when we assume that a sharply reduced purchasing market would have no impact on the price and supply of publications. Publishers are similarly fanciful when they assert that they could append cataloging, dissemination, and preservation to what they already do. Other ideas are even more expansive, for instance in proposing that universities could retain copyrights for local academic products which their libraries would then publish and market.

There is no doubt that libraries, publishers, and scholars themselves are caught in a vise. Researchers' diminishing ability to manage the glut of overpriced research resources that libraries themselves can neither afford nor control coincides with the scholarly trend—most marked in the humanities—to exalt the writer's subjectivity. Postmodernism and deconstructionism, among their other virtues and vices, have in many instances encouraged researchers to select idiosyncratic and unilateral frames of reference. It may not just be chance that the sheer mass of materials makes once-standard bibliographic trenchwork ever less appealing.

Money is a marker of institutional vitality understood by publishers, booksellers, and libraries alike. Explanations of change based on the "crisis of scholarly communication" are therefore founded first and foremost in economics. Simpleminded economicism nonetheless carries some danger of reducing a very complex reality to a single dimension. Some analyses also acknowledge the actors in the process of scholarly communication. It is still fairly uncommon, however, for these actors to be appreciated as mutual stakeholders rather than autonomous (and usually competing) agents within an increasingly dysfunctional system.

Analyses of change that are cast in terms of the crisis of scholarly communication can have varying effects. Those that reflect only one actor's perspective and interests are incomplete, divisive, and necessarily unworkable. Other approaches espouse grand transformations that would rebuild the system from the ground up: the risks of irrelevance are high. Frustration over our intractable dependency upon an increasingly shaky structure is a third response. The solutions that eventually emerge will probably look different from any of these.

C. The Peopling of Change: Transformation through Demography

Three related explanations locate the sources of change in scholarly communications and academic libraries within the dynamics of academic life. The first emphasizes the demographics of higher education; the second, the academy as social and political system; the third, the dynamics of inquiry within each scholarly field. We will examine each in turn.

Our first explanation based in the academy, and the third overall, focuses on demography. Academic fields continue to produce new PhDs. Fledgling scholars, whose job prospects depend upon their publications, join with veterans in writing new texts. Qualified faculty, as they scatter more widely, also draw new students to their fields and (whenever they can) establish new research programs. The demographic base for scholarly inquiry continues to expand, even as funds for higher education level off and the professorate ages. Slow growth and intensifying competition for entry-level positions may themselves, rather perversely, have increased the pressure to publish.

This analysis, while cast in terms of actors and groups, is rooted in Malthusian economics. The processes of academic specialization and overpopulation face few obvious limits. In the broadest terms, there is a finite reservoir of potential students. Developed-world institutions are resourceful in ferreting out "non-traditional" and international clienteles, but universities' expansion must sooner or later slow. Cash-flow economics, at the level of individual institutions and as public support ebbs, is playing a more obvious role: academic downsizing has become a real possibility. Such constraints are only beginning to have an effect on research publications.

Libraries have next to nothing to say about academic demographics and the associated supply of publications. At first blush, this line of analysis thus seems to accentuate our dependence. Further discussions usually follow one of two streams. Technology enthusiasts often perceive the current constraints of scholarly communication as entirely artificial: the Internet, which allows everyone to be his or her own publisher, will obliterate an entirely unnecessary competition for outlets. This vision unfortunately overlooks such additional (and essential) systemic functions as selection, validation, organization, and preservation.

Arguments that locate the engine of change well outside the library's purview can invite another sort of response as well. The circumstances that lump publishers, booksellers, and libraries together as potentially superfluous players also make them probable partners in facing the future. Coordinated efforts can enable libraries (and other actors) to recognize and assert their common interests. Explanations founded in academic demography parallel Malthusian economics in foreseeing a necessarily bleak future. But technological change and organizational transformation have generally postponed Malthusian predictions for the world as a whole. The scholarly sphere may find similar relief.

D. Scholarship and Society: Academic Bureaucracies, Commercialized Campuses, Instrumental Knowledge

Scholars, popular myth notwithstanding, rarely inhabit isolated ivory towers. The academic community instead very much reflects the broader society. At one level, colleges and universities have established large bureaucracies for such varied ends as safe working environments, health care, affirmative action, cash management, record-keeping, and so on. The enterprise of higher education must concern itself with a host of matters that are peripheral to scholarship. These obligations have in and of themselves expanded the limits of academic concern.

Society's intrusions are more subtly, though perhaps more profoundly, affecting the very nature of the academy. Public subsidies for higher education are under fire. As higher tuitions and corporate and alumni support fill the gap, a logic of costs and benefits is ever more frequently invoked. Programs and courses are judged for economic return as well as academic rigor. Entrepreneurial academics, partnerships between universities and industry, and sponsor-defined research are all in ascent. An emphasis on instrumental knowledge translates into good jobs for graduates, programmatic support for professors, and black ink for administrators.

American higher education has always been pragmatic as well as theoretical, utilitarian as well as idealistic. The tilt may now be more pronounced, while non-instrumental fields of inquiry and the pursuit of knowledge for its own sake seem increasingly anachronistic. Some fields that were once thought rarified to the point of irrelevance have become politicized. One explanation may lie in the consequent intensification of their connections to the larger society: stronger links make them more competitive within the academic marketplace.

This commercialization of academic life has been complemented, and perhaps partly balanced, by concerns for public policy. The place of minorities and the marginalized, the needs of a graying population, environmental activism, "traditional" values and neoliberal economics—all have provoked scholarly inquiry. Questions of globalization, international relations, and the policy implications of economic and technological change have likewise found academic homes. Many research projects grapple with these issues, which again privilege instrumental knowledge. These broad questions have also encouraged scholarship to become ever more eclectic and interdisciplinary.

Changing agendas for research and teaching, like shifts in academic demography, are largely beyond libraries' reach. The changes again leave room for individual and collective action. In this case, however, the shifts favor certain types of instrumental inquiry and the associated research services. They also suggest new alliances that may in some cases too readily focus on economic rather than academic returns.

E. The Dynamic of the Disciplines: Research as Its Own Reward

Our final explanation for change, both among the three that look to the academy to find its driving force and the five overall, focuses on specific academic fields. Several models would explain the scholarly process. Thomas Kuhn's The Structure of Scientific Revolution proposes an elegant dialectic through which a field's theoretical constructs induce a "normal science" of experiment and refinement.[2] This process generates data which, inevitably, do not all fit. The anomalies gradually build to a dissonant crescendo, provoking a disciplinary crisis that is ultimately resolved by formulating a new theoretical synthesis. The dynamic is essentially internal to each field, though external elements—for instance improved technology (as with the telescope in astronomy)—can accelerate the process.

Kuhn's model has sparked widespread debate. While it fits some fields quite well, others diverge. Another approach looks to the psychology, sociology, and politics of scholarship to suggest a sequence that is neither so efficient nor benign. Petty interests, arbitrary decisions, and convenient accommodations in fact prevail. Whichever the preferred explanation, many commentators agree that specific scholarly inquiries are framed in terms of questions and concerns that have emerged from within each discipline or field. New starting points may be provoked by social change, technological advance, or arbitrary mandate, but the research process is essentially one of ongoing refinement and reiteration. Day-to-day scholarship reflects a context determined by the fields themselves.

The language used to characterize some areas of scholarship suggests continuing progress toward answers that are ever more truthful and complete. Analysts who focus on the social constructedness of knowledge instead perceive a process rooted in power and politics. The first explanation is idealistic, the second sociological and political. In either case, scholarship responds to dynamics well removed from both libraries and processes of scholarly communication: the models simply assume these underlying structures of support.

Even though these explanations overlook the relationship between research and scholarly communication, it is not too hard to fill in the blanks. Ongoing investigation—Kuhn's "normal science"—requires ready access to other research results and to the synthetic literature in which a specific inquiry is given its place. Timely and comprehensive coverage of relevant resources is critical; informed engagement with each field of inquiry indicates where "relevance" is to be found.

III. LIBRARIANS IN CHANGE; LIBRARIANS IN CHARGE

Academic libraries, whether as individual entities or as a collective actor, are at once limited and empowered by their place within universities and within the structure of scholarly communication. These contexts are in flux, and we have considered five of the most popular explanations for change. None of the explanations is sufficient unto itself. Equally important, none is neutral in its implications.

Our vision of library purpose and possibility will reflect the explanations, facts, and circumstances that we find most pertinent. Interpreting change is an active process through which we create our story and our role. Our choice of analysis and rhetoric will have a strong effect on the institutions that we build.

As we have seen, current explanations for change are diverse and sometimes contradictory. This range of interpretation can be useful in inhibiting premature commitment to any single course of action. With the stakes so high, delayed consensus may work to our advantage. On the other hand, moving from broad generalizations about "scholarship" or "the academy" to the more specific frameworks of individual topics and disciplines should give us a greater sense of our prospects. Focused initiatives are likely to follow.

The Diversity of Scholarship and the Causes of Change

Academic libraries are charged with supporting local scholarship, a concept that combines the concrete needs of flesh-and-blood users with the more abstract requirements of each scholarly field. A library's users are of course unique. Academic disciplines, and the associated patterns of research and communication, are in flux. However, different fields reflect different combinations of the explanatory arguments outlined above. Library responses to change must be founded in these particularities rather than one-size-fits-all prescriptions.

One possible starting point for analysis and action thus works from specific scholarly topics and disciplines, exploring their dynamics in their own terms and also assessing them against the general explanations for academic change. This sort of exercise should suggest the library initiatives that are most appropriate to each field. A few examples will illustrate how the process could work.

Research in most of the hard sciences—fields like particle physics or human genetics—is international, fast-paced, and heavily subsidized. Scholarship is linked to commerce and defense. Its institutional base includes the corporate sector, the military, civilian agencies of the government, and universities. Research, which often requires very expensive equipment, is frequently conducted by teams whose membership can cut across many institutions. Scholarship itself seems a fairly clear-cut cumulative process in which new questions emerge out of previous efforts. Most analysts perceive an enterprise moving steadily toward understanding, and further expect that new knowledge will translate into practical applications.

Current information, which is crucial, is provided through the "invisible college" of personal contacts and also through electronic resources. Scholarly communication is heavily dependent upon digital technology. Paper publication is slow, expensive, and mostly useful for its historical or archival function of documenting past findings.

This characterization has various implications for libraries. Research takes place within a quickly moving and well-financed world of exotic equipment and electronic information. Libraries are peripheral to most original scholarship, despite their utility in providing background, organizing and preserving the historical record, and orienting newcomers to particular topics and fields. As Don Waters suggests, librarians may have become unnecessarily obsessed with the expensive hardcopy journals and reports whose scholarly uses are secondary.[3] All the institutions concerned with these scientific fields, whether as producers, chroniclers, or users of research, might together explore alternatives. Such unified action could also resolve some of the many unanswered questions associated with long-term support for and access to digital information. In time, the "crisis" of scientific serials might even resolve itself.

Science and technology are fields in which research appears objective, knowledge is instrumental, and the library's functions in scholarly communication may bear a second look. Patterns of research, the nature of the scholarly community, and the process of scholarly communication are all quite different in some other areas. The implications for libraries and librarians are likewise distinct.

Policy-oriented scholarship, for instance concerning immigration and immigration reform, is again instrumental. In this case, however, inquiry is informed by a chaotic jumble of facts and figures, testimonials and posturings, ideologies and prejudices. Scholarship tends to be eclectic, interdisciplinary, and interested. Its institutional base includes universities, but also think tanks and some government agencies. Studies are conducted by both research teams and individuals. Academic discourse, for the most part pitched to the political sphere, has generated little sense of accumulating wisdom: partisan scholars rather seem to address only their own camp. Areas of concern likewise appear to advance and recede as events bring topics in and out of the public eye. Research resources run the gamut from electronic data files and computerized opinion polls to broadsides and screeds, from Internet discussion lists to talk radio and broadcast TV. While current information is at a premium, the complete range of relevant sources is immense.

Libraries face at least two challenges as they address public policy scholarship. Local researchers may encourage collections that entirely omit some issues, and that also address only certain aspects of the questions considered central. Moreover, the sheer mass of sources renders comprehensive coverage almost impossible. In the future, scholars seeking to understand the issues and discourse of our time will require a full representation of both argument and source. Libraries, probably working in concert, must document the complete process of scholarship and debate. With a little luck, such coverage might even improve the arguments that we hear today.

Literary scholarship affords a third academic case study, this time from a discipline with a particularly fascinating recent history of change. Literary criticism was traditionally viewed as a quintessentially academic endeavor, probing Beauty and Truth at a safe remove from everyday life. Authors and topics could be studied, and studied again, until their significance within a canonical structure became clear. Occasional critical innovations would provoke a ripple of refinements and new research. Inquiry within this humanistic enterprise, while bounded by a broad consensus concerning ends and approach, reveled in the particulars of human expression. Individual scholars, normally attached to universities, carried the torch. Their goal was understanding, rather than either instrumental knowledge or control.

As new students sought fresh subjects for their work, literary research naturally tended toward ever more esoteric writers, themes, and works. Trivialization has (arguably) been held at bay as a result of larger trends within the academy and within society as a whole. In the largest sense, the transformations of the twentieth century have also transformed literary scholarship. Women and minority scholars have taken the lead in identifying groups excluded from the canon and elevating them—or at least representative champions—to their own canonical status. New questions, as well as new groups and writers, have emerged as different understandings of truth and human experience have come to the fore.

Perceptions of a thoroughly apolitical enterprise have simultaneously given way before a pervasive sense of ideological and political struggle. Humanity has engendered many visions of truth. Each reflects a particular mix of history, possibility, and chance, and all are equally worthy of contemplation and support. Multidisciplinary inquiries are combining the insights of anthropology, history, and other fields with those of literary criticism under the rubric of "cultural studies." New theories of reading and interpretation, finally, have elevated subjective dialogues between readers and works to an acceptable scholarly form. Through all the change, the traditional streams of textual analysis and criticism continue as well.

Scholarly consensus concerning literary criticism's meaning and goals has long-since vanished. Digital technology, while useful for some specific research projects (particularly in the relatively apolitical subfield of textual analysis), is for the most part largely irrelevant. Academic debate is often intense, but research rarely requires very rapid access to either sources or results. Specific research sources may be difficult to obtain because they are obscure or scarce, but the field as a whole—perhaps because it remains an area in which individuals can make a mark, perhaps because its many facets make it attractive to a great many people, perhaps because publications are relatively cheap—has been only marginally affected by the "crisis of scholarly communication." On the other hand, the battles for control are noisy, often nasty, and laden with instrumental overtones.

The shifts within literary scholarship in some ways parallel those within policy studies in their implications for libraries. For instance, ideological and political agendas may both shape local research priorities and skew the corresponding library collections. In contrast to scholarship in either the hard sciences or public policy, however, literary criticism is comparatively relaxed in locating resources and disseminating the results. Costs also remain within bounds. Hardcopy materials predominate, and a traditional mix of local acquisitions and simple cooperative programs still provides adequate coverage.

These three sketches suggest a kind of subject-specific analysis that could both be made more precise for these very broad fields and also extended to other topics. The general lesson should be clear: Most of us are fairly good at determining what our local scholars would like to see, even if our resources can't satisfy their needs. We are less adept at tracing and then responding to each field's research agendas and patterns of scholarly communication. Our strategies need to identify the variations among fields and also to recognize the consequences for local and cooperative action.

Library Solutions and the Causes of Change

The intersection of libraries, scholarship, and scholarly communication can be considered from other vantages as well. Those who are concerned with whether and how libraries can continue to serve scholarship have sponsored repeated studies, meetings, and reports. They have also launched a variety of projects designed to explore longer-term solutions. How well do these address our needs?

Two approaches are particularly prominent. The first, most fully articulated by the Association of Research Libraries, seeks to establish "networked, distributed" collections of foreign materials. This effort, which focuses on cooperative collection development and linked bibliographic access, is complemented by related initiatives to develop significantly quicker and cheaper systems for document delivery and to clarify copyright as we enter the "digital age." While ARL has taken a lead role in improving our approaches to resource sharing and cooperative collection development, local and regional consortia are active as well.

A second thrust centers on digitization per se. Many basic questions have not yet been answered, and current efforts serve more to probe a grab-bag of very specific concerns than to fulfill any clear-cut strategy. Numerous projects are nonetheless either under way or under consideration. The appeal of flexible electronic files, instantly and ubiquitously at hand, is immense.

Resource sharing and digitization respond first and foremost to the increasing pressures upon libraries as they struggle to meet their mandates. Both approaches seek to replace a system characterized by redundant acquisitions and inefficient access with one of minimal duplication and seamless document delivery. The history and rhetoric of both solutions reveal strengths but also shortcomings.

Projects to share resources are the brainchild of libraries. Perhaps as a result, their goals and procedures are almost always framed in terms of publications. Efforts like the Farmington Plan sought to ensure the fullest possible representation of the world's scholarly resources within American libraries. Subsequent cooperative programs have likewise focused on specific sets of materials. We habitually discuss cooperative collection development only in terms of research materials, even though many of these efforts also address scholarly agendas.

The three pilot projects that are now taking shape around the Association of Research Libraries' Foreign Acquisitions Project reflect this more inclusive approach. The effort which has advanced the furthest concerns Latin American materials and encompasses three separate components. Several sets of Argentine and Mexican government documents are being digitized and made available over the Internet; a cross-section of serials from Argentina and Mexico has been identified for distributed acquisitions among the more than thirty participating institutions; and the same libraries will collect comprehensively from selected Argentine and Mexican Non-Governmental Organizations.

The Latin Americanist Project's Advisory Committee, which includes both scholars and librarians, identified these target categories. Project priorities, for instance the NGO reports so crucial to public policy research, thus reflect needs identified by researchers themselves. The Advisory Committee has also sought to ensure truly effective scholarly access to project resources. The results include a new online index for the project serials and detailed cataloging for NGO publications.

These concerns notwithstanding, the Project's rhetoric may have understated its sensitivity to scholars and to research agendas. Public statements and internal reports generally describe its ambitions in terms of categories of materials—"serials," "documents," and "NGO publications,"—rather than as responses to scholarly priorities. The rhetoric of many other cooperative efforts is similarly flawed.

A second shortcoming involves the relationship between libraries' plans to share resources and the interests of all the players concerned with scholarly communication. Publishers and booksellers rely on sales to stay in business. A shrinking market is likely to provoke higher prices and, further down the road, a reduction in both products and outlets. Mutual efforts that involve all the actors may, in the long run, prove less disruptive than initiatives based solely in libraries. At the very least, it behooves libraries to explore the long-term, systemic implications of their single-sector endeavors.

The Association of Research Libraries, following years of study as well as the three pilot projects concerned with foreign materials, has promulgated a "Strategic Plan for Improving Access to Global Information Resources in U.S. and Canadian Research Libraries."[4] This "Strategic Plan," which anticipates a comprehensive panorama of electronically-linked collections that will ultimately merge into the "North American digital library," captures an emerging consensus in support of strengthened foreign holdings. Its formal adoption by the ARL membership is a landmark in and of itself.

The Strategic Plan nonetheless repeats some of the rhetorical and conceptual errors of other cooperative efforts. Most narrower initiatives are grounded in specialist librarians and scholars who, at least implicitly, recognize at least some of the dynamics of research resources and scholarly communication. Explicit acknowledgment becomes more important as the scope of action increases and the discussion becomes more abstract. The "Strategic Plan," however, focuses almost exclusively on libraries as agents and actors. It recognizes scholars and scholarly communications only in passing, and altogether ignores publishers. The rhetoric is monolithic, unilateral, and unambiguous. A statement based in specific disciplines and referring to the several collective actors in the structure of scholarly communication would provide a more solid foundation.

Libraries are also responding to changes in scholarship and scholarly communication through digitization projects. Many of these have been conceived as narrow experiments to resolve specific technical or logistical issues. The community as a whole, however, remains susceptible to an overwrought rhetoric of urgency and of opportunities slipping past. Nuance is an inevitable casualty in the face of such aggressive argumentation.

Many digitizing experiments have been devised with reference to types of materials rather than scholarly uses or needs. Technical issues alone—choosing among binary, gray-scale, or color scanning; determining appropriate resolutions; assessing image files versus ASCII or marked-up text; managing the size and physical characteristics of different sorts of originals—justify a large array of initiatives. Some projects have also sought to probe how users approach electronic products, or to develop mechanisms to recover costs. A consensus on how—or even whether—to establish digital priorities that reflect scholarly needs has not yet formed.

One can nonetheless imagine digital initiatives, framed in terms of scholarly priorities, that not only reflect but also advance academic agendas. Some projects might assist other actors in the structure of scholarly communication as well. For instance, we earlier described the communications pattern in some hard sciences whereby current research results are disseminated electronically. The same fields produce (very expensive) journals in order to authenticate and enshrine these findings. Digital projects to systematize and save electronic pre-prints might assist scientists by adding depth to the electronic resources that are already central to their work. They could at the same time provide librarians with a new handle on one of the most problematic areas of the "serials crisis."

CONCLUSION

Libraries are vitally connected to both scholars and scholarship. Research and scholarly communication are in a period of rapid change. Circumstances, possibilities, expectations, and demands are all in flux. But we can only understand and respond to the shifts as we analyze each separate field. The same process will allow us to exploit fully our room to create. The challenge is immense, and also immensely promising.

ENDNOTES

1. Vannevar Bush, "As We May Think," The Atlantic Monthly 176 (July, 1945), p. 101–108.
2. Thomas S. Kuhn, The Structure of Scientific Revolution. 2nd ed. (Chicago: University of Chicago Press, 1970).
3. Donald J. Waters, "Realizing Benefits from Inter-Institutional Agreements: The Implications of the Draft Report of the Task Force on Archiving of Digital Information." Insert in The Commission on Preservation and Access Newsletter, #85 (January, 1996).
4. The "Strategic Plan" is reproduced in Jutta Reed-Scott, Scholarship, Research Libraries, and Global Publishing: Final (Unpublished report by the Association of Research Libraries, 1995), p. 141–148. The document as a whole summarizes the full range of ARL's efforts concerning foreign materials.

Traditional Library Services and the Research Process: Are Social Sciences and Humanities Faculty Getting What They Need?

By Linda Lester and Karen Kates Marshall
University of Virginia

INTRODUCTION

With an emphasis on implementing the virtual library at the University of Virginia, staff, dollars, and space are being directed to highly visible electronic initiatives and are being diverted away from traditional reference and instructional services. User surveys, observations, and informal conversations indicate that information technology is changing the nature of research and teaching in a positive way. What is not apparent, however, is whether faculty still perceive a need for the more traditional library activities and resources to teach effectively, conduct their own research, and supervise the research of their graduate students. Are faculty noting the erosion of these traditional services? Are they receptive to the trade-offs between traditional services and new technologies? We set out to answer these questions by interviewing our own faculty. We focused our attention on the traditional services relating to research and reference, instruction, and the physical library vs. the virtual library.

BACKGROUND

The University of Virginia Library consists of fourteen libraries serving all areas of undergraduate and graduate study with the exception of graduate business, the health sciences, and law. The library has been reorganizing, reengineering, and restructuring itself around direct customer needs with a focus on technological initiatives to meet those needs. Electronic centers for text, digital images, social science data, geographic information, digital media and music, and special collections attract international attention. The library's user education program was strengthened with the appointment of a library-wide coordinator and the initiation of a Short Course Series offering frequent sessions on topics from Internet Basics to Advanced HTML. Two library classrooms with electronic capabilities for teaching and hands-on practice are in use much of the semester.

At the same time we are promoting new technologies, we are seeing trade-offs. Like other research libraries, we face a continuously declining budget for materials, coupled with increases in materials costs, especially for serials. Our stacks are crowded, and some public reading and study areas have been converted into electronic centers. To address the dilemma of diminishing resources and the cancellation of a large number of serials approximately five years ago, the library created a campus-wide delivery service, LEO—Library Express On-Grounds. LEO delivers books and photocopies of journal articles both owned by the library and requested on interlibrary loan directly to faculty in their academic departments. Turnaround time is often no longer than forty-eight hours. Off-site stacks were built two years ago and now hold over five hundred thousand volumes of infrequently used materials with the collection growing as rapidly as staff can identify, prepare, and transport materials there. The effort of retrieving and returning titles to that building is labor intensive, and although the facility addresses overcrowding, it also reduces the ability to browse for materials in the library's main collection. To begin to assess services and collections from a user viewpoint, large-scale surveys of faculty and students have been conducted over the past three years, with a new faculty survey now under way. A student advisory group meets regularly with library administrators and public service department heads.

With user-directed goals of additional transparency and more rapid response time during busy periods, Alderman Library services to the humanities and social sciences (its primary clientele), have been restructured. The former reference and circulation departments were combined to include most of the front-line services in the building. The reference desk and a small ready reference collection were moved to the library's main lobby which also houses the circulation desk and many Internet/Web, networked CD-ROM, and OPAC workstations. The reference room no longer houses a reference desk. The space formerly occupied by that desk now is used for public workstations and staff offices. Cross training of staff involved in providing information, reference, and circulation services is ongoing. Circulation periods have been liberalized and standardized to include an unlimited loan period and no limits on the number of volumes that can be checked out to faculty. Recognizing the importance of tying materials' selection more closely to academic user groups and strengthening links between the collection building program and academic departments, collection development functions were restructured to create two new departments: Humanities Services and Social Sciences Services. Previously these areas of the collection had been built by geographic area with professional bibliographers whose primary function was selection. Now department level teams focus on user education and electronic information services in addition to their selection responsibilities. Approval plans are now used extensively.

INTERVIEWS

To become more familiar with faculty needs for traditional library services, we talked to twenty faculty members in humanities and social sciences departments. We selected faculty we know to be users of at least some of the services we were interested in researching. The group included department chairs, graduate advisors, departmental library representatives, and both tenured and junior faculty. We sent each faculty member, in advance, our proposal for this Finding Common Ground conference paper, along with an outline of the topics we wanted to cover in our discussion. By way of introduction, we asked them what they need from the library for their research, teaching, and supervision of their graduate students, what they see as the library's role in supporting their work, and how the library measures up to their expectations. Then we sought comments on their needs in the following specific areas: research and reference service, staffing, telephone service, instructional activities, physical and space needs, ambiance, comfort, library hours, and virtual library and technology, but we did not restrict their comments to these areas. The talks were strictly informal. We met either in their offices or in the library, and each interview lasted approximately one hour. We both participated in each interview. In the discussion with the Chair of the Anthropology Department, he suggested that our research was like Ethnography, and that these interviews were our field work.

FACULTY'S DESCRIPTION OF THEIR WORK AND THE LIBRARY'S ROLE IN IT

As one of the historians said, if the documents are not there, we can't do history. Faculty talked to us about what they need to do their work. The History faculty are reliant on primary sources which are not yet digitized, and still must travel to manuscript repositories for their research materials. The classes that they teach are often driven by what is in print, and they place a higher value on microforms than on Web or Internet sources. They frequently teach from microfilm sets, and sometimes an entire class is using the same set for their course assignments. History graduate students are still choosing traditional research topics, and with the highly efficient Interlibrary Loan service that the library now enjoys, students can successfully embark on significant semester-long projects, and be assured of getting the materials they need on time.

The philosophers said they spend more time with periodicals, and less time with books. Economics is not a library-using department, according to one of its members. They use preprints and personally subscribe to the journals they need. The sociologists said they need statistics and government information sources, and items that don't circulate, e.g., CD-ROMs. The Web is of great value to students and faculty in Government and Foreign Affairs, and offers them access to constitutions, trea-

212   *Finding Common Ground*

ties, and documents. My research demands that I get ideas, said a Religious Studies professor, and I can't get them from a computer. An awful lot of what faculty do, claimed an English Department faculty member, can be done sitting in a room with a book. Another member of the English Department expressed his need for the physical book as artifact, complete with book jacket, covers, etc., and his concern that important elements of the book were often lost when it went through preservation microfilming or binding. An art historian said his work was with books and slides, and that the digital image was becoming significant to him. He also said that he wants less information so that he can think, and that he finds the fanatical futurism at the library to be an impediment to his scholarship.

Many faculty talked about the interdisciplinary nature of their work, and how important it is to have an accessible collection of books, periodicals, and reference sources for browsing and consulting outside their areas of specialization. Some found that our decentralized system made this difficult in areas such as family research, human evolution, and history of the mind. They stressed their reliance on having a "real" library with a "real" collection when they are starting research in new areas, as well as for graduate students for whom presumably most research is new. It was frequently mentioned that the ease of doing electronic bibliographic searching frees up time for other aspects of research, and replaces the need to maintain and archive personal bibliographies, which can now be updated frequently by doing a search of the OPAC or a CD-ROM. With all of these electronic tools and access, there is now no excuse for reinventing the wheel, and for writing articles that have already been written.

We heard predictions that the nature of the Academy is changing, with an increasing emphasis placed on undergraduate education, and a decreasing emphasis on publishing. Faculty are now forced to produce books to justify their tenure, and libraries are forced to buy them, although these books are not necessarily the tools of anyone else's research or scholarship. Departments such as English are concerned about the unavailability of jobs for their graduates and are looking at the World Wide Web as a way of enhancing their students' skills. They are using the Web as a pedagogical tool, and are requiring use of it in their students' projects. The Ph.D. degree is overkill for anything beyond academia, but coupled with Web savvy, students become more marketable. The Web will get people jobs, it was suggested.

Faculty perceive the library's role as supporting the university's mission of producing and disseminating knowledge. It is seen as the key institutional unit, with its strong role in building and maintaining the research collection; in providing efficient means to access it; and in providing the instruction needed to utilize it fully. The center of what we all do is the library, it was said, and for that reason the faculty must be involved with it. The library is seen as a culturally rich significant place, but also a place where technology is being taught and learned. It was said to be the crown in the recruiting process.

REFERENCE SERVICE AND SUPPORT

Reference is the heart, the nerve center, the gateway to the library, we were told. On the whole, faculty reported to us that they need and use reference service and are satisfied with the results. They especially need reference librarians for help in negotiating the information highway. We found little difference in the opinions and patterns of reference use among the various departments. Most commented that we have a knowledgeable and helpful staff, seen as enjoying their search for information, described by one faculty member as detective work. Another said that reference was a great secret and that he hadn't known what reference librarians would do for him until he watched a colleague receive extensive reference assistance. A few told us that they do not make use of reference service at all.

Faculty offered many reasons for seeking reference assistance. These included seeking help with factual or verification questions, locating a specific known item, and conducting elaborate data searches that they either cannot do in their offices or do not have the expertise to do. Reference is the place some come to find out about new services and products in their areas of research. One faculty member said she wants to tell a reference librarian what information she needs for her research, and be told where the information resides, and what's the quickest route to get to it. Some faculty indicated that they try to take care of their own research needs and consult reference staff only in areas outside their specialization.

Faculty also mentioned some obstacles to using

reference services and materials. One said he doesn't ask many questions because he doesn't think he should, and he compared his behavior to men not seeking directions. A similar comment was not wanting to admit ignorance in an area in which the faculty member is supposed to be an expert. One sociologist said his use of reference service is hindered because he no longer knows the reference staff the way he used to when he practically lived in the library, before the days of remote access. There was also mention that staff just look too busy to take questions. Ongoing reorganization of the reference department has resulted in a number of major shifts in the reference collection layout. Some faculty who know their way around the reference room find these changes to be bothersome and disorienting. Don't keep shifting the reference books around, we were told. The perceived spirit of religious zealotry over computer technology in the reference department was seen as off-putting to one faculty member who claims he has been forced to use computers by the scruff of his neck.

Even faculty who use reference services only infrequently, or not at all, do encourage their students to use them. They want the reference staff and collection to be a resource for their students. A History faculty member mentioned that graduate students don't seem to have the research skills they used to have, and she suggests that they go to reference staff for help. Some faculty structure assignments to ensure that their students, who may be too embarrassed or intimidated to ask questions, consult with librarians to get help. It was suggested that graduate students can feel like they're cheating if they ask reference questions. For the most part, they say their students who do seek service are treated well and are satisfied with the results. One faculty member, whose students don't use reference resources, teaches from primary sources and doesn't require them to use the library at all.

It's the staff that makes this library great, said one senior English department faculty member. The effectiveness and strong customer service attitude of staff were mentioned frequently, and in an overwhelmingly positive way, by faculty in all disciplines. More than ever they see a need for sympathetic helpful humans at the reference desk. A number said we need well trained staff and a better system of referral for in-depth research questions than we now have. Some faculty have determined that certain staff are more effective in providing knowledgeable assistance, and they make a point of seeking out those staff with their own research level questions and also refer their students to them. If the most knowledgeable person in an area isn't present, most will ask informational queries of anyone at the desk rather than taking the additional time to seek out a specific librarian or returning at another time. The accessibility of reference service is important to these faculty, and they want staff present at a service desk without having to seek them out. Faculty value the availability of staff at the reference desk and don't want to see it diminished. It may be arrogant on my part, said one, but I am used to it and still want it. One suggested that more and more people in the library should be directly involved in giving customer service. People tucked away in offices should also be dealing with the public and finding out what they need. Faculty members perceive the camaraderie, the cooperative spirit, and the dearth of hierarchy in the library as positively contributing to the good service they receive.

For many years the Alderman reference staff has included doctoral graduate student assistants with significant teaching and research background in the humanities and social sciences disciplines. For the most part faculty seem pleased with the assistance these students provide. Even so, a noticeable difference in the level and quality of reference service between full time staff and these student assistants was noted. Some said that late evenings and weekends, when their students are most likely to do their work, are often the times when they will receive the least knowledgeable service since these are the hours that the desk is normally staffed by graduate student assistants. It was suggested that student assistants need more training.

The physical environment in which reference service is provided was a topic in many of our discussions. When reference service moved into the main lobby to join circulation, the original reference desk (an imposing presence in the Reference Room since 1938 when Alderman was built) was dismantled. Relocating reference service received rave reviews from some faculty while others opposed the decision. Even within the same academic department there were varying opinions on the usefulness of the new service point. For some, moving reference to a central busy area put the service at the place where it is needed, making it more visible and more accessible, with staff more readily available to spot bewildered people who need help. The new location puts service at the place where it's most useful. Others disagreed, noting that staff are now physically distanced from the reference room collection, and are no longer well located for just pointing people to resources. Although they do take researchers into the reference room while assisting them with a query, the impression is that it is a problem for staff to leave the desk unattended. The dignity of reference service has been diminished by the rearrangement of the service area, it was said; it's now betwixt and between, and it is more difficult to find a librarian now that you're out in the hall.

Although remote access to reference service is available, telephone reference service is used by only a few faculty and e-mail reference is used by even fewer. In the instances in which telephone service was said to be used, it was reported to be very satisfactory. One person told us that when he is asking a question at the desk and the telephone rings, staff seem to be unclear about which service has priority. He expressed strong sentiment that telephone reference service shouldn't have priority over someone standing at the desk. If the telephone cannot be picked up on first ring, have the call diverted elsewhere, he suggested.

PHYSICAL LIBRARY AND VIRTUAL LIBRARY

I'd sleep better at night knowing that the library was building and strengthening its collections, one faculty member told us. Clearly, the purchase and maintenance of our print collection of books, journals, and microforms is of the utmost importance to the scholars we interviewed, and faculty take pride in the strengths of the collection. Although we had not suggested the library's general collection as a topic of discussion, the faculty were eager to talk about it. Some were unhappy that we no longer can collect at the level we formerly did, and are finding holes in the collection that were once not so evident. One said he doesn't want to see incomplete runs of journals in the stacks; the library should make a strong effort either to fill in the gaps or remove the bits and pieces. Another suggestion was that when journals must be canceled or we are unable to subscribe to new titles, provide adequate table of contents access to them and publish that service. There was recognition that although there is a cost to the collection in shifting the library's emphasis to electronics, the cost is a bargain. For many, the collection remains viable in support of their work. The erosion of service was also mentioned in relation to the collections. A sociologist told us that he would not want a first class collection if it meant that he would get only third class public service, whereas a government professor said he would be willing to sacrifice library hours, staff, and technology in the interest of maintaining a first class collection.

For some the trade-off between purchasing books and providing rapid efficient interlibrary loan and delivery is a reasonable one. Others said that ILL is not an effective trade-off because books obtained this way cannot be kept long enough to meet their research needs, and a high level of borrowing activity reduces the library's image. Not owning books was seen as more serious than not owning journals, because through table of contents and indexing and abstracting services, faculty said they could see what is inside a journal without having to hold it in their hand. They could then receive photocopies of the articles through LEO and not have to return them. The LEO service for the delivery of materials was spoken of in laudatory, almost reverential terms. It makes the process of obtaining needed resources transparent and allows increased time for actual research.

The process of selecting materials for purchase is one in which some faculty want to participate, while others simply want the books to be on the shelf when they need them. They do want to be consulted about possible serial cancellations. Some have found the bureaucracy of the library's collection development process daunting and don't know whom to approach in the library when they want to have a book purchased. Others seem pleased with the relationship they have established with a particular bibliographer.

We asked our faculty, who now have the potential for increased remote access to our services and collections, if they still value coming to the physical library and working in it. For many it remains a rich cultural center, a delving place, a community of scholars. Faculty are often isolated by the nature of their work, and even more so by use of the virtual library, and they value the social and scholarly intercourse of humans taking place within the physical library. Browsing the stacks is still seen as very pleasurable and important for locating material for new courses, learning about an unfamiliar topic, and finding books on the same subject as a known item. Browsing leads to interesting discoveries, they said, and they fear losing this ability.

Some of them who once spent a great deal of time in the library find themselves coming there less frequently, thereby browsing in the stacks less frequently, as well. They regret this, but also enjoy the ease of locating specific titles in the catalog from their own desktop and requesting the items to be delivered. Others do not see browsing through a call number or subject index in the catalog as a comparable alternative to browsing in the stacks because there is value in actually opening the books on the shelf. Browsing was also seen by many to be less productive since our off-site closed stacks became operational.

In addition to browsing the stacks, faculty said they enjoy hanging out in the current periodicals room and the special collections reading room. However, the library is increasingly becoming a place for lightning-strike visits to pick up a fact or a book when there is not enough time to wait for a LEO delivery. It was noted by some that the library is starting to look different and have a different feel to it. It looks increasingly like an equipment-driven place with fewer books and staff in evidence, and fewer study and lounge areas. It was suggested that we need a coffee stand, more plants, more couches, better climate control, more comfortable chairs, more study carrels and work areas, better light in the stacks, more short term parking, better drive-up access to book drops, and longer hours during intercession. The resources and comforts of the physical library, it was pointed out, are even more important for graduate students who frequently live in the library.

Most faculty are acutely aware of the positive things that the virtual library offers them, and are enthusiastic that the library is cutting edge in so many areas. The academy is experimental right now, and it is expected that the library should be as well. There was a strong desire voiced, however, to keep things in perspective. Dissatisfaction was expressed with the mindless rhetoric, hype and posturing surrounding technology, and the fact that increased information and access could not take the place of critical thinking. There was also concern with access issues. Many of the CD-ROM databases networked from the library are not accessible in faculty offices. The Web is still seen as slow, unpredictable, and barren by many. As more faculty are putting their courses on the Web and requiring class participation through the Web, the library and the computer labs are hard pressed to meet the demands for high end student workstations. Although the faculty are excited about full-text being delivered to their desktops, they still want to read print journals from comfortable chairs. There was nostalgia expressed for the library of the past (the way you have nostalgia for LPs or typewriters, said a young assistant professor), but most accepted that trade-offs are necessary, and that technology is here to stay and has significant positive impact on scholarship and teaching.

USER EDUCATION

Librarians will inherit the earth since they can teach others how to retrieve and filter information, was the way one faculty member put it: It is the opinion across departments that need for library instruction is significant. With technology on the one hand presenting increased opportunity for access to information; for many it also presents a challenge in learning new methods which are frequently changing, and in dealing with personal workstations not always equipped to take advantage of these new technologies. I don't have time for change, was the way one woman stated her problem, and many despaired that they don't even have sufficient time to learn about change. Everything is a problem in the computer world, said another. Many of the faculty who had sought help with technology from our university's computing facility were disappointed, and felt that they were given the run-around, or that the help desk staff were so technical that it posed communication problems. As one complained, they can't even figure out what we don't know. A number of university-wide opportunities for faculty to learn how to use technology in their research and teaching have been set up in the hopes that faculty would return to their departments as missionaries and spread their new knowledge and skills to their colleagues. This "seed" method of teaching technology is not working as well as had been hoped. We heard that often the few in each department who are sophisticated in their use of technology are too busy to teach the others, and that it is difficult to communicate with colleagues who have left the world of the book.

To some it seems as though there is a world out there with no set of instructions. The Information Superhighway is seen as vast and disorganized, and the library is seen as an inviting place to get help using it. Faculty value a versatile library staff, well-trained in new technologies, but also conversant with traditional print sources. Many revealed that they don't like to admit their ignorance, or to appear incompetent. Ideally they want individualized help with technology where and when they need it, and would particularly appreciate instruction at their own workstations in their own offices, rather than instruction out of context, such as attending classes or reading documentation. Some no longer have the time or the skills to help their students with their library research, and appreciate the library's instructional role.

The Short Course Series in electronic information offered by the library got good reviews, although some suggested that the courses would be more beneficial if directed more specifically to skill levels or subject areas, and that they would like to see more short courses created for individual departments or disciplines. Course-related instruction is regarded as invaluable for demystifying the library and for acquainting students with possibilities for research. It is also valued for facilitating good relationships between the students and the highly qualified library staff, and for letting students see the relationship the library has with the faculty at this university. Many faculty expressed concern that traditional bibliographic instruction of print resources be retained. We need to stress the bifurcation of print and electronic sources in our sessions, as students are too apt to settle for what can be found on a computer, thereby ignoring relevant print sources.

To publicize new products and services, the library typically has been sending e-mail notices and instructions to academic departments. We also use our newsletter, LIBRA, which goes out in print to all faculty, and is also available on the Web. Faculty seem pleased that we are providing these services, but are also overwhelmed with the amount of information coming to them from the library and elsewhere. With thirty or forty e-mail messages appearing in faculty mailboxes each day, it was suggested that unsolicited messages start to look like junk mail and can be irritating. People tend to learn ad hoc, and if you don't need the service or product at the time you are reading about it, you don't remember it. A number of faculty mentioned that they learn about new library resources through their relationships with library staff, and often come to the library to learn more about products they have read about through our publicity or their professional reading. The advice was to keep the messages brief and to the point, explain why you would consult the new database or service, what the search results would look like, and then offer to demonstrate it. A sociologist told us that eighty percent of all possible uses of a product or service could be met by twenty percent of the product's features, e.g., eighty percent of us use only twenty percent of the functions in a word processing program, and that a maximum of two pages of documentation should be enough to take care of most people s needs. It was also suggested that when products change, or are no longer available, faculty want to hear about it as much as they want to learn about new products.

We are right now in the process of creating library Web pages for each academic department that we serve, and it was agreed that they would be a good venue for announcing and archiving information about new products, for providing documentation and online help for existing services and products, and for offering access to selective relevant Web sites and Internet resources. One professor mentioned that VIRGO, the library catalog system, is the most universal link to the library, and that maybe new services and products should be announced in banners on the opening screen.

CONCLUSION

The faculty that we interviewed still value traditional library activities and resources. Above all else they value the collection and want to maintain its strengths. They see as important personal contact with service-oriented staff. They recognize the library's instructional role, and want to continue to receive assistance and support from well-trained librarians familiar with the research process and traditional sources, and with the new technologies. When they find aspects of the virtual library to be irritating or daunting, they want individualized help, especially at their own workstations, rather than attending classes or reading documentation. They have noticed some erosion in traditional services and in the physical library, but, on the whole, they see the new technologies and initiatives at the library as having positive impact on their work and that of their students. They are not seriously troubled by the trade-offs.

Through our discussions we learned that if the

library is to respond to faculty needs, it must sustain traditional services while supporting new initiatives. Our new model of collection development integrating subject selection with liaison, instructional, and technical support activities is designed to deliver materials and services to faculty where and when they need them, and should accomplish this goal. Training of library staff, particularly in electronic services, should be ongoing, and public service desks need to be staffed with people who know how to navigate the information network, but who are also familiar with the research process and can communicate effectively with both faculty and students. We need to maintain, if not improve, comfort levels and ambiance in the physical library while at the same time work toward making remote access to the virtual library more transparent and more dependable. What we heard clearly in these discussions is that it is vital that faculty and librarians talk. When we asked an anthropology faculty member what he perceived as lacking in the library, the answer was: meetings like these. We recommend ongoing dialogue between the library and the faculty so that well-informed decisions about resource allocation can be made and we can target our resources and services to faculty teaching and research.

Twenty-first Century Scholarship: Expertise, Energies, and Expenses: A Four-Part Discussion

Part 1:
Expertise in Electronic Scholarship: Psychological Factors in Individual Inquiry Development

By Patricia O'Brien Libutti
Fordham University

SCHOLARSHIP AND SCHOLARS: TAKING SEMANTIC SNAPSHOTS

We are all scholars, inquirers by profession. In thinking about the essence of the work we do, it seems that both "Scholar and "Scholarship" are key descriptors. So looking at the Person labeled a "Scholar" and the Process "Scholarship" defined is our beginning point. Merriam-Webster's Unabridged Dictionary, Third Edition (1971) provides the description of a scholar as: "2a: One, who by long systematic study (as in a university) has attained a high degree of mastery in one or more of the academic disciplines; esp. one who has engaged in advanced study and acquired the minutiae of knowledge in some special field along with accuracy and skill in investigation and powers of critical analysis in interpretation of such knowledge (a noted Shakespeare ~.)"

Further description includes personal characteristics of a scholar: "2b: a learned person; esp. one who has the attitudes (as curiosity, perseverance, initiative, originality, integrity) considered essential for learning." (p.2030, col. 3).

Two juxtaposed definitions of scholarship provide a perspective to assess common ground and significant chasms. Beyond the granting of funds or the recognition of character, scholarship is recognized as a describable entity. The process described by both Webster and OCLC provides the following: "Scholarship: . . . 3. the body of learning and esp. of research available in a particular field. syn. see knowledge." (p.2031, col. 1.) The innovations involved in the advent of technological applications termed Electronic Scholarship are part of the description in OCLC's posted WWW advertisement for its services.

NEW ELECTRONIC SCHOLARSHIP

Under the new electronic models of information management (and according to OCLC), the following definitions apply:

1: Scholarship: the application of the digital electronic computer and telecommunications networking to study, instruction, research, and experience.
2: Research: to use electronic means to find specific information from a large body of information.
3: Homework: a student's work or activity done on a computer or computer network.
4: Writing: the process by which an author prepares a work for publication.

5: Electronic Journal: the digital version of a printed book or serial.
6: Electronic Library: organizing, storing and providing access to information and knowledge in electronic form.
7: Information Superhighway: electronic communication over the Internet and World Wide Web.
8: a way of life syn see Scholarship. (http://www.oclc/define.html)

Electronic Scholarship as sketched above primarily outlines the way information work is done, although the secondary definition is of an entity: (library, journal). It is notable that a crucial shared aspect with Webster's definitions of scholar is OCLC's fusions of the definitions of Scholar and Scholarship: "8. A way of life. syn., see Scholarship." The first aspect, that of work process, is the primary focus in this part of our discussion. The next three parts look at the reality embedded in such imagery: in instruction, costs, and institutional organization. This discussion will address the following questions: Is the inquirer motivated by technology-driven information work? Will the speed of fiber-optically transmitted information change: how we learn? how we understand? how we evaluate information?

There are issues beyond the individual inquirer's immediate concerns that will have an impact on inquiry in general. Answers that evolve to respond to the following questions will alter the very nature of scholarship, and, possibly, relate to the quantity of those who choose to dedicate themselves to the lifestyle of a scholar. What is the meaning of production of knowledge when difficulty of transmission is not an issue? What value is there in pursuing a line of inquiry? What motives would make such be one's chosen work? New technology brings with it old anxieties. Experiences with electronic searching include getting lost in links with texts of uncertain lineage and mutations This problem aroused in many the predictable resistance that has accompanied each major movement in knowledge transmission (Rogers 1983).

One couldn't argue in person with a written text—but one could continue to do so in print long after the original disputant was no longer vocal. One could not have the elegance and beauty of the scripted word on vellum with the printing press (Trithemius, 1462–1516)—but so many could read and use what was printed. With The Press, The Word as Art continued to be true: witness Text as Art in everyday twentieth century design.

We are familiar with the expressed loss of The Book in its sensory glory: (the smell of a newly opened one, the joy of opening a well designed text is unlikely to be such a loss). Isn't it likely that the same aesthetic urge that gave us beautiful book design will lead to design/art not yet seen? And is it not true that all of the prior forms of expression: Oratory, Calligraphy, Textual and Visual Book Design—are likely to continue, co-exist, as have many other technologies? Although "deep-reading" is seen as a necessary loss in the highly technological environment (Birkerts 1994), it is much more likely that speed and deep reading will co-exist as methods used for appropriate tasks. Any scholar will continue the development of self-regulation of stimuli (sometimes called critical thinking).

Similarly, it seems just as likely that the scholarly person will continue to be an essential member of society—and that scholarship as both process and product will evolve, as it always has with new methodologies opening inquiry. The Last Librarian Who Knew Every Book, just like The Last Person Who Knew Everything (Gumpert 1987) disappeared with increasing information. A scholar evolved into a professional inquirer rather than a depository of knowledge.

THE INDIVIDUAL INQUIRER MOVING THROUGH CONCEPTUAL SPACE

How does an inquirer gain expertise in today's electronic information? We might well look at ourselves learning on the job: we did gain expertise to operate in our work environment that changed so fast in the last decade. The Digital Library (Marchionni 1995, Purves 1990) has been experienced, examined and evaluated as a significant advance as a place for learning. This "advance" involves the usual civilization dance: "Hazard yet Forward yet Backward".

The master-apprentice model seen in universities (past and present) is recognizable in the best computer mediated instruction, programs that have been designed from the study of human tutoring skills (Lepper et al. 1993). Lepper's study found that recognizably expert human tutors stressed positive affect and consistent progress monitoring with their students. The implications of these findings are important for any instruction that will be relegated to a computer interface.

We need to go beyond electronic search skills for inquiry to happen. Looking at how one moves through conceptual space from individual inquiry to using information can be seen as "layers of learning", illustrated in Figure 1. These "layers" mark progress in conceptual knowledge emanating from the individual with the question (Carr 1988). Technology, originating in the Greek: "techne": to make, is applied in the making of knowledge, no matter what the tools. The card catalog, the shelving code, and the arrangement of the physical space all formed the technology used to craft scholarship. The addition of electronic search and communication tools enlarges and compresses the learning task for any level of scholarship, as described in each layer needed to move from concept to communication which takes on a pattern of its own for each individual.

These Layers Of Learning in an electronic environment begin at the Individual Inquiry Level, within that One Inquiring Individual. The Inquirer (whether preschooler or professor) first recognizes the need for information, and then conceptualizes that need by framing a question. That question extends into other questions, enlarging the language of inquiry. The inquirer individualizes a quest, constantly re-orienting within the flow of information, keeping the essence of the question intact.

THE INQUIRER IS WORKING IN AN ENVIRONMENT

The Library Layer (whether digital or physical) demands that the individual go outside his own thinking into that environment and describe an information need in the context of that environment. That description, that initial articulation, may be with a person or an electronic interface. The essential feature is that this articulation becomes part of the inquiry. Beyond philosophers, whose primary mode of inquiry involves highly internal reflection, this beginning dialogue is essential in shaping an inquiry that becomes part of a larger process, larger than internal cogitation. The inquiry takes on a public aspect, although much of the thought process will, wonderfully, remain private. In that information environment, recognizing format distinctions and applying location descriptions is part of the work. The Inquirer navigates the environment from citation to access.

The Technology Layer has become an integral part of that Library Layer, requiring the extension and transfer of skills needed to gain information. The Inquirer is required to translate the question into search structure protocol, and accurately apply search protocol for particular databases. Using multiple computer literacies, such as searching, word processing, file transfers, and presentation programs become part of the work (McClure 1994). Specific transfer of previously learned reading tasks involve decoding electronic text (Costanzo 1988, Landow 1992). Learning the physical operations with computers and peripherals until there are patterns established similar to driving operations is still another part of the learning tasks for the Inquirer.

The Scholarly Layer is the level in which the information becomes meaningful in the context of the communication of the findings to an identified audience. To be effective as a scholar, the Inquirer needs to recognize data as data by defining "information" as changing his thinking. The Inquirer essentially "has a dialogue" with represented point of view (whether in print, pixels, or in person) and reflects on diverse points of view, holding onto ambiguity and tension while examining evidence She examines individual pieces of literature, developing a pattern of inquiry across all literature examined on a topic. To do this adequately, the Inquirer uses metacognitive strategies to regulate learning, searching and production of information, synchronizing all the diverse parts of an inquiry.

HYPERTEXT: THE DEFINING POINT IN INQUIRY CHANGES

The combination of both older and newer learning tasks with print and electronic resources puts our Inquirers in much the same positions we have been in, learning the technologies while keeping a perspective on that which existed and was valuable to maintain. The crux of the exponential jump in information availability for the scholar has been the emergence of hypertext, leading to developments in what a scholar can DO with hypertext that cannot be done with print resources. It is possible to transcend Place, to follow threads of discourse, ideas, concepts, etc. that would, at best, have been tedious, and, in many instances, unlikely (Landow 1992). Time as a variable in access is compressed, although the impact of reduced time on comprehension and use of information has yet to be fully explored.

We, as librarians, have been familiar with hypertext for a long time, perhaps longer than we consciously know (Kerr 1991, Costanzo, 1988). Our physical work patterns are different: our eyes have subtly responded to the non-standard terminal screen displays, we moved from grasping a writing instrument to pressing and coordinating a keyboard and peripherals. We have gone through so many physical changes that we provide a large customer segment for ergonomic consultants.

Our intellectual information work has changed: we have expanded into new areas; we have taken on new tasks—needs became obvious. We have interpreted methodology to inquirers not familiar with nonstandard reading patterns. Screens rarely conformed to what we learned in this culture's kindergartens: we read from left to right, top to bottom. Cursors, hot links, and multi-screen segments have presented us with both the necessity of self-directed learning and the task of designing library instruction modules on How To Read Electronic Text. It is likely that such experiences have reinforced what we have known: learning is rarely linear, often episodic, and marked by critical moments. Cavalierre's study of the Wright Brothers' invention and its precursors in concepts and contacts shows the impact of information brought together in ways we have seen in our reference work (Cavalierre 1991).

ELECTRONIC SCHOLARSHIP: NEW WORKFLOW PATTERNS

The interactions of changing information areas have many implications bringing out both the Optimists and Pessimists in each library Futurist discussion. Inquiry could be enlarged by the novelty of technology, even sparked by what can be done. Library information structure and technology methodologies are likely to merge, becoming even more transparent, resulting in scholarly work being closer to the inquirer.

As the layers between traditional library information organization and technology speed blur, that individual inquirer faces stimuli that call for internal filtering—or the Great Overwhelm will squelch questioning for fear that the answers are too much to handle. (The "Great Overwhelm" is David Carr's current expression for the phenomenon.) Further, the concern that the information is not absolutely guaranteed to be as represented is an integrity-testing problem, as seen in this "caveat emptor" now placed on a Large University's opening screen to Internet access:

> This program will attempt to connect you to various information sources via the Internet.
> Some services may not be available at all times. THE SERVICES OFFERED ARE CREATED AND MAINTAINED BY VARIOUS ORGANIZATIONS AND INDIVIDUALS. UNIVERSITY LIBRARIES CANNOT GUARANTEE THE ACCURACY OF INFORMATION PROVIDED BY THESE SOURCES.
> please wait . . . .

The warning above will disappear. Much of what is the medium of scholarly work in the electronic learning environment will be more transparent. Our Common Ground in pursuit of individual inquiry—and the facilitation of that—lies in recognizing human attributes above all else no matter what electronic resources shape the inquiry. Donald Norman (Norman 1993) titled his book Things That Make Us Smart: Defending Human Attributes in the Age of the Machine. John Dewey's observations in 1927 anticipated the same value: a basis on inquiry as a human activity, directed by the Inquirer: "The highest and most difficult kind of inquiry and a subtle, delicate vivid and responsive art of communication must take possession of the physical machinery of transmission and circulation and breathe life into it. When the machine age has perfected its machinery it will become a means of life and not its despotic master. Democracy will come into its own, for democracy is a name for a life of free and enriching communion. It had its seer in Walt Whitman. It will have its consummation when free social inquiry is indissolubly wedded to the art of full and moving communication." (Dewey 1927, 184)

Despite dramatic differences, we are still producing human enterprises, and need the same curiosity, persistence, and artfulness to do what is now and what will be scholarly work.

REFERENCES

Birkerts, S. 1994. The Gutenberg elegies: The fate of reading in an electronic age. Boston:Faber.

Figure 1. Layers Of Learning In Research In An Electronic Environment:

Inquiry Skills Needed for Scholarly Work

Individual Inquiry Layer

Recognizes the need for information
Conceptualizes questions, extends questions into language
Individualizes an inquiry and directs it appropriately
Re-articulates inquiry in the light of information

Library Layer

Using an electronic interface
Recognizes and applies the classification of information used in the information environment
Recognizes format distinctions
Knows and applies location descriptions
Navigates the environment from citation to access

Technology Layer

Translates own question into search structure
Applies accurately search protocol for particular database
Uses multiple computer literacies (McClure 1994)
Decodes electronic text(Costanzo 1988, Landow 1992)
Operates computer and peripherals

Scholarly Layer

Recognizes data as data
Defines information as changing his thinking
Has a dialogue with a represented point of view (whether in print, pixels, or in person)
Communicates discoveries, findings, to identified audience
Reflects on diverse points of view, holding onto ambiguity and tension while examining evidence
Develops an individual viewpoint, relationship to the literature.
Examines individual pieces of literature and develops pattern of inquiry across all literature examined on a topic
Uses metacognitive strategies to regulate learning, searching and production of information

© Libutti and Blandy. As the Cursor Blinks: Electronic Scholarship and Instruction, Presentation: Westchester Library Association, April 28, 1995

Carr, D. 1988. The situation of the adult learner in the library. In Proceedings of the Sixteenth Annual LOEX Conference, (Bowling Green, Ohio). 35–43. Ann Arbor, MI: Pierian Press.

Cavalierre, L. 1991. The Wright Brothers Odyssey: Their Flight Of Learning. Presentation at Thomas Edison College, New Jersey, June, 1991.

Costanzo, J. S. 1988. Reading the electronic text. In The electronic text: Learning to write, read, and reason with computers. 37–63. Englewood Cliffs, NJ: Educational Technology Publications.

Dewey, J. 1927. The public and its problems. 184. Athens, OH: Swallow Press. Reprint, 1954.

Gumpert, G. 1987. The last person who knew everything. In Gumpert, G. Talking tombstones and other tales of the media age. 140–166. New York: Oxford University Press.

Kerr, S. 1990. Pale screens: teachers and electronic texts. In From Socrates to software: The teacher as text and the text as teacher. Yearbook of the National Society for the Study of Education, ed. P. Jackson. 88:2, 202–22. Chicago, IL: NSSE.

Landow, G. P. 1992. Hypertext: The convergence of contemporary critical theory and technology. Baltimore, MD: Johns Hopkins Press.

Lepper, M. et al. 1993. Motivational techniques of expert tutors. In Computers as cognitive tools. ed. S. P. Lajoie and S. J. Derry, 75–105. Hillside, NJ: L. Erlbaum.

Marchionni, G., & Maurer, H. 1995. The roles of digital libraries in teaching and learning. Communications of the ACM, 38:4, 67–75.

McClure, C. R. 1994. Network literacy: a role for libraries? Information Technology and Libraries, 13:2, 115–126.

Norman, D. 1993. Things that make us smart. Defending human attributes in the age of the machine. Reading, MA: Addison-Wesley.

Purves, A. 1990. The scribal society: An essay on literacy and schooling in the information age. New York: Longman.

Rogers, E. M. 1983. Diffusion of innovations. Third edition. New York: Free Press.

Trithemius, J. [1462–1516]. De laude Scriptorum (In praise of scribes). Vancouver: Alcuin Society, Reprint, 1977.

Part 2:
Energies in Electronic Scholarship: A New Path for Library Instruction

By Eleanor Langstaff
Baruch College

A. The blending of traditional print sources and new electronic resources creates a different and unique perception of library instruction.

After years of concentrating on marketing the hidden and esoteric bibliographic skills that are the hallmark of the mature scholar and that equally come to the aid of the neophyte, as rubbing alcohol to the athlete, those of us engaged in library instruction find ourselves treated with new respect. And to what do we attribute this new image? Is it the information explosion, the Internet, the computer? Of course, but that learners hang upon our every word is due, rather, to the cloak of invisibility that surrounds digital information. A somewhat uninformed stumble among the stacks results in some good material; the analogous fumble in the digital world may result in a cornucopia of full texts, charts, maps, or provoke a family conference about the telephone bill, while leaving the student without a fact upon which to pin an opinion.

The non-electronic library world has similar situations. In libraries where there are closed stacks, the imperative to do searching based on surrogates of one kind or another impels the users to avail themselves of whatever instructional devices are at hand. In many respects the coming of the online catalog, with the raised expectations brought about by the new electronic formats effectively closed the stacks. The library user assumed the electronic resource would give him the fullest access to the collections. I see this as comparable to finding information on the Internet. Suddenly a vast panoply of information was out there—somewhere—for the taking. But just what is there and what is retrieved is dependent on some factors controllable by the student or faculty member and other factors outside their control that put these users in a precarious position as far as their success in amassing the right material is concerned. What I most bless information technology for is that sooner or later it leaves its users with a wonderfully sharp awareness that they lack a full understanding of information and of its technology, whether old, as in codex, or new, as in hypertext. The relationship between information and its technology adds a dimension to understanding of a subject domain that is, or should, or could be, part of the research picture, and its invisibility, or rather the uncompromising digitality of this information turns the user to the experts in his search for wisdom.

B. The current changes in technology present library instructors with a vast array of choices when implementing a library instruction program.

Information for a New Age: Redefining the Librarian published last year by ALA's Library Instruction Round Table addresses what it sees as the true role of Bibliographic Instruction, which focuses on the need to make library patrons become more proficient in locating and using information, as a major contributor to information literacy. The selection of papers and essays in this volume describe approaches to proactive interaction with library users with the single goal of achieving an information literate society. Many of the papers address technologies, from the political, technical and psychological aspects, following a trend brought about by the common accessibility to the Internet that students and faculty typically enjoy. Coping with the new and the unknown blurs the instructional vision to a degree. In the summer issue of RQ Lori Arp points out that of 711 articles indexed in Library Literature under Internet, a mere 41 also include material about teaching or instruction. The thrust is to inform about the new technology. Implications for teaching will follow. Even teaching will follow. This is not the whole story, of course, because the Internet has brought its own modes of communication which are not necessarily indexed in the older bibliographic tools. The Nettrain discussion list, for instance, addresses just those issues of teaching the Internet, ranging from a discussion of fuzzy logic to heated exchanges about the value of a projector versus a liquid crystal display panel, from business and research sites to what you teach students at the elementary and high school levels.

What is both curious and refreshing about the situation is that both students and teachers become active and reactive learners. That technology equals tool is a commonplace; that it has shaken the foundations of the lecture method of imparting knowledge and has democratized the learning space is refreshing and invigorating. It may not, however, change its goals.

At Baruch College, City University of New York, the objectives with which the undergraduates are challenged in the 3–credit 15 week Information Research core elective courses are these:

1. To acquire lifelong proficiency in handling information quickly, efficiently and effectively.
2. To work with varied information forms and practice presenting findings in an organized manner.
3. To plan and conduct information searches.
4. To understand and evaluate information from a variety of sources.
5. To obtain a sense of the history of and current developments in information sources in the key disciplines of the social sciences and humanities.

Although no mention is made here of the technology by which these objectives are achieved, the course is pursued in a state of the art library, classroom, and library media center. Central to the course, from its design in the eighties, is that although information is, for the most part transmitted within and among disciplines as text, and although scholarly discourse is text based discourse, it is packaged in many forms. Because texts were once all tangible artifacts, they came to be seen and to be managed as commodities. We taught that information is expandable, and paradoxically, compressible into summaries; that information substitutes for capital, labor or physical materials, that information is transportable—how clear that is today—and it is also diffusive, and above all, information is a resource that, when shared, is not consumed. (Harlan Cleveland's list developed in the early 1980's is repeated in the Mellon Report (104–05).

All information theorists are not agreed as to its nature. We also had to teach that in law information is seen as a consumable, and that the producer of information has property rights in his contribution to the knowledge base. What has happened is that one kind of library research has not replaced an older model, but that one has, at the very least to be superimposed on the other, and at best merged with the other, because both beginning and advanced researchers have to deal with the artifacts but also the elusive electronic and invisible materials essential to their work. Instruction can only be improved because we are forced to teach at the level at which these formats share common characteristics, whether print or e-text, whether retrieved by precoordinate indexing, or Boolean, or fuzzy logic. And the need to teach so much, means teaching better, more efficiently, and that brings us back to the role of technology.

C. Computer-assisted instruction programs and effective use of multi-media products such as Power Point are just a few of the new issues facing library instruction.

Cerise Oberman urges us to strive for balance in the use of technology. "In teaching balance means striving towards a philosophy that encourages students to appreciate the look and feel of books while understanding the role of electronic texts; to understand that much of the world's information is not online, while being comfortable using the Internet" (Oberman 36).

Ideas about bibliographic instruction that should wear into the next century when, it is probable, much of the world's current information will be online.

1. IT is a democratizing tool. Student and teacher may necessarily learn together; an enriching experience. When the teacher is also the learner, the process remains always in the conscious.

Learning how to learn, to seek for analogies among the tools in use, all are important, if non-traditional. An ideal test of self-learning would be a log detailing the first experience with an unknown source, with reference to the qualitative clues seen in the object and categorized by the items provided in the theoretical part of the course.

2. The systems model of input, process and output must be expanded to show links. Analysis of the value added at output is essential and leads back into the process and input to examine the nature of this particular information. Linking of system to system necessarily follows. What linked system, as a student develops his information web, will explain the difference between an article published in one periodical and a seemingly similar one in another? How in the digital world does one replace the contextualizing materials of masthead and editorial, of sponsorship and author's biographical notes? These are the key questions that must be supplied by the information specialist. As we master efficiencies in teaching the technology, we must also develop means to transfer this information.

3. The need to concentrate materials, so as to include both past and present. We fin de siecle librarians find ourselves stretching out hands to the past and to the future. In the same course students may be equally enthralled with a tale of bibliographic scholars determining the urtext by comparing copies of a manuscript book and downloading a favorite work from Project Gutenberg on the Internet and running it through a concordance package.

4. The need to tailor materials to groups increasingly more diverse in background, in motivation, in experience. The use of those software applications designed first for the business community enable more customizing of material within a realistic timeframe. Publication on demand of handouts, taking a basic presentation and substituting one set of examples for another—both are realizable because of IT.

5. The need to provide instruction for a geographically distributed population. Distance learning has been in use since the British began to establish colonies. The leapfrog effect of needing to move on to new material while waiting feedback on a previous lesson has been removed by IT. Email provides a forum for immediate query and answer between learner and instructor. The Web provides a multimedia environment for both presentation of materials and an interactive venue for problem solving and testing. Retention that results from direct application of what is just learned to problems testing the theory. Earlier materials lacked part of this system, or were too cumbersome to maintain and update.

D. Current energies and trends in library instruction programs will be responsive to new needs; the task of the next decade is to integrate the new gracefully with the old to meet the newer conditions of scholarship and learning.

A publication for a general audience called The Futurist hosts articles by many of the social and technical thinkers of our age. It constituted one of the fora of the oft quoted Harlan Cleveland who has written so much about the nature of the future and the need for public policies that address issues that will be important in it. A recent article by Edward Cornish in the same publication gives a laundry list of projected changes due sometime during the next thirty years. In general it highlights the unprecedented power to do whatever we want to do that information technology provides. It further suggests that we do not know how to use our growing power wisely. Our Apollos may have gone from fire bringer to arsonist with no intervening step.

Many of the changes that Edward Cornish suggests would already be recognized by librarians today. For instance: "The Internet will allow people easy access to stupendous quantities of information on innumerable subjects, allowing them to become far better informed than in the past." We now experience the first part; we have yet to experience the second part of that assertion. Again Cornish writes "The global network of interconnected computers and telecommunications links is already the biggest machine ever built . . . and will grow larger." True. He continues by noting that the costs of this technology are rapidly plunging. Cornish thinks that the day will come when computers will be given away to get consumers to buy attractive but expensive peripherals.

Further, the stupendous increase in the knowledge available in libraries and databases will pose an increasingly critical question: What must be in the curriculum, what must be in the canon? And how do we teach students and researchers to develop their own approaches to culling from these riches?

These are, I think, the challenges that the next century poses for bibliographic instruction, end user training, information studies components and other current modalities of learning to manage information and its retrieval.

First, what role does bibliographic instruction play in the global university. Of what should it consist, and how is it to be taught? With this virtual seat of learning connecting students, lecturers, and researchers in many nations via computer networks, satellite television, how will they all learn about the nature of information, learn to form qualitative judgments and the like. If, as at my institution, there is some concern for a professional future where the teaching comes from St. Elsewhere, the librarians are also concerned at the increasing responsibility they must shoulder for all this inundating information and all the classless students participating in distance learning who need their tuition.

Once a modus, such as the one outlined in the previous section, is developed, it may be that there will be no time to catch our breaths. Cornish further proposes the idea that education may become compulsory for adults as well as children, in a general way, similar to that enjoined by the various medical boards. The employer may provide but the employee will be responsible for staying au courant. BI in this context, it would seem, will rely heavily on the technology to facility retailoring of materials to suit niche markets. Whatever else happens in the next century, it is clear that lifetime learning will be a part of it.

REFERENCES

Arp, Lori. "Reflecting on Reflecting: Views on Teaching and the Internet." RQ 34(no.4):453–457.

Cornish, Edward. "The Cyberfuture: 92 Ways Our Lives Will Change by the Year 2025." Futurist 30(n1)(Jan/Feb. 1996): SS1–SS15.

Cummings, Anthony M. and others. University Libraries and Scholarly Communication. A Study Prepared for the Andrew W. Mellon Foundation, 1992

Information for a New Age: Redefining the Librarian. Chicago: American Library Association, Library Instruction Round Table. 1995.

Oberman, Cerise. "Unmasking Technology: A Prelude to Teaching." Research Strategies 13(Winter 1995):34–39.

Part 3:
The Bottom Line:
Expenses Involved in Electronic Scholarship

By Lois Cherepon and Karen Svenningsen
St. John's University/College of Staten Island, City University of New York

"If cost accounting sets out, determined to discover what the cost of everything is and convinced in advance that there is one figure which can be found and which will furnish exactly the information which is desired for every possible purpose, it will necessarily fail, because there is no such figure. If it finds a figure which is right for some purposes it must be necessarily be wrong for others."[1]—*John Maurice Clark, 1923*

The development of electronic scholarship in academic libraries has created an environment of economic complexity for librarians who are charged with the difficult task of selecting new electronic resources while continuing to develop traditional print research collections. Although the new electronic medium of scholarship has many advantages, financial issues about implementing new technology are yet to be fully resolved. The financial impact of acquiring electronic resources while developing print reference collections has affected the public and technical service library departments while fostering new affiliations among librarians and others throughout the campus community. Electronic publishing is having an impact not only on the way scholars conduct their research but also on the selection process of these products and the budgetary considerations in selecting print or electronic, or in some cases several versions of the same source. This paper focuses on the relationship between the university's mission statement and the use of cost-benefit analysis in selecting both traditional and electronic reference research sources. There is a need to align the selection of research formats with the university's mission statement while considering the budgetary realities of the institution. Through inter-departmental communication with teaching faculty and university administrators, librarians can utilize cost-benefit analyses that will meet the user's needs, support the institution's goals, and provide a rationale for purchasing which will reflect the library's mission statement.

OVERVIEW

In Peter Young's 1994 article in *Information Technology and Libraries*, he discusses new roles for librarians and outlines a fundamental change in the economic structure of information access. Young cites the changing nature of scholarship and the emergence of information as a commodity—goods or a service with economic value. Included in his discussion are issues relating to the economics of the product or service and the hardware to support that product in electronic formats. This shift from the traditional, or past practice of viewing information as a public good, which is accessible to anyone who could obtain the hard copy, has forced information professionals and those involved in the administration of library collections to reevaluate the way we do business daily and collect scholarly materials. Young presents insights into the changing economic structure of libraries' service to their clientele. He gives a detailed analysis of networks and their impact on the fee-vs-free debate. Young stresses the need for creating a new paradigm—new roles for libraries and librarians, with a definite focus on the need to evaluate resources, both print and non-print, as commodities and products which are quantifiable.[2]

This view may create some difficulty for information professionals who must now view scholarly resources in a new, non-traditional light, as commodities. We should no longer think of information and informational services as free and non-quantifiable, but analyze them as products or services which possess monetary economic value. *HarperCollins Dictionary of Economics* defines goods or commodities as—"any tangible economic products (washing machines, soap powders, tools, machines, etc.) that contribute directly or indirectly to the satisfaction of human wants . . . Economic goods are goods that are (a) scarce goods or (b) desirable goods that one would buy more of if one could."[3] The difficulty for many information professionals in academe is that with the introduction of electronic reference sources we must now shift our traditional view of scholarship from one in which information cannot be measured or quantified to a view which asks us to measure not only the set price of a published item but also the total cost of all the elements of electronic scholarly sources.

Tightened budgets have forced the understanding of economic commodities into *everyone's* conscience. Information resources, or commodities, should be evaluated on an economic basis, as opposed to the traditional method of viewing information resources as non-quantifiable. This viewpoint requires examining a source or product as an economic commodity regardless of whether that source is a book, CD-ROM, or an online product. The issues of collection development and reference budgeting become complex when librarians are faced with many choices of the same, or very similar, products available in different formats. There are so many varieties of formats in which a reference source is produced, or in which the information commodity is available, that the decision making process becomes increasingly complex. Within the framework of viewing an information resource as an economic commodity, we could simplify the task of reference collection development by utilizing cost-benefit analyses for the selection of information resources.

Current economic uncertainty facing many academic communities requires a close examination of the reference resource budget and collection development policies. While libraries continue to function in an environment where technology is accelerating at what sometimes seems to be the speed of light and budgets are decreasing at a similar rate, our users' demands continue to increase. This scenario presents a quandary—the need for additional reference materials in various formats—both print and electronic—and resource budgets which are inadequate to meet these needs. We are playing a balancing act with our collections, trying to keep up with technology and the new electronic resources yet continuing to develop our print collections. This balancing act is especially difficult because there are areas where technology may not have kept pace with the subject matter, such as history and literature. These subject collections must continue to grow, yet some of the funds traditionally budgeted for print sources are now being funneled into the growth area of electronic resources, such as the science and business areas.

Librarians purchase reference books through the general book allocation. For example, business materials are usually purchased for the business collection, not necessarily for reference collection development. Many librarians purchase serials and non-print resources in the reference area through the serials budget lines, not a separate reference serials line. Because reference does not typically have a separate line item budget and because electronic resources may force us into areas of technology beyond our expertise, the selection of non-print resources presents librarians with a new or unique situation. We must now coordinate our purchases not only with librarians and library administrators but also with administrators and professional staff from other units. Reference collection development, once the domain of the reference department, has taken on a new direction, one which requires a consorted effort among librarians, teaching faculty, administrators, and technology professionals.

Electronic resources compound this issue by bringing other factors into the analysis. In the evaluation of electronic reference resources, not only the usefulness of the item, but many other cost factors accompany the resource. These cost factors such as hardware, maintenance, and updating of the equipment and the resource are both hidden and apparent. Maintenance of print and non-print reference resources have traditionally been factored into the budget of the institution. An example is the projection of additional support personnel responsible for maintenance, updating, weeding, shelving, and repairing of print and non-print reference sources.

In the absence of a separate reference line budget and in the midst of electronic scholarly resources, librarians must learn to build new bridges among library departments and between the library and other academic units. Librarians can no longer afford to operate within a self-contained unit or department. Lines of communication must be fostered and cultivated, so that collection development librarians in the acquisitions department and librarians in the reference department consciously seek to work together on the process of selecting research materials regardless of the format. Librarians, both public and technical service, must then move beyond the library's walls and seek active roles on university-wide committees and task forces. Jerry Campbell proposes a transitional library model or TLM for libraries faced with the changing parameters of technology. In his article "Getting Comfortable with Change: A New Budget Model for Libraries In Transition," he places an emphasis on teamwork stating that "a library in transition must find a way to escape the rigidity and inflexibility of the divisions within the existing library model . . . to redesign the library on the basis of a team approach."[4] Through active roles on campus, librarians will gain a better understanding of scholarly research needs, make contacts with technical support personnel and increase the knowledge and will also gain the technical support and knowledge necessary to make informed purchasing decisions.

Those responsible for selecting and developing the reference collection should have a working formula. This formula would help in the decision making process by clearly defining how the product or service would meet the mission and goals of the institution. Because every discipline is unique in its needs, this working formula of materials selection and collection development should encompass a functional definition of information resources, a clearly stated consensus which could be cited throughout the university or college. If the ultimate goal is to find a common ground among the various formats of scholarly reference resources, then information specialists must establish a common definition of information resources, one which would create a baseline to employ in all discussions pertaining to the library, as far reaching as the university's strategic plan and as local as library committees. The definition needs to encompass print, non-print, and electronic reference resources and all of the fixed, variable, and foreseeable hidden costs. Information resources as defined in ARL Spec Kit No. 166 (1990) includes those funds used to acquire and lease materials with funds used for the following: books, serials, government documents, microforms, videos, sound recordings, maps, manuscripts, computer files (PC-based diskettes, mainframe tapes, CD-ROM), resource sharing agreements, binding, preservation and conservation, consortia memberships, remote database sharing, bibliographic utility memberships and transaction fees, computer hardware to manage computer files, computer file processing and servicing, interlibrary loan and document delivery.[5] It is imperative that the academic community agree to a working definition of information resources, or as in our specific example, to reference information resources, if the mission of the institution and the library's collection development policy is to remain unified toward a common goal. The definition forms the basis of selecting scholarly materials and serves as a point of reference for all academic units.

This partnership and exchange of information should be an ongoing process, as in traditional collection development procedures. Information, in whatever format, be it a book, CD-ROM, multimedia or future trends not yet fully examined, remains the basic economic commodity of the academic library community. Just as the influx of technology has expanded the paradigm of scholarship from a local community to a global environment, the administrators and faculty who serve as guardians of scholarship in their institutions must also collaborate in a new atmosphere, beyond departments, library walls, and self-serving constituents. Jane Dysart and Rebecca Jones in their article "Tools for the Future: Recreating or 'Renovating' Information Services Using New Technologies" encourage librarians to "Review, Refocus, Redefine, Relate, Revamp, and Recreate"[6] their framework for providing information services within this new transitional environment, which encompasses print, non-print, and electronic scholarly resources: "Your mandate or mission is the framework within which all decisions concerning products, services, service levels, staffing, and resource allocation are made."[7]

MISSION STATEMENT

The library's mission statement should support the university's strategic plan and should be broad and directional in focus, providing purpose and general guidelines for the existence of the library as an academic unit. Librarians should be able to develop objectives and anticipate future areas of growth based on the directional guidelines of the library's mission statement. The library's goals and service are defined by its mission statement. A cost-benefit analysis should be charted within the framework of the library's mission statement. In *Creating a Financial Plan: How-To-Do-It Manual for Librarians*, Betty Turrock discusses the importance of financial planning as part of the overall strategic plan of the institution. She refers to the "The New Age Library Mission Statement" and describes it in the following way: "The fundamental purpose of the New Age Library is to provide our community with the right information, in the right form, at the right time, while insuring the most cost-effective use of resources. The library acts as a conduit to and from other external information sources and services."[8] Turrock goes on to say "The library's mission statement gets its roots from the mission statement of its parent organization: . . . the university if it's an academic library."[9]

When collaboration between the library and other academic units exists, the library's goals are clearly represented and the university's mission statement serves as the guideline for all units. Together they will decide the details on how to implement "the right form" and "the right time" and "the most cost-effective use of resources." As Betty Turrock comments, the mission statement should also clearly define "Who we are? Why we are here? and What is our business? . . . As a result, both the library's mission statement and that of its parent institution are operatives in financial planning, and both are points of reference for library managers in their day-to-day work and in moments of crisis."[10] A clear mission statement, one that encompasses all types of information formats and a clear financial plan within the institution's goals and objectives, should form the basis of decision making in the library.

Similarly, GraceAnne Andreassi DeCandido in an editorial from the now defunct *Wilson Library Bulletin* emphasizes that a mission statement as

> A statement of purpose . . . should be straightforward and memorable—the kind of thing any staff person can state clearly and concisely and can internalize readily . . . Once a library articulates its mission, it should be disseminated everywhere, in all the places where staff and patrons can see it daily. The mission statement informs the choices for collection development, acquisitions, reference services, community information provision—in short, for everything the library does . . . Mission statements need to be revisited regularly, too. Times, needs, missions change, and statements of purpose must also. Without an understanding of the mission, a librarian doesn't know whether to put the money into picture books or romance novels, hard rock CD's, or poetry on tape.[11]

Reference tools must be purchased with this vision at the center or core of the rationale for purchasing the product or service.

In Michael Gorman's article "Five New Laws of Librarianship," he presents several hypotheses. "Another aspect of this law (Ranganathan's Five Laws) is its emphasis on humanity—our mission is both to the individual seeker of truth and to the wider goals and aspirations of the culture." In the academic institution, the mission of the university or college is the wider goal, which encompasses library's goals and serves as the basis of the library's mission statement. Gorman goes on to state that "with a sense of history and a knowledge of enduring values and the continuity of our mission the library can never be destroyed."[12] Active participation of librarians both within their unit and beyond will ensure the "continuity of our mission."

Larry Benson has written about the need for a philosophy to support our purchases of books and periodicals, most recently in his article "Scholarly Research and Reference Service in the Automated Environment," which appeared in *The Reference Librarian*. He states "there will always be a gulf between our philosophy of the service we would like to render and the reality of the service we can provide . . . In spite of the challenges, we must maintain our resolve to narrow the distance between the two by creating opportunities to influence scholarly research through a librarian-faculty team effort."[13] He stresses the need for reference librarians to create their impact on scholarly research through the development of better relationships with teaching faculty, which will help ease the selection process by providing the librarian or information professional with a detailed picture of the true needs of scholars. We propose that librarians should take this strategy a step farther and go beyond the librarian-faculty team to become active on committees which encompass faculty, librarians, and administrators. Regardless of the organizational structure of the institution, communication must take place among all of the units and divisions. Mutual recognition of skills, the sharing of ideas, and the articulation of needs and goals must be communicated throughout the institution.

Ralph A. Wolff notes that the library, technology, and the critical thinking skills of the students are all intertwined in the mission statement of the library, or at least ideally they should be intertwined.[14] The goal of the library's mission statement is that it should focus on this connection among the students, the faculty, and the means utilized by the library to assist in the learning process. The costs and benefits of utilizing both print and electronic scholarly resources in reference to foster the critical thinking skills necessary for this learning process become a pivotal point of concern in the overall discussion of the library's mission statement. It is through the tools employed by the reference librarians that the scholarly research process takes on new directions and new avenues of thought processes. Reference librarians must guide the scholar, both student and faculty, to the most appropriate scholarly resource. They must also guide them in the use of these sources. It therefore becomes the role of the reference librarian to study the costs and benefits of these sources and recommend which items will best serve patrons. Reference librarians can no longer sit back and decide which item to purchase based on a consensus of reviews, be it book reviews or technology reviews.

Librarians must examine the services, the products, the hardware or facilities, and recommend the purchases based on a critical analysis of cost-benefit factors in conjunction with the library's mission statement. Purchases of products, such as books or subscriptions or services, will be based on the cumulative study of the products themselves, the needs and mission of the institution, and the best analysis of how these products will serve our library today and in the years to come. Will the products or services purchased today fulfill the objectives of the library and institution in the future? Will they be as useful, or more importantly, will products purchased this year be accessible five years from now given the swift and frequent software changes and hardware configurations? These are some of the questions reference librarians should be asking vendors when they are considering replacing or supplementing a current print product with an electronic version of the same source. Several electronic versions of a source may exist; for example, ERIC is accessible in many formats including: CD-ROM subscription, direct online access via fee-based services such as Dialog, or Internet access. A cost-benefit analysis would assist librarians in organizing all the positive and negative elements of the product under consideration.

COST BENEFIT ANALYSIS

Many librarians refer casually to cost and benefit analysis, but few in the library community understand the intended method for application. Cost-benefit analysis as defined in *HarperCollins Dictionary of Economics* is "a technique for enumerating and evaluating the total social costs and total social benefits associated with an economic project."[15] Jose-Marie Griffiths and Donald King offer a library perspective as stated in their manual *Library Cost Benefit Analysis*,

> Cost and benefit analysis is one form of economic evaluation that is designed to provide information and a rationale for making decisions . . . to continue or discontinue certain operations, systems, services or products . . . to choose among alternative equipment or methods or performing system functions . . . to charge for services or not and, if so, how much or . . . to allocate resources among alternatives. To make such decisions one must know how possible outcomes of decisions will affect the object of the decision (e.g., a service or product) as well as other participants in the environment within which it resides.[16]

Griffiths and King continue,

> Cost and benefits should be described in terms of the unfavorable (i.e., costs) and favorable (i.e., benefits) outcomes of input and output and consequences such as effectiveness . . . If the outcome of the comparison is favorable it is recorded in a benefit column. The trade off between cost and benefit can be made by comparing all the items in the cost column against the items in the benefit column. The outcome of choosing between each alternative can be described in terms of their costs (i.e., dollar amounts associated with resource expenditures

and other quantifiable and non-quantifiable detriments that occurs as well), and benefits (i.e., dollar amounts associated with the favorable outcomes or consequences of choosing an alternative and other quantifiable or non-quantifiable benefits). Thus, cost and benefits (of a component, activity, service or product, function or library) are expressed in terms of input expenditures and other resources, and output results in terms of performance, attributes, and effectiveness.[17]

Cost benefit analysis attempts to decide whether the outcome is worth the expense. In simplest terms, the resource that expedites or is favorable to the process is worth spending budget dollars on, and the resource that impedes should not have a place in the budget.

A decision to change a technological function in one area of the library will not only affect that particular function, but may also affect an entire library operation. For example, a decision to purchase an index service with document delivery capabilities will not only affect reference service and patrons' expectations but also change the number of interlibrary loan requests. Although not a recent article, an excellent overview of cost-benefit analysis can be found in the Thompson Cummins article "Cost-Benefit Analysis. More Than Just Dollars and Cents," which appeared in the 1989 issue of *The Bottom Line*. Cummins presents a succinct definition and a "how to do it" summary of cost-benefit analysis. He states that "The concept of cost-benefit analysis is best appreciated if its motivation is understood. The key is whether reallocation of resources results in being better off and certainly not being worse off. The simplest way is to ask those who will be affected; for example, library patrons might be polled on whether they would be willing to pay for a new program and, if so, how much. Cost-benefit analysis is not an attempt to convert decision making into a formula, but it does provide a framework for decision making—a method of listing and quantifying the pros and cons of a problem or opportunity in order to weigh the importance of each. As a tool for better fiscal control, it supplements but does not replace judgment or political acumen."[18]

Cummins goes on to list the five basic steps in conducting a cost-benefit analysis.[19] The following explanation employs his five step process.

Step #1) Establishing Objectives

In selecting reference resources, the first step is to list the benefits gained from purchase of the source. The librarian needs to be able to track or trace the objective for selecting the resource. This objective is a clearly defined outcome of the product under consideration. The objective designates a kind of test, as a true-false test, that reduces subjective factors in answering and prioritizing. Two criteria should be listed, the content and the format of the product under consideration. For example, selecting ERIC on CD-ROM creates a positive-negative scenario. This format of ERIC provides enhanced citation retrieval, diminishes long term shelf space, research time, and maintenance. Negative attributes include limited number of users at any given time, the need for additional equipment and increased user instruction. Therefore, the objective would be stated as the product being purchased to save shelf space and maintenance while enhancing retrieval results, something that would be impossible to achieve with the present print version of this product. One common objective in analyzing the product might be to determine to what extent the researcher's needs are inherently part of the library's and university's needs. How can the greatest amount of information available to the scholar given budget constraints and the institution's goals? The strategy is to create a foundation for recommending the purchase based on the strategic plan or goals of the institution.

Step #2) Establishing the Program's Impact on Those Objectives

The reference librarian selecting a product, must determine the impact of the selection on the objectives of the selection. If the objectives are to save space, reduce maintenance, and enhance searching capabilities, then the impact on these objectives can be described as how the saving of space, time, and staff labor cost would affect, either positively or negatively, the function of the component, the reference area, the entire library, and finally the institution as a whole. Griffiths and King clearly define how the various levels need to be brought under consideration, even for seemingly small purchases, if we are to use this method of analyzing and thus justifying the purchase.

Step #3) Determine Costs

After careful analysis of the product selection's impact on the objectives, one must calculate the dollar worth of that impact and the costs should be calculated in real numbers when possible. Common units of cost among different formats of reference resources, including but not limited to the following:

- initial product or service fees
- hardware and software
- professional and support personnel
- training investment
- dissemination of information in various formats—print, disk, faxes, data transfer, etc.
- overhead (building maintenance, lighting, climate control, electric power, security, etc.)

These common units of cost include fixed costs (both one time purchases and recurring fixed costs), variable costs, and hidden costs. For example, fixed costs could include the hardware, setup, manuals, furniture, and training. Recurring fixed costs might include subscription fees, maintenance of hardware and software, and in-house created training and instruction materials. Some examples of variable costs could include labor costs, telecommunications, supplies such as ink, ribbons, paper, etc... There are also costs generated which are unique to a particular format. These unique costs can include storage cabinets for microform products, shelving space for books, CD-ROM drives for CD-ROM formats, telecommunication cables and connections for online service. As Cummins states in his overview, "An estimate of the total cost of a program includes any and all capital costs as well as operating costs for the life of the program. As the total amount cannot always be definitely determined, the important cost becomes the opportunity cost of the program, which is the cost loss of alternative programs not pursued."[20]

An example of this would be selecting the CD-ROM version of a resource as opposed to the online version. With the CD-ROM product, one can serve many researchers at one time if it is networked or connected to a local area network. The online version (i.e., fee based services such as Dialog) would allow access to only one user at a time, unless the product subscription is specified as multi-user, which in turn would incur multi-site licensing fees and the need for multiple work stations. Down time and currency would also differ between the two products. An example of opportunity loss cost would include analysis of these differences, as previously stated.

Step #4) Discounting Costs and Weighing or Establishing Benefits

Since the costs and benefits of any particular product do not always occur within one fiscal year, Cummins cites what he describes as the discount rate, which is "a process of converting a flow of returns or costs incurred over a number of years to a single present value... Since many programs and services involve multiple-year decisions, the returns are compounded over several years. Discounting simply adjusts sums expected in the future to their present value equivalent."[21]

He cites the benefit analysis in the following definition: "The additional value of goods and services that could be produced is measured against the increase in expenditure of resources. The difference is net benefits."[22] Cummins presents the weighing or establishing of benefits as the decision criteria, in which the two basic criteria include the benefit-to-cost ratio and the net present value of the resource selected. The product selected is analyzed by giving the present value of the benefits less the present value of the costs. If the ratio is positive, the product selected would then be considered cost efficient. The "benefits" category is perhaps the most difficult to define in terms of library service because of the hidden variables, which cannot always be weighed or measured in economic terms. An example of this would be the benefit gained in providing the product through an online system, which could theoretically be accessible 24 hours a day from on-site or off-site locations. Measuring benefits in terms of convenience is difficult because how could one measure the time saved or ease of accessibility for the researcher? A user survey might help one justify the expenditure by providing the hard numbers or percentages of satisfied scholars researching with such a system.

Step #5) Summarizing the Findings

In summarizing the results of the analysis, the librarian must decide if the outcome of the selection is worth what it cost to provide. Do the benefits outweigh the cost? Are expenditures budgeted with the objective of providing the greatest value to as many users as possible? Since the benefits portion of the analysis is difficult to measure in terms of service provided, then the answer to this question may not be as definitive as the economic model suggests. As Carol Tenopir states, "... one problem lies in that it is, moreover, often difficult to determine exactly what coverage is provided in any database."[23] F.W. Lancaster also stresses this point in his book, *If You Want to Evaluate Your Library*: "Cost-benefit analyses are very difficult to perform in the information service environment and perhaps no study of this kind has ever been fully credible."[24]

Alison Keyes evaluates methods which can be used to justify the value of special libraries. She explains the application of cost benefit analysis and states, "Cost-benefit analysis is one technique to demonstrate the positive benefits of certain expenditures (costs) on information services."[25] The cost-benefit ratios table she presents can be easily applied to different reference resources. Estimated benefits of ERIC on CD-ROM as opposed to the online source can be measured in terms of a comparison between the recurring fixed costs of the two products. Prior to determining the costs of the two products, one should first establish the objectives and the impact of those objectives on the program or service selected. Following a determination of the costs, one must then discount the costs and weigh or establish the benefits of that particular product. The final step is to summarize the formula's outcomes.

Using ERIC as an example, one objective might be to increase accessibility of this resource to library patrons. The librarian must study and weigh the impact that the various formats of ERIC will have on the library patron including performance, ease of use, currency, information integrity, and availability. Other objectives would constitute listing different considerations; for example, if the objective is to save space in the library then the considerations might include hardware, equipment, and facilities.

In determining the costs, both variable and fixed costs need to be examined. Citing ERIC selection as an example, recurring fixed costs include subscription fees, online access and password fees, maintenance and training. These costs can be projected over a given time span to illustrate the differences in choosing one product over another. In this projection, the current inflation rate can be factored into the analysis. The discount rate which Cummins cites is the projected expenditures over a number of years adjusted to its present value. A summary of the findings would include an analysis of the products' considerations and the determined costs.

Although the benefits may be difficult to measure or quantify, cost-benefit analysis is still a useful tool to employ in selecting reference materials and force the selector to make purchasing decisions in compliance with the goals of the institution. This compels the selector to review not only the concrete data but also the other variables, including fixed costs (both one-time and recurring), hidden costs and variable costs. Diane Tebbetts says in "What Library Services Really Cost," "Cost analysis is, therefore, a powerful analytical tool for the systematic study of the library's operations. It is, of course, only one part of the local picture ... quality and effectiveness as related to the mission of the library are still of paramount importance."[26]

In today's rapidly changing information environment, scholarly resources cannot always be strategically analyzed. Some librarians incorporate a cost benefit analysis model in their daily operations, but they may not be examining the factors in precise economic formula. Librarians may follow a cost-benefit formula in decision making but applying this method intuitively rather than systematically. Although a true cost benefit analysis is often time consuming, it may be worth the extra effort to justify purchasing decisions. Larry Benson states, "we must become more knowledgeable about complex technologies, more creative in promoting new electronic systems, and more energetic about working with our clienteles or we will lose our opportunities to teach faculty and graduates about the new programs from which they may benefit ... "[27] It is imperative that librarians examine the basic elements of costs and weigh each against the benefit of that particular format. The goal should be to use the library's mission statement as a foundation for analyzing costs and benefits of a particular product or service, one that would best serve the library and the institution's mission. The debate in electronic scholarship will intensify as library service moves and transcends the walls of the building. The common ground is to do the most 'good' with our limited resources and in so doing, examine, analyze, and weigh the costs and benefits.

ENDNOTES

1. J. Maurice Clark, *Studies in the Economics of Overhead Costs*, (Chicago: University of Chicago, 1923): 14.
2. Peter R. Young, "Changing Information Access Economics: New Roles for Libraries and Librarians", *Information Technology and Libraries* 13 (June 1994): 109.
3. Christopher Pass, *Harper Collins Dictionary of Economics*, (New York: Harper Collins Publishers, 1991): 220.
4. Jerry D. Campbell, "Getting Comfortable with Change: A New Budget Model for Libraries in Transition", *Library Trends* 42 (Winter 1994): 454.
5. Peggy Johnson, *Materials Budget in ARL Libraries: Spec Kit 166*, (Washington, DC: Association of Research Libraries, Office of Management Studies, 1990): 10.
6. Jane I. Dysart and Rebecca H. Jones, "Tools for the Future: Recreating or 'Renovating' Information Services Using New Technologies", *Computers in Libraries* 15 (January 1995): 16.
7. Ibid.
8. Betty J. Turrock and Andrea Pedolsky, *Creating a Financial Plan: A How To Do It Manual for Librarians*, (New York: Neal-Schuman Publishers 1992): 11.
9. Ibid.
10. Ibid.
11. GraceAnne Andreassi-DeCandido, "Your Mission Should You Choose to Accept It", *Wilson Library Bulletin* 69 (March 1995): 6.
12. Michael German, "Five New Laws of Librarianship", *American Libraries* (September 1995): 784–785.
13. Larry Benson, "Scholarly Research and Reference Service in the Automated Environment", *Reference Librarian* no. 48 (1995): 67.
14. Ralph A. Wolff, "Using the Accreditation Process to Transform the Mission of the Library", in *Information Technology and the Remaking of the University Library*, ed. Beverly P. Lynch (San Francisco, Calif.: Jossey-Bass, Inc.): 85.
15. Pass, *Harper Collins Dictionary of Economics*, 100.
16. Jose-Marie Griffiths and Donald W. King, *Library Cost Benefit Analysis: A SUNY/OCLC Workshop Manual* (Albany, New York: SUNY/OCLC Network Office of Library Services, State University of New York, 1983): 2.
17. Ibid.
18. Thompson R. Cummins, "Cost Benefit Analysis: More Than Just Dollars and Cents", *The Bottom Line* 3 (1989): 19.
19. Ibid.
20. Ibid., 20.
21. Ibid.
22. Ibid., 19.
23. Carol Tenopir, "The Same Database on Different Systems", *Library Journal* 116 (May 1991): 59.
24. F.W. Lancaster, *If you Want to Evaluate Your Library*—2nd Edition. (Champaign, Illinois: Graduate School of Library and Information, University of Illinois, 1993): 304.
25. Alison M. Keyes, "The Value of the Special Library: Review and Analysis", *Special Libraries* (Summer 1995): 177.
26. Diane R. Tebbetts, "What Library Services Cost", *The Bottom Line* 6 (Spring 1992): 24.
27. Benson, "Scholarly Research and Reference Services in the Automated Environment", 68.

REFERENCES

Bauer, Benjamin F. "Balancing Your Database Network Licenses Against Your Budget". *Searcher* 3 no. 2 (February 1995):48–52.

Beiser, Karl. "CD-ROM by the Numbers". *Online* 19 no. 5 (September/October 1995):102–105.

Benson, Larry D. "Scholarly Research and Reference Service in the Automated Environment". *The Reference Librarian* No. 48 (1995):57–69.

Bickner, Robert E. "Concepts of Economic Cost." In King, Donald W., Nancy K. Roderer, and Harold A. Olsen (eds.) *Key Papers in the Economics of Information*. White Plains, NY: Knowledge Industry Publications, Inc., 1983, pp10–49.

Birdsall, William F. *The Myth of the Electronic Library: Librarianship and Social Change in America*. Westport, CT: Greenwood Press, (1994).

Budd, John M. and Karen Williams. "CD-ROMs in Academic Libraries: A Survey". *College & Research Libraries* 54 no. 6 (November 1993):529–35.

Campbell, Jerry D. "Getting Comfortable with

Change: A New Budget Model for Libraries in Transition" *Library Trends* 42 no.3 (Winter 1994):448–59.

Clark, J. Maurice. *Studies in the Economics of Overhead Costs*. (Chicago: University of Chicago Press,1923):234.

Cummins, Thompson R. "Cost-Benefit Analysis: More than Just Dollars and Cents" *The Bottom Line* 3 no. 2 (1989):18–21.

DeCandido, GraceAnne Andreassi. "Your Mission, Should You Choose to Accept It." *Wilson Library Bulletin* 6 (March 1995):6.

DeLoughry, Thomas J. "Remaking Scholarly Publishing". *Chronicle of Higher Education* 40 no. 17 (December 15, 1993):A15–A17.

Dowlin, Kenneth E. "Distribution in an Electronic Environment, or Will There Be Libraries as We Know Them in the Internet World?" *Library Trends* 43 no. 3 (Winter 1995):409–417.

Dubbeld, Catherine E. "CD-ROM—A Viable Alternative to Online Searching for Academic Libraries" *Electronic Library* 9 No. 4–5 (Aug-Oct 1991):245–50.

Dunn, John A.(Jr.) and Murray S. Martin. "The Whole Cost of Libraries". *Library Trends* 42 no.3 (Winter 1994):564–578.

Dysart, Jane I. and Rebecca J. Jones. "Tools for the Future: Recreating or 'Renovating' Information Services Using New Technologies". *Computers in Libraries* 15 no. 1 (January 1995):16–19.

Ekman, Richard H. and Richard E. Quandt. "Scholarly Communication, Academic Libraries, and Technology". *Change* 27 no. 1 (January/February 1995):34–44.

Fine, Sara. "Change and Resistance: the Cost/Benefit Factor." *The Bottom Line* 5 (Spring 1991):18–24.

Gorman, Michael. "Five New Laws of Librarianship". *American Libraries* 26 (September 1995):784–785.

Green, Kenneth C. and Steven W. Gilbert. "Great Expectations: Content, Communications, Productivity, and the Role of Information Technology in Higher Education". *Change* 27 no. 2 (March/April 1995):8–18.

Greenberg, Douglas. "Get Out of the Way If You Can't Lend a Hand: The Changing Nature of Scholarship and the Significance of Special Collection". *Journal of Library Administration* 19 no. 1 (1993):83–98.

Griffiths, Jose-Marie and Donald W. King. *Library Cost Benefit Analysis Workshop Manual*. Albany, New York: SUNY/OCLC Network Office of Library Services University of New York. 1983.

Gross, Robert A. and Christine L. Bergman. "The Incredible Vanishing Library" *American Libraries* 26 no.9 (October 1995):900–904.

Harloe, Bart and John M. Budd. "Collection Development and Scholarly Communication in the Era of Electronic Access". *Journal of Academic Librarianship* 20 no. 2 (May 1994):83–87.

Horton, Forest Woody, Jr. *Analyzing Benefits and Costs: A Guide for Information Managers*, (Ottawa,ON: International Development Research Centre, 1994)

Johnson, Peggy. *Materials Budgets in ARL Libraries*. Washington, D.C.: Association of Research Libraries, Office of Management Studies. 1990.

Kaser, Dick. "Paradigm Rift: When Print-Based Institutions Fight for Survival in the Electronic Age". *Computers in Libraries* 15 no. 6 (June 1995):6–8.

Keyes, Alison M. "The Value of the Special Library: Review and Analysis". *Special Libraries* 86 no. 3 (Summer 1995):172–187.

Lynch, Beverly P. (ed), *Information Technology and the Remaking of the University Library* New Directions for Higher Education No. 90 Volume XXIII Number 2., California: Jossey-Bass, Inc. 1995.

Martin, Murray S. *Collection Development and Finance: A Guide to Strategic Library-Materials Budgeting* (Chicago: American Library Association, 1995)

Metz, Paul. "Revolutionary Change in Scholarly and Scientific Communications: The View from a University Library". *Change* 27 no.1 (January/February 1995):29–33.

Miller, William. "Electronic Access to Information Will Not Reduce the Cost of Library Materials". *Library Issues* 15 no.6 (July 1995):1–4.

Nahl-Jakobovits, Diane and Carol Tenopir. "Databases Online and on CD-ROM: How Do They Differ, Let Us Count the Ways". *Database* 15 no.1 (February 1992):42–50.

Nelson, Michael L. "Database Pricing: A Survey of Practices, Predications" *Online* 19 no. 6 (November/December 1995):76–86.

Pass, Christopher. *HarperCollins Dictionary of Economics* New York: HarperCollins. 1991.

Pastine, Maureen and Carolyn Kacena. "Library Automation, Networking, and Other Online and New Technology Costs in Academic Libraries". *Library Trends* 42 no. 3 (Winter 1994): 524–536.

Reynolds, Judy. "A Brave New World: User Studies in the Humanities Enter the Electronic Age". *The Reference Librarian* no. 49/50 (1995):61–81.

Rogers, Michael. "Database Site Licensing Usage Rises 67 Percent Since 1994". *Library Journal* 120 no. 16 (October 1, 1995):23

Rowley, Jennifer. "A Comparison of Pricing Strategies for Bibliographical Databases on CD-ROM and Equivalent Printed Products". *Electronic Library* 12 no.3 (June 1994):169–75.

Salomon Condic, Kristine and Frank J. Leplowski. "Attitudes of Academic Librarians Toward CD-ROM Indexes and Print Cancellation". *RQ* 34 no.1 (Fall 1994):48–58.

Shreeves, Edward. "Embracing the Inevitable". *Journal of Academic Librarianship* 20 (July 1994): 136–7.

Sisson, Lorene and Donna Pontau. "The Changing Instructional Paradigm and Emerging Technologies: New Opportunities for Reference Librarians and Educators". *The Reference Librarian* no. 49/50 (1995):205–216.

Tebbetts, Diane R. "What Library Services Really Cost". *The Bottom Line* 6 no. 1 (Spring 1992):19–25.

Tenopir, Carol and Ralf Neufang. "Electronic Reference Options: Tracking the Changes". *Online* 19 no. 4 (July/August 1995):67–73.

Tenopir, Carol. "Internet Issues in Reference". *Library Journal* 120(October 1, 1995):28–30.

Tenopir, Carol. "The Same Databases on Different Systems" *Library Journal* 116(May 1, 1991):59–60.

Turrock, Betty J. and Andrea Pedolsky. *Creating a Financial Plan: A How-To-Do-It Manual for Librarians*. New York: Neal-Schuman Publishers, Inc. (1992):11+

White, Herbert S. "The Cost of Knowledge and the Cost of Ignorance". *Library Journal* 120 no. 11 (June 15, 1995):48–49.

White, Herbert S. "Hiding the Cost of Information" *The Bottom Line* 4 no. 4 (Winter 1990):14–19.

Wiedemer, John David and David B. Boelio. "CD-ROM Versus Online: An Economic Analysis for Publishers". *CD-ROM Professional* 8 no. 4 (April 1995):36–42.

Wood, Wendy D. "A Librarian's Guide to Fee-based Services" *The Reference Librarian* no. 40 (1993):121–129.

Wulf, Wm. A. "Warning: Information Technology Will Transform the University". *Issues in Science Technology* 11 no. 4 (Summer 1995):46–52.

Young, Peter R. "Changing Information Access Economics: New Roles for Libraries and Librarians". *Information Technology and Libraries* 13 (June 1994):103–14.

Zakalik, Joanna and Sara Burak (eds.) *Gale Guide to the Internet Databases* Detroit, MI.: Gale Research, Inc. (1995).

Part 4:
A Case Study In Electronic Scholarship Development: Meeting the Challenges of the Changing Face of Research

By Ree DeDonato
Columbia University

My role in this discussion is to describe some of the activities taking place at Columbia University which demonstrate how the library is in the forefront of development and leadership for the emerging electronic scholarship. Librarians at Columbia are not alone in their interest in shaping the teaching/learning/research environment in academe as is evidenced by all of us attending this conference. Some of the activities taking place at Columbia, however, are unique in the way Columbia's libraries, computer services and academic departments are working together designing programs to incorporate technology into the present and future directions of scholarly endeavors. I hope that by describing our efforts to you, we may discuss their implications and all come away with new insights for these and future initiatives.

Columbia is fortunate in that it has a well-established and widely used campus network from which to build on and to extend the libraries' outreach in the realm of electronic information delivery. For years, the libraries and AcIS (the Academic Information Services) have worked together. AcIS and the libraries report to the Vice President of Information Services and University Librarian. This organizational structure has enabled ongoing collaboration and promoted sharing of expertise in providing library and computing resources to the Columbia community.

From this working partnership, it became clear that a first step for enabling the library to exercise its leadership role in the emerging electronic scholarship is to ensure that its staff understand and are adept at using the developing technological innovations. Thus was born the Internet Training Program (ITP) for the library's professional staff. ITP was designed by a small core of Columbia library and AcIS staff in 1992 and "graduated" its first class in December 1993. Since then, the ITP has been offered each semester through the summer of 1995. Nearly 90 of us have taken the 16 week course taught by a changing team of 8–12 previous graduates. ITP's objective is to equip its students with the computer skills necessary to become competent users of the growing number of electronic resources and services encountered in our daily jobs and to be able to help others—fellow staff and library users—with their mastery of the world of electronic scholarly communication.

The course covers a variety of topics: everything from Telnet, to listservs, newsgroups, ftp, cunix (Columbia's UNIX system), gophers & veronica, wais and the web. Included in ITP are supplementary readings placed on course reserves, a rather hefty notebook of training documents and practice exercises, and weekly written evaluations. There are even prerequisites for enrollment (e.g., demonstrated basic computer literacy and competencies in email and kermit) in addition to one's individual project proposal which was part of the application to take ITP.

The class met once a week for 2 hours in a library training classroom where a combination of formal lecture, demonstration, hands-on practice and individual exercises were completed. A feature of the course which I particularly appreciated was that the alternating week's class time was designed as a "lab." Therefore, built into one's schedule were 2 hours to complete the prescribed hands-on exercises, review previous training topics and work on individual pathfinder projects all with a trainer present. ITP labs guaranteed that each of us could work at our own pace but still have the benefit of fellow learners and a trainer on hand to do some of our own collaborative learning. "I'm too busy with my job" excuses for those of us tending toward not doing our homework fell on deaf ears in the ITP structure!

The library administration, by supporting ITP fully, demonstrated its commitment to giving staff ample time to learn and master what was being taught. Each semester, ITP represented a major investment of staff resources engaged in formal training. This is not always the case for many of us learning new skills—on the job, on the fly or on our own. When taking the course, ITP was fully part of our job and it received the serious attention it deserved and required to be a success.

Completing ITP, in turn, helped us create the various Internet guides and subject resources in LibraryWeb or CLIO Plus as well as workshops we offered to students and faculty. It gave us a first-hand understanding of how important the learning process is which helped us design better instruction activities ourselves. And, as the number of ITP trained staff grew, we had more input to help identify new training issues. It became apparent, for example, that to keep ITP relevant greater emphasis on web related topics (e.g., HTML mark-up, web browsers) and a mechanism for refresher or advanced training workshops were needed.

A "2d Generation ITP" task force has submitted a proposal which completely redesigned the course. Instead of the full semester course model, ITP is now structured around beginning, intermediate and advanced series of classes. There will be 30 modules which staff can mix and match based on topic of interest and level of training need. We are looking forward to piloting the new ITP this year.

Another example of staff training activity evolved as an extension of the ITP; it is our weekly Friday afternoon open house in the library's computer training facility. During this regularly scheduled 2 hour block of time with a system's staff member present to serve as on-site consultant, staff can drop-in to seek help to resolve a specific problem or just to have access to a fully outfitted workstation to work on a project. (Not all of us have personal desktop access to full range of computing power available in the training room.)

The third key staff activity which supports training is the library/AcIS Web Users Group. WUG as it is known, began as rather informal meetings open to anyone working on Internet projects or interested in learning about various web developments, such as comparing web browsers, or understanding SGML or HTML mark-up, or how to use various web search engines. It quickly became the most timely brainstorming opportunity for the near daily development occurring in Columbia's LibraryWeb. WUG now meets monthly and is the forum where many ideas for adding new services or modifying the design of our homepages are shared and shape the practice and policies underlying the delivery of web based resources. It is not uncommon to have discussed a neat new service or design feature at WUG and find it available on screen later that day when browsing LibraryWeb. WUG has also "spilled over" to topical brown bag lunches where further exploration of a specific application is the focus. WUG is truly a grassroots movement of self-selected individuals (whether they are cyberexperts or devoted lurkers) whose suggestions directly shape what the public sees when using our electronic services.

ITP, the weekly open house and WUG are highlights of activities focused on developing staff expertise and promoting staff input to the technological applications changing the face of daily life at Columbia libraries. I mention these first as a way to underscore the importance of investing in our own human resources. If we are to help lead the way on our campuses, we have to have both a sound knowledge base and the freedom to exchange ideas and try things out.

Turning now to library activities which are focused on resources and services for our user community, I'd like to describe a few of the projects which fall under the umbrella concept of the Columbia Digital Library.

In Columbia Libraries' past few annual strategic planning retreats, technology in general and the idea of building a digital library in particular have become central to the continued refinement of our strategic plan. I'd like to share with you a brief section of a working document called "Strategic Planning for Integrated Delivery of Networked Information Services at Columbia University: the Columbia Digital Library" because it sets the stage for the outward focus of our efforts to contribute to the electronic scholarly environment on campus.

Columbia's digital library is a collection of information tools and resources made available to the Columbia community over the network in an organized, well managed and well supported manner. The contents of the digital library include research, instructional, administrative and student information in a variety of forms, including full text, images, indexes, catalogs, databases, multi-media resources, geographic and numeric datasets, and links to selected services on the Internet. The digital library organizes and delivers this content through powerful search and retrieval mechanisms, and it provides a wide array of tools and applications for users to manipulate and employ the content they retrieve. The University is allocating resources to building the infrastructure, the content, and the tools of the digital library, and in a program of research that will enable the digital library to evolve continually in step with changes in the information infrastructure. Current investments build upon other technology initiatives that led to installation of the fiber-optic network, authentication systems, and network management systems.

What is the content of and what are the tools and applications of our digital library today? How are we adding value to the existing electronic scholarly environment and making the digital library a real presence in real time for the students and faculty at Columbia.

The Online Books Evaluation Project is one of our digital library initiatives. My colleague Mary Summerfield, the Project Coordinator, has a paper in these proceedings; I hope you will read it. The Online Books Evaluation Project is supported by a three year, $700,000 grant from the Andrew W. Mellon foundation. There are 3 major areas of focus in the project: 1) our user community's adoption of and reaction to various online books and delivery system features provided by the libraries, 2) the relative lifecycle costs of producing, owning and using online books and their print counterparts, and 3) the implications of intellectual property rights and commercial traditions for the online format.

Nineteen ninety-five was the first year of the project and like many new initiatives, it had its share of fits and starts and delays. Progress has been made, however, in several areas. One of the components of the project in which I have been involved in my capacity as Undergraduate Librarian, is using online books in the Columbia College Core Curriculum. I have been working with selected teaching faculty to help integrate the use of online texts into "Contemporary Civilization," one of the required Core Curriculum classes taken by all Columbia College undergraduates. Contemporary Civilization, or "CC" as it is known, is a 2 semester course whose objective is "to help students 'to understand the civilization of their own day and to participate effectively in it'... to study and reflect critically upon the major ideas, values, and institutions that have helped shape the contemporary Western World." Authors read in CC include Plato, Aristotle, Machiavelli, Hobbes, Locke, Rousseau, Kant, Smith, Marx, Darwin, Nietzsche, and Freud. Students usually take CC in their freshman year.

We are currently using the Past Masters electronic full-text versions of titles which match the CC reading list to deliver online books to students. Selected titles have been mounted on the campus network within the "digital collections" section of LibraryWeb and appropriate site licensing is in place. These online books can be accessed via Lynx or Netscape and we are adding various searching capabilities to them. In addition, nearly 100 Past Masters titles in political and economic philosophy which relate to the broader curriculum are available in CD-ROM for use in the libraries Electronic Text Service.

An interesting thing about this particular part of the Mellon funded online books project is that it is aimed at beginning undergraduate students not faculty subject specialists or graduate students. Increasingly, Columbia's undergraduates arrive on campus fairly computer literate and pretty well wired. But at the same time we're finding that this does not mean they have used computers in what we typically call "serious research" much less are they accustomed to using electronic books in a scholarly context. It's quite a leap from *Myst* to John Stuart Mill's *On Liberty*. Also, if these selected online books become a successful teaching tool, they will generate a lot of traffic on our network as the target audience is large (over 40 sections of CC are offered each semester). How undergraduates will use online books, how will the availability of online books impact on the instructors teaching, how will online books relate to printed texts are some of the questions we hope to begin answering in this study.

While library and AcIS outreach to CC faculty and students has been modest to date, we continue to schedule online books demonstrations and meet to discuss ways to integrate the project into the curriculum. Some of the issues raised in this process have included questions of translations and editions used and the relationship between the digital and printed text, various needs for printing and/or downloading, designing meaningful course assignments which take advantage of the digital format, and of course, user training. We are working to "scale up" our outreach efforts and see a substantial increase in student use of the CC online books in the coming school year.

The last example of digital library developments I'd like to address concerns the use of images. Here again, the library is playing a leading role in the creation and delivery of a new service to enhance the teaching and learning experience through the innovative use of technology.

Masterpieces of Western Art or "Art Humanities" is another requirement in the Columbia College Core Curriculum. The Columbia College Bulletin describes the course as "an analytical study of a limited number of major monuments and images in Western art . . . to provide students with a foundation in visual literacy." The Parthenon, the Gothic cathedral of Amiens, works by Raphael, Michelangelo, Bruegel, Rembrandt, Bernini, Goya, Monet, Picasso, Frank Lloyd Wright, and Le Corbusier are studied. Beginning undergraduates enroll in this one semester course which incorporates the traditional lecture/slide presentation along with various field trips. (About 30 sections are offered each semester.) Until the debut of the "Art Humanities Image Reserves Database" this Fall, students relied on a printed compilation of 5x7 inch black and white reproductions either sold through the campus bookstore or available in the library's college reserves unit to study and review the art works presented in class. Neither the Art Department or the libraries have a slide library open to general student use.

Librarians and AcIS staff worked closely with the Chair of the Art Humanities Program and other faculty to identify the specific works to be digitized for the project. Some 1200 images were targeted and the library went about acquiring as many as possible from a variety of sources—sometimes slides taken by the faculty, sometimes CD-ROM images available from commercial suppliers like Saskia, Ltd. Appropriate permissions for networking was received for any commercially obtained images. Much of the digitizing was done by Columbia's AcIS staff for display on 19" color monitors. Procedures were implemented to add a catalog record for each image to the library's OPAC. At the same time, the Art Humanities homepage was designed and linked prominently to both the LibraryWeb and ColumbiaWeb. A thumbnail of each web image and caption listing creator, title of the work, date, location, brief description and 2 choices of image size is displayed. The full course description, syllabus, directory of instructors, and brief information on NYC museums were added to the homepage as well.

Hands-on workshops were offered first to those teaching Art Humanities and then to any interested students enrolled in the course. Through the instructional workshops we learned that students were eager to try their hand at manipulating the images even if they had never used a mouse or worked with online visual resources before. Intuitively, students sensed that this technology ought to put them in control. Almost immediately the questions started: how do I zoom-in on a section of the painting; can we put two views of the same building on screen side-by-side; can I download this image on to my "Mac" back in the dorm.

As the weeks passed, the use of the image database grew, hitting its high point not surprisingly in the three weeks before final exams. (Use statistics went from an average of 1500 per week to over 16,000!) By the opening of this Spring semester, a newly formed group of Art Humanities instructors added links to remote websites which contained additional images of the art works covered in class. This allowed us to begin filling-in the gap for those works for which we were unable to secure a site license for use on the network. Several instructors are creating individual homepages for their sections with information on specific assignments, class discussions and links to "personal favorite" websites.

As a library "high tech" service initiative, the Art Humanities Image Reserve Collection is clearly a success. It has enhanced the students' ability to review and study material presented in class and has encouraged an exciting working collaboration among the teaching faculty, librarians and AcIS staff. User training has been manageable and even has allowed us to expand our instruction to other relevant topics in the "ArtHum OnlineWorkshops."

We have, however, encountered a weakness in using the images in relation to their usefulness as a classroom teaching tool. For while the quality of the digitized image (e.g., resolution, color balance) displayed on the desktop monitor is very close to the original source (e.g., a slide), the image quality degrades when transmitted through an RGB projector onto the wall. We had originally hoped to see classrooms equipped with workstations so instructors would have the flexibility to tap into the full collection of images on the spot and in any order instead of relying on trays of 35mm slides and two projectors. But at present, the computer projected images are not acceptable substitutes for the slides shown in the classroom. Let's just say this presents us with another challenge to meet in the changing face of research in the electronic environment.

There are many other activities taking place at Columbia to make the digital library a reality for our community of users. Investing in staff to strengthen their skills and capitalize on their expertise, engaging in dynamic, collaborative projects with faculty and computing professionals, and producing results which directly benefit the teaching and learning process have characterized our efforts thus far. It is an exciting, sometimes exhausting effort, but one which is creating wonderful new services, resources and interpersonal contributions to Columbia's scholarly environment.

Columbia is one of the seven universities and seven museums participating in the Museum Education Site Licensing Project (MESL), a Getty Art History Information Program and MUSE Educational Media project. MESL hopes to explore and promote the educational benefits of digital access to museum collections from campus networks and assess the legal, administrative and technical mechanisms in doing this. MESL is a large project which is only now getting under way.

REFERENCES

Columbia University. "The Core Curriculum." Columbia College 1995–96: Columbia University Bulletin 20, no. 1 (May 22, 1995).

Columbia University Libraries. Internet Training Program Notebook. 1993–95.

Columbia University Libraries. Strategic Planning for Integrated Delivery of Networked Information Services at Columbia University: The Columbia Digital Library. (rev. 1/22/96)

Columbia University Online Books Evaluation Project: Annual Report to the Andrew W. Mellon Foundation, January 1995–January 1996.

'No Bar-Rooms or Theatres or Idle Vicious Companions': Criteria For The 21st Century

By Patrick Max
Castleton State College

This paper is organized under two general rubrics:

1. The title of the conference—"Finding Common Ground: Creating a Library of the Future Without Diminishing the Library of the Past," and
2. The title of my own paper—"'No Bar-Rooms or Theatres or Idle Vicious Companions': Criteria for the 21st Century."

Let me begin with the former, the title of the conference, and attempt to unravel the rather complex mystery that it suggests. Regarding "Creating a library of the future without diminishing the library of the past" I would say I think that we cannot create the library of the future without significantly altering the library of the past by focusing on new goals, new values, new visions of the profession. I suspect that we cannot make progress without challenging our past vision of the profession. We will inevitably relinquish long held practices and goals as we already have. The commonplace, "you can't make an omelet without breaking a few eggs," is operational here. However, since in a few moments I will feel constrained to claim that I am not a Luddite, let me say that the "egg breaking" should be a thoughtful process that carefully weighs past and present values, not a blind leap into an overmarketed and insubstantial future. Nevertheless, I feel very comfortable with my "the future-is-bound-to-require-change" beginning. Having said this, I would also say that I have little insight into, and no clear vision of, the library of the future. My reading of Macbeth suggests to me that we are punished for thinking that we know the future even when it is foretold to us by three witches, or Jeanne Dixon, or Nostradamus, or any of those misguided prophets who call themselves "futurists." My horoscope has never helped me with a market investment. Jean Dixon did not predict that OCLC would market a ghost product called CD450 in the 1980's and neither Nostradamus nor the CIA could predict the imminent collapse of the Soviet Union even a few hours before it happened.

But in the interest of titillating the techie lurking somewhere in my psyche, let me indulge momentarily in the language and vision of the futurists among us.

The library of the future has been variously described as a "high speed, high bandwidth network" of communication with a "shifted locus of information control" replete with "effortless interfaces," a veritable "digital magic carpet" in a restructured "virtual world." It is a world, we are told, where "collection developers" will be "needed for value-based privileging more than demand-based decisioning" and in which we can do "12 cool things on the Internet." Evidently the net effect of all of this has been to make us "the first nation in cyberspace" and to enable us to avoid the humiliating fate of low tech societies such as the Soviet Union. Finally we are told that our high tech era is "quite literally the age that humanity has looked forward to since the dawn of time." We are said to be "reaching a threshold, a line of demarcation, and on the other side of that line we will finally confront the true nature of Man."[1]

Wow. Captain Kirk is talking to Earth and I'm back in my dinosaur of a traditional library trying to save a few warehoused "passive objects" from imminent budget cuts.

Frankly, based on such discussions, the "common ground" in our conference's title appears to be a field of fire where the warring parties have nothing in common. And unfortunately for me, such descriptions of the virtual library have virtually nothing to do with my experience of libraries in real time—in the interesting but quite messy and flawed present. It seems to me that if we are going to find common ground, the search must begin with a clear and critical analysis of the present:

Who are we?
What are we doing?
What is changing about what we are doing?
How can we make a significant contribution to the life of our community?

Now, earlier, after saying that you have to break a few eggs to make an omelet (i.e. that real change is required to step into the future), I said that sooner or later I would have to claim that I was not a Luddite. Well, I am not a Luddite. (I say this fully recognizing that some will see a certain kinship here with Richard Nixon's "I am not a crook" speech.) I have worked with, spoken of and written about the new technology on numerous occasions, frequently indicating my appreciation of some current practices and my rather substantial hopes for the future of the new technology. (You may have read an article on the "Point of View" page of the Chronicle of Higher Education that was more or less aimed at rebutting Nicholson Baker's anti-electronic card catalog article in the New Yorker.) From my perspective, clearly, the profession has in its possession some marvelous new tools for meeting its social goals. I would further say that in some few ways these are not just tools but ideas and processes that may enable us to identify new and significant goals for the profession.

But we cannot move into the future with a distorted notion of progress—one that values this technology only because it is new and different and is perceived as a means to enhance personal prestige. I feel that the "techie as guru" approach to the future has little to offer the profession. It is not clear to me what the techies see in the present that warrants their apocalyptic predictions. We don't have perfection in practice, and they certainly don't have a vision of the profession that will enable us to judge the past and the present without distorting language and prejudices. Moreover, with the latest powerful tools of the new technology have come problems:

1. on the business/marketing end, vendors often have little understanding of their products, make extravagant marketing claims and have no notion of fair price. These extravagant claims are further inflated by those in the profession seeking to enhance their own prestige;
2. there has been sloppy design and/or creation of products that perform no real service (the electric hand-dryer syndrome);
3. the profession has adopted a set of criteria that validate only high tech services, goals, etc.;
4. the computer has become the paradigm for the human thought process.

Most significantly, as a result of our professional futurism, we have forgotten who we are and where we have come from.[2] Perhaps to begin to understand who we are or are not, a reference from Steven Spielberg's Empire of the Sun would be useful. In that film, a young abandoned English boy is depicted in a Japanese internment camp in China during World War II. The young boy is enchanted by airplanes. His attraction reaches a feverish pitch when the camp is attacked by U.S. planes. The boy rushes to the upper level of a tower, and, placing himself in harm's way, runs about hysterically shouting, Mustang P51, "Cadillac of the skies." Rushing to his rescue, the camp doctor is finally able to calm the boy by grabbing him and telling him to "stop thinking." The boy immediately calms down, and in tears, says that he cannot remember the color of his mother's hair, but then proceeds to recall several intimate experiences with his mother.

Like the boy in Spielberg's film, in our single minded enthusiasm for technology (in this case the Mustang P51, the "Cadillac of the skies"), we have distorted our identity; we have substituted one of our legitimate endeavors for the whole, a sort of professional synecdoche. We have forgotten our origins (our mothers) and thus lost a sense of our identity. Our professional dreams are filled with shiny "things," not human goals. So I believe that any common ground, any common understanding of the profession that will permit us to move into the future, can only be found in 1.) a clear and honest discussion of the present state of the profession and 2.) our memories of the "color of our mother's hair," that is a sense of the identity and purpose of the past. However critical the last decade has been in our professional lives, we would be ignorant and careless to ignore the preceding few hundred years.[3]

Over the past five to ten years I have become increasingly persuaded that many of our most important professional goals (goals which provide us with meaningful criteria with which to judge progress) are to be found in our uncool, interfaceless, undigitalized earlier history. So let's go back a couple of centuries to see what we can learn from America's first electrified (and electrifying) librarian, Benjamin Franklin. It might be useful for us all to reexperience that point in our collective history when American libraries were getting born. (I have come to listen to accounts of the founding of early libraries with the same reverence that fundamentalists reserve for the book of Genesis.)

In the late seventeenth and early eighteenth centuries, America was a cultural crossroad, an information highway if you will, at which met the rights of the individual, the printing press, democratic forms of government and Benjamin Franklin. Larzer Ziff says of this time, "Benjamin Franklin was a printer and beyond others in his day, even of fellow printers, he comprehended the change in consciousness that print was effecting. Printing, to be sure, had been established centuries before Franklin took up the trade, but in his America print was spreading from centers of learning and population into the countryside of towns and hamlets with rapidity unmatched in Europe. The printing press followed the flow of settlement as an institution of the common life."[4]

"Franklin sought to develop print's potential to create communities of readers from across the boundaries of a community previously defined by class, religious belief, or occupation." As Ziff says, Franklin, in fact, fostered a "revolution in perception, a revolution without which political revolution would not have occurred."[5] Clearly it was only a matter of time before the Library would be added to the symbiotic "printing-press-democracy-U.S.-Franklin" mix.

In the fall of 1727 Franklin gathered a group of young men (mostly tradesmen) in a club dedicated to "mutual improvement," to the "sincere Spirit of Enquiry after Truth" and to their legitimate claim to their full rights as human beings and citizens of a democratic society. Books far from being thought of as "passive objects" that could not "speak" to one another, were seen as the very "soul" of a culture. They were rightfully viewed as the process through which a society could examine its image and come to a new understanding of its future. And so very soon after the Junto was formed, Franklin proposed: "that since our books were often referr'd to in our Disquisitions upon the Queries, it might be convenient to us to have them all together where we met, that upon Occasion they might be consulted; and by thus clubbing our Books to a common Library, we should, while we lik'd to keep them together, have each of us the Advantage of using the Books of all the other Members, which would be nearly as beneficial as if each owned the whole."[6]

And thus a truly American library was born. As Franklin said later, "I shall always be ready with Pleasure to promote so good and necessary an Under-taking, as erecting a Publick Library in this City."[7]

"The nineteenth century mechanics and mercantile libraries echoed Franklin's call to the democratic table and the life of the human spirit. When the labor of the day is over, instead of the apprentice scouring the streets, visiting bar-rooms or theatres, mingling with idle, vicious companions, he takes his seat in this library with a rich intellectual repast before him, or, being privileged to take a book home with him, he trims his lamp and reads aloud to his little brothers and sisters, scattering good seeds among them to take root hereafter...."[8]

Although I must say that a Blackbush neat and a few idle companions always seemed to me to be part of a rich cultural stew, the point is that libraries were a critical part of an effort aimed at providing free and open access to the language and ideas that shaped a fledgling democracy. Moreover in Myths, Dreams, and Mysteries, Mircea Eliade says that reading is the magical way in which a culture creates a new vision of itself in order to meet new and different challenges. He says, "reading replaces not only the oral folk traditions, such as still survive in rural communities of Europe, but also the recital of the myths in the archaic societies. Now, reading, perhaps even more than visual entertainment, gives one a break in duration, and at the same time an escape from time. Whether we are 'killing time' with a detective story, or entering into another temporal universe as we do in reading any kind of novel, we are taken out of our own duration to move in other rhythms, to live in a different history."[9]

In On Learning to Read, Bruno Bettelheim says, "literature in the form of religion and other myths was one of man's greatest achievements since in them he explored for the first time his existence and the order of the world. Learning to read, then, appeals to the highest and the most primordial aspects of the mind."[10] The issue here is not "reading" in the narrow sense, i.e. reading a book, rather it is gaining access to the significant debate that shapes the future of the culture.

So it is very important for us to remember that the library is not merely a series of "high speed" "high bandwidth," "effortless interfaces," no matter how utterly "cool" it may be to think of it that way. In the end I am convinced that our common ground for moving into a very complex future must be the "intellectual advancement of the whole community,"[11] "the life-long education of the whole people."[12]

An 1852 report by the committee of the newly formed board of trustees appointed to establish a public library in Boston states: "For it has been rightly judged that,—under political, social and religious institutions like ours,—it is of paramount importance that the means of general information should be so diffused that the largest possible number of persons should be induced to read and understand questions going down to the very foundations of [the] social order, which are constantly presenting themselves, and which we, as a people, are constantly required to decide, and do decide, either ignorantly or wisely. That this can be done,—that is, that such libraries can be collected, and that they will be used to a much wider extent than libraries have ever been used before, and with much more important results, there can be no doubt."[13]

Our goals must reflect our collective commitment to creating an open and freely accessible learning environment (real and "virtual") that enables people to fully exercise their rights and responsibilities as citizens, and permits individuals to reach their full human potential.

ENDNOTES

1. These quotations, aimed at characterizing the future of the library, are taken from a number of different sources. Among them are included the Washington, D.C. conference, "Challenging Marketplace Solutions to Problems in the Economics of Information," an article by Maurice Line reprinted in OCLC Systems and Services (vol.11, no.4). Several articles from the December, 1995 issue of Information Technology and Libraries (vol.14, no.4) are also quoted. See also Fred Moody's description of Microsoft's projects, "Encarta" in I Sing the Body Electronic for examples of high tech product development and jargon.
2. Clifford Stoll's Silicon Snake Oil (Doubleday, 1995) generally echoes these sentiments. He talks about the false promise of technology and quotes Thoreau: "Our inventions are wont to be pretty toys, which distract our attention from serious things."
3. In The Gutenberg Elegies (Faber and Faber, 1994) Sven Birkerts talks about the way in which "electronic postmodernity" causes "a divorce from the past." He also says "that what distinguishes us as a species is not our technological powers, but rather our extraordinary ability to confer meaning on our experience and to search for clues about our purpose from the world around us."
4. Larzer Ziff, "A Silent Revolution: Benjamin Franklin and Print Culture," in Publishing and Readership in Revolutionary France and America (a Library of Congress Symposium), ed. Carol Armbruster (Westport, Connecticut: Greenwood, 1993), 45,46.
5. Ziff, 55.
6. Benjamin Franklin, "The Autobiography" in Margaret Korty, "Franklin and the Library Company of Philadelphia," in Reader in American Library History (Washington, D.C.: NCR Microcard, 1971), 34.
7. Benjamin Franklin in The Papers of Benjamin Franklin, L.W. Labaree, ed., in Reader in American Library History (Washington, D.C.: NCR Microcard, 1971), 38.
8. New York Daily Tribune, September 24, 1850, p.1 in Reader in American Library History (Washington, D.C.: NCR Microcard, 1971), 74.
9. Mircea Eliade, Myths, Dreams and Mysteries (New York: Harper Torchbooks, 1967), 34–37.
10. Bruno Bettelheim and Karen Zelan, On Learning to Read (New York: Knopf, 1982), 49–51.
11. "Report of the Trustees of the Public Library of the City of Boston," (July, 1852) in Robert Lee, The People's University—The Educational Objective of the Public Library," in Reader in American Library History (Washington, D.C.: NCR Microcard, 1971), 119.
12. Jared Heard, "Origin of the Free Public Library

System of Massachusetts," in Reader in American Library History (Washington, D.C.: NCR Microcard, 1971), 118.

13. "Report of the Trustees," in Reader in American Library History (Washington, D.C.: NCR Microcard, 1971), 120.

Research across the Curriculum: Integrating Our Teaching with Our Institution's Academic Goals

By Steve McKinzie
Dickinson College

Professional papers at traditional library conferences such as this one tend to fall into two broad categories. (We cannot say that this is always the case, but it is generally true.) The first category consists of descriptive, practical, and largely self-congratulatory narratives. Such papers catalog the successes and triumphs of the profession. They follow a pattern that runs something like this: here is how we approached a major difficulty at Dickinson College, or here is how we did it at Harvard. These papers are the scholarly lifeblood of the discipline. We need them. And we need good ones.

Then there is the other, smaller group of papers that analyze major problems and offer tentative solutions. Sometimes such papers complain about libraries. Sometimes they lament the shortcomings of librarians. Unlike those in the first category, such papers aren't really practical or down-to-earth, and they are often written by people who seem to enjoy abstraction or by people who like to talk about crises. These kinds of presentations (however much they may whine about things and however much they may arrogantly pontificate on the way things ought to be) are really quite necessary. They serve to give us a collective jolt—a sort of professional kick in the pants.

My paper falls within the confines of this second generic group. I can only hope that my analysis doesn't appear overcritical or unduly pessimistic about academic librarianship. I am actually neither. I applaud the energy of my fellow academic librarians, and I have a great deal of respect for many of the things that are going on in the profession.

But I do think that we have some serious problems. One of the larger ones involves teaching research, that is, instructing people how to use the library (virtual, real or otherwise) in today's fast-changing information environment. Whether we call this teaching "information literacy," "bibliographic instruction" or just "teaching research," we need to make some drastic changes in our thinking.

Now, it isn't that we have taught our patrons poorly. We have some great teachers in the field, and librarians in general may be among the better educators in the academic enterprise. Nor have we skirted the technological demands of the information age or failed to give due consideration to the political dimensions of our profession's place in the global information marketplace. We are high-tech, politically active, and pedagogically astute. (Or we are at the least doing what we can to be this way.)

No, our problem is that we have allowed ourselves to be hamstrung by a piecemeal, truncated, almost parochial approach to teaching. What we have taught, we have taught well. But we have done too little of it, and we have done it generally outside the broader concerns of the academic community. Proof of this assertion is in evidence in almost every facet of American scholarly life. Academic administrators, boards of trustees, faculty committees of whatever variety see the kind of instruction that we do as librarians as largely a peripheral service,—something that is nice to have but something that you can do without. Library instruction is wonderful but unnecessary, valuable to some degree but not essential.

This present malaise is largely our own doing. We have blundered in our attempts (if we have indeed made any attempts at all) to make the case that learning how to do research in today's fast-changing information environment is part of what it is to be an educated person. We have never succeeded in implementing in any more than a few institutions of higher learning a campus-wide academic program of research. We have failed to demonstrate that research is an integral part of the learning process.

What should we do about the present predicament? How should we rectify the current malaise? I suggest that we begin now to insist that our instruction of students in how to navigate the internet, how critically to evaluate sources, and how to master the research tools of a specific discipline is essential to an institution's academic mission. We must, in fact, begin to teach research the way college and universities already have been teaching writing—across and throughout the curriculum.

If anyone should think that I have exaggerated the academy's present state of affairs or that I offer solutions that are too far reaching or unnecessary, just consider this all too-typical scenario in the average college or university. Most of the class-specific instruction that is done, librarians do by invitation only. Sometimes faculty forget about research altogether or foolishly assume that their students know all about it anyway. More enlightened professors may rave about the research dimensions that librarians may bring to their classes. General Education committees even may commend the efforts of librarians to make students information-literate, but few of our colleagues in administration or among the faculty demand that their students know how to research in a given discipline or know what it is to function in the information world.

The academy values solid research. It wants students to engage in the analysis and retrieval of sophisticated data.. But making certain (with clearly-articulated policies or agreed-upon mandates from the administration) that that kind of research ability is mastered by a college's graduating students or insisting that the university turn out scholars with a minimal ability to perform research is another thing altogether. That kind of articulation of and implementation of policy is costly. It is labor-intensive, and the goal of making students master research has never been recognized as an actual goal of America's institutions of higher education.

In fairness to the nation's colleges and universities, we should remember that these institutions really do want to improve the research capacities of their students. They certainly value the scholarship and good academics. But the academy has never really contemplated what it is going to take to ensure that that occurs. America's colleges and universities are like that middle-class family shopping for real estate. They really want that loan to go through on the prospective purchase. They want a very nice place to live. But they don't want to be saddled with a mortgage payment.

This present reluctance to address the problem of teaching research in academic institutions and the concomitant lack of adequate research abilities among undergraduate students has a fascinating parallel in an earlier area of inadequate student writing—but a parallel that to date has had a very different outcome. When an ever-increasing number of incoming freshman students began to evidence an inability to write solid English prose several decades ago, literature departments took an interesting tack. They jettisoned the English composition course. They recognized that teaching writing couldn't and shouldn't be attempted in isolation to the larger curricular needs of the academy.

Note that they didn't implement a program that advocated a basic grammatical literacy. They wanted students to employ good grammar and to write in complete sentences, but they didn't make this their purpose. Unlike librarians, they recognized that learning how to write well involved more than stressing some sort of minimal requirement (as in the case of information literacy). They began, as I noted earlier, by eliminating the single freshman composition course that was supposed to teach everyone how to write effectively in seven or so easy compositions—a program similar to many library's bibliographic instruction course. Everyone knew that the freshman composition course wasn't going to accomplish much, just as everyone now knows that the introductory bibliographic instruction course isn't going to accomplish much.

Most importantly, literature departments realized that they would never be able to improve the writing of a generation of students if their vision of writing remained one of higher education's peripheral goals. They knew that they had to push their vision to the forefront. They had to make writing a major priority of the college—or a major facet of the university's mission.

This newly-articulated importance placed on writing several decades ago and the courage of administrators to put these new ideas into practice achieved remarkable results. Literature departments established writing centers throughout the nation, and they created a program called "writing across the curriculum"—a program that has probably done more to improve the writing of students than anything else in this century—a program that took as its premise the notion that you couldn't learn to write in a single class or in a single session. The new movement insisted that learning to write well takes practice. Teaching students to write well takes an institutional commitment to see that every student has multiple opportunities to learn how to communicate effectively and convincingly.

I submit that this recent piece of academic history could serve as a model for academic librarians and our very similar responsibility of teaching people how to do research. Learning research is very much like learning to write. It takes effort and it takes commitment. Forget about mastering research in a fifty-minute library session. Banish from your students' minds any notion that they can learn all they need to know about it in a three-hour freshman library instruction course. No, if today's students are going to learn how to do research well, they are going to have to practice it (like writing, let us say) in a great many contexts and in a great many educational environments. They are going to have to engage in research throughout and across the curriculum.

For librarians, the present juncture is clear. The choices are obvious. We can cling to our older notion of making our research instruction an invitation-only academic additive—something that is useful but not altogether necessary. This is the present state of affairs. Or we can begin to insist that learning how to do research is a fundamental skill—something that every student needs and something that no student can do without.

If librarians have the boldness to grasp this later option, we might be able to create a new consensus about research in the academy. Such a new consensus won't be easy to establish (they never are), but even the mere articulation of a new vision can sometimes accomplish more than one might expect.

If librarians in cooperation with others in our institutions develop effective strategies to create this kind of paradigm about research—a paradigm that would entail teaching research across and throughout the curriculum—some startling things could occur. Let me suggest three. First, the new vision would mean that colleges and universities would take the extra steps (steps similar to what they have done in the area of writing) to insist that their students really learn how to do research. Second, they could commit themselves to making the mastery of research skills one of the competencies that they demand of their graduates. Most colleges and universities already have clear competencies that they demand of their students. A mastery of research skills should be among those competencies. Thirdly, deans and curricular committees would learn to query departments about the research dimensions of their majors. They could begin to exercise a measure of oversight that would demand high standards for research and high standards for the librarians and professors who teach it. Faculty might even start insisting (rather than merely asking) that librarians have a larger part in teaching their students how to navigate the internet or to evaluate sources.

Academic librarians have the skills and the abilities to teach the coming generation of students how to function in a new age of information. Our approach to that teaching should mirror the importance that we place on it. Our teaching should be within the broad context of the academic enterprise. We need to link our pedagogy to the broad mission and goals of our institutions. We should abandon the current status quo of intervention only, very-nice-if-you-can-have-it-but-it-isn't-necessary instruction. We must teach research throughout and across the curriculum.

Ways of Working and Knowing across Boundaries: Research Practices of Interdisciplinary Scientists

By Carole Palmer
University of Illinois at Urbana-Champaign

CHANGES IN THE STRUCTURE OF KNOWLEDGE AND THE CONDUCT OF RESEARCH

If we could map how the entire stock of knowledge has grown over the past half century, we would see considerable expansion of the exterior boundaries and a striking change in the internal geography. Knowledge has been in a state of flux, a continual process of reconfiguration, with existing subject domains merging and seceding, and new ones emerging. A visual representation of the structure of knowledge would reveal an intricate web of connections between countless new territories.[1]

A number of models have been proposed to represent the dynamics of contemporary knowledge development. According to Chubin (1976) each discipline is centered around an intellectual core, and these domains overlap through scatter. Dogan and Pahre (1990) assert that during the twentieth-century knowledge has been reorganized through a "specialization-fragmentation-hybridization" process. As these new hybrid units of knowledge develop, they take form in various informal and institutionalized structures, ranging from cross-disciplinary interpersonal networks to interdisciplinary research organizations. Campbell's (1969) fish-scale model of omniscience represents a shift from isolated islands of specialization to overlapping layers of knowledge that encourage communication across disciplines and the development of new combinations of competencies.

Given the increase in both the scope and specificity of knowledge, we must also recognize the considerable impact this has on the way research is conducted (Roederer 1988). Turner (1991) notes that path-breaking ideas within any specialty usually come from cross-referencing ideas from other disciplines, and Fuller (1988) describes disciplinary boundaries as the fault lines that conceal future scientific revolutions. Established disciplinary frameworks bear ever less resemblance to the way researchers actually work and group themselves. The lines that separate scholars run at "highly eccentric angles," and disciplinary categories obscure what is "really happening out there where men and women are thinking about things and writing down what they think" (Geertz 1983, 6–7). While the structures that support research may not be adapting to the situation, it appears that researchers are. Increasingly, they import and export information, techniques, and tools across disciplinary boundaries, and people from different backgrounds work together to solve problems.

As research becomes more interdisciplinary,[2] current organizational frameworks become increasingly ill-suited to the conduct of research. Searing (1992) contends that academic librarians are at odds with scholars whose attempts to integrate across disciplines call into question our verbal, numerical, and spatial systems. Information professionals are participants in the networks of research activities, and according to Wilson (1981), they are responsible for providing information that is in alignment with the "user's life world."[3] As users extend their range of inquiry into multiple domains, interpreting their worlds becomes much more difficult, complicating the task of fitting information to the needs of the individual. We need to understand the activities and patterns involved in the cross-disciplinary research process before we can provide support systems that adequately reflect the needs of contemporary researchers.

In this paper I draw from my recent study of scientists at an interdisciplinary institute to explain how researchers cross borders to solve research problems.[4] The institute, referred to hereafter as "the Center," is devoted to the study of "living and non-living systems of increasing complexity." It houses programs that span the physical sciences, engineering, computational science, the life sciences, and the behavioral sciences. While I used both quantitative and qualitative methods during the course of the project, this report relies primarily on the analysis of data collected through interviews with twenty-five members of the Center.

CHARACTERISTICS OF BOUNDARY-CROSSING RESEARCH

The researchers at the Center are not comfortable with disciplinary, interdisciplinary, or multidisciplinary classifications of what they do. They describe their work as "problem-centered" research. As one physicist explained:

"The world doesn't know about physics, chemistry, and biology. The world's problems developed independently of them, so to solve them you really have to try to go at it from all angles. The strategies that researchers use to gather and disseminate information across disciplinary boundaries are constructed around the problem they address. In their attempts to 'go at it from all angles,' researchers communicate through formal and informal channels and take advantage of written, oral, and electronic information formats. They seek, gather, and probe for information, accumulating knowledge through many types of exchanges. The information they receive is acted on, translated, or converted in some way, and then sent back out to be reacted to again.[5] In order to understand the information use of boundary crossing scientists in full, the entire process of knowledge accumulation must be taken into consideration.[6] The structures and organizations where the exchange of information takes place are as important as the tools and techniques used for passing information back and forth."

The picture of research work that grew out of my data was complex, yet there were important patterns that ran across the sample. The researchers exhibited two overlapping cross-disciplinary orientations in their work approach. These orientations are best thought of on a continuum of interaction, with specialized participatory researchers at one end and individualistic generalists at the other, with the orientations merging in the middle. Along this continuum, researchers apply different strategies to accomplish boundary crossing research work.

Two practices were common across approaches: the use of personal contacts for gathering information and participation in problem-centered meetings, rather than large disciplinary conferences. Personal networks continue to be a dominant research component because they are a highly effective forum for research related interaction.[7] They seem more like invisible constituencies than invisible colleges, however, providing information and support from multiple disciplines, with limited hierarchical control or domination by elites.[8] Two problems were also prominent in the researchers' cross-disciplinary information work. Language complications and information overload were experienced by all of the scientists, regardless of their research orientation.

Interestingly, researchers at the far ends of the continuum tend not to base their research projects at the Center. While they benefit from the facilities and the prestige of being Center members, they configure their own intellectual communities through local collaborative projects and personal networks. The researchers in the middle of the continuum, those who combine participatory and generalist approaches, spend most of their time at the Center, taking full advantage of its resources. These scientists provide the best model of cross-disciplinary research because they manage to do integrative work while maintaining an adequate level of productivity. They employ a range of boundary crossing methods that assist in managing the tensions involved in the cross-disciplinary research process. Participatory generalists alter their levels of information dependence and independence as they balance breadth and focus and perform information work in core and peripheral knowledge domains.

Highly participatory researchers tend to cross boundaries through consultation and collaboration, while generalists concentrate on learning. I refer to the information work associated with learning activities as "information probing." Probing is investigative in nature. Researchers probe widely to broaden their perspective and to generate new ideas, and they also probe deeply to upgrade knowledge in peripheral subject areas. The infusion of new knowledge can further complicate information routines by causing a shift or expansion in a researcher's problem scope.

Support systems for cross-disciplinary research need to be designed to sustain both participatory and generalist research approaches. Problem-centered research does not fit neatly into any one framework of inquiry. Solutions are woven together from multiple knowledge domains by researchers who not only vary in their work styles and preferences, but who change their approach based on the problem being investigated. The multiplicity of these individuals is also reflected in the many types of information they use in their work. Published research reports are no more valuable to them than the raw results found at conference meetings, the "know-how" absorbed through teamwork, and the concepts offered by broadly based scientific authors.

KNOWLEDGE LEVELS

Since interdisciplinary researchers are often confronted with new situations, it is crucial that they know how to learn. They need to know "what information to ask for and how to acquire a working knowledge of the language, concepts, and analytical skills pertinent to a given problem, process, or phenomenon" (Klein 1990, 183). Despite their complex information needs, interdisciplinarians continue to rely on standard disciplinary forms of communication. Electronic mail has changed the way researchers do business and collaborate, but personal networks, conferences, and the published literature are still the primary sources of information.

How much does a scientist need to know about another discipline in order to successfully incorporate it into their research process? Petrie (1986) suggests that researchers must acquire an interpretive level of tacit knowledge to do interdisciplinary work.[9] He describes the minimum amount of learning required for interdisciplinary work as follows: knowledge of another discipline's observational categories and understanding of the meaning of key terms. However, these two criteria convey an overly simplistic idea of how knowledge is developed and applied in scientific interdisciplinary research.

For researchers with a generalist orientation, comprehension seems to involve much more than understanding terms and categories. On the other hand, participatory researchers often work across disciplines with less than Petrie's minimum level of knowledge. For example, a device physicist explained that he uses work done in chemistry without interacting with chemists or their literature. "I am not so concerned about understanding exactly what they are doing as long as there is a link in between which, you know, is going to feed the information. I just need the results. I just need to know exactly what is important, and they will tell me what is important. It is a good way to collaborate in the sense that I don't need to micro-understand everything. I just need to get the right amount."

His strategy is to locate knowledge that has already been interpreted and applied in a way that is useful for his purposes. It is important for him to understand how the connection was made, but he "takes for granted that they know what they are talking about."

A bioenergetics specialist with a background in biology offered a very different notion of what it means to "know enough." She must be able to communicate successfully with those in other scientific communities, particularly physicists. Understanding terminology and results is not sufficient; it is necessary to comprehend the meaning from the other's theoretical perspective. "I couldn't do a quantum mechanical computation, even the kind that they did on the backs of envelopes 40 years ago. This is just something which I never tried to do. But what I have done is try to understand the formulas and the meaning, if you like—the theories. And I think you have to do that in order to be able to communicate with the people who very often are injecting the novel ideas into the field."

A photosynthesis specialist, who manages a multidisciplinary laboratory, described the necessary level of knowing in yet another way. For him, knowing enough is being able to recognize when something is inconsistent with all the possible hypotheses in a problem area. "The beginning of knowledge is the recognition of ignorance.... The things that you understand, even though they might be the basis of most of your research, are not the interesting things. The most interesting things are the ones you don't understand.... The trick is knowing enough to see when something is interesting for the right reasons." He believes that to do interdisciplinary science you must be able to recognize an opportunity for discovery when you are confronted with it.

These examples show how different work approaches are associated with varying levels of knowledge development in outside subject areas. The device physicist is a participatory researcher who relies on being able to identify and apply connections that have already been established by others. As a generalist, the bioenergetics specialist needs a deeper level of knowledge that allows meaningful dialogue between various subject areas. The functional level of knowledge described by the managerial photosynthesis specialist requires enough depth and breadth to understand the complex of overlapping principles surrounding a problem and the potential implications. Furthermore, researchers sustain multiple knowledge bases. Some areas need to be more extensively developed than others, and some are more difficult to maintain than others. An animal learning specialist thinks of it as a literacy issue. His competency in molecular biology requires constant work because it is a topic that he has just recently begun to incorporate, and it is a science that is "exploding" with new knowledge. Neuroanatomy, however, is a relatively low maintenance literacy for him because he has built up his knowledge over time, and it is a much more static science.

Cross-disciplinary communication is complicated by the fact that any given audience is likely to have a very small base of common knowledge. A neurophysiologist discovered that it is risky to make assumptions about what appears to be a homogeneous audience. The first talk he gave to a group of complex systems researchers was "a disaster." "I started out talking about linear control systems theory and stuff like that. And like I say, I'm not a mathematician. So I thought these guys are all mathematicians and they are going to know what this stuff is, but they didn't. It's not that it was beyond them. It certainly wasn't. But, it was a use of complex numbers that they weren't familiar with. I didn't know that one group of mathematicians understood what another group didn't."

Researchers employ various techniques to reach their diverse constituencies. Participants tend to write for multiple audiences, while generalists compose reports for broader groups, "backing up to where any scientist can understand" what they are talking about.

STRUCTURAL AND CULTURAL INFLUENCES

As we consider the approaches researchers use to gather and disseminate information and knowledge, we must also take into account the context of these activities. The structures in which scientists situate their work, and the work conditions in those places, are an integral part of the research process. As Fisher (1990) notes, although boundary crossing is carried out by individuals, it simultaneously involves institutions and the social structures that surround people and their work. One of the reasons members of the Center succeed at crossing boundaries is because they are situated in multiple research structures. They belong to numerous groups, ranging from loosely arranged project teams to stable fields that are "embodied in university departments and professional societies."[10]

Problem-centered researchers configure their memberships and places of practice to accommodate their boundary crossing activities, but they continue to struggle with disciplinary forces that regulate what they study, how they study it, how they talk about it, and how they disseminate it. Each new territory that they explore has a different set of cultural norms. As researchers adapt to the new cultures, they can maneuver more freely between what are often competing jurisdictions.[11] The scientists in this study attest to just how burdensome this process can be.

As White (1987) suggests, perhaps fields of study should be thought of as force fields, in order to accurately capture the aggressive nature of academic life. One researcher described what it is like to pursue interdisciplinary work at a university that is highly respected in conventional disciplinary areas of study and research. The departments function like "black holes." "It is a gravitational force that can overpower you. The departments are entrenched in what they are good at, what they do well, and it works to suck you down into these big holes. The force pulls you back into working within the areas that have been done so well for so long."

Once researchers break free of these centripetal forces, it takes considerable time, effort, stamina, and humility to become a recognized member of a new scientific community. It took more than ten years for one researcher to feel accepted into a circuit of scientists in his new research area. In some ways, gaining entrance into a new group is like starting a new career or developing a new professional identity.[12] There are few incentives for giving up the respect associated with being an expert in a specialization to become a novice in a new field, except the opportunity to learn how to do better science.

The cultural differences between groups are most apparent in their inability to understand each other's dialects. Researchers experience serious language barriers in all types of cross-disciplinary activities, including information gathering, collaborative work, and informal discussion. An artificial intelligence specialist offered examples of how language hinders communication across relevant intellectual communities. Although he shares a common problem interest with a particular group of philosophers, it took him a year to read one of their books, because "they have such a completely different style of writing." He found writing for them equally challenging.

"These people who I consider philosophers wrote this book [on AI], and they asked me to write a chapter on epistemic aspects of databases. I went to the dictionary and looked up epistemic. I could not figure out for myself what the epistemic aspects of databases were. After thinking about it for awhile, I figured out what I thought they must have meant, wrote a chapter and sent it off.... but you see, they had to suggest a title. I would never ever have titled anything I wrote something like that."

He had the knowledge needed to complete the task, but the terminology used by the other group had no meaning for him. The language complications experienced by the researchers were frequent and varied in complexity. In one case, a linguist described an interaction where he identified five meanings for a word that had a single meaning for a geneticist colleague. A few of the researchers believe that the export of information across disciplinary boundaries could be greatly enhanced by the field of library and information science, especially if it can find a way to translate jargon into terminology that is meaningful across sciences.

INFORMATION INITIATIVES

From the outset of this paper I have argued that information professionals are part of the research process, and as such, that they are in a position to support cross-disciplinary inquiry. I propose that in order to facilitate boundary crossing research we must first understand the information work involved in knowledge accumulation, and then design systems and services that accommodate divergent research orientations and foster communication across cultures. Moreover, since the essence of interdisciplinarity appears to lie in the dialectic work accomplished through multiple group memberships,[13] we must be able to identify and provide services for the groups that are meaningful to researchers. This study confirmed one of our field's greatest challenges—the individual and situational nature of information needs.[14] While we can strive to create adaptable systems that can be customized to personal profiles, it is more realistic, and perhaps more productive for the dialectic process, to organize around aggregations based on information use patterns—that is, groups of users from different subject backgrounds who have similar information routines and common goals. Having identified the participant / generalist continuum as one important variable of user behavior, what other practice based differentiations can be made?

Physics, chemistry, and psychology are not particularly meaningful classifications of knowledge for researchers at the Center, and academic departments and Ph.D. specializations are not valid or complete descriptions of any of the areas in which the scientists work. Furthermore, the Center's official research groups are just one of many affiliations in a given scientist's circle of memberships. The problems that scientists work on, however, are germane. Researchers converge—through their work the Center, through e-mail, and at seminars and conferences—as they try to solve problems characterized by subjects such as light, membranes, and oscillation. Groups form in many informal and unrecognized pockets within the academic setting and in professional worlds outside the university. Problem areas are both realistic and meaningful domains for organizing research and the information related to the conduct of research.

Brown and Duguid (1991) have shown how the detection and support of emergent communities in the workplace can foster working, learning, and innovation. Research is a type of work, and learning and exploration play a particularly significant role in problem-centered inquiry. Researchers cross boundaries to explore and develop new and better ways to do their science. The informal structures that support work, learning, and discovery provide important guides for organizing information and information services. While the many local, national, and international emergent communities are too numerous to allow each to be addressed as a separate user group, these units can be combined into larger overlapping domains. Mapping of problem areas can be done locally or more globally through co-word analysis of literature or other scientometric measures. Inventories of conference attendance and correspondence based networks would also reveal an accurate, and more current account, of how researchers link together, creating a relevant framework for developing user oriented information systems and services.

At the local level, research libraries and information centers can identify the shadow structures[15] that form around problems and develop liaison with hybrid research units as they emerge. Then, features can be introduced into our information environments to support these working user groups. Collections and information tools need to support rather than deter integrative inquiry. We have seen that researchers have independent and dependent ways of gathering information from multiple domains. Individuals rely on other people's knowledge in different degrees, and a researcher's level of dependent knowing varies from project to project. For some purposes, it may be adequate to know an expert in an area and depend on that person for consultation. Another project may require recruiting a collaborator as a full member of a research team. Dependent knowing is an important strategy for combating information overload. It is also a practice that can be supported by librarians. Current awareness programs can concentrate on the information activities that researchers find the most difficult, the seeking and probing that takes place in new peripheral areas. Researchers can be informed of new work, as well as pertinent people, places, and activities in the subjects that feed into their central problem areas.

Generalists tend to be self-contained knowers. They are likely to do fairly extensive reading or attend a seminar before consulting a personal contact about specific details. Independent knowledge base development is a key component of their research process, therefore their information environment needs to be conducive to learning. Fortunately, addressing the important role of faculty learning in boundary crossing research should enhance rather than detract from the pedagogical aspect of academic library services. In some ways, the information needs of generalists parallel those of students who are developing background in new subjects. Derivative works, such as textbooks, handbooks, and review literature are important counterparts to the masses of scholarly research reports, although they remain low on the list of collection priorities in many research libraries. These types of materials are studied and consulted frequently, making them good candidates for working digital collections that can be shared by many and accessed remotely.

Another type of knowing that has not yet been discussed is what one researcher referred to as "knowing what to forget." She suggested that in order to battle overload we must develop our "forgeteries" at the same time we build our memories. In a similar sense, we can build filters into our information systems to conform to a memory / forgetery model. As we study scientists to find out what is currently important, we must also take cues from them about what can be preserved in the archival forgetery. Problem-centered electronic information sources can be developed in layers. For instance, on a cross-disciplinary web page on computer vision, applicable information from artificial intelligence, graphics, and psychophysics can be emphasized in the foreground, while disciplinary root material from computer science, engineering, and physiology can be receded into the background. This arrangement retains the core and its ancestral categories of knowledge in the forgetery, allowing the emergence of the new hybrids in the active memory.

Interdisciplinary research progresses through the exchange of information across boundaries. Problem-centered systems and services can create valuable information leeway for researchers. As we work to organize knowledge in meaningful units and maintain open channels between them, we are taking on a portion of the boundary crossing burden. Moreover, creating cross-disciplinary thesauri and building conceptual links between disciplinary sources can help dismantle the language barriers that divide scientific cultures. Supporting the work practices, research orientations, and the multiplicity of individuals should be the guiding principles for the creation of cross-disciplinary information environments. Attention to these aspects of the research process will do more than satisfy the explicitly stated needs of interdisciplinary scientists—it will enable the ongoing boundary crossing dialogue that generates new knowledge. The libraries and information centers that apply these principles will make a significant contribution to the dialectic process that facilitates the synthesis of knowledge and will help clear the path for future scientific discoveries.

ENDNOTES

1. Recent knowledge mapping research addresses these dynamics. See, for example, Robert R. Bramm's (1991) Mapping of Science: Foci of Intellectual Interest in Scientific Literature and Callon, Law, and Rip's (1986) Mapping the Dynamics of Science and Technology: Sociology of Science in the Real World.
2. Klein (1996) presents a panoply of claims that knowledge is becoming more interdisciplinary. Twentieth-century assertions date back to the Social Science Research Council in the 1930s and the Manhattan Project. After a resurgence of interest in the 1960s and 1970s, the importance of interdisciplinary approaches is now widely acknowledged. As Klein points out, even the New York Times periodically heralds "new research developments under the banner of interdisciplinarity" (13).
3. Wilson defines this as the "totality of experiences centered upon the individual as an information user" (6). He calls attention to the need to explore the role of information in the user's organizational and social settings, rather than studying information sources and systems.
4. The comprehensive results of this project appear in my 1996, Practices and Conditions of Boundary Crossing Research Work: A Study of Scientists at an Interdisciplinary Institute. Ph.D. dissertation, University of Illinois.
5. Latour (1987) points out that this translation process is different from diffusion. The concept of diffusion recognizes the movement of facts but not what happens to those "facts" as they are passed from person to person. Translation is best thought of as how scientists convince others that they have solved one of their problems—the actions they take to turn their claims into facts.
6. Latour's (1987) definition of knowledge as a cycle of accumulation incorporates the many dimensions of knowledge development. He explains that "knowledge cannot be defined without understanding what gaining knowledge means. Knowledge is not something that could be described by itself or by opposition to ignorance or to belief, but only by considering a whole cycle of accumulation: how to bring things back to a place for someone to see it for the first time so that others might be sent again to bring other things back" (220).
7. Scientists' use of informal channels of communication have been of interest since the important APA (1963) reports, and Price (1961) and Crane's (1972) recognition of the invisible college.
8. I would further suggest that as hybrids become stabilized within institutions and as highly influential figures emerge, the loose constituencies will develop into more stable college-like networks.
9. Petrie develops his notion of interpretive knowledge from Broudy's (1970) study of learning and Polanyi's (1958; 1966) concepts of tacit and focal knowledge.
10. Messer-Davidow, Shumway, and Sylvan (1993) describe disciplines, subdisciplines, and specializations as embodied in "otherwise disparate elements: objects of study, methods of analysis, scholars, students, journals, and grants." Lenoir (1993) includes textbooks and lab manuals in his notion of disciplinary embodiment.
11. Abbott (1988) develops a competitive model of jurisdictional negotiation between the professions that has been referred to in the literature on interdisciplinarity by Klein (1993) and others.
12. Lave and Wegner (1991) claim that "the development of identity is central to the careers of newcomers in communities of practice," and that learning and identity are inseparable.
13. Davis (1978) describes the method of interdisciplinarity as a dialectic process, and Klein (1996) expands on this notion in her analysis of interdisciplinarity as communicative action.
14. See Dervin (1977) and her (1983) review of research on specific needs of users and the kinds of knowledge that meet those needs.
15. This term is adopted from Charles C. Lemert's (1990) "Depth as a Metaphor for the Major: A Post Modernist Challenge." Association of American Colleges meeting, San Francisco, 11 January; quoted in Klein (1996).

REFERENCES

Abbott, Andrew Delano. 1988. The System of Professions: An Essay on the Division of Expert Labor. Chicago: University of Chicago Press.

American Psychological Association. 1963. Reports of the Project on Scientific Information Exchange in Psychology. Washington, D.C.: APA.

Bramm, Robert R. 1991 Mapping of Science: Foci

of Intellectual Interest in Scientific Literature. Leiden, Netherlands: DSWO Press, University of Leiden.

Broudy, Harry S. 1970. "On Knowing With." In Proceedings of the Philosophy of Education Society, Studies in Philosophy and Education, Southern Illinois University, Edwardsville, IL.

Brown, John Seely and Paul Duguid. 1991. "Organizational Learning and Communities-of-Practice: Toward a Unified View of Working, Learning, and Innovation." Organizational Science 2: 40–57.

Callon, Michael, John Law, and Arie Rip. 1986. Mapping the Dynamics of Science and Technology: Sociology of Science in the Real World. Basingstoke, Hampshire: Macmillan.

Campbell, Donald. 1969. "Ethnocentrism of Disciplines and the Fish-Scale Model of Omniscience." In Interdisciplinary Relationships in the Social Sciences, ed. Muzafer Sherif and Carolyn Sherif. Chicago: Aldine.

Chubin, Daryl E. 1976. "The Conceptualization of Scientific Specialties." Sociological Quarterly 17: 423–441.

Crane, Diane. 1972. Invisible Colleges. Chicago: University of Chicago Press.

Davis, Walter A. 1978. The Act of Interpretation: A Critique of Literary Reason. Chicago: University of Chicago Press.

Dervin, Brenda. 1977. "Useful Theory for Librarianship: Communication not Information." Drexel Library Quarterly 13: 16–32.

___. 1983. "Information as a User Construct: The Relevance of Perceived Information Needs to Synthesis and Interpretation." In Knowledge Structure and Use: Implications for Synthesis and Interpretation, ed. Spencer A. Ward and Linda J. Reed. Philadelphia: Temple University Press.

Dogan, Mattei and Robert Pahre. 1990. Creative Marginality: Innovation at the Intersections of Social Sciences. Boulder, Colo.: Westview Press.

Fisher, Donald. 1990. "Boundary Work and Science: The Relation between Power and Knowledge." In Theories of Science in Society, eds. Susan E. Cozzens and Thomas F. Gieryn. Bloomington and Indianapolis: Indiana University Press.

Fuller, Steve. 1988. "Disciplinary Boundaries: A Conceptual Map for the Field." In Social Epistemology. Bloomington and Indianapolis: Indiana University Press.

Geertz, Clifford. 1983. Local Knowledge: Further Essays in Interpretive Anthropology. New York: Basic Books.

Klein, Julie Thompson. 1990. Interdisciplinarity: History, Theory, and Practice. Detroit: Wayne State University.

___. 1993. "Blurring, Cracking, and Crossing: Permeation and the Fracturing of Discipline." In Knowledges: Historical and Critical Studies in Disciplinarity, eds. Ellen Messer-Davidow, David R. Shumway, and David J. Sylvan. Charlottesville and London: University Press of Virginia.

___. 1996, forthcoming. Crossing Boundaries: Knowledge, Disciplinarities, and Interdisciplinarities. Charlottesville and London: University Press of Virginia

Latour, Bruno. 1987. Science in Action: How to Follow Scientists and Engineers through Society. Milton Keynes, UK: Open University Press.

Lave, Jean and Etienne Wegner. 1991. Situated Learning: Legitimate Peripheral Participation. Cambridge: Cambridge University Press.

Lemert, Charles C. 1990. "Depth as a Metaphor for the Major: A Postmodernist Challenge." Association of American Colleges meeting. San Francisco, 11 January.

Lenoir, Timothy. 1993. "The Discipline of Nature and the Nature of Disciplines." In Knowledges: Historical and Critical Studies in Disciplinarity, eds. Ellen Messer-Davidow, David R. Shumway, and David J. Sylvan. Charlottesville and London: University Press of Virginia.

Messer-Davidow, Ellen; David R. Shumway; and David J. Sylvan. 1993. "Disciplinary Ways of Knowing." In Knowledges: Historical and Critical Studies in Disciplinarity. Charlottesville and London: University Press of Virginia.

Palmer, Carole L. 1996. Practices and Conditions of Boundary Crossing Research Work: A Study of Scientists at an Interdisciplinary Institute. Ph.D. dissertation, University of Illinois.

Petrie, Hugh G. 1986. "Do You See What I See? The Epistemology of Interdisciplinary Inquiry." In Interdisciplinary Analysis and Research: Theory and Practice of Problem-Focused Research and Development. Mt. Airy, Md.: Lomond. Reprinted from Educational Researcher 5 (February 1976): 9–15.

Polanyi, Michael. 1958. Personal Knowledge: Towards a Post-Critical Philosophy. London: Routledge and Kegan Paul.

___. 1966. "The Logic of Inference." Philosophy 40: 369–86.

Price, Derek and J. de Solla. 1961. Science since Babylon. New Haven, Conn.: Yale University Press.

Roederer, Juan G. 1988. "Tearing Down Disciplinary Barriers." Astrophysics and Space Science 144: 659–667.

Searing, Susan E. 1992. "How Libraries Cope with Interdisciplinarity: The Case of Women's Studies." Issues in Integrative Studies, no. 110: 7–25.

Turner, Ralph H. 1991. "The Many Faces of American Sociology: A Discipline in Search of Identity." In Divided Knowledges: Across Disciplines, across Cultures, eds. David Easton and Corinne Schelling. Newbury Park, Calif.: Sage.

White, James Boyd. 1987. "Intellectual Integration." Issues in Integrative Studies 5: 1–18.

Wilson, Thomas D. 1981. "On User Studies and Information Needs." Journal of Documentation 37, no. 1: 3–15.

The Changing Face of Social Science Research: Building and Protecting Gateways between the Past and the Future

By Mary J. Reddick
University of Utah

INTRODUCTION

There is no question that technology has changed, and is continuing to change, the basic nature of academic research. This paper is primarily addressed to librarians who are attempting to facilitate the transmission of learning in institutions of higher education by interpreting and managing the changes in social science research brought about by technology. The paper discusses these changes in the context of the blurring of the traditional boundaries of the social sciences. I approach this topic in three parts.

I. Technology and the Organization, Retrieval, and Dissemination of Social Science Research

Technology has helped to reclassify the subject matter of social science by virtue of computerized search strategies and concepts. The ability to limit searches according to specific fields and formats, and to narrow and broaden searches through the use of Boolean connectors, has provided researchers with multiple access points to records in a variety of formats. Since computerization has enabled people to search for records that may not be defined according to vocabulary-controlled or subject heading classifications, it has opened up the possibility for retrieving a much wider and richer range of records and texts on any given subject.[1] This opening up process has alerted people to the ways in which subject classifications may be transcended. Researchers have been empowered with the autonomy to rearrange for themselves the classification scheme that traditionally dictates the organization of materials. In so doing, it has become easier to recognize that there always has been a variety of materials indexed in paper indexes and catalogs, including specialized ones, that research has missed because of the way it was classified and because it was not accessible by so many different entry points.

In addition to reclassifying the subject matter of research, technology has had an impact on the retrieval and dissemination of social science research. Not only have computers helped to reduce the time between the publication of articles and books and their appearances in abstracts or indexes but, assuming the computers are up and working, it is often less time consuming for a researcher to search a database than a traditional index. Researchers have been enabled to browse online tables of contents of journals and books, and to order material directly from their work stations. In some cases, moreover, access to full text documents has rendered obsolete the need for the use of indexes and abstracts. Technology has provided the means for more expedient document delivery and a wider dissemination of available resources. Through such services as online databases and the Internet, researchers are given immediate access to a world wide gold mine of information.

The advantages of these capabilities reinforce a reliance on computer-assisted research, which tends to diminish the use of many resources that constitute a traditional research library—paper indexes, reference materials, and even journals and books. The extent to which computers are not only supplementing but replacing such traditional library resources and, by implication, libraries themselves, is a question that parallels one at the heart of the debate over the future of the university. As Stanford University President, Gerhard Casper, put it: "Will technological substitution be complete, or will the university as a physical space continue to attract students?"[2] In light of the increasing commercialization of knowledge, the question of the relationship between computers, libraries, and research seems inherently to raise a larger question of the relationship between computers, libraries, research, and learning. As Casper concludes, the university—and I would add, the library—is still a space for intellectual interaction. As a physical space both will remain attractive only if they are viewed as "valuable to people to interact personally and face to face in learning and research." This is a traditional view of libraries, and it remains appealing for a variety of reasons.

The President of the Andrew W. Mellon Foundation alludes to some of these reasons when he speculates why libraries have such a hold on so many people: "because of their ambiance, the sense they give of the power of ideas and the luxury of being stimulated and encouraged to think for one's self." "Libraries are humbling places," he continues, "because they remind us of the vast store of knowledge which we can approach but never really control." And, he says, libraries "are humanizing places, because we are brought into contact with so many lives lived in the past as well as in the present. They are symbols of the continuity of learning."[3] The appeal of this view remains forceful, but the image it portrays is no longer sufficient. As universities compete for scarce resources in a global political economy, they are under increasing pressure to account for and justify the quality of services they provide for students and the public at large. University libraries are symbols of such quality. They must be viewed as integral both to the university curriculum and to the life-long learning experience of those whom they serve. The traditional view of university libraries will remain appealing only so long as librarians find ways to integrate the demands of the university curriculum and the goal of life-long learning into the plethora of exploding technological services and networks that are transforming our society.

II. Technology and the Traditionally Defined Disciplines of the Social Sciences

While there are certainly controversies brewing over the uses of the words, "interdisciplinarity," "multidisciplinarity," "cross-disciplinarity," and "transdisciplinarity" in academic writing, there is nevertheless a considerable amount of attention being directed toward scholarship and programs that are traversing or redrawing the traditional boundaries of disciplines in colleges and universities. There are now programs on many campuses such as American Studies, Cultural Studies, Ethnic Studies, Folklore Studies, Gay Studies, Environmental Studies, and Women's Studies that intersect at the crossroads of several disciplines. The process of hybridization, in which specialized knowledge from different subfields is combined as a result of the overlapping of two or more fringes from different formal disciplines, has compelled an advocacy for the use of the terms "trans-speciality" or "polyspeciality."[4] This process has created such fields as child development, Indo-European studies, criminology, artificial intelligence, not to mention some of the longer standing established subfields such as cultural, economic, philosophical, and physical anthropology; historical, industrial, international and labor economics; human, cultural, regional, and urban geography; cultural, economic, intellectual, and psychological history; American, comparative, international political science, political theory and political thought, political economy, and public administration; animal, clinical, behavioral, cognitive, educational, political, social, and transpersonal psychology; and demographic, group, historical, and political sociology.[5] The common element in these and many other such subfields is that they have affinities to their parent discipline as well as to at least one other subdiscipline of another field. And, in all of these cases, technology is playing a central role in making it easier to conduct research.

Some writers, such as English Professor Richard Lanham, argue that it is necessary to modify departmental and disciplinary structures to take account of the influence of the "electronic text." Lanham argues that the university's departmental, disciplinary, and administrative structures commonly work to discourage both the influence of electronic texts and a much needed university-wide conversation about this influence.[6] Others, such as Political Scientists Mattei Dogan and Robert Pahre, find no need for administrative reorganization due to the fragmentation, specialization, and hybridization of the social sciences. The boundaries are moving anyway, they argue, and technology is one of the most important influences of this movement.[7] Steve Fuller, a British sociologist of science and social epistemologist, has been collaborating with a group of like-minded colleagues in an attempt to help transform both the structure and the purpose of the university curriculum. He has been working:

> to foster closer cooperation between humanists and social scientists in the emerging interdisciplinary complex known as Science and Technology Studies (STS), a field that is capable, I believe, of not only redrawing disciplinary boundaries within the academy but ultimately, and more important, of making the academy more permeable to the rest of society.[8]

For the time being anyway, the idea that the social science disciplines are distinctly subject based seems to remain relevant to the way in which the administrative structure and organization of the university curriculum have been conceived, but it nevertheless appears to be the case that academic trends away from monodisciplinary research are becoming more pertinent to a variety of ways that researchers investigate subjects across the university curriculum.

Technology has provided quicker and more comprehensive access to traditional subject based social science research, but also it has helped to integrate previously peripheral, multidisciplinary based research into mainstream curricula. Technology has enabled specialists in subfields of one discipline to have easier access to the work of others in relevant subfields of different disciplines, thus encouraging greater multidisciplinary awareness.

III. Technology, the Reconfiguration of Social Science Disciplines, and the Work of Instruction Librarians in Academic Libraries

In a recent editorial in Behavioral & Social Sciences Librarian, Michael Winter recounts his experience at a conference on the future of scholarship and libraries, noting his confusion that resulted from the frequent references to the interdisciplinary character of recent literatures.[9] In subsequent pursuit of this line of thought, Winter came to realize that the term "interdisciplinary" has been used to convey a variety of meanings, but the two meanings he found most useful to distinguish from each other were drawn by analogy to Isaiah Berlin's distinction between "hedgehogs" and "foxes." The hedgehog is a systemic kind of thinker who attempts to know one big thing, whereas the fox, making no pretense at grand synthesis, is content merely to know many little things. Winter admits that most of us are foxes today, yet he senses an element to librarianship that requires a certain appreciation for hedgehog mentality. Librarians, concludes Winter, are hedgehogs who deal with foxes as clients: the more specialized the literature, the more the need for librarians to generalize to cover all of the specialties. A university library is based on a grand and systematic classification scheme that deems the organization of knowledge to be reliant on the interdependence of each and every individual classification scheme. Perhaps one of the biggest tasks facing instruction librarians today is to find interesting and challenging ways for students to learn about their chosen fields of study by comprehending the interrelationships between various subfields of knowledge.

Richard Lanham sees libraries as a vital component in the modification of university administrative structures: "Librarians of electronic information," he writes, "find their job now a radically rhetorical one—they must consciously construct human attention-structures rather than assemble a collection of books according to commonly accepted rules." "They have, perhaps unwittingly," he goes on to say, "found themselves transported from the ancillary margin of the human sciences to their center."[10] Lanham thus looks to the library or the library school as a logical place for the necessary conversation about the influence of the electronic text to begin taking place. Dogan and Pahre maintain that the skills of librarians and information specialists are required to help scholars in their specialized fields keep abreast of developments in relevant subfields.[11] Steve Fuller takes issue with the view that library work is purely reactive to the current trends in scholarship. In advocating a view of knowledge in terms of its positional rather than its public value, Fuller argues that the value of a piece of knowledge cannot be determined without knowing how many people have access to it and to other pieces of knowledge. Thus, the value of knowledge "is continually changing in ways that may not be apparent to the average researcher, who typically lacks an overview of the entire knowledge system."[12] What this suggests to Fuller is that librarians and informational professionals should play a major role in any university planning policy, but to do so they must become more proactive than their traditional image as "guarantors of free access to information" suggests. What this also seems to suggest is the need for more collaboration among instruction librarians themselves to foster a better appreciation for the importance of maintaining an overview of the entire knowledge system.

Now, while it may be admitted that Lanham, Dogan and Pahre, and Fuller might not fall into the mainstream of their professions, I see no reason for instruction librarians not to seize the opportunities provided to them by the blurring of the traditional disciplinary boundaries. After all, it was the President of Duke University, Nannerl O. Keohane, who recently remarked that "teleconferencing and electronic mail have accelerated communication, knowledge is spilling over traditional boundaries, and new investigative tools have suggested the possibility of asking new questions."[13] It is precisely these kinds of new questions that the hedgehogs can ask of the foxes. By so doing, instruction librarians can begin to undermine from within what one writer refers to as the dominant, positivist, and mechanistic image of the modern research library as an impersonal depository of objective knowledge. We can begin, in short, to make "the creation of new knowledge possible at its most fundamental level."[14]

Instruction librarians can employ a variety of strategies to achieve the twin goals of ensuring the library's place in the university curriculum and enhancing the life-long learning experience of library users. As such, they can enrich the research process for students in the social sciences. In the remainder of this paper, I would like to spell out briefly four premises in teaching social science research which, I believe, when given due attention can lead students to fruitful paths of discovery both in the social sciences and in the real world.[15] These premises should be viewed in conjunction with an approach to teaching social science research that strives to incorporate the bibliographic dimension of discipline-related knowledge into the epistemological, sociological, and historical dimensions of the social science disciplines.[16] Such an integration can contribute to an understanding of the process of disciplinary scholarship that is central to reliable inquiry, and hence to the effective use of library resources. The premises are thus intended to bolster an approach to social science research that is both substantive and contextual; that is, that encourages the development of a framework of concepts about disciplinary structures, research processes, and the individual and society in social science inquiry:[17]

DISCIPLINARY ASSUMPTIONS.

With the exception of the material taught in a few courses, most undergraduate students are not fully exposed to problems and issues in the philosophy of social science. Even though recent scholarship in social science bears witness to an increasing methodological awareness among social science practitioners, the problems addressed in the literature are sufficiently complex and obtuse to render adequate treatment of them impossible in anything more than senior and graduate level seminars.[18] Yet it is not that difficult for undergraduate students to come to understand that disciplinary assumptions of the social sciences contain epistemological, sociological, historical, and bibliographic dimensions that dictate the way social science inquiry is conceived and conducted. In understanding these dimensions of disciplinary assumptions, students should see what is distinct about the modes of inquiry within a particular discipline while recognizing the degree to which the subject boundaries of each discipline are arbitrary. This recognition should enable students to see the connections between or among the disciplines and the ways in which each discipline can illuminate the others.

Instruction librarians can draw on available resources to help students become more aware of the importance of disciplinary assumptions in the social sciences. Students can benefit from reading a selection of articles whose authors are cognizant of and articulate about the nature of this phenomenon.[19] Such authors illustrate, by cases from anthropology, science, and ethnic studies, the ways in which the reconfiguration of social thought is affecting attitudes about traditional conceptions of the classification of knowledge into discrete subject matters.[20] Professors may be invited to class to discuss the role of their own disciplines, their connection with other disciplines, their understanding of the assumptions guiding various types of social science inquiry, and the reasons for the persistence of contending factions of social scientists. This provides them with an opportunity to reflect more openly than normal on the state of their own disciplines, and to engage in multidisciplinary interaction with librarians and students. Students can be assigned readings about issues in the social sciences that are presented by adherents from each of the disciplinary perspectives emphasized in the course.[21] This permits students to examine critically the separate perspectives while keeping their attention focused on the subject of disciplinary assumptions.

DISCIPLINARY SUBFIELDS

An awareness of the existence of disciplinary assumptions requires understanding the interrelationships between or among different subfields in the social sciences. This implies that students can be taught to recognize which subfields are most closely allied, and which subfields in other disciplines are most pertinent to their own fields of investigation. Making explicit the implicit connections to the journals and books in relevant subfields of different disciplines can facilitate a greater awareness that the determinant of disciplinary boundaries is more a question of conceptual framework than subject matter.[22]

Instruction librarians are in the unique position of being able to spend time exploring these interconnections with their students. In consultation with the instruction librarian, students can be asked to formulate a research question that deals in some way with issues pertaining to the individual and society. Over the entirety of the course, students can compile a bibliography consisting of relevant citations to sources from a wide variety of paper and computerized indexes, abstracts, and full text documents. The theory here—and it seems to apply in practice—is that for most social science topics that the student is researching, relevant sources can be found in almost all of the various indexes—general and subject-specific—in the social sciences and, depending on the topic, in the humanities, fine arts, and sciences. Since there is enough variation in the titles of the journals included in indexes, abstracts, or full text sources, the student's own specialized bibliography produced by this research is inherently a result of the blurring of traditional disciplinary boundaries. Toward the end of the class, students can present orally the answers they are tentatively formulating in response to their research questions. Class discussion and constructive criticism of each research question can help to clarify and refine the original questions as well as provide the grounds for the formulation of new research questions that may extend into fresh domains of inquiry.

Self-sufficiency. Quicker and more comprehensive access to an ever increasing number of academic resources available on the information superhighway may be desirable to students, but information overload can have a stifling effect on curiosity. Teaching students the concepts behind traditional controlled-vocabulary and key word or subject heading searches, combined with the essential concepts of Boolean searching and of software based computerized indexes, can help students reduce the problem of information scattering. The essential concepts behind traditional and computerized search strategies, in conjunction with an appreciation for differences in individual learning styles, can encourage students to learn how to become self-sufficient in libraries.

Traditional and computerized library sources need not be divided into subject-specific categories to be taught effectively. Information sources may be grouped into such categories, depending on the library's holdings, including but not limited to: a) controlled-vocabulary paper indexes; b) paper key word and citation indexes; c) computerized indexes by software, such as SilverPlatter indexes, Information Access Corporation indexes, FirstSearch indexes; full text databases; and other specialized indexes; and d) Internet sources such as national and international library catalogs, Gophers, and the World Wide Web. Students cannot reasonably be expected to remember the names and contents of so many research sources, but if they have been taught the basic search strategies and concepts, their potential for learning the skills necessary for self-sufficiency in libraries will be enhanced greatly. It is important to foster the kinds of skills and abilities that can be generalized and transferred successfully to new information problems so the students on their own can construct new questions, and formulate and discover new problems.

TECHNOLOGY AND SOCIETY

There are many recently published books and articles that offer pro and con perspectives on the virtues and dangers of an information society.[23] These views can be complemented by discussing current controversies in postmodernist interpretations of university undergraduate and liberal education curricula.[24] The repeated use of technology in library research should naturally raise questions in students' minds about the role and use of technology in society. Besides being asked to reflect critically on these issues, students can be asked to offer assessments about what information, technology, knowledge, and education in general mean or might come to mean to themselves and others in today's rapidly changing world. Students will begin to see the relationship between their understanding of the strengths and weaknesses of technology and their understanding of themselves in their quest for a deeper understanding of the world.

CONCLUSION

As the above remarks indicate, I believe that there is room in a university library instruction program for courses that offer students substance and context to library research. A library instruction class based on the premises spelled out here seeks to encourage students to develop an appreciation for the necessity of maintaining a balance between technological know-how and the intellectual exploration and development of ideas. If the father of the learning to learn movement, John Dewey, was right when he wrote that "the aim of education is to enable individuals to continue their education," then the changing face of social science research must accompany the need for Janus-faced librarians to build and protect gateways between the past and the future.[25]

ENDNOTES

1. Thomas Mann, Library Research Models: A Guide to Classification, Cataloging, and Computers (New York: Oxford University Press, 1993), 107.
2. Gerhard Casper, "Come the Millennium, Where the University?" Speech given at the Annual Meeting of the American Educational Research Association, April 18, 1995. San Francisco. Provided by University Communications, Stanford University. Located in "Casper Speeches" in Stanford's Portfolio Home Page (WWW).
3. William G. Bowen, "The Broader Role of the Library," Foreword to University Libraries and Scholarly Communication: A Study Prepared for the Andrew W. Mellon Foundation, by Anthony M. Cummings, et al. (Published by the Association of Research Libraries for the Andrew W. Mellon Foundation, November, 1992), xi.
4. Mattei Dogan, "Fragmentation of the Social Sciences and Recombination of Specialties Around Sociology," International Social Science Journal 139 (February, 1994): 29.
5. Mattei Dogan and Robert Pahre, Creative Marginality: Innovation at the Intersections of Social Science (Boulder: Westview Press, 1990).
6. Richard A. Lanham, "Electronic Textbooks and University Structures," in The Electronic Word: Democracy, Technology, and the Arts (Chicago: University of Chicago Press, 1993), 135.
7. Dogan and Pahre, Creative Marginality, 230, 141–42.
8. Steve Fuller, Philosophy, Rhetoric, and the End of Knowledge: The Coming of Science and Technology Studies (Madison: University of Wisconsin Press, 1993), xii.
9. Michael F. Winter, "Specialization and Interdisciplinary Growth in the Social Sciences," Behavioral & Social Sciences Librarian 10 (1991): 1–7.
10. Lanham, "Electronic Textbooks," 134.
11. Dogan and Pahre, Creative Marginality, 235.
12. Steve Fuller, "Why Post-Industrial Society Never Came: What a False Prophesy can Teach Us About the Impact of Technology on Academia," Academe (November-December, 1994): 27.
13. Nannerl O. Keohane, quoted in "Academic Disciplines Increasingly Entwine, Recasting Scholarship," The New York Times (March 23, 1994): 19.
14. Gary Radford, "Positivism, Foucault, and the Fantasia of the Library: Conceptions of Knowledge and the Modern Library Experience," The Library Quarterly 62 (October, 1992): 412, 419.
15. These premises, in part, have guided my efforts to design and teach a three credit, three hundred level University Writing Program course entitled "Researching the Social Sciences."
16. Michael Keresztesi has identified these dimensions as follows: epistemological refers to the creation of knowledge in a discipline, including subject matter, structure, scope, boundaries, methodologies, and paradigms that set the direction for the discipline's quest for knowledge; sociological aspects of the discipline as a group and organizational phenomena, including the institutionalization, status, and structure of the profession; historical dimension of a discipline, including its origin, development, and transformation; and bibliographical dimension, including the research, communication, and dissemination process of a discipline. See, Michael Keresztesi, "The Science of Bibliography: Theoretical Implications

for Bibliographic Instruction," in Theories of Bibliographic Education: Designs for Teaching, Cerise Oberman and Katina Strauch, eds. (New York: R. R. Bowker Company, 1982): 21–23.

17. Topsy N. Small and Stephen H. Plum, "Teaching Library Researching in the Humanities and Sciences: A Contextual Approach," in Theories of Bibliographic Education.

18. A comprehensive reader has been published in response to what the editors view as the reemergence of this "vibrant and exciting field of philosophical inquiry." See, Michael Martin and Lee C. McIntyre, Readings in the Philosophy of Social Science (Cambridge: MIT Press, 1994), xv.

19. For an excellent bibliographic overview of interdisciplinary research in the social sciences and humanities see, Julie Thompson Klein, "Finding Interdisciplinary Knowledge and Information," in Interdisciplinary Studies Today, Julie Thompson Klein and William G. Doty, eds. (San Francisco: Jossey-Bass, 1994), esp., 22–27.

20. See, for example, Clifford Geertz, "Blurred Genres: The Refiguration of Social Thought," in Local Knowledge (New York: Basic Books), 1983, 19–35; Richard Rorty, "Science as Solidarity," in The Rhetoric of the Human Sciences: Language and Argument in Scholarship and Public Affairs, John S. Nelson, ed. (Madison: University of Wisconsin Press, 1987), 38–52; Robert Boynton, "The New Intellectuals," Atlantic Monthly (March, 1995): 53–70.

21. William H. Newell, "Designing Interdisciplinary Courses," in Interdisciplinary Studies Today, 47.

22. Dogan and Pahre, Creative Marginality, 84.

23. On the role of technology in society see, for example, Peter F. Drucker, "The Age of Social Transformation," Atlantic Monthly (November, 1994): 53–80; Adam Jones, "Wired World: Communications Technology, Governance and the Democratic Uprising," in The Global Political Economy of Communications: Hegemony, Telecommunication and the Information Economy, Edward A. Connor, ed. (New York: St. Martin's Press, 1994), 145–164; Richard Lanham, "Operating Systems, Attention Structures, and the Edge of Chaos," in The Electronic Word, 225–257; Howard Rheingold, "Disinformocracy," in The Virtual Community: Homesteading on the Electronic Frontier (New York: HarperPerennial, 1994), 276–300; Theodore Roszak, The Cult of Information: A Neo-Luddite Treatise on High Tech, Artificial Intelligence, and the True Art of Thinking, 2d ed. (Berkeley: University of California Press, 1994); Herbert Schiller, "The Global Information Highway: Project for an Ungovernable World," in Resisting the Virtual Life: The Culture and Politics of Information, James Brook and Iain A. Boal, eds. (San Francisco: City Lights, 1995), 17–34; Frank Webster, Theories of the Information Society (London: Routledge, 1995); Langdon Winner, "Citizen Virtues in a Technological Order," in Technology and the Politics of Knowledge, Andrew Feenberg and Alastair Hannay, eds. (Bloomington: Indiana University Press, 1995), 65–84.

24. For a postmodernist perspective of liberal education, see Jean-Francois Lyotard, The Postmodern Condition: A Report on Knowledge, Geoff Bennington and Brian Massumi, trans. (Minneapolis: University of Minnesota Press, 1984). For a critique of postmodernism and a defense of liberal education see, Linda Ray Pratt, "Liberal Education and the Idea of the Postmodern University," Academe (November-December, 1994): 46–51.

25. John Dewey, Democracy and Education: An Introduction to the Philosophy of Education (New York: Macmillan, 1916; the Free Press, 1944), 100.

Librarians Are from Venus, Scholars Are from Mars

By William Z. Schenck
Library of Congress

Let me begin with apologies to John Gray, the author of *Men Are from Mars, Women Are from Venus*, for making a somewhat scrambled use of his title. I do not mean to imply that librarians and scholars inhabit different parts of the solar system; it is just that sometimes the two do not always appear to be on the same wave-length. Certainly their needs and goals are not always the same. And, to be honest, it never hurts to have a catchy title for an essay.

I also need to clarify the authorship of this paper. Originally, William Sittig, then the Director of the Collections Policy Office, and I planned to co-author it, using our experiences with the Case Studies being done at the Library of Congress. However, last October Mr. Sittig was named Chief of the Science and Technology Division of the Library and, as a result, his involvement with the Case Studies diminished as he had to spend more time with administrative matters in his new position. Therefore, we decided that I would prepare this paper alone. However, I want to acknowledge his contributions to the case studies, as well as those of Prosser Gifford, the Director of Scholarly Programs (who also serves on the Case Study Steering Committee) and his assistant, Lester Vogel. However, I assume all responsibility for the comments and opinions in this paper.

What I plan to do is to provide a general description of the Case Study project, with a brief description of the six case studies, and then focus on one of the six, the one on Social Science Studies in 20th-century China. I will explain how it worked, what it did, and highlight some of its recommendations, concluding with a general overview of the Case Studies themselves. As I know you are more interested in theory than practical applications to the Library of Congress, I will focus more on the process than on the results.

THE CASE STUDY APPROACH

The Library of Congress has a long tradition of working with scholars who use its collections. In some cases this meant formal evaluations; in others it was a few suggestions from someone who had been here using our collections, often in rather specialized (some might say esoteric) areas. In addition, individual Library staff in reference or in area studies have always worked closely with visiting scholars (and scholars from institutions in the region) to identify specific gaps in the collection. But these were usually isolated instances, dependent on the motivation of the Library staff and the willingness of the user to take the time to discuss problems. More importantly, these isolated evaluations were not large-scale, systematic examinations and there was little or no follow-up.

When the present Librarian of Congress, James H. Billington, was appointed in 1987, he expressed as one of his goals the need to bring outside scholars and Library staff closer, building on the expertise of both groups to improve the quality of our collections. The Case Study Project is an outgrowth of that concept. Instead of more conventional collection evaluations, with which we are all familiar (and which the Library also does), the case study technique was used as a way to focus on major issues facing the Library. Six areas were selected for in-depth study:

- African-American Materials
- Business and Economics

- Social Science Studies in 20th-Century China
- Environmental Policy
- Hispanic and Hispanic-American materials
- Islamic materials

A diverse, but not a randomly selected group, they were chosen to represent areas of importance to Congress and the nation as well as (and this was a major consideration) areas of changing scholarship and emerging trends of research. They are also areas where resources are being greatly affected by the increased availability of new electronic formats. It is also important to note what these are not. They do not necessarily represent the only areas of high priority to the Library, to Congress, or to the nation; nor do they necessarily represent problematic areas at LC.

These areas were not to receive classic evaluations in the traditional sense we are used to. Instead, each case study group was asked to focus on strategic questions, both specific to their area and general to all six areas. The general questions were:

- What resources do Congress and the Federal government need to function?
- What is intrinsically important to scholarship in the broadest sense?
- What is unique about the Library of Congress collection; what is the unique configuration of this collection within the field as a whole?
- What are the trends in scholarship in this field and how do our collections support them?

Teams were then selected to examine each area. There were five to six Library staff selected for each team, with an attempt to represent those areas of the Library with a vested interest in the study. Thus the five-person China team had representatives from the Law Library, Acquisitions Directorate, Asian Division, Congressional Research Division and the Federal Research Division (an LC division which contracts to perform specialized research for Executive Branch agencies—you are probably familiar with their Country Guide series). Administratively, the team members were approved by the Collections Policy Committee after consultation with the appropriate division chiefs. A four-person Case Study Steering Committee coordinated the overall activities of the teams, meeting (usually) monthly with the chairs of each team. The Steering Committee reported to the Collections Policy Committee (CPC), a high-level committee that coordinates and recommends collection building policy issues to the Associate Librarian for Library Services.

The Case Studies were supported with funding from the Madison Council, a private group whose members generously support innovative Library projects. Additional funding came from the Andrew W. Mellon Foundation. Funds from Mellon were used primarily to focus on electronic resources, especially to study the availability of such resources and the relationship between access and ownership, especially in view of the Library's archival responsibilities. Funds assisted some team members to attend professional meetings to discuss their project (as members of the China Team did when the Association of Asian Studies met in Boston in March, 1994 and at the AAS meeting in 1995) and to contract with outside scholars to examine specific issues and comment on changing research trends.

I need to mention that as of March, 1996, the Collections Policy Committee had received the reports from all six teams but had not yet discussed the reports and their recommendations. Thus it has not yet been determined, at the time of this writing, which of the recommendations the Library will implement.

A CASE IN POINT: THE CHINESE SOCIAL SCIENCE COLLECTION

While it may appear obvious that 20th-century Chinese social science resources are an important area to study, let me quote from their final report: "If the twenty-first century is indeed going to be the 'Pacific Century' and if China becomes the major world power it hopes to be, then the Library of Congress—in serving the information and research needs of the United States Congress, the United States Government, and the nation—must move with diligence and dispatch to return to a position of preeminence in the field of China studies."

In addition to the overall strategic questions, each case study team developed strategic questions that focused on their specific area and subject. Here are the seven questions from the China Team:

- What are the emerging research trends in this area, given current political developments in China?

- How are the Library's collections adapting to or preparing for foreseeable political change in China?
- What collection resources should the Library have to serve the needs of the Congress and the Federal government?
- What use do the Congressional Research Service and the Federal Research Division make of the Library's collections of Chinese social science materials?
- What use do other federal agencies make of the Library's collections of these Chinese materials?
- Are there other libraries or resources to which users turn because the material they seek is unavailable at the Library?
- What measures might be taken by the Library to supply these materials directly?

I will not go into the methodology the team used to answer these questions; instead I will focus on the use the team made of outside scholars. I use the term "outside scholar" intentionally as I do not mean to imply that LC does not have scholars on its staff. In fact, four of the five members of the Chinese Team have doctorates.

The team engaged six expert consultants to assist in its deliberations, selecting each consultant with the aim of finding the best qualified person who could operate within the (rather broad) time constraints. The funds available were sufficient to attract top people. We were fortunate, I might add, in that some of our experts lived in the region. For example, Dr. Anna Shulman, who surveyed the Western-language sources in all formats, and who is the editor of the Bibliography of Asian Studies, lives in the region.

Other consultants included Dr. Tai-loi Ma (East Asian Library, University of Chicago) who examined the Chinese-language collection; Dr. June Teufel Dreyer (University of Miami) who focused on national security issues; Ms. Madelyn Ross (a China business consultant) whose field is business and economics; Dr. James Feinerman (Georgetown University Law School) an expert in Chinese law; and Dr. Jonathan Ocko (North Carolina State University) who examined electronic media covering this area.

Each consultant met with the members of the China Team. A written contract specified the type of report wanted and the deadline for submission. To the best of my knowledge, all reports from consultants in all the teams, with one exception, met or exceeded the contractual obligations.

The reports submitted by these outside scholars to the China Team were both complimentary and, when necessary, critical. This was especially important, as we didn't want to have people just tell us we were doing a good job—we needed and wanted to know where we could improve.

The China Team then took the six consultants' reports and used them, plus their knowledge of the collections and problem areas, to prepare a short (twenty-six page) report. Instead of simply supplying a laundry-list of recommendations, the Team evaluated each recommendation and grouped them into four distinct subjects. It is important to note that not all the recommendations from the consultants were adopted by the China Team. For example, several scholars complained about decreased access to the stacks. However, knowing the overriding security concerns in the Library, the Team did not directly endorse these comments but instead recommended the Library "enhance electronic bibliographic access to all printed and special format China-related material owned by the Library."

Because, as I mentioned, the Library has not yet discussed implementation of the recommendations from the six teams, it is premature to describe the overall project except as a work-in-progress. But, from my personal perspective, I will provide some comments on the strengths and weaknesses of the overall case study project.

The scholars were all enthusiastic about the project. The only problems were ones of schedules—not everyone was available at specific times. This interest was true regardless of the status of the scholar—from full professor to independent scholar.

Secondly, the scholars provided a valuable perspective. Those of us who work in an institution the size of LC too often get used to current procedures without getting information from our ultimate users on how well these procedures work.

Thirdly, the consultants were not afraid to be critical when that was justified. For example, Dr. Ocko's report pointed out the need to improve the collection of electronic resources relating to China; few are currently owned.

And fourth, the project brought together staff working in various areas of the Library and encouraged them to work together as a team. In fact, one of the China Team's recommendations is to "establish a permanent China Working Group . . . to effect better coordination among LC staff building and using the collections."

There were also some problems with the project, foremost of which was the time of staff involved in the process. The financial picture has changed in Washington over the past two years; it proved difficult for many staff to give this project a high priority at a time of decreasing resources. Thus the burden of work was often unevenly divided among team members.

Secondly, some of the consultant's recommendations are unrealistic, given the current budget which LC (and other research libraries) face. For example, one consultant wrote that "to keep abreast with law developments, the Library must increase acquisitions, processing, and user-services budgets." Who could disagree with that logic, but it isn't going to happen. I would categorize these recommendations as fiscally unrealistic; I had personally hoped for more recommendations that would look at different and unusual solutions to such problems.

Thirdly, it proved difficult for the outside scholars to locate some material which we in fact did own, leading to mistaken assumptions that we did not have the item when we actually did. This, of course, does highlight a different issue—one of the ease of use of our bibliographic data. But it does reduce the usefulness of some of the consultant's conclusions.

In conclusion, the Case Study methodology proved a useful way to match outside scholars with inside staff in a way that resulted in a valuable analysis of our collections and how those collections can and will meet the changing research needs of our users into the next century.

Changing Materials, Changing Economies

Elsewhere in the Forest: The Place of U.S. Government Information in Libraries of the Future

By George D. Barnum, Margaret S. Powell, and Mary Webb Prophet
Case Western Reserve University / The College of Wooster / Denison University

Soon after its inception, the American federal government began to form what we would identify in our time as information policy. Constituents clamored for information on the actions of the new government, and members of Congress began to find ways to inform them. Initially, each bill or other document was separately authorized by resolution, but by 1813 this gave way to more regular and routine arrangements whereby copies of documents were regularly sent to libraries and academies.[1] As Carroll W. Pursell points out, "The revolutionary generation of Americans was born in a country which labored with a medieval technology in a colonial economy. By the time its work was done, it had deliberately borrowed the new European industrial technology and rejected the Old World's political control."[2] The emergence of the American experiment in government, with its emphasis on an informed electorate, neatly coincides with expansion in American technology and the industrialization of American society. The role of the government in informing its citizens grew up beside and ultimately became inextricably entwined with the development of bigger, better, and faster printing presses.

The spirit that moved legislators to print and publish also created an impetus to disseminate, and the rise of libraries in the 19th century added another strand to the thread of government information in the libraries of today. During the first Congresses, copies of the journals and other printed documents of both chambers were distributed beyond the limits of the Congress by special resolution. By the 13th Congress, a joint resolution established a set sum of 200 copies to be distributed to officials, colleges and universities, and historical societies in each state and territory. Ultimately, the number of copies grew, and finally, the formalized system of deposit was born of three acts of Congress between 1857 and 1859. The acts gave members of Congress power to designate depositories and assured geographical dispersion of government information in a growing nation.[3] These acts laid the foundation of the depository system as we know it today.

Two more administrative developments cemented the future of government information in U.S. libraries: the centralization of government information dissemination activities in the Government Printing Office (GPO) by the Printing Act of June 30, 1860, and the landmark Printing Act of 1895. The 1860 act brought all government printing under the centralized authority of the Public Printer of the United States, ending the system of private contracting and political patronage that had dogged the Congress since colonial times. In 1869, the position of Superintendent of Documents was created within the Government Printing Office to oversee all dissemination activities, including distribution to depositories. The Printing Act of 1895 established the structure of the Depository Library Program which remained basically unmodified until 1962, when it was further broadened into the program of today by expanding geographic coverage and mandating "full" or comprehensive collections in each state.

The basic operational principles of the Federal Depository Library Program (FDLP) may be summarized as follows:

1) All publications of the government from all three branches are to be included in the program, except those which are strictly internal in nature, are classified for reasons of national security, or which depend on sale to the public to cover the cost of their publication.

2) The copies to achieve this distribution are pro-

duced at Congressional expense for the program.
3) Libraries which meet certain minimum guidelines including geographical criteria may be designated by Congress as depositories.
4) Depositories must make publications freely available to the general public without impediment or charge and retain them for a specified period.
5) Depositories must meet various performance standards, which are assessed in periodic inspections.[4]

These principles flesh out the intent of the Congress to create and maintain a steady channel through which government information is made widely available to the electorate and for improving commerce. As long as the sole medium for the dissemination of information was printed documents, the concept and operation of the program were simple. GPO did the government's printing, usually on state-of-the-art equipment, and included in any appropriate printing order enough copies above the request of the publishing agency to distribute the document to depository libraries. The prevailing technologies for printing and distribution served the FDLP reasonably well, far into the 20th century.

In the last 20 years, however, various pressures have come to bear on the operation of the program. As government has grown in size and complexity, its output of information has grown in like manner. Internally, GPO has had to adapt in the way it conducts business in order to handle the sheer volume of printing. By the 1990s GPO has become as much a procurement agency as a printer, with the majority of non-Congressional production being obtained under standing contracts through GPO with the private sector.[5] These developments have exacerbated the long-standing problem of documents that qualify for the program, but by oversight or intentional agency noncompliance are not made available for GPO to distribute. Libraries have increasingly found themselves in the position of having to pursue this "fugitive" information actively from individual agencies and from private sector vendors in order to offer comprehensive collections to their users.

In the early 1980s, as government sought ways to control costs, paper documents were converted to microfiche format, the first move away from dissemination of ink-on-paper. Although the introduction caused some consternation among librarians and users (and despite ongoing questions of the appropriateness of diazo fiche for long-term preservation) this first shift in technology was relatively easily assimilated into the operation of the FDLP and depository libraries. In almost every respect, except its use by the reader, it is produced, disseminated, and collected just like printed matter, and despite its negative attributes, significant savings of both cost for GPO and storage space for libraries were achieved. The move to fiche did make librarians aware, however, that in the era of cost/benefit analysis, the FDLP was under scrutiny, and that it was no longer possible to rely on the ideological goodwill of a benevolent Congress. Microfiche was but a harbinger.

In 1988, GPO distributed its first Compact Disk/Read Only Memory (CD/ROM), a pilot project from the Census Bureau. This shift resembled the microfiche transition in that GPO was still shipping a physical object, an "information product," to libraries. Here, however, the similarities ended, and the conflicts for libraries and the FDLP began in earnest. As with the first fiche, many depository libraries were unprepared for electronic distribution. Users who had access to appropriate equipment were met with a medium that required a completely new sensibility for use and which carried with it little or no assistance in the way of documentation or instruction. And it was only the tip of a rapidly emerging iceberg.

With the new administration elected in 1992 and the new majority in Congress in 1994, government has been pulled very rapidly into the electronic age. By the early 1990s, GPO had grappled with attempts by the Reagan and Bush administrations to privatize many of its functions. Integral to this struggle was the question of whether or not online information falls within the legislative parameters of 44 USC—in effect whether there is some distinction between "information products" and "information services" when the definition hinges on the presence or absence of a physical object.[6] This trend was part of a larger phenomenon during those 12 years that saw less and less government information available through many channels. The administration sought to alter and consolidate a variety of administrative and regulatory practices that controlled the public's access to information, including revisions to the Paperwork Reduction Act and to Office of Management and Budget guidelines on information policy. It has become more and more widely accepted since

1992 that the distinction between product and service was largely artificial and served the commercial ends of private sector firms involved in marketing government information better than the public at-large. We have witnessed, with the headlong proliferation of electronic resources, the growth of the notion (which librarians probably held all along) that access to government information should not be ruled by the format or medium of that information. Currently, the atmosphere for government information in libraries is being formed by two strong ideological strains which seem to be, to a greater or lesser extent, shared by both the Congressional majority and the administration. Not surprisingly, however, the two camps have not found a common ground for implementation of their ideas.

The first of these strains is that government should, for a whole host of economic and ideological reasons, be made smaller and more efficient. There is consensus on both sides of the aisle that the federal bureaucracy has grown too large and too inefficient. Vice President Al Gore conducted an extensive study at the beginning of the Clinton Administration which proposed the "reinvention" of government, a government that "works better and costs less."[7] The implications of this line of thinking for GPO have been serious. Although the actual functions of printing and the wide spectrum of information dissemination have grown apart very rapidly, GPO has remained philosophically and practically a largely print-based operation despite tremendous strides forward in becoming a multi-medium disseminator of information. There have been repeated moves to shrink the GPO radically or eliminate it entirely in favor of individual agencies procuring printing services on their own, with a depository library system administered by some other agency such as the National Telecommunications and Information Administration, the National Technical Information Service, or the Library of Congress.

The other, complementary strain that has come into prominence since the election of a new majority in Congress in 1994 is the move to economize in all federal programs more stringently than ever before in an attempt to balance the federal budget. The Congressional leadership, in particular that of the House of Representatives, has a broad belief in the ability of technology to economize bureaucracy and reform society simultaneously. Thus, the three years since President Clinton took office have been highly uncertain for GPO generally and the FDLP in particular.

During this period of advancing uncertainty, librarians began to discuss their vision of a "reinvented" FDLP. A large group of concerned documents librarians met in mid-1992 in Washington to begin to articulate this vision. This "Dupont Circle Group" stimulated a discussion in the professional community of documents librarians and ultimately arranged a conference, held in Chicago in October, 1993. The reports of the Chicago Conference emphasized the essential features of a program of free and open dissemination of government information and defined a framework that posited a partnership between the public, libraries, government agencies as producers of information, and a "central coordinating government authority" to disseminate and ensure access to information.[8] The results of the conference were a substantive document, which has formed the basis of much of the discussion surrounding the future of government information since, and a core of approximately 150 librarians thoroughly briefed on the issues facing the FDLP. The conference reaffirmed that:

no-fee access to government information is a right;

government information's role in daily life is multi-faceted;

a central coordinating authority will provide the most complete and efficient dissemination services;

the program should facilitate a partnership between its constituents.

The future of the FDLP is being shaped by a legislative climate of budgetary austerity and a shift to technology to create cost efficiencies. Even as the Chicago Conference was in session, Congress received from the Executive Branch a proposal to reduce the size of GPO severely and reorganize the FDLP.[9] The proposal was modified when the House Administration Committee reported it on November 15, calling for the elimination of GPO and the transfer of the Superintendent of Documents operation (including the FDLP) to the Library of Congress. House Report 3400, the initial legislative proposal for the implementation of the National Performance Review, passed the House by a wide margin but ultimately died in committee in the Senate.

The debate continued and crystallized in 1995 around budgetary issues. In the first draft of their appropriation for GPO for fiscal year 1996, the House of Representatives proposed a cut in the funding of the FDLP of nearly 50% from the FY 1995 level of $32 million.[10] This measure would have specifically altered the fundamental principle that non-classified, non-sensitive material produced at taxpayer expense is included in the program at Congressional expense regardless of format. By requiring that only the production and distribution of information produced in electronic form would be paid for by Congress, the cost for the production of depository copies and the overhead costs for distribution in the FDLP would be charged to the agency. This action is referred to as an "incentive" to stimulate agency conversion of electronic dissemination formats.

The Senate took a more moderate approach, restored the funding at the 1995 level, but inserted language in their report which was eventually retained in a House/Senate Conference report. This directed the Public Printer to undertake a study that:

> examines the functions and services of the Federal Depository Library Program;
>
> surveys current technological capabilities of the participating libraries in the Federal Depository Library Program;
>
> surveys current and future information dissemination plans of executive branch agencies;
>
> examines and suggests improvements for agency compliance of relevant laws, regulations, and policies regarding Government information dissemination;
>
> identifies measures that are necessary to ensure a successful transition to a more electronically based program;
>
> identifies the possible expansion of the array of Federal information products and services made available to participating libraries;
>
> ensures the most cost-efficient program to the taxpayer.

The study shall include a strategic plan that will assist the Congress in redefining a new and strengthened Federal information dissemination policy and program.

In conducting the study, it will be important for the Public Printer to work closely with the respective oversight and appropriation committees, executive branch agencies, other distributors of Federal documents and information products, the Library of Congress, the depository library community, the National Technical Information Service, users, the information industry, and other appropriate organizations. The completed study shall be available to Congress by March 1996.[11]

The Legislative Branch Appropriation became law on November 19, 1995, restoring FY 1995 funding levels to the FDLP and retaining the conference language intact.[12]

This "Public Printer's Study"[13] was undertaken in two parts: a strategic plan, in December, 1995, and the full report, due in March, 1996. As the outlines are currently drawn, we can foresee two divergent futures for the FDLP. These two futures are the extreme ends of a spectrum within which government information dissemination policy will actually fall. By defining the environment at these extremes, we may provide a context for local and regional responses that will shape the access that library users will have to government information in libraries of the future.

THE FIRST FUTURE: AN ELECTRONIC FDLP

The Public Printer's Study is predicated on four broad assumptions[14]:

> The FDLP will be primarily electronic.
>
> The law [Title 44 United States Code chapter 19] will be revised so that electronic information is clearly in scope for the FDLP. Agency participation in the FDLP will be required.
>
> These factors will lead to changes in the structure of the FDLP.
>
> The funding available to the FDLP from the legislative branch appropriation will not exceed the current level.

When the Transition Plan was published, further assumptions were added:

> The existing GPO Access service will provide the basic platform for online services.
>
> In the transition period, priority will be given to achieving electronic access for information already in the program, followed by electronic

information not currently in the program, and with retrospective data receiving lowest priority.

GPO will attempt to fund "technology grants" to libraries, to assist in the transition that will help to assure geographic dispersion.[15]

The Transition Plan describes a program altered at all levels: Congressional, GPO, and local library. The roles and responsibilities of all program constituents are redefined, and relationships shift. Historically, the FDLP has been central to the information dissemination functions because of its location within GPO. The inclusion of information in the FDLP was accomplished as a part of the printing and distribution of documents. The effectiveness of the program at providing a comprehensive selection of government information has been seriously eroded over time as agencies have bypassed GPO, turning either to other contractors or to in-house operations as desktop publishing and large scale duplicating capabilities became commonplace. When GPO was providing a service that proved advantageous for agencies, the FDLP functioned smoothly. Now agencies do not need GPO to produce information products for distribution on CD/ROM or mounting on the World Wide Web, even though a variety of these services are readily available from GPO. Consequently, the structure of the FDLP must be altered radically to enable it to fulfill two continuing functions: the obligation and/or statutory requirements of agencies to provide information to the public; and, perhaps more importantly, the right of citizens to information by and about their government. The Transition Plan and its assumptions speak to that alteration.

Under the GPO plan, the FDLP will be primarily electronic by the end of FY 1998, with the exception of a few select titles which must always remain in paper. The costs of this transition will be met by reducing or eliminating the production and distribution of paper and microfiche for the FDLP. This entails an almost unimaginably aggressive program of conversion to electronic formats both at the production level, where new products are created in a standardized format, such as Standard Generalized Markup Language (SGML), and at the distribution/dissemination level. Agency products received by GPO in ink-on-paper format are to be converted to digital form at GPO. The first of these changes has been in use at GPO for some time and parallels a trend throughout the printing and publishing industry. A text no longer moves from manuscript to type to printed page but instead from manuscript (which may itself be electronic) to digital text which may then be printed or mounted on a server. This shift in the origination of digital data will be pivotal. In the interim GPO will convert printed documents to electronic form by means of optical scanning. It is not clear at this point if these scanned files will remain as digital images requiring special software for viewing as well as the more traditional processes of description and cataloging or if there will be an attempt to convert the files to searchable text.

The assumption of a totally electronic future for the FDLP carries several possible consequences for libraries and users. To begin with, no project has been attempted on this scale to provide information electronically without regard to its manner of origination or production. William Saffady lists a wide range of digital library prototype and pilot projects.[16] None approach the scale or complexity of the GPO proposal nor have demonstrated a production methodology for such a high volume of information. Likewise, there is little available data on actual costs of digital library implementations. Saffady observes, "As with other aspects of library automation, economic concerns are often ignored by technology enthusiasts; cost calculation, affordability issues, and justification parameters are rarely examined. . . . "[17]

A consideration that may be overlooked in the headlong rush to convert sources to electronic form is that the bulk of costs associated with producing a print run of documents is incurred in the stages leading up to actual printing, i.e., the generation of the information and its synthesis into publishable form. This cost is likely to remain relatively constant regardless of the form of dissemination. Marks has estimated that for commercial scientific journals, "The cost of printing, paper, and binding, excluding subscription, fulfillment, and mailing costs, is in the range of $10 to $40 a page. . . . On this basis the first copy cost represents 82 to 86 percent of the total cost. The first copy cost is the investment necessary to produce an electronic digitized version of each page."[18] Within the context of the way government information is produced, the bulk of this cost falls to the agency, since GPO only provides printing and dissemination services. The remaining 14 to 18 percent of the cost goes to distribution and represents the funding GPO expects to make available for the transition as ink-on-paper work declines. Presumably, the transition will require significant capital outlay for GPO as they move into a completely new field of production with scanning and, perhaps, optical character recognition technology. There will also be a substantial expense for retraining and redeploying the skilled workforce that will remain at GPO. It remains unclear whether the net savings GPO achieves by reductions to the paper and microfiche program will cover the costs of conversion to electronic distribution.

The interim step of scanning materials on a large scale may introduce inconsistencies over time. In terms of searchability, texts originated in digital form are still somewhat superior to scanned texts. While the technology for optical character recognition has advanced, machine conversion of text from images to a fully digitized text is still problematic. Thus a highly inferior interim product may result, with no control on the part of the originating agency, since the conversion will be undertaken by GPO for the sole purpose of distribution to the FDLP.

It might seem reasonable at this point to question why, with the mass of information GPO proposes to make available through networked or networkable channels, the nation needs a depository library program anyway. Certain factions in Washington might argue that we do not, and the effects of that argument are explored below. The answer that comes forth again and again from documents librarians and others in the profession is that electronic formats are among the least egalitarian with respect to individual readers. While we hear constantly that the number of personal computers in homes is growing at an astonishing rate, these are, in general, in homes of a particular income level. With the coming expansion of competition in the telecommunications industry, the Internet is likely to become more and more a marketplace. Libraries generally and depository libraries in particular must continue to provide a bridge between information and inability to pay.

The revision of the law to embrace electronic information resources within the scope of the FDLP must necessarily address not only the issue of defining government "publication" or "information product/service," but compliance by agencies as well. The model for the program being suggested in the Transition Plan makes the inclusion of information in the FDLP a far more conscious or voluntary act on the part of agencies than the current law outlines. Currently, agencies are expected to obtain their printing through GPO, at which point GPO adds or "rides" sufficient additional copies for depository distribution. In cases where agencies are not obtaining printing through GPO, there is an expectation that appropriate titles will be made available for distribution, either by reprinting or by other means such as micrographic reproduction. Agency history on compliance with this expectation is spotty at best, and the so-called "fugitive document" problem has grown in scope and seriousness in recent years. There is every reason to assume that this problem will increase and that valuable information, regardless of format, will continue to elude the net of depository distribution, thus contributing to an even greater reduction in public access to information.

Although libraries will, presumably, think more and more along the lines of access and less of local ownership and collections, having access to comprehensive and consistent collections and databases will determine the success or failure of an electronic FDLP. Acceptance of an access-based model of library use may be influenced more by reliability of access and consistency of available data than by the speed of access.[19] The future FDLP will need substantial powers of enforcement to assure compliance with statutory depository requirements, given the relative ease and speed with which information can be produced and distributed by agencies themselves to their own constituencies.

Changes in the structure of the FDLP will also occur at various levels. The most radical change, and the most potentially worrisome, is the shift in the fundamental role of GPO and the FDLP from central distributor and administrator to disseminator and repository. Until the early 1970s GPO did maintain a collection of those documents that had been cataloged in the FDLP but did not operate it as a working collection for service to librarians or end users. The Transition Plan states that "This electronic FDLP model replaces the geographically-dispersed collections of books and microfiche with connections to a number of on-line electronic services operated under authority of the SOD [Superintendent of Documents]. The responsibility for ensuring long-term access shifts from the [depository] libraries to the SOD. . . . To provide long-term access to data in SOD facilities, the SOD assumes such costs as data preparation for mounting, maintenance, storage, and ongoing costs to minimize deterioration and assure technological currency. The SOD will work with the National Archives and Records Administration (NARA) to ensure that electronic information which no longer has sufficient usage to warrant maintaining it at a SOD site for the FDLP is permanently preserved."[20]

It might be argued that this misstates the case. What the new model actually replaces is not the depository library but the GPO distribution and shipping operation. GPO and the depositories will share the responsibility for long-term access, and ultimately, the best scenario is a redefined partnership between libraries and GPO. To depository librarians in institutions that are operating at a high level technologically, there is no small irony in the above statement coming from an agency that has made advances in technology erratically at best. Expecting GPO, and therefore Congress, to assume the responsibility for ongoing access to information and reducing the depository to a kind of filling station ill serves both user and GPO, and leaves the program vulnerable to severe damage as congresses come and go.

A related concern for libraries is the issue of electronic capabilities and revised technical requirements for the FDLP. Preliminary results from the fall 1995 *Biennial Survey of Depository Libraries* indicate that, among the 1400 depository libraries presently in the program, only 516 (37.6%) offer Internet access to the public with a graphical user interface.[21] The Transition Plan optimistically projects that "GPO intends to expend up to $500,000 in FY 1997 for 'technology grants' . . . intended to ensure reasonable public access and proximity to at least one electronically-capable depository in every Congressional district."[22]

The Transition Plan was conceived in part as a point of departure from which concrete discussions might begin. The first organized response to the plan was a resolution by the Government Documents Roundtable (GODORT) of the American Library Association, which was adopted at the 1995 ALA midwinter meeting and which is generally supportive of the notion of the electronic depository but expresses concern about the two-year time frame and recommends a " . . . realistic 5 to 7 year time-frame for the transition."[23]

With the present state of technology, a 5 to 7 year transition may be more realistic for implementation of any project approaching the magnitude of the Transition Plan. Desire may be strong from Congress, GPO, and at least a segment of the library community for the transition to electronic media, but conversion is time-consuming and ultimately costly. Conversion offered as a cost-saving measure for the short run may well be a disappointment.

THE SECOND FUTURE: A DISPLACED FDLP

The legislative language which sparked the Public Printer's Study was the Senate response to more extreme language from the House at the beginning of the FY 1996 budget cycle. H.R. 1854 was the most recent attempt to alter the FDLP radically by cutting funding for inclusion of paper documents in the program as an "incentive" for agencies to move to electronic dissemination. It has been observed that such initiatives point out "what little understanding members of Congress have of the public's use of government information."[24] While the program received a "stay of execution" in the form of the Senate's insistence on its language in conference and on its directive for the Public Printer's Study, the reality persists that the FDLP continues to come quite close to serious reorganization or even extinction.

In the bipartisan frenzy to reduce the size and complexity of government, GPO and its centralizing functions have repeatedly been a target in a mistaken understanding of GPO's mandate as a monopoly. The National Performance Review and various legislative proposals since have expressed a desire to see all government printing privatized, with procurement for that printing handled individually by each agency. While none of these proposals has received broad enough support to prevail, several of them have had hearings held and one, H.R. 3400, passed the House before languishing in committee in the Senate.

The fate of GPO's primary functions in these bills is clear: all printing is to be done in the private sector and centralized procurement of services eliminated. What is less clear is the fate of the FDLP in such a scenario. No proposal thus far has called for its outright elimination. The general tone of the National Performance Review, as well as various of the Congressional proposals, is that the program be relocated within another agency. H.R. 3400 directed that its operations be moved to the Library of Congress; and the National Archives, National Technical Information Service, Office of Management and Budget, and National Telecommunications and In-

Changing Materials, Changing Economies

formation Administration have also been mentioned. Any such scenario has serious and potentially difficult, if not fatal, side effects for the FDLP.

In such a scenario, proposed in the very generalized terms that have been forthcoming to this point, the FDLP is left without the organizing principle that drives its daily operations, and without the legislative mandate that assures what success it has. The twin expediencies of the FDLP's presence within the printing/distribution process and with the definitions established by 44 USC for eligibility, which makes agency participation in the program a statutory obligation, have served the FDLP remarkably well. The shift away from printed media has made the universe of information that can and should be within the scope of the program vastly larger, but it has not obviated the need for the program to be a centralized point of collection and dissemination, nor the need for statutory "teeth" in accomplishing the mission of providing no-fee access to the citizenry.

Over the past several years the problem of so-called fugitive documents has grown steadily. Such documents are eligible for the FDLP but, through a variety of circumstances ranging from ignorance to avoidance of the requirements of 44 USC on the part of agency administrators, are not included in the program. The problem has become more acute as agencies have at their disposal desktop publishing software, high-speed, high-volume copiers, and now access to the Internet and the wide-ranging possibilities it provides. In a future in which the FDLP is removed by its new enabling legislation from a coordinating function and in which it is not given authority to pursue agency products actively, there will be no imperative and probably very little actual incentive for agencies to participate.

Over the years the U.S. government has been recognized as the largest publishing concern in the world. While we are in highly charged and rapidly changing times, it seems unlikely that electronic information will entirely replace every agency's printed products. By imposing a penalty on agencies for having printed products in the FDLP (thus in effect a penalty on printing regardless of any factor such as intended audience, ultimate use, or appropriateness for electronic dissemination), and by scattering the FDLP's coordinating function to the wind, libraries will have less and less reason to accept the obligations of depository status, since Depository Libraries will be in little better position than non-depository libraries to be assured of comprehensive access to information. Libraries with a commitment to including government information in the menu of information they offer to their users will necessarily have to increase the allocation of staff time devoted to seeking and obtaining information from agencies individually and will be forced to increase expenditures for acquisition of such material.

No proposal for the "reinvented" or moved FDLP deals with the vast treasure of information that is already available in the depository collections of today that exists because of the guidelines defining the program to this point. Retention requirements and the system for disposal of materials ensure that significant retrospective collections will exist and that a certain built-in overlap and redundancy will protect them. These collections, in the absence of the FDLP, would be far more subject to the stresses of shrinking budgets and other exigencies in local institutions. Likewise no proposal puts forth any scenario for the long-term preservation and accessibility of electronic information.

THE MIDDLE GROUND: LOCAL RESPONSES AND THE FUTURE

In outlining these two extreme scenarios above, only one thing is clear: the Federal Depository Library Program will look quite different at the beginning of the new century. The area between these scenarios is the ground in which the reality of the future FDLP will exist. Beginning with the appropriation cycle for 1997 and the reception accorded the Public Printer's Study, Congress will forge, from the materials at hand, a new program that will address expanding electronic technology. But the government's role is only a part of the picture. Such change has been understood as inevitable in libraries for some time, and various solutions have already been implemented in libraries to address the problems and challenges that the changes to the FDLP merely restate.

LIBRARY SERVICES TO USERS

Collection development, bibliographic control, and reference service are continuously adjusted by library staff members to accommodate constantly changing information environments. No matter where in this spectrum of possibilities the future of depository libraries actually falls, government information will still be needed at the local level. Many of the sources to be converted in the next two years will be acceptable in electronic format; but some of these materials, especially those which fall outside of GPO's core list, will be found to be unsuitable for electronic distribution and use. Libraries will be forced to acquire these sources in print form in order to maintain appropriate levels of service and continuity in existing collections. Government sources in electronic formats may neither supersede nor enhance and extend corresponding material in older or more traditional formats nor do they always eliminate the need to retain earlier print editions of the same material.

Existing traditional depository collections, which have been developed in designated libraries for over a century, will continue to be needed and used by agencies, scholars, and the public. The increasing number of online government information sources, such as those available through GPO ACCESS; the growing amount of government information posted directly to the Internet by agencies or by agreements between libraries, educational institutions, private organizations, and commercial firms; and the large number of sources converted to CD/ROM or other electronic formats may lessen the demand for paper and microfiche documents but are unlikely to eliminate that demand in the near future. Although electronic services, online catalogs, and computerized literature searching have become established parts of library services in the past fifteen years, libraries have only recently begun to deal with the provision of electronic information products and services such as e-mail and Internet access to end-users with or without intensive training and direct staff mediation.

The movement of information to electronic format is not a new phenomenon. The development of computer mainframes in the late 1950s made possible the storage on tape of massive amounts of data, such as that collected in the 1960 Decennial Census. OCLC and the origins of online public access library catalogs emerged in the early 1970s. During this same period, online government bibliographic databases such as ERIC and MEDLINE were made available in libraries and, though brokered through commercial computerized bibliographic search services such as DIALOG and BRS, began to provide improved bibliographic access to government information in limited areas. This trend continued into the 1980s with the appearance of informational databases like CENDATA, which was produced by the Bureau of the Census. By the mid-1980s, these online services had become commonplace in most large libraries and many small and mid-sized academic libraries. As the online versions became familiar, some libraries dropped both subscriptions to the corresponding print editions and depository selections of such sources as *Resources in Education*, *Index Medicus*, and other print indexing and abstracting services. On the other hand, data sources, such as the comprehensive Census publications, were generally retained by libraries in more traditional formats.

Electronic bibliographic indexes, data disks, and full-text CD/ROM products had become a fact of life in most libraries by 1990. Depository libraries received their first government disks in 1988, inaugurating a flood of these products which has continued unabated to this day. Access to electronic bulletin boards (bbs), the use of file transfer protocol (ftp) for downloading electronic information, the provision of modem-accessible data direct from government agency computers, and the riches of the Internet were quickly incorporated into discussions of library policy and services. These tools and sources are frequently characterized by unique access procedures and individual search protocols. Most libraries struggled through a gearing-up period while hardware and software were acquired and librarians became computer-literate. Since the first appearance of computer-assisted services, the pace of computerization in libraries has generally reflected the headlong rush of technological advance. In order to offer these phenomenal new products and services to their users, some libraries have been forced to institute user fees to offset the necessary equipment costs and online charges, which are not insignificant. The debate over free public access continues to rage in libraries today and is strongly felt in depository libraries which have pledged to honor the no-fee access philosophy for government information.

If the implications of this transition to electronic media for basic reference services are impressive, the impact of electronic sources on documents reference service is staggering. One significant difference between the two service areas is that standard electronic reference sources from commercial sources are publicized and supported by the publishers and vendors. Libraries will not buy products they do not know and cannot evaluate. For documents librarians, however, the workload has been significantly increased as agencies have migrated to the use of electronic media and information simply disappears from standard print sources, often with little or no advance notification. Monitoring e-mail discussion groups such as GOVDOC-L for postings on changes in the status and format of information or in the operation and use of specific products helps the depository library community significantly but the list discussions are eclectic, covering only information about which GPO has been informed or that which librarians have discovered and wish to share.

Many federal offices, commissions, and programs are now accessible through World Wide Web (WWW) sites associated with universities and colleges. Individual libraries have also established useful web sites, both by themselves and in collaboration with government agencies. The Martin P. Catherwood Library at the School of Industrial and Labor Relations, Cornell University, for example, offers an Internet site for the publications of the Glass Ceiling Commission, the Child Labor Study produced by the Bureau of International Labor Affairs, and the Task Force on Excellence in State and Local Government through Labor-Management Cooperation.[25] Each of these partnerships involved a government effort of limited duration, making the size of the information package provided relatively small and the archiving responsibilities assumed by the library reasonably manageable. The Department of State Foreign Affairs Network (DOSFAN), a much larger cooperative initiative between the Department of State and the library of the University of Illinois at Chicago, provides Internet access to official documents and publications on the foreign affairs of the United States. The home page states that the site is "an official U.S. Government source for information on the WWW."[26]

Point-and-click government information on the Internet does not, however, guarantee that users will be able to locate the information they need easily. It is relatively easy to locate general WWW, gopher, and ftp sites for government agencies, but it is extremely difficult to locate specific publications by title, specific data sets, or materials which have been produced by individual offices or divisions within the agency which operates the web site.[27] Librarians can approach this problem by designing local home pages, which point to electronic sources of government information and resources and will direct users quickly to frequently requested information sources.[28] Others, including government agencies, are in the process of designing electronic pathfinder systems to lead the user to the electronic version of products which are no longer published in print form. An example of this technique is the information on the Current Population Reports (CPR) series provided by GPO[29] and enhanced by Larry Schankman on his home page at Mansfield University.[30] This Census documents area includes information about the CPR and provides links to the information from these reports which is available on the Internet. Even with this type of assistance, however, it is not always easy to find a particular bit of information which had once been published in a well-known print source. For example, the quintile data from the CPR P-60 report series entitled *Money Income of Households, Families, and Persons in the United States* was last issued in print form in 1992. Schankman's home page informs the user that no reports have been published in this series since 1992, not even in electronic form, and that the Census Bureau had planned to publish two reports in 1995. A hot link is provided from the home page to the history files for the P-60 series. What is not readily apparent is that the quintile data for 1992 can be found in those history files, and there is also no indication that 1993 data is currently available from the Census Bureau upon request.

In addition to electronic information available on the Internet, the distribution of electronic information takes place most often in the form of CD/ROMs and floppy disks. While libraries can select commercial CD/ROM and other disk products with the goal of minimizing the number of different software protocols staff must learn, this is not the case with disk products received from the federal government. Although the CD/ROM industry has agreed upon certain standards, the form and format of government data and text files vary with the software used and the agency producing it. To date, government agencies have operated somewhat independently and with little agreement on broad standards for operating platforms, file formats, or search and retrieval software packages. The information specialist must have a basic understanding of computers, a facility for learning several computer operating systems, and be versed in a multitude of ways to navigate this bewildering variety of technical settings in order to give users anything above minimal assistance. Minimal depository requirements for software include: a database program capable of handling dBase and/or ASCII comma delimited files; a spreadsheet such as Lotus or Quatro Pro; word processing software; some form of communications software (ProComm, Kermit, XMODEM); software for Internet access (telnet, gopher, WAIS); and a WWW browser such as Mosaic or Netscape.[31] Most of these packages must be purchased or acquired by the local library. Additional software such as GO, Extract, Adobe Acrobat, Personal Librarian, I-Search and others are provided on or with government disk products.

The ALA statement, "Access to Electronic Information, Services, and Networks; an Interpretation of the Library Bill of Rights" states that "Libraries have an obligation to provide access to government information available in electronic format. . . . Users also have a right to information, training and assistance necessary to operate the hardware and software provided by the library."[32]

The impetus for inclusion of electronic sources in library collections and services has come both from within through collection development and from without as users discover the existence of these sources and their utility. Bibliographic instruction, already a catch phrase by the late 1970s and an integral component of library services since then, is gradually ceasing to be just bibliographic. This change has paralleled the increasing availability of electronic information in depository collections and goes hand in hand with the steady increase of computer literacy and sophistication on the part of both library staff and user. The use of LCD panels and well-equipped portable workstations has virtually replaced the loaded book truck of sample sources for classroom instruction or public demonstration. While these supporting levels of technology and technological expertise are already present in major research libraries and even in many mid-sized academic libraries, many small academic and public libraries have not yet acquired either the required basic hardware or developed the necessary staff expertise. Notwithstanding computer literacy or GPO's toughening of its technical guidelines (soon to become requirements) many electronic applications function best with the background skills of an experienced documents librarian who understands the organization of government and its information products.

Once bibliographic indexing is computerized, users at all levels will line up to use that source, despite the availability nearby of the printed version.

CD/ROM products with full-text capability such as the National Trade Data Bank (NTDB) and full-text materials available on the Internet by ftp made computer instruction and computer search techniques an essential component of traditional bibliographic instruction. The proliferation of gophers and web sites has also necessitated instruction programs in their use. Full electronic classrooms, outfitted with equipment once reserved for computer science majors, have spread from science and mathematics to economics, sociology, political science, and other academic disciplines which rely heavily on literature searching, graphic and mapping capabilities, or data manipulation for research projects. This same electronic classroom, now in place or proposed for library information resources programs, may provide everything from e-mail to advanced statistical and geographic information system (GIS) packages.

Library users, particularly youthful ones, are delighted to find and explore materials in easily identifiable electronic formats. The new sport of "surfing the Net" has activated confirmed "couch potatoes" and may be reaching addictive levels in the population. Yet however long people are willing to sit in front of the flickering screens, most still prefer to take the information found with them in print form. At present, printing costs for materials downloaded from electronic sources are still assumed by many libraries; the cost of photocopies from print or microfiche documents, on the other hand, is usually borne by the patron. It is obvious that public demand will continue to exist for hard copy, even in the all-electronic environment forecast by Congress and the GPO Transition Plan. Libraries will be forced to foot the bill (not just for hardware and software but also for paper, toner, and service) or attempt to recover that cost in some way. As mentioned above, this poses serious questions about "no-fee public access." The American Library Association policies oppose "the charging of user fees for the provision of information by all libraries and information services that receive their major support from public funds."[33]

Some may propose that free access standards could be met by allowing patrons to download data to their own floppy disks with charges levied only to those requiring paper copies. Although this policy would certainly save the library paper and toner costs, it would place the cost burden for acquiring copies of government information on that segment of the population which can least afford it and/or those who do not own a computer and are not likely to purchase one.

Access to information by computer has become an easier and faster method for research and retrieval for many people, and the omnipresent printer has all but eliminated the tedious tasks of copying out citations and making notes from texts by hand. It is unfortunately already possible to see evidence that scholarship published before the magic date when electronic translation begins may be simply ignored by some users because it is "more difficult to access," i.e., not in the computer. Librarians, by their very enthusiasm for the improved access provided by the computer, may even unintentionally foster this computer-age mind set.

To counteract this trend, librarians have become engaged in a number of pilot projects to provide computer access to older materials. Project JSTOR, a pilot project initiated and funded by the Andrew W. Mellon Foundation, has recently created electronic versions of virtually complete historical backfiles for ten core journals in history and economics. Although the project stops short of providing the most current volumes, JSTOR adds recent volumes to the backfiles on a rolling basis each year. The database consists of two linked files: a digitized bitmap file and an optical character recognition (OCR) file, which were created by scanning and digitizing each page. The OCR file is searchable and provides multiple access points to the information for the user; and the digitized file is used to produce prints on demand which are exact replicas of the original journal pages, including charts, illustrations, and unusual type fonts.[34]

JSTOR, now a nonprofit organization in its own right, is currently exploring the possibility of expanding the original base of core journals by digitizing complete runs of older federal publications which would benefit from this type of electronic access. While there are other services that provide online access to electronic journals and full-text documents, JSTOR is unique, at the moment, in providing access to entire backfiles. Projects like JSTOR will enable libraries to provide reliable, searchable access to complete retrospective collections, a task which may be difficult or impossible to achieve in existing print collections.

The maintenance and preservation of collections to assure availability for future generations has been a major concern in libraries throughout history. Each format, from manuscript to the printed page, audio visual materials, microfilm, microfiche, and electronic information in various forms, presents unique challenges and requires the invention and application of creative conservation methods and techniques. Heavy use, accidents, natural disasters, and neglect provide abundant laboratories in which to test these methodologies. Traditionally, conservation and preservation techniques were limited primarily to materials in special and rare book collections. As late 19th-century paper aged, became brittle, and crumbled away by the mid-20th century in what the Library of Congress described as "slow fires," the emphasis has shifted to the massive job of preserving and conserving library collections and materials in general. The emergence of materials in a variety of electronic formats has presented very different, but nonetheless pressing, preservation issues for the foreseeable future

CONSERVATION AND PRESERVATION OF ELECTRONIC MATERIALS

At the request of the U.S. National Archives and Records Administration (NARA) in 1986, the National Research Council (NRC) formed the Committee on Preservation of Historic Records to study solutions to the deterioration of their paper records. The Committee, composed of experts on paper, microfilm, and electronic storage methods, produced a report which called for "the use of paper of better quality by the Federal Government and for research into how the microenvironment within a container in which a document is stored can best be controlled to ensure long life."[35] For documents which were already brittle, the recommendation was preservation photocopying or microfilming. Electronic storage of information for archival purposes was considered "inappropriate at the present time."[36] It is questionable whether technology has advanced enough in the ten years since the NRC report to make any of the various available electronic storage media appropriate for the long term preservation of historic documents.

There are currently four basic types of storage for electronic data in active use: magnetic tape, videotape, magnetic (floppy) disk, and CD/ROM. Predictions on the time that each of these media will store data without significant loss vary from one year for magnetic tape to thirty years for CD/ROMs.[37] New storage technologies include CD/R (rewritable disk) and magneto-optical media. Literature on CD/R from the 3M Company recommends that disks be stored in a "cool dry environment away from the direct light"[38] and predicts that "Disks stored below 30° C. (86° F.) should last 100 years."[39] Documentation on magneto-optical storage media is even more optimistic, proclaiming "Archival Storage: Over 300 Years Under Long-Term Controlled Storage Conditions - 25° C. (77° F.) and 50% relative humidity . . . the evidence suggests that under harsh storage conditions . . . [in] a test environment of 30° C. (86° F.) and 90% relative humidity there is a 95% probability that 3M magneto-optical media will survive approximately 68 years without suffering data loss."[40]

We know that low-acid/high rag content paper will last 400 years, medieval vellum manuscripts have survived longer still, and even the poor-quality paper from the World War II era has lasted more than 50 years before becoming too brittle to use. We have not yet had the advantage of hindsight for the longevity of the various electronic storage media, but even the most optimistic predictions look somewhat worse than the track record demonstrated by paper.

Technology is changing at such a rapid pace, however, that obsolescence may be more of a problem than loss of data due to the failure of a storage medium. There are predictions that the most commonly used electronic storage media of today, including the CD, will be obsolete in ten years.[41] There have already been several near disasters, the most infamous of these being the near loss of the 1960 Census data. At the time this data was rescued, there were only two machines in the world that could read the tapes—one was at the Smithsonian and the other in Japan.[42]

Reading data, however, is only half the battle as there must also be a way to interpret it. Electronic data is stored as a "bit stream," a series of 0s and 1s. The number of bits which make up a character may vary from one data storage method to another. A key is sometimes provided at the start of the data but this key, too, must be read by a machine. The only way to guarantee proper interpretation of a bit stream is some form of documentation which can be read by a human being.[43] These keys, both human- and computer-readable, may be lost as software becomes obsolete. H.R. 101–978 includes a number of examples of valuable federal government data in danger of being lost because the hardware, software, or data storage medium had become obsolete. These included the Herbicide File from the National Military Command Center Information Processing Center, which was needed by the Agent Orange Taskforce to analyze the impact of the use of Agent Orange during the Vietnam War, and 4,000 reels of census data produced prior to 1989. At the time of the NRC's report in 1986, NARA was also dealing with some 249 government studies whose data had been stored in multipunch format, i.e., on Hollerith cards.[44]

The NARA procedures for long-term preservation of electronic records stipulate that documents be accessioned in ASCII format only. Because ASCII is relatively software-independent, it is an excellent storage medium for text. Numerical data, however, presented in tabular format or information designed for use with a specific spreadsheet program such as Lotus 1–2–3 are definitely software-dependent, and even though NARA accessions ASCII versions of the data file, actual use of the information may become difficult or impossible. The preservation of all graphic information, whether from pictures, photographs, drawings, graphs, or tables, is also software-dependent and presents additional problems for preservation. NARA only accessions print formats of works containing important graphic elements.[45]

There are two ways graphic materials may be preserved. First and most obvious, the necessary software can be preserved along with the data. Software, however, is often hardware-dependent and may be written for use with specific families of machines or operating systems. Programs written for the DOS operating system, for example, will not run on Apple computers without the intervention of some conversion routine, and there is always a risk of losing data or formatting during this conversion. Consequently, it is not always sufficient just to preserve the software with the data; the future use of historic materials may also require preservation of the correct hardware.

A second and even more labor-intensive approach over time involves translating the document upward through a series of programs. For example, a document produced in WordPerfect 5.1 can be read by WordPerfect 6.1 As each new version of WordPerfect is released the document must be translated again. If WordPerfect should cease to be produced, the document must be transferred into another word processing program, if such exists, which recognizes WordPerfect documents. As in translation of text from one language to another, each time an electronic translation is made, there is the risk of losing information or introducing errors; but saving the file in a new format generally prolongs its usefulness.

In order to preserve electronic information both from constantly changing technology and from decay of the storage medium, it must be copied into a new software and/or hardware environment on a regular basis, a highly repetitive and labor-intensive process. "Future access depends on an unbroken chain of such migrations, frequent enough to prevent [storage] media from becoming physically unreadable or obsolete before they are copied."[46] Considering the sheer volume of material stored in electronic form (as with the 4,000 Census tapes mentioned earlier), preserving this material will require a Herculean effort and substantial funding over time. The very real danger is that, even with workable procedures, the data may be lost in times of tight budgets.

Rapidly changing technology, loss of data in translation, the volume of data to be copied, and software problems are huge obstacles to the preservation of electronic information, and these are problems which arise in a stable and relatively peaceful world. Preservation of electronic information is highly dependent on a solid technological infrastructure which insures a reliable supply of electricity, a stable telecommunications system, and a populace with computer and information skills. In times of civil unrest or war, all of these ingredients would be at risk. "One reason why information systems may become targets of the disaffected elements in society is the growing gap between the 'information rich' and the 'information poor'."[47] The supply of information-literate people might also be at risk from natural disaster or disease, as portrayed in the recent movie, *Outbreak*, with a resultant catastrophic loss of much common knowledge.

In addition to all the issues which might lead to loss of information, we may also be sacrificing future ease of access. Material posted by government agencies on the Internet is often available for six months or less. GPO's requirements for retention of distributed materials in depository libraries have insured that information remains available throughout its life cycle, permanently in regional full depository libraries, and for at least five years after distribution to selective depository libraries. The Transition Plan states that GPO will maintain electronic files for public access during a period of potential use. It is not clear how this period of use will be determined or by whom. After file access is discontinued by GPO, the sources will apparently revert to the original issuing agency whose responsibility it will be to deposit the files following NARA's guidelines for archival preservation. This procedure is still too broadly outlined and seems to lack the teeth necessary to insure proper permanent disposition of materials or to assure free public accessibility to the data beyond its apparent popular life cycle.

Stuart M. Basefsky suggests that "Only by collaboration among libraries can the public be assured of free access to government information in the present and the future."[48] His vision calls for libraries to do with federal electronic information exactly what libraries do with other materials: collect, catalog (provide access to), archive, authenticate, and make available to the public. Some of the new technologies should make this easier. With print materials as well as electronic materials, libraries must also repair (copy, update, and upgrade) and occasionally replace individual items to ensure a useful, vital collection. With electronic information, the library will need to keep links and pointers (addresses) current and to upgrade equipment and storage media. Coordination among libraries on collections can allow significant duplication to avoid loss in most disasters (flood, fire, civil disorder) and still avoid wasteful duplication.

LIBRARY COOPERATION AND CONSORTIAL INITIATIVES

Cooperation among libraries is not a new idea; it probably arose naturally as soon as there were two libraries providing service to users. Interlibrary loan is perhaps the oldest form of resource sharing. History records that the library at the Priory of Henton loaned 20 books in 1343.[49] The very first issue of *Library Journal* published a letter about interlibrary loan.[50] By 1910 the Library of Congress was already producing both cataloging records and printed cards for library catalogs of the world and had spearheaded the creation of a Union List of Serials so that others might know who had what, where, and how much. By 1912 lending policies were being published, and at ALA midwinter in 1916 the Committee on Coordination presented the Code of Practice for Interlibrary Loans.[51] Resource-sharing among libraries is a pragmatic recognition that no one library can ever be completely self-sufficient and is a practical way to extend collections and service.

Since 1962, the Depository Library Program system of regional full/complete depository collections, approximately one library for each state, has provided a safety net for all depositories. If a source is identified but found missing in the local library, it can probably be borrowed from a larger library collection nearby or from the regional depository. In addition to assistance with resource sharing, there are many ways in which regional libraries can and do assist the depository library community from provision of missed shipping lists or replacement of a publication in fiche to training, support and constructive advice during the inspection cycle. The weeding and withdrawal of depository materials, which have been housed for the statutory five years in a selective depository collection, for example, have been placed under the watchful eyes of the regional. The regional libraries take first crack at a disposal list hoping to fill the gaps which might lurk in their "complete" collections. The rest of the depository community may take the second chance to reap a harvest from another library's pruning.

Because of the nature of the charge to depository libraries and the structure of government information in a large government bureaucracy, an unusually strong and supportive bond has developed among depository library staff. United by the same challenges and problems, we have created informal and formal support groups both independently and in collaboration with other national groups. These include the Depository Library Council to the Public Printer; ALA's GODORT; similar state and regional documents organizations, for example, GODORT/Ohio and the Northeast Ohio Government Documents Interest Group; and GOVDOC-L. These groups provide a forum for the exchange of ideas and information, foster mentoring relationships among their participants, suggest answers to difficult reference questions, and share advice on diverse issues of depository library operation and policy. In recent years, focus in these forums has been on fast changing issues related to the electronic transition: workstation configuration requirements, purchasing computer hardware, solving the challenges of individual CD/ROM products and sharing the solutions, tracking down technical documentation or identifying sources for software upgrades and support. Since 1992 staff at GPO, especially those in the Library Programs Service, have monitored GOVDOC-L, contributing timely information to the list discussions. The Internet has provided a powerful and almost instantaneous medium to facilitate and strengthen the network already in place.

Another more recent approach to some of the problems discussed here, and one by no means restricted to government publications and depository libraries, makes use of the old idea of economy of scale. In June 1995, a new consortium was formed to promote effective intercollege cooperation and resource sharing and achieve cost savings for the individual institutions as a result of this cooperation. This consortium, modeled loosely on that of the Five Colleges of Western Massachusetts, includes five of north central Ohio's private undergraduate liberal arts colleges: Denison, Kenyon, Oberlin, Ohio Wesleyan, and Wooster.

During a study and planning period, various committees, including one for Government Publications, were formed to explore the possibilities for cooperation in traditional areas of library administration and operations. The Government Publications Committee produced a comprehensive report which included a detailed statistical portrait and the current status of the five depository collections along with several recommendations for cooperation, including the following: "The depository collections at each college should be evaluated specifically for gaps as well as for duplications in holdings. A determination should be made of the relative importance of materials held in each collection as well as a prioritization of gaps to be filled. With increased awareness of the sources available and their location in the consortium, we can weed collections of little used or unimportant sources more intelligently and consolidate or distribute important holdings to strengthen collections at one or more appropriate sites."[52] At the present time the depository staff from each college are meeting to begin the detailed collection analysis necessary to implement these recommendations.

This concept of consolidated and shared collections has already been extended to electronic sources. The consortium has implemented a shared selection and housing arrangement for the 900 Digital Raster Graphics CDs. Earlier, several Ohio depositories organized a similar selection and housing agreement to assure one complete set of the 3,000 Digital Orthophotoquad disks in the state. Although this plan was later rendered unnecessary by the agreement of the regional library to house the entire set, it nonetheless provided a model for future action. Consortial arrangements such as these may be an excellent way to coordinate electronic collection and archiving activity.

In 1991 the member institutions of OhioLINK began to construct what has become the largest shared library system in the nation, merging the online catalogs of nearly fifty public universities and colleges in the state. Invitations to join have been extended to those private academic libraries who also have Innovative Interfaces' INNOPACs. In addition to facilitating user-initiated lending ("270,000 requests since January 1994"), supported by a daily delivery system, OhioLINK also offers full-text document delivery electronically, delivering "hundreds of thousands of full-text journal articles from a wide variety of journals" from such sources as the UMI PowerPages on CD/ROM and Periodical Abstracts on FirstSearch.[53]

THE MIDDLE GROUND: WHAT NEEDS TO REMAIN

As librarians begin to grapple with the implications of an electronic future which is not so far away, traditional organizational structures in their libraries have begun to bend and shift to accommodate the changes. Traditional job descriptions will become blurred or blended; education in the library and information sciences will continue to prepare students for broad, general competence in library organization, administration, and services with a comprehensive core curriculum which is inclusive of the challenges of all formats. Reference librarians, for example, will be increasingly concerned with acquisition, "cataloging" (pathfinding), and archiving issues as well as the usual reader/user services functions; many have already assumed titles like Electronic Reference Services Specialist to reflect the new focus of their duties. Depository librarians, who have traditionally worn many hats in library operations, may ultimately break depository bonds and become more involved in the general effort to identify, capture, and interpret electronic sources.

The House report "Taking a Byte out of History" begins "Long after Federal agency records are needed for current operations they remain useful in other ways. The records are source material for agencies, historians, political scientists, genealogists, and other students of the United States, its Government, its foreign relations and its people. Federal records document the history and intent of public policy and form the basis of our national history."[54] The electronic age presents new challenges for the preserving and providing access to all records of human endeavor.

Regardless of the shape of a new FDLP, a few principles have appeared repeatedly in the responses of documents librarians to the government's proposals:

> There must be a commitment to geographically dispersed no-fee access to government information through depository libraries.
>
> Information should be available in a format and medium most appropriate to content, use, and audience.
>
> Definitions used in enabling legislation must be broadly inclusive of all types of information in all formats and media.
>
> There must be authority vested in the depository program by which agency participation is assured.
>
> Funding must be provided by Congress appropriate to the revised goals of the FDLP.[55]

Two extremes are delineated by the GPO Transition Plan and the opposite alternative of a displaced FDLP. The future of government information in academic libraries will be defined by libraries' continuing responses to government's initiatives.

The time approaches
That will with due decision make us know
What we shall say we have, and what we owe.
Thoughts speculative their unsure hopes relate;
But certain issues strokes must arbitrate:
Towards which advance the war. [Exeunt, marching]
(Macbeth, Act V Scene iv)

ACKNOWLEDGEMENTS

The collaborators acknowledge with gratitude the contributions of the following individuals: Mary Alice Baish, Cheryl Burden, Joan Cheverie, Matt

Finckel, Sheila McGarr, Colleen Parmer, David Powell, Virginia Saunders, Kyle Strohm, Julia Wallace.

ENDNOTES

1. Miller, 1989 (pt. 1) 29
2. Pursell, 1990, 1
3. Morehead & Fetzer, 1992, 48–9
4. Adapted from 44 USC ch. 19
5. Di Mario testimony, 1994
6. The oft-used test ran that "information products" could be dropped in a mailbox, "information services" could not.
7. National Performance Review, 1993
8. Chicago Conference, Executive Summary, 1993
9. H.R. 3400 (103/1), 1993
10. H. Rept. 104–141, 1995, 31
11. S. Rept 104–114, 1995
12. P.L. 104–54, 1996, 514
13. "Study to Identify Measures Necessary for a Successful Transition . . . ", 1996
14. "Assumptions", 1995
15. Transition Plan, 4
16. Saffady, 1995, 230–38
17. Ibid., 238
18. Marks, 1995, 86
19. Truesdell, 1994, 203
20. Transition Plan, 1995, 8
21. Biennial Survey Update, 1996
22. Transition Plan, 1996, 14
23. Tulis, 1996
24. Baish, 1995, 231
25. Basefsky
26. http://dosfan.lib.uic.edu/dosfan.html
27. Basefsky
28. An excellent example is the Duke University Public Documents Team page at http://www.lib.duke.edu/pubdocs.html
29. "Population",1995, 16
30. http://www.clark.net/pub/lschank/web/cendoc.html
31. "Recommended Minimum Technical Guidelines", 1995, 5
32. American Library Association Council, 1996
33. Ibid.
34. Bowen, 1995
35. "For the Record." 1987, 60
36. Ibid.
37. Rothenberg, 1995, 44
38. Maray, 1995.
39. "3M Magneto-Optical Media," 1993, 3
40. Ibid., 2
41. Rothenberg, 1995, 44
42. House Rept. 101–978, 1990, 23
43. Rothenberg, 1995, 45
44. House Report 101–978, 1990, 23.
45. "FDLP Study: Task 8D", 1996
46. Rothenberg, 1995, 45.
47. Harbour 1994, 46
48. Basefsky
49. Johnson, 1965, 112
50. McMillen, 1928, 81
52. Powell, 1995, 6
53. INNOPAC, 1996, 1, 4
54. House Report 101–978, 1990, 1
55. These are broadly adapted from ALA/GODORT Resolutions reported by Tulis (1996), the "New Universe" document (1995), and the final report of the Chicago Conference on the Future of Government Information (1993).

REFERENCES

American Library Association Council. "Access to Electronic Information, Services, and Networks: An Interpretation of the Library Bill of Rights." 1996 (gopher://ala1.ala.org:70/00/alagophx/alagophxfreedom/electacc.fin)

Assumptions About the Future of the Federal Depository Library Program, October 4, 1995

Baish, Mary Alice. "Washington Report." Documents to the People 23 (December, 1995): 231–4

Basefsky, Stuart. Special Library Collaboration with Government Agencies to Collect, Disseminate, and Archive Publications in Electronic Form: A Case Study in Privatization. Typescript

Bowen, William G. JSTOR and the Economics of Scholarly Communication. Andrew W. Mellon Foundation, October 4, 1995. (http://www.mellon.org/jsesc.html)

Chicago Conference on the Future of Federal Government Information, Chicago, October 29–31, 1993, Executive Summary, November 2, 1993. Documents to the People v. 21 (4) (December, 1993) 234

Di Mario, Michael F. Prepared Statement Before the Committee On Rules And Administration, U.S. Senate, Thursday, February 3, 1994

Electronic Federal Depository Library Program: Transition Plan, FY 1996 - FY 1998. Administrative Notes 16(18)(December 29, 1995): 3–25

"For the Record," Scientific American 256 (January 1987): 59–60.

Harbour, Robin. "Is the Pen Still Mightier than the Sword," New Scientist 143 (September 3, 1994): 45–46.

"INNOPAC Powers Document Delivery: Ohio LINK-An Evolving Mission" INNTouch January 10, 1996: 1,4

Johnson, Elmer D. A History of Libraries in the Western World. New York: Scarecrow Press, 1965

"Legislative Branch Appropriations Act, 1996" (P.L. 104–53, 19 November 1995) 109 United States Statutes at Large 514

Maray, William P. "3M CD-ROM Life Expectancy" 3M TSPB No. CDR-10, June 10, 1995.

Marks, Robert H. "The Economic Challenges of Publising Electronic Journals." Serials Review 21 (Spring, 1995):

McMillen, James A., ed. Interlibrary Loans. New Yrok: H.W. Wilson Co., 1928

Miller, Sarah Jordan. "Producing Documents for Congress and the Nation: Government Printing in the United States, Past and Present, Part I." Printing History 11 (1989): 27–41

Model for "New Universe" of Federal Information Access and Dissemination: Preliminary results of Forum on Government Information Policy, July 20–21, 1995 Sponsored by the American Library Association (Working documents: 4 August 1995)

Morehead, Joe and Mary Fetzer. Introduction to United States Government Information Sources, 4th ed. Englewood, CO: Libraries Unlimited, Inc, 1992

National Performance Review (U.S.). From Red Tape to Results: Creating a Government That Works Better and Costs Less: Report of the National Performance Review. Washington: Office of the Vice President, 1993.

"Population" Administrative Notes 16 (October 15, 1995):16–18

Powell, Margaret S., ed. Prophet, Mary Webb, et al. Mellon Planning Grant. Library Cooperation Among Five Ohio Colleges. Report of the Subcommittee on Government Publications. 1995

"Public Printing and Documents" Title 44 United States Code sec 1901 et seq., 1988 ed.

Pursell, Carroll W. Jr. Technology in America: A History of Individuals and Ideas. 2nd edition. Cambridge, MA: The MIT Press, 1990

"Recommended Minimum Technical Guidelines, Federal Depository Libraries. Revised, January 1995" Administrative Notes 16 (January 15, 1995): 5

Reinventing Access to Federal Government Information: Report of the Conference on the Future of Federal Government Information, Chicago, Illinois, October 29–31, 1993. Documents to the People 21 (4)(December, 1993) 235–246

Rothenberg, Jeff. "Ensuring the Longevity of Digital Documents." Scientific American 272 (January, 1995):42–47

Russell, Judith C. (1996, February 4) FDLP Study: Task 8D: OTA Web. Govdoc-L Listserver February 4, 1996

Saffady, William. "Digital Library Concepts and Technologies for the Management of Library Collections: An Analysis of Methods and Costs." Library Technology Reports v. 31,no. 3, May June, 1995. pp. 221–380

Schankman, Larry. Electronic Data Dissemination of Census Publications, 1995 (http://www.clark.net/pub/lschank/cendoc.html)

Tenopir, Carol and Ralf Neufang. "Electronic Reference Options: Tracking the Changes". ONLINE (July/August 1995): 67–73.

Truesdell, Cheryl B. "Is Access a Viable Alternative to Ownership? A Review of Access Performance." The Journal of Academic Librarianship v. 20 no. 4, September, 1994, pp. 200–206

Tulis, Susan E. "Summary-Midwinter GODORT : GPO's Electronic FDLP Transition Plan Dominated Midwinter 1996 GODORT Meetings" Message posted to Govdoc-L listserver, 29 January 1996

U.S. Congress. House. 101st. Congress. 2nd Session. Taking a Byte Out of History: the Archival Preservation of Federal Computer Records. (H. rept.101–978). Washington: Government Printing Office, 1990. (Serial Set 14027. 1992)

U.S. Congress. House. 103rd Congress. 1st Session. H.R. 3400 To Provide a More Effective, Efficient, and Responsive Government, November 15, 1993

U.S. Congress. House. Committee on Appropriations. Legislative Branch Appropriations Bill (H.

Rept. 104–141). Washington: Government Printing Office, 1995 (Y 1.1/8:104–141)

U.S. Congress. Senate. Committee on Appropriations. Legislative Branch Appropriations Bill (H. Rept. 104–114). Washington: Government Printing Office, 1995 (Y 1.1/5:104–114)

U.S. Department of State. U.S. Department of State Foreign Affairs Network (DOSFAN). (http://dosfan.lib.uic.edu/dosfan.html)

Young. M.O. "Theory and Practice of Interlibrary Loans in American Libraries" in McMillen, James A., ed. Interlibrary Loans. New York: H.W. Wilson, 1928, 13

3M Magneto-Optical Media: Aging Test Supports Increased Archival Life Expectancy. 3M No.778. (December 12, 1993)

"1995 Biennial Survey Update" Administrative Notes 17,(2)(January 15, 1996): 9

Wave of the Future: Supporting Interdisciplinary Collaborations

By Stella Bentley
Auburn University
(formerly at the University of California at Santa Barbara)

Interdisciplinarity has been described as the complex endeavor that seeks to explicate relationships, processes, values, and context using the diversity and unity possible only through collaborative approaches [Stember]. Even a casual observer of the academy will notice that there is considerable interdisciplinary research today, and there is every indication that this trend will continue to grow in the future. The academy is being forced to make some changes in order to accommodate and encourage interdisciplinary research. The principal method of organization in the academy at the base level is the academic department (English, political science, chemistry, etc.). The norm is for the department to determine its direction, select faculty to provide the range of expertise that is thought necessary to cover the discipline, and to assess the work of each faculty member in terms of his or her contributions to the discipline. Most of the professional associations are also discipline based (e.g. MLA, ACS, IEEE, APA, etc.).

Research, however, does not always fit nicely into the neat categories of our academic departments. Particularly in the sciences, but also increasingly in the other disciplines as well, we are seeing that interdisciplinary research, which integrates the contributions of several disciplines to the study of a problem, is becoming very widespread, and at times the predominant method. "Many life scientists point out that the widespread use of new molecular techniques has continued to blur the lines among many disciplines. Geneticists use molecular biology and chemistry techniques, chemists use molecular biology and genetics, plant pathologists need to know molecular biology..."[Benowitz]. Biomedical engineering, based on the collaborations of biologists, chemists, physicists, engineers, and physicians, is a booming field, and just one example of a plethora of such collaborations in the sciences.

Benowitz, writing recently in *The Scientist*, points out that "there are institutional roadblocks to interdisciplinary collaborations—most universities remain bound by traditional departmental structures for administrative and curricular purposes, including peer review, tenure, and promotion." More and more, though, we see universities are taking steps to encourage or enhance interdisciplinary efforts in a number of ways. Programs drawing on faculty from existing departments are established to enable individuals from a variety of disciplines to bring their perspectives to emerging areas, boundary spanning problems, or multidisciplinary approaches. At my own institution, for example, we have eight programs in the humanities and social sciences, some with a few faculty for which the program is their "home", and all with affiliated faculty who have a regular "home" department—comparative literature, East Asian languages and cultural studies, film studies, environmental studies, Latin American studies, law and society, medieval studies, renaissance studies, and women's studies. To give an idea of the mix of interdisciplinarity involved in these programs, the law and society program has faculty from the history, political science, sociology, communication, anthropology, and economics departments, while the medieval studies program has faculty from the history, French, English, art and architecture, Spanish, religious studies, music, and dramatic art departments.

We also have eight Organized Research Units (ORUs) which have been established to provide opportunities for basic and applied research in a variety of disciplines, often including humanities, social sciences, and sciences. One of these is the Community and Organization Research Institute (CORI), which promotes interdisciplinary basic and policy research focused on global issues. Investigators are from the social and behavioral sciences, the humanities, and those sciences involved with environmental issues. Areas investigated range from archeology in the Americas, how health care data are acquired and used in research, the economics of criminal justice, and the linguistics of almost extinct and modern languages, to the sociology of religion and the globalization of industry. Another ORU is the Institute for Crustal Studies, whose purpose is to increase our understanding of the earth's crust and lithosphere, including the portions below the sea floor. Its research agenda includes tectonics, crustal structure and materials, earthquakes, and hazardous waste disposal, and faculty from the departments of biological sciences, engineering, geography, geological sciences, mathematics, and physics participate in the Institute's activities. It is quite common now to have some form of an interdisciplinary humanities center on university campuses to promote collaborative research and teaching projects that overlap traditional humanities disciplines. Social science inquiry often overlaps into the various social science disciplines, and much applied work draws on multi-disciplinary approaches.

Another campus and national effort to encourage interdisciplinary inquiry in the sciences and social sciences is the establishment of National Research Centers. At UCSB, for example, we have six National Research Centers, funded principally by the National Science Foundation, which engage in specialized research in a multidisciplinary environment. The National Center for Geographic Information and Analysis (UCSB, SUNY Buffalo, and University of Maine), for example, brings together researchers in geography, surveying engineering, computer science, sociology, political science, linguistics, and psychology to focus on developing and promoting the use of geographical information systems (GIS) in the natural and social sciences and in the applied, planning, and engineering sciences. QUEST, the Center for Quantized Electronic Structures, focuses on microelectronics—the investigation and development of materials containing features known as quantum structures. Crossing the boundaries of traditional disciplines, the Center is composed of faculty from chemical and nuclear engineering, chemistry, electrical and computer engineering, materials, and physics.

While some funding agencies have been oriented to a discipline-specific academic model and find it difficult to handle collaborative research proposals, others encourage and even expect interdisciplinary approaches to problems. NSF, as noted above, has funded many National Research Centers to work on multidisciplinary problems. A program at Penn State, funded by NSF, is training students across several fields—including ecology, plant physiology, biochemistry, and molecular biology—to study how plants interact with their environment. The NSF/ARPA/NASA Digital Libraries Initiative, announced in late 1993 for projects to begin in mid 1994, sought proposals from multidisciplinary teams. Project Alexandria, the DLI project at the University of California, Santa Barbara, includes teams from computer science, geography, electrical engineering, education, and the library, as well as commercial hardware and software vendors and a variety of federal agencies.

Just as the research university and funding agencies have had to adapt to accommodate and encourage interdisciplinary research, the library needs to insure that its collection development efforts are organized so that the interdisciplinary materials that faculty and researchers need are available. In some cases, the boundaries that once delineated the disciplines have become blurred, and it is difficult to separate the frontiers of one from another. Furthermore, as Osburn has pointed out, academic research in the late twentieth century has become more focused on practical applications to societal problems of the present and the future, and the "use of quite current information of a highly interdisciplinary nature has increased very substantially."

Regardless of how we have structured our collection development efforts, the key features of most efforts to establish a division of labor among selectors have been to base decisions on one or more of the following criteria:

- university departments or programs
- subjects or disciplines
- language group and area of the world.

Metz and Foltin have ably described the gaps that can develop under each of these with an analogy to football defenses:

1. Assigning selection responsibilities by academic department is like the use of a man-to-man defense, where selectors attempt to chase their departments all around the field of knowledge. In doing so, selectors may be easily deceived about the directions of those they are assigned to cover, and they risk colliding fairly frequently with other selectors as they cross and recross the field.
2. Assigning selection responsibility by subject or discipline is like a zone defense. Selectors cover an area, and in effect build collections for the use of whoever may enter that area. There are invariably gaps between the various zones of responsibility, and whole areas of knowledge may fall outside the scope of a discipline as we have defined it.
3. Making assignments in a hybrid manner of the two noted above—with elements of the academic department and the discipline present in the assignment of collecting responsibilities (e.g. the selector is assigned a discipline, but expected to support the research or instructional needs of the department's faculty in that discipline). When I arrived at UCSB, I found that this was the case. It did not mean that we were avoiding gaps in the collections, but the hybrid method was used to determine which fund paid for an item if it was requested by a professor before a collection manager had purchased it— if a professor in department A recommended a book in subject B, the subject selector for A was expected to purchase the item, or wheedle the B selector into buying it.

We have tried to compensate for the gaps that can inevitably develop in these schemes by insisting that:

- selectors keep on top of what is going on in the discipline as a whole and with our faculty in the discipline;
- the disciplines be defined so that emerging or interdisciplinary areas are covered. We often rely on assignments by LC classification to do this, which can cause problems in itself: *Biochemistry*, which we purchase for chemistry, is classified in QH301 (biology), *Analytical Biochemistry*, purchased for biology, is classed in QD1 (chemistry), and both *Journal of Biochemistry* (purchased for biology) and *Biochemical Journal* (purchased for chemistry) are classed in QP1 (physiology).
- selectors talk to each other to insure that the needs of those professors who cross over the disciplinary lines are met.

My experience as the CDO in two different libraries with collection development organized in very traditional ways with the hybrid structure (i.e., the combination of man to man and zone defenses that is fairly common in research libraries) is that we recognized that there were interdisciplinary gaps in our collections, we would often discuss as a group the importance of acquiring appropriate interdisciplinary materials, and we talked about taking the needed steps to make sure that we avoided gaps because of areas that fell between our collection development assignments. We would stress again and again that selectors needed to talk to each other, and work together to avoid coverage gaps. Despite these efforts, we still were finding gaps in our collections, either because no one felt that the materials really fell within his/her purview, or because each person thought someone else was taking care of an area until we discovered we had missed something that we really should have acquired.

During the past three years, though, selectors have been working together to address interdisciplinary needs. What changed? As a result of a significant downsizing of our professional staff during 1991–93 (approximately 25% of our librarians retired and were not replaced), we had to reassign the responsibility for many collections, and we reorganized both public services and collection development. We wanted a more collegial environment, with individuals assuming more responsibilities and working together in a team environment. A major goal of the reorganization for collection development was to increase the interaction among selectors, thus increasing our capability to acquire appropriate interdisciplinary materials (i.e., setting up our defense in such a way that there would be fewer gaps). For the purposes of collection development, all librarians with selection assignments (which includes all public services librarians and some from technical services and administration) were organized into teams, with one team set up for each of the broad areas— humanities, ethnic/gender/area studies, sciences, and social sciences. Each librarian was assigned for the purposes of our review process to one particular team, but many participate in more than one team because of their multiple collecting responsibilities.

The assignment of the "home" team was a somewhat arbitrary process to set up fairly equal base groups so that each team coordinator would be responsible for serving as the review initiator for the same number of individuals in our formal review process for librarians. Nine of the 24 individuals with collecting assignments participate in more than one team. One collection manager, for example, is responsible for women's studies and sociology; her "home" group is the Ethnic/Gender/Area Studies Team, but she also participates in the activities of the Humanities and Social Sciences teams. The major outcomes, with so many people participating in more than one team, have been not only a considerable increase in communication among selectors within each team but also much more communication between and among the teams because of the great extent of cross-fertilization. To further encourage the teams to address interdisciplinary materials, we have allocated a small permanent fund to each team (this is in addition to the allocation each selector has for his/her subjects), and all one-time supplementary allocations each year are made to the teams. The only restriction that I have placed on how the team allocates these funds is there can not be any sort of across-the-board allocation. While teams have used the one-time funds to supplement individual subject allocations, they have also allocated funds for interdisciplinary needs within their own group (e.g., the humanities group set up a separate fund for popular culture materials last year—each member of the group recommends materials to be purchased with these funds, and the group decides what to buy; the EGA group set up a fund for materials on the social aspects of AIDS, and designated one person to be responsible for the fund). In some instances, the teams have also gone in together to fund multidisciplinary efforts involving two or more groups (e.g., the social sciences and sciences teams jointly funded an effort to procure materials on women's health issues). A further outgrowth of the work in collections teams is that individual selectors have been cooperating more with each other to address interdisciplinary areas—there have been quick agreements reached, for example, to go in together to purchase an electronic data file, to add a journal subscription, to select materials for an interdisciplinary WEB page, or to pool funds to purchase interdisciplinary monographs.

Interdisciplinary collaborations are the wave of the future. Just as the research university is undergoing changes not only to accommodate such research but also to encourage interdisciplinary collaborations, the research library also needs to take appropriate steps to insure that its collection development efforts support interdisciplinary collaborations.

REFERENCES

Benowitz, Steven. "Wave of the Future: Interdisciplinary Collaboration", *The Scientist* 19:1,4 (June 26, 1995).

Graham, Peter S. "Research Patterns and Research Libraries", *College and Research Libraries* 50:433–440 (July 1989).

Metz, Paul and Bela Foltin, Jr., "A Social History of Madness—or, Who's Buying This Round?", *College and Research Libraries* 51:33–39 (January 1990).

Osburn, Charles B. *Academic Research and Library Resources: Changing Patterns in America.* Westport, CT: Greenwood Press, 1979.

Stember, Marilyn. "Advancing the Social Sciences Through the Interdisciplinary Enterprise", *The Social Science Journal* 28:1–14 (1991).

Reference and Electronic Document Delivery: A Marriage Made in Heaven or Hell?

By Cynthia Coccaro and Joseph Straw
University of Akron

INTRODUCTION

Full-text electronic document delivery is increasingly becoming an option for a greater number of library users. Immediate access to information is freeing many patrons from the need to find materials in hardcopy. The proliferation of automated full-text resources are involving traditional public service areas more and more in the document delivery process. An example of these trends can be found at the University of Akron's Bierce Library. Bierce has recently implemented the PowerPages system. PowerPages is offered as a full-text supplement to a select group of UMI bibliographic databases. This service is made available through OhioLINK (Ohio Library and Information Network), a statewide library system. During the first five months of service, starting June 13, 1995, PowerPages was administered by the library's reference department, which absorbed the full initial impact of this new service.

Some of Bierce Library's experiences with PowerPages will be described in the paper that follows. The first part will examine the history of electronic document delivery, its migration into the reference setting, and OhioLINK. Next, a case study of Bierce's experience in using the PowerPages system will be presented. The location, staffing, use, benefits and limitations of the system will be assessed and analyzed. Lastly, the appropriateness of providing an electronic delivery service in Bierce's reference department will be examined.

HISTORY AND BACKGROUND

Full-text databases and document delivery systems grew out of the application of computers to information systems which began in the 1950s. Early computerized information systems were first used by a number of government agencies to index and store the results of defense related research. In the 1960s, the development of machine readable bibliographic databases allowed for the electronic reproduction of common print indexing and abstracting services. The emergence of the National Library of Medicine's MEDLARS system in 1964 created a huge collection of bibliographic databases that expanded the availability of information to a much broader segment of the scientific community.[1] The MEDLARS system has been the model for the development of other government and commercial online services such as STN, STAR, DIALOG, and BRS. In the latter part of the 1960s, online services migrated from exclusive laboratories and national research libraries into a wider variety of public and private organizations. Many of these online services were commercialized and made available to libraries and private subscribers.[2]

The ability of libraries to access bibliographic records and compile bibliographies was revolutionized by these online services. By the early 1970s, all types of libraries were using online databases as part of the regular reference process. While researchers could obtain citations with greater speed and efficiency, the process of producing full-text records still depended on traditional delivery sources. The exponential growth of scholarly literature, particularly technical literature, created a demand for the application of computer technology to reproduce full-text bibliographic records.[3]

Databases with full-text capabilities were first mounted in the late 1970s. Many of these were quickly made available to all types of libraries. These databases were first offered through online services such as DIALOG and BRS. By the end of the 1980s, several thousand full-text titles were made available. More recently, CD-ROMs have become a popular format for full-text materials. This method of access saved libraries from incurring online print charges, decreased time pressures for the searcher, and enabled libraries to search the same database without additional charges. In the 1990s, an ever growing number of libraries have the technology to access full-text databases through an online service or by CD-ROMs.[4]

As full-text options become more common, a number of online and CD-ROM database choices emerged. The types of databases that have come into use are those having full-text and hybrids, combining features of full-text with traditional indexing and abstracting services. Full-text products now available in the current market include UMI's Full Image ProQuest, Information Access's InfoTrac - Expanded Academic ASAP, Ebsco's MasterFILE, and hybrids such as UMI's PowerPages, and PTS PROMPT.[5]

The evolution of full-text databases has implications in the reference area of libraries. Full-text data can be made available online, at stand alone workstations, and through a local or wide area network. It is possible for certain types of library transactions to be started and completed from a single public service point. Thus, reference work is evolving from merely providing bibliographic citations to the actual delivery of materials.

OHIOLINK

A practical application of full-text access can be found in the state of Ohio's consortium of academic libraries called OhioLINK. OhioLINK emerged in the mid 1980s in response to a rising number of requests for new library buildings. Rather than build new facilities, the Ohio Board of Regents proposed to more cost effectively utilize the state's existing resources. In 1989, the founders of OhioLINK decided to build a statewide automated system with Innovative Interfaces, Inc. that consists of universities, two-year colleges and regional repositories. The main goal of the system is to "maximize the utility of the state's major investment in library resources through improved access and delivery mechanisms."[6] This goal is being obtained through the continued development of the state's automated network.

OhioLINK is made up of forty-one college and university libraries including the State Library of Ohio. Some of the services OhioLINK provides to enhance statewide access consist of a shared online union catalog, cooperative collection development, online borrowing of monographic resources, and the coordination of database services. OhioLINK's mission is to provide services that will allow students, faculty, and other researchers the opportunity to borrow materials in the shortest time possible.[7]

In providing timely access to materials, document delivery plays a central role across the OhioLINK system. OhioLINK's approach to document delivery is not based on a single service "but on the integration of all forms of document delivery compatible with OhioLINK."[8] These various services include "home library go-to-the-stacks use, patron-initiated OhioLINK borrowing, traditional interlibrary loan to non-OhioLINK institutions, use of commercial document supply services, and local or remote electronic storage and delivery."[9] The aforementioned are presently available at all of the member institutions.

While the emphasis is on the integration of all elements, the electronic delivery elements have been significantly improved. An important recent enhancement is the addition of PowerPages, which has been offered to OhioLINK member institutions. PowerPages allows online full-text access to a select group of magazine and journal titles through the ABI/Inform and Periodical Abstracts databases. UMI produces the ProQuest PowerPages system, from which full-text articles are provided through OhioLINK's wide area network.

Primary components of PowerPages include the Network IMAGEserver (NIS), the Remote Image PRINTstation (PRS), and the Image FAXserver.[10] The NIS includes the following:

> . . . . a high-end PC [personal computer], Kubik CD-ROM jukeboxes and proprietary software that is responsible for receiving, queuing and processing article requests from users at workstations linked together on a network. The NIS locates the article image(s) from the appropriate UMI full-image database and routes the article image(s) to a user-requested destination service for output.[11]

OhioLINK's NIS is located at Wright State University. There are four personal computers and four sets of six CD-ROM jukeboxes to increase the speed of article delivery. An additional jukebox for the most current full-text articles will be added early in 1996, making the total four sets of seven.[12]

The second component is the Remote Image PRINTstation, a print element that receives articles from the NIS for the remote OhioLINK sites. PRS consists of a personal computer, software, and a laser printer. All of the OhioLINK institutions with PowerPages who expect a volume of at least thirty article reprints per hour are required to have this unit.[13]

The last PowerPages component is the Image FAXserver. This unit receives images of articles and converts them into a facsimile format. The images are then sent to a fax machine or personal computer with a fax card. The Image FAXserver gives users the option of having articles printed "at a location that is not linked to a network".[14] PowerPages sites are required to have this unit if they do not expect more than thirty articles per hour.[15]

In 1995, twenty-eight OhioLINK sites had fully implemented PowerPages. In 1996, more sites are expected to begin this new service. System enhancements such as ASCII full-text for ABI/Inform and Periodical Abstracts, and the linking of non-UMI databases to UMI full-text articles are also being developed.[16] The continued evolution of PowerPages will add a powerful component to OhioLINK's document delivery options, and enable users to obtain information with greater speed and efficiency.

METHODOLOGY

This case study of the University of Akron's experience with OhioLINK's PowerPages employed several sources of evidence. Statistics were gathered at various service points. If patrons had questions concerning PowerPages, or were introduced to PowerPages, it was requested of the staff and student assistants working these service points to tally the number of such transactions. These statistics were collected and totaled on a weekly basis during the 1995 Fall Semester.

Other data collection methods included the printing of Bierce's UMI PowerPages statistics from July 31st to December 18th, monitoring OhioLINK's UMI electronic discussion group, and ascertaining the student staffing pattern at the information desk from July to December 1995 compared to the previous year. In addition, various OhioLINK committee minutes from the past three years were examined. Lastly, personal observations and comments of Bierce Library staff responsible for PowerPages were noted.

POWERPAGES AT BIERCE LIBRARY

The University of Akron is an OhioLINK member institution. This northeastern Ohio university, located in the heart of downtown Akron, is known worldwide for its College of Polymer Science and Engineering.[17] Degrees can also be obtained from the Colleges of Arts and Sciences, Education, Business Administration, Engineering, Fine Arts, and Nursing. The University of Akron is the third largest university in Ohio, and currently enrolls approximately 28,000 students.[18]

The research needs of the university community are met mainly by Bierce Library, a four-story building centrally located on the University of Akron campus. The ground floor of the library houses the bound periodical collection, microforms area, government documents, ground floor reference desk, photocopy center, and audiovisual services. Located on the first floor is the main entrance, circulation department, acquisitions department, cataloging department, collection management department, curriculum collection, reference collection, first floor reference desk, information desk, and part of the circulating collection. Most of the circulating collection is housed on the second and third floors. Bierce's total collection is estimated at 900,000 titles.

The library's reference department is unique in that duties and domain are split between the first and ground floors. This department is made up of eight librarians, five staff members, and approximately thirty students. Reference's responsibilities are divided among four previously mentioned service points: the first floor reference desk, ground floor reference desk, microforms area, and information desk. General and telephone reference questions are answered at the first floor reference desk. Most government documents and periodical questions are answered at the ground floor reference desk. The microforms area is responsible for distributing microfiche or microfilm, as well as providing assistance for viewing and printing these resources. Lastly, services made available at the information desk include answering directional questions and providing general assistance with the online public catalog.

Other reference department duties include specific document delivery responsibilities. These consist of collecting interlibrary loan forms, searching DIALOG for newspaper interlibrary loan requests, distributing microforms, and providing full-text CD-ROM databases through a local area network or at a stand alone workstation. The full-text databases provided by the reference department include Compact Disclosure, Ethnic Newswatch, Broadcast News, and government document CD-ROM products.

From the middle of June to the end of November 1995, the reference department was assigned another important document delivery responsibility. Due to insufficient space in the circulation area, the reference department was given the responsibility for administering the PowerPages service. These new duties consisted of sorting articles, stapling them together, alphabetically arranging them into bins by the patron's last name, and handing them out. The distribution point was located at the information desk, which is centrally located near the entrance to the library, and a seemingly logical access point.

The information desk is triangular in shape, with openings at two of its points. Located between these openings is the service counter, which has a computer terminal and telephone for staff use. Three online catalog terminals are positioned on each of the other two counters. The Remote Image PRINTstation was located at the inside apex of these two counters, behind the service point. Bins for sorting the full-text articles were located on the service counter of the information desk.

The University of Akron's online public catalog, ZipLINK, provides patron access to a select number of databases from OhioLINK. Of these databases, Periodical Abstracts and ABI/Inform indicate full-text articles to patrons by having the following statement at the bottom of the screen:

Full Text Available
1> Request printed copy of this article

By typing the number one, the process for obtaining an article reprint is begun. Next, patrons are asked to identify their institutional affiliation from a numbered list of OhioLINK institutions. A prompt then instructs patrons to enter their name and barcode number. Another screen provides the print destination options. The last screen advises patrons of the amount being charged and gives them an opportunity to cancel the article request. If they decide to proceed, the system informs patrons that the request has been accepted. It can take approximately five to ten minutes for a request to be printed in full.

PowerPages is presently a fee-based service. Starting with the Fall Semester 1995, a ten cents per page charge is attached to patrons' circulation records. Payment for the articles is collected at the circulation desk. Patrons have the option of paying immediately or waiting for a bill at a later date. The circulation system does not allow fines or charges to accumulate past twenty dollars, thus library privileges will be blocked until a portion of the owed amount is paid.

Providing access to PowerPages at the information desk uncovered problems with security, staffing, and funding. The open design of the information desk left articles within patrons' reach. When an employee working the information desk was absent for any reason, patrons were instructed, as indicated by signage, to go to the reference desk and ask the librarian to retrieve their articles. However, patrons were still known to go behind the desk and retrieve articles themselves. This created the potential of having articles stolen that were already charged to patrons' records.

Open access to the information desk also compromised the safety of the PowerPages' equipment. The Remote Image PRINTstation was vulnerable to accident or manipulation by patrons going behind the desk to pick up articles. It was not uncommon to see users handling trays, changing paper, and pushing buttons at the PowerPages printer. Such unauthorized use was a constant concern while the system was located at the information desk.

Secondly, staffing the information desk was not an easy task. Prior to PowerPages, the information desk was staffed Monday through Friday, 7:30 a.m. to 3:00 p.m. during the summer, and from 7:30 a.m. to 5:00 p.m. during the Fall Semester. It was not staffed on the weekends, nor during the intercession between the Summer and Fall Semesters. The installation of PowerPages meant a need for increased student staffing at the information desk. Staffing levels were increased to provide coverage during the evenings, weekends, and intercession. Compared to the previous year, student hours more than doubled at the information desk. In 1994, a total of 650 hours were scheduled from July to December. In 1995, this total increased to 1484 hours for the same period.

To make up for this increase, more student staff were hired and additional training duties were assigned to the reference staff.

Lastly, PowerPages required additional funding for both staffing and supplies. In order to meet increased student staffing needs, the library administration agreed to increase the student assistant budget. One thousand dollars was immediately allocated for additional student assistants.[19] From July to December 1994, coverage of the information desk by students cost the reference department $2,071. Following the implementation of PowerPages, student coverage costs rose to $4,730.

Supplies for PowerPages also proved to be very costly. The Hewlett Packard Si4 laser printer is designed to provide uninterrupted printing during the day and night. This unit prints with a tray holding one ream of paper and a reserve tray which holds another four reams. During the first six months of service, PowerPages generated 15,293 articles, using 52,325 sheets of paper. This is approximately 105 reams, consisting of 500 sheets each. At an average cost of two dollars and forty cents per ream, the cost of paper was approximately $250. Toner cartridges for the laser printer cost $108 each. Twenty cartridges were ordered for $2,160 when the printer was located at the information desk.

It was envisioned that PowerPages operating costs would be recovered by the fees assessed for articles. During the Fall Semester, approximately $4,413.80 was billed to patrons for articles. However, these monies went into the University's general fund and not into the library's budget. Hopefully, when the general fund is allocated, the library will be awarded some or all of the amount collected.

POWERPAGES USE ANALYSIS AT BIERCE LIBRARY

PowerPages became operational at Bierce on June 13, 1995. In the first six weeks of service, there were a small number of article requests. Reasons for this include that it was a new service, there is typically lower enrollment during the summer, and the project was not well-advertised. During the first two weeks of August, use exceeded the total of the previous six weeks. Reasons for this increase are due to the end of a summer session, increased student knowledge of PowerPages, library staff introducing the service, and the fact that the service was free.

During the first weeks of the Fall Semester 1995, a decrease in article printing was evident. Causes for this decrease include the start of a new semester, students not having their course assignments, a lack of advertising, and fees for articles requested. At the beginning of October, there was a noticeable increase in the average number of articles printed per day. This was in the midst of bibliographic instruction sessions where PowerPages was introduced. Signage was also introduced in this period and helped to increase awareness of PowerPages. Additionally, students were beginning to work on their papers and were telling their peers about this new service. Most articles were printed from November 11th to December 4th, when papers are typically due. The peak usage period was the first four days of December when nearly 600 articles were printed. Lastly, during exam week, there was an expected seventy-five percent drop in articles printed.

Tally sheets also reflect the aforementioned Fall Semester trends. Increased use during the months of October and November were duplicated in both tables. A noticeable difference in service points tallies compared to articles printed was evident. There was a greater number of articles printed than service point tallies. Reasons for this difference include the user friendly front-end of Innovative Interfaces, repeat PowerPages users, and remote access patrons.

An analysis of the tally sheets also reveals various activity levels at the reference department service points. Toward the beginning of October, there was a noticeable increase in tallies at the ground floor reference desk. This is due to the installation of four additional workstations capable of accessing PowerPages. The first floor reference desk had more tally marks than any other service point. Reasons for this include that most terminals accessing PowerPages are located on the first floor, and two or three people usually staff this desk. The microforms area had few questions concerning PowerPages because there are no public terminals in the area, and patrons are usually only looking for microforms. Lastly, the information desk had a surprisingly small number of tally marks. This is presumably due to a lack of participation on the part of students, a misunderstanding of what was expected, or an increased workload at the information desk.

Another use issue is that articles were not being picked up at the distribution points. The number of unclaimed articles reached high levels during the Fall

Semester. For example, during the month of October, over 200 articles were not claimed. This indicates some confusion as to the pick-up location for articles. Although there were six seminars teaching PowerPages during the Fall Semester, they were sparsely attended. These unclaimed articles could be seen as a need for better screen messages on the public catalogs or more vigorous instruction.

Bierce Library's experience with PowerPages revealed some solid benefits. One obvious advantage is its full-text coverage of a select group of periodical titles. Any type of full-text service is bound to have a built-in audience of users. For many, a full-text delivery option is a much more attractive alternative than finding the article themselves.

Another benefit of the service is that it provides almost immediate delivery of requested articles. This feature allows users to avoid many of the delays associated with other forms of document delivery, such as interlibrary loan and commercial delivery services. Such capabilities promise a sense of "instant bibliographic gratification" in which users can type in a few words and obtain an article in a matter of minutes.[20] The ability to obtain rapid access to information instills in the user a strong sense of success and empowerment in reaching their information goals.

PowerPages allows for the delivery of articles not carried by Bierce Library. The ability to obtain these materials helps shift the library's emphasis from ownership to access. Having the chance to acquire this information frees users from depending on their libraries' ability to provide or borrow from distant collections.

While by no means negating the systems benefits, the use of PowerPages has exposed some limitations. One disadvantage of the system is its insufficient backfiles of periodical articles. In Periodical Abstracts, the average coverage per full-text title is only 1.19 years, while the coverage per full-text title in ABI/Inform is 6.54 years.[21] These figures highlight the bias toward very recent research or current events. For many researchers at Bierce, this is not enough coverage to be helpful. Users wanting more retrospective information still must find the full document using traditional delivery methods.

Another weakness of the service is its failure to incorporate all titles indexed. In Periodical Abstracts, there are 1600 periodicals covered, and 512 periodicals have partial full-text coverage. ABI/Inform includes articles from 1625 periodicals, and 570 have partial full-text coverage. A user is confronted with citations in which the text can be obtained through PowerPages, and with citations that have to be located by other means. Patrons must be prepared to obtain articles from the computer, interlibrary loan, or the library's collection. The hybrid nature of PowerPages does not allow for one stop bibliographic searching. Unfortunately, this has been a source of confusion and frustration for many users at Bierce.

Performance factors have also limited the use of PowerPages. Image processing problems, article printing delays, the inability to print articles, multiple printings of articles, central site shutdowns, output quality, and paper jams all conspired to weaken the efficiency of this service at Bierce. These problems are always a source of delay and frustration for library users and staff. Problems are to be expected from any new system and will be resolved as the service evolves. Troubleshooting thus plays a role in keeping the system running efficiently.

The inability to search or display articles proved to be a serious drawback for the system. PowerPages can only print out the full-text articles that it offers, and no other text manipulations can be performed. The citation and abstract is not always enough for a patron to determine the relevance of a potential article. Thus, patrons were known to make costly print requests without knowing the research value of the article.

Fees have limited some choices in the use of PowerPages. The imposition of fees restricts the inherent benefits of the service to those who are able to pay. Patrons must look at their financial resources in planning to obtain documents from this service. The reality of fees forces users to consider and choose a document delivery option that may not meet their needs.

Illustration and graphics issues have also limited the effectiveness of PowerPages. Many Bierce patrons have requested articles that have poor illustrations. PowerPages, along with many other full-text options, often fail to produce quality graphics. Unavailability of color printing, poor quality graphics, and blurred pictures leave many patrons with information that may be unusable.[22] For research that requires a high degree of graphic and textual accuracy, the full-text article offered by PowerPages may not provide a substitute for the original.

Finally, the potential for instant gratification can

also be a temptation in which users only take advantage of PowerPages' full-text capabilities. The quality of research could be compromised by researchers abusing this service. PowerPages is just one tool that helps patrons achieve their information goals. The ease of full-text access should not dictate the use of this abstracting tool.

APPROPRIATENESS OF POWERPAGES IN REFERENCE

Bierce Library has wrestled with the question of finding the right location within the institution for PowerPages. Bierce's experience with PowerPages, as part of its reference department, has revealed an interesting two fold legacy. First, the responsibility for delivering PowerPages articles appeared to be incompatible with the reference department. Second, the effect of continuing PowerPages service has remained to impact reference service at Bierce.

The delivery of documents proved inappropriate for the reference setting. It was decided by the library's administration that because of problems with security, funding, and staffing, PowerPages would be better handled in the reserve room. The reserve room is managed by the circulation department. This department's primary function is document delivery, and thought better suited for this aspect of PowerPages service. PowerPages' printer and article storage bin is now located behind a confined service desk, greatly enhancing the security of the system. Staffing is normally constant from the time the library opens until it closes, thus additional staffing and funding should not be necessary. These factors appear to make the reserve room a more natural place for the PowerPages operation.

Secondly, despite its move into the reserve room, PowerPages is still a part of life in the reference department at Bierce. PowerPages, in conjunction with bibliographic searching, must be taken into account by librarians working reference. The significant growth and use of the service has highlighted the roles of reference librarians as instructors and advocates.

Reference librarians have the duty of teaching PowerPages to patrons. This includes introducing, explaining, and demonstrating the service. The need for this instruction provides an excellent opportunity for reference librarians to interact individually with users. One-on-one instruction from the reference desk provides a chance to present a new tool to patrons when it is most beneficial.

These instructional challenges highlight the reference librarians' role as patron advocate. PowerPages is just one more choice in an ever expanding information universe. Patrons are faced with many different avenues to obtain the same materials. Options for patrons include printing from PowerPages, an interlibrary loan request, or ascertaining if the University of Akron or another local library owns the article. Once apprised of possible accessibility and charges involved, patrons can then make their own informed decision.

CONCLUSION

In attempting to answer the question, "Reference and Electronic Document Delivery: A Marriage Made in Heaven or Hell?", we found that the answer was not clear cut. Securing, stapling, sorting, and distributing documents was clearly an incompatible union with reference functions. However, the responsibility of teaching PowerPages to patrons, and introducing document delivery options to them, is an appropriate addition to the reference department's duties.

Bierce Library's experiences may be helpful for other institutions planning to establish an electronic full-text delivery service. Institutions considering a system which is not end-user driven need to examine closely the missions of the departments being considered for its placement. Staffing patterns, funding needs, security of expensive parts, and the service point's primary purpose should be analyzed. Reference departments and library administrators may consider end-user delivery of text, such as Ethnic Newswatch or Broadcast News, as appropriate for the reference area. Finally, full-text delivery services requiring an intermediary, such as PowerPages, is better suited for a department whose primary function is document delivery.

ENDNOTES

1. Lancaster, 6.
2. Ibid., 7.
3. Gillikin, 27.
4. Hearty, 135.
5. Everett, 24.
6. *OhioLINK Operating Plan 1994*, 2.
7. Ibid.

8. *OhioLINK Document Delivery Task Force.*
9. Ibid.
10. *Proquest PowerPages*, 2.
11. Ibid.
12. Anita Cook, interviewed by Cynthia Coccaro, telephone, 5 January 1996.
13. Ibid.
14. *Proquest*, 2.
15. Anita Cook, interview.
16. *1995 III Development Summary.*
17. *College Blue Book*, 629.
18. Division of Student Affairs, 25.
19. Budget Office, 4.
20. Pagell, 33.
21. *ABI/Inform Global; Periodical Abstracts Global.*
22. Siddiqui, 369.

REFERENCES

1995 III Development Summary to the Library Advisory Committee, Bierce Library, University of Akron, (September 9, 1995).

ABI/Inform Global - list of publications. Ann Arbor, Michigan: UMI, July 1994.

About OhioLINK [library guide]. (June 1993).

Budget Office. The University of Akron Unrestricted Fund Departmental Budget Statement 12 Months Ended 06/30/95. Akron, Ohio: The University of Akron, July 28, 1995.

College Blue Book: Narrative Descriptions. New York:Macmillan Library Reference USA, 1995.

Division of Student Affairs. *The University of Akron Undergraduate Bulletin 1995–96.* Akron, Ohio: The University of Akron, 34 (July 1995).

Everett, David. "Full-Text Online Databases and Document Delivery in an Academic Library: Too Little, Too Late?" *Online* 17, no. 2 (March 1993): 22–25.

Evolution of the OhioLINK Vision [library guide]. (June 1993).

Gillikin, David P. "Document Delivery from Full-Text Online Files: A Pilot Project." *Online* 14, no. 3 (May 1990): 27–32.

Hearty, John A.; Rohrbaugh, Valerie K. "Current State of Full-Text Primary Information Online with Recommendations for the Future." *Online Review* 13, no. 4 (April 1989) 135–140.

Lancaster, F.W. *Toward Paperless Information Systems.* New York: Academic Press, 1978.

OhioLINK Update 1, no. 1 (January 1995).

OhioLINK Update 1, no. 2 (August 1995).

OhioLINK Operating Plan 1994, 4/18/94 to the Library Advisory Committee, (April 22, 1994).

OhioLINK Document Delivery Task Force, 11/10/93 to the Library Advisory Committee, (December 17, 1993).

Pagell, Ruth A. "Searching IAC's Full-text Periodicals: How Full is Full?" *Database* 10, no. 5 (October 1987): 33–36.

Periodical Abstracts Global - list of publications. Ann Arbor, Michigan: UMI, November 1994.

Power Pages Implementation (Update:9/12/95) to the Library Advisory Committee, (September 9, 1995).

Proquest PowerPages Remote Image PRINTstation. Ann Arbor, Michigan: UMI, 1994.

Siddiqui, Moid A. "Full-Text Databases." *Online Review* 15, no. 6 (1991): 367–372.

Just in Time vs. Just in Case: An Alternative to Traditional Collection Development and Interlibrary Loan

By Judie Malamud and Florence Schreibstein
Albert Einstein College of Medicine

Rising journal prices in the biomedical sciences coupled with decreasing budgets has necessitated a reassessment of the traditional selection, acquisition, storage and provision of the journal literature in a research library. Alternative models must be looked at. Considerations should include cost, ease of access to documents delivery time, future access, copyright, user expectations, and institutional politics. The use of a commercial document delivery provider offers an option that may meet the changing milieu of a research institution.

BACKGROUND

The Albert Einstein College of Medicine has, from its opening in 1955, been an intensely research-focused institution. Funds received from the National Institutes of Health (NIH) have ranked the school among the top twenty NIH recipients of medical schools in the U.S. Much of the operating funds for the institution come from the overhead associated with NIH grants. Over the last few years NIH funds, both competing new grants and non-competing renewals, have become more difficult to obtain. Institutional overhead rates have been re-negotiated downward with NIH. New junior faculty find it harder to get that first grant that will establish a track record that will assist with future funding. Last year the school had a $3 million deficit and this year it will be at least $9 million. All departments are being forced to retrench. This has affected the library, particularly in the book/journal funds available, the largest portion of the budget after personnel. The library's book/journal budget for 1994 had only a 7.5% increase after a decline from the year before. Increases in prices were projected at 10–15%. As journals are the core of a biomedical library, a new plan of action needed to be implemented to maintain access to journals and documents needed.

In May, 1993, I had chaired a session at the Annual Meeting of the Medical Library Association focusing on options for new forms of document delivery. Having done a review of options currently available[1] the interlibrary loan staff, both professional and support, were receptive to trying a new approach to collection development, cost containment and enhanced document delivery. In a recent paper[2] that validated our decision in 1993, arguments are made for the use of a commercial document delivery provider in four areas: as a selection tool to assist in the decision to acquire new subscriptions; in lieu of new subscriptions too expensive to purchase; in lieu of current subscriptions; and to supplement interlibrary loan service.

After discussing the features of various vendors the decision was made to set up an account with UnCover. Reasons for using UnCover included a) Internet access to their database, b) holdings that included titles we needed, c) routine use of fax for 24–hour turnaround time, and d) charges that were competitive with other vendors.

PROJECT INCEPTION

In August, 1993, a new junior faculty person in the Department of Physiology and Biophysics came to the library with a request to purchase four very expensive titles outside the field of biomedicine. The department was changing research interests and had brought in several new junior faculty members and graduate students the year before. It had just assumed, without talking to us, that we would take care of any journals needed to support research efforts. The cost of the four journals came to almost $9,000. If the titles had been added to the collection, by 1996 the cost would have been over $14,500, a 63% increase in just 3 years.

When the new faculty member was queried as to why he had not approached us when he first came, he replied that he had come to us from Princeton, he and his wife still had a lot of friends in Princeton whom they visited every few weeks, and when he went to visit he would spend time at the Princeton library where they had all his journals!

The library could not afford the four titles. In lieu of subscriptions, a counter proposal was made. The library was already receiving Current Contents-Life Sciences on Diskette which was updated weekly. Current Contents -Physical, Chemical, and Earth Sciences on Diskette (with abstracts, $840 for 1994) would be purchased and loaded on the same 286 PC as the Life Sciences section to which we had already subscribed. About a month's worth of tables of contents of each of the two sections would be loaded and searchable at any one time. All faculty interested could search the tables of contents, identify potentially useful articles, and the library would provide these, at no charge to the users, from a commercial document delivery provider within 24 hours. If more than 70% of the cost of a subscription to a title was spent in document delivery, that title would be reconsidered for the library's subscription list the following year. The faculty member agreed but asked if we'd like a new, fast 486 PC for just the Physical, Chemical, and Earth Sciences section. We would then be able to keep six months of tables of contents loaded at any one time. The library accepted the offer, and the 486 was purchased and installed in the library within a month.

RESULTS

During the remainder of the year we had requests for five additional new titles that totaled $5,953, added on to $8,956. Declining to subscribe to these titles too, the Interlibrary Loan Office was instructed to add them to the UnCover list should requests come in for them. By the end of the 1993-1994 year, 42 requests had gone to UnCover and 41 had been filled for a cost of under $500. Clearly we had come out ahead financially. All requests were received via fax within 24 hours. About 75% of these requests were completed within four hours. We had no further requests to purchase the original list of titles and knew of no complaints.

For the 1994-1995 year another two titles that had been requested for purchase were added to the UnCover list along with two titles that had been canceled in the 1970s and 1980s. The number of requests filled by UnCover totaled 47, at a cost of $996 or $21.20/article. Totals for the four titles, had we subscribed, would have been $13,289.

The cost for 15 documents from July, 1995-November, 1996 has been $267.50 or $17.83/article. As of January 11, 1996 we had turned down requests to purchase seven new titles ($3,517), but promised to provide them via UnCover. Two of the faculty were upset this year and said we were thwarting the research effort at Einstein.

DISCUSSION

Cost savings have been substantial. In addition to the subscription cost, other savings include: service fee to the subscription agent, labor/time savings for check-in, processing, claiming, binding, shelving, and storage.[3] The ILL Department can process an UnCover request more quickly than a traditional ILL request as there is less paperwork and/or computer time used. Turnaround time is within 24 hours, significantly faster than traditional ILL. In a biomedical setting, speed in obtaining a document is of the utmost importance. There is no need to worry about exceeding copyright as the cost of a document includes the publisher's copyright fee, sometimes quite high. Some feel that the increasing use of commercial document delivery providers will translate into publishers' receiving less subscription income, and this may lead publishers to increase subscription rates which would lead to further cancellations and loss of revenue. Eventually, publishers can be expected to offset the decline in subscription income by raising copyright royalty fees.[4]

Disadvantages of using a commercial provider include an alteration in the integrity of a collection. Under the traditional model of collection development many purchases were made so materials would be available "just-in-case" a user needed an item. Research libraries can no longer afford this luxury. Libraries are moving to spend more on access to information, or the " just-in-time model," instead of the "just-in-case" scenario, and less on ownership of information.[5] Users who would come to the library to browse the latest issues of the important journals in a field will now have to do much of the browsing electronically. Social and scholarly interaction that always took place in the library with one's colleagues will take place via e-mail.

The library has budgeted more in the interlibrary loan/document delivery line while only small increases have been incurred in the journal/book line. Overall dollars spent have been reallocated and reduced, which was a major part of the initiative. As the library has been using a commercial provider for only two years, the long-range implications are as yet unclear. For now the information needs of our users are being met.

Note: As the final draft of this manuscript was being prepared, the authors saw posted on a six-week-old listserv[6] a description of a project with UnCover. The University of Kansas has allocated $25,000 to pay for subsidized articles in FY96 for faculty and graduate students. UnCover will be the document delivery provider. Kansas has taken advantage of some enhanced features of UnCover that Einstein as yet has not chosen. The experiment will be evaluated in May or June and a decision made whether to continue or not.

ENDNOTES

1. Malamud, J. and Levine, L. 1994. DocuShock: options for document delivery in the nineties. Bull. Med. Libr. Assoc. 84:161–87.
2. Coons, B. and McDonald, P. 1995. Implications of commercial document delivery. C & RL News 56:626–31.
3. Lawrence, G.S. 1981. A cost model for storage and weeding programs. C & R L 42:139–47/
4. Carrigan, D.P. 1995. From just-in-case to just-in-time: limits to the alternative library service-model. J. Scholar P. 26: 173–82.
5. Ibid.
6. Miller, R. 1995, January 25. UnCover experiment at Univ. Of Kansas [Discussion]. Document Delivery Discussion List [Online]. Available e-mail docdel-l@dynamic3.ebscodoc.com.

Having It All: Strategies for Providing Monographic, Serial, and Electronic Resources in Tight Budget Times

By Chestalene Pintozzi
University of Arizona

BACKGROUND

Over approximately the past two decades academic libraries have been battered by converging forces that have eroded buying power and made it increasingly difficult to provide the information resources needed to support our customers' curricular and research needs. One key factor has been static or decreasing library funding, in relation to funding for other areas, from parent institutions. As noted in the Mellon Report on university libraries and scholarly communication, the share of educational and general expenditures going to the Research I libraries included in the study rose from the mid-1960s through 1971, then remained level until 1980 when a rapid decline began that continued through 1990.[1] Many state university budgets have suffered also in recent years as the result of external forces including economic difficulties such as recessions, tax cuts, and competing needs such as the demand for more prisons and higher state costs for medical care. In Arizona, a complicating factor has been decreasing regard for higher education on the part of many legislators and public officials. The state's three universities have been characterized as bloated and inefficient by our Governor and the Auditor General's office and state mandated new costs have exceeded budget increases for the past several years.

Another key factor has been the rapidly increasing cost of information resources. Serial prices, in particular, have skyrocketed, fueled by the falling value of the U.S. dollar in relation to European currencies, increasing page counts, paper and postage costs, and what many librarians believe to have been exorbitant price increases by large commercial publishers.

At the same time, the quantity of information being created, published, and marketed has been expanding rapidly, particularly in the sciences, during the Twentieth Century. For example, in 1935 the American Chemical Society published 4,500 pages of research in its journals. In 1995, the Society published over 125,000 pages.[2] New fields of research such as biotechnology have sprung up and others such as materials science have grown dramatically. New journals have started up and old titles have split into two or more parts to help accommodate this information explosion. A contributing factor has been the need to "publish or perish" that drives some faculty and researchers to publish more and more articles in support of their quests for tenure, promotion, or grant funding. An additional complication, albeit a wonderful development, is the flood of electronic publications now reaching the market.

We librarians have found ourselves caught in the middle. Faculty, students, and researchers are demanding more information resources to support their work and learning. Legislatures and parent institutions are allocating the same, less, or in the best cases, slightly more money for materials while costs and the marketplace continue to expand at a rapid pace. This situation demands strategic planning, difficult choices, and creative solutions. At the University of Arizona Library we are successfully employing the following four strategies to make the most effective use possible of existing resources and to find new ways of meeting customer needs.

STRATEGY ONE: SERIAL CAPS AND MANAGEMENT OF SERIAL COSTS

Our first strategy was to gain control over and manage serial costs on an ongoing basis. During fiscal years 1993 and 1994 we canceled almost $700,000 worth of serial subscriptions. Our approach was to target for cancellation those titles whose costs were increasing the most rapidly. Any title increasing in price 25% or more from 1990 to 1992 was reviewed by the appropriate librarian(s) and faculty and many were subsequently canceled. This process reduced the overall rate of inflation of our serial subscriptions significantly and it remains approximately five percentage points lower than the average for academic libraries nationwide.

In order to manage ongoing serial costs more effectively and ensure that funding for needed monographic materials is available, we have instituted serial caps. We have defined caps as the ratio of serial to monograph expenditures deemed appropriate for each information access budget line. They are based on the ratio of the dollar value of worldwide serial to monographic publishing, within subject areas, with adjustments made as necessary based on analysis of local needs. Some approaches used to justify local adjustments include citation analysis of works by University of Arizona authors, interlibrary loan statistics, and ratios of graduate to undergraduate students in departments known to use materials purchased through each budget line. Librarians assigned responsibility for managing budget lines are responsible for working with faculty and other customers to keep subscription costs at or below the set cap. This means that cancellations are not made across-the-board, but are driven by costs and funding for given lines and that cancellations may be necessary if new titles are to be added or if costs of existing subscriptions rise.

STRATEGY TWO: ALTERNATIVES TO OWNERSHIP

A second strategy has been the identification and use of access as an alternative to ownership of information resources when feasible. During the serials cancellation project cooperative agreements were developed with the libraries at the other Arizona Regents' universities to provide priority delivery of articles among the schools. This enabled the development of resource sharing agreements providing for retention of subscriptions to some low-use or high-cost journals at only one school while permitting access by the others.

Commercial document delivery services are also being utilized to meet customer needs for serial publications. We have been supplying articles through UnCover at no cost to faculty and graduate students for around three years. Availability of journal articles from UnCover was a criterion used in cancellation decisions. Use statistics of current periodicals in the Science-Engineering Library were analyzed to identify titles where document delivery would be a cost effective alternative to local ownership. This year we are instituting free access to articles through EbscoDOC for all our primary customers including undergraduates. This service is configured to permit direct online ordering by and delivery to end users and should both reduce time from ordering to delivery and limit workload increases for our ILL staff. Use of these commercial services increases the quantity and variety of resources available to our faculty, students, and researchers while limiting our costs and permitting us to retain subscriptions to high use titles.

Other uses and enhancements of access that we have implemented increase the variety, scope, and availability of electronic indexing and abstracting services and full-text resources available to our customers. We provide free access in the library to the 450+ Dialog databases utilizing the Classroom Instruction Program package through a program we call QuickSearch. In this program we provide training sessions to teach search protocols and strategies to end-users, provide workstations and space, and employ library school students as monitors to assist searchers with use of the hardware and software. We make selected FirstSearch databases available free of charge to our primary customers from their offices, dorms, or homes by purchasing quantities of searches and providing passwords and instructions for use.

Enhanced availability, including remote access and extended hours of access, is provided through Sabio (our integrated library system) to ten commercial databases including Expanded Academic Index (index and full-text), Current Contents, BIOSIS, ERIC, INSPEC, PsycINFO, and ABI/Inform (index and full-text). This permits remote customer access to these databases almost 24 hours a day. A gateway to Encyclopedia Britannica is also provided through Sabio. In-library and remote access to approximately twenty additional databases is available through our CD-ROM network.

STRATEGY THREE: DEVELOPMENT AND PARTNERING

Our third strategy has been the implementation of an active fund raising and partnering program targeting both on-campus and off-campus funding sources. While many private and some public universities and libraries have been quite active in this arena over the years, many librarians, including some at the University of Arizona, have felt that it is not a productive endeavor, one that they were comfortable with, or that external funds are simply not readily available. While we have not yet developed endowments to rival Harvard's or funded a Gutenberg Bible through our efforts, they have resulted in the addition of resources that make a difference to our customers.

We have increased our efforts substantially over the past five years and have had a full-time Assistant Dean for External Affairs who focuses on these activities on the staff for just over a year. Our Dean of Libraries actively supports and participates in development efforts. Income from fund raising and grants library-wide has increased from $124,373 in FY1991 to $918,462 in FY1995. A good deal of this income has been earmarked for information resources.

Following are some examples of successful initiatives in support of information resources acquisition. During FY1995 we raised a total of around $150,000 in contributions from two separate external donors and from the Colleges of Business and Public Administration, Agriculture, and Science to purchase equipment, software, and databases needed to make BIOSIS and ABI/Inform (index and full-text) available via a server to customers at remote sites as well as within the Library. Another development initiative last year resulted in the establishment of the $30,000 Della Cole Distler Endowment to fund purchase of information resources in the areas of humanities, fine arts, the Southwest, and Special Collections. Ongoing gift solicitation efforts resulted in gifts of books and other materials worth approximately $117,000 last year.

The Library also collaborates with various groups that are actively involved in fund raising on behalf of the Library. The University of Arizona Alumni Parents Association Bookplate Program usually generates at least $25–30,000 annually for purchase of materials. During one two-year period this group contributed $75,000 that the Library was able to use to purchase $150,000 worth of equipment to support access through collaboration with IBM. The Friends of the Library undertake various fund-raising events and manage the Library's annual book sale that brought in around $11,000 last year that was used to purchase library materials.

A consortium with our local community college and public library system to provide access to Expanded Academic Index has resulted in savings of several thousand dollars per year that can be used to support other undergraduate needs. Partnering with our computer center, academic departments, and individual faculty members provides reduced cost or free access to several serial subscriptions. For example, we share the cost of an Association of Computing Machinery membership with our computing center with the publications being placed in the library and we receive several Japanese technical journals free from a faculty member in the Department of Computer Science who scans contents pages into an Internet server as part of a grant-funded project.

In addition to the acquisition of the resources mentioned above, we have heightened awareness on the part of all librarians that fund raising is an activity that is crucial to meeting our customers' information needs and to the development of high quality collections of specialized materials such as photographic archives for our Center for Creative Photography.

STRATEGY FOUR: NEEDS ASSESSMENT AND CUSTOMER EDUCATION

A fourth, and critical, strategy is ongoing needs assessment and customer education. In order to make the most effective use of our limited information access budget we must fully understand the true information needs of our faculty, students, and researchers. We no longer have the luxury of having enough money to build collections based on a "just-in-case" philosophy. We must make strategic decisions based on knowledge of what information our customers need, how they use it, and the options that are available to provide that information to them.

Systematic, ongoing customer needs assessment and evaluation is a focal point of our organization. Techniques we are employing to understand customer needs include focus groups to identify critical issues, surveys of faculty and students, and such traditional activities as one-on-one liaison work by librarians and visits to departmental meetings as well as feedback from service points such as reference desks and InterLibrary Loan. Additional approaches include the previously mentioned citation analysis studies to determine which types of publications support which departments and colleges and use studies of current periodicals such as the one currently under way in our Science-Engineering Library and soon to be implemented throughout the Library. An equal part of this strategy is an active, ongoing program of communication with, and education of, our customers. All librarians involved in public service and the selection of information resources are expected to participate in what we call connection development. This means that we actively identify our user communities and develop effective means of communicating with faculty, students, and researchers in our assigned subject areas in order to maintain current awareness of developing programs, changing information needs, and to provide them with information regarding our services, trends in publishing, new options for provision of information, and results of our needs assessment analysis.

CONCLUSION

Each of these strategies alone provides some benefits to the Library and our customers. Using all four enhances results. Use of alternative means of access to information supports our ability to manage our serials budget. Managing our serials budget through the use of caps frees up funding for the acquisition of needed monographic and electronic materials. Development efforts help provide funding to enhance access and fund acquisition of rare or specialized materials that help develop some excellent local collections to meet identified goals. Needs assessment and education efforts ensure that the information resources purchased support the curricular and research needs of our customers and help those customers better understand and utilize the resources provided.

Implementation of these strategies has not been easy. Difficult decisions were made to cancel some core journals and more, equally difficult decisions surely await us. We are in the process of learning what it means to be a user centered rather than a collections centered library and how to make document delivery and other alternative means of access work to provide information on a "just-in-time" basis. We are finding that we need to spend a great deal of time communicating with and educating our customers. We must overcome our own, often unfounded, assumptions and reluctance to become involved in fund raising efforts. But the result of our efforts is that we are maintaining and enhancing our ability to meet our customers' information needs even in these tight budget times. We expect that these benefits will increase over time as we become better at these activities. We also must continue to focus on the future, to make hard choices, and to develop new or different strategies as new or different needs, issues, problems, and opportunities arise.

ENDNOTES

1. "Growth of Library Expenditures," in Cummings, Anthony M. et al. University Libraries and Scholarly Communication: A Study Prepared for The Andrew W. Mellon Foundation. Washington, D.C.: Association of Research Libraries for the Andrew Mellon Foundation, 1992, 23–40.
2. Will Science Publishing Perish? The Paradox of Contemporary Science Journals. Washington, D.C.: American Chemical Society.

Online Books: What Role Will They Fill for Users of the Academic Library?

By Mary C. Summerfield
Columbia University

INTRODUCTION: THE COLUMBIA UNIVERSITY ONLINE BOOKS EVALUATION PROJECT

As the Libraries and Academic Information Systems at Columbia University have proceeded with a pilot project[1] to provide the Columbia community with a substantial collection of online books and to evaluate the reactions of scholars to those books, it has become clear that a basic understanding of how scholars interact with various classes of traditional print-on-paper books is necessary for optimal design of the various facets of a system for intellectual and physical access to online books, for assessing the value of various components to the academic community, and for successful selection of books to be included in online collections. However, the library-related literature on the use of books by scholars has focused largely on issues related to the overall demand for collections rather than on how scholars select books to review or read or ultimately employ books in their work. Similarly, the psychological and ergonomic literature on how people read has focused on concepts which have little to do with the place of books in scholars' work or how scholars manipulate books in that work.[2]

In the Columbia University Online Books Evaluation Project, several programs of research have been undertaken to date in an effort to develop this understanding: 3 focus groups of faculty and graduate students; 28 interviews with faculty and graduate students; and a review of literature on the use of books by scholars and on human-computer interaction and the implications for use of online books. Among the issues that this research is exploring are the following: What constitutes use of a book for scholars? Do various disciplines use books differently? How do scholars locate and select various types of books? How do scholars manipulate various types of books as they use them? How much of a book do scholars review or read? Are those segments typically together or scattered through the book? What constitutes an episode of using a print-on-paper book? How do scholars absorb the information in the books they read and take it into their own scholarship or teaching? Are scholars equipped to use online books? How do scholars react to the concept of online books; are they likely to adopt them readily? If not, what are their doubts about the concept?

What follows is a brief description of the discussions undertaken at Columbia University in 1995 as well as an analysis of the findings from that original research. There is also related information from the literature reviews and conclusions flowing from these findings about the design of online books delivery systems and collections and the steps necessary to introduce the scholarly community to this new format.

DISCUSSIONS WITH THE COLUMBIA UNIVERSITY COMMUNITY

In late spring 1995, three focus groups were convened at Columbia University. Two were comprised of scholars (faculty, researchers, graduate students) in neuroscience-related disciplines; one of scholars in the humanities.[3] (These disciplines were chosen because books in these fields will be part of the pilot project.) The discussions centered on the scholars' current use of computer-assisted communication and research, their expectations for the online book format and their use of it, and design features that they would value.

In fall 1995, a program of individual interviews with faculty members and graduate students was undertaken.[4] A key focus was on the neuroscience and humanities disciplines, but a wider range was sought in order to discern patterns that might apply more broadly. In particular, social science representation was sought; political science was the discipline used.[5] A total of 28 interviews were conducted.[6]

The interviews included a one page questionnaire (Exhibit 1) which the scholar was asked to fill out at the beginning of the session[7] and a discussion based on an outline. In some cases, the scholars began the session with their thoughts on the use of books or related topics, so the outline was used in only a general way. The sessions lasted twenty minutes (when a scheduling conflict cut the discussion short) to an hour. The interviews were distributed by discipline (Table 1), University status (Table 2), and years in the discipline (Table 3) as follows:

Table 1. Interview Distribution by Discipline

Discipline	No. Interviews
Political Science	11
English & Comparative Literature	5
Psychology	4
Philosophy	2
Religion	1
Chemistry	1
Biology	1
Astronomy	1
Physics	1
Chemical Engineering	1

While the concentration in political science is considerable, those individuals were distributed across the quantitative, historical and philosophical aspects of that discipline, bringing a variety of scholarly practices.

Table 2. Interview Distribution by University Status

University Status	No. Interviews
Professor	13
Assistant Professor	9
Associate Professor	1
Graduate Student	5

Table 3. Interview Distribution by Years In Discipline

Years in Discipline	No. Interviews
31 or more	4
21 to 30	6
11 to 20	9
6 to 10	6
2 to 5	2
Not Determined	1

As noted above, all of the interviewed scholars had email accounts and used them; this combination indicates at least a moderate sophistication with computer-assisted communication as some Columbia faculty members and graduate students scholars do not have email accounts and not a few of those who have accounts use them little or not at all. All of the scholars interviewed reported ready access to a personal computer with access to the Columbia campus network. On average, they had access to 22 such computers in their homes, offices, labs and other sites. Only one of these scholars reported no access to a computer that can access the graphical Worldwide Web. On average, they had access to 17 such computers. The humanities scholars seemed to have the most limited access to personal computing resources. Some mentioned that their computers are quite old or that they do not keep computers in their campus offices as both security and modem and network connections are inadequate.

Use of computer-assisted communication and research varies considerably among the scholars interviewed. Several noted that they are relatively new in doing anything with computers besides word processing and searching the online library catalog and bibliographic indexes. One scientist said that he had been a leader in using computing in research several years ago, but that he relies primarily on his younger colleagues to pursue the advances now. Several others are quite sophisticated and extensive users of the Internet in all its facets.

SCHOLARS' USE OF BOOKS

Each scholar has his own ways of approaching the literature in his field. However, in general the steps involved in scholars' use of books, either for a specific research problem or in maintaining awareness in a field, might be defined as: selecting books to review,

Exhibit 1. Book Use Study

Columbia is studying how scholars use books in order to assess how online books might serve the academic community. Your assistance is critical to success in this study. Thank you for answering the following questions and participating in the discussion.

1. What is your primary discipline?

2. If you have a significant secondary discipline, what is it?

3. About how long have you been working in this discipline?

Computer Access and Online Activities

4. Please check all locations at which you can use a computer attached to the campus network (by modem or direct link) whenever you want.
A. None ___ B. Office ___ C. Lab ___ D. Home ___ E. Other (describe) _____

5. Please check all locations at which this computer can access a graphical Worldwide Web.
A. None ___ B. Office ___ C. Lab ___ D. Home ___ E. Other (describe) _____

6. On average how many hours a week do you use a computer in total:

7. On average how many hours a week do you use a computer in each of the following online activities:
____ Email   ____ Listservs & Newsgroup   ____ CLIO Plus
____ Text, Image or Numeric Data Sources   ____ Other WWWeb

8. Please rate your level of expertise by checking the appropriate boxes below.

Activity	Low						High
General computing	1	2	3	4	5	6	7
Online activities	1	2	3	4	5	6	7

Book and Journal Use

9. On average how many books (not journals or bibliographic tools) do you use in any way each month from each of these sources:

Number of Books	Columbia Library	Own Collection	Colleague's Collection	Other Library	Other Sources
For scholarly research					
For teaching support					
For other reasons					

10. On average how many journal issues do you use in any way each month:

For scholarly research	
For teaching support	
For other reasons	

11. Typically for what share of the monographs or textbooks that you use do you look at each of the following percentages of the book? (Answers in each row should sum to 100%.)

Reason For Book Use	1-20%	21-40%	41-60%	61-80%	81-100%
For scholarly research					
For teaching support					
For other reasons					

Department: Status:

Changing Materials, Changing Economies

obtaining books, sifting books to review, choosing books to browse and to read at length, reading, and retaining and using the books' contents. Patterns of behavior accompanying each step, as determined in the Columbia interviews and in the literature on scholarly use of books, are summarized below.

SELECTING BOOKS TO REVIEW

Each scholar uses several methods to gain intellectual and physical access to books that might support his work. These vary depending on the nature of the use, e. g., whether the scholar is keeping up with developments in his field, pursuing a specific research project in a known field or in a new field, or supporting teaching. Among those commonly cited for keeping up with the new books in a field are:

> Reviewing publishers' catalogs, advertisements and tables at conferences. Scholars tend to have strong opinions about various publishers' programs in their fields and pay most attention to the new books from those they most respect.[8]
>
> Reading book reviews, journal lists of new books or reviews of recent work;
>
> Browsing in bookstores;
>
> Browsing new books' shelves in the library or reviewing lists of a library's new acquisitions;
>
> Seeking and following up on recommendations from colleagues.

Scientists report that they use their colleagues to help them decide which of the new publications that they need to read in part or entirely so as not to be overwhelmed by the enormous flow of scientific information.[9]

Among the most commonly cited methods for locating books as part of research in a known field (besides those listed above) are:

> Following chains of citations and bibliographic entries in the literature, and then perhaps moving to a citation index to go further forward and backward. When a book is identified, it is sought in the local library catalog and then on the library shelf. Surrounding books are likely to be included in the next review step.
>
> Seeking the work of researchers known to be active in the field in bibliographic indexes, library catalogs, and Books In Print;
>
> Searching bibliographic indexes and library catalogs by subject or key words;
>
> Checking the relevant stacks of a library to see if any books address the issue at hand.

Scholars tend to use the same reference books repeatedly; however, many will request reference librarians' assistance in finding others that might answer a question.

Among the methods cited for pinpointing useful books in an unfamiliar field, besides the uses of indexes and catalogs cited above, are:

> Seeking recommendations from colleagues who are active in that field;
>
> Reviewing textbooks in the field;
>
> Reading journal overview articles about that field.

In a study of British philosophers, 45 percent reported that they went to colleagues first when trying to identify useful materials to use in research on a new topic and 55 percent reported browsing after getting colleagues' advice.[10]

In general, the Columbia interviews and other scholars' research finds that scientists and social scientists do not seem to have dramatically different information-seeking behavior.[11] In the Columbia interviews, similar methods were described across the disciplines. Humanities scholars focus more on primary sources, which are eclectic and which may be very old, but employ the same steps as the scientists and social scientists in reviewing modern literature.[12]

OBTAINING BOOKS

Some of the methods described for selecting books also involve physical access to the books, e. g., browsing library shelves or bookstores. However, others are simply means of intellectual access, e. g., bibliographic indexes or library catalogs, and the scholar must still obtain a copy of the book itself in order to determine whether it has value for his work. Doing so may be difficult. His library may not have ordered it. In such a case, requesting ordering may not be viable, e. g., the book might be out of print, and would certainly take time. Borrowing it from or using it at another library would also require considerable time.

If the library has ordered it, it may not have arrived. If it has arrived, it may not have been cataloged and processed. If the book has reached the library shelf, someone else may have checked it out, or potentially worse, simply removed it from the shelf so that it is not available. If it is checked out, the scholar could ask for a recall or a hold to be put on the book. However, if it is a popular title, someone else might already have a recall or hold on it; or it might be on reserve and not readily available.

These problems lead scholars to want to own books that may be central to their work. Many scholars, even graduate students who have less disposable income than faculty members, reported that they buy or are given dozens of books each year. Others said that they buy any book that looks valuable. Many would buy even more books if they were available for purchase or if they did not feel that they were overpriced.[13]

However, scholars do recognize problems with owning books; the scholar must house and organize the books so that they can be located when they are needed. Their information must still become known to the scholar; records must be made so that it is accessible when needed. Most scholars obtain books from the library themselves often or always. Relatively few reported that they delegate this effort to assistants—either because they do not have such an assistant or because they feel that browsing the shelves and doing initial reviewing at the library are important parts of their research.[14]

The scholars interviewed use libraries at all times of the day, week and year. Some noted that they do most of their heavy research during breaks from the teaching year, but others try to fit it in throughout the year or use the library for teaching support during the semester. A few noted that they would have liked to use libraries at hours that they were closed. One noted that she sought to use the library when students were least likely to be there as they tended to interrupt her work with questions otherwise. Scholars tend to check out library books that they wish to use extensively. Hardly any reported the library as a site at which they commonly read books.

REVIEWING BOOKS

The first step in using a book is that which makes the scholar decide whether to seek the book on the library or bookstore shelf and to move beyond cursory review. In general, this centers on the credibility of the book as well as its potential value. Credibility is determined by the author—his education, mentors, employer, and previous work; the publisher's history in this field, and the research design. An initial determination of potential value is made by scanning some combination of the Table of Contents, the index, chapter headings, the preface, introduction and conclusion, the citations and bibliography, graphical material and mathematics.

Scanning, flipping, paging, leafing, browsing are terms used commonly to describe this initial review of a book to determine whether it warrants closer attention. It is a physical process of handling the book and a visual process of moving quite quickly over its contents while looking for the nature of the analysis, highlights, and the utility to the scholar's own work.

Sometimes the scholar is seeking to find nuggets of information relevant to his work; in such cases the index, the Table of Contents and headings are very important.[15] If the scholar believes that the research the book is presenting may be interesting as a whole, he typically scans the introduction, graphics, mathematics, and perhaps the conclusion to discern if that is true.

In her work on the information needs and habits of humanities scholars, Rebecca Watson-Boone observed that such scholars typically work alone and make personal interpretations of material. They graze material, their colleagues' minds and texts, accumulating, selecting, and interpreting information and transforming it into knowledge. Thus, doing their own searching and working with materials in a wide range of subjects is important to their method of creating knowledge.[16]

READING BOOKS

More often than not, scholars and students do not read books in their entirety. In some cases, only a few facts are needed. In some others, the book is comprised of distinct thematic chapters, essays or papers presented at a conference, and only one or a few are pertinent. In yet others, the scholar does not need to read the whole book to understand as much of its argument as she needs. However, reading part of a book does not necessarily mean reading a single segment, such as an entry in an encyclopedia or a chapter in a monograph. As noted above, a scholar may look widely within a book to locate the elements that are valuable to her work. In their study of the use of circulating non-fiction humanities and social science books at Ohio State, Prabha and Rice found that 75 percent of such uses were for the purpose of obtaining specific information (defined as one or more ideas or facts); in almost half the cases the user read no more than a quarter of a book; in only a quarter of cases did she read more than three-quarters of the book.[17]

In the Sabines' study of heavy users of scientific and technical information, 18 percent reported reading at most one percent of the book about which they were being interviewed and 62 percent read ten percent or less of that book. Only 11 percent had read the whole book.[18] Asked how much of a book they usually read, 77 percent reported small parts, 14 percent sometimes parts/sometimes all, and nine percent all.[19]

The Columbia research confirms that in relatively few cases do scholars read whole books and in many cases they read a relatively small section of a book.[20] The questionnaire (Exhibit 1) asks scholars to distribute their book reading for scholarly research and for teaching purposes over quintiles of the whole book read. For example, if a scholar reads over 80 percent of a quarter of the books he uses, then he was to write 25% in the 81–100% box. Unfortunately, in ten of the 28 cases, the scholar checked one box as representing his central tendency of use rather than giving a distribution across the quintiles. As a result, analyzing the resulting data was not straightforward. The following table gives a few indications of the tendencies that scholars reported. Clearly, reading full books is not the norm and reading quite small segments is common.

Scientists reported that they often use handbooks or books comprised of essays or conference papers in which they are interested in only a few of the essays or papers. As a result, they tend to be reading a relatively small percentage of the book. Seldom do scientists choose to read entire monographs as they feel that few valuable ones are published in their fields. Scientists report that the papers or essays that they read are typically located by reviewing the Table of Contents. Reading scientific monographs and such papers and essays involves absorbing not only the text but the illustrations, mathematics, tables, graphs and other such materials. The reader generally refers back and forth from text to graphical materials, often flipping pages in so doing.

Table 4. Percentages of Books Read By Scholars

Share Reading	Scholarly Research	Teaching Support
20% or Less of Book in 1-35% of Cases	21%	25%
20% or Less of Book in At Least 50% of Cases	39%	36%
Over 80% of Book in 1-40% of Cases	39%	25%
Over 80% of Book in At Least 50% of Cases	7%	0%

Other scholars noted that they often are seeking relatively precise information as defined by Prabha and Rice, for example, insights on a period or a personality, rather than the totality of a book. Or they find that reading just the introduction and conclusion and perhaps some of the middle of the book gives them as much of the flavor of the research as they can afford the time to attain. Often they read only the parts of a book they deem pertinent to their work, whether that be paragraphs, pages or chapters. These elements, which may be widely separated in the book, are found by reviewing the Table of Contents, the index, and chapter headings, and by general scanning of the text and any graphical elements. These scholars tend to read fully only those monographs that were authored by noted scholars or that they feel present important research in their fields. Humanities scholars also read fully the primary works of their fields be they novels and plays, philosophical works or documents.

Asked how many books they use on average each month for their scholarly research and teaching, the Columbia scholars gave widely varying counts. In general, scientists use far fewer books than social scientists or humanists.[21] Six of nine scientists reported that they used fewer than eight books a month for research; only one reported use of as many as 56 books a month. For teaching, scientists reported roughly the same levels of book usage. Over 45 percent of the political scientists used more than 40 books a month for research; only one (9 percent) used as few as eight a month.

One political scientist used more than 40 books a month for teaching; four used eight or fewer. About 43 percent of the humanists used nine to 24 books a month in research; 29 percent used 41 to

75 books a month; and 29 percent used over 75 books a month. Humanists' book use for teaching clustered in the nine to 55 book range.

Scholars have widely varying patterns for where they read books, but these do not seem related to discipline. Over 55 percent of interviewed scholars reported that they do most of their reading of monographs at home; 22 percent reported both home and office; 14 percent home, office, and library; and seven percent home and library. Library books are more often used in the library or the office for 44 percent of respondents. The rest reported that the ownership of the book did not affect where they read it. Scholars have preferences for when they read books, but they vary widely over time of day and time of year. Some reported that they regularly do their reading at home in the morning before coming to campus or at home in the evening. Others reported that they read books whenever they can in the day, week, and year, often with teaching-related reading being predominant during the term and research-related reading during academic recesses.

For the majority of the interviewed scholars (59 percent), the number of sessions required for reading a book varies by the amount of the book being read or the density of the argument. Another 33 percent said that they always spent more than one session on a monograph.

ABSORBING A BOOK'S INFORMATION

A key component of the process of using a scholarly book is making its contents available for one's scholarship, whether that be by making a bibliographic entry that the book was reviewed and put aside as lacking relevance or by taking substantial notes about it. Effective scholarship and teaching support requires the reader to have a system for information transfer.

Scholars report a variety of methods of information transfer; many admit to frustration with their systems. Most keep lists of the books that they have reviewed; some in computer databases, others in notebooks or on notecards. Nearly half write in books that they own or on photocopies of sections of books that they have borrowed—underlining, margin notes, topical indexing at the front or back. A few reported adopting Post-Its as flags, with or without notes.

The majority make paper notes on sheets of paper or note cards; 29 percent use the computer for such notes or for topical databases. However, one scholar commented that she finds writing on paper focuses her mind and helps her understand the topic at hand, in a way that typing does not. Others noted that they generally read away from their computers, so taking notes on a computer during a reading session would require changing reading habits. Virtually everyone (93 percent) makes photocopies of parts of books, from a chart to a whole book, either occasionally or often. Occasionally a whole book is copied because the scholar believes it is important, wants to have it at hand, and finds it to be out of print or unacceptably expensive. More often a few pages or a chapter or two are copied.

Scholars use these photocopies in various ways: annotating them, filing them by topic or book, or incorporating them into classes through a lecture note, an overhead projection transparency, a handout, a coursepack or a reserves item. Several noted that coursepack use has diminished as the need to obtain copyright clearance has become clear. Filing systems fail in many cases as piles of papers accumulate on a floor or table.

POTENTIAL ADVANTAGES & DRAWBACKS OF ONLINE BOOKS & DESIRED FEATURES

The facets of the use of online books on which discussion has focused are searching, browsing, obtaining, reading, printing, and annotating books and accessing the system itself. The advantages and drawbacks that scholars foresee for online books are discussed below along with some of features that they consider necessary or desirable.

Searching

Searching has two aspects: (1) looking across a collection to find books relevant to the topic at hand, and (2) looking within a book for pertinent information. Traditionally, scholars have accomplished the first by reviewing a library's catalog, a union catalog, bibliographic indexes, and the like, with subjects, key words, and authors as search criteria. Reviewing Tables of Contents and indexes and scanning the text and graphical features are the chief methods of searching within a book.

Scholars find the concept of searching in an online library for concepts, names, or period-specific information appealing, but they stress the need to be able to focus the search, especially within a subject-specific collection, so as to minimize hits on irrelevant books. Once that search has been completed, the scholar must be able to move smoothly, and with clarity as to where he is, in a book and between books. Scholars assert that searching across books online would be more appealing the greater the size of the online collection. If it were small, the scholar would have to search the print collection anyway so little efficiency would be gained by taking the effort to learn to manipulate the online system and then actually using the online collection. Absent a critical mass of books in their fields, many scholars would not adopt the system. That critical mass need not be the entirety of a collection, but if it is just new books, the greater the coverage of new books the better.

Browsing

Scholars feel that browsing in an online book could have great utility but that the online system must mimic the way in which users browse print books, e. g., to page smoothly and quickly through a book or to focus on a graphical element and read the material on the pages around it. Equally the user should be able to move quickly, preferably with a clicking feature, from the Table of Contents to a chapter or from an index to a point referenced there. Browsing would be enhanced by enriching Tables of Contents with chapter headings and the titles for graphical elements and the ability to click on an entry in that Table of Contents and to move smoothly to it. Several noted that they would find an online books system that included new publications an improvement over publishers' catalogs, advertisements, and conference tables in determining which books were worth buying or borrowing from the library. The searching and browsing capabilities would allow the user to focus more quickly and more closely on the books and their value to his work.

Obtaining

One of the greatest complaints of scholars about use of libraries is the inconvenience or impossibility of obtaining books that they have identified as being of interest. Even if the scholar is on campus; the library is open; and the library has purchased and processed the book, he will often find that the book is circulating, simply not on the shelf, or on reserve. Reference books seldom have the availability problems of circulating monographs, but going to the library to look up a relatively small amount of information is an inefficient use of a scholar's time and may be impossible if the scholar is off campus or the library is closed. The constant availability of online books (absent system overload or breakdown) is one of their most appealing aspects.

Many scholars like to own books that are important to their work; they consider a system for ordering copies of books that are in the online library a convenience, especially if prices are discounted. In the same way, a networked printing service is viewed as a convenient way to obtain a partial copy of a book as long as the price is reasonable compared to that for photocopying or that for the whole book. Scholars also want to be able to download or print small selections from a book for use in their research or teaching.

Scholars are intrigued by the possibility that an online books collection might include books that are out of print but not out of copyright and others that are out of copyright as well. They lament that some modern works that they would like to use in teaching are no longer available for students or the library to purchase.

Reading

While most of the scholars interviewed see potential value in browsing a book online, hardly any are eager to read more than a few pages online. They explained that they find reading online tiring to the eyes and to the body; that they like to be comfortable when they are reading; that they like to work with the printed page; that they often read books when they are away from computers. They also expressed concern about the layout of the online book, the ease of moving across pages and of referring back and forth among pages, and the quality of the images.

In thinking about how they would work in a system with online monographs, they concluded that once they had browsed a book online and found that they wanted to read more than a few pages, they would purchase the book, borrow a print copy from the library, or use the networked printing service to have a copy made of the parts that seemed most interesting. On the other hand, scholars recognized that their use of reference books might be confined to the online editions as they would be reading only a small amount at any time. As noted earlier, research shows that in a large share of cases scholars read only a small portion of a monograph as well. Thus, it may be that scholars will often find that online monographs and reference books are sufficient for their use, that they have no need to obtain the print book or a photocopy.

Annotating/Bookmarking/Linking/ Enhanced Books

As noted above in the discussion of methods of absorbing information from a book, some scholars are frustrated with their systems and all acknowledge that keeping track of their reading is a challenge. They are intrigued by the possibility that in using books online, they might be able to manage the inflow of facts and ideas better, thus making themselves more efficient and effective researchers. The mechanics are not clear, but the ability to keep citations and clips from books in files in their computers is appealing. Similarly, scholars would value the ability to bookmark books or pages to which they would like to refer again.

Scholars see value in a system that would allow them to link online course syllabi directly to components of books that students are to read. Several scholars noted that enhanced book formats, such as hypertext links within books that allow readers to follow various paths, the ability to review and manipulate datasets, updating as information evolves, links to relevant material outside the book, and multimedia content as appropriate, are key to substantial value in online books. These capabilities are particularly valuable for text books, but they would also allow reference books and monographs to evolve into richer tools for scholars.

Accessing the Online Books System

Using online books requires access to a computer connected to the appropriate network, sufficiently high monitor quality to make browsing and reading online viable, preferably computer power and software allowing use of a graphical Worldwide Web interface, and a sufficiently robust campus network and system of incoming modems that scholars can reach the online books when they wish to use them. If scholars are in disciplines which rely on books containing photographs and other high resolution images, monitor quality is particularly important and the ability to make fine color printouts is also desirable.

Scholars are concerned about how members of the academic community will obtain access to the hardware, software, communications linkages, and training to use online books. Will users need to have their own high quality systems in their residences and offices or will their institutions provide them in sufficient quantity in public and private locations?

Scholars note that they have had problems dialing in to the campus network from home as demand on that system has grown and that it is often difficult to find an unoccupied computer in the library on which to access the current online resources. They worry that the demands on the campus network and the online books system would be so high that accessing and using online books would be frustratingly slow.

Scholars who live outside the local telephone district are concerned about the cost of dialing in to use online resources, including books. A lengthy session online becomes quite costly if one does not have an Internet account with a local provider. Similarly, using online resources over even a relatively high speed modem can become tedious, especially if graphics are involved. These problems lead some to suggest that a scholar should be able either to borrow a CD-ROM version of an electronic book or to download an online book to his computer's hard drive.

Although they acknowledge that online books may have advantages over print-on-paper books, many scholars are concerned that learning to use the system fully will be difficult and that they will not receive sufficient personal or on-line assistance in doing so. Many recall difficulty in setting up computer systems in their homes and offices and lament the scarcity of assistance for such tasks. Many do not have graphical Web interfaces, especially at home, at this time, in some cases because their computers are not sufficiently powerful but in many cases largely due to the difficulty of setting them up.

Scholars express concern about how online books will be purchased, whether they will be a complement or a substitute for print copies, and the conditions of use. They do not want to pay to use library books or to be forced to use the online versions. Similarly, they believe that a certain amount of printing or downloading should be allowed as fair use.

BEST BOOKS TO BE ONLINE

Although scholars use a vast range of types of books and eras of scholarship, they agree somewhat on the best books to go online. In general, they feel that reference books would be most useful in that format. The combination of the need to look up information quickly and the relatively small quantity of information sought make online access particularly appealing. Types of reference works mentioned include general and specialized encyclopedias, dictionaries, historical timelines, handbooks, factbooks, commentaries on classical texts.

Columbia College students take a set series of courses in the humanities. Supporting those courses with online texts and related materials would be a service to a large part of the community. Scholars are frequently frustrated by an inability to obtain copies of out-of-print books that they would like to review or to use in classes. They would value online access to such books.

CONCLUSIONS: DESIGN STRATEGIES FOR MAKING ONLINE BOOKS ATTRACTIVE TO SCHOLARS

As both the discussions with scholars and Andrew Dillon's summary of the relevant ergonomic and psychological literature emphasized, the academic community is accustomed to patterns of making physical, perceptual, and cognitive contact with various types of documents. Having a mental model (schematic representation) for a certain family of books enables a scholar to move around in a book of that sort with ease. Being able to predict the organization of text elements facilitates comprehension of the material. At this point in time, online books lack schemata and frequently they are not presented as print-on-paper books, e. g., with information on publication, date, length, amount of use. A lack of standards and cues on using these books has hindered the development of such schemata within the scholarly community. [22]

Few scholars will be eager to learn the new patterns of presentation and use that come with online books; most will find that the process requires a time investment and initially slows their work. In order to encourage use of online books, early designers of online books systems must strive to make them as close to print-on-paper in look, feel, browsing, searching and other utilities as possible, while also providing obvious advantages to users. Institutions providing online books to their communities must ensure that scholars can readily access these books and that use will be as smooth as possible. If these conditions cannot be met, scholars may attempt to use online books, be frustrated, and be reluctant to try again even when they have been assured that the system has been improved.

Scholars gave several specific suggestions for ways to make online books attractive: the ability to browse and order partial or full copies of new publications in one's field online would be useful. The greater the number of publishers represented and the more promptly the books are available after publication the more valuable the collection would be. If only a few books, especially monographs, were available in their disciplines, some scholars doubt that they would use the online system. The greater the coverage and the more important the books to their work, the more likely scholars will make the effort to learn to use the system effectively.

The sponsors of the online books system must communicate about its holdings directly with the community members who might find them most useful. In addition, instructions on how to use the system must be provided to these individuals. Similarly, scholars need assistance in configuring their computer systems to work with online books optimally and in learning how to use online books, e. g., to search, browse, annotate, bookmark, provide syllabus links and the like.

Library and academic computing staffs should work together to ensure that such assistance is provided efficiently. Capacity for accessing the system must ensure that potential users do not get busy signals—find that they cannot get on a terminal in a library or other public location when they want to or that they cannot reach the server when they dial-in or that the book they want is not available or using it is unacceptably slow. The online books system should have an attractive interface that provokes interest in the potential user. Many scholars find an aesthetic pleasure in working with books; the online book system from interface to book should be designed to provoke a similar reaction.

Online books have the potential to provide substantial service to the academic community and to derive substantial usage from its members. However, in order to do so in the early years, librarians and their colleagues in academic computing must focus carefully on the issues delineated above and provide books that will have the greatest utility in the online format to selected user groups with interfaces and functionalities that are both easy to use and valuable to the scholar. To move in a less deliberate fashion is to risk alienating the academic community.

ENDNOTES

1. The Andrew W. Mellon Foundation has given Columbia University a grant of $700,000 to support a three year project of evaluating online books. The evaluation focuses on three elements: (1) user adoption of and reactions to online books, (2) lifecycle costs of producing, owning and using online books and their print equivalents; and (3) intellectual property issues.
2. See Andrew Dillon's excellent *Designing Usable Electronic Text: Ergonomic Aspects of Human Information Usage* for a summary of this work.
3. Librarians in the subject disciplines recommended individuals to be invited to participate in the focus groups based on their knowledge of who was active in the field and who might be interested in the topic. As the focus groups were held at the end of May and beginning of June, many faculty members were not on campus. The first group was comprised of five individuals from the Psychology and Biology Departments, the second of two from the Germanic Languages and English and Comparative Literature Departments and the third of three involved in Neuroscience at Health /Sciences.
4. Jan Olsen's *Electronic Journal Literature: Implications for Scholars* provided inspiration for this program of interviews and the design of the questions.
5. This choice is fortunate as Columbia University Press has now agreed to provide political science titles to the pilot project.
6. Librarians were asked for recommendations of individuals who might be willing to participate in an interview on the topic of their use of books. In disciplines in which the librarians were unable to supply enough names, names were selected from the University course catalogs or recommended by others who were interviewed. Each of these individuals (a total of 63) was sent an email message describing this research effort and requesting their participation in an interview. Individuals who did not have email accounts were eliminated from the roster. This procedure resulted in a sample that included only scholars who are sufficiently aware of the value of computer-assisted communication and research to have an email account. Persons who did not respond to the message within a few weeks were sent a reminder message.
7. However, in a few cases, he/she did not want to take the time to do so at that point or the scholar began the discussion such that it would have been disruptive to go back to the questionnaire. In those cases, the questionnaire was left behind or sent later with a note requesting that it be completed and returned. In only one case, did the scholar neglect to do so.
8. Scholars also have strong opinions about which publishers sell their books at prices they are willing to pay.
9. Rice and Tarin, p. 162.
10. Watson-Boone, p. 206.
11. See, for instance, Ellis, Cox and Hall for a report of a comparison of physicists, chemists and social scientists.
12. See both Wiberley and Jones papers.
13. These factors lead some scholars to photocopy whole books on occasion.
14. Richard Hopkins (page 114) noted that humanities scholars are reluctant to delegate research activity as serendipity is important. Similarly, he found that hesitation about using online searching stemmed from fear that serendipitous finds would be lost. However, they did admit that they often located sources too late for them to be of use with their traditional searching techniques.
15. As Liddy and Jorgenson noted in their study of the use of book indexes, we need greater insight into the physical and cognitive behavior of users so that electronic information-accessing systems will facilitate not hinder users' searching. (p. 188).
16. Watson-Boone, p. 213.
17. Prabha and Rice, p. 147.
18. Sabine and Sabine, p. 402.
19. Ibid., p. 403.
20. Making generalizations about reading habits from the few Columbia interviews is not scientifically valid. However, the reported reading patterns are consistent with the research done by others.
21. Scientists report that the bulk of scholarship in their disciplines is produced in papers published in journals.
22. Dillon, pp. 42, 54–56.

REFERENCES

Beheshti, Jamshid. "A Cross-Sectional Study of the Use of Library Books by Undergraduate Students." Information Processing & Management 25, no. 6 (1989): 727–735.

———. "A Longitudinal Study of the Use of Library Books by Undergraduate Students." Information Processing & Management 25, no. 6 (1989): 737–744.

Broadbent, Elaine. "A Study of Humanities Faculty Library Information Seeking Behavior." Cataloging & Classification Quarterly 6, no. 3 (Spring 1986): 23–37.

Chen, Ching-chih, and Peter Hernon. Information Seeking: Assessing and Anticipating User Needs. New York: Neal-Schuman Publishers, Inc., 1982.

Dillon, Andrew. Designing Usable Electronic Text: Ergonomic Aspects of Human Information Usage. Bristol: Taylor & Francis Inc., 1994.

———, John Richardson, and Cliff McKnight. "Towards the Development of a Full-Text, Searchable Database: Implications from a Study of Journal Usage." British Journal of Academic Librarianship 3, no. 1 (Spring 1988): 37–48.

Ellis, David, Deborah Cox, and Katherine Hall. "A Comparison of the Information-Seeking Patterns of Researchers in the Physical and Social Sciences." Journal of Documentation 49, no. 4 (December 1993): 356–369.

Getz, Malcolm. "Petabytes of Information: From Authors to Libraries to Readers." Advances in Library Administration and Organization 12 (1994): 203–237.

Hopkins, Richard. "The Information Seeking Behavior of Literary Scholars." Canadian Library Journal 46, no. 2 (April 1989): 113–115.

Kent, Allen, Jacob Cohen, K. Leon Montgomery, James G. Williams, Stephen Bulick, Roger R. Flynn, William N. Sabor, and Una Mansfield. Use of Library Materials: The University of Pittsburgh Study. New York: Marcel Dekker, Inc., 1979.

Kuhlthau, Carol Collier. "Longitudinal Case Studies of the Information Search Process of Users in Libraries." Library and Information Science Research 10, no. 3 (July 1988): 257–304.

Liddy, Elizabeth D., and Corinne Jorgensen. "Modeling Information Seeking Behavior in Index Use." Proceedings of the ASIS Annual Meeting 1993 30: 185–190.

Lougee, Wendy P., Mark Sandler, and Linda L. Parker, "The Humanistic Scholars Project: A Study of Attitudes and Behavior Concerning Collection Storage and Technology." C&RL 51 no. 3 (May 1990): 231–240.

Metz, Paul. The Landscape of Literatures: Use of Subject Collections in a University Library. Chicago: American Library Association, 1983.

Nilan, Michael S., Robin P. Peek, and Herbert W. Snyder. "A Methodology for Tapping User Evaluation Behaviors: An Exploration of Users' Strategy, Source and Information Evaluating." ASIS88: Proceedings of the 51st ASIS Annual Meeting 25 (1988): 152–159.

Nunberg, Geoffrey. "The Places of Books in the Age of Electronic Reproduction." Representations 42 (Spring 1993): 13–37.

Olsen, Jan. Electronic Journal Literature: Implications for Scholars. Westport: Mecklermedia, 1994.

Pinelli, Thomas E., "The Information-Seeking Habits and Practices of Engineers." in Information Seeking and Communicating Behavior of Scientists and Engineers. Cynthia A. Steinke, editor. New York: The Haworth Press, 1991, 5–25.

Prabha, Chandra G., Duane Rice, and John Bungee. "Access to the Full Text of Nonfiction Books: Design Considerations from a Study of Public Library Users." ASIS87: Proceedings of the 50th Annual Meeting 24 (1987): 196–200.

Prabha, Chandra G., Duane Rice, and David Cameron. Nonfiction Book Use by Academic Library Users. Dublin: OCLC Online Computer Library Center, Inc., 1988.

Prabha, Chandra G., and Duane Rice. "Assumptions About Information-Seeking Behavior in Nonfiction Books: Their Importance to Full Text Systems." ASIS88: Proceedings of the 51st ASIS Annual Meeting 25 (1988): 147–151.

Rice, Ronald E., and Patricia Tarin. "Staying Informed: Scientific Communication and Use of Information Sources Within Disciplines." Proceedings of the ASIS Annual Meeting 1993 30 (1993): 160–164.

Sabine, Gordon A., and Patricia L. Sabine. "How People Use Books and Journals." Library Quarterly 56, no. 4 (1986): 399–408.

Simpson, Annette. "Academic Journal Usage." British Journal of Academic Librarianship 3, no. 1 (Spring 1988): 25–36.

Watson-Boone, Rebecca. "The Information Needs and Habits of Humanities Scholars." RQ 34, no. 2 (Winter 1994): 203–16.

Wiberley, Stephen E., Jr., and William G. Jones. "Patterns of Information Seeking in the Humanities." C&RL 50, no. 6 (November 1989): 638–645.

———. "Humanists Revisited: A Longitudinal Look at the Adoption of Information Technology." C&RL 55, no. 6 (November 1994): 499–509.

Working Together on the Global Electronic Library

By Kerry Adrian Webb
National Library of Australia

Geoffrey Blainey is an Australian historian who coined the phrase "the tyranny of distance" to refer to the problems encountered by a country such as ours, remote in geography and in time from the major centers with which we wanted to deal, notably Europe (particularly Britain) and North America. Since the improvements this century in transportation and telecommunications, this has been less of an issue and with the past few years' experience of the Internet it has virtually disappeared.

Libraries in many countries have suffered from the same tyranny, having to battle on in often remote locations, being somewhat aware of what was going on elsewhere, being pretty sure that someone else had that extra bit of information that was needed by their patrons, and wishing they could get it now. We overcame this by using whatever technology presented itself (like fax machines for document delivery), and by cooperation. In many ways, the Internet is just a big extension of this. It is a new technology that libraries have embraced, and we are cooperating, but for a number of reasons cooperation is more needed than ever.

The reason for this is that we are being presented with the opportunity to build a global library that will be able to meet the needs of our patrons at a cost that is reasonably affordable. But if we don't work together, we will be wasting not only the opportunity but also the money which is being made available for a number of significant projects at present. I'd like to talk about some of these projects from a global perspective, looking at how cooperation is happening and how they may serve as models for further work.

G7 ELECTRONIC LIBRARIES PROJECT

The first and most extensive is the G7 Electronic Libraries Project, which is part of the G7 Information Society Program. This was discussed at a conference in Brussels in February 1995, which examined how emerging global communications technology can be best utilized for the benefit of society. That conference focused on regulatory frameworks and competition policy, implementation of information structures and accessibility for citizens, development of applications, and social and cultural aspects of the information society.

The Conference endorsed 11 pilot projects to demonstrate the potential benefits of the information society and stimulate its deployment, covering areas such as education, telemedicine, government information online and electronic libraries. The Electronic Libraries Project will be based on earlier work called Bibliotheca Universalis, which proposed a number of initiatives:

- establish an international steering committee ensuring international liaison between the relevant nominated national/regional/local agencies in the area of library and information networking;
- the steering committee should define a memorandum of understanding which can be broadly accepted by all participants;
- the steering committee should propose for decision taking a planning structure and timing based on the work already initiated in G7 countries;
- it will look after the coherence of the digitized collections. The selection of actual documents

to be compiled into databases will be left to each country's choice;
- it will give statements on technological solutions to ensure systems interoperability;
- it will focus on coordination with other G7 initiatives.[1]

Based on other projects within the Information Society Program, the way that this is likely to be implemented is that the steering committee will call for proposals for specific activities. It will decide on which of these proposals will be funded, and then call for tenders for implementing the proposals. The funds for all of the projects will come from the European Commission and they are substantial, running into many millions of dollars.

The point to be stressed in looking at how this will work is that it needs cooperation, and cooperation at a number of levels - within a country, between countries, between groups of countries (non-G7 countries have been invited to participate in the projects), and between the different projects. At the same time, the planners must be sensitive to the needs and aspirations of individual countries in considering "the coherence of the digitized collections." I'll return to this later.

Of course, it is a very bureaucratic approach - understandable when you consider that the process originated in the government sphere and will involve spending of large amounts of public money. But I doubt if it could be done in any other way, taking into account the large number of stakeholders. What is more difficult is using today's technology to make this sort of cooperative structure work. Much can be done with the use of e-mail for private messaging or distribution of documents, and we all appreciate the benefits of this, but in projects of this magnitude there is no substitute for getting on a plane and flying to a meeting to sit across the table from your colleagues. And that's where smaller, remote countries are again at a disadvantage.

JOINT ELECTRONIC DOCUMENT DELIVERY SOFTWARE

A project of a different kind is the Joint Electronic Document Delivery Software (JEDDS), involving the academic communities of Australia and the United Kingdom, and the National Libraries of Australia and New Zealand, with the cooperation of the Research Libraries Group in the US. JEDDS aims to develop electronic document delivery software that will give library users in the various countries greatly increased access to electronic information. The partners have agreed to jointly develop document delivery software which has a MIME-compliant delivery system. It will have the ability to interface to Interlending and Document Request Management Systems (IDRMS) through standard interfaces such as the international Interlibrary Loan protocol (ISO 10160/10161).[2]

The software to be developed will enable products to be delivered to most hardware platforms available, and will make use of the facilities within the Windows environment to allow streamlined or transparent interworking between the document delivery system and IDRMS, and associated software. It will also provide an ability for the end user to receive electronic documents via MIME mailers, and view and print documents on a variety of platforms.

The project partners have identified the enhancement of an existing document delivery product, Ariel, developed by RLG, as the preferred option for development. It also has links to work done by the Group on Electronic Document Interchange (GEDI) based in Europe and the US.

The reason that the National Libraries of Australia and New Zealand are involved together is that they are in the middle of a major development called the National Document and Information Service (NDIS), which is a bibliographic utility comprising advanced text database management and retrieval facilities and a range of document delivery services.

The management of the JEDDS project, with fewer participants than the G7 projects, is much simpler. Face-to-face meetings are occasionally necessary, but communication by phone, fax and e-mail is providing sufficient flexibility and functionality to enable considerable progress to be made in a short time. In JEDDS, the project is quite focused and the stakeholders have no trouble in sharing a common vision, so decision making is much simpler

OCLC METADATA

One project area where there is some concern about the lack of cooperation is in the mammoth task of creating the catalog of the Internet. OCLC is a leader in these developments, with its work on "persistent URLs" (PURLs) and especially on metadata, following its successful Metadata Workshop in March 1995. In the PACS-L list on 11 January, Karen Coyle said: "The results from the OCLC metadata workshop are being taken very seriously in the Internet Engineering Task Force world, one where librarians previously had no influence. But the work of a number of different groups on all or part of this 'catalog' seems to be going on without any overall coordination. My fear is that standards will be set in place through channels like the IETFs or other standards organizations without full discussion of all of us who have a stake in this."[3]

Mindful of this concern and the possibility of wasted resources in excessive duplication, organizations are having to build into their plans a degree of publicity to ensure that others are aware of their general developments. This won't always be possible. Commercial developers will not be sharing their plans and secrets with anyone, for obvious reasons, but those of us whose projects are publicly funded owe it to the community (and by this I mean the global community) not to duplicate our efforts.

So for the big projects in creating the infrastructure and the tools at the core of the global electronic library, there's no doubt that cooperation is necessary, but as the number of primary stakeholders increases and the difficulty of getting a shared vision grows, the cooperation is more difficult to accomplish. This is most obvious when we consider the creation of content for the global library. We do need to cooperate in this area too, but the big question is how to do it.

The Internet, with its easy access to publishing tools and relatively cheap storage costs, has been the prime example of the principle, "Let a thousand flowers bloom." Thus we see dozens of Home Pages featuring the biographies of Mulder and Scully from the "X-files" (each with its very artistic background images), a score of Simpsons' archives, and so on. I hesitate to make such criticisms, as my country has three "official" Federal Government Home Pages, each containing pretty much the same links to departments and agencies.

But that works for small activities, or those taken on by enthusiastic amateurs. With the sort of projects that will be going on for the electronic libraries, there's big money involved. I was asked recently to give a rough estimate for the cost of digitizing the complete collection of the NLA - it came to A$15–20 billion. (Our annual total budget is around A$50 million, and last year we spent less than A$100,000 on digitization.) When you're talking about that sort of figure, you'll be looking at all opportunities for cooperation, and not just with libraries. Developments in recent years have meant that we have access to a wide range of resources which are outside libraries, outside the control of libraries, and in many cases outside the knowledge of libraries.

Large organizations tend to start their digitization program with their "crown jewels," like the Library of Congress with its superb collection of Civil War photographs and the drafts of the Gettysburg Address, and the British Library's Electronic Beowulf project. You will also find that when a sponsor is involved, there is added pressure to make such a project a "blockbuster." Of course, there's nothing new in this—before the age of the digital library, there were always sponsors with great ideas for the most appropriate subjects for their donations.

And there is nothing wrong with using the initial funding (wherever it comes from) to make a splash, at the same time demonstrating what the new technology can deliver and giving the library staff some experience in using new tools and concepts. But the time must come when the pilot projects have made their mark and the real work of building the global library must begin.

THE NATIONAL DIGITAL LIBRARY FEDERATION

In this context, it's interesting to note the goals of the National Digital Library Federation, in the agreement signed in May 1995, specifically:

- The implementation of a distributed, open digital library conforming to the overall theme and accessible across the global Internet. This library shall consist of collections—expanding over time in number and scope—to be created from the conversion to digital form of documents contained in our and other libraries and archives, and from the incorporation of holdings already in electronic form.

and

- The formation of selection guidelines that will ensure conformance to the general theme, while remaining sufficiently flexible and open-ended to accommodate local initiatives and projects;

and to ensure that the digital library comprises a significant and large corpus of materials.[4]

Here is the basis for the global digital library (albeit with a US orientation), in line with the "coherence of the digitized collections" referred to in the G7 Electronic Libraries document referred to earlier.

So far, the selection guidelines for most institutions have been based on what is most attractive and what is easiest to manage. But has there been much thought given to what the public wants to see in the digital library? Talk to historians, and they'll confirm that of course the public wants to see the Civil War photographs, or images of paintings from the Australian goldfields of the 19th century, and they'll refer to the "educational market." But I'm not convinced. I have a feeling that what the public wants to see is an online version of a guide to Movies on Video or recent textbooks in popular subjects.

COPYRIGHT ISSUES

The problem with these suggestions is, of course, copyright. The public may want to see this material online, but in the absence of any simple way of charging per view (and it must be simple if it is to be widely accepted and implemented), the copyright holders will not be allowing online access. By a remarkable coincidence, the crown jewels that have been chosen so far are out of copyright.

At the National Library of Australia, we've had some experience of this with our Portraits Digitization project. In this, we've identified around 1300 portraits in our collection, photographed them where we don't already have a transparency and then scanned them at three resolutions—one thumbnail size for display on a Web page, one larger size for better display on the Web, and one of sufficient resolution for reproduction, to be supplied on demand for a reasonable charge. A major aspect of the project has been tracking down the copyright holders and gaining their permission for this. It has taken considerable time and most people have given their permission without any trouble. But that is quite a different issue from a copyright holder giving the same approval for a print publication to be accessed freely throughout the Internet.

The whole issue of copyright is one which will benefit from a coordinated approach. If we can work together in negotiating with the major publishers nationally and preferably internationally, we'll be better off. It's a big IF. What's more likely is that in each country, the local publishers' representatives will do their best to get a favorable result, with little regard for what has been done elsewhere. And the publishers being aware of the global nature of the collections that we're trying to build will be unwilling to make it too easy for one organization to put material online if that can then be accessed from anywhere else. It really is a global problem.

BUILDING COHERENT GLOBAL DIGITAL COLLECTIONS

But eventually we'll have to address the "coherence" issue. In a global electronic library, there should be a minimum degree of duplication, a maximum degree of access, and the greatest spread of subjects that we can achieve. How can this be done?

First, the duplication. I'm not saying there shouldn't be any, just that it needs to be minimized. To a certain extent, the crown jewels policy works well in this regard, as few of the documents and images which are the basis of these initial resources are duplicated. The important decisions come in the next step, in the acquisitions policies. Within organizations such as the National Digital Library Federation there can be broad agreement on such policies, but there does need to be wider consultation if we are to achieve a truly global library.

The best way to do this would be to encourage similar bodies to be set up in other countries, with the charter of arranging the digitization of those countries' resources in such a way that we can achieve coverage without unnecessary duplication. In coming to agreements between these organizations there would have to be trade-offs, based on expected patterns of usage and the access to the resources in question.

The access question is important. In the same way that you may not presently be able to rely on interlibrary loan from a particular library or region because of the other library's lending policies or unreliable postal services, so in the digital library there may be technical or organizational barriers to the access that you and your patrons may require. In that case, it may be necessary to have duplication of all or part of another library's collections.

There may be political questions on access. For example, the Library of Congress has for many years provided services to the world as a by-product of the services which it gives to the American community. Let's hope that it and the other great libraries continue to do the same in the digital world, but we can't rely on this. What is needed is a realization that each country needs to contribute to the global library as soon as it can. In this way, not only is the global collection enriched but the principles of sharing information can be strengthened.

In the arguments for building the national information infrastructures (NIIs), much is made of the benefits of information access to something called "competitiveness." A narrow interpretation of this concept may see barriers to international communication of information which is freely available in one particular country. This is surely not the aim of the architects of NIIs, and we need to work to ensure that access to information is not restricted in this way.

It's much more likely that the barriers to access will be technical, whether because of limitations in the communications infrastructure in a particular region or because the level of access to resources on a system is greater than that envisaged by the system planners. In the former case, there's not much to do except wait until things improve. Currently, many countries throughout the world look with envy at the communications possibilities in North America, Western Europe and even Australia, but it won't always be like that. Step by step, these countries will develop their facilities so that they can join the fun.

The latter case—user overload—is harder to deal with. We've seen many cases on the Internet in the past couple of years where a useful (or at least highly popular) resource has been put online only to disappear a short time later with the explanation that the usage was too much for the system to bear. This is particularly noticeable when the system owner is charged for data transmitted as well as received. When this sort of problem occurs, if you can't negotiate a better arrangement with the service provider, the best thing to do is consider mirroring the data at another site.

The final "coherence" issue will be to address the need for a wide range of subjects in the global electronic library. This will be the biggest challenge of all. As the goal of the National Digital Library Federation says, we need to remain "sufficiently flexible and open-ended to accommodate local initiatives and projects." How do you convince an organization that it should move in a direction not of its choosing? You can talk of accommodating local initiatives and projects, but decisions on who takes on responsibility for the major themes in the global collection will require plenty of negotiation.

One thing is sure—it can't be mandated from some "higher authority." If it is to be achieved somehow, it will have to be done in a spirit of cooperation. I suggest that we have a good model for this in existence—the Conspectus. Although there is some work relating to digital collections at present in the context of preservation, it is surely applicable also in this area of electronic collection development. And by extending the model to other countries, we will be able to get a truly global perspective on the issue.

Different types of projects involve different types of stakeholders and different types of cooperation. What works for one will not necessarily be suitable for all others, and we need to recognize this at the start. Even within a group of projects the management tools and styles will change as the projects progress. The "crown jewels" concept makes sense when things are starting out, but this needs to be changed as the projects mature and different outcomes are required. In this, as with everything else, we need to be flexible.

REFERENCES

1. "Initiatives." Bibliotheca Universalis. http://www.culture.fr/culture/bibliuni/engbu6.htm (24 January 1996).
2. "What is JEDDS." http://www.gu.edu.au/alib/iii/docdel/whatjedd.htm (24 January 1996).
3. Coyle, Karen. "Re: PURLS" PACS-L@UHUPVM1.UH.EDU (11 January 1996).
4. Peters, Paul Evan. "National Digital Library Federation Agreement Signed" http://solar.rtd.utk.edu/friends/telecomm/natl.digital.library.fed.html (24 January 1996)

The Future of Intellectual Organization

Reducing Complicity in Bibliographic Systems: An Exercise in Collaboration

By Judith R. Ahronheim, Kevin L. Butterfield, and Lynn F. Marko
University of Michigan

The bibliographic aspects of librarianship represent a long tradition that has been automated but not necessarily rethought. The networking of libraries with other information providers in a virtual universe presents us with opportunities to remodel our practices. Academic libraries increasingly form a part of campus, state, national, and global information systems. These systems represent differing communities and traditions of bibliographic access and retrieval. The academic research library, due to its size and mission, must stand ready to serve varying needs and constituencies within the university community. With the expansion of services into the realms of electronic texts and digital access, the library has had to both broaden its perspectives and narrow its focus—broadening in the sense that these new arenas require not only serving many diverse constituencies but working with them to develop content and access models; and narrowing in the sense that, while still serving the university community at large, specific paradigms of electronic access need to be developed with the distinct constituencies they are created to serve. Specific projects, specific users, and specific goals equal success in digital projects. On our campus, we have had the opportunity to test some of these assumptions.

In 1991 the University of Michigan Libraries, the University's School of Information and Library Studies, and the Information Technology Division began collaborating on the development of university-wide policies and structure to support the provision of access to electronic information and technologies. The initial collaboration on a "campus dialogue on the challenges of electronic information" has, at present, grown into the University of Michigan Digital Library. This is an umbrella name for a wide variety of projects that are associated with the delivery of digital information to users and that are administered and staffed jointly by members of all three organizations.

The Monographic Cataloging Division at the Hatcher Library has participated in both planning and production stages of several of these projects:

- The design of the prototype for the University's home page, the University Gateway, involving the collection, description, and organization of University related web pages, gopher sites, and databases.
- The standard cataloging, as well as provision of Text Encoding Initiative (TEI) headers, for the Humanities Text Initiative American Verse collection, a collection of digitized texts scanned from the University's paper collections and intended to be distributed through the University of Michigan Press. The Monograph Cataloging Division has established standards and practices for uniform TEI headers and for creating catalog records for both the SGML and HTML digital forms. We also have been involved in discussions on how these documents can best be accessed.
- The Michigan NSF/ARPA/NASA Digital Library grant that is focusing on the development of intelligent agents to aid in electronic resource discovery and retrieval. Catalogers have been involved in the design of the "conspectus," a standard for the description of electronic collections; in the development of attribute lists; in the creation of an ontology used to define the terminology employed by the Library's automated agents; and in advising on potential pitfalls in database maintenance.

In all these projects, working catalogers have labored alongside computer programmers, information scientists, and faculty members. The result has been a broadening of horizons on all parts. Our experience as library representatives in these collaborative efforts to organize and provide access to electronic forms of information has provided us with ideas on the nature of the changes now stirring in our field of endeavor and a vision of how these changes may affect the methods libraries use to serve their publics.

In an effort to serve these publics, modern academic libraries increasingly form a part of campus, state, national, and global information systems. These systems represent differing communities and traditions of bibliographic access and retrieval. The intent is that the resultant networking of libraries with these other information providers will be seamless to the user. Such a seamless environment presents us with opportunities to reconsider our cataloging practices in light of this shared information provision. That collaborative provision will press us to review the underlying economy of the services we deliver and the bibliographic models we use to deliver them. As we struggle to integrate our services with those of other providers, we will have the opportunity to participate in the cooperative design of more broadly based means of arranging and retrieving data and, thus, to embrace a more diverse set of bibliographic traditions in addition to our familiar ones.

Library practice has striven for a clear universal description and analysis of information. The forms and quantity of bibliographic objects that we need to describe have grown and diversified. In response, our practices of thorough and compulsory description have grown increasingly detailed and complex. Different communities have different conceptions of what and in what detail an object is described in a digital library. Their community of interests dictates the level of detail and description which they perceive as needed. Librarians can provide a valuable tempering influence as we participate in metadata use and development across communities. Many metadata systems are concerned with present day or timely description. We have experiential recognition of the fact that material thought to have little value twenty years ago is extremely important to research now. A librarian's perspective would add that while some information diminishes in value over time, the value of other information increases radically. Allowing only those influences in operation at the point of description to determine the describing and presenting of information may be a disservice to generations to come. We can be advocates for those future generations.

Grant-seekers and future-predictors have latched on to the phrase "digital library," but they do not necessarily mean the same set of services and concepts that we associate with "traditional" libraries. In fact, many of their notions of the "digital libraries" to come partake of traditions very different from those we associate with our own libraries. The concept of the library, as we know it presently, is that of a discrete set of controlled physical objects with controlled, pre-coordinated access. We provide this access through online catalogs that retain mostly paper functionality, albeit with keyword and remote access to other listings and catalogs. We traditionally offer this access to a wide population in a manner we expect to be universally understood. In contrast, the new world of the web and of many other information repositories is based on a more free and open flow of information, where "library" can mean a depository where information is placed (and removed) by contributors, rather than a selected set of objects chosen by collectors.

At present, serendipitous discovery is more common than is the focused searching or browsing done in traditional catalogs. Many of the database designers and programmers working to control this new world of information come from a tradition of service to known and limited, often specialist, populations. Where catalogers try to provide control to information at the front end (at the time an item is entered in a collection) through cataloging and authority work, other communities may prefer to control it at the back end (at the time of search) through the use of automated search agents and linguistic manipulation. Where traditional libraries have focused on describing the containers of information, these programmers often focus on accessing individual facts. Neither approach, the traditional library or the search agent in a hypertext environment, has been successful in making large quantities of electronic information accessible.

As we have participated in collaborative projects, we have begun to realize that working catalogers can provide a number of skills and perspectives of unique value to our engineer and researcher collaborators.

a) First and foremost is a production-oriented point of view. We are accustomed to making things work in volume and over time. b) Adjusting to a more experimental mode of operation, where not everything has to work in order to be of value, can be difficult. c) And yet, the importance we place on providing a useable product can help keep the rest of a team effort "honest" and focused on the final purpose of the effort at hand. d) In addition, those of us who work with large systems—in the range of millions of records—have a special perspective on the problems of scale-up and maintenance of these systems and can offer suggestions that, when applied at the design end, could make life easier for those who will have to keep the system useable, perhaps for decades to come.

The collaborative environment in which the Humanities Text Initiative operates illustrates these principles. It has provided, for catalogers, the opportunity to participate in the development of electronic textual access, as well as an opportunity for the exploration of additional alternative means of access and description for electronic humanities texts using the TEI guidelines. Collaborative endeavors combine to both broaden perspectives and throw new light on past practices. Ours is not the only community attempting to arrange a disordered information universe.

Our longer perspective may be one of the most valuable things we can bring to digital library design. Our hundred-year experience with naming conventions, authority control, and upgrading to meet new standards can provide designers of new systems with specific instances of challenges met and problems solved (not to mention problems unsolved). Our use of controlled vocabularies to manage language drift is an issue which frequently must be sold to computer system designers. In the case of Michigan's NSF Project, and after much discussion and debate, designers finally decided that controlled vocabulary may be the most efficient way to provide the kind of consistent access they wanted. The focus of development could then move to designing automated ways of controlling and incorporating controlled vocabularies into the database.

As catalogers, we stand at one point in a long continuum of database development, beginning with the invention of catalogs. To date, that development has produced a set of conventions that people learned as children and whose performance has been fairly predictable over long periods of time and over various cultures. Our commitment to retaining that fidelity, consistency, and predictability, even if the mechanisms of providing it change, is a value of our profession.

Catalogers are accustomed to scanning an object, distilling from its content a few general concepts, and relating those concepts to models of human knowledge that have been building since the time of Linnaeus and the Encyclopedists. New indexing methods, new search engines, and new theories of knowledge and chaos may significantly change those intellectual models, but the human need to orient oneself in relation to the information one seeks remains constant. Our wealth of experience in this distilling and relational process has yet to be analyzed or duplicated by automation specialists. As new models of information relationships develop, the input of catalogers can help keep these new models consistent and general enough to be understood by a wide range of users, as well as flexible enough to allow for the variation in manifestations we have encountered in our working lives. As we struggle to integrate our services with other information providers, the opportunity arises to design cooperatively a simpler, more broadly based means of arranging and retrieving data. The challenge for librarians over the next several years will be to forge, with these other information providers, a method of associating a variety of systems in such a way that consistent universal access can be provided.

Librarians always have been mediators of information. Through our contributions to the emerging information environments and through the development of skills with a number of information systems, we can return to our view of preserving our long-standing goal of universal access, albeit not necessarily through a universal system. As information mediators and service providers, we can continue through our mastery of content and of a number of metadata information systems to provide collocation of information from disparate resources and sources. In this effort, we need not make other information systems conform to MARC but rather, we need to understand the philosophy and design constructs other communities require in their information systems. Librarians/catalogers have the potential to participate in both the creation and mediation service sides of information delivery. In other words, librarians will provide service by integrating different resources into a coherent service whole, not necessarily a coherent system whole. Another aspect of service is the continuing support of controlled subject access in all information systems to assure vocabulary keeps pace with changes in technology. It is possible to conceive a system that allows for differing levels of description such that the access that is provided by others assures continuous utility.

The challenges are exciting and many. We have come to the obvious conclusion that the universe, in which we who are accustomed to organizing information work, is changing dramatically. Rather than being intimidated by these changes, we are asking our community to reconsider our traditional role and the service that we have provided in a new light. This may result in some redefinition and refining of our skills, but the path is there. We hope to participate in the excitement, respecting both the past and the future, while working toward reducing the complexity of our processes.

Cataloging for a Worldwide Digital Library: A Proposal for Organizing Ephemeral Metadata Information

By Peter D. Ciuffetti
SilverPlatter Information, Inc.

INTRODUCTION

Here at the dawn of digital libraries, library patrons seeking answers to questions navigate vast bodies of metadata, or "data about the data" looking for candidates. The importance of catalogs as an end-user tool has clearly surpassed the importance of their historic role as an administrative tool for inventory control. Yet catalogs of library collections are not sufficiently oriented with this important role in mind. Oddly enough, the bodies of metadata covering digital collections, which some might presume, given their high-tech profile, represent a "future of the cataloging art" are even less useful though they serve no other purpose than as searchable indexes to online material. What the world lacks is a practical approach to bibliographic description which transcends the incidental characteristics of the materials being described. We need to recognize the role of library professionals and the automated tools which they use to create the map of the world's knowledge while at the same time recognizing the needs of end users and the automated tools they use to find information.

This paper proposes a practical re-orientation for these catalogs which places emphasis on their fundamental use as a search tool for end users, in effect making a proposal for a new type of catalog which would better serve the emergence of a worldwide library. The proposal borrows a main perspective from computer science (which is my background) with a goal of stimulating thought among those who have library science as their primary background. Following the proposal is a brief summary of some current projects and proposals which include new approaches to cataloging. From these I extract characteristics which contribute to the overall theme of end-user navigation of metadata worldwide.

INFORMATION ATTRIBUTES WHICH INFLUENCE PRESENT CATALOGING

Not surprisingly, the characteristics of present catalogs are evident from the problems they first were designed to solve. The attributes of the information they describe led to the design of the catalog itself. There's one prevailing design for books in a library and another prevailing design for documents on a web site. These characteristics have endured despite the evolving nature of catalog use and the type of information they are responsible for describing. The following outlines the more obvious differences between prevailing catalogs of collections of physical artifacts and those organizing digital information. In this outline, I'm contrasting traditional catalogs found in library settings and the searchable indexes like Lycos and Alta Vista found on the web. Even though both are "digital" in how the information is stored, I'll call the former "library catalogs" and the latter "digital catalogs" giving emphasis to what is described, not how. The list below is not an attempt to contrast specific examples of these but rather to summarize the typical differences.

The scope of the catalog. Library catalogs describe primarily what is "held" by one or more institutions. Digital catalogs tend not to have institutional boundaries and they rely on the publisher/author to hold the item.

Professional imprimatur. An artifact described in a library catalog has quite often gone through a rigorous selection process and has been determined by a professional to be "worthy" in some respect, not the least of which is that the artifact has been "published", which is itself a complicated selection process. Digital catalogs tend to boast about their volume rather than their substance describing much material that is loosely published or not published at all

Extent to which the artifact is static. Digital artifacts are changeable and can be rendered to users in a variety of ways. Library catalog records assume that the artifact described will not/does not change.

Value added during cataloging. With human-generated classification and subject encoding, library catalogs add value through their descriptions. This is at best approximated by the automatic procedures which generate digital catalog records.

The unit of description. Library catalogs have well defined (though often local) rules for determining what constitutes a describable unit. Digital artifacts, particularly those exploiting hyperlinks, do not have readily identifiable boundaries. The tools used to generate descriptions of these artifacts may not attempt to discern the artifact's true boundaries, resulting in descriptions of incomplete items and single descriptions for what may be several items

The locus of the catalog. Digital catalogs are more likely to be hosted in a distributed fashion; the catalog itself may not live in one place.

Person or software as primary consumer. While both have ways of describing computer files, traditional descriptions of computer files are organized to assist human users while digital catalog records have fields designed to directly assist the computer processes which will use the item.

Presence of bibliographic information in the content. Either through Cataloging-in-Print (CIP) or other common approaches to print publishing, the metadata of traditional library materials is more readily identified. While bibliographic elements are difficult to determine from digital artifacts, cataloging tools have access to and might be able to analyze the full text.

Format variety. In describing a digital artifact, the cataloger may not have the software tools needed to render its content. Automatic digital cataloging tools must stop at hypertext links leading to documents in formats they do not understand (for example PDF). This is less of an obstacle in library catalogs, perhaps with the exception of foreign language materials.

Rate of new material, Rate of change of existing material. Web catalogs are dealing with an explosion of material that frequently changes.

This list is not exhaustive but it does illustrate how library catalogs and digital catalogs can be so different. A similar list could be developed for the differences between library catalogs and commercial bibliographic databases indexing and abstracting journal literature, since the attributes of the journal literature have led to unique processes for encoding that metadata. The resulting world of metadata, though rich and encompassing is at best hostile to the end user, yet without it I am sure to be lost. A library patron standing in the midst of a well-connected library with a question, might find the answer in a book, a journal article or a document on the Internet. If it is a complex question, one may need input from all three sources. Agonizingly, the metadata is organized in ways that create artificial boundaries between information of differing publication types. Clearly any system providing access to metadata summaries for only one or two of these sources either denies access to relevant materials or at best insists that the user employ multiple systems.

It would be folly to assume that a single system could, by itself, overcome the characteristic limitations which require one catalog use one format and construction process and another catalog use another format and construction process. A more relevant proposal would be to adopt a holistic approach to the organization and content of catalogs and A&I databases without compromising their primary design objectives.

WHAT I WANT FROM MY WORLDWIDE LIBRARY CATALOG

For the moment, I'll take an unabashedly end-user centric view of the requirements for a worldwide library catalog.

I want my library to "acquire" relevant digital material as well as physical material. In fact, the format and location are not the issues here as much as the notion of offering preservation for relevant digital works in light of web site instability. I want a single query mechanism to retrieve references to monographic, serial and electronic literature independent of the item's location. I want the result set to be oriented toward the most relevant materials that are the most readily available. Emphasizing quality over quantity; organizing duplicates in a way that limits the clutter they can represent. I want instant delivery of electronic material when available, converted as appropriate to formats I can deal with.

For physical items, I want assistance in finding a copy; any organization that is willing to show it to me, lend it to me or sell it to me. I want access to it from whatever desktop machine I am currently using, emulating the universal readiness of web catalogs. None of this is rocket science. Many individual systems, some described below, have successful implementations of subsets of these features.

GUIDING FACTORS TO THE APPARENT DESIGN OF A CATALOG

If the incidental characteristics of library materials are not adequate determining factors for the design of a catalog, what are? What's important in my end-user-centric view of a catalog is its apparent design, that is, the one that shows up while I am using it. If underneath, there are legacy systems using MARC and AACR2 and which constrain themselves to describing physical materials found on the shelves of some identified building, then fine, as long as this does not automatically constrain my search result sets.

The apparent catalog should be one that:

Describes items I can obtain nearby or from where I sit or can be obtained by the community I am a member of. Describes items deemed important by authoritative sources. Alerts me to items that are available were I willing to pay for them or go through some other procurement process (walking, driving, phoning, translating, whatever) to get them. Given the above criteria, this body of metadata might no longer fit the current definition of a "catalog." What I am really describing is the set of metadata the library has organized for the patron's benefit as a tool for finding answers to questions. Somewhere in the internals of this superstructure, a librarian might recognize the familiar catalog used for inventory control of the local items.

AN IMAGINARY PROCESS WHICH FEEDS THE WORLDWIDE LIBRARY WITH METADATA

The time is the future. Publishers or authors understand the importance of and play a role in the generation and distribution of quality metadata. This is linked to the item and, like CIP, coeval with the item. Publishers having a web presence also act as the distributor of the metadata. National libraries or other intermediate organizations like OCLC, RLIN and A&I services make up the difference for those publishers not participating in CIP. Collection development staff make judgments based on what web crawlers dig up. These web crawlers are programmed to find data conforming to some broadly expressed selection criteria. (This is in addition of course to all the other sensory data collection development staff use to determine what is to be held.)

Cataloging systems collect headers in their available format as the items are nominated for inclusion in the library's metadatabase. These are loaded into the catalog immediately. For all the serials a library chooses to subscribe to, the bibliographic A&I databases which index those serials are configured as "relevant" into their catalog so that catalog searches will encompass article level metadata and not just journal title metadata. Using a pay-per-view business model, this does not involve a purchase at the time of acquisition unless of course the library staff has determined that pre-payment or other bulk purchases are more cost-effective.

The value-added process of conversion to a local format, local classification, subject encoding and other content addition is more of a process of improving or adjusting the content of native headers in situ once they reside in the local catalog. Annotations are made using revision control technology. Users themselves have tools to attach private annotations to the descriptions. The amount of human attention a unit of metadata receives has more to do with the present perceived importance of a work not its orientation in a stream of newly acquired items. This allows the value added process to be applied to selected articles and electronic files as well as monographs; even older material if for some reason it returns to vogue.

What makes this process imaginary is the fact that much of this metadata is in different formats, and uses different controlled vocabularies, and some of it is free and other of it is not, and we know pub-

The Future of Intellectual Organization 339

lishers won't participate and librarians want the quality of local cataloging, and a host of other problems. What makes this process practical is that it preserves the cataloging value addition in a greatly expanded environment of metadata without requiring that individual cataloging staffs take upon themselves acquiring and cataloging everything.

Most of this proposed process has already been suggested by programs such as IFLA's Universal Bibliographic Control (UBC) and by Lorcan Dempsey who described an "all-through" system in 1991[1]. What I have added is the notion of eliminating the artificial boundaries which currently separate the metadata for journal literature and electronic files on the Internet.

TRANSITORY STRUCTURE OF METADATA

Given the data flow described in the previous section, we need to look at how it is all made searchable. In the spirit of the requirement that the end-user perceive a metadata navigation system encompassing monographs, serial and electronic publications, the metadata will need to be made searchable in one of two ways: either it will need to be configured into the local catalog in a format the navigation system can handle, or the navigation mechanism will need to seamlessly interoperate with the metadata where it resides in some remote system. As primarily a practical matter, I have above implied a two-step search process which emphasizes a "local" result set. That is, when I do a query of the catalog, I am first made aware of material which I can obtain locally that has been deemed worthy of local description by collection development staff. This local orientation further implies that the metadata included in this result set has been configured into the catalog.[1] If the result set obtained in this first pass does not satisfy me, then I employ an extended query mechanism. This extended query simultaneously searches some number of remote catalogs, perhaps hierarchically situated, that are maps of institutions capable of lending or selling information to me. The two step process allows for better performance in the normal case where the local collection will suffice. Any habitual multi-database searching of remote systems does not qualify one for good network citizenship so it is important to reduce the need for it.

In order to accommodate the local queries, some metadata will pass from an alien system to the local system and it may need to change formats and evolve in content to accommodate local requirements. A common theme of UBC, CIP, the Text Encoding Initiative (TEI) and many Internet-based digital library metadata approaches is the notion of metadata being available with the publication itself. Architects working on current digital library projects have proposed a variety of metadata formats designed for specific types of electronic data, with varying emphasis on ease of creation and richness of content. Others, notably Heaney [2], have proposed to re-architecture metadata to overcome the limitations of current cataloging processes thereby improving the service of catalogs to end-users and reducing the maintenance costs of catalogs for library staff.

CURRENT CATALOGING PROJECTS AND PROPOSALS

For the rest of this paper, I will shift focus to looking at metadata proposals and attempt to draw from them characteristics which I believe address the requirements of a broader scope end-user-oriented worldwide library catalog. In outline, here are the noteworthy proposals and works-in-progress I will analyze:

OCLC Intercat and CATRIONA
The Dublin CORE
TEI Headers
Object-oriented Cataloging
Z39.50 Explain
The Harvest System
ALIWEB and ROADS

OCLC INTERCAT AND THE MARC 856 FIELD

OCLC Intercat which uses the Library of Congress, Guidelines for the use of Field 856 [3] is an excellent example of a set of metadata that would fit well into existing catalog systems and search paradigms. Records in it are compatible with MARC-based systems, and use the AACR2 cataloguing rules. Intercat uses PURLs (Persistent URLs), a nice feature that assists with the maintenance of volatile location information for electronic resources. With the benefit of MARC and AACR2 though come the costs. The production of MARC records would not be simple (or even possible) for non-librarians. In the data-flow of metadata proposed above, I think of MARC records with an 856 field as a late-stage metadata effort; one that applies for important material where exerting professional effort is cost-justified or where the library intends to acquire the item.

A similar initiative to Intercat is the British Library's "CATaloguing and Retrieval of Information Over Networks Applications" (CATRIONA). "CATRIONA is a 6 month feasibility study funded by the British Library Research And Development Division. The purpose behind the CATRIONA project is to investigate the technical, organizational and financial requirements for the development of applications programs and procedures to enable the cataloguing, classification, and retrieval of documents and other resources over networks, and to explore the feasibility of a library system supplier led collaborative project to develop such applications and procedures and integrate them with one or more existing library housekeeping systems and associated OPAC interfaces." [4] The model CATRIONA intends to employ is one where Internet-accessible items are described by the library staff. The records themselves would be stored in traditional catalogs allowing users to search simultaneously for books and internet-accessible items.

THE DUBLIN CORE

The OCLC/NCSA Metadata Workshop report [5] defines a very brief set of metadata. It was designed to be concise and understandable by non-librarians. The description itself is syntax independent which allows the concepts of a core set of metadata to be applied to a variety of encoding mechanisms (as long as the encoding mechanism itself is generalized or readily extensible). The report proposes an SGML encoding although one could imagine a set of keyword=value pairs in a simple ASCII encoding. What looks like a useful feature of the Dublin Core is the ability to encode a hierarchical relation. For example, the metadata for an item could specify a relationship with another item like "Contained.In", "Is.Part.Of", "Child" and "Parent" (among others.) The Dublin Core is attractive as a suitable goal for author/publisher-generated metadata; a low-cost entry-point in the world of metadata for items in the early stages of release or where the life-span of the item is likely to be brief.

THE TEXT ENCODING INITIATIVE—TEI HEADERS

The Text Encoding Initiative [6] has taken a robust perspective on the importance of metadata. TEI headers in the SGML syntax allow a rich encoding of metadata accommodating details important in scholarly analysis of materials. Using SGML mechanisms, the header can either be separate from or attached to the work itself. In a publishing environment which uses SGML to encode the item, the TEI header would be a compatible way to include the metadata with the item without introducing foreign encodings. As such, one could imagine it being the "Cataloging in Print" of an electronic work. Since it uses SGML instead of MARC, it inherits flexibility and extensibility characteristics that elude the MARC format.

OBJECT-ORIENTED CATALOGING

Using object-orientation, Heaney [2] at Oxford has proposed a structure of the catalog that would enhance end-user searching and reduce duplication in the maintenance of the metadata. In the proposal, the metadata describes entities which have properties and perform roles. The entities can be the physical volume holding the content, the intellectual property inside it, the publisher, etc. Whereas a MARC record for an item concatenates into single record properties of all these entities, an object-oriented approach separates them into classes. Each entity then has a set of metadata [properties] relevant to the role the entity plays. These properties can be inherited by instances [e.g. editions] of the item when, as is usually the case for an item, one edition of an item has only a few variant characteristics but is otherwise identical, at least content-wise, to an earlier edition. Object-orientation also allows hierarchical classes of items where the properties of several related classes have been aggregated. This proposal improves the utility of a catalog for end users since searching for metadata falling into one class produces a result set that is not cluttered by duplicate records which vary only by some arbitrary (to the user) metadata detail in some other class.

Z39.50 EXPLAIN

The Z39.50 retrieval protocol [7] has an elaborate function called Explain which is a metadata solution for very complex objects such as databases. Through Explain, Z39.50 allows what I'll summarize as two realms of metadata: 1) metadata useful to the retrieval software so that it can discover databases and learn about retrieval capabilities of those databases and 2) metadata that allows the retrieval system to describe the database and its characteristics to the end-user. You can think of the former as a help system for the client software and the latter as a help system for users.[2] This is an important distinction and one that must prevail in any robust metadata system. Some metadata designs inadequately address one or the other whereas Z39.50 is rich in both areas.

In a retrieval session using Explain, a short, but intricate conversation goes on between the Z39.50 client software and the server software while they determine if they interoperate. This all happens in the background unknown to the end user. The conversation is one of a series of "can you...?", "yes, I can..." questions and answers which determine common capabilities. This is metadata passing back and forth and, for practical reasons, it must conform to a precise and efficient protocol language. Metadata which affects the internal logic of retrieval software cannot be encoded in the vagaries of natural language.

Similarly, end-users deciding on the appropriateness of a database cannot be expected to understand terse controlled-value labels or tags. To be helpful this type of metadata must use natural language. Explain provides a wide array of information such as database descriptions, disclaimers and coverage information as human-readable strings intended to help the end-user.

THE HARVEST SYSTEM AND THE GATHERER

The Harvest System [8], developed at the University of Colorado, is an automated process for gathering metadata for Internet-accessible resources. It uses a strategy for organizing the metadata called the Summary Object Interchange Format (SOIF) [9]. Content summaries in the SOIF format are generated by an automatic process called the Gatherer [10]. The Gatherer is configured at the host site to identify which sites contain relevant resources; it "provides a content extraction system that allows users to customize what data are gathered; whether data are gathered locally (which is more efficient but requires site cooperation) or remotely (which allows data to be gathered via the standard FTP/Gopher/HTTP protocols); how data are typed; what types of presentation-layer encodings (such as compression and network data representations) are handled; what data will be extracted into content summaries; and how data are extracted." [11]

A key feature in the Gatherer is that it will timestamp the content summaries. The system can then uses these timestamps to automatically control the frequency with which the content summaries are refreshed. It will also generate a hashing code called a "message digest" that systems can use to determine the authenticity of an item. If any bit is manipulated in an item, its message digest will no longer match the one recorded in the content summary.

ALIWEB AND ROADS

ALIWEB or "Archie-like Indexing for the Web", developed by Nexor in the UK, emphasizes the role of the host site in providing metadata [12]. Each host site using the ALIWEB model provides metadata in a format called an IAFA Template (Internet Anonymous FTP Archive) [13]. IAFA Templates and SOIF content summaries are similar, but the former are typically generated by hand. The tradeoffs of hand-generated templates versus automatically generated content summaries include speed, accuracy and cost.

The ROADS project "Resource Organisation and Discovery in Subject based Services" in the UK intends to use the IAFA template strategy: "The ROADS project will investigate the creation, collection and distribution of resource descriptions, to provide a transparent means of searching for, and using resources. The object is not to create an individual and idiosyncratic system but to draw on, and help create, standards of good practice which can be widely adopted by subject communities to aid and automate the process of resource organisation and discovery."[14]

SUMMARY

The following outline summarizes from these seven proposals characteristics which I feel are appropriate to consider and preserve in a holistic view of a worldwide library catalog:

OCLC Intercat and CATRIONA

MARC and AACR2 quality for important items
PURLs address volatility of URLs
Records stored as part of the traditional catalog

The Dublin Core

Brief, creator-friendly format for lesser importance items
Syntax independent
Hierarchical relations
More cost-effective to generate when the item count is high

TEI Headers

The CIP of electronic publishing

Object-oriented Cataloging

Efficient description and storage of similar items
Same principles of AACR2 but oriented toward end-user searching

Z39.50 Explain

Metadata for complex items
Record formats suitable for both human and software system consumption

The Harvest System

Automated generation and update
The ability to "look inside" binary formats when searching for metadata
Message digest stored with the metadata as a security mechanism

ALIWEB and ROADS

Host operators play a role in metadata preparation and maintenance

Given a superstructure which incorporates, in a convenient fashion, these characteristics in addition to journal literature metadata, then library patrons would have a truly useful tool for navigating the world's knowledge.

ENDNOTES

1. It bears emphasis that it is not a requirement that the metadata for important article literature and important web literature be physically loaded into one extended local catalog. Instead, a result set of this scope could be achieved by simultaneously searching a small set of systems; for example, a traditional catalog, a small set of journal indexes and a web catalog created and maintained locally.
2. While I describe these as two "realms", there are actually 17 different Explain record types which mix the metadata from the two realms together in a way that's convenient for the protocol. The two realms I describe are not actually specified in Z39.50 as separate systems of information.

REFERENCES

1. Dempsey, L. 1991. "Publishers and libraries: an all-through system for bibliographic data?" International Cataloguing and Bibliographic Control. 20(3), (Jul/Sep): 37–41. http://ukoln.bath.ac.uk/ukoln/publications/ubcim.rtf
2. Heaney, M. 1995. "Object-oriented Cataloguing." Information Technologies and Libraries 14(3), (Sep): 135–153.
3. Library of Congress, 1995. Guidelines for the use of Field 856. (March) http://www.nlc-bnc.ca/documents/libraries/cataloging/marc856.txt
4. CATRIONA; http://www.bubl.bath.ac.uk/BUBL/catriona.html
5. Weibel, S.; Godby, J.; Miller, E.; Danial, R.; 1995. "OCLC/NCSA Metadata Workshop Report" (March) http://www.nlc-bnc.ca/documents/libraries/cataloguing/oclcmeta.htm
6. Sperberg-McQueen, C.M.; Burnard, L. eds. 1994. "Guidelines for Electronic Text Encoding and Interchange." Chicago and Oxford, ALLC/ACH/ACL Text Encoding Initiative (May)
7. Information Retrieval (Z39.50): Application Service Definition and Protocol Specification (ANSI/NISO Z39.50-1995) Bethesda, MD: (NISO Press.) 1995 http://lcweb.loc.gov/z3950/agency/1995doce.html
8. Bowman, C. Mic; Danzig, Peter B.; Hardy, Darren R.; Manber, Udi; and Schwartz, Michael F. 1994. "The Harvest Information Discovery and Access System." Proceedings of the Second International World Wide Web Conference, Chicago, IL. (Oct): 763–771.
9. For information on the Harvest Summary Object Interchange Format (SOIF), see http://harvest.cs.colorado.edu/Harvest/brokers/soifhelp.html

10. Hardy, Darren R. and Schwartz, Michael F. 1995. "Customized Information Extraction as a Basis for Resource Discovery." Technical Report CU-CS-707–94, Department of Computer Science, University of Colorado, Boulder, March 1994 (revised February 1995). To appear, ACM Transactions on Computer Systems.
11. For information on the Gatherer, see http://harvest.cs.colorado.edu/harvest/technical.html#subsystems
12. For information on ALIWEB, see http://www.nexor.co.uk/public/aliweb/doc/introduction.html
13. Deutsch, P.; Emtage, A.; Koster, M.; Stumpf, M. 1994. "Publishing Information on the Internet with Anonymous FTP." Internet Draft http://www.nexor.co.uk/public/aliweb/iafa/rfc/iafa.txt.
14. Hiom, D.; Dempsey, L.; Norman, F. 1995. "ROAD to Resource Discovery" Library Association Record, 97(7), (July): 134. http://ukoln.bath.ac.uk/roads/pub/lar.html

Lessons Learned from the Development of a Global Information System

By Christopher Davis and Cheryl J. Burley
Consortium for International Earth Science Information Network (CIESIN)

INTRODUCTION

Since its founding in 1989, the Consortium for International Earth Science Information Network (CIESIN) has been building a global information system related to human interactions with the environment. CIESIN's Information Cooperative Program, a globally distributed information system that allows major international data archives and resource centers to catalog and share information electronically, has required establishing relationships with many organizations worldwide ranging from the National Library of Estonia to the World Bank. The international, interdisciplinary issues associated with information access among this diversity of geographically-distributed organizations has required development of a flexible toolbox of Internet-based systems for data and information dissemination. In addition, it has required active participation in groups developing standards for cataloging diverse, distributed, on-line information resources. The distributed, collaborative organizational model utilized to implement the Information Cooperative is a pioneering example of the potential of the Internet to provide infrastructure to link the resources of individual institutions and expand the range of users, and highlights the importance of information brokering expertise and services in successful information initiatives.

BACKGROUND

CIESIN was formed with the mission to provide access to and enhance the use of information worldwide, advancing understanding of human interactions in the environment and serving the needs of science and public and private decision-making. CIESIN is intended to serve as a bridge between the natural sciences and social sciences to enable a more informed understanding of the interactions between human activity and the environment. To accomplish this, CIESIN seeks to identify key data and information resources focused particularly in the social sciences and to provide access to these resources.

While no existing data archive offers a collection that spans the interdisciplinary needs of CIESIN, many individual organizations provide access to relevant data. In many cases, these organizations are data archives or libraries for specific disciplines, but in other cases the organizations are governmental and non-government organizations that have collected data and information resources for administrative and other purposes.

One approach to enhancing access to these resources would have been development of an interdisciplinary, centralized data archive and library by replicating the data holdings of these other organizations at CIESIN. This approach would have been not only labor and equipment intensive, it lacked political feasibility. Organizations are very protective of the data and information they provide, and CIESIN has had only limited success in the instances where they sought permission to distribute data from other organizations. These realities combined with the evolution of the Internet in the early 1990s lead CIESIN to develop alternative strategies for data archiving based on a distributed network of data provider nodes.

The core of these strategies is the Information Cooperative, a network of organizations worldwide, joined by agreements with the common goal of data and information sharing. The Information Cooperative provides an institutional mechanism for linking the distributed and interdisciplinary capabilities of a global collection of organizations into a virtual data archive and library. As of early 1996, the Information Cooperative partnership had over seventy members, spanning every continent except Antarctica (see Appendix A: CIESIN's Network of Organizations and Data Centers). Partners include traditional data archives, governmental agencies, multilateral and non-governmental organizations, universities, and libraries.

Parallel to the development of the institutional relationships of the Information Cooperative, has been the development of an electronic information system to enable the location and access of data resources available through the Cooperative. Initially, the primary component of this information system was the CIESIN Gateway, an information access system developed by CIESIN to enable parallel searching of distributed, heterogeneous metadata databases over the Internet. (Cicone and Abreu, 1995) More recently, the World Wide Web (WWW) has also played an increasingly important role as an enabling technology for the Information Cooperative.

The potential for the Information Cooperative to serve as a model for the future of digital libraries, is indicated by the external recognition that CIESIN has received. The CIESIN Gateway won the 1995 Computerworld Smithsonian Award for information technology in the area of Environment, Energy, and Agriculture. The Information Cooperative program itself was a finalist in the 1995 National Information Infrastructure Award Program. CIESIN has also been designated by the International Council of Scientific Unions (ICSU) as a World Data Center (WDC-A) for Human Interactions in the Environment.

These achievements and successes have not been without setbacks and CIESIN has learned much from them. There are five key lessons that may benefit others and that point to a vision of the future of information dissemination and the role of information intermediaries in the digital arena.

Lesson #1:
The Benefits of Centralized Decentralization: Broker information services for information users and providers

One of the great assets of the Internet is its distributed architecture. Any organization on the Internet is free to make its information available in the manner appropriate for the organization and its users. This strength, though, is also a weakness. It contributes to the difficulty of information discovery described previously, and it also results in information being made available in an inconsistent fashion across sites, causing search and retrieval difficulties for users. CIESIN's Information Cooperative provides an institutional response to this problem by acting as an information intermediary or broker between data providers and users (see Figure 1). As the Information Cooperative has developed, the need for several types of information brokering services has emerged, such as:

- Insuring that information access is provided to users regardless of location and limitations of network access, such as low bandwidth;
- Understanding user needs and responding with access tools and applications which allow users to effectively filter the ever-increasing volume of available information;
- Developing and maintaining catalogs of resources which facilitate information location;
- Developing, maintaining and promoting the use and benefits of standards for information description to insure that users continue to have access to useful, quality information content; and
- Training both information providers and users about effective information description, organization, management and access techniques.

Successful information brokering services are provided by professionals such as data and information specialists and librarians, with information management expertise and knowledge of user communities and needs; combined with the expertise and skills of professionals such as computer scientists, systems analysts and engineers. Organizations and institutions which incorporate this expertise and position themselves as information brokers will be providing needed information services to both information users and providers. As more and more individuals and organizations use the Internet to disseminate information, the information broker and the services provided will be increasingly important. This expertise and these services are at the heart of the emerging digital library.

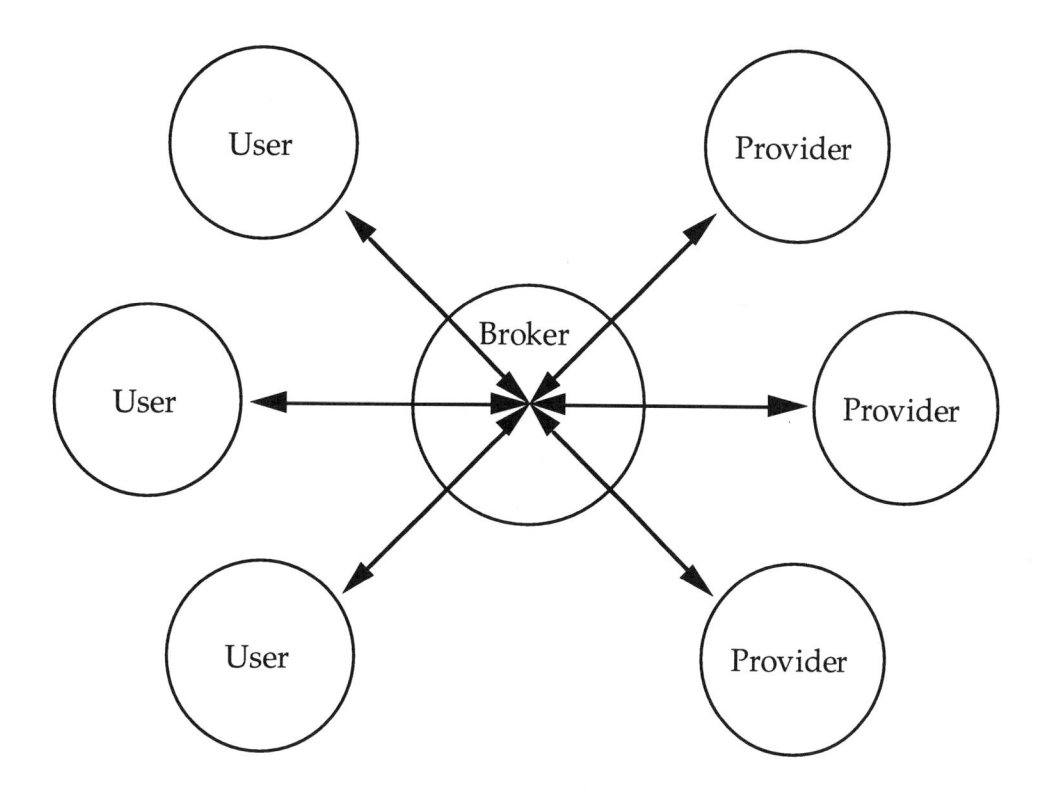

Figure 1. User-Broker-Provider Model

Lesson #2:
The Problem of the Information Explosion: Facilitate information retrieval through integrative searching

The explosion of the Internet and WWW has created a new venue for data and information scavenger hunts. While this may be entertaining, it does represent a problem for a user in search of relevant information for a practical purpose. Retrieving large quantities of information is relatively easy; filtering this for precise information is typically more difficult.

To find information on a specific topic, users have two primary on-line search approaches available. One approach uses a topical or subject index, where the user can select from an organized list of categories. Yahoo! (Yahoo! Corp., 1996) is an application implemented in this way. This approach is limited by the categorization scheme used by the list creators, the amount of descriptive information presented about a particular resource (often only a title or brief excerpt), and at the end of the search, the user may be confronted with a long list of resources to examine individually for relevance. The other approach is to use one of the several query tools that will perform an automated search of a subsetted index of the WWW, such as Lycos (Lycos, Inc., 1996) and Infoseek (Infoseek Corporation, 1996). This approach leads to similar results: a long list of links with little distinguishing information and which likely includes everything from personal home pages to scientific articles. Either approach forces the user to personally examine each link very closely, and even then the relevant information may be buried several layers deep in a specific site.

CIESIN's Gateway provides a hybrid approach. Gateway users search indexed descriptions of resources (metadata) organized in a catalog, rather than an index of the resources themselves. The catalog is geographically distributed, and the Gateway conducts searches across the multiple metadata collection sites. Resources have been selected based on the criteria appropriate to the Information Cooperative and other anticipated users, which provides an initial filter. Metadata are created as structured text containing descriptive abstracts and additional access points, such as subject and geographic index terms. The metadata support searches of specific attributes, or free text searches of the metadata record if desired. These search options provide more flexibility to the user to select search methods and construct search strategies most appropriate to meet their needs (Lancaster and Warner, 1993). For example, when conducting free text searches users are not bound by a categorized list of subjects which may or may not be meaningful. Alternatively, because the search target is typically structured metadata to which index terms have been added, the user may more easily narrow a search by using controlled index terms or select specific attributes to search. While the user still retrieves a list of items, these items are metadata rather than the resources themselves. The metadata are typically brief and reasonably uniform, thus the user is able to more easily scan a large number of items and identify those of interest. Descriptions also contain access instructions for obtaining the resources and, whenever possible the CIESIN Gateway supports direct access to on-line resources by linking to URLs embedded in the metadata.

Lesson #3:
Dealing with the Burden of System Heterogeneity: Address access issues associated with system and organizational heterogeneity

CIESIN's Information Cooperative is composed of many different types of organizations, each with a unique collection of data and information resources (Burley 1995). These organizations employ a variety of methods for accessing and disseminating their resource collections. Integrated access to heterogeneous collections can be problematic and CIESIN has focused its efforts toward improved access on the integration of metadata catalogs. CIESIN has examined several approaches to catalog integration or interoperability which are currently in use and employs a combination of several.

One approach is to establish a common standard for describing and accessing catalogs. The U.S. Government Information Locator Service (GILS) (United States Geological Survey, 1994) is an example of this approach. A related approach is to establish a common standard for describing resources themselves, such as Anglo-American Cataloging Rules (AACR) (The Joint Steering Committee for Revision of AACR, 1988) or the Federal Geographic Data Committee's (FGDC) Content Standards for Digital Geo-spatial Metadata (Federal Geographic Data Committee, 1994). Many descriptive standards exist, and while they may be appropriate for describing particular information resources and useful to specific user communities, they may be inappropriate for other uses and users. To be successful, effective use of a common standard may require participating organizations to adopt the selected standard and either abandon existing systems or support multiple standards and systems. Either approach may require substantial efforts which are likely to be expensive for participating organizations.

Another approach is to use the lowest common denominator of description or access mechanisms across a shared catalog system. For descriptions, this may mean using a very brief metadata record containing only those attributes upon which participating organizations can agree (Wood, Bhatia, and Burley, 1995). This agreement is not only difficult to negotiate, it may result in the loss of much potentially valuable metadata in favor of a minimal record presented to users at the end of a catalog search. For search systems, the lowest common denominator may only allow a free text query with little means of filtering or narrowing a search.

To resolve issues associated with system heterogeneity, organizational heterogeneity must be addressed. CIESIN has worked with two general types of organizations: those which focus on disseminating information, and those which focus on generating or collecting data and information.

Data centers where the primary purpose is the dissemination of information may already have a significant investment in existing catalog systems and are usually unwilling or unable to adopt new descriptive standards. Typically, these organizations require catalog interoperability through the lowest common denominator in order to make use of existing resources. Data centers which lack local catalog systems, are generally open and receptive to a standardized approach. In fact, for this type of organization, a standard and proven approach to catalog access and interoperability is often desired.

Organizations which generate data as part of their primary function, including many government agencies, typically have minimal interest in cataloging their information resources. These organizations generally view information dissemination as low priority and cataloging an even lower priority, especially when their catalog may consist of only a few items. Providing access to resources at these organizations may be accomplished by conducting catalog development and maintenance functions on their behalf.

These examples demonstrate the need for diverse approaches to catalog development and interoperability. Rather than selecting a single specific approach, CIESIN has implemented its systems to accommodate this organizational heterogeneity, premised on the belief that institutional autonomy and organization-specific requirements should be supported, rather than subsumed, by the Information Cooperative whenever possible. Thus the Information Cooperative employs different description and access options based on the specific needs of the participating partner organization.

To illustrate, the CIESIN Gateway employs the Directory Interchange Format (DIF) (NSSDC, 1993), initially developed by NASA, to provide the basic structure of metadata records. Metadata elements within the format are fairly general and organizations can add more specific elements as needed. Systems based on DIF, or approximating DIF, can be searched using attributes through the CIESIN Gateway. Systems not using DIF can be searched using a simple free text search simultaneously. This implementation presents several alternatives to suit specific Information Cooperative partner needs.

Another method employed by the Information Cooperative to promote catalog integration is offering common information management software which allows organizations without existing catalog systems to develop and maintain one. Specific written guidelines (CIESIN, 1995b) and an indexing vocabulary (CIESIN, 1995a) have been developed to assist organizations in creating metadata. These aids may be used with CIESIN's specialized software or with other cataloging tools. Training in standardized methods of information description, metadata management, and system administration is available to Information Cooperative partners as needed. These approaches help to increase standardization and contribute to a similar look and feel across sites while simultaneously allowing local flexibility as appropriate. Meeting the individual needs of each type of organization is an important key to success in developing a distributed information system.

Lesson #4:
The Perils of Software Development: Consider alternatives to custom software development

The development of customized software solutions has allowed CIESIN to design systems tailored to specific user requirements. However, this flexibility comes at a price. For example, in the early 1990s when CIESIN began development of the CIESIN Gateway, a long list of requirements and features was developed. As time went on, this list was amended and added to, resulting in a very long development cycle. During that time, the Internet was transformed through the development of the World Wide Web. The software and standards underlying the WWW are relatively simple and in many ways not very efficient, but this simplicity allows for flexibility and rapid deployment of applications and information. Many organizations give up functionality in favor of speed of availability. CIESIN has now adopted a strategic approach of integrating the customized CIESIN Gateway and the WWW. For example, the CIESIN Gateway provides access to URLs contained in structured catalog records, and a WWW interface to the Gateway is being tested.

A lesson learned is to carefully weigh the trade-off of time versus functionality. A simple system may be available quickly and provide needed momentum for an idea or project. Customized systems take more time, and users and providers may not be willing to wait. In instances where custom system development is required, prototyping and rapid application development can reduce the risks of system development and increase user involvement in development projects. Large development projects can also be broken down into smaller, tangible components, facilitating management and user involvement.

Another important lesson is the importance of the systems requirements process. Users and developers must both have an agreed, clear understanding of requirements at an early stage in the development process. Prototyping and mock-ups can facilitate communication and enhance the design process, reducing the risks of re-design at later stages in the development process. System development can also be implemented in an incremental process. Rather than meeting all requirements in version 1, some functions can be implemented as enhancements in later versions. Changes in requirements in the middle of system development inevitably lead to increases in the time and cost of development. These changes can also be incorporated in planned future releases. A staged development process also builds in the opportunity to take advantage of new technologies at each incremental stage. System development is an evolutionary process. Rarely will it be done right on the first try, and significant lessons can be learned through successive approximations of the ideal system.

Lesson #5:
Limits of Internet Infrastructure: Accommodate the needs of low-bandwidth users

The explosive growth of the Internet provides the infrastructure for a major transformation in the way that information is disseminated. The emergence of the WWW as a flexible, widely available, and easy to use technology fuels this fire. Both organizations and individuals can easily use the WWW and Internet to make a wide array of information available to a sizable audience. Information published on the Internet is immediately accessible around the world 24 hours a day, 7 days a week. This creates the potential for anyone with Internet access to become an information publisher.

Despite the potential of these technologies, they have important limitations. First, the Internet is not a global information infrastructure, and Internet connectivity does not guarantee efficient access to available resources. Even in industrialized areas such as North America, Internet access is limited to a relatively small community of the technological elite with a fairly substantial computing and telecommunications infrastructure. Also, many Internet users who have a computer, modem, and telephone line are limited to slow speed connections that restrict access to e-mail and similar services. This problem is even more significant throughout the rest of the world, including Western Europe. These limitations can create a substantial barrier to the use of on-line information.

To overcome this barrier, CIESIN has developed e-mail interfaces to WWW resources and the CIESIN Gateway and is researching how to use similar techniques to provide access to on-line databases (Davis, 1995). In addition to developing WWW-based services, information providers should also consider the use of e-mail interfaces to services. This approach enables access to a wide range of users worldwide who lack the Internet connectivity to use WWW but can easily send and receive e-mail. At a minimum, designers of WWW pages should keep in mind potential network bandwidth limitations of users before publishing large, graphic-intensive pages.

CONCLUSION

The growth of the Internet, the emergence of the World Wide Web, and the proliferation of information access applications are significantly reducing barriers to widespread information dissemination. As a result, the potential for improved access to distributed archives and libraries is greatly increased. However, the rise of distributed digital libraries is also accompanied by organizational and operational changes for information intermediaries, such as libraries, information access organizations, and the librarians and information specialists which staff them.

As an organization whose primary role is to provide access to digital data and information, CIESIN is attempting to incorporate and extend previously successful information provision models into its operations and organizational structures. For example, the Information Cooperative is conceptually similar to cooperative cataloging and cooperative collection development initiatives, but operates in a primarily decentralized, digital environment. Also, primary access to Information Cooperative data and information collections is provided through standardized catalogs of metadata, but usefulness and flexibility of these catalogs is extended using improved indexing and retrieval tools which support multiple metadata standards and user needs. The lessons learned using these access models and techniques to build a distributed information system are helping to identify appropriate future directions and needed services for information intermediaries. More importantly, they have reinforced the need for institutions and individuals with expertise in information organization and access, to position themselves as intermediaries or brokers between information users and providers, and to build organizations and cooperatives which provide these increasingly valuable information brokering services.

REFERENCES

Burley, Cheryl J. 1995. "Socioeconomic and geo-spatial metadata access: Issues in compliance and interoperability." Paper presented at Science Information Systems Interoperability Conference, November 6–9, 1995, College Park, MD. (For abstract see: http://hollywood.gso.uri.edu/sisic/burley.html)

Cicone, R.C. and V.J. Abreu 1995. "Data sharing: an information co-operative." In TERRA 2 Understanding the Terrestrial Environment: Remote Sensing Data Systems and Networks, ed. Paul M. Mather, pp. 93–102. West Sussex, England: John Wiley & Sons, Ltd.

Consortium for International Earth Science Information Network (CIESIN). Metadata Administration. 1995b. CIESIN Metadata Guidelines. University Center, Mich.: CIESIN.

Consortium for International Earth Science Information Network (CIESIN). Metadata Administration. 1995a. CIESIN Indexing Vocabulary. University Center, Mich.: CIESIN.

Davis, Christopher. 1995. "Electronic mail access to on-line science resources." Paper presented at Science Information Systems Interoperability Conference, November 6–9, 1995, College Park, MD. (For abstract see: http://www.ecologic.net/mjk/sisic/S3_CDavis.html)

Federal Geographic Data Committee (FGDC). 1994. Content Standards for Digital Geospatial Metadata (June 8). [online] Washington, D.C.: FGDC. http://geochange.er.usgs.gov/pub/tools/metadata/standard/metadata.html

The Government Information Locator Service (GILS). 1994. [online]. N.p.: United States Geological Survey (USGS). http://www.usgs.gov/public/gils/gilstoc.html

Infoseek Corporation. 1996. Infoseek. [online]. Santa Clara, CA: Infoseek Corporation. http://www.infoseek.com

The Joint Steering Committee for Revision of AACR. 1988. Anglo-American Cataloging Rules. 2nd ed., 1988 rev. Prepared by the American Library Association, the British Library, the Canadian Committee on Cataloging, the Library Association, and the Library of Congress. Edited by Michael Gorman and Paul W. Winkler. Chicago: American Library Association, London: Library Association Publishing Limited, Ottawa: Canadian Library Association.

Lancaster, F. Wilfred, and Amy J. Warner. 1993. Information Retrieval Today. Arlington, VA: Information Resources Press.

Lycos, Inc. 1996. Lycos, Inc. : The Catalog of the Internet. [online]. N.p.: Carnegie Mellon University. http://www.lycos.com

National Space Science Data Center. 1993. Directory Interchange Format Manual: Version 4.1. Greenbelt, Maryland: Goddard Space Flight Center, NASA.

Wood, L., M.T. Bhatia and C.J. Burley. 1995. "The challenge of metadata development in a multi-disciplinary environment." In TERRA 2 Understanding the Terrestrial Environment: Remote Sensing Data Systems and Networks, ed. Paul M. Mather, pp. 123–128. West Sussex, England: John Wiley & Sons, Ltd.

Yahoo! Corp. 1996. Yahoo! [online]. Sunnyvale, CA: Yahoo! Corp. http://www.yahoo.com

APPENDIX A:
CIESIN'S NETWORK OF ORGANIZATIONS AND DATA CENTERS

I. Partners

Administrative Center for China's Agenda 21 (ACCA21), China

The Agency for Toxic Substances and Disease Registry (ASTDR), U.S. Department of Health and Human Services, USA

Biotech Consortium India Ltd. (BCIL), India

Center for Indigenous Knowledge and Rural Development (CIKARD), USA

Center for International Research and Advisory Networks (CIRAN), Netherlands

Center of Information and Communication of the Environment of North America (CICEANA), Mexico

Chiang Mai University, Thailand

China in Time and Space Project (CITAS), USA

Chinese Academy of Sciences (CAS), China

Chinese Academy of Surveying & Mapping (CASM), China

Chinese Economic Monitoring Center (CEMC), China

Chinese Ecosystem Research Network (CERN), China

Chinese Population Information & Research Center (CPIRC), China

Commission for Integrated Survey of Natural Resources (CISNAR), China

Consultative Group on International Agriculture Research (CGIAR), USA
Department of Social, Labor and Institution Statistics of Canada, Canada
Earth Resources Observation System (EROS) Data Center (EDC), U.S. Geological Survey, USA
Economic and Social Research Council (ESRC) Data Archive, United Kingdom
Environmental Protection Agency (EPA), USA
Estonian Interuniversity Population Research Center, Estonia
Food and Agriculture Organization (FAO), Italy
Global Change Research Information Office (GCRIO), USA
Harris Center, Institute for Research in Social Science (IRSS), USA
Human Dimensions of Global Environmental Change Programme (HDP) of International Social Science Council (ISSC), USA
International Centre for Research in Agroforestry (ICRAF), Kenya
International Crops Research Institute for Semi-Arid Tropics (ICRISAT), India
International Institute for Applied Systems Analysis (IIASA), Austria
Inter-University Consortium for Political and Social Research (ICPSR), USA
International Development Research Centre (IDRC), Canada
International Programs Center (IPC), USA
IUCN - The World Conservation Union, Switzerland
Keio University, Japan
Leiden Ethnosystems And Development (LEAD), Netherlands
Millenium Institute, USA
National Technical Information Centre (OMIKK), Hungary
NERISENA, Lithuania
Organization of American States (OAS), USA
Pan-African Development Information System (PADIS), Africa
Peking University, China
Polish Academy of Sciences (PAS), Poland
Population Reference Bureau (PRB), USA
RIVM (National Institute of Public Health and Environmental Protection in the Netherlands)
The Roper Center for Public Opinion Research (Roper), USA
South African Data Archive (SADA), Africa
Swedish Social Science Data Archive (SSD), Sweden
SWIDOC, Steinmetz Archive, Netherlands
Thane Belapur Industries Association (TBIA), India
Third World Network of Scientific Organizations (TWNSO), Italy
United Nations Development Programme (UNDP), Ukraine
United Nations Development Programme/Sustainable Development Networking Programme (UNDP/SDNP)
United Nations Educational, Scientific, and Cultural Organization (UNESCO), France
United Nations Environmental Programme (UNEP), Kenya
United States Department of Agriculture (USDA), USA
University of Latvia, Latvia
Warsaw University, Poland
WETV Global Access Television Service (WETV), Canada
World Bank, USA
World Conservation Monitoring Center (WCMC), United Kingdom
World Health Organization (WHO), Switzerland
World Resources Institute (WRI), USA
Zentralarchiv fur Empirische Sozialforschung (ZA), Germany

II. Pending Partners

Arab Academy for Science and Technology (AAST), Egypt
Asian Institute of Technology (AIT), Thailand
Center for Agriculture and Biosciences International (CABI), United Kingdom
Griffith University, Australia
International Fertilizer Development Center (IFDC), USA
Institute for Graduate Studies and Research (IGSR), Egypt
Instituto Nacional de Ecologia (INE), Mexico
Instituto Nacional de Estadistica, Geografia e Informatica (INEGI), Mexico
Norwegian Social Science Data Services (NSD), Norway
Regional Environmental Center (REC), Hungary
Regional Information Technology and Software Engineering Center (RITSEC), Egypt
Tropical Soil Biology and Fertility Programme (TSBF), Kenya
World Engineering Partnership for Sustainable Development, USA

Unique Permanent Identifiers for Management and Retrieval of Distributed Digital Documents

By Rebecca Lasher
Stanford University

INTRODUCTION TO URNS

Most Web users know about URLs (Uniform Resource Locators). These are locations that browsers use to find and display networked resources. URLs look like this: http://www.server.edu. Web browsers retrieve URLs by looking up the IP address in Domain Name Servers (DNS).

> In Domain Name Servers
> http://www.server.edu = IP: xxx-xx-xx

The problem with location dependent identifiers is that the files move around. They move because new versions of applications may change the file structure which in turn changes all of the machine addresses. Files move from magnetic to optical disks. Files move when computers are replaced.

The solution for web masters and library catalogers creating bibliographic records that name electronic resources is a permanent unique identifier. The Internet Engineering Task Force (IETF) has been working for several years to come up with such an identifier. These permanent unique identifiers, often called Uniform Resource Names, (URNs) will work with a mechanism like the DNS table lookup above to resolve the identifier to a URL.

URNs are being defined by a URI (Uniform Resource Identifier) working group. URNs fit within a larger Internet information architecture, which in turn is composed of, additionally, Uniform Resource Characteristics (URCs), and Uniform Resource Locators (URLs). URNs are used for identification, URCs for including meta-information, and URLs for locating or finding resources. It is provided as a basis for evaluating standards for URNs. (Sollins 1994)

URNs according to an Internet document called RFC1737 (RFC=request for comments) must meet several requirements: requirements for functional capabilities (global scope, global uniqueness, persistence, scalability, legacy support, extensibility, independence, resolution); requirements for URN encoding (single encoding, simple comparison, human transcribability, transport friendliness, parsability) (Sollins 1994).

There is no shortage of proposals for URN schemas. The various proposals and their criticisms can be found in Internet working drafts. See the reference section below.

Most groups working on this problem agree that several types of URNs will be needed to meet multiple needs of divergent groups. There is agreement on the general form of a URN but there is not agreement on implementation.

Format of a URN:

URN: <scheme> : < naming authority> : <arbitrary string>

ISBNs and ISSNs would work well as unique identifiers for publications and in particular the content of publications.

Example: URN: isbn: isbn.org:1234567890

Example: URN: issn: issn.org:12345678/v.12/no.5/pg.21

The naming authority can assign any string it likes as long as it is unique, making the URN unique in its entirety. There is an interesting debate in the Internet community about the importance of semantics of the arbitrary string. The naming authority can have software assign an accession number or a semantic string as long as the string is unique for that naming authority.

There are two types of difficulties in designing URNs which are why the IETF is having a difficult time converging on a single URN standard: 1. name assignment & ownership 2. name resolution.

NAME ASSIGNMENT & OWNERSHIP

1. Who can create and update a URN?
2. Who can create a naming authority?
3. What syntax is necessary?

NAME RESOLUTION

1. What mechanism will work?
2. Where will the URN resolution servers reside?
3. Local or international?
4. How does the URN work with the URC (meta information)?

Four or five URN schemas (depending on currency) have been proposed as IETF Internet drafts. The details of these URN schemas with their pros and cons are beyond the scope of this paper. Please see the individual Internet drafts (cited at the end of this paper) for details, summaries, and/or criticisms. This paper will instead focus on the Handle System developed by CNRI.

THE HANDLE SYSTEM DEVELOPED BY CNRI

The Corporation for National Research Initiatives (CNRI) has implemented a URN scheme called handles. The development of the Handle System was part of the Computer Science Technical Report (CSTR) project. Five academic institutions were funded by ARPA to research digital libraries and mount computer science technical reports on servers (Anderson 1995). The results of the debate about name space for digital libraries is summarized in a document on distributed digital object services, also called the Kahn/Wilensky paper (Kahn 1994).

The most important concept in the Kahn/Wilensky paper is the creation of a handle or a permanent unique identifier for every document. The handle is used to name the document on a server. A handle server maps the permanent unique identifier to the machine address. The handle server is now available at CNRI and the handle functionality is being integrated into WWW browsers.

HOW THE HANDLE SYSTEM WORKS

The Handle System provides identifiers (handles) for digital objects and other resources in distributed computer systems. The system ensures that handles are unique and that they can be maintained over long time periods. Since the system makes no assumptions about the characteristics of the items that are identified, handles can be used in a wide variety of systems and applications. (Arms 1995)

The Handle System contains the following parts.

- Naming authorities are entities authorized to create new handles and store them, with their associated handle records, in handle servers.
- Handle generators create new handles on behalf of naming authorities.
- Handle servers store handles and provide a service to resolve them. There is a single global handle server and many associated local handle servers.
- Client software is used for user applications to communicate with handle servers.
- Caching servers are used to provide fast resolution of handles for clients and to minimize the frequency with which client software accesses other handle servers.
- Proxy servers permit Web browsers and other clients to resolve handles.
- Administrative tools create naming authorities which create, modify, and delete handle records, and create and maintain administrative groups.

HANDLE SYNTAX

Handles meet all of the requirements as defined in RFC1737.

A handle has the form:

n/d

Where n is a naming authority and d is an arbitrary string. The string d is unique for that naming authority. Handles are case insensitive.

example: URN:: hdl:stanford.cs/stanford.cs/tr-95–1234

example: URN:: hdl:stanford.cs/berkeley.cs/tr-95–4321

example: URN:: hdl:stanford.cs/tr-95–1234

The above examples show how a library might use the arbitrary string to give the handle semantic information. Stanford.cs is the naming authority, but it can assign handles to documents from other institutions. In the first example, stanford.cs assigns the string "stanford.cs/tr-1234 to indicate the report is a Stanford report. In the second example, stanford.cs assigns the string "berkeley.cs/tr-95–4321" to indicate the report is a Berkeley report. The report numbers are not necessarily unique across institutions so assigning the publisher institution and department (cs) as a string guarantees uniqueness.

RESOLUTION OF HANDLES

Resolution of handles is carried out by handle servers, at the request of a client. To resolve a handle, a handle server receives as input a handle and returns some or all of the fields of typed data in the corresponding handle record. The typed data will usually be a URL but is extensible. It could be a URC (meta information) or information on the naming authority for the handle or some other as yet to be defined data.

Handle resolution is fast because the architecture uses a transport protocol called User Datagram Protocol (UDP), but some firewalls do not pass UDP packets. Therefore, the slower Transmission Control Protocol (TCP) is provided as an option. (Arms 1995)

FEATURES OF THE HANDLE SYSTEM

- URCs are not required for the Handle System to work. Many of the URN proposals require that the URN return information about the resource but not the resource itself. This requirement seems very restrictive and implies that the URN naming authority must maintain all of the meta information as well as the URLs. It is likely that libraries will choose to create their own meta information and for that purpose will want a URN that identifies the resource itself.
- Local Handle Servers allow flexibility. The Global Handle server is publicly accessible, highly secure, fault tolerant, and designed to run continuously. Local Handle servers are not publicly available. Currently access control is by the IP address of the client. Local Handle servers allow naming authorities, repositories, or others to create handles for local use. These local handles do not have to go into the Global Handle server.
- The Handle System has been developed to scale up. The researchers at CNRI were aware from the start that the Handle System must scale to millions of handles. The System takes full advantage of caching and the UDP protocol for fast processing. The System was also built for flexibility. The philosophy was to build general purpose system components that will support a great variety of systems and applications. A handle is a pure name: no assumptions are built into the system about the type of object, the use made, or the applications.

For more detailed information on the Handle System see http://www.cnri.reston.va.us /home/cstr/handle-intro.html

CONCLUSION

Uniform Resource Names (URNs) are a critical part of digital library development. The URN working group should be applauded for their hard work on this complex problem and encouraged to converge on a set of solutions. Once browsers, like Netscape and Mosaic, know how to deal with URNs, a user/client with a unique identifier will be able to send a message to the resolution server that will know on which document server the document resides. The client will then go to the document server using the URL or machine address. No longer will Web servers contain false links because the resolution servers can update in real time. In addition, libraries will be able to catalog electronic material using unique permanent identifiers which will not change. Unique permanent identifiers, URNs, that are known worldwide and automatically map to the machine address using resolution servers will be a very powerful tool for libraries.

REFERENCES:

Internet Drafts and Request for Comments can be found at http://www.ietf.cnri.reston.va.us/home.html. Use the RFC index or the Internet-Drafts index on this home page.
Anderson, Greg; Rebecca Lasher; and Vicky Reich. The Computer Science Technical Report (CS-TR) Project Considerations for the Library Perspec-

tive, July 1995. Available from http://elib.stanford.edu.

Arms, William; David Ely. "The Handle System A Technical Overview", June 23, 1995. Internet draft = draft-ietf-uri-urn-handles-00.txt. Available from http://www.ietf.cnri.reston.va.us/home.html. See note above.

Duranceau, Ellen Finnie. "The Balance Point: Naming and Describing Networked Electronic Resources: The Role of Uniform Resource Identifiers," Serials Review 20 (4): 31–44 (1994). Articles include: Alan Emtage. "The Way and What of URLs and URNs"; Karen R. Sollins. "The Hard Problems are Not All Solved"; Rebecca Lasher. "New Model Needed for Locating and Describing Networked Information"; Clifford Lynch. "Uniform Resource Naming From Standards to Operational Systems."

Kahn, Robert; Robert Wilensky. "A Framework for Distributed 'Digital Object' Services." version 5.3, dated 5/13/95. Available from http://www.cnri.reston.va.us.

Madsen, Mark. "A Critique of Existing URN Proposals," July 14, 1995. Internet draft = draft-ietf-uri-urn-madsen-critique-00.txt. Available from http://www.ietf.cnri.reston.va.us/home.html. See note above.

Shafer, Keith E.; Eric J. Miller; Vincent M. Tkac; Stuart L. Weibel. "URN Services", July 1995. Internet draft = draft-ietf-uri-urn-resolution-01.txt. Available from http://www.ietf.cnri.reston.va.us/home.html. See note above.

Sollins, Karen; Larry Masinter. "Functional Requirements for Uniform Resource Names", December 1994. RFC1737. Available from http://www.ietf.cnri.reston.va.us/home.html. See note above.

Providing "Services" to the Electronic Library: The Role of Technical Services: A Four-Part Discussion

Part One:
Introduction

By Janet McCue
Cornell University

David Levy, a computer scientist at Xerox PARC, studied the history and culture of cataloging. He lurked on library listservs, worked with an original cataloger, and researched the anthropology of the book and the foundations of cataloging. Levy embarked on this study in order to examine the question of cataloging in the digital world. Is there a role for cataloging in this new electronic library or will sophisticated search tools and intelligent agents ferret out all the information a person will require? The conclusion he reached was that " . . . the work of stabilizing and maintaining digital collections will require a great deal of systematic human activity."[1]

It is assumed that these humans will be public services librarians who will provide knowledgeable assistance to users, collection development officers who will evaluate and select information resources, and computing professionals who will develop and sustain the technical infrastructure required for this digital world but will these humans also include technical services librarians?

"Should technical services be involved in the creation and maintenance of the digital library?" This question is regularly posed in library listserv discussions. Debates abound on whether technical services staff should monitor hypertext links on web pages, catalog Internet resources, or check-in electronic journals. Judging from the rhetoric, the role of technical services in this evolving world is still somewhat unclear. Will the activities in Technical Services be outsourced and the staff laid off or transferred to other units? Or, will cataloging and acquisitions staff take on new roles and activities related to the digital library?

These papers will address this persistent question by showcasing the real "services" which cataloging and acquisitions provide in the electronic library. They will review the new roles and responsibilities of technical services staff, the organizational issues related to training and retooling, and the strategies for balancing the demands of the print collection and the growing responsibilities of the electronic library. The three papers will cover the following topics:

- New Breed of Cataloging Librarian: bushwhackers or evolutionary deadends? Several institutions, including Yale University, the University of Rochester and Cornell University, recently recruited "Cataloging Librarians for Networked Information Resources." In each of these positions, Cataloging Librarians are being asked to assume a leadership role in the organization of electronic information. What are the responsibilities of these Cataloging Librarians? What impact have they made in the realm of organizing and providing access to networked information resources? Matthew

Beacom, the Cataloger for Networked Information Resources at Yale University will describe his transformation from Rare Book Cataloger to Internet Bushwhacker.
- Acquiring the Virtual Library: oxymoron or reality? Institutions are providing access to a variety of electronic resources—from titles mounted locally to "pointers" on homepages. Each of these means of access provides different challenges for acquisitions staff. How do acquisitions staff order, receive and process networked resources for the electronic library? Bill Kara, Acquisitions Librarian at Cornell University's Mann Library will summarize the activities of acquisitions staff in providing access to electronic files and the skills which his staff have developed to handle these new responsibilities.
- The Culture of Technical Services: information agility vs. risk aversion? As technical services departments provide service to both the print and the electronic library, many organizational questions must be addressed. Perhaps the most important question is how to change the organizational culture in Technical Services in order to stay in the mainstream. Gillian McCombs, Assistant Director for Technical Services in the University Libraries at the University of Albany (SUNY) will explain how we can remain nimble and quick in this changing environment. She will discuss the concept of "information agility" in Technical Services and how changing the culture allows one to make a difference and effect change.

ENDNOTE

1. David Levy, a computer scientist at Xerox PARC, delivered a paper for the Digital Libraries '95 conference entitled "Cataloging in the Digital Order" in which he discusses the future of cataloging and catalogers in the digital world. After studying the role and history of cataloging and evaluating the future of intelligent agents, Levy suggests that there will still be a role for human catalogers in providing and maintaining intellectual access to information resources—whether print or electronic. Although it is unclear what this role will be or how Technical Services functions will change, Levy suggests that catalogers have done important work which is often not generally understood nor fully appreciated. See "Cataloging in the Digital Order" by David M. Levy pp. 31–37 in *Proceedings of Digital Libraries '95*, The Second Annual Conference on the Theory and Practice of Digital Libraries, June 11–13, 1995 Austin, Texas, edited by Frank Shipman III, Richard Furuta, and David M. Levy (College Station, TX: Hypermedia Research Laboratory, 1995). The proceedings also are available on the Web at: http://csdl.tamu.edu/DL95/.

Part Two:
The Catalog Librarian in the Age of the Smart Machine

By Matthew Beacom
Yale University

Janet McCue asked me to discuss a new breed of cataloging librarian and to answer the question, Is this new breed of cataloger a bushwhacker or an evolutionary dead-end? Well, I am one of the new breed, and my answer may not surprise you. For I think those catalog librarians who are now cataloging Internet resources, organizing new-born digital libraries, managing Campus-Wide Information Systems (CWIS), or working to create protocols, rules, standards, etc. for information distributed through digital networks are cutting paths that the next generations of librarians and information professionals will follow. I'll begin with a little current and historical context to situate these new-breed librarians and their opportunities. Then I'll attempt to describe the new breed of catalog librarians and discuss what needs to be done to nurture them and put them to good use.

We know that the whole business of publishing is moving from print or analog products to products created and distributed on digital information networks and that scholarly communication and research libraries are moving on the same tide. (I think I'll have died from old age long before this transformation is complete.) Since the advent of the phrase "information superhighway" and the World Wide Web, the movement to digital networked information is causing more uncertainty and anxiety than ever. Words like "outsourcing" and "obsolescence" sound ominously in our ears. Publishers, academics, and librarians are all concerned about what this change will do to them and to the people who buy their products or services. But the change from ink and paper to digits and networks has been happening for some time. Indeed, the digital libraries we hear of so frequently now are not new. They are the second generation of digital libraries. And the new breed of catalog librarian that I am talking about today is also of the second generation. To know this new breed, we'll look first to their professional "parents."

The librarians who first made digital libraries digitized the metadata, the information about scores, archives, maps, books, journals, and other document-like objects that libraries collect. They converted catalog records from cards to digital form. They were wise. We know this story. We lived it, or the people who hired us did. Catalog librarians did more than make bibliographic and authority records, they were high among the dreamers and the toilers in this effort. They created online catalogs for individual libraries and online bibliographic utilities such as WLN, RLIN, and OCLC. They created MARC: a standard for the exchange of digital information. They and their colleagues used these tools to advance great collaborative projects such as shared cataloging and Inter-Library-Loan. Librarians didn't do it by themselves. It was, then as now, a cross-profession collaboration. But catalog librarians played a decisive role in the achievements of the first generation of digital libraries.

Their achievements were not just technological wonders. For they transformed how we do our work and how we organize ourselves to do it. The librarians who developed the first generation digital libraries altered the structure and culture of the workplace within libraries. We are living with its effects now—good and bad. Library management systems and the networked computer and communication systems that linked and supported them drew library staff, processes, and functions into a more integrated whole. Boundaries that traditionally separated cataloging, collection development, and reference services began to change and fade. The need for intra-library cooperation and consultation increased. Formal and informal re-organization of libraries followed. And the online catalog became a more valuable and potent tool for providing information services than the card catalog could ever be. For the online catalog had become the database supporting integrated library services. The next generation of the new breed may use the catalog as the key database supporting integrated networked information services.

After all the generation of librarians who digitized metadata did, they deserved a day of rest. Well, praise—and new opportunities for interesting work—will have to do for them, because instead of rest, the Internet happened. The Internet is called by some a web, by others a cloud, by everyone else a superhighway. Whatever metaphor is used, we know it's chaos time. We're in awe of the Internet's power, its speed, its growth, its potential. We wonder. What will we do with it? What will it do to us? We don't know whether to tame the Internet or surf it. We doubt that either can really be done, but the second generation of the new breed of catalog librarian is now trying to do both. And our mentors from the first generation have given us a double legacy—their own example as innovators and the digitized metadata tools they created.

Today's digital libraries and this generation of the new breed must build upon the great works of the first generation and integrate those achievements with the new networked, digital initiatives that are revolutionizing the publishing industry, academia, and scholarly communication. Many projects now under way in libraries and universities—lists of Internet resources, WWW pages for individual libraries or departments, CWISs, a book digitized, a journal brought online, etc.—are divorced from the online catalog. They are related to one another, if at all, by the tenuous grasp of a search strategy and the engine-of-the-week, the surprise of a web link, or a tortuous path through an array of lists within lists. These efforts are often praiseworthy, but in the aggregate they tend to dis-integrate metadata and data (full text, images, etc.) In the rush to put full text online or use full text resources, we too often neglect existing metadata structures, practices, and concepts.

Other projects—WWW versions of online catalogs, attempts to catalog Internet resources, the efforts of task forces and working groups to create order through developing and adopting standards, protocols and rules—adapt the library catalog for the Internet or adapt the Internet to the information organizing culture of institutions such as libraries. These efforts, though limited, tend toward integrating metadata and data. (Another, the Technical Services Workstation, puts the necessary computing and communication tools in the hands of catalogers and other catalog librarians.) Existing metadata resources are used, adapted, imitated, or ported to add the value of organized access to clouds of document-like information objects. WWW-aware online catalogs are now among the best available instruments for integrating metadata with data on the Internet. With such library catalogs, we are able to both organize intellectual access and deliver physical access to the body of knowledge present on the Internet. For such efforts, catalog librarians are among the mission critical staff. For without the catalog librarian, there is no library catalog.

To understand who the second generation new-breed catalog librarians are (and will be), we can look at a few individuals, read a few job descriptions, and guess. But we'll start with a backward glance at the first generation. I'm sure we all know some examples. One librarian I know is a typical case. As head of the circulation department, he wrote the spec for moving the data in one vendor's circulation system to another's integrated library management system. With an integrated library management system in place, the library reorganized the technical service division, and he became the head of the database management unit. In a subsequent reorganization, he moved to the library's information technology unit as the chief database administrator. Now as the head of the library's information technology unit, he is directing development of the library's WWW-aware online catalog and many other digital networked projects.

The next generation of the new breed will create themselves in the same way. Catalogers or acquisition librarians or other librarians who have taught themselves to know computers, networks, and protocols will come forward into positions of responsibility and leadership. Library systems staff such as database administrators, programmers, or workstation support specialists (these may not be graduates of library schools) who have imbued the values of librarianship will enlarge their scope of action with libraries and the emerging world on networked digital information services. And recent graduates of library schools who at best combine the disciplines of computer science and library science will apply for jobs that promise opportunity and intellectual excitement. It's this group that I believe will be the true new breed: Generation-X digital catalog librarians. Will their CCQ look like Wired?

Will such library school graduates even be attracted by the jobs we offer in Technical Services? They will apply for the jobs we offer in technical services only if those jobs offer opportunities to play a decisive role in creating full-scale digital libraries. Will their teachers and fellow students say in shock, "You're going to apply for a cataloging job?" This was the response given to one new-breed catalog librarian. Will they have taken a course in cataloging? Will the new breed graduate from library schools? I think they will only if library schools offer the right preparation: one that builds a foundation for growth in traditional library skills and the skills needed for the new networked digital information environment. I don't know enough about what our library schools are doing to give an assessment. CRISTAL-ED, the collaborative project at the University of Michigan's School of Information and Library Studies offers some hope that information science and library education will be re-invented in ways that build on past achievements and values while reaching out to realms formerly consigned to Computer Science or Business School programs. But we have counterexamples of good schools closing altogether. And not every library school has the resources of the Michigan school. Adapting library school education to a communications and publication environment of digital, networked information is one of the critical challenges for our profession. If library schools do not prepare students to add value to services and products in a digital networked information environment, then librarians—meaning "graduates of library schools"—will not be a part of scholarly communication.

What skills do we expect to see in the new breed? We expect them to have the usual bibliographic skills and comparable computer skills. While such a combination is rare now, it will become less so. A student on the rare book cataloging team at Yale, now off to graduate school at Harvard for study in 17th century English history, was our team's UNIX resource person and WWW guide. The Yale web-master majored in Political Science and graduated in 1994. A Yale undergraduate psychology major who works part-time for the library is a terrific web site designer and html tag writer. Young men and women such as these are of the generation that will be our pool of potential colleagues. Well, they might not go to library school . . . So will we ask that in addition to excellent English and two other European or Asian or African languages, the ideal candidate know programming languages such as C++ or Perl or Java? Will we ask that in addition to years of experience cataloging, the ideal candidate have years of experience producing networked information resources? That will narrow the candidate pool some. And what would we have to pay to attract a candidate with an MLS and an MS in computer science? As you might think, organizational and cultural changes in the library as a workplace are not at an end.

Cornell University's Mann Library has had some experience writing job descriptions that aim to attract the new breed. Elements common to qualifications in the job description for the Catalog Librarian for Networked Information Resources and the Metadata Specialist (these tend to be common to other library's job descriptions I have reviewed) include an MLS, knowledge of information retrieval software, experience with various computer systems and their programming languages, one or more foreign languages, cataloging experience or interest in "metadata, cataloging, and full-text retrieval." I see Mann Library's experience as instructive in many ways. In particular, it shows that one perfect new-breed staff member is not likely to be found. Once one hires a really terrific candidate who does a great job, one new-breed librarian will not be enough. The skills needed to organize access to information in the digital library environment must be well-distributed throughout the technical services units of the library. One other role for many of the new breed is as a trainer or mentor for other staff. Your first hire of this new breed should have the instincts if not the experience of a teacher. One of the best systems librarians I've ever met used to teach elementary school. Such experience or talent is critical to successful innovation. As an organization, the library will gain new skills in two ways—by recruiting new talent and by re-training the old.

What are the new breed doing? They are cataloging Internet resources, writing C, Perl, or Java programs, creating and managing lists of Internet resources, designing and managing WWW sites, writing HTML, developing library policies for organizing and delivering networked resources, consulting on library WWW, SGML, and other digital initiatives, working on teams developing and managing Campus-Wide Information Systems, and developing and supporting Technical Services Workstations. And they are contributing to the development of metadata standards that may structure not only library catalogs but the Internet itself.

How do we nurture this new breed? If you've been listening you know already that I'll say we nurture the new breed the same way we did the old. We create opportunities for interesting work. We also offer cross-unit responsibilities within the library, research and development projects, and links to faculty and campus information technology units. Money, toys, and status never hurt. We must support their professional growth by sending them to conferences, seminars, and back to school. And we should support their participation in the wide world of the networked digital information industries through such groups as the ALCTS Taskforce on Meta Access, IETF working groups, and other library and information technology professional groups.

What lies ahead for us, for librarians, for academics, and for publishers really is unknown territory. I have insisted today that the past is prelude and that librarians—in particular catalog librarians—will be vital to scholarly communication in the age of smart machines, an age of networked information and digital libraries. But it isn't necessarily so. And it won't happen by itself. Being vital to a great enterprise is not like falling off a log. If catalog librarians are going to play a decisive role in the creation of full-scale digital libraries, then we will have to make it happen. If by collaborating with allied information professions catalog librarians are able to help solve vexing problems of organizing access to networked information, then we will have earned a place of importance. We will have created things of value. But such collaboration and achievements will force organizational and cultural changes on libraries, universities, and publishers. As the online management systems we created for libraries allowed a greater integration of library services, so the management systems we are creating for networked information may support a greater integration of libraries, universities, and publishing. What that integration may look like is impossible to predict—we may speculate—and it is a long way off. But the boundaries between institutions and between professions are beginning to change, and my speculation is that librarians, especially catalog librarians, will significantly shape that change.

Part Three:
Acquiring the Electronic Library:
Implications for Acquisitions

By William J. Kara
Cornell University

Acquisitions units have important roles to fulfill as the electronic library evolves. In these units reside the skills and the experience for acquiring and processing items for the collection. That experience can and should be applied to items in different electronic formats. If not, acquisitions staff will fail to stake their claims in the future of their own units, in technical services and increasingly, in the electronic library.

To illustrate this transition, I will briefly review some of the changes technology has brought to acquisitions and their impact on the Acquisitions Unit at the Albert R. Mann Library. In somewhat more detail I will discuss the processing of electronic files which is handled by the Acquisitions Unit. These nearly 300 separate titles produced by the U.S. Dept. of Agriculture and processed by the acquisitions staff have required the greatest changes to the Unit's staffing and skills. Although this example is the most significant new responsibility integrated in the Unit's daily routine, it is only one change among many.

CHANGES IN ACQUISITIONS

Acquisitions staff are not strangers to change. Procedures and entire workflows have evolved considerably with automation. Although there are still some libraries that do some or much of their processing off-line, this is increasingly the exception. Automation has enabled acquisitions units, including those processing serials and monographs, to more efficiently accomplish their core tasks electronically. On-line ordering, claiming, receipt, and payments are all part of the daily routine of most organizations. Increasingly, some of these activities are even finally being done with less paper as more library systems are able to interface with vendors' on-line systems. Acquisitions has moved from typewriters, to "dumb" terminals, to computers, to workstations. The workstation provides access to the library's on-line system, standard software packages, specialized resources or files, and the ability to tailor commands to facilitate processing. With the continuing development of workstations, acquisitions and serials control systems, vendors on-line resources, and EDI (electronic data interchange), acquisitions will certainly continue to evolve.

The same technology that is making the automation of acquisitions procedures a reality, is also providing new opportunities and demands on acquisitions. Print publications have been the mainstay of acquisitions programs and are likely to remain important for a very long time. Predictions regarding the imminent demise or decline of print publications have varied considerably, but acquisitions librarians know that print publications are still important for any collection. Print resources remain the dominant materials processed for the library, yet gradually, perhaps in fits and starts, electronic publications are becoming increasingly numerous and essential to any up-to-date collection. Some types of publications, including bibliographic and numeric files and those needing immediate dissemination, are more suited for the electronic environment which permits more efficient searching and manipulation of data. There are also some publications which are not available in print and others for which it is more cost effective to produce and distribute the electronic version. For example, in the December 29, 1995 issue of *Administrative Notes* it was reported that one of the Government Printing Office's goals was to change the Federal Depository Library Program to a "predominately electronic program by the end of Fiscal

Year (FY) 1998."[1] For these increasingly numerous and varied electronic publications acquisitions can continue to play important roles.

Electronic publications will still need orders, payments, and subscription maintenance. They will also often need contracts. These important business functions have been and should remain part of the acquisitions process. Acquisitions units also have traditionally supplied the basic bibliographic record to track in-process items for the collection. These activities are true even if an item is only available electronically and no local receipt or processing is necessary. One recent example of serials maintenance involved free online access to the electronic versions of several publications that the Library subscribes to in print. On January 1 our account and passwords for these five titles expired. After a call to the publisher it was found that the renewal information for our print subscriptions failed to be properly relayed to the office handling electronic access. Our account and passwords were quickly reactivated, but it was the serials staff who needed to react quickly. This particular example did not require any special computer skills, but used very traditional acquisitions and business skills for subscription maintenance.

CHANGES AT MANN LIBRARY

The acquisitions staff at Mann Library are also responsible for the actual processing of an increasing number of monographs and serials in electronic form. Some background information about Mann Library might give some perspective. The Albert R. Mann Library is the second largest library in the Cornell University Library system and serves the College of Agriculture and Life Sciences, the College of Human Ecology, and the Divisions of the Biological and Nutritional Sciences. Approximately 10% of our annual expenditures (from a 1.2 million dollar materials budget) goes to electronic resources, whether these are received and processed locally or only accessible remotely. In addition to the titles and access which are purchased, free internet-accessible resources are carefully selected and made accessible through the Gateway. Mann Library's Gateway provides a single point of access to approximately 500 titles, whether they are mounted locally or available remotely, and whether they are purchased, leased, or free.

These titles have required significant flexibility on the part of acquisitions staff. This flexibility not only includes a willingness to become involved, but flexibility in regard to learning and applying new skills. Early in the development of Mann Library's electronic collection, it was decided that the different divisions and units of the Library all had skills and experience to contribute to its development. It was also clear that any unit left out of the process might increasingly become marginalized. In Technical Services, acquisitions staff acquired the items and the catalogers described them using both traditional and innovative means. As staff developed their skills much of the processing or preparation of electronic files also moved to Technical Services, much of it, but certainly not all. Staff from our Information Technology Section still maintain the computers and servers and do most of the programming to support different activities. The routine processing and maintenance, and increasingly more difficult problem solving, however, has moved to Technical Services. In addition, programming that has facilitated our processing has also moved to Technical Services. One might look at these new responsibilities as a burden on already busy staff or as an opportunity to learn new skills, or both. As managers, acquisitions librarians need to explore options and plan for these changes. While doing the work of the present, an eye needs to be focused on the future.

PROCESSING ELECTRONIC FILES IN THE ACQUISITIONS UNIT:

Approximately 300 of the titles presently available on the Mann Library Gateway are published by the U.S. Dept. of Agriculture (USDA) economic agencies (Economic Research Service, National Agricultural Statistics Service, and the World Agricultural Outlook Board). These USDA economic agencies and Mann Library entered into a partnership that helps ensure timely and free access to hundreds of their publications, both monographs and serials. The first files were loaded in December 1993 and the service, the USDA Economics and Statistics System, was significantly expanded in April 1995. It is Mann Library's responsibility to mount and maintain access to these electronic titles for the public. This responsibility, more than any other, has required the Acquisitions Unit to develop a new outlook and new skills.

Processing the USDA files is the most significant

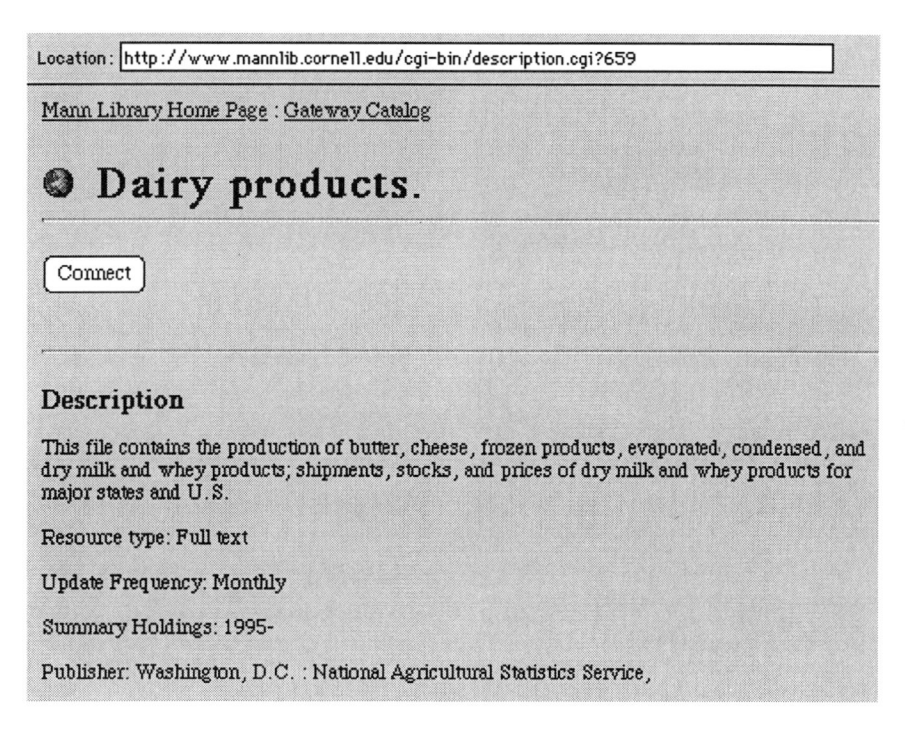

> Location: http://www.mannlib.cornell.edu/cgi-bin/description.cgi?659
>
> Mann Library Home Page : Gateway Catalog
>
> ● **Dairy products.**
>
> [Connect]
>
> **Description**
>
> This file contains the production of butter, cheese, frozen products, evaporated, condensed, and dry milk and whey products; shipments, stocks, and prices of dry milk and whey products for major states and U.S.
>
> Resource type: Full text
>
> Update Frequency: Monthly
>
> Summary Holdings: 1995-
>
> Publisher: Washington, D.C. : National Agricultural Statistics Service,

Figure 1. Gateway Catalog description page

new responsibility undertaken by the acquisitions staff. These titles are core to our collection in the agricultural sciences and present a unique opportunity for Mann Library. Included in this collection are statistical datasets and full-text reports. Many of the full-text reports are time sensitive and need to be posted as quickly as possible after receipt. Staff work from a schedule, retrieve the files, rename them using standardized guidelines, and move them to their correct directory location on the Library's server. These full-text reports are comparable to any group of print serials; many, in fact, are electronic versions of titles received in print. There are weeklies, monthlies, quarterlies, semiannuals, and annuals. In addition, no print or electronic serials collection would be complete without a few special supplements and irregular publications.

Below is an example of one of the titles received from the USDA. Each title can be accessed from the Mann Library Gateway via an alphabetic list or by subject categories. Titles and database descriptions are also accessible via keyword searching. The Gateway catalog record (Figure 1) utilizes many key fields from the MARC bibliographic record.

After choosing to connect to a title, the user can choose the year containing the issue he or she would like to read. After selecting "1995" the user is presented with a list of issues in chronological order for that year (Figure 2).

When a specific issue is selected, the full-text of that report will appear. Figure 3 shows a small portion of the April issue of this monthly report. During the last half of 1995, approximately 7,000 uses of the "USDA Economics and Statistics System" were recorded each month. In addition, approximately 1,500 users subscribe to individual reports (or several reports), which are automatically e-mailed to them as part of the acquisitions processing.

Receiving these reports electronically is, of course, considerably different from checking in a print issue. Yet there are similarities. Each issue is still received (or retrieved) in the Library, recorded on our on-line check-in record, and processed for the collection, albeit differently. Instead of marking the item with a LC call number, the item is renamed in a standard format and then moved to the correct directory location for that title and issue. To post the issues staff need to have a knowledge of FTP, UNIX, directory structures, and electronic mail.

Despite these new and different computer skills, the process still incorporates many of the traditional acquisitions skills. Was the correct issue received and is it readable? If not, the staff need to quickly request a replacement. Has the expected issue been re-

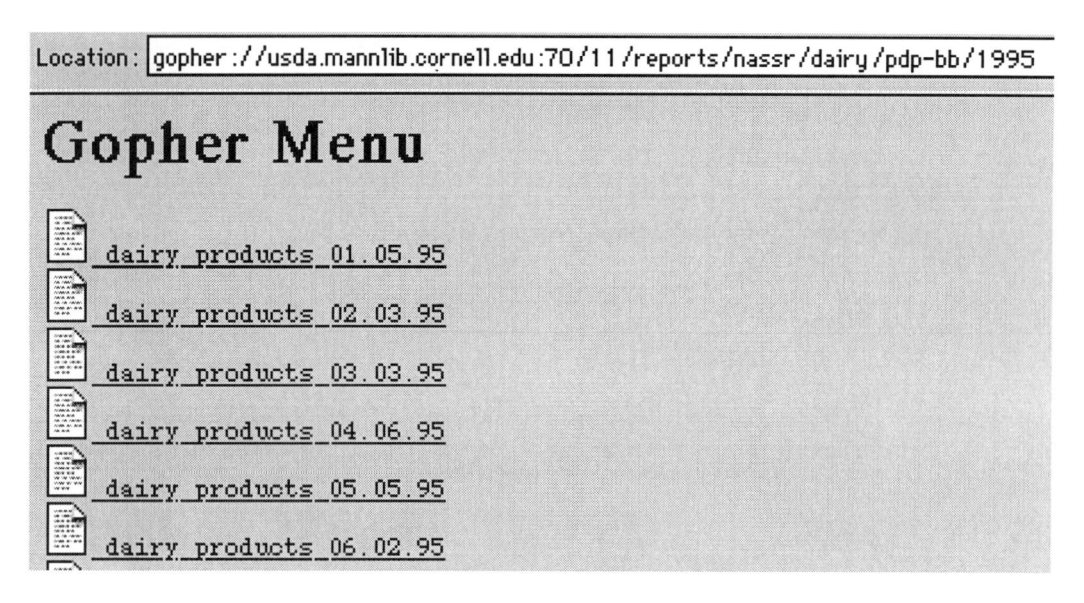

Figure 2. List of *Dairy Products* issues received

ceived? If not, the staff need to claim the item—usually by phone, but sometimes by electronic mail. There are bibliographic and processing questions raised when new titles or special supplements are received. Much of acquisitions work demands attention to these many details involving the purchase, receipt, and bibliographic control of items processed for the collection. For processing electronic files, additional technical skills need to be used in conjunction with these already existing skills which are used in processing print titles for the collection.

Undertaking this new responsibility initially involved some trepidation on the part of many staff. Very different tasks needed to be done in the Unit and not just by one staff member. For every primary function of the Unit it is important to build in some redundancy. This is also true and especially important for processing the USDA reports. Approximately 10–12 new issues are received every week, scheduled for different days and different times. Many of these reports contain information of time-sensitive economic value on the cost and production of different agricultural products. The time-sensitive nature of the reports is sometimes an extra burden, but it helped to instill a sense of importance and greater commitment to the process. Reports are usually posted within ten minutes of their availability to the acquisitions staff. Our processing couldn't be taken lightly. In order to successfully integrate these new responsibilities into the Unit there needed to be planning and plenty of training.

Fortunately, due to the many changes during the last few years, all staff had some familiarity with various computer applications. Additionally, some more specialized computer skills already existed in the Unit. Mann Library's Government Information Librarian, who is part of the Acquisitions Unit, first developed his own skills and was able to effectively transfer many of those skills to other staff. Staff also had a series of more formal training sessions. This combination of one-on-one and group training helped to develop the basic skills.

Routine use of these computer skills and experience with the reports over the last year has proved invaluable in developing staff confidence. Increasingly staff have been able to resolve many problems involving the receipt and display of these reports. Although the Government Information Librarian no longer receives reports on a daily basis, he is still a resource person for technical and processing questions from other acquisitions staff.

Processing USDA full-text reports and datasets is just one of many significant changes in Mann Library's Acquisitions Unit. This is not a project, but part of the Unit's ongoing responsibilities. Although staff had and have different skills and assignments, we've been fortunate that all have shown flexibility and an interest in these new activities.

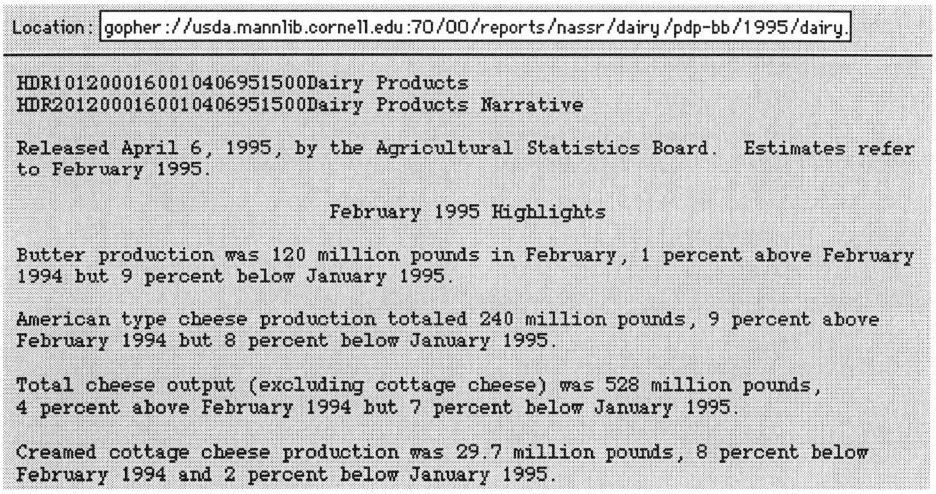

```
Location: gopher://usda.mannlib.cornell.edu:70/00/reports/nassr/dairy/pdp-bb/1995/dairy

HDR1012000160010406951500Dairy Products
HDR2012000160010406951500Dairy Products Narrative

Released April 6, 1995, by the Agricultural Statistics Board.  Estimates refer
to February 1995.

                          February 1995 Highlights

Butter production was 120 million pounds in February, 1 percent above February
1994 but 9 percent below January 1995.

American type cheese production totaled 240 million pounds, 9 percent above
February 1994 but 8 percent below January 1995.

Total cheese output (excluding cottage cheese) was 528 million pounds,
4 percent above February 1994 but 7 percent below January 1995.

Creamed cottage cheese production was 29.7 million pounds, 8 percent below
February 1994 and 2 percent below January 1995.
```

Figure 3. Beginning of the April 1995 issue of *Dairy Products*

CONCLUSION

In the evolution to the electronic library, much can be written about staffing and training needs and about who should do what. Each organization is different and will have different missions and priorities. I concentrated on only one initiative at Mann Library to provide an example of how our roles and responsibilities have changed. Certainly other libraries would not have the interest or the need to process and maintain large, unique electronic collections in the agricultural sciences. There are, however, increasing opportunities and demands to provide more information electronically. Libraries will increasingly subscribe to many of their journals via on-line services. Even if only access is acquired and there is no physical processing of the items, there will remain important order and maintenance activities.

Acquisitions librarians and staff have much to offer in fast-changing times. We need to be aware of these changes and be educated consumers. It is essential that we become full participants in the process and develop our skills. Acquisitions units will continue to evolve. As managers of those units we will need to adapt, be prepared for new responsibilities and opportunities, and help shape the future of our profession.

ENDNOTE

1. For changes to the Federal Depository Library Program, see: "The Electronic Federal Deposi-tory Library Program : Transition Plan, FY 1996 - FY 1998," *Administrative Notes : Newsletter of the Federal Depository Library Program* 16:18 (Dec. 29, 1995)

FOR MORE INFORMATION

Access instructions to the "USDA Economics and Statistics System": World Wide Web:

> http://usda.mannlib.cornell.edu/usda
> Gopher: Host=usda.mannlib.cornell.edu
> Port Number=70
> Telnet: Host=usda.mannlib.cornell.edu
> User ID= usda <lower case>
> FTP: Host=usda.mannlib.cornell.edu
> User ID=anonymous
> Password= <your e-mail address (optional)>
> (After logging in, change the directory with the following command: cd usda)

For more information on changes in Mann Library Technical Services and processing the USDA reports, see:

> Janet McCue, "Technical Services and the Electronic Library : Defining our Roles and Divining the Partnership," *Library Hi Tech* 12:3 (1994):63–70.
> William J. Kara, "Acquisitions in Transition: On the Road to the Electronic Library," *Continuity & Transformation : The Prom-*

ise of Confluence, Proceedings of the 7th National Conference of the ACRL, Pittsburgh, Pennsylvania, March 29–April 1 1995 (Chicago : ACRL, 1995), p.203–207

Marijo S. Wilson, "Mainstreaming Electronic Numeric Data Files : The Impact on Technical Services," *Continuity & Transformation : The Promise of Confluence, Proceedings of the 7th National Conference of the ACRL, Pittsburgh, Pennsylvania, March 29–April 1 1995* (Chicago : ACRL, 1995), p.267–271

For information on the changing roles of acquisitions, see: Ross Atkinson, "The Acquisitions Librarian as Change Agent in the Transition to the Electronic Library," *Library Resources and Technical Services* 36:1 (January 1992):7–20.

Part Four:
'Jack Be Nimble, Jack Be Quick':
The Concept of Information Agility in Technical Services

Gillian McCombs
University at Albany, State University of New York

Technical Services has not, in the past, been noted for its agility. This is exemplified by the following description of a two-day institute entitled "The Catalog in the Age of Technological Change," which addressed the "vast potential in on-line computerized catalogs, but warned that it will be necessary to 'cultivate a more positive attitude' toward the new technology if this potential is to be realized." One speaker stated that "what is needed is to break out of the circle of endless discussion of cataloging rules and to initiate serious research in the way library catalogs are approached and used." The list of speakers included Michael Gorman and John Byrum. When was this institute held, last year? Sadly, this was an institute held 20 years ago in 1977, when Michael Gorman was still at the British Library, and when John Byrum was chairing the American Library Association (ALA) Resources and Technical Services Division (RTSD) Catalog Code Revision Committee (Ricard 1977).

I would like to propose an agenda for change that will enable Technical Services librarians to recover their position of centrality in the mission of the library as well as the university. This agenda will allow them to remain true to themselves; that is, retain what they do best—organizing and providing access to large bodies of information for current and future researchers—while at the same time preparing them to take on new responsibilities in the electronic era. In order to keep themselves in the mainstream, Technical Services librarians need to change their organizational culture. I do believe that one of the key concepts which will aid them in doing this is AGILITY!

'Agility' as a management concept is the ability of an organization to adapt proficiently in a continuously changing environment - in a word, be agile (Zannetos and Cashman 1995, 14). The November 27 issue of PC Week brought this concept to my attention in a series of articles in the "PC Week/Executive" section. The concept of agility was described in both business and educational contexts, together with an enumeration of the hallmarks of agility - flexibility, critical thinking and teamwork (Crowley 1995). The URL address was given (http://absu.amef.lehigh.edu) for the Agility Forum's Web page, the Agility Forum being a national center for research on this topic established at Lehigh University in 1991.

All this information on agility was ready to be filed away as related but not central to my focus when I logged into my Email and read the November issue of the E-News for ARL Directors. The very first item of news was the notification of the topic for the next Association of Research Libraries (ARL) membership meeting in Vancouver in May 1996 "to explore approaches to creating change-oriented organizations. The leadership . . . (is) planning a program that will focus on the broad theme of creating new organizations that are AGILE, resilient, and responsive in turbulent environments." So of course, I retrieved the URL for the Agility Forum home page and launched a search for more information on the concept of agility.

Previous attempts to change the way we do business in Technical Services have focused on systems and structure. The impact of early technology on Technical Services has certainly changed how we do things - cf. the earlier illustration describing the impact of online catalogs (OPACs). But OPACs have remained very much an 8"x11" online representation of the 3"x5" catalog card. We have not rethought how information should be organized or accessed in the online environment (De Klerk and Euster 1989). There has long been a focus on trying to change the organizational structure of academic libraries, to blur the lines between Technical Services and Public Services (Larsen 1991). More recently this equation has included Collection Development (McCombs 1992). There have also been numerous attempts to break down barriers between the traditional departments within Technical Services - Acquisitions and Cataloging - and to function according to various matrix-like organizational structures (Gomez and Harrell 1992). However, many leaders in the field of organizational change believe that, in order to effect change, the focus must be on the organizational culture of a unit or institution (Schein 1992, xii).

ORGANIZATIONAL CULTURE

How do we change the organizational culture of Technical Services? First, we need to understand what organizational culture is and why it is so important. The organizational culture of a particular institution, profession or group of people is a system of shared meanings and beliefs, a way of looking at life together (Schein 1992, 12). Organizational culture represents the unwritten, feeling part of the organization and provides the members with a sense of original identity, generating a commitment to beliefs and values that are larger than themselves. Some cultures have several sub-cultures embedded within them. A library may have its own culture within a university, and within that there may be a variety of sub-cultures such as Technical Services, Public Services, support staff and computing professional cultures. Culture can be broken down into four nested layers going from the most explicit, such as rites and symbols, through norms of behavior and basic values to the implicit core assumptions (Connor 1994).

Culture can change in two basic ways. First there can be a natural evolution which can take the form of a specific adaptation or can appear as the cumulative effect of incremental change. One example of this would be the changing role of reference librarians to include computer and technical activities such as online searching, and handling hardware malfunctions at the CD-ROM stations. Second, there can be a managed evolution, to be thought of as "organizational therapy" which is probably closer to the process that most of us will be engaged in (Schein 1992, 307). This managed evolution comprises planned change and organizational development strategies. There are a number of different factors which can drive or spark the change process. These can include dynamic leadership, (such as that of Carol Mandel, Deputy University Librarian at Columbia University); a technological catalyst which seduces the user - such as the development of the World Wide Web; the use of 'hybrid' librarians in key positions, librarians who possess skills in other areas than Technical Services. Similarly, the infusion of outsiders - whether professionals from outside librarianship, such as computing professionals, or the addition of a substantial block of new hires from within the profession - can drive change. The use of turnaround/or coercive persuasion has also been noted, as in successfully 'making the case' for a radical shift in gears, selling the shift in how things are done.

To manage this cultural change, a number of major steps need to be taken. We need to assess the existing culture, perhaps by doing an ethnographic study or a cultural analysis of the organization (Kunda 1992, 23). We need to tease out and discuss the existing norms and then work on establishing the desired norms. This is crucial, for if base values continue to be those respected during the initial establishment of the culture, then changes in culture will not occur. There is a need to differentiate between the espoused values - what people SAY they believe in - and real values, what people ACTUALLY believe in (Schein 1992, 27). We also need to identify culture gaps - for instance training or technological empowerment may be an issue - and then close these gaps with actions - such as buying more PCs or setting up more training classes. Above all, we need to sustain the cultural identity, continue to reinforce the new values and be consistent. It is no good expecting librarians to get up on the Internet if they have not been provided with 486 PCs, Ethernet connections, adequate browsing software and the time to learn how to use all this equipment. This will only lead to frustration and a reinforcement of the old culture.

What are the commonly agreed upon values of a standard Technical Services culture? The need for stability, standards and consistency, the importance of thinking things through, due process, following the rules, controlling the environment and the need for precedents (Benemann 1993). Change is considered bad, the status quo is paramount, risk aversion is a predominant trait. The desired norms that we would like to move to include agility, flexibility, a willingness to do new things, the ability to change quickly, the ability to prioritize, to know when to follow the rules and when not to, the ability to be proactive, creative, and innovative (Mandel 1992).

On the surface it would seem that the traditional values of Technical Services are in direct contrast to those needed to become more nimble. However, a recent article in Library Quarterly reported on a study of 101 librarians which tested individual differences considered important to enhanced use of the Internet (Finlay and Finlay 1996). It was found that high levels of the personality trait "innovativeness," or being positively disposed toward novel stimuli, is positively related to overall attitudes toward the Internet. Among the variables tested which had no significance were job position, job location, and education - all factors which might have shown Technical Services librarians as a group not well disposed toward the Internet, or as not being in possession of this particular personality trait. This is good news, because it shows that, irrespective of library calling, there is an innate quality or factor which can determine how staff will approach the digital future.

This all sounds well and good, but how do we ACTUALLY get Technical Services librarians to develop a new, more agile value-system that has an increased emphasis on change and flexibility, and a decreased emphasis on protecting the status quo? How do we move from controlling the environment to enabling change, from reactive to proactive mode - all without losing those very qualities of attention to detail and consistency which allow us to succeed at the task in hand - the task of organizing large bodies of material so as to be accessed both now and in the future by current and potential users, the task of both preserving the record of scholarship and the raw materials for future scholarship?

I do not put forward this agenda for change as a flip or facile suggestion that changing the culture can be accomplished as easily as waving a wand. A managed change process takes years to accomplish (Bridges 1991, 6). But we do need to start somewhere, and so I have developed this agenda as an attempt to iterate some specific changes that must occur in order for us to have a chance at effecting cultural change in Technical Services.

AGENDA FOR CHANGE

1. Leadership

There must be leadership from the top, from the Assistant Directors, from the Heads of Cataloging and Acquisitions. As leaders, we must learn to develop 'strategic' arguments, so that instead of asking for more catalogers to allow us to keep on doing what we have always done, we request more staff to enable us to add new services, refocus our cataloging expertise, and add value for the users. We also need the ability to develop strategic arguments for assigning scarce resources to maintain the integrity of current bibliographic databases, a much less popular need.

As proponents of this cultural change, we ourselves need to be open and flexible, to act as role models and use the technology ourselves. If this is to be a 'managed change process' someone needs to 'manage' it, so we must be prepared to spend a considerable part of the rest of our lives on this process. Do not delegate this responsibility. Michael Gorman states bluntly that "an inefficient or unproductive cataloging department is a failure of management. Libraries that do not devise means to use the accumulated expertise of their catalogers in innovative ways are wasting an invaluable human resource," (Gorman 1995, 33). The buck very much does stop here, at the desk of the Assistant Director for Technical Services.

Not only do we have to sell this agenda for change to our Technical Services staff, but to our library directors. They must also be convinced so that they in turn can sell the desired agenda for change to their bosses. If we had done a better job of 'coercive persuasion,' then perhaps there would be fewer articles such as that of Ellen Waite, who responded to Michael Gorman by calling attention to the "stagnant administration of catalog and technical services departments, and . . . rigid professional standards," (Waite 1995, 36). Waite lists three features of Technical Services departments "which do not mesh well with the new environment: they are expensive, they are slow, and they do not meet the information needs of our patrons," (Waite 1995, 36), thus indirectly calling for a refocused agenda which embodies the very qualities of nimbleness and agility we are looking for.

2. Continuing Education

Go back to school, send your staff back to school. One of the factors that did influence positive Internet use was knowledge (Finlay and Finlay 1996, 80). This was not necessarily defined as training or education - in fact, the authors see the topic of education as another research question to explore, 'how does this knowledge happen?' (Finlay and Finlay 1996, 81).

The number and type of learning opportunities need to be expanded. This includes nuts and bolts courses, like Windows training and html/SGML classes, but also in-depth courses on the organization of information in a digital environment. One such example of the latter is the recent workshop taught by Elaine Svenonius at the Digital Libraries '96 Conference, held in Bethesda, Maryland, in March 1996.

3. Rethink the Concept of Organization of Information

We need to rethink and expand the concept of 'organization of information' in the digital age. Organizing information is what we do best. However, we have over the years allowed our skills there to deteriorate into 'following the rules,' whether those rule books be Library of Congress Rule Interpretations or AACR2. The above-mentioned presentation by Elaine Svenonius, which covers principles and methods used to design systems for organizing information, is one way to get back to the basic principles. Our library schools need to take some responsibility in this area. Concern has been voiced in many arenas that the teaching of cataloging and classification needs to be both revamped and re-emphasized (MacLeod and Callahan 1995). We need to add to current syllabi new modules which focus on information retrieval and scholarly communication in the context of digital access.

We must learn the different ways in which hypertext is marked up and hyperstacks are constructed. We need to understand the differences that searching the Web mean for the user. Hypertext is based on the understanding that human idea processing occurs through association, which is considered to be the framework for effective communication of knowledge, a very different concept than our previous training in controlled vocabulary systems and pre/post-coordinate subject searching comparisons. Hypertext allows one to overcome the limitations of the linear nature of printed text, and allow for three dimensional navigation through a body of data. There are numerous design issues with which to be concerned, such as nonlinearity, presentation of information, the problem of losing the navigator in hyperspace and the need to compensate for the lack of preconditions that accompany hypertext (Al-Hawamdeh et al. 1991). There have been a number of experiments to upgrade bibliographic access over the years such as creating user pathways, establishing pathfinder headings and enhanced access (Mandel 1986). But we need to have a better understanding of the principles that make these strategies successful, or not, and work with both Public Services staff and our users and learn from their experiences.

3. Support Systems

We need to provide a nurturing environment for innovation in our home institutions. Finlay and Finlay call attention to the fact that, once knowledge and innovation have combined to deliver the positive attitude, then, after knowledge, the other factor that had a noticeable effect, was the provision of a supportive environment (Finlay and Finlay 1996, 81). This was defined as having an encouraging supervisor and sufficient opportunity to learn to use the Internet. At the same time, supervisors must encourage their librarians to take risks, 'to break out of the box,' to do things differently (McCombs 1994, 170).

4. Flexibility

We do have to 'give' a little. We need to realize that - just as in the past - there will never be enough resources to 'do it right.' As Intner noted "a mountain of problems stands between their [catalogers] ideals and their results" (Intner 1994, 3). In this era of shrinking resources, we do have to do things differently. There are hard choices to be made. We need to develop our own triage methods, figure out how to delegate down, how to have tasks performed by the lowest level staff possible so we can save that high-quality cataloging skill for more complex tasks in areas that can add value. Some examples are developing home pages, organizing campus wide information systems (CWIS), providing access to electronic resources BEFORE we have a national MARC format, becoming partners with network services librarians or computing professionals, and teaching people how to use the Internet.

5. Rethinking Job Descriptions

Catalogers need to rethink and rewrite their own job descriptions. The recent job advertisement for a metadata specialist at Cornell's Mann Library asks for a "creative librarian to provide leadership in the development and use of metadata. In this context, metadata is data used to describe information objects. The metadata, which may take the form of a MARC record, a TEI header, or a customized format for spatial data, provides intellectual and physical access to information resources," (American Libraries 1996, 128).

A recent article in CIO predicts that "the most dramatic improvements in knowledge management capability over the next 10 years will be human and managerial.... They [knowledge managers] will manage all stages of the knowledge management process from creation to use.... Categorization and organization of knowledge will be a core competence for every firm. This will require strategic thinking about what knowledge is important; development of a knowledge vocabulary (and a thesaurus to accommodate near misses); prolific creation of indices, search tools and navigation aids; and a constant refinement and pruning of knowledge categories, (Davenport 1995, 32). The article goes on to state that the skills to perform these tasks are most commonly found among librarians and print journalists! At the same time, we need to make smart hiring choices, examine the innovation quotient in our candidates and make sure that we do not hire according to the old value system (Rapp 1990).

6. Value-Added Services.

Although we are not accustomed to thinking about 'the competition,' in fact, we should be. We are competing both against the ability of vendors to deliver the same services we provide, and against Public Services units who currently have a very high profile and need increased resources to deliver many of the new Internet services. We need to determine our competitive edge. Is it cost, speed, quality of products, superiority and ease of management, off/onsite responsiveness? The OCLC Internet Cataloging Project is a case in point. The OCLC Office of Research and the OCLC Internet Cataloging Project have recently announced the development of Persistent Uniform Resource Locators (PURLS) (http://www.oclc.org:6990). The standardized use of PURLS would address some of the general concerns voiced about resource stability as we look to provide access to networked resources (Graham 1995, 331).

CONCLUSION

In closing, I want to state very clearly that I see a key role for Technical Services librarians to play in the Digital Age. This role may not be the one which Technical Services librarians imagined ten or fifteen years ago, but it is a role for which we have received ample training and for which we most certainly have the skills and innate abilities. It will take courage to rethink and reinvent the Technical Services culture, to develop new skills and to take that giant step away from the comfort of our rule books and our codes into the digital age. In order for us to counter articles such as that by Ellen Waite calling for a reinvention of catalogers, we need to reinvent ourselves first. We need to change before we have to, and while we still can.

REFERENCES

Al-Hawamdeh, S., R. de-Vere, G. Smith, and P. Willett. 1991. "Using Nearest-Neighbor Searching Techniques to Access Full-text Documents." Online Review 15:173–192.

American Libraries, 1996. 27:128.

Benemann, W.E. 1993. "The Cathedral Factor: Excellence and the Motivation of Cataloging Staff." Technical Services Quarterly 10:3,17–25.

Bridges, W. 1991. Managing Transitions: Making the Most of Change. Reading, MA.: Addison-Wesley.

Cargill, J. 1989. "Integrating Public and Technical Services Staff to Implement the New Mission of Libraries." Journal of Library Administration 10:21–31.

Connor, P.E. 1994. Managing Organizational Change. Westport, CT.: Praeger.

Crowley, A. 1995. "Kids Are More Agile than You'd Think." PC Week 12:47,11.

Davenport, T. 1995. "Think Tank: The Future of Knowledge Management." CIO Dec.15 1995/Jan.1 1996:30–32.

De Klerk, A. and J.R. Euster. 1989. "Technology and Organizational Metamorphoses." Library Trends 37:457–68.

Finlay, K. and T. Finlay. 1996. "The Relative Roles of Knowledge and Innovativeness in Determining the Librarians' Attitudes Toward and Use of the Internet: A Structural Equation Modeling Approach." Library Quarterly 66:59–83.

Gomez, J. and J. Harrell. 1992. "Technical Services Reorganization: Realities and Reactions." Technical Services Quarterly 10:2,1–16.

Gorman, M. 1995. "The Corruption of Cataloging." Library Journal 120:Sept. 15, 32–34.

Graham, P.S. 1995. "Requirements for the Digital Research Library." College & Research Libraries 56:331–339.

Intner, S.S. 1994. "Outsourcing - What Does It Mean for Technical Services?" Technicalities 14:3–5.

Kunda, G. 1992. Engineering Culture: Control and Commitment in a High-Tech Corporation. Philadelphia, PA.: Temple University Press.

Larsen, P.M. 1991. "The Climate of Change: Library Organizational Structures, 1985–1990." The Reference Librarian 34:79–93.

MacLeod, J. and D. Callahan. 1995. "Educators and Practitioners Reply: An Assessment of Cataloging Education." Library Resources & Technical Services 39:113–216.

Mandel, C. 1986. "Enriching the Library Catalog Record for Subject Access." Chapter in Improving LCSH for Use in Online Catalogs. Littleton, CO.: Libraries Unlimited.

———1992. "Library Catalogs in the 21st Century." ARL: A Bimonthly Newsletter of Research Library Issues and Actions 164:1–4.

McCombs, G.M. 1992. "Technical Services in the 1990s: A Process of Convergent Evolution." Library Resources & Technical Services 36: 135–148.

———1994. "The Internet and Technical Services: A Point Break Approach." Library Resources & Technical Services 38:169–77.

Rapp, J. 1990. "Personnel Selection for Cataloging." Library Resources & Technical Services 34:95–99.

Ricard, R.J. 1977. "ISAD/RTSD Institute on the Catalog, New York City, April 22–23, 1977." Library of Congress Information Bulletin 36:430–32.

Schein, E.H. 1992. Organizational Culture and Leadership. 2nd ed. San Francisco, CA.: Jossey-Bass.

Waite, E.J. 1995. "Reinvent Catalogers!" Library Journal 120: Nov.1, 36–37.

Zannetos, C. and P.M. Cashman. 1995. "Balancing an Agile Infrastructure." PC Week 12:47,14.

Archiving the Content of Print and Electronic Reference Works in the Digital Age: An Analysis and a Proposal

By Jean C. McManus
Tufts University

What happens to old print reference books? What will happen to old editions of digital reference works? Starting from these questions, I propose to examine the following interrelated concepts: the potential archival value of certain reference books; the dilemma of deciding what to preserve in research libraries; the role of cooperative collection development and cooperative retention in serving the historical needs of many fields, and how the principles behind collection management can make the transition from the print environment to the hybrid print/digital library.

This paper will address the problems of overlapping print and electronic libraries and, more concretely, will consider certain "classic" reference works, look at how reference librarians and scholars value these, and examine what libraries are doing to retain them. Starting points will include James Rettig's *Distinguished Classics of Reference Publishing* and core lists of reference sources. A regional consortium of academic libraries will be surveyed on retention history and decision-making relating to core reference books, and these results will be presented as a case study of current practice.

Finally, this paper will make suggestions for cooperative reference retention projects with attention to the following details: identification of materials with potential use; location of projects within library consortia, and consideration of mechanisms for recording retention decisions. By looking at both the print and electronic realms I will attempt to give practical shape to the issues of preservation, retention, and archiving in the complex environment of the print and digital library.

CRISIS: WHERE DOES THE ARCHIVAL FUNCTION FIT IN THE ELECTRONIC LIBRARY?

Bart Harloe and John Budd write, "for collection managers, especially, the language of crisis is upon us."[1] The "crisis" is the intersection of print and electronic information in every library and the need to maintain both of these systems. The "serials crisis" and the larger "crisis of scholarly communication" arise from this juncture. These writers expect to see a gradual migration in libraries from owning materials to accessing content. This change, from the "just in case" approach to collection development that emphasizes an archival collection to a "just in time" approach that emphasizes reliance on document delivery, is taking place already and works well for many library transactions.

We would do well, however, to recognize the diversity of users for whom we plan this library of the future. One large distinction that can be made in the academic library is between humanists and scientists, who have different patterns of research, different modes of intradisciplinary communication, and different collection needs. Humanists have unique requirements for texts that are stable, authentic, and in an authoritative form—they need, in other words, to know what editions they are using.[2]

The discussion of the importance of "editions" of electronic resources has begun to take place. Recent library conference panels have raised the question of what should be "archived" by libraries, whose responsibility it is, and how to do it.[3] The essential question of what the library's role in preserving knowledge, or at the very least, preserving contents, should be arises in both the print and the digital library.

Certain research trends bring new uses of library materials. Historians and philosophers, for example, are now greatly interested in old encyclopedias as a means of tracing the history of ideas.[4] Archivists, genealogists, and historical researchers in many disciplines make use of directory information in telephone books, industry directories, and association publications. Such secondary uses of reference materials (both print and electronic) are not possible without recognition of the archival value of materials and taking steps towards their retention. Reference works include things that become instant classics, but also many standard reference sources that are usually considered most useful when new, such as directories. The first unanswered collective question is this: what are libraries keeping? The second question is whether libraries can arrive at some means of prioritizing the tasks of decision-making and preservation in the hybrid print/digital age.

Ross Atkinson sees a particular library responsibility to humanists in this changing environment: "However this [transition from paper to online environment] evolves, an essential role of collection development in this process will be to ensure that those disciplines which lag behind, and which abandon the primarily paper phase more slowly or reluctantly, are adequately serviced."[5] He notes also that: "Because any publication or human creation can have research potential, humanities scholars—and the information service professionals who support them—have become increasingly unwilling and incapable of coming to terms with what should be collected and maintained, and what should not. This would be less of a problem if the humanities, like the sciences, were capable of endorsing the withdrawal of older secondary materials; or if the humanities were able to summarize effectively earlier publications. But the humanities can do neither. Older secondary materials cannot be discarded because, as we know so well in research libraries, the second a critical work is no longer in fashion, it becomes as valuable—or more valuable—as a primary work, to be used in the study of the history of the field. For this reason alone, history remains probably the most expensive 'subject' the library supports—probably much more expensive in the long term than the notoriously costly natural sciences."[6] The "archival" function of the academic library will persist into the future, as a service to certain users, particularly humanists, and also to insure the integrity of the intellectual record. The challenge will be to find efficient ways to serve diverse needs.

For much of this paper, I will talk about and around reference works, especially those reference works that are so commonly regarded as core that they are ubiquitous. To return for a moment to the "language of crisis" that is upon collection managers, the situation I describe is not necessarily a crisis at this time. The fate of reference works does bear thinking about, and solutions imagined here can be extended to other "crises" in the hybrid print/digital library.

TYPES OF REFERENCE WORKS AND THEIR RETENTION

Reference works can include the following types: encyclopedias and dictionaries (e.g., *Encyclopaedia Britannica*, *Dictionary of American Biography*), authoritative texts (e.g., the Bible, the Talmud), fact books and directories (e.g., *Encyclopedia of Associations*, *Statistical Abstract*), and pointers or bibliographic sources (e.g., indexes and abstracts, bibliographies).[7] Many titles in these categories are ubiquitous reference works, held by most academic libraries. Local practice and collection development policies suggest that many old reference works are retained in libraries, although often not as part of the reference collection. An informal survey, described below, showed much duplication of effort in acquisition and in retention of reference titles of certain types. However, some materials, though cherished when new, are rarely held when no longer current.

College libraries and research libraries vary in their retention of reference works. The college library justification for keeping the latest edition only of reference works often implicitly includes an expectation that some regional research library will retain the materials. That assumption is one that needs to be examined in the context of growing interdependency among libraries.

ACCOUNTING FOR THE VALUE OF REFERENCE WORKS

Reference works are just one part of the library collection and are often distinguished from other library materials by the type of use they receive, however imperfect that distinction might be. Reference works represent a monetary investment, especially over time, as they claim more valuable space on library shelves and take valuable staff time for tasks that give context to works, such as authority control and classification. One can claim two types of use for reference works, primary and secondary research uses. Primary use is made of a reference work when it is current, and secondary use is made when the work is "out of date," when it has historical rather than reference uses. One study assessing the monetary value of print library collections established the "useful life" of encyclopedias as five years, and that of almanacs, yearbooks, and statistical handbooks as three years. While this study applies accounting principles to print collections, it is nevertheless interesting that works of literature rated a "useful life" of twenty years.[8]

RESEARCH POTENTIAL AND "ADDED-VALUE" IN REFERENCE WORKS

In thinking about the value of reference works, research potential also has to be considered. Reference books of all types include information that might be found in monographs, periodicals, or government documents; however, by virtue of its format, the creator of the reference work has added value to the information by organizing, summarizing, ranking, or translating it. This "added-value" makes the work valuable when current, but also makes it a useful primary source when "outdated," as a pointer to a community, tradition of thought, collection, or country at a particular point in time. As Douglas Badenoch puts it: "One way of valuing information assets would be to calculate how much it would cost to re-create this information now, or how much it cost to create the information in the first place."[9]

Insuring access to old editions of reference materials is part of the intangible charge of libraries, but it is a task that is not easily supported by user statistics or citation indices. Citation indices, for instance, will not reflect those uses of reference works for fact-finding and other uses that do not need to be documented.[10]

BLC CASE STUDY/INFORMAL SURVEY

Prompted by questions received at the reference desk and a general curiosity about the availability of old editions of reference books, I decided to investigate the retention of ubiquitous reference books in the libraries of the Boston Library Consortium (BLC), a regional consortium of 16 academic libraries. Taking as a starting point the *Distinguished Classics of Reference Publishing*, titles from another core list described by Richard Hopkins were added,[11] as well as some directory titles that are widely held (see Appendix). The titles were checked for holdings and evidence of retention decisions against the BLC Union List of Serials, online library catalogs of the member libraries, and, for comparison, the Harvard University catalog, and the Center for Research Libraries catalog. The results were sometimes inconclusive, but interesting.

The majority of titles included in this eclectic list are retained by most of the academic libraries within the BLC. Reference types, including encyclopedias and dictionaries, and "pointers" or bibliographic sources (e.g., indexes) are retained by almost all libraries, from the smallest college libraries to ARL (Association of Research Libraries) institutions. "Fact books" containing statistical or tabular information, such as the *World Almanac* and the *Guinness Book of Records*, are generally retained.

The one category that is not apparently routinely saved by libraries in this group is directories, the best example being the *Encyclopedia of Associations*, which is retained in all its editions by only two institutions within the consortium, the Boston Public Library and one college library, Wellesley. That decision to retain the *Encyclopedia of Associations* at the college library shows the value placed on the work, but is hard to justify in terms of the use it receives. Outside the consortium, the Harvard University Library retains old editions of the *Encyclopedia of Associations* only in remote storage. The Center for Research Libraries in Chicago, of which several consortium libraries are members, does not have any holdings of that title.

DIRECTORIES IN PERIL!

The real message from the informal survey described above is not that our directories are in peril; rather, it appears that within this particular region/consortium, most of our needs for retrospective reference materials can be met in a minimal way with existing collections. The decisions made at individual institutions to retain certain reference materials, however, are not explicit. Information recorded in the Union List includes summary holdings and messages denoting "latest edition only retained," but no conclusive or consistent indication of retention decisions. Two different conclusions might be drawn from these notations in the Union List: the retention decisions of libraries in this group may reflect an assumption that the research libraries will keep everything; or, the lack of retention of certain types of reference materials may reflect the thinking that those titles are not important. In the electronic environment, these positions may come under more careful scrutiny as research libraries become more stretched, and frank discussions of the value of masses of written material (hopefully) take place. A different kind of cooperation might result.

At the same time that some types of retrospective reference works are undervalued within the consortium, other works are retained everywhere. Another question left unanswered in the print environment is "how many copies of a work do we need?" Or in the words of archivist Andrea Hinding: "... one colleague asked several years ago, more than a little seriously, how many Valentines are enough? How many Valentine cards have to be saved by how many repositories in order to understand what Valentine's day meant in our culture?"[12] Although this discussion concerns reference works, not Valentines, the question remains pressing and will be asked as well in a distributed network environment or a CD-ROM library. As a group, the consortium libraries might save library space and binding, reformatting, and maintenance costs by coming up with a cooperative retention plan for old reference books that would, over time, result in adequate resources for the many, while relieving the research libraries of the job of saving titles that may, in an increasingly use-driven system, be hard to justify.

ELECTRONIC CONSIDERATIONS

As reference works become available in CD-ROM format and over the Internet, issues surrounding access and preservation get more complicated. The questions of whether to and how to save and make available variant editions of works, reference and otherwise, have not been solved in the print environment, so it is no wonder that they persist in the electronic environment. Internet documents, reference or otherwise, may truly be the new "gray literature"; with scarce guarantees of authenticity, no indication of edition, and fleeting (perhaps) availability, such documents present a dilemma, or maybe several, for the collection manager. Reference works in electronic format may also be available only through a limited license, and not for ownership. Insuring access to retrospective reference works for historical research, therefore, may be difficult.

In addition to the adjustments collection managers must make to a new medium, there are new attitudes to contend with—those of publishers, users, and librarians. Publishers of electronic works might be said to be more distant from their products, in the sense that they put the work of gaining access to the content (from disc to screen) on the user or librarian.[13] Users' queries reflect the expectation that everything is available somewhere on a computer, relying on libraries to archive and locate materials. Librarians too sometimes have the dangerous attitude, an expectation carried over from the print world, that the large research libraries will continue to acquire and archive those things that become research materials. The electronic environment offers an unprecedented opportunity for cooperative collection development. If access agreements can be worked out to the satisfaction of consortium members and vendors, the previously knotty problem of where to locate jointly purchased materials is a moot one. What the electronic environment removes is the certainty of the thing itself (the multi-volume set, the drawers of microfiche). Cooperating libraries now need to ask explicitly, not only about costs for licensing, but also about availability of backfiles, and the terms for access to such materials.[14]

CAN WE PLAY WELL TOGETHER?

Cooperation among libraries is a necessary strategy for coping with the transition from ownership to access. Collection managers need to learn from, and form alliances with, other library and information experts in devising successful cooperative collection agreements. Archivists, catalogers, preservation librarians, and humanists are among those groups who can help.

Archivists have developed an approach to collection development of archival materials termed "documentation strategy." This approach brings together interested parties in a region or discipline to come up with a plan for deciding what to save and includes a reporting structure and opportunities for fine-tuning the strategy.[15] Archivists have also long dealt with data archiving and record sampling, areas that librarians may seek to learn about in the near future as local archiving of electronic documents becomes a necessity. Catalogers are at the forefront of developing "metadata" elements that will describe materials in the new electronic media as well as traditional resources such as books, journals, and videos. A dialogue begun now between collection managers and catalogers could insure the inclusion of non-bibliographic information in the record, that is, the record of decisions made about a resource, as well as its description and URL. Preservation librarians grapple routinely with decision-making for preservation. Collection managers have the opportunity to make retention (a.k.a., preservation) decisions about materials before or as they are acquired, whether the decision is local or cooperative. Our users, especially humanists but also scientists, complete the circle of expertise, with their subject knowledge, practical experience using the collections, and interest in the future availability of research materials. All of these experts—who are often represented in our libraries now—could effectively be involved in cooperative collection development projects, along with collection managers and systems librarians.

IN CONCLUSION

Old editions of reference books will, with time, become historical records that point to past communities. Unlike archival materials, this universe of reference works is manageable. If librarians can find ways to save sufficient numbers of enough editions of these works, humanists, genealogists, and librarians of the future will be glad they did.

ENDNOTES

1. Bart Harloe and John Budd, "Collection Development and Scholarly Communication in the Era of Electronic Access," *Journal of Academic Librarianship*, (May 1994): 86.
2. Ross Atkinson, "Humanities Scholarship and the Research Library," *Library Resources and Technical Services* 39(1) (January 1995): 81.
3. Peter Graham, "There's Gold in the Stacks," presentation at ALA/ALCTS President's Program, "The Importance of Print Collections in the Digital Age," ALA Annual Meeting, June 26, 1995.
4. For example, see several of the essays contained in *Revolution in Print: The Press in France 1775–1800*, ed. Robert Darnton and Daniel Roche (Los Angeles: University of California Press, 1989); and Alasdair MacIntyre, *Three Rival Versions of Moral Enquiry*, (Notre Dame: University of Notre Dame Press, 1990), on the *Encyclopaedia Britannica*.
5. Ross Atkinson, "Access, ownership, and the future of collection development" in *Collection management and development: issues in an electronic age* (ALCTS Papers on Library Technical Services and Collections, no. 5) edited by Peggy Johnson, and Bonnie MacEwen (Chicago: ALA, 1994), 104.
6. Ross Atkinson, "Humanities Scholarship and the Research Library," *Library Resources and Technical Services* 39(1) (January 1995): 81–82.
7. After Christopher Nolan, "The Lean Reference Collection: Improving Functionality through Selection and Weeding," *College and Research Libraries* (January 1991): 84–87.
8. Edward Marman, "A Method for Establishing a Depreciated Monetary Value for Print Collections," *Library Administration and Management Association* 9(2) (Spring 1995): 95.
9. Douglas Badenoch, et al., "The value of information" in *The value and impact of information*, ed. Mary Feeney and Maureen Grieves (New Jersey: Bowker Saur, 1994), 28.
10. Richard L. Hopkins, "Ranking the Reference Books: Methodologies for Identifying 'Key' Reference Sources," *The Reference Librarian* 30 (1991): 77–102.
11. James Rettig, ed., *Distinguished Classics of Reference Publishing* (Phoenix, Arizona: Oryx Press, 1992), and Richard L. Hopkins, "Ranking the Reference Books: Methodologies for Identifying 'Key' Reference Sources," *The Reference Librarian* 30 (1991).
12. Andrea Hinding, "Toward documentation: new collecting strategies in the 1980s" in *Options for the 80s: Proceedings of the second national conference of the Association of College and Research Libraries (Foundations in Library and Information Science Volume 17 Part B)* (Greenwich CT: JAI Press, 1982), 537.
13. Tom Clark, "On the Cost Difference between Publishing a Book in Paper and in the Electronic Medium," *Library Resources and Technical Services* 39(1) (January 1995): 28.

14. For a good discussion of questions to ask when acquiring electronic resources, see Cheryl LaGuardia and Stella Bentley, "Electronic Databases: Will Old Collection Development Policies Still Work?" *Online* 16(4) (July 1992): 60–61.
15. A detailed discussion and case study are in Larry J. Hackman and Joan Warnow-Blewett, "The Documentation Strategy Process: A Model and a Case Study," *American Archivist* 50 (Winter 1987): 12–47.

APPENDIX

Titles in *Distinguished Classics of Reference Publishing*

Baedeker's Guidebooks
Bartlett's Familiar Quotations
Black's Law Dictionary
Brewer's Dictionary of Phrase and Fable
Chicago Manual of Style
Dictionary of Modern English Usage
Dictionary of National Biography
Dissertation Abstracts International
Encyclopaedia Britannica
Encyclopedia of Associations
Etiquette (Emily Post)
Granger's Index to Poetry
Grove's Dictionary of Music and Musicians
Guide to Reference Books
Guinness Book of Records
Moody's Manuals
National Union Catalog
New York Times Index
Oxford English Dictionary
Pollard and Redgrave's and Wing's Short-title Catalogue
Readers' Guide to Periodical Literature
Robert's Rules of Order
Roget's Thesaurus of English Words and Phrases
Science Citation Index
Statesman's Year-book
Strong's Exhaustive Concordance of the Bible
Times Atlas of the World
Merriam Webster dictionaries
Who's Who
World Almanac
World Book Encyclopedia

Other Reference Titles

Ayer Directory of Publications (now: Gale Directory of Publications and Broadcast Media)
Acronyms, Initialisms and Abbreviations Dictionary
Books in Print
Forthcoming Books
Hotel and Motel Red Book
Magazines for Libraries
Paperbound Books in Print
Peterson's Guide to Colleges
Publisher's Trade List Annual
Rand McNally Commercial Atlas and Marketing Guide
Reader's Adviser
Select Phone (on FirstSearch or CD-ROM)
Standard Directory of Advertisers
Subject Guide to Books in Print
Thomas Register
Ulrich's International Periodicals Directory
Value-Line

A Picture Is Worth a Thousand Words of Bibliographic Description

By Russell Owen Pollard
Harvard University

The capability of linking bibliographic records and images in the online catalog provides a solution to a traditional problem in the bibliographic description of rare books; namely, how to represent in as much detail as possible the actual appearance of a rare book title page. Current standards for the bibliographic description of rare books represent an uneasy compromise between the needs of bibliographers and the expense of cataloging. This paper will chronicle the tradition of title page transcription for rare books and consider how developments in online catalogs, particularly the World Wide Web and its hypertext links, combine with developments in imaging technology, particularly scanning, to provide a new possibility for realizing the long standing goal of rare book bibliographers and catalogers to use title page images for identification and access. It will report on a modest home grown prototype designed to demonstrate this capability, and on what was learned from experimenting with it. Finally it will suggest ways that image-enhanced cataloging might contribute to the development of more convenient and informative online catalogs.

THE PROBLEM OF "U'S" AND "V'S"

One minor episode in the development of standards for the transcription of rare book title pages serves to illustrate the problem and the need. In 1981 the Library of Congress published *Bibliographic Description of Rare Books* (BDRB), an interpretation of *Anglo-American Cataloging Rules, Second Edition* for this special class of materials. This publication, along with *International Standard Bibliographic Description for Older Books (Antiquarian)*, promulgated by the International Federation of Library Associations, marked the beginning of the most recent phase in the standardization of rare book cataloging. Rare books, for the purposes of these standards, were considered to be those produced during the era of the hand press, or generally prior to 1801.

The transcription of the letters "u" and "v" has long been an issue for rare book catalogers. Prior to the mid seventeenth century they were considered to be two forms of the same letter and there was no distinction between "u" as a vowel and "v" as a consonant. Current practice requires that words on the title page be capitalized as they would be in a sentence in the language of the title, rather than as they might in fact appear on the title page. Since words on rare book title pages were often printed in all capitals, or began with capitals as a stylistic device for the title page, catalogers often need to change case. The rules for this transcription specify that the practice of the book's printer for upper/lowercase "u's" and "v's" be followed, so that in effect the letter used when changing case is the one the printer would have theoretically selected. When it is not possible to discern a printer's pattern from other words on the title page or within the text, a rule is applied that is based on the most common practices of the time. The common practice was to always use "V" in uppercase, "v" in lowercase at the beginning of a word, and "u" in lowercase in the middle.[1]

The current rule for this transcription first appeared in BDRB, 1981, as the now infamous Rule 0H.[2] It was unclearly written, often misunderstood and probably frequently misapplied. When preparation began for the revision of BDRB, Rule 0H elicited more comments, complaints and questions than any other.[3] So with the publication of a revised edition in 1991, which bore the revised title *Descriptive*

Cataloging of Rare Books (DCRB), the rule was completely rewritten and additional information on early printing practices was made available in an appendix. Meanwhile however, a decade of confusion had passed. For many shared records created during that time it is impossible to surmise what actually appeared on the title page. Whether the transcription "ubiquitate" appeared as "Ubiquitate," "Vbiquitate," "vbiqvitate," "UBIQUITATE," or "VBIQVITATE" would need to be verified by checking the title page itself. If the image of the title page were readily available to verify the transcription, this poorly written and inconsistently applied rule would not be so problematic.

FROM QUASI-FACSIMILE TO CALCULATED RISK

The idea of using images of title pages as an adjunct to rare book description is certainly not new. It has a long tradition, first in analytical bibliography, and later in descriptive cataloging. It grew out of the tradition of "quasi-facsimile" transcription. In quasi-facsimile different type fonts are used to represent the type styles—roman, italic, or gothic—that appear on the title page. Many other details such as contracted forms, ligatures, line endings, punctuation and ornaments are also represented. In short, quasi-facsimile is an attempt to depict the *form* of the title page in type fonts as much as is possible.[4]

The bibliographers Edward Capell in the eighteenth century and Falconer Madan in the late nineteenth were advocates of this method. Each in his own way worked to "help the reader visualize the title—an antiquarian interest for Capell, a desire to show changes in layout in historical perspective for Madan."[5] W. W. Greg and his disciple Fredson Bowers, two great twentieth-century bibliographers, were very strong advocates of quasi-facsimile as the best way to achieve Capell and Madan's goal of visualizing.

While quasi-facsimile was an appropriate ideal for printed bibliographies, it was soon recognized to be impractical for typed cards in catalogs. For that purpose a version of quasi-facsimile was developed which employed conventions such as underlining and dots to represent the type fonts of italic and black letter respectively. In this way the detail of quasi-facsimile was preserved, in so far as possible, on typed cards.[6]

In his classic *How to Catalog a Rare Book,* Paul Shaner Dunkin offers two alternatives to quasi-facsimile. One, known as "full content" transcription, makes the typing easier by eliminating any attempt to represent type fonts. Everything is typed entirely in roman. Further, capitalization is transcribed as it would be in a sentence in the language and not as it appears. Otherwise the content is as "full" as it would be in quasi-facsimile.[7] The other, known as "calculated risk" transcription, is a more radical departure. In calculated risk transcription line endings and insertions are eliminated, lengthy titles and other lines are shortened by using the marks of omission, roman numerals are changed to Arabic. The result is a short bibliographic sentence that appears much the same as a modern transcription done for a contemporary book using current rules; in fact, it is probably even briefer. The "risk" that is calculated is that simpler, briefer transcription will occasionally fail to be sufficient to identify an edition or issue, but studies have indicated that this would only be true for a very small percentage of cases.[8] Dunkin had one other proposal for transcription: photographic reproduction. Photographic reproduction would remove the risk from calculated risk.

Dunkin argued: "Photographic reproduction saves a great deal of time; it is accurate; it more exactly shows the kinds and relative sizes of type and ornaments, and there is no need to agonize over what to omit from a transcription. With photographic reproduction of the title and collation by gatherings and pagination, the cataloger has done all he can short of handing the reader the book itself."[9] And he concludes: "Quasi-facsimile or full content only are traditional, and they offer many advantages, but they are costly. Calculated risk transcription is much cheaper and does almost as complete a job. Photographic reproduction seems best of all."[10]

Even while strongly favoring quasi-facsimile, Bowers also conceded that photographic reproductions are useful additions to transcription. But he did so only begrudgingly. First he argued against J. M. Osborn's proposal to eliminate quasi-facsimile altogether in favor of photographic reproductions. Then he rehearsed a litany of potential problems with photographic reproductions, noting among other things that the reproduction of an imperfect copy, or poor inking, might cause textual distortions; that imperfections on the paper may appear to be punctuation; and that manufacturers might corrupt plates by retouching them.[11] These are mentioned because, as will be seen, they are also valid considerations in the production of title page images using technology that is available today.

The development of rules for the transcription of rare book title pages moved from the ideal of representing the title page in as much detail as possible to much simpler representations that would be greatly enhanced by photographic representations. The desire to be able to "see" the title page remained throughout, but the catalog transcription was simplified in the interest of saving time and money. While current rules permit an even more lengthy transcription than calculated risk, a so-called "faithful transcription," they do not reproduce any of the detail of the typography and page layout characteristic of quasi-facsimile or full content. Of course not even quasi-facsimile could reproduce all the details of typography and page layout. Printers' marks and other illustrations could not be represented for example. Only an image of the title page would enable bibliographers and catalogers to realize the goal of being able to see the title page detail that is preferred.

THE NEW POSSIBILITY

Efforts to apply existing technology to integrate title page images within the catalog are also not new. One experiment reported in 1968 involved the mounting of photographs of title pages directly onto catalog cards.[12] It is even reported that some cards in the old catalog in Widener Library at Harvard had microfilmed images of rare book title pages affixed.[13] Now a combination of new technologies provide a new possibility. Developments in the online catalog, especially the emerging Web catalogs with hypertext links, and developments in digital imaging technology, especially scanning, are the new components.

With the increasing popularity of the Web, we are beginning to see the development of both Web gateways for providing Web access to online catalogs and Web-based catalogs or "webcats" or "webpacs."[14] Webcats are designed so that hypertext links, one of the most appealing features of the Web, are fully integrated.

Hypertext Markup Language (HTML) is the common encoding standard for documents displayed on the Web. HTML is a close relative of Standard Generalized Markup Language (SGML) which is one of the most common standards used in electronic publishing today. HTML makes it possible for Web browsing software such as Mosaic or Netscape to display text and graphics. Moreover, it provides the coding for hypertext links to other electronic documents and images by accommodating Uniform Resource Locators (URL's), the computer addresses of linked files or sites. In the Windows environment, the click of a mouse on a highlighted phrase or graphic brings the linked document or image into display. Hence a bibliographic record coded in HTML can contain a link from the title, which would be highlighted or underscored, to an electronic file of the image of the title page.[15]

Another possible way to create such links would be to use field 856 in MARC records. Field 856 was created specifically to locate and retrieve a wide variety of electronic data on the Internet, including electronic documents and images.[16] Here is an example of an 856 taken from Harvard's HOLLIS catalog: 856:7 : $u http://listserv.american.edu/catholic/church/papal/jp.ii/jp2evanv.html $2 http. The field is part of the local holdings data, and generates a public display something like: To access use URL: http://listserv.american.edu/catholic/church/papal/jp.ii/jp2evanv.html. In future editions of the online catalog, especially those based on client/server architecture, such a link will become "hot" and provide basically the same functionality as described for HTML links above. (You might have guessed that this particular one will link a record for a papal encyclical to a digitized text of the encyclical.)

However, to use field 856 to link to images of rare book title pages would require revision of the current guidelines, since the field is designed to provide access to documents that are described by the record, but not to ones that are serving as adjuncts to the descriptive cataloging itself. The subfield 3, "Materials specified," might be appropriated for this purpose, since it contains information specifying that only a part of the bibliographic item is being linked. For example, if the record is for a collection of someone's papers and a finding aid is mentioned in a note, subfield 3 can be used to indicate a link to the finding aid. Thus "$3 Title page" might be used, but even this would be a stretch of the intended definition. A new subfield specifically designed for descriptive cataloging information would better serve to create the link to the title page image.

Scanning documents into computers for storage and retrieval has become almost commonplace in the banking, credit card and insurance industries, as well as in other businesses that involve large amounts of paperwork. In libraries most applications so far have been developed for the preservation of brittle materials or for the wider distribution of local use materials such as archives and microfilms.[17] For example, Cornell has experimented with the scanning of brittle books and Yale with microfilms. These experiments have involved the use of raster type scanning devices, or devices that capture images as patterns of dots so that the image is represented in much the same way as a pointillist painting. Pages of text are scanned so the resulting image is an image of a text, or an image of a mixture of text and illustrations, but it is a digitized image, not an ASCII or character-coded text.

The dots captured by the scanner are converted into numerical sequences or bitmaps that can be manipulated, stored and transmitted by a computer. The numerical sequences code information about the lightness/darkness of a particular dot, its location in the image and, perhaps, its color. In general the quality of the image is directly related to the number of dots that are captured and stored: the more dots, the better the image. This measure of quality is called resolution and is usually given in dots per inch (dpi). Already experiments such as the one at Cornell have led to the recommendation of 600 dpi for preservation purposes.[18]

A big problem, however, is that the higher the resolution, the larger the electronic file that is created, and consequently, the more memory that is required to store it. Color images, which require even more bits to record the color information, are huge. The storage capacities for large scale projects are being estimated in quantities of hundreds of megabytes or several gigabytes. Another problem for large files of data is the time it takes to transmit across a network, as any PC user who has attempted to download a color image file can attest. Transmitting a 1 megabyte digital image at 9,600 bits-per-second takes 17.4 minutes.[19] These problems of size are considerable challenges for those developing library applications, but they are not so problematic for the purposes of rare book cataloging, as will be explained in the observations and conclusions regarding the following experiment.

A MODEST EXPERIMENT

In order to test the applicability of the technologies described above to the linking of bibliographic records and images of rare book title pages, a modest prototype using the hardware and software conviently available in my library was set up.

The equipment included: (1) Microtek's ScanMaker IIsp, a relatively inexpensive flat bed scanner with a glass platen size of 8.5 x 11.69 inches. (2) Image Star II image processing software, provided with the scanner, and Lview Pro, a shareware image display and editing software. Both products were also used to convert file formats. (3) 486 PCs with SVGA monitors (8 bit/256 color), Windows 3.1 and Netscape.

Title pages were scanned in color, grayscale and line art. Images were edited for legibility or to reduce the file size and were saved in various raster type file formats (e.g. TIFF, BMP, and PCX), but were ultimately converted to the Graphic Interchange Format (GIF). The GIF file format allows high-quality, high-resolution graphics to be displayed on many different types of hardware, and it is especially suitable for inexpensive PC monitors that are limited to 256 colors. GIF files are typically used for hypertext-linked images in the network environment.[20]

Bibliographic records were cut from HOLLIS, Harvard's online catalog, and pasted into a Windows Notebook. Simple HTML codes were supplied, including the "A HREF" code which created the link between the book's title and the title page image. The file was then saved as an HTML document (with the file extension ".htm") for retrieval using Netscape. After opening the file containing the bibliographic record, a simple mouse click on the highlighted and underlined title brought up the image of the title page.

Observations and Conclusions

Although only a modest experiment using a relatively unsophisticated prototype, it does demonstrate that the concept works. Legible title page images were produced, hypertext links created and the results could be viewed in Netscape. Putting it together led to the following conclusions, observations and recommendations:

(1) Image Resolution and File Size

Although image scanning for preservation purposes requires high resolution (a recommended 600 dpi in some cases), images suitable for SVGA display can be created at a much lower resolution and file size, since these monitors only display at 70 to 150 dpi.[21] Color images in this experiment were produced in the range of 100–200 kilobytes, far below the image sizes of preservation applications. Moreover small file sizes mean that transmission rates fall within acceptable ranges: seconds rather than minutes. These images were considered to be satisfactory because the type fonts were legible enough to distinguish between "u's" and "v's," determine line endings, view printers' marks and generally view title page elements of interest to bibliographers. No attempt was made to accurately reproduce the color of the paper.

(2) Size of Original and enhancements

One way to preserve the integrity of the original is to maintain the same ratio of height to width so that the sizes of type fonts and spacing between lines of type remain in the same proportions. Most image editing software, such as the products used here, include settings which maintain these proportions. So while the actual size might be changed in the interest of greater legibility, it would be theoretically possible for bibliographers to reconstruct the page in its original size if the original height and width were also reported. One recommendation therefore is that this information be provided along with the image display.

The image editing software can make changes in lightness/darkness, blurring/sharpening and background contrast, among many other things. All this can produce greater legibility, but the end result must be a faithful reproduction. A faithful reproduction is one in which no type element that was on the original is removed and nothing that appears to be a type element introduced. A faithful reproduction is necessary to address the concerns expressed by Bowers (see above) regarding distortions on photographic reproductions.[22]

The scanner that was used cannot accommodate an original larger than 8.5 x 11.69 inches, which is a typical platen size for business applications. This limitation means therefore that many of the folio or other large size rare books would need a scanner with a much larger platen.

(3) Conservation

Conservation is of course an overriding priority in the handling of rare books and it is perhaps the greatest obstacle to the idea proposed here. Not only is the equipment too small to accommodate many rare books, but it is also poorly designed to facilitate scanning without possible damage. The current products are designed basically the same as standard photocopiers and therefore present the same threats to the physical condition of the pieces. While some photocopiers have been designed with special cradles for fragile materials, no scanners equipped with cradles are currently marketed. It might be possible to photocopy and then scan the photocopies, but that is less than ideal because of the increased risk of introducing distortions. Digitizing cameras might also provide a solution. Equipment that addresses conservation concerns is needed to facilitate any wider implementation.

Conservation concerns also limit the portability, or transportability, of rare books. They normally cannot travel far and handling needs to be minimized. Therefore the images will need to be produced locally, either within the cataloging department itself or at a nearby image services lab.

(4) Workflow and Expense

Who would produce these images and at what point in the cataloging process? The best images naturally are produced by operators familiar with the equipment. Scanning equipment involves the use of complicated settings for best results. Since it is unlikely that most rare book catalogers will be either skilled or equipped to do the scanning, the image will need to be produced either before or after cataloging. Operators would need guidelines regarding proportionality and faithful reproduction and catalogers should probably check the image to guarantee that it truly enhances the bibliographic record without misleading the bibliographer.

Beyond that the process would not require any more of the cataloger's time. In theory it could save time, since it should make it possible to adopt minimal level cataloging standards for the description.[23] In reality, though, this is highly unlikely, since most pre-1800 books have already been cataloged and shared MARC records are readily available. Further, in many settings there would need to be a retrospective project to add images to existing cataloging.

Therefore it is doubtful that any time would be saved in practice. Also, the costs of scanning, as well as storing and retrieving the images, would be additional. It would, however, save the time of scholars and bibliographers by lessening the amount of travel and correspondence necessary to identify and distinguish editions. And if images are increasingly integrated into future versions of online catalogs, it might be possible to incorporate the production of rare book title page images in the same workflow without much additional cost. Library administrators will need to weigh these costs against the benefits to bibliographers.

IMAGE ENHANCED CATALOGING

Linking scanned images of rare book title pages to bibliographic records is a specific application of the more general concept of using images to enhance cataloging in online catalogs. There are a number of other ways that the concept might be applied to solve cataloging problems or to add useful information.

> Links to title pages in nonroman script or title pages with characters that cannot be otherwise reproduced. (The development of UNICODE, a universal MARC code that accommodates nonroman scripts may also provide a solution to this cataloging problem.)
>
> Links to images of tables of contents, indexes and summaries.
>
> Links to personal and corporate author information such as that found on authority records, e.g., information about pseudonyms or other name forms; institutional histories; biographical information; explanatory information.
>
> Links to portraits and illustrations mentioned in the description.
>
> Links to online exhibits which provide further historical context for the piece, e.g., a link from a rare book record to an online exhibit which includes the cataloged book.
>
> Links to citations (MARC field 510).

The online catalog itself can become a virtual hypertext encyclopedia. Image enhanced cataloging will enable us to jazz up the catalog with images in useful ways so that future online catalogs are more convenient, informative and interesting to researchers.

ENDNOTES

1. For background on the printer's use of "u" and "v," see *Descriptive Cataloging of Rare Books,* 2nd edition (Washington, D.C.: Cataloging Distribution Service, Library of Congress, 1991), 6–7 and Appendix B.
2. *Bibliographic Description of Rare Books* (Washington: Library of Congress, 1981), 7.
3. Laura Stalker and Jackie M. Dooley, "Descriptive Cataloging and Rare Books," *Rare Books & Manuscripts Librarianship*, 7:1 (1992): 19.
4. For details about quasi-facsimile transcription, as well as other alternative transcriptions, see the following: Fredson Bowers, *Principles of Bibliographical Description*, Reprint of the 1949 edition with introduction by G. Thomas Tanselle (New Castle, Del.: Oak Knoll Press, 1994), 135–184; Ronald B. McKerrow, *An Introduction to Bibliography for Literary Students*, Reprint of the second impression, 1928 (New Castle, Del.: Oak Knoll Press, 1994), 145–151; Philip Gaskell, *A New Introduction to Bibliography* (Oxford: Clarendon Press, 1974), 322–328; Paul Shaner Dunkin, *How to Catalog a Rare Book*, second edition, revised (Chicago: American Library Association, 1973), 17–40.
5. David F. Foxen, *Thoughts on the History and Future of Bibliographical Description* (Berkeley: University of California Press, 1970), 18.
6. Dunkin, *How to Catalog a Rare Book*, 17–21.
7. Ibid., 21–36.
8. Ibid., 36–40.
9. Ibid., 40.
10. Ibid., 40.
11. Bowers, *Principles of Bibliographical Description,* 135–136.
12. Philip J. Weimerskirch, "The Use of Title-Page Photography in Cataloging," *Library Resources and Technical Services,* 12 (1968): 37–46.
13. Reported by Michael Fitzgerald, Research Librarian for Data Organization, Retrieval and Access, Widener Library, Harvard University.
14. For examples of webcats, try the following

URL's: http://www.iii.com/screens/opacintro.html; http://www.sirsi.com/webcattoc.html; http://webpac.als.ameritech.com/; and http://www.dra.com/opener.html. Also see Tim Kambitsch, "Mainstreaming Our Library Catalogs," in American Theological Library Association, *Summary of Proceedings, Forty-ninth Annual Conference* (Evanston, Ill.: American Theological Library Association, 1995): 121–132.

15. There is an abundance of information available on HTML, including documents available on the Internet. Most of this information is from "The Basic HTML Home Page Workshop," presented by Michael R. Leach, Harvard University, January, 1996.

16. See "Guidelines for the Use of Field 856," prepared by the Network Development and MARC Standards Office, Library of Congress, March, 1995. Available at URL: gopher://marvel.loc.gov/00/.listarch/usmarc/856_guidelines.

17. For a wealth of information about scanning technology and library applications, see *Digital Imaging Technology for Preservation, Proceedings from an RLG Symposium held March 17 and 18, 1994, Cornell University, Ithaca, New York*, edited by Nancy E. Elkington (Mountain View, Cal.: The Research Libraries Group, 1994). See also: William Saffady, "Digital Library Concepts and Technologies for the Management of Library Collections," Library Technology Reports, 31:3 (May/June 1995): 219–380 and Richard W. Boss, "Imaging for Libraries and Information Centers," *Library Technology Reports*, 28:6 (Nov./Dec. 1992): 637–723.

18. Shari L. Weaver, "Quality Control" in *Digital Imaging Technology for Preservation...*, 91.

19. Howard Besser, "Image Databases," in Online Computer Library Center, Inc., *Annual Review of OCLC Research, July 1990–June 1991* (Dublin, Oh.: Online Computer Library Center, 1991): 49.

20. For file formats see Pamela R. Mason, "Imaging System Components and Standards," in *Digital Imaging Technology for Preservation*, 30–31. See also Allison Zhang, "Multimedia File Formats on the Internet," URL: http://ac.dal.ca/~dong/contents.htm.

21. Mason, "Imaging System Components and Standards," in *Digital Imaging Technology for Preservation...*, 38.

22. Bowers, *Principles of Bibliographical Description*, 135–136.

23. For guidelines for minimal standards, see *Descriptive Cataloging of Rare Books,* Appendix D, 75–76.

Common Good: Cataloging Operations and Electronic Text Processing

By Jackie Shieh
University of Virginia

INTRODUCTION

Consider the following: what does electronic text mean to the academic research environment? Is it the latest novelty to be shown off? Isn't this quite similar to what Mortal Kombat is to boys, and Barbie dolls to girls: an absolutely necessary thing to own, but what should really be done with those things? It usually takes a little while to figure it out. So, too, is the case of electronic texts.

Catalogers were, and still are, the people who make sure materials that come in unorganized go out with tracking devices attached. Catalogers are the people who have a very definite mission in mind, a sense of what sort of impact they contribute to the general and research community. So what do cataloging operations have in common with the processing of electronic texts? What is it that cataloging and electronic texts share in regard to the vision of organizing library collections, accurate data retrieval, and information dissemination?

This paper explains the development of the cooperative relationship between the Cataloging Services Department and the Electronic Text (ETEXT) Center at the University of Virginia, and, in so doing, provides an answer to the questions posed in the paragraph above. The cooperation involved in this project has produced a decentralized, but highly efficient, cataloging operation that makes use of shared technology and expertise. The rapid cataloging of electronic texts and the immediate retrieval of information on the library's online catalog is a direct result of this collaboration.

The Original Cataloger for Electronic Resources catalogs the remote-access computer files and coordinates the cataloging of electronic texts. Cataloging electronic texts is a joint effort among some of the original catalogers and the Original Cataloger for Electronic Resources. As part of her coordinating responsibilities, the Original Cataloger for Electronic Resources acts as the mediator between the Cataloging Service Department and the ETEXT Center. She disseminates work among the original catalogers of the ETEXT cataloging team to create MARC records. Various procedures have been developed and documented in the departmental manual.[1] Having adequate procedures ensures that materials are still cataloged despite changes in personnel.

The cooperation between the ETEXT Center and the Cataloging Services Department has evolved in three phases. Phase I: The Cataloging Services Department had the overall responsibility for creating both headers and MARC records. Phase II: The ETEXT Center took over the creation of headers, and the Cataloging Services Department continued creating original MARC records by the manual transfer of data from the header to the MARC format. Phase III: The ETEXT Center continues to create the texts and headers. The Cataloging Services Department implemented a conversion program, called TEI2MARC to transfer automatically the header data to MARC format. TEI2MARC has dramatically reduced inputting error rates.

PHASE I:

The Cataloging Services Department began cataloging electronic texts in 1992. The staff in the Library's ETEXT Center provided basic bibliographic description in a provisional header attached to the electronic text. Catalogers used that information to create a TEI-conformant bibliographic header, following the rules stated in the Anglo-American Cataloging Rules 2nd ed. 1988 Revision (AACR2 R),[2] and a full MARC record for OCLC. The headers used SGML with OTA.DTD (Oxford Text Archive document type definition). Over time, the process of creating TEI-compliant headers was standardized so that the staff in the ETEXT Center were able to create the TEI-header themselves.[3]

The header information was exchanged between the two units by means of a shared directory on the ETEXT Center's RS6000 server. Headers were deposited to a directory from which the cataloging staff reviewed them for consistency of description and access points and then created MARC records. After the MARC records were created on OCLC, the headers were then parsed by a Cataloging staff member. Patrons are then able to retrieve the information via either the ETEXT Center's Web home page or the library's online NOTIS catalog, VIRGO.

PHASE II:

The ETEXT Center began creating TEI-conformant headers for cataloging purposes in late November 1994. The Center created three subdirectories in its server to facilitate communication and editing of the headers for cataloging. These subdirectories are headers.incoming, headers.unparsed, headers.parsed.

The newly created headers are deposited in the headers.incoming directory. Catalogers who retrieved the assigned headers from the directory would transcribe the data and record them in the OCLC Computer File MARC format. The catalogers would then create MARC records on OCLC and download the records to VIRGO via NOTIS GTO data transfer. After the MARC record was created for the header, the header would be moved from the directory, headers.incoming to the directory, headers.unparsed. The ETEXT Center staff would parse the headers from the unparsed directory. At this point, the patron is able to retrieve information via either the ETEXT Center's Web page or VIRGO.

As this procedure was being implemented, both the ETEXT Center and the Cataloging Services Department determined that it was very difficult for staff without cataloging training to apply AACR2R standards to headers. It has taken professional catalogers years of training and experience to choose entries correctly, and formulate the bibliographic description. Since the majority of ETEXT Center staff consists of student employees, it was not a wise use of time and energy to have them learn how to apply AACR2 standards to headers. The first solution to this problem was to implement a mentor-mentee program which mapped one original cataloger to a ETEXT staff or student employee. After a couple of months, it appeared to those involved that this mentor-mentee mapping did not work as well as originally hoped for. It became apparent that having a cataloger complete the header was the most effective solution. Thus, the Original Cataloger for Electronic Resources began job-sharing with the ETEXT Center in April, 1995, to edit the headers in accordance with AACR2 Revised standards. This procedure has expedited the process of cataloging electronic texts, so they are available to users in little time.

PHASE III:

To make bibliographic records available on VIRGO, the data in the TEI-header were manually transferred to MARC record format. Over time, the catalogers did this in different ways. At first, the MARC record was created on a form in VIRGO using a cut and paste technique, then a staff member would enter the bibliographic data onto OCLC (as OCLC does not accept computer files tapeload from local online catalogs). At a later time, the catalogers inputted the record directly into OCLC and downloaded it via NOTIS GTO to VIRGO. VIRGO templates and OCLC / PRISM constant data were established to facilitate the creation of MARC records and the data transfer.

No matter which method was used, however, the activity was still quite labor intensive. The cut and paste technique of transferring data from headers to MARC records did not give the catalogers an opportunity to exercise their unique specialties, wealth of knowledge and skills. At this time, most headers do not need subject headings assignment as the ETEXT Center's collections consist primarily of literary works (traditionally, Library of Congress subject headings are not assigned to most literary works). The ETEXT Center is expected to broaden its online collection, so the need to assign subject headings to facilitate access is definitely imminent. The catalogers will undoubtedly find many occasions to perform complex cataloging activities.

The less editing done to a record, the more reliable the information will be. When the data are moved among various utilities or platforms, excessive human manipulation of the data is more likely to cause inevitable errors. Ideally, one set of raw data ought to be manipulated only once when being created and edited.

Beginning in the Fall of 1995, the procedure for cataloging electronic texts was dramatically simplified by the implementation of the TEI2MARC conversion program.[4] TEI2MARC is in PERL programming language for UNIX, RS6000 server, and based on the ETEXT Center's most current document type definition (DTD), TEILITE.DTD. It reads in a header element by element, stores its readings in USMARC format, and creates an output file following the MARC computer file format setup field by field. TEI2MARC also creates a log file recording the conversion activity that has taken place previously.

In the past, there have been several DTD files for the electronic text collection: OTA (Oxford Text Archive), UVA, and now TEILITE. Modifications and changes will be needed for TEI2MARC as the ETEXT Center's DTD file evolves.

What the TEI2MARC conversion program achieves is transferring all data found in a TEI-header to a MARC record with all related fixed and variable fields filled in. TEI2MARC is designed to read in headers, which are created in English language on TEILITE.DTD and give the output in a bare-bones setup for MARC computer file format. Because the Library is participating in OCLC's Internet Cataloging Project (known as InterCat)[5] the converted records will be sent to OCLC's union catalog via FTP. The TEI2MARC conversion program is derived from a similar program developed at the University of California at Berkeley.[6]

The limitation on TEI-conformant header is that detailed information cannot be sufficiently represented in accordance with MARC format. The TEI2MARC cannot identify an element which is not defined in the TEI-conformant header. As a result, some transferred data to MARC format do not have the coded fields attached which are required for MARC. Take, for example, the author Anna Barbauld. The established author entry for her is "Barbauld, Mrs. (Anna Laetitia), 1743–1825." It is entered in header: <author>Barbauld, Mrs. (Anna Laetitia), 1743–1825</author>. In MARC it is transcribed as: 100 1 Barbauld, Mrs. $q (Anna Laetitia), $d 1743–1825. Another example is Pope John Paul. Pope's entry in cataloging is "John Paul I, Pope." In the header, it is entered: <author>John Paul I, Pope</author>. In MARC, it is: 100 0 John Paul $b I, $c Pope. There is no unique character inside the element <author> to assign various subfield codes required by the MARC format. In addition, the establishment of analytical entries is another area in which the machine cannot make intellectual discernments.

What catalogers will need to do is review, add appropriate indicators, subfield codes, and additional access points for the MARC record when necessary. Time saving? Yes. Labor intensive? No. Is it the best use of the catalogers' skills and knowledge?—Undoubtedly, yes.

CONCLUSION

The hottest toys for sale today will be nothing like the toys of tomorrow. When the fever and interest for the toys disappear, so does the potential legacy. Electronic texts, the 'hot' toys of the day, provide information in a manner and format of which no one had ever dreamed before. Without catalogers arranging the information, users will be forced to search results and retrieve what they want in an inefficient manner. This 'hot' toy of the day will quickly disappear in the abyss of the information jungle. Retrieval will become a routine frustration and unnecessary disappointment. The process described above, which organizes the new 'toy on the block,' is good for the electronic text, catalogers, and users. It is for the common good, indeed.

ENDNOTES

1. Cataloging Services Department, University of Virginia Library, "Chapter XII: Computer Files Cataloging. Part B, Electronic texts," in Cataloging Procedures Manual. (Charlottesville, Va.: University of Virginia Library, 1995); available from http://www.lib.virginia.edu/cataloging/manual/chapxiib.html; INTERNET.
2. Anglo-American Cataloging Rules, 2nd ed. 1988 Revision. (Chicago: American Library Association, c1988).
3. David Seaman, Electronic Text Center, University of Virginia. The Electronic Text Center Introduction to TEI and Guide to Document Preparation. (Charlottesville, Va.: University of Virginia Library, 1993–); available from http://

www.lib.virginia.edu/etext/tei/uvatei.html; INTERNET.
4. TEI2MARC, Rel. 1. Jeff Herrin, Library System, University of Virginia Library; available from ftp://ftp.lib.virginia.edu/utilities/tei2marc/; INTERNET.
5. OCLC Online Computer Library Center, Inc. Internet Cataloging Project; available from http://www.oclc.org/oclc/man/catproj/catcall.htm; INTERNET. Project Coordinator, Erik Jul; available from mailto: jul@oclc.org; available on newsgroup, news:INTERCAT@oclc.org; send subscription request to: LISTSERV-Request @oclc.org; INTERNET.
6. Jerome McDonough, School of Library & Information Studies, University of California at Berkeley developed programs that convert SGML texts based on USMARC.DTD to USMARC format and vice versa, sgml2marc, marc2sgml. These programs are available by contacting the author; available from mailto:jmcd@lucien. Berkeley.EDU; INTERNET.

Organized Access to Engineering Internet Resources Using Indexing Principles

By Lynn Silipigni Connaway and Danny P. Wallace
University of Denver and Kent State University

This research project is partially funded by the 1995 American Library Association Carroll Preston Baber Research Grant and a 1995 University of Missouri Alumni Association Faculty Incentive Grant.

INTRODUCTION

The vast international conglomeration of electronic resources known as the Internet has presented unprecedented opportunities for enhanced access to a vast array of information. The casual researcher, scholar, business person, student, or citizen can establish direct access through a desktop computer to millions of machine-readable files linking thousands of computer networks and millions of network users. The result is a cooperative system that constitutes a world encyclopedia, a global library, a messaging network that transcends the most distant possibilities of traditional postal services, an international bulletin board, and more.

The opportunities granted by the Internet do not, however, come without corresponding limitations. The electronic mail, file transfer, and remote logon protocols that made the Internet successful assumed that the user knew in advance what information was available and how to gain access to that information. Although various directories and listings of sources of information and their electronic addresses have circulated formally and informally since the Internet's infancy, they have acted only as a partial solution to providing effective access to network resources.

The more complete solution lies in the development of sophisticated navigational tools to guide the user through the maze of the Internet. The key word in the preceding sentence is sophisticated. Although several navigational tools have gained popularity, none of them is more than a simple, preliminary, experimental approach to a complex, long-term problem. Archie, designed to act as an index to FTP (File Transfer Protocol) archival files, is based on a very rudimentary approach to analysis of the nature of the files available at those sites. The Internet Gopher provides a menu system for identifying documents, transferable files, and remote systems, but movement through the networks can be tedious and confusing. Veronica, designed as an index to Gopher sites, is crude at best and misleading at worst. WAIS (Wide Area Information Server) systems combine the potential of relevant feedback with the inherent limitations of keyword retrieval. Mosaic and other Web browsers provide visually satisfying interfaces to Internet functions via WWW (World Wide Web), but add nothing tangible in terms of effective utilization of network resources.

Recently there has been agreement and much discussion among Internet users on the lack of organization and the poor quality of the indexing of the vast amount of information available on the Internet (Quittner, 1992). Snyder (1994) states there will be "too much information too poorly indexed [on the Internet] to be of any use to anybody." He believes that people will stop using the Internet if they cannot readily retrieve the information they need. In response to the WWW, Vaughan-Nichols (1994) states that the " ... data is not organized ... , and finding specific information can be frustrating."

Response to the Internet and its potential has generally been more emotional than analytical. A typical remark comes from David Churbuck (1993), writing in Forbes: "Full-text retrieval, still very limited at this point, is around the corner. When it comes, the local library as we know it all but disappears. In lieu of librarians we will have programmers and database experts." The naiveté of this and similar statements is initially disturbing, but implies an unexpected compliment to the library profession. Librarians have done their jobs so effectively, have made their libraries so usable that educated, reasonably intelligent individuals, such as Churbuck, fail to understand that any work has been done at all. This is the epitome of the transparent, user-friendly interface. The reality, of course, is that professional librarians are database experts at a level that is incomprehensible to the mainstream of computer science. Library and information science has historically concentrated on intellectual access and usability. The former is typically treated as irrelevant to the design of computer databases. The latter is addressed primarily in a mechanistic manner that concentrates on hardware and software features at the expense of attention to human characteristics.

One of the oldest retrieval mechanisms is organization by commonality. Objects are often organized by their likeness to each other and then by their relationships to each other. This type of organization or grouping expedites the retrieval of objects (Soergel, 1985). This systematic organization that allows for the retrieval of related objects by cross references and relational grouping is the basic premise of indexing. Library and information professionals create directional cues by indexing resources for users of electronic information systems. Sophisticated indexing principles have not yet been fully utilized to expedite the retrieval of Internet resources.

The popular analogy of the Internet as an "information superhighway" is appealing, but is also an invitation to negative analogies. The problem is, you have to find your own way and it is not easy going. Signposts are few and often seem to point back upon themselves. The Internet isn't exactly the Clinton administration's idealized electronic "superhighway," at least not yet. The highway is there but there are no road maps, no rest stops and few on-ramps, and the surface is positively littered with potholes (Lindman, 1993).

This is due to the limited access to the files and documents available on the Internet. At present, keyword and hypertext searching are the best approaches that have been offered as ways to navigate the Internet and its innumerable resources. This approach, however, is not sufficient to provide for the complex navigation that would make the Internet fully usable. The best of freetext retrieval systems requires an unacceptable amount of processing time and tends to produce an excessive volume of return (Salton, 1993). There has been more than ample research to demonstrate the limitations of keyword searching and the advantages of the deliberate application of carefully developed systems for describing the contents of databases. Svenonius (1986) reviews this literature in detail.

The difference between keyword searching and controlled vocabulary searching is the distinction between mechanistic access to isolated terms and intellectual access to unified concepts. This is the key to the utilization of the Internet. Controlled vocabulary searching is not always implemented in an optimal manner. Effective use of a controlled vocabulary retrieval system requires substantial expertise on the parts of the architects of the vocabulary and those applying that vocabulary to a body of literature. Despite these drawbacks, it is clear that the presence of a controlled vocabulary greatly enhances the usability of any information retrieval system.

Controlled vocabularies take one of two basic forms: classification schemes and indexing languages. Classification schemes, such as the Library of Congress Classification and the Dewey Decimal Classification, offer either a hierarchical or enumerative arrangement, or a combination of both. They typically organize sets of classes identified by symbolic names usually referred to as call numbers.

Indexing languages describe concepts by using a natural language modified to produce a reduced vocabulary and simplified syntax. A good indexing language provides for hierarchical links among concepts and thereby facilitates both generic and specific searching. Indexing languages have the advantage of being relatively easily understood, since they use elements of natural language rather than symbolic codes to represent ideas. Indexing languages may easily be designed to represent a combination of subject terms and proper names.

The major disadvantage of controlled vocabularies is that their development and application requires substantial, expert human effort. Although there have been many experiments with automatic classification and automatic indexing, none has been especially successful, and no automated approach to classification or indexing has found its way into general acceptance or widespread use. The success of automatic indexing is dependent upon the consistency of source document and query formulations (Salton, 1989). The design and application of controlled vocabularies is the province of library and information professionals.

To the extent that these professionals have been successful, they have built a truly transparent, moderately user-friendly system of libraries and related information services that provides effective access to an array of information that greatly exceeds the current offerings of the Internet in volume, scope, variety and especially in organization.

OBJECTIVES OF THE RESEARCH

Because of the heavy traffic on the Internet, locating potentially useful information is a matter of concern among researchers and information specialists. Ann Eagan (1993) discusses the challenges of identifying science resources on the Internet. John Maxymuk (1994) identifies some special Internet resources in certain scientific fields and details how access to these resources may be attained. Gail Clement (1994) focuses on science journals available electronically and discusses the problems associated with the access and usability of these electronic documents. These writings indicate both the great number of electronic science sources available and the difficulties facing researchers and information specialists regarding the identification of these sources and the access to these sources.

Engineering researchers often need the most current information in their discipline and the Internet is often the best source of the most current engineering resources. Thomas P. Dowling (1994) identifies a plethora of engineering resources available on the Internet, with no systematic method of retrieval available for these resources. This research project explores the feasibility of utilizing systematic indexing techniques as organizational tools for navigating engineering Internet resources. Specific objectives of the project include: 1) retrieval of engineering resources and samples from the Internet; 2) classification of the engineering Internet resources by non-subject parameters, i.e., document and site types; 3) selection of random proportionate samples of engineering Internet resources from the non-subject parameters of document and site types; 4) classification of the samples of engineering Internet resources by other non-subject parameters, i.e., date, language, format, location code; and 5) application of two subject indexing languages, Ei Thesaurus (Ei) (Milstead, 1995) and Medical Subject Headings (MeSH) (1995), to describe the samples of engineering Internet resources.

METHODOLOGY OF THE RESEARCH

An indexing language can be based upon the language used by experts in a particular intellectual domain. This is referred to as scholarly usage (Svenonious, 1990) or as intellectual warrant. It is also possible to think in terms of adopting or adapting an existing indexing language. This approach is valid when the existing language is of acceptable quality and the need for a new retrieval system is reasonably similar to the need that led to the development of the adopted or adapted language.

The adoption of an existing indexing language provided the basis for the research project. The Ei was constructed to provide subject access to documents specific to the engineering discipline. Specific aspects of the engineering discipline also overlap with the vocabulary developed for the G, J, and L trees of the MeSH list. MeSH is a very tightly structured language that includes an annotated alphabetic list, tree structures, and a permuted list, combining hierarchy, trees, and classification. For these reasons, terms from both the Ei and MeSH were assigned to the proportionate sample of engineering Internet resources.

The project began with a detailed, analytical, functional analysis of the types of engineering information being provided through the Internet. Gopher site addresses were obtained from engineers and from searching the Internet. The engineers are the expert panel for this study. Documents from the Physical Sciences menu items in Information by Subject Area as it was on March 30, 1995 were selected. Each menu item was followed to the end of the menu and every third document located at Rice was downloaded. Documents from the following Rice servers were downloaded: riceinfo.rice.edu, is.rice.edu and belladonna.rice.edu. Three hundred documents were downloaded to the project mainframe UNIX account. The gopherlink information was then saved in a separate file. The documents were printed and the gopherlink information was attached to each document.

Using a sample of the different types of documents, the descriptive non-subject parameters were developed. The non-subject parameters were also developed in part by a research project by Dillon, Jul, Burge and Hickey (1993). After the relevant non-subject parameters were identified, the document indexing coding form was devised. See Appendix A.

The document type non-subject parameter was then assigned to each of the 300 documents. The document type non-subject parameters used are: announcements; bibliographic information; course descriptions; directories; electronic conferences; inventory lists; journal articles; listservs; manuals; newsgroups, discussion groups, Usenet; questions/answers; research reports; software; and statistical information. The documents were divided into groups by the document type non-subject parameter and every third document within each group was selected for the sample of 100 documents. The documents were indexed by the non-subject parameters, Ei, and MeSH. At least two indexers indexed the documents as a measure of inter-coder reliability and as a quality check measure for subject indexing, since one of the indexers has an engineering background. The selection and indexing of Web documents has also been completed. In addition to the URLs for Web documents obtained from engineers, a random approach to searching the Web was used. Yahoo, WWW Virtual Library, etc., were used to identify Web documents. The search terms used were engineering, chemical, civil, medical, materials, as well as terms from the thesauri, i.e., sheer strength, cold climate, etc.

This method is different from the method used to select the gopher documents. The Web document sample is non-scientific and is not an exhaustive sample. If a Web document was substantive enough to apply topical indexing terms, it was selected as part of the sample. The goal was very different from the selection of gopher documents. Basically, the gopher documents were limited to a sample of 100. One hundred Web site documents were actively sought to be consistent with the number of gopher documents analyzed.

PROBLEMS ENCOUNTERED DURING THE PROJECT

It is difficult to retrieve Web documents that contain substantive information. The searches for both gopher and Web documents retrieved irrelevant sources, e.g., advertisements for departments, individuals, corporations, associations, societies. Gopher sites had many questions/answer, inventory lists and manuals that did not deal with engineering specifically. Web sites each had many links to other corporations, associations, societies, etc. They were primarily links to more links. The Web searches retrieved many announcements of Web sites advertising their existence.

It is also often difficult to establish a document as a single document in Web sites since it can be composed of multiple files and hypertext links to other documents and document sites. This is very different from the gopher environment where either a menu or a document is retrieved. Web menus can be Web documents.

The gopher and Web sites are ephemeral. Names, content, and location may change or cease to exist at any time. When gopher or Web addresses change there are often references to the new addresses. This takes much time to continually update. This is why the documents were downloaded and the date of downloading was documented. Initially, file size was included in the non-subject parameters, but as Web documents were retrieved, it was discovered that file size was practically impossible to document. The numbering of the file size was renumbered with each file included on that site. GIF and JPEG files and text files were all individually numbered so it was very difficult to document the total file size unless someone sat and documented each file size as the system displayed this information. Even when an individual tried to document file size, the information was displayed on the monitor very quickly, making it very difficult to observe and document. In Gopher a single document was one file and all text. When a Web document was accessed, a document was usually composed of multiple files, some of which are not textual, such as icons, images, illustrations, sound, etc. It is unfortunate that it was not possible to develop a method for documenting file size since some users may not want to wait for large files to be downloaded and would like to know the size of the file before initiating the download process.

CONCLUSIONS

Throughout the research project, it became obvious that one must be willing and open to revision when working with electronic data. For example, the researchers revised the non-subject parameters several times throughout the project. The document type, research report was added; file size was eliminated;

and the category, other, was added to domain. It is possible to organize the information on the Internet, but not all of the information. First, the existence of the information on the Internet must be identified. After the information is identified, it must be evaluated in terms of the users and the existing library collection, indexed, and organized in a form that can be incorporated into other electronic retrieval systems. If this type of information is linked to other electronic retrieval systems, the information will have to be continually monitored and updated.

TARGETS FOR FUTURE RESEARCH

This research project will result in a model for the application of indexing language principles to organization and retrieval of engineering Internet resources. A prototype retrieval system will be designed using a text management program. The prototype will be based on evolving approaches to navigating the Internet and may be based on existing structures or on a newly developed structure. The prototype will be deliberately designed to utilize existing navigational tools. The current rivalry among different approaches to navigating the Internet makes it difficult to select a particular navigational approach in advance. It is possible that a totally new navigational tool will be developed to support the non-subject parameters and indexing languages.

The research project includes no specific examination of user behavior in relationship to an Internet navigational system based on indexing language principles. A logical next step would be to examine the distinctions among user approaches to such a system and user approaches to existing navigational tools. Following the implementation of the prototype system, testing will be conducted to compare use of the indexing language approach to alternative, available approaches to identify and retrieve engineering information through the Internet. Comparative analysis will be achieved by constructing a set of typical information-seeking profiles and executing each profile using each of several navigational tools, including the indexing language approach accessible through the prototype retrieval system. Success will be measured in terms of the total time required to achieve an acceptable result, the number of steps required to achieve an acceptable result, the volume of information produced by each search and the relevance of the information retrieved.

REFERENCES

Churbuck, David C. 1993. Good-bye, Dewey Decimals. Forbes 151 (Feb. 15): 204.

Clement, Gail. 1994. Evolution of a Species: Science Journals Published on the Internet. Database 17(October): 44–54.

Dillon, Martin, Erik Jul, Mark Burge, and Carol Hickey. 1993. Assessing Information on the Internet: Toward Providing Library Services for Computer-Mediated Communication, Results of an OCLC Research Project. Internet Research 3(1): 54–69.

Dowling, Thomas P. 1994. Internet Resources for Engineering. C&RL News (July): 352+.

Eagan Ann. 1993. Order Out of Chaos: Science Databases on the Internet. Database 16(December): 62–67.

Lindman, Peter. 1993. Confessions of a Techno-Anarchist. Minneapolis-St. Paul Magazine 21 (October): 86.

Maxymuk, John. 1994. Science Resources on the Internet. Science Librarian 41/42: 81–98.

Medical Subject Headings. 1995. Bethesda, MD: National Library of Medicine.

Milstead, Jessica L., ed. 1995. Ei Thesaurus. 2nd rev. ed. Hoboken, NJ: Engineering Information.

Quittner, Joshua. 1992. Getting Up to Speed on the Computer Highway: Overcoming Real Problems in a Virtual World. Newsday (Nov. 3): 51.

Salton, Gerard. 1989. Automatic Text Processing: The Transformation, Analysis, and Retrieval of Information by Computer. Reading, MA: Addison-Wesley Pub., 275.

_____. 1993. Talk at Louisiana State University, February 26, 1993.

Snyder, Joel. 1994. Internet: Going South. Internet World 5(8): 94.

Soergel, Dagobert. 1985. Organizing Information: Principles of Data Base and Retrieval Systems. San Diego: Academic Press.

Svenonius, Elaine. 1990. Design of Controlled Vocabularies. Chap. in The Encyclopedia of Library and Information Science. New York: Marcel Dekker.

_____. 1986. Unanswered Questions in the Design of Controlled Vocabularies. Journal of the American Society for Information Science 37(5): 331–40.

Vaughan-Nichols, Steven J. 1994. The Web Means Business. Byte (Nov.): 27.

APPENDIX A

Document Indexing Coding Form

1. Document ID number:

2. Document type: Announcements, Listservs, Bibliographic information, Manuals, Course Descriptions, Newsgroups, discussion groups, Usenet, Directories, Software, Electronic conferences, Statistical information, Inventory lists, Questions/Answers, Journal articles, Research reports

3. Site Type: Gopher, FTP, WWW

4. URL:

5. Document author:

6. Document title:

7. Dates:

    Dates covered: Date of production: Date of latest update:

8. Language: Programming language: Language:

9. Presentation format: Text, Hypertext, Numeric, Multimedia

10. Downloading format: ASCII, Binary, L8

11. Geographic location: Country: State: Institution:

12. Domain: edu   org   gov   com   us   mil   net   Other:

13. Subjects:
    Mainframes   Microcomputers   Networks
    Personal computers   MacIntosh

14. *Ei* Terms and Classification Numbers

15. *MeSH* Terms and Classification Numbers

Bibliographical Metadata; or, We Need a Client-Server Cataloging Code!

By Gregory James Wool
Iowa State University

This paper addresses the topic of library catalog records, the standards used in their creation, and the impact of online technology upon them. It does so by examining two concepts, each of which combines the traditional and the trendy: "bibliographical metadata" and "client-server cataloging code."

WHAT IS (OR ARE) BIBLIOGRAPHICAL METADATA?

Priscilla Caplan, formerly at Harvard and now at the University of Chicago, probably said it best: "Metadata really is nothing more than data about data; a catalog record is metadata; so is a TEI header, or any other form of description."[1] In this sense, the phrase "bibliographical metadata" seems almost a tautology, but the term "bibliographical" does narrow things down a bit by specifying data, or information, about data-bearing objects (such as books), or about identifiable collections or presentations of data. Again, we are talking about library catalog records, but also about records in online periodical indexes, as well as documentation for a wide variety of computer files.

At the same time, however, the word "metadata" is quite new, and in fact was coined to refer not to bibliographic records, but to machine-readable documentation of machine-readable data files.[2] In an environment quite different from that of libraries and card catalogs, these metadata records, though functionally similar to card-catalog records, nevertheless took on a different structure. Whereas catalog cards—like records in printed bibliographies—present their data in a compact paragraph-style citation form, metadata records, constructed using database management software, are tables of attributes (or file characteristics) and their values. Whereas catalog cards include a separate set of filing elements that repeat, in a somewhat different form, much of the information in the main part of the record, metadata records seldom contain any such redundancy. Whereas most of the data on catalog cards serve either as descriptive information or as index entries, all the information in metadata records serve both functions.

It is, at the very least, an interesting coincidence that in nearly all online library catalogs, the records take the form not of an annotated bibliographic citation, but of a labeled list of document attributes. In these catalogs, much (if not all) of the descriptive information is indexed for keyword searching, while the added-entry headings are no longer isolated from the record in a sort of appendix, but appear and function as part of the description.[3] Because of this, at least some of the transcribed information or notes used under AACR2 to justify those access points are missing from the records we see online. In other words, libraries have traded in their card-catalog records for—bibliographical metadata!

WHAT IS A CLIENT-SERVER CATALOGING CODE, AND WHY DO WE NEED ONE?

In networked computing, client-server architecture separates the functions of data storage and data access; one machine (the "server") stores the data, while the machine accessing the data (the "client") houses the software which does the searching, retrieving, and presentation. Compared to mainframe-based models, client-server computing not only distributes the workload of data provision more efficiently, it also gives the end user greater control over what he sees.

The way bibliographic records are made available in online catalogs—in the form of bibliographical metadata—can be seen as a kind of client-server process. A MARC record created by one library may be downloaded by hundreds of other libraries without significant change. However, each library's set of decisions about which fields to display, what order to display them in, what labels to use and which fields go with which labels will be distinctive. Z39.50 clients take the process a step further, by transferring this control over retrieval and display from the library itself to the remote user.

The trouble is, these bibliographical-metadata records have been created—and continue to be created—using rules designed for the production of catalog cards. AACR2 defines two types of catalog data: descriptive information and access points, and contains separate sets of rules for the two (rule 0.3). Moreover, by prescribing that all headings be based on information in the description (rule 21.29F), it for all practical purposes mandates duplication of data. Descriptive data are organized into eight areas (rule 1.0B), and a paragraph-style arrangement is mandated, with ISBD punctuation separating the data elements (rule 1.0C). A particular order of data display is at least assumed, as can be seen in rules governing the structure of entries (rule 0.6) and abbreviation of publisher's names appearing elsewhere in the record (rule 1.4D4).[4]

But while AACR2 is rightly considered the first cataloging code to take into account the automation of the catalog, one aspect of automation its developers seem to have neglected is the atomization of the catalog record made possible by the MARC format. A MARC record brings together description and access elements in a single structure, with a much finer granularity than AACR2's eight areas of description. With the help of online catalog software, this has made it possible for libraries to take apart and reassemble their records in ways scarcely envisioned by the framers of the catalog code. While cataloging input (what gets recorded) continues to be governed by AACR2, cataloging output (what the library user sees) is a veritable garden of experimentation. Data elements are displayed selectively, subject and name headings are presented as part of the description, and labels provide an added interpretive dimension.[5]

Such manipulation of cataloging data may well seem harmless, but in fact it often distorts their meaning and compromises their integrity. What displays beside the label AUTHOR, for example, is the content of the MARC fields that have been mapped to it. Since headings for co-authors share the same MARC field with headings for editors, festschrift honorees, and anyone else deemed worthy of an added entry in the card catalog, OPAC displays can be quite misleading to anyone inclined to take the word "author" literally. At the same time, because this information (author label plus name headings) is functionally similar to the "statement of responsibility" transcribed from the title page as part of the title statement, some libraries have chosen not to display the latter in their catalogs—inadvertently suppressing, in many cases, valuable information not found elsewhere in the record.

Speaking more generally, this type of "machine translation" of card-style data to labeled-list formats carries with it three problems:

1) Rearrangement of data destroys the context in which the data were recorded and which helps make them intelligible (much like scrambling the words of a sentence).
2) Brief, jargon-free labels (which form the new context) represent radically simpler bibliographic concepts than those defined in AACR2 and the MARC field definitions.
3) Mixing descriptive data and access points in a record creates clutter and encourages confusion.

Despite these problems, the simple fact is that today's catalog records are modular in nature. In order to expedite record creation, ensure data integrity and make records easier to understand, we need a cataloging code which recognizes this fact and explicitly separates recording decisions from display decisions. This need will intensify as the development and growing use of Z39.50 browsers shifts display decisions, in effect, from libraries to end users. Z39.50 represents the advent of client-server computing, in which an end-user at a PC uses her own software to search and retrieve information stored at a remote site, as a means of catalog access. A client-server cataloging code, by defining data elements which could be displayed selectively and in any sequence, and labeled with a minimum of ambiguity, would produce server-based records intelligible to a wide variety of clients.

OK, HOW DO WE GET THERE?

There are at least four requirements for a client-server cataloging code. First, it should be catalog-format-neutral; the rules should neither prescribe nor assume a particular mode of display. Second, it should, as far as possible, define data elements independently of one another. Third, it should simplify data categories to facilitate unambiguous labeling. Fourth, it should set up a workable relationship between description and access in online catalogs.

We could easily meet at least some of these requirements by revising what we have rather than by tearing down and starting over. The rules governing display, as well as the context-sensitive definitions for descriptive data, are few and could be cut out or rewritten without affecting the other rules. But the big obstacle to an AACR for modular catalog records is the separation of description and access; most online catalog software essentially ignores this distinction, resulting in "dueling definitions" in several data categories. The goals of modularity, simplicity, consistency, and intelligibility would be furthered above all by redefining the relationship of description and access in terms of how online catalogs work, as well as what they could be made to do. But any redefinition goes to the very heart of AACR2, and would require widespread changes.

There are two directions the library community could follow in rethinking description and access. One is to formally abolish the distinction between them. Though there are several ways one could do this, the most obvious is to abandon transcription from the item in most cases, in favor of a well-labeled list of searchable terms either chosen from, or created for, an authority file. Such an approach fits well with current practices in data storage and manipulation. It would at once simplify record creation and increase cataloger responsibility (as it would make a cataloger's work more purely interpretive). However, it could also undermine database consistency in a shared cataloging environment, and make catalog records less useful for identifying specific bibliographic items.

The other direction would be to preserve the distinction, and force descriptive data and access points to be treated differently from one another in online databases. This approach would require few if any changes to AACR2, but a virtual reinvention of MARC. Michael Gorman's HYPERMARC and Barbara Tillett's MARC III are two models of how this could be done. The basic idea is that while only descriptive data would be displayed in a record, these data would be linked to the authority-controlled index terms providing access to the record. Such a development would also facilitate instant access to other works by a given author or on a given subject.[6]

Different as they are, either of these approaches would bring cataloging standards closer to the world of relational database design. Other ideas of this sort are being advanced as well. Gregory Leazer, in a 1992 article, presented a relational database analysis of the MARC formats, which revealed a high degree of data element redundancy.[7] More recently, Michael Heaney of Oxford's Bodleian Library has proposed the use of object-oriented modeling as the basis of cataloging; this would involve simple descriptive records with coded links showing relationships between bibliographic entities (works and editions, for instance).[8] At the same time, a task force of the International Federation of Library Associations (IFLA) is using entity-relationship modeling as the basis for a baseline study of "The Functional Requirements of Bibliographic Records." This approach is significant in that, while based on current cataloging standards, it conceptualizes the catalog record as a table of attributes and values.[9]

Meanwhile, a working model for attributes-and-values cataloging can be found in the Text Encoding Initiative (TEI), which has developed a standard for creating "headers" for digitized texts based on Standard Generalized Markup Language (SGML). Such a header is both part of a text file, functioning as a sort of title page, and a structured and searchable description which can also be converted by software into a MARC record.[10] The use of text markup to encode bibliographic data opens up a new realm of possibility for incorporating cataloging into the publishing process, as well as for creating data to function effectively both as description and as access points. Turning possibility into reality, however, requires a universally-accepted set of data definitions.

A promising initiative to meet this need was launched last year at the NCSA/OCLC Metadata Workshop, where representatives from a wide variety of information access providers and developers put together a set of 13 core elements for resource description (known as the Dublin Core). These core elements are meant to be simple enough for authors and publishers to use, functional in all software platforms and compatible with all record formats. They are also meant to form a common basis on which particular interest groups can construct their own specialized—but mutually compatible—metadata schemes.[11] A Dublin Core extension for library cataloging may well be the client-server cataloging code we need!

CONCLUSION

As the online database has become the predominant form of library catalog (at least in North America), the table of attributes and values (characteristic of computer-file metadata) has become the primary record display format. However, standards for record creation have yet to catch up with this trend, resulting in translation problems which compromise the integrity and reduce the usefulness of records. The modular nature of online records and the migration of record-formatting capability to remote catalog users (via Z39.50 clients) demands a client-server cataloging code for the bibliographical metadata users have come to expect. Such a code, integrating relational database design and text markup with traditional cataloging, would rationalize and simplify data definitions and in the process, redefine the relationship between resource description and indexing. As part of a larger effort to develop metadata standards, it would also extend the reach of bibliographic control deep into the future of digital information resources.

ENDNOTES

1. Priscilla Caplan, "You Call It Corn, We Call It Syntax-Independent Metadata for Document-Like Objects," The Public-Access Computer Systems Review 6, no. 4 (1995), paragraph 3. URL http://info.lib.uh.edu/pr/v6/n4/capl6n4.html.
2. Cf. Leo Mark and Nick Roussopoulos, "Metadata Management," Computer 19, no. 12 (Dec. 1986), 26–36; Stephanie Cammarata et al., "A Metadata Management System to Support Data Interoperability, Reuse and Sharing," Journal of Database Management 5, no. 2 (spring 1994): 30–40.
3. Gregory J. Wool et al., "Cataloging Standards and Machine Translation: A Study of Reformatted ISBD Records in an Online Catalog," Information Technology and Libraries 12 (Dec. 1993): 394, 396.
4. Anglo-American Cataloguing Rules, 2d ed., 1988 rev. (Chicago: American Library Association, 1988).
5. Cf. Gregory Wool, "The Many Faces of a Catalog Record: A Snapshot of Bibliographic Display Practices for Monographs in Online Catalogs," submitted for publication 1995.
6. Michael Gorman, "After AACR2R: The Future of the Anglo-American Cataloguing Rules," and Barbara B. Tillett, "Future Cataloging Rules and Catalog Records," in Origins, Content, and Future of AACR2 Revised, ed. Richard P. Smiraglia (Chicago: American Library Association, 1992).
7. Gregory H. Leazer, "An Examination of Data Elements for Bibliographic Description: Toward a Conceptual Schema for the USMARC Formats," Library Resources & Technical Services 36 (Apr. 1992): 189–208.
8. Michael Heaney, "Object-Oriented Cataloging," Information Technology and Libraries 14 (Sept. 1995): 135–153.
9. IFLA Study Group on the Functional Requirements of Bibliographic Records, "Functional Requirements of Bibliographic Records: Report" (draft July 31, 1995; Parks Library, Iowa State University, Ames, photocopy).
10. Richard Giordano, "The Documentation of Electronic Texts Using Text Encoding Initiative Headers: An Introduction," Library Resources & Technical Services 38 (Oct. 1994): 389–401.
11. Caplan, "You Call It Corn."

Our Individual and Collective Futures: The Library as an Organization

An Organizational Model for Library Faculty and Staff Involvement in the Development of New Electronic Services

By Julie Bobay
Indiana University

It is increasingly evident that there is no "right" answer to how a library should be organized to respond to fundamental and rapid change. What I hope to learn from this conference is how my colleagues' approaches have allowed them to meet new demands for electronic resources while still providing excellent print-based collections and services. In this spirit of shared experiences, I will describe how, at Indiana University Bloomington, a new department was created to provide the support, coordination and leadership to enable librarians and staff to find the proper balance between electronic and print scholarly communications. Our decentralized approach was consciously chosen in the belief that there are probably several "best" answers for us, varying by discipline, department and mission, and that these various answers are best discovered by librarians and staff throughout the Libraries who are empowered to do that.

In the library management literature, there is widespread agreement that research libraries must become flexible organizations that encourage risk, innovation and teams that span departmental and hierarchical structures. There is also some agreement that libraries need to develop partnerships and collaborative projects with the scholars who are their primary users, especially as the scholarly publication system undergoes radical changes with the advent of new technology. Large, multi-disciplinary research libraries with extensive print collections must take special care to ensure that new electronic resources and services complement and build upon their vast printed collections. Most of our primary users, especially those in the humanities and some social sciences, depend on print collections and services. They will continue to do so for many years as the economic, intellectual property and archival issues inherent in electronic publishing remain unsolved. It is critical for us to incorporate electronic resources and services into what is perceived by many as our greatest strength—our ability to closely match our resources and services to the needs of our users. Note that the goal here is to incorporate electronic resources, NOT replace, compete with, or supersede, printed resources. At Indiana University, as I'm sure is true at other research institutions, the Libraries' credibility among scholars was earned, in large part, by librarians' knowledge of each discipline, their ability to build a library collection that truly meets the needs of scholars, and of the rest of the library's ability to order, receive, organize, process and provide services.

Incorporating electronic resources in a distributed technical environment into the fabric of a large research library that has been built around a stable publishing paradigm, (one in which we have operated for decades and will continue to operate,) is much more complex and challenging than creating a separate institution with new employees and a clear mission. "Incorporating" means persuading, cajoling, encouraging, supporting and, at times, catching up with a large and diverse library faculty and staff with wide-ranging skills, interests, and foci. We believe, however, that these librarians and staff are in the best position to select resources and appropriate means of delivery, and make appropriate links to print and media resources.

In order for librarians and staff to be able to respond effectively to this new challenge, they must be granted the authority, responsibility and means to do so. Several years ago, the IUB Libraries reorganized the libraries in order to distribute responsibility and authority more widely, to integrate key operations, and encourage quick and effective responses to the changing environment.[1] The associate dean positions for public, technical and collection development services were eliminated and replaced with twelve departmental heads, each reporting directly to the dean of libraries. At the same time, librarians and staff began experimenting with new information technologies such as gopher and the World Wide Web (WWW). As technology became more accessible to librarians and staff, our dependence on technologists to design and implement new resources and services began to decrease. For the first time, tools for distributing access to information were, in large part, within the technical grasp of librarians and library staff.

Given the broad distribution of authority and responsibility brought by the reorganization and the accessibility of distributed technologies for providing information resources, the IUB Libraries recognized that newly-empowered librarians and staff needed new types of support if they were to be successful in incorporating electronic information resources into already over-full jobs. These included central WWW services on which departments and individuals could build; specialized training; more sophisticated hardware and software; and leadership and coordination in areas that did not even exist a year ago.

In order to provide leadership and support, Jim Neal, Dean of University Libraries, created a new experimental unit called "CBRST: Computer-based Resources and Services Team." CBRST was subsequently enlarged, (currently including myself, an instruction librarian, a graphic artist, and a librarian with a technical services background,) and renamed "Electronic Resources and Services Dept. (ERSD)." What we do, sometimes so amorphous as to be almost indescribable, is to identify and implement programs that empower librarians and library staff to embrace and incorporate new tools such as the WWW into their everyday work of collection development, reference, instruction and cataloging. ERSD is not in charge of innovation; we do not schedule flashes of brilliance for the library. We do not have technical staff, nor do we have operational responsibility for any production service. While our interactions with a wide range of departments, librarians and other organizations sometimes give us a broad perspective, we do not see ourselves as implementing our vision of the "electronic library of the 21st century." We believe that the librarians and staff in the best position to dictate those changes are those who have a clear understanding of the needs of our users at a discipline-specific level and who have the necessary support and infrastructure to implement those changes. Even though the name of the department suggests we are only interested in electronic resources and services, I'd like to emphasize that is not true. The department was created on the premise that the print collection and services provided by the IUB Libraries is central and fundamental and that the way to preserve them is to provide support for librarians and library staff to incorporate electronic resources when and where they see a good fit.

Implementing WWW services is an example of the importance of a unit such as ERSD in a decentralized organization. In a more centralized organization, WWW services might be managed by an editorial committee responsible for all content and design for the "Libraries Web." This has the advantage of informed, consistent design and selection, and presents users with a single face for the library. In our decentralized organization, however, we chose to decentralize responsibility, authority and credit for developing WWW services and resources, vesting these rights with individual departments. Theoretically, this model takes advantage of many librarians' and library staffs' perspectives and knowledge and incorporates electronic services and resources into the work of existing departments and staff. At the same time, however, it gives the library much less control over the content and design of services and resources.

ERSD was able to play an important role in minimizing the problems inherent in this model. It took responsibility, with the advice of a broad-based committee, for central Web resources such as library hours, connections to dozens of networked databases, etc. ERSD also led in the development of policies, procedures and guidelines to encourage library units throughout the libraries to participate in Web development. Any library unit that agrees to adhere to three design guidelines (the IUB Libraries banner must appear on the home page, the page must be dated, and the page must include a facility for users to send comments) is authorized to present, in the format they decide, any information they deem useful to the users of their services and resources. In addition to mandating three guidelines, ERSD provides support such as guidelines for page design, HTML training, and consulting on graphic design issues.

There are many examples in which a unit such as ERSD can provide leadership and support for library units. One of the challenges of a large, complex organization is communication across units, particularly in a chaotic electronic publishing environment. Many issues that arise in the electronic environment do not fit easily into the traditional library departmental structure and lack a clear organizational home. One example of this is access to electronic journals, which has tremendous implications for most areas of libraries (collection development, technical services public services, preservation and technology) but no clear coordinating body or mechanism. A "neutral" department like ERSD can take the lead on these issues that span traditional library departments, communicating about and coordinating them as each department explores ways of fitting it into their mission and work. Another area in which a department like ERSD can be useful is conceiving and coordinating an overall computer training and development program for librarians and library staff. As an active participant in electronic initiatives throughout the libraries, the department is in a unique position to understand and implement training programs that are meaningful to librarians and staff with a wide range of needs. Another need faced by all research libraries today is to monitor the ever-changing commercial electronic publication scene of new systems, new databases and ever new pricing mechanisms.

WHAT WE'VE LEARNED

Through the work of librarians and staff, we've made significant progress on many fronts: a rich array of WWW resources and services reflecting the expertise of a wide range of librarians and staff; networked access to more than twenty commercially-available index and full-text electronic databases; links to a wide range of electronic resources in a meaningful context of library resources; creation of specialized databases such as the Index to the Lilly Library Chapbook Collection and the Victorian Women's Writers Project, and many others. The creativity, enthusiasm and energy that have come from empowering individuals and providing them with appropriate support mechanisms are just beginning to be evident and are growing daily. The range of these services and resources, and the decisions made in context of an existing print-based library, would not have been possible with a small, centralized technology-focused structure.

As these initiatives grow in number and in scope, however, the challenge of integrating them into the routines of the libraries also grow. Lack of effective communication is always lurking as a potential problem. With many initiatives happening at the department level, effects of decisions are sometimes not widely discussed or understood. With dozens of autonomous units authorized to design and select their own WWW content, it is very important to persuade information providers to abide by standard design guidelines to avoid a very confusing and inconsistent set of services for our many user groups. Our choice to provide support for those units who want to participate in electronic initiatives results in uneven progress across the library, depending on the initiative, opportunities and inclination of individuals. We see spectacular, pioneering accomplishments in some areas, and absolutely no electronic presence in others. We have not mandated any level of participation, and some individuals have chosen not to participate thus far.

Although the existence of a coordinating/leading/supporting department like ours is absolutely critical in a decentralized organization, the mere existence of such a department will not ensure success. The key element is that individuals throughout the libraries share common goals and values and are committed to working together to find the best way to accomplish them. We have not had to face the potentially disastrous question, "What if Department X chooses to embark on an initiative that follows the letter of your guidelines, but is not in the best interest of the libraries as a whole?" Such a confrontation could be very harmful in an environment where we strive to grant autonomy and responsibility across the organization.

While I don't know if this particular organization is an appropriate model for other libraries, I believe our department has been successful in encouraging librarians and library staff in the IUB Libraries to become active participants in electronic information projects. We believe our emphasis on supporting librarians and library staff has resulted in a growing array of electronic resources and services that meet real needs of researchers who coexist in print and electronic worlds.

ENDNOTE

1. James G. Neal and Patricia A. Steele, "Empowerment, organization and structure: the experience of the Indiana University Libraries." Journal of Library Administration, 19(3/4) 1993, 81–96.

The Evolution of the Roles of Staff and Team Development in a Changing Organization: The University of Arizona Library Experience

By Bob Diaz and Shelley Phipps
University of Arizona

FIRST TWO YEARS: 1992–94—LAYING THE FOUNDATION FOR THE RESTRUCTURED ORGANIZATION: TRAINING PLANS

In 1992, the University of Arizona Library undertook a major organizational self-study. The reasons for doing this were simple and straightforward: shrinking funds from both the University and the State, rising costs for materials (especially serials), and a rapidly changing technological and vendor environment. The writing was on the wall—it was time to stop and reassess how we went about our business. The results of this study prompted us to conclude that we needed to change how we were organized to accomplish our work so that we could continue to provide access to materials, moving from an ownership model of delivery, while at the same time improving and increasing services for our customers.

Our solution to this challenge lay in making a bold and daring decision: to restructure completely the Library from a traditional hierarchy to a team-based structure that held the customer as the central focus. As this new structure was designed, many challenges arose, one of the toughest being staff training and team development. What follows is an overview of what we at the University of Arizona have learned from three years of experience in attempting, through training and development, to change our work processes and organizational culture.

Before embarking on a description of the kinds of training and programming that we undertook, a brief snapshot of the entire restructuring process is in order. It started in 1992 with a steering committee that was charged by the Library's Administrative Group (The Dean of the Library and three Assistant University Librarians) to study various organizational models and to offer three alternative models for staff perusal. The Steering Committee was assisted by Susan Jurow of the ARL Office of Management Services. Staff feedback was critical to which model was chosen. Once the model was chosen, Design Teams were put into place. The charge of these teams was to design workflow that was customer focused.

When this phase was completed, the Operational Adjustment team was formed. This group represented members of the original Steering Committee and the Design teams. Their task was to take the workflow of the four Design teams and to identify and describe the functional teams and determine how they would work together. This team created the new organizational chart. It was at this point in the process that the Dean of Libraries first became involved in the design of the new organization.

Finally, "Implementation Teams" were formed to further refine the work of the design teams. This work included identifying key work activities within each team and making full time personnel allocation recommendations. After all this was accomplished, several other major tasks needed to be taken care of, including interviewing and hiring team leaders and reassigning staff to teams.

During this year and a half process, the library needed to identify its new values and philosophical framework. What kind of organization did we want? What did we aspire to be? What was our mission? How did we want to organize our work? Based on our study of trends in the business world and an environmental scan, we determined that a team-based organization would allow us to focus on customer needs. We also wanted to foster and promote diversity in staffing as well as in our collections and services, and we wanted to empower people to openly communicate and make decisions more appropriate to their level of responsibility to customers. In addition, we chose to adopt total quality management techniques to improve work processes and increase accountability to serve customers. We aspired to become a learning organization to ready ourselves for unknown future challenges.

While all this was fine and dandy in theory, how to get from "a" to "b" and all the way to "z" was another matter. What kinds of teams did we want? What was the role of team leaders? Of team members? What new skills were required? What was the role of support/administrative positions? And finally, how the heck were we going to train people to develop these new skills and learn these new concepts?

OUR APPROACH TO TRAINING IN THE FIRST TWO YEARS:

There were very few libraries that had undertaken the kind of restructuring to a team-based environment that we had chosen, so we had no library models to follow. Instead, we relied heavily on advice and guidance from a number of consultants.

These included the Association of Research Libraries Office of Management Services staff, the University of Arizona Continuous Organizational Renewal Office (CORe), the INTEL Corporation, and trainers from the University's Employee Development and Training and Employee Wellness departments. The Library's Staff Development librarian (whose title was later changed to the Assistant to the Dean for Staff Development, Recruitment and Diversity), and the Assistant University Librarian for Branch Services (who later became the Assistant Dean for Team Facilitation) worked with these consultants and trainers to identify areas of need and to coordinate and implement training plans for the transition. The Library's Staff Development Committee, a cross section of Library staff composed of librarians and career staff, also helped coordinate numerous in-house programs.

The need for training was the constant theme in all our discussions with consultants. Therefore much of the staff's time in the first two years in the new structure was spent in training. Topics covered dealt with three major themes—dealing with change, team leader development, and team development. What follows are more in-depth descriptions of some of the sessions held and what we learned from them.

DEALING WITH CHANGE:

Because we knew that we would be undertaking major changes throughout the organization, some of the first training sessions held were on coping with organizational change—what to expect and how to take care of oneself in a time of uncertainty. While it was a noble effort, this and subsequent sessions on dealing with change yielded mixed reactions. When the first session was conducted, for example, nobody knew what kinds of changes were going to take place or what kind of impact these changes would have on individuals. This left staff feeling vulnerable and afraid, the opposite of what we wanted to accomplish.

Yet we continued our efforts, addressing the issue of uncertainty and fear by involving as many staff in the actual design and implementation processes as possible and by sponsoring more sessions and resources for the staff at different points in the process. One such session all staff were invited to attend covered organizational values and the issue of trust. Much brainstorming was done, but since not all staff participated and because consensus on these values was not reached, a shared understanding did not occur at this point, even if it was clearly apparent that there did indeed exist shared values within the organization. Other sessions held that dealt directly with change included stress management, time management, conflict resolution training and goal setting training.

Major changes in positions occurred during the staff reassignment process. As a precursor to this, several training sessions were held on the topic of negotiation. Our intent was to provide staff with some basic negotiation skills that they could use during the reassignment process, as there was flexibility built in so that staff could apply for and prioritize which positions they wanted.

Because we wanted the reassignment process to be fair and equitable, 6 staff members (elected by their colleagues and the library's leadership group) served as "ombudspeople" after they received training in effective listening and problem solving. Ombudspeople provided neutral mediation for staff who felt they were not being heard or given a fair shake in the reassignment process.

Since we wanted to increase the numbers of diverse staff on board in addition to raising awareness of diversity issues across the organization, we also provided numerous opportunities for the staff to learn about other cultures and traditions. Many of these events were celebratory occasions that included the sharing of food, music and a presentation by a guest lecturer. A number of technology-related workshops and other events were held for the staff during this time period. Several sessions were held on e-mail and its use, for example, as were two videoconferences on new technologies.

In retrospect, our expectations were high. We thought we could easily manage to implement successfully a change in the structure of the organization and create a new culture while also undergoing budget cuts, cuts in serials, and the implementation of a new integrated library system. We challenged ourselves and the staff to capacity (and in some cases beyond capacity) to absorb and turn the training they received into learning by practice. This resulted in some resistance to the restructuring. It also, in some cases, resulted in a negative reaction to participation in training.

We have learned that training alone does not insure a successful change process. An understanding of the reasons for and a willingness to accept and embrace change have to be continual as does the practice of new skills and behaviors. Training is a starting point, but that's about it. There has to be follow through, reflection, feedback and practice over a long period of time for real change to take root.

Finally, we have found that venturing into new territory is challenging and can be lonely. Because we had no other library models to go by, we learned by doing. In retrospect, we have learned that when undergoing change it is important to work with people where they are in their own development and to be convincing, clear, and positive about the need for change and the vision of the future. We are in the process of practicing the team-based model, and are fine tuning it as we learn what does and what does not work.

TEAM DEVELOPMENT:

In order to follow the team model which the study committees had chosen, our consultant from ARL/OMS, Maureen Sullivan, introduced the concept of teams and team development to staff members (roughly one third of the entire staff) involved in the design and implementation phases of the restructuring process. Included in these sessions were an overview of teams—what they were and how they differed from committees—and an introduction to the stages of team development. To assist these teams in their work, the consultants also offered training in workflow charting and encouraged the teams to gather data to drive their decision making. In addition, several assessment instruments such as the Personal Style Inventory and the Parker Team Player Survey were used to help the staff assess their own preferred work styles and to assess how their fledgling teams were operating.

Once teams had been put into place, our OMS consultant recommended that the entire library staff take the Myers-Briggs Personality Inventory (MBTI) so that each team could identify differences and commonalities among team members during team building, thus fostering a shared understanding of individuals' preferred modes of communication and work styles. The MBTI became the foundation for future teambuilding sessions aimed at members increasing mutual understanding and valuing of differences.

At approximately the same time that the Library began the restructuring process, the University of Arizona implemented a program called Continuous Organizational Renewal (referred to simply as CORe), the purpose of which was to provide training and resources for campus units undergoing change to a total quality management model. CORe partnered with the INTEL Corporation, which in turn provided a full time consultant and some of the training modules used in the CORe curriculum. These included courses on effective meetings, facilitation skills, management by planning, and basic quality tools.

Because we planned to move toward implementing total quality principles and process improvement, we were invited to participate in some of this training. We chose at first to send staff to the sessions on effective meetings, since the CORe program was more comprehensive than some of the training we had previously offered on the same topic. We "strongly encouraged" all staff to attend these sessions because we felt that everyone in the organization needed to develop a common understanding of basic techniques for running meetings. (These techniques included agenda setting, tracking group memory, developing action/decision charts, and assigning responsibility for follow-up as well as an overview of the scope and contents of different kinds of meetings, such as mission meetings and process meetings).

While the material covered was viewed by most of the staff as very useful, there was some resistance to the notion that staff were "strongly encouraged" to attend these sessions. Practice of these techniques was not uniformly implemented in team meetings. In addition to having access to consultants, funding was available for staff attendance at conferences and workshops that helped us learn more about total quality management, teams in organizations, needs assessment and other related issues. We also invited a number of outside "experts"—librarians from other institutions—to talk about some of these issues. In sum, we spent approximately $30,000 on these efforts.

As we engaged in this work, we learned that library leadership's (including ours) participation was vital to the success of the restructuring process. We learned that we need to be anticipators, assessors, organizers, matchers of need to trainers, identifiers of training opportunities, counselors and coaches. Little did we know, however, that over time our own roles would evolve and change along with the rest of the organization.

Looking back, we were very successful in attaining basic conceptual understandings and some follow-up practice of the skills and values we had identified as being key to our success. While we could have chosen a method other than the top down model to attain this success, we believe this approach was necessary because leadership, commitment to change and perseverance were critical elements in this phase. The top down approach allowed us to move forward quickly and allowed us to contribute to the provision of these necessary ingredients.

TEAM LEADER TRAINING:

The reorganization reduced 17 departments to 11 teams. The evolution into teams meant we no longer had positions available for our excellent department managers, rather we needed the positions of coaches and mentors. All team leader positions became open and any qualified staff could apply. Once team leaders were hired, several training sessions were provided by the UA Employee Development and Training Department that included an overview of team development and dynamics as well as an exploration of what the roles of leaders in a team-based environment should be.

Participants also worked together to brainstorm first steps in the team formation process, addressed barriers to effective communication and explored various models of decision making and effective meeting planning. While these first sessions were a helpful start, there clearly was lots more to learn and much more to do in subsequent months, including bringing line supervisors, (later referred to as "work team leaders") into the leadership group and working together to learn these new skills and behaviors.

Diversity training was offered at least twice to the Dean's Cabinet, (comprised of team leaders, the Dean, the Assistant Dean for Team facilitation, the Assistant to the Dean for Staff Development, Recruitment and Diversity, and representatives from the Library Faculty Assembly and the Staff Governance Association). The intent was to help the library leadership gain a better understanding of diversity issues and to gain commitment to promoting diversity within the Library's teams. The sessions focused mostly on individual perceptions of differences, as well as how culture influences one's world view. Little time was given to actual exploration of real life case scenarios in which diversity was the issue. This missing ingredient contributed to these sessions being only marginally successful.

In retrospect, we assumed that team leaders had, through the training they were provided, a strong enough foundation quickly and easily to tackle the process of developing their teams. We were naive about how much time it takes to learn coaching skills, new ways of running meetings, and new ways of communicating with people at a time when everyone is involved in a change process. Early on, we were forewarned by our INTEL consultant that the kind of change we were embarking upon would take up to ten years. We quickly realized that this was indeed the case.

SUMMARY:

Even though the above modules did give a foundation upon which to move forward, the real team work of forming, storming, norming, and performing lay ahead. Especially difficult in the early stages of team development were issues of communication, including conflict resolution and decision making. Sharing and building upon a common understanding of terminology also became critical to teams' success. In some cases, terms like "empowerment", "consensus", and "dialogue" became buzzwords that easily lost their impact and true meaning. Teams had to grapple with these concepts and define them so that all team members understood what they meant within a team context.

Overall, the first two years of the restructuring were ones of experimentation, excitement, and major change for the staff of the University of Arizona Library. In our roles as catalysts for change, we did our best to provide staff with a basic understanding of what they needed to know and do to make the transition successfully to a team-based organization. While there were probably many things we could have done differently, in hindsight, we accomplished a great deal and succeeded in laying a foundation upon which to learn and grow as we continued building the new organization.

3RD YEAR: 1994/95—DEVELOPING STRATEGIC ANNUAL PLANS TO CREATE AN EFFECTIVE ORGANIZATION: FOUNDATION BUILDING, TRAINING AND STAFF/TEAM DEVELOPMENT PROJECTS

As previously noted, the Intel Corporation shared a number of their training modules with CORe, and in turn, with the Library. One of these—Management By Planning—a strategic planning method developed in Japan and adopted by Intel, became the model we used to develop our annual plan for the 1994/95 year. Briefly, management by planning is a tiered system designed to frame annual planning to move forward towards key long range strategic directions. Included in this tiered framework are the formation of strategic objectives, strategies, tactics, and projects. Teams are structured to build upon each other's work from the top (the strategic objective level) down (the project level). Emphasis throughout is placed on using data to analyze the current environment and track future trends.

THE PROCESS:

As we began fiscal year 1994/95, the Strategic Long Range Planning Team (SLRP), consisting of 3 librarians, 3 support staff, 1 team leader and 2 student customers, learned and began use of the "management by planning" model. Based upon careful analysis of available data and trends, SLRP decided that one of our priority 5 year strategic objectives would be:

> To create a Library environment and culture that supports the research and education needs of a diverse, ever-changing University community.

SLRP appointed another team, consisting of a cross section of professionals and career staff (called the Strategic Objective 4 team) to guide this strategic objective to completion and success.

This team then chose the strategy:

> To build an effective organization where the library faculty and staff are committed to excellent service, diversity, empowerment, shared responsibility, mutual respect, trust, and continuous learning.

From there they in turn appointed another team, referred to as the Stratactic 4.1 team (consisting of the Assistant to the Dean for Staff Development, Recruitment and Diversity, the Assistant Dean for Team Facilitation, one librarian, and two career staff members), to develop tactics and projects that would move us forward in reaching this strategy. The Stratactic 4.1 team then embarked on an exercise called the matrix evaluation process to select those "critical few" Tactics that would be developed into year-long projects. The tactics chosen were:

Tactic 1: Develop Appreciation for Diversity as a Strength
Tactic 2: Structure and Initiate Effective Communication Mechanisms
Tactic 3: Develop Clear Understanding of Mission and Define Day-to-Day Work Processes in Relation to Mission
Tactic 4: Train for Skills and Abilities Needed for Priority Work
Tactic 5: Align Reward and Recognition Systems with Contribution to Teamwork and Goal Achievement

The Stratactic 4.1 team continued to use the tiered Management by Planning model, and created 18 projects to complete the Tactics. Each project was appointed an owner (similar to a committee chairperson) who in turn was asked to take individual responsibility or work with a team to complete the projects. The Stratactic 4.1 team then became the Management Review Team for each of the project owners and teams.

THE TACTICS AND THEIR PROJECTS:

Listed below are Tactics identified by the Management Review Team and the projects that were developed to complete the Tactics.

Tactic 1: Develop Appreciation for Diversity as a Strength

The University of Arizona Library values diversity and understands the difficulty in developing support for our diverse staff—to be appreciated, treated fairly and equally, and encouraged to participate fully in the shared leadership of the organization.

Project: Diversity Awareness Training

Two projects were designed to strengthen our appreciation of diversity. A national diversity training group, the Equity Institute, was hired to conduct 2 two-day training sessions that focused on broadening our understanding of what it feels like to be a minority in our society and in the workplace, and on how members of the dominant culture could become allies for people of color and others outside the mainstream in battling various forms of oppression. These sessions were evaluated positively, unlike those designed and facilitated by campus trainers for the Dean's Cabinet.

Our Library Diversity Council also continued its programming and training efforts, sponsoring several informal sessions focused on introducing staff to each other's cultural and ethnic traditions. Some of our most memorable events included: a lecture, open to the entire campus, on Yaqui Easter traditions; a roundtable entitled, "Not So Straight, A Dialogue with Your Gay, Lesbian and Bisexual Colleagues"; and a Juneteenth celebration in which a local dance troupe performed and presented information on traditional African dance. In all, 41% of the staff attended a formal diversity training session, with many more attending the more informal programs.

Project: Cross-Cultural Communication

Twenty-five percent of the staff attended training sessions in cross-cultural communication. The sessions were designed specifically to enable our public services staff to serve our diverse clienteles better. The first workshop yielded mixed evaluations. However, the trainers used the data gathered from these to revise the program, leading to more positive evaluations in subsequent sessions. This particular training program was later integrated as a standard offering in our information and reference service training programs.

Our goal to have 80% of our public services staff (75% of our total staff) participate in this training was too ambitious. Staff readiness to commit time to this competed with other priorities. In addition to having to deal with the challenges associated with the change process, everyone was busy learning new jobs and how to work in teams. First time public service desk employees felt especially stretched with having to learn an array of new skills and behaviors.

Tactic 2: Structure and Initiate Effective Communication Mechanisms

Three projects were planned to help us deal with the lack of a hierarchical communication structure. However, one project was abandoned, because one of the project teams did not recommend formal training, as we expected they would. Therefore, the two projects listed below describe our strategies to increase our skills in openly, honestly talking and listening to one another in our teams and across the organization.

Project: Organizational Communication

The first project in this area was to study present modes of communication and to recommend improvements and changes. Although the project team did not complete its work until late in the Fall of 1995, their work resulted in a number of changes. As the project unfolded, this team realized that analyzing organizational problems by survey can be very complex. They discovered that because there exist a wide array of individual styles, needs, and goals for communication, preferences for communication mechanisms are varied and contradictory, rendering any one system incomplete. The rapid development of electronic communication without much protocol or evaluation (here or in the literature) didn't help matters any. It contributed to our difficulty in determining which changes would yield positive results.

By recognizing the difficulties associated with lateral communication, we were able to bring attention to a number of problems that had been created when the hierarchy was dismantled. In January, we began a new structure for Team Reports (abandoning a required report format that included Highlights, Lowlights, Issues and Plans in favor of leaving the format up to teams) and designed them as Team Reports to the Library rather than to the Dean's Cabinet. The Dean's Cabinet was also renamed the Library Cabinet to reflect its reporting relationship to the whole Library, not JUST the Dean. Cabinet members have also been challenged to play a greater role in team to team communication.

Teams have been empowered to choose what they think are the most appropriate ways to communicate their progress and problems. At the same time, however, they have been asked to be open to constructive feedback. The new Team Reports process and formats will be evaluated by the Library Cabinet during 1996.

E-mail etiquette was reinforced by a list of do's and don'ts that this team asked be developed, and the paper copy of the Library Newsletter was eliminated as this team discovered that staff reported being on "information overload."

The team recommended that the Dean continue her monthly report to the staff that outlined her activities and efforts on behalf of the Library. This helped staff stay informed of campus developments, national developments, and the Dean's interactions with faculty and administrators.

Project: Interpersonal Communication Training

Another project laid the foundation for understanding the complexities involved in interpersonal communication. We offered Interpersonal Communication and/or Conflict Management training to those permanent functional teams who identified this as an issue in their team assessment. One hundred thirty-five individuals, or 68% of the staff, participated in sessions offered to the teams by local expert trainers.

Through this training, teams and individuals have been exposed to interpersonal communication differences, problems, and barriers. Some of these barriers include how we filter communication, how we ascribe roles, how we speak from positions rather than explore interests, and how we have mastered debate rather than dialogue as a way of exploring ideas that can lead us to good decision-making. Many of our staff now appreciate the complexity of valuing supportive, open, honest communication.

Tactic 3: Develop Clear Understanding of Mission and Define Day-to-Day Work Processes in Relation to Mission

Five projects were created to support this strategy, which in turn was designed to realign the work of individuals with team priorities.

It was clear that in the previous organizational structure, the culture of the workplace was such that jobs and individual work assignments had become ends in themselves. As we implemented the new structure, we set out to realign the work of the teams so that our customers' needs determined what kinds of work would take priority. Job descriptions would be written with this goal in mind.

Project: Quality Dialogues

An overview of total quality management tools designed to increase staff awareness of Quality concepts and what it means to be a Quality organization was designed. An outside Quality consultant, (who we also contracted to work with our Process Improvement Teams), led dialogue sessions that focused on Deming's Four Quality Principles and related management concepts. These included a brief history of Total Quality Management, an overview of economic threats to the Library, and a look at the importance of understanding customers, innovation and success. Small groups then discussed these principles and how they applied to the Library. Transcripts of the dialogue portion of each session were distributed to all participants.

Fifty percent of the staff attended one of these sessions, which yielded overwhelmingly positive evaluations. The "dialogue" approach was especially appealing to staff. We felt this was due to small group discussions that supported inclusiveness and allowed participants to engage in creative thinking when addressing the application of quality ideas.

The sessions also served to connect what the Library was doing with what was happening in the outside world, particularly in business and industry. This helped to dispel some perceptions that we were just doing restructuring to do it, or to be new.

Project: Mission, Vision, Aspiration Statements

The second project under Tactic 3 included several components: to develop new vision, aspiration and mission statements for the Library and to have the mission statement widely disseminated so that staff would understand it and strive to align their daily work to it. (A hoped for by-product was that staff would eliminate work that did not meet the mission). Unfortunately, the project stalled because it was assigned to the Strategic Long Range Planning Team (SLRP), who had more than enough tasks and deadlines to deal with already. Even so, by the end of the year, SLRP did manage to come up with four draft statements that reflected library-wide input. Involvement of the staff was a successful part of this incomplete project. However, SLRP ran out of time and as a result was not able to make a decision about which statement to adopt.

Further exacerbating these problems was our one attempt at "lightheartedness"; it failed miserably. Specifically, we stated that the final outcome related to the goal of widely disseminating the mission statement would be that "100% of the staff could recite the mission on demand." We had good intentions—to keep the mission statement succinct and to make it widely available. However, our humor was not appreciated. Some individuals thought we were brainwashing, lobotomizing, and otherwise forcing staff to fit a new, unwanted mold. We felt that this perhaps was a sign that staff were stressed out from having to learn so much and make so many changes. We learned from this. Humor under such circumstances is very difficult to practice without offending or fostering negative reactions.

Project: Team Objectives

This project involved the design and development of a methodology for developing customer focused team objectives. Teams leaders were provided training materials and offered facilitation support to help their teams clarify their team mission, identify customers, outputs, inputs and processes, and develop priorities.

Even though it took longer than planned (six months), every team did develop a set of objectives for the year. To foster team accountability, progress reports on these objectives were to be included in each team's monthly report to the Dean's Cabinet. However, quantifying objectives, learning how to develop timelines and Gantt charts, and staying customer/product focused—all elements of our newly adopted cultural expectations—proved to be a surprisingly difficult challenge for the teams. At times this meant that some teams did not report any progress at all. Staff had difficulty letting go of old habits. They were accustomed to doing work without prioritizing it, and had no previous experience in improving processes and making changes based on customer feedback. Nor were they accustomed to being held accountable in a data-based way for what work had been accomplished throughout the year. Furthermore, there existed little data to describe what priorities teams should focus on. Consequently, many objectives were staff-focused—on training, learning, and developing the new techniques needed to become customer focused.

Project: Position Descriptions

The purpose of this project was twofold: to revamp both the generic portion (that part that outlines the qualities and expectations that apply to all employees) and the more specific portions of our job descriptions, so that they would reflect the new organizational expectations and mission of the Library. The first piece was developed by the three person team that owned this project, and the second developed by individual staff and team leaders (see appendix for generic portion). The campus Human Resources Department was kept informed on a regular basis of the progress made and approved all changes.

Tactic 4: Train for Skills and Abilities Needed for Priority Work

In order to achieve this very ambitious tactic, we created six projects, too many to achieve in a year's time. In hindsight, we should have identified first steps in some of these areas and settled for that, but in our efforts to move forward in turning the direction of the staff toward priority work, customer service and quality training, we bit off more than we could chew. We made some progress, but we still have a long way to go.

Project: Assessing Customer Satisfaction

Our first project was to develop a methodology for assessing customer satisfaction and to have every team conduct an assessment with their primary customer group. This latter piece proved unfeasible. The four member project team did accomplish a great deal, however. They learned about customer satisfaction surveying, how to do it and what not to do, and they created a "generic" survey for teams to adapt.

Five teams (three cross-functional and two regular) have adapted and utilized this survey. It is interesting to note that during the 94/95 project year there was pressure to try it and utilize the data. Several teams did this. However, since the 94/95 Strategic Project year is over, we have noticed that no one has utilized the survey instrument since. Our intent was to provide teams with a foundation experiment, a tested methodology, and a commitment to gather data. Only the tested methodology has been successful. Assessing customer satisfaction seems to be viewed as unnecessary and cumbersome—though we still believe it to be critical. This is an area in which we need to do more walking of the talk.

Project: Customer Service Training

This project proved successful, though not as we originally designed it. The campus Employee Training and Development Department, in its efforts to support Quality, developed a Customer Service Training Program module that was adapted to meet each team's needs. The module introduced attributes of good customer service, and led teams to develop their own customer service goals. Participants evaluated the training well—BUT, no team has yet developed and published their customer service goals or operating principles. So, although the content and presentation of the training was seen as successful at the time, formal follow-up has not occurred. We can only hope that individual learning took place and that our interactions with customers have improved.

Project: Training the Trainers

Anticipating that we needed to develop and/or improve the training ability of team leaders and work team leaders, we hired a consultant to design training modules that would accomplish this. Two modules were created, one for experienced trainers and the other for beginners. While 40 staff members attended one of these sessions, there existed a number of challenges or problems that stunted the success of this project.

For starters, we found that work team leaders and team leaders weren't necessarily the right target group. We lacked information regarding how on-the-job training was organized and accomplished within each team. To rectify this situation, we eventually invited any and all trainers to attend one of these sessions, regardless of their position.

Still, there was resistance. We learned that staff are not generally aware that the ability to teach or train others requires the development of a number of skills, including an awareness of adult learning theory and its application to work processes and an ability to adapt training methodology to learners' styles. We don't think this is unique to our organization, but it reflects how library workers have been trained in the past. Although most training did not change immediately, there are signs that integration of adult learning techniques is taking place in some areas of training this year.

Project: Assessing Staff Training Needs

This project, designed to identify skills and abilities needed by members of each team, grew out of a very strong concern that we had put people on new teams and expected them to learn new skills without providing the necessary training. Since we knew that this was a major problem, we set out to identify those areas of need and to follow up with the appropriate training.

Nineteen of our 25 work teams completed a skills and abilities inventory, but we know of no team that followed up on their inventory in a formal manner to design a training program for team members. We assume that either the training got provided as a matter of course, or the work was not as new as expected.

Although the project was completed as designed, it was done so under duress and without much understanding about how and why it should be accomplished. While we never evaluated why it encountered so much resistance and misunderstanding, a number of things could have contributed to this phenomenon—there may not have been a need to do this, the reasons behind it were not communicated well to teams, or the inventory itself did not suit our needs.

In hindsight, rather than appointing one individual to accomplish a project of this magnitude, we probably should have created a team and charged them to accomplish two things: to assess the utility of this kind of project, and once that utility was established, to communicate its importance to each team.

Project: Training Documentation

This is another project that was only marginally successful. While its purpose was to have each team create training documentation and make it available so that cross training and enhanced teamwork would occur, little time was spent communicating this to teams. Consequently, each team met only the minimal expectations, by developing check-lists of procedures. Many of these were helpful training guides, created to help individuals learn new tasks, but others were merely hastily put together lists.

Project: Teambuilding

This project was designed to support teams in their developmental stages, and to help them learn teamwork concepts and skills. Our goals were to have each team complete a teamwork assessment instrument and to have each of them go through two teambuilding sessions. While 23 of 25 work teams completed the assessment instrument, only 17 of them completed the two teambuilding sessions.

Most of these sessions included a getting to know each other exercise (either through the sharing of individuals' Myers Briggs Type Indicator profiles or a similar sharing exercise) and an experiential problem solving exercise designed to help team members get a taste for team-ness and the stages of team development. Some of the sessions addressed barriers to effective team work, including issues of communication, goal orientation, and differing work styles. In order to help teams address some of these concerns, they were introduced to a number of group problem-solving and decision-making techniques.

Most sessions were evaluated positively. In fact, several teams have made it an objective to continue teambuilding sessions this year. Overall, this project was very successful in helping to build the team foundation. All team assessment, individual assessment evaluation with the team leader, and "just-in-time" teambuilding were key to the teams' readiness to learning.

Tactic 5: Align Reward and Recognition Systems with Contribution to Teamwork and Goal Achievement

Project: Conduct a Review of Current Salary, Classification, and Reward Systems for Alignment with Principles of a Team-Based Organization. Identify Key Issues and Develop a Timeline of Addressing Those Issues.

Our first project in this area proved to be too ambitious and was side-tracked when the University first agreed to, but then withdrew support for hiring a consultant to study team-based classification systems. However, discussion of the need to address this situation occurred throughout the year. Strategic budget decisions were made which increased staff salaries and a "career progression" fund was created that supported staff in learning and applying appropriate new skills needed to meet changing customer expectations. This project also illustrated the need to design a team-based performance evaluation system and this is being pursued by this year's strategic planning project team.

Project: Teams Share Celebration Options and Activities with Each Other

Our second, and last project under Tactic 5 was created to increase our efforts at recognizing and celebrating staff accomplishments. All Library teams were asked to share how they were currently doing this and a compiled list was distributed to all teams in hopes they would be inspired to find new and creative ways to reward hard work, commitment to change, and project accomplishment.

The Dean of the Library has also made an effort to include more celebratory occasions by sponsoring all staff recognition meetings, special dinners for teams completing major projects, and by providing cups, tee-shirts, and calculators as gifts to these teams. Informal recognition still needs to be encouraged however, since work and task focus seem to take over too easily.

REFLECTIONS: WHAT WORKED AND WHAT WE HAVE LEARNED

Involving Staff in the Creation and Implementation of Training and Effective Team Support Processes.

Widening the circle of responsibility is key to developing awareness of accountability and self-responsibility for success. The staff involved learned through practice, which greatly facilitated the development of the skills and knowledge they needed to complete their projects.

There was a clear agenda for supporting training and skill development related to the organizational structure and its new requirements. Our plan was evident and our project goals known by the entire staff. Regular reporting requirements also kept us on track in planning, designing and offering the training and support embedded within each project.

Training for staff and team development was integrated into the Strategic Plan and well supported with additional funds. The difficulty of change and constant new learning were acknowledged, and organizational resources were shifted to provide resources (time and money) to help staff begin this journey. In sum, $28,900 was provided for the accomplishment of these projects. Our efforts, resources, and goals were all focused and aligned with the Library's long range strategic goals.

Quantifiable goal setting helped us work hard to achieve the expected result and created tensions at the same time. Giving ourselves a one-year time frame in which to complete our projects misguided us. Instead, we should have planned to reach these goals over a two- to three-year time frame. Knowing that we were only a one-year team (we would no longer exist at the end of the year) contributed to our uncertainty that what we designed would be followed up on and expanded to staff who did not participate.

We chose 14 of the 28 areas of need and called them the "critical few." We felt we needed to address all of these because we knew that the beginning stages of implementing a total restructuring process and culture change required an overwhelming number of things to do. We used our own accumulated wisdom, reactions from all staff, and data gathered from a staff development needs assessment survey to determine the annual projects and their goals. This led us to select too many projects and to ignore the concern expressed by the Strategic Long Range Planning Team that we had lost focus on the "critical few."

In our Strategic Planning process, we were guided to set numerical/quantifiable indicators and goals so we could measure our success or lack thereof at the end of the year. This was incredibly useful, but, again, in our enthusiasm to make great progress, we set unrealistic goals for staff participation. It was hard to see where training only some staff in skills would have the appropriate "foundation-building" effect. And, although we calculated that the actual amount of time that our projects would take staff was an estimated 5% of their total time, their reaction to MORE things to learn was a barrier.

Although the goals we set were considered "too high," setting them this way motivated us to continue our efforts to achieve them creatively. This was key to our learning and to our ability to increase our capacity to juggle multiple projects with regular work. We knew the importance staff learning would play in making the new organization a success, so we came up with innovative ways of using consultants, designing sessions, partnering with others, marketing training, and discovering new ways of assessing and implementing. All in all, we came close to achieving many of the critical goals. Our own learning was also vastly increased.

Deeper Analysis Needed/Too Many Projects

We did not know which were the key "foundation" areas or "drivers" that would yield us the biggest impact. We had not learned ID Graphing, a planning tool that would have greatly aided us in narrowing the areas of need to the critical few, but we did use a Prioritization Decision Matrix, using a set of criteria that may not have been the best.

Clearly Written Charges

In some cases, we did not communicate as clearly as we could have with the project owners about our expectations for each project. However, demonstrating their own fortitude and intelligence, some teams set their own goals and parameters as they learned more about the issues related to their projects. Still, lack of written charges that could be revised along the way resulted in some confusion and time-consuming meetings.

Leadership Support

Although the projects we identified and set out to accomplish were approved for full budget support by the Planning and Budget Advisory Group and the Dean's Cabinet, there remained a lack of dialogue between the Management Review Team and the rest of the staff, especially the leadership group. This led to a lack of commitment to achieving all our project goals.

This came from several sources: a lack of understanding about our thinking and how it related to the whole library restructuring, the number of overwhelming challenges faced by team leaders and staff during this year in learning new work and new roles, a lack of shared vision of the need for and importance of these projects, a reluctance on the part of some team leaders and staff seriously to commit to the new organization concepts, and disagreement on content, design, and participation goals we had set. Communication about the myriad issues that developed was challenging and incomplete.

Our strongly-held belief in the value of completing these projects also proved to be a barrier to true dialogue. We were resistant to being criticized, especially after we put in so many hours of hard work. We were only slightly open to having our assumptions questioned.

Management Review/Guidance Team Concept

While this first year had its successes and problems, we learned a great deal about how to share responsibility widely. We had to learn how to give constructive, thought-provoking feedback to another team without taking over their work or creating communication barriers. The goal of a Management Review Team is to support teams as they solve their own problems. As a Guidance Team, our own members' commitment waxed and waned as other priorities came up. Ownership of results and shared concern for success continued, however, throughout the year.

First Year of Staff-Driven Strategic Planning

We experienced a reaction similar to that experienced by other Strategic Planning Tactic Teams in that in this first year of 30 or more annual projects, organized separately from regular team work, staff often felt as though these projects were "additional" and "not as important" as what had been called their "key" work (the functions assigned to the team that directly served the customer) activities. They felt that we had created new "competing" pressures on their time, and that we were going against our renewed focus of customer service. In general, they were often unwilling and unprepared to reprioritize their work in order to focus on developing skills and capabilities for a new future.

The conflict between the offering of current, unexamined services and preparation for the future, which involves studying processes and developing new skills and capabilities, is real and difficult to address.

Summary:

We have concluded that we had a successful year for a number of reasons. We began to build a foundation of understanding amongst the staff of a number of key concepts—those principles, tools, and values necessary to build an effective organization for the future. We also readied the staff and ourselves for a deeper understanding and appreciation of the challenges of becoming continuous learners. Finally, we set the stage for expanding the responsibility for learning through our use of the Strategic Planning process as a vehicle for setting the team and staff development agenda.

OTHER INITIATIVES:

Funding Support:

While most of our efforts focused on these strategic projects, we continued to support staff travel to workshops and conferences they or we identified as key to developing our organizational capabilities. Many of these included trips to conferences such as Educom and other forums that introduced new technologies. Staff were also supported with funding for attendance at workshops that introduced them to new software, that helped them deal with stress and conflict, and that exposed them to new concepts such as Peter Senge's theory of the learning organization.

New Staff Orientation:

Other initiatives undertaken this year included the development of a new staff orientation program which included a number of training modules, (effective meetings, Myers-Briggs Type Indicator, Customer Service training, and a review of the reasoning and philosophy behind the restructuring) and the creation of a new staff handbook.

Team Leader and Cabinet Training:

Dean's Cabinet also continued to receive training in leadership skills and communication skills. Newly hired Cabinet members were integrated into the group through teambuilding. Work team leaders were also included in some of these sessions.

Facilitation Skills:

Facilitation skills training was offered to "volunteer facilitators." This workshop was useful in introducing basic facilitation tools and techniques. Participants found that practice was key to developing successful facilitation skills. Follow-up sessions where ideas and tools were shared helped further to develop these individuals skills.

Changing Role of the Staff Development Committee:

The Staff Development Committee found that its role was diminishing, since most of the training that took place was now coordinated by the Assistant Dean for Staff Development, Recruitment and Diversity, the Assistant Dean for Team Facilitation and two half time support staff. Toward the end of 94/95 the committee was abolished and a new group, the Staff Development Advisory Board was created to help the Assistant to the Dean for Staff Development Recruitment and Diversity provide information about training opportunities to each team and to conduct team needs assessment. This group is different from the former Staff Development Committee as it does not get involved in the coordination of training. Members also consist of representatives from each team, unlike the former Staff Development Committee.

Process Improvement in the Library:

We also worked closely with the experimental Process Improvement Teams that were formed to address other strategic initiatives. It was here that much of our learning took place. We learned the importance of just-in-time training, of learning by doing meaningful and challenging new work, and about the importance of the relationship of individual skill and team development to overall success. We've learned that empowering teams in a structured, guided, accountable, and supported mode is key to their success.

Working closely with teams that were actually changing the overall current processes intended to meet and exceed customer expectations gave us the chance to learn how to better prepare the entire Library for understanding, accepting, and embracing change. We have learned that the best way to do this is to charge a team with discovering the need to change and then to give them the tools and the expertise (through training and the application of new skills) to analyze and develop the data that will drive the change. Empowering them to develop and choose, through a structured, scientific process, the best ways to change processes and develop technological innovations was a successful learning experience. Giving them responsibility for implementation increased their commitment to take pride in their solutions.

Summary:

Of our 18 strategic projects, seven achieved the goals originally specified or modified by the team in charge; another seven achieved an estimated 60–80% of their defined goal; and four did not achieve their goal in any substantive way. Staff who attended training and teambuilding sessions evaluated them positively directly after the sessions, but successful transfer of skills and new behaviors may or may not have occurred.

Understanding of concepts and terminology, utilization of analytical tools and approaches, and development of interpersonal capabilities has increased dramatically, as has individual teams willingness to take responsibility for continued learning.

In spite of our many shortfalls, we have taken major steps in further laying the foundation for building an effective organization in which staff are committed to our future success "in supporting the research and education needs of a diverse, ever-changing University community,"—our 1994/95 Strategic Objective.

FOURTH YEAR: 1995/96—DEVELOPING STRATEGIC ANNUAL PLANS TO BECOME A LEARNING ORGANIZATION: EMPOWERMENT OF TEAMS AND STAFF

In our fourth year, we have continued our efforts to learn how best to foster a supportive, learning environment while continuing to focus on serving customer needs and providing the necessary training staff need to accomplish this. We are fine tuning what works, looking for new strategies and deeper understanding, and letting go of what does not. Many of the initiatives taken on this year are similar to last year's, but there are some new developments taking shape.

The Strategic Long Range Planning Team

Once again, the Strategic Long Range Planning Team was charged to develop five key strategic objectives that would enable the Library to move forward and at the same time be in alignment with the University's strategic directions. This year, the group continued its use of the management by planning model, but modified it somewhat. The team learns as it goes, through the current situation analysis process, through coordination of the annual strategic objectives setting process, and through its attempts at creating a staff driven mission statement. The team is just about ready, in fact, to share a draft of the Library mission statement with the rest of the Library. Interestingly, SLRP has learned that the Mission must not only be clear and brief, but that it does not stand alone—vision and values are key ingredients in completing the overall picture of the Library's purpose and role in a University setting.

The Annual Plan

Last year's strategic objective dealing with the Library environment and culture was re-worded. Whereas before it read:

> To create a Library environment and culture that supports the research and education needs of a diverse, ever-changing University community.

It now reads:

> To transform the library environment and culture to improve the way the staff are supported in their achievement of the library's goals.

This reflects the clearer understanding of our transformational imperative to change a culture, not just build our organizational effectiveness, and it is a vital revision of our direction and scope in developing staff and teams and their future success.

Among the many changes that occurred this year, one was that SLRP used a modified version of the management by planning model to design the Library's strategic initiatives. In a reaction to the cumbersome effect of the tiered, "waterfall-like", process one of these modifications included the elimination of the tactic level of planning. Instead, as part of the above strategic objective, a team was formed to develop the following strategies and projects. Project teams were then formed to carry out these projects:

1: Provide an Environment Which Encourages, Supports, and Respects All Staff

Project A: Identify values, communicate vision, hold leadership accountable for modeling desired behaviors

2: Support Staff Development Through Continuous Learning, As Well As Training, to Meet Changing Work Requirements

Project A: Shift the Library's focus from training to learning

3: Address the Human Resource Needs of the Staff Through Policies, Procedures, and Structures Developed by the Staff.

Project A: Designing a fair and equitable performance evaluation system for all staff.

Project B: Study the human resources issues in the Library, identify problems, and recommend solutions

Teams have been formed, charged and are working on these projects now, but it is too early to predict their success. However, what we do know is that involving a new and different set of staff (the Dean for Team Facilitation and the Assistant to the Dean for Staff Development, Diversity and Recruitment were not involved in designing the projects this time around) did mean that there was little time and formal opportunity to dialogue about what was learned the previous year. This year's teams have also decided to organize themselves and their charges more loosely than last year's team, i.e., most have no quantifiable goals or indicators. This year's teams are more exploratory, involving a new group of staff in developing ideas for how to increase the learning capability of the organization.

As for our own roles as Assistant to the Dean for Staff Development, Recruitment and Diversity and the Assistant Dean for Team Facilitation, it is assumed we will continue with our responsibilities, building on the previous year's experiences and changing our approaches as needed. We are engaged in a number of initiatives outside the Annual planning process. What follows are descriptions of some of these:

Using a bottom-up approach to provide needs-based, just-in-time training:

The Staff Development Advisory Board plays a key role in encouraging their respective teams to take ownership of team training and learning needs. This year, members were guided to encourage their teams to address learning/training needs during the objectives setting process early in the 95/96 fiscal year.

In contrast, the role we play is to guide and assist teams in the needs assessment process and to design appropriate learning activities, interventions and formal training. We are also encouraging staff to communicate their needs to us regularly through the Staff Development Advisory Board and through the use of "request for facilitation forms," so that just-in-time training and team building can take place.

More teambuilding offered to cross functional teams and more back-up trainers available to do this.

As more and more cross functional teams are formed throughout the Library, we have found it necessary to provide them with initial training in the team process in order for them to begin development as a team. To help us meet this need, we have trained a group of over fifteen backup volunteer facilitators from throughout the Library in the principles of teamwork and the use of problem solving and prioritization techniques. The challenge for these facilitators is to be prepared to know what to do, to do good assessment of issues, and to design appropriate learning opportunities that will move each team forward.

Continuation of new staff orientation program

As we continue to hire new staff, we think it is imperative that for them to be successful here, they learn about our organizational structure, philosophy, and related concepts and practices. For this reason, the new staff orientation program continues and is widely supported. Modifications from last year include the alignment of the library-wide new staff orientation program with orientation taking place within individual teams. In addition to providing training on the basics of customer service principles, effective meetings, and total quality concepts, we continue to provide offerings on the Myers-Briggs Type Indicator and a review of the restructuring. This year, we will also be including for the first time a module on diversity.

Continued Diversity Initiatives

Diversity programs and visits by guest speakers continue. A new group of staff members has joined the Library Diversity Council, which has made plans to continue our tradition of offering thought-provoking, fun and celebratory programs for the staff. Included in this year's offerings was a site visit by the Association of Research Libraries Diversity Consultant, Kriza Jennings, Library co-sponsorship of a number of campus programs, including a very well-attended and -received presentation by Cornell West, and a videoconference on affirmative action. In the coming months, we plan to offer a Chinese New Year celebration and a workshop on homophobia in the workplace.

Revised Objectives Setting Process

This year we decided to redesign the training session on developing team objectives for Team Leaders and volunteer facilitators. Overall, a more extensive process of objectives development was pursued as we learned from last year's mistakes. Even so, the process this year was successful in some teams and seen as a barrier in others. Needs assessment data is still unavailable (except in one team) and learning of project management skills, prioritization skills, and owner responsibility is slow in occurring. In 95/96 we asked teams to align their projects with the strategic plan. Team objectives and Library Strategic Objectives are still seen as not in alignment, although some progress has been made. There is also overlap between team objectives and some cross-functional team goals. We will continue to re-think this important process.

Process Improvement

We continue to provide support for our crucial Process Improvement Teams as they learn and train others in the analytical techniques and teamwork necessary to make transformational improvements in process effectiveness, cost reduction and customer satisfaction.

We have also developed a Change Management Support Program for teams affected by the radically changed work processes that result from Process Improvement (now called Business Process Re-engineering). This program is designed to expose affected staff to: the reasons for studying their areas—the budget, technological, and competitive environment in which we operate, and to the techniques being used by the Process Improvement Team to study their processes. We hope this will help the staff prepare for inevitable changes designed by their teammates and other staff in the Library. The goal of this program is to encourage staff to conduct their own assessment of their skills and abilities and to identify future capabilities needed by the Library. If we are successful, the Library will then offer training in learning new skills and support for staff who will be dislocated. We hope that this partnership of organizational and individual responsibility will increase the desirability for and commitment to continuous learning.

Learning Through Regular Work

Teams are still experimenting and looking for ways to be successful, as they are challenged by their new roles. While at times learning teamwork can be painful, most real learning is occurring in the day-to-day team process. Our role is to offer focused support, encouragement and appropriate resources to these teams as they grow and mature.

New Partnerships:

This year, the campus Human Resources Department began its own restructuring process, and as a result has offered to continue to provide assistance and support to the Library in a number of innovative ways. These include the development of a partnership program with the Library, whereby members of the Human Resources Team participate as full members of some of the Library's annual project teams. In addition, trainers from the former Employee Development and Training Department, rather than merely responding to needs with training, have begun to assist teams in assessing and identifying true needs. Since this is a brand new initiative, the success of these efforts has yet to be determined.

Continued Offerings That Support Staff Well-Being

We continue to offer a number of programs that assist staff in their general well being. Some of those that have already taken place this year include training sessions on the use of CPR, computer ergonomics and workplace safety. A health screening program offered in conjunction with the campus Employee Wellness department is in the planning stages.

CONCLUSIONS

In conclusion, we have learned a great deal and have made an incredible amount of progress these past four years. While we have had our share of blunders, many of our initiatives have been quite successful. Process improvement for example, has yielded incredibly positive results. Teambuilding efforts are also successful in many cases. Development of training needs from the ground up has led to team "ownership" of needs, another positive step. Finally, we have learned that change is constant. The challenge is to anticipate it, be open to it and flexible enough to be able to embrace and learn from it and further develop our organizational and individual capabilities to respond to it. This is our goal as a learning organization.

Critical Thinking in Future Libraries: Re-Inventing Staff Development Programs

By Craig Gibson and Allan Bosch
George Mason University/Library Building Consultant

Libraries worldwide are reeling from the impacts of technological change, shrinking budgets, proliferating user demands, and questions about their very future. It has become a truism that change is the only constant in the library and information world; in fact, it is almost a certainty that librarians, in order to have more than a diminished future, will have to internalize the principles of "lifelong learning" that they espouse for library users in many instances.

The real question is not whether to respond to change, but how to do so effectively. Many programs at professional conferences and meetings in the field highlight this problem. Topics such as technostress, the most crucial or salient points for library managers to understand about technology, the changing workforce (with emphasis on increasing diversity among library patrons and library staffs alike), changing institutional mandates about assessment, and changing organizational patterns and structures are now commonplace. These programs offer valuable support and advice for librarians and library staffs attempting to cope with the rapid changes both inside and outside their workplaces. However, such programs often address symptoms and do not necessarily serve as continuing education in the fullest sense of that term.

For the library profession to grasp control of a seemingly uncontrollable future, continuing education and staff development programs in libraries will need to address many of the stresses and impacts due to technologies, changing institutional frameworks, shifting organizational patterns, and more diverse patrons—but with a disciplined approach to individual and organizational learning not heretofore evident in the profession. Staff development programs in libraries of the past have often focused on either narrow "micro-skills" needed to improve job performance, or on humanistic issues related to improving working relationships among colleagues. Such staff development programs, while often worthwhile, are reactive, merely responding to immediate problems in the local environment. Future staff development programs in libraries, intended for everyone in the organization, whether Associate Directors, Team Leaders, or classified staff working groups, should focus on developing the thinking skills of all. The new staff development paradigm transcends "training" because it raises the development of each library employee to a higher cognitive plane.

"Training programs," which often focus on communicating the latest set of technological changes in particular libraries, are obviously essential. Everyone must learn new CD-ROM software, new online service protocols, new downloading capabilities, new cataloging rules, new acquisitions routines. Much library work and staff learning is procedural and will remain so. The new staff development paradigm, however, folds such training into a more disciplined approach to learning throughout the organization. The synergy achieved through a critical thinking approach to staff development will make the rhetoric of the "learning organization" a reality because the quality of learning must grow out of the quality of thinking throughout the organization. Training programs in this paradigm become occasions for continuous learning and a disciplined approach to solving ongoing problems, rather than mere "one-shot" sessions to address specific concerns and needs.

FUTURE STAFF DEVELOPMENT PROGRAMS AND THE LEARNING ORGANIZATION

The major challenge facing libraries now is the need to take planning and strategizing beyond a reactive response to a deeper, more thoughtful level. All too often, the current information environment and rapid technological change militate against thoughtful planning for the future; libraries engage in "planning" and staff development that does not improve the ability of their personnel to engage the future in a strategic, thoughtful way. Quick solutions to temporary problems are the norm. Stephen Covey, a leading management thinker and consultant, describes the same problem in the business world:

"People are intrigued when they see good things happening in the lives of individuals, families, and organizations that are based on solid principles. They admire such personal strength and maturity, such family unity and teamwork, such adaptive synergistic organizational culture. And their immediate response is very revealing of their basic paradigm. 'How do you do it? Teach me the techniques.' What they're really saying is, 'Give me some quick fix advice or solution that will relieve the pain of my own situation.' They will find people who will meet their wants and teach these things; and for a short time, skills and techniques may appear to work. They may eliminate some of the cosmetic or acute problems through social aspirin and band-aids. But the underlying chronic condition remains and eventually new acute symptoms will appear. The more people are into quick fixes and focus on the acute problems and pain, the more that very approach contributes to the underlying chronic condition. The way we see the problem is the problem."[1]

Covey's description of our need for short-term solutions to difficult, knotty problems should sound familiar to many in the library and information profession. When libraries institute "quick fix" training or staff development programs to respond to new technologies, to enhance sensitivity to diversity issues in the workplace, to improve working relationships among various library units, the "problem," whatever it may be, is viewed superficially. The real challenge is to transform the library organization into a synergistic environment where high quality thinking occurs regularly, where staff members challenge each other to find better solutions to problems, where there is an unwillingness to accept mediocrity or "quick fixes." The library, in short, must become a learning organization.

The burgeoning literature on the "learning organization" suggests crucial elements of future staff development programs. Peter Senge, the originator of the current concept of the learning organization, discusses five "core disciplines" of the learning organization: personal mastery, mental models, shared vision, team learning, and systems thinking.[2] All of these elements of the learning organization are holistic, somewhat utopian, and difficult to implement without a realistic assessment of a library's current organizational culture. The difficulties of making teams work in libraries is a good example: team members must be highly responsible, mature individuals who continually place the good of the organization and the clientele above individual interests and goals. Yet the team concept must include ample opportunities for individual learning and self-fulfillment. Team decision-making may be agonizingly slow in an information environment that often requires quick, yet thoughtful responses. Teams require much intra- and inter-team communication, and the team leader must be an expert facilitator of process and a constant nurturer of people.

Senge's "core disciplines," however, all elucidate what is most important in the capacity of a library organization, or any other organization, to respond to the demands of the future: cognitive growth and intellectual discipline throughout an organization. Personal mastery, mental models, shared vision, team learning, and systems thinking all require high levels of creative and critical thinking. Just a few examples will suffice to point out the necessity of disciplined thinking in libraries, according to Senge's model:

- Personal mastery—the "technostress" we hear about continually definitely points out a sense of loss of mastery on the part of librarians. Until about 1980, libraries operated primarily in a print environment, with a few libraries having automated circulation systems and basic OPACs. Libraries offered librarian-mediated searching of DIALOG databases and within a few years started offering end-user training on some systems. CD-ROMs began appearing about 1985, starting a process that continually accelerates, with more and more choices in the form of online services, full-text databases, image databases, Geographic Information Systems, and Internet resources. Librarians feel overwhelmed, as do patrons.

A sense of personal mastery is problematic for librarians in a constantly changing information environment unless these elements of critical thinking are incorporated into their professional lives: a tolerance of ambiguity; an understanding of paradox; and a sustained focus on learning underlying concepts rather than rote procedures.

- Mental models—these are the mental images that individuals and groups hold of the world. Librarians hold many traditional images of their organizations, their services, their teaching and learning strategies in instructional programs, even their library buildings. These images may inhibit cognitive change, which in turn may forestall necessary changes throughout a library's programs and services. Relying on a "one-size-fits-all" reference desk model is one example of a deeply imbedded mental model in the library profession. Teaching a linear search strategy, based on the exclusive print environment of the past, is another example of a deeply imbedded, and obsolescent, mental model. Library buildings themselves embody "models" or mental images in librarians' minds; the traditional emphasis on vast, monolithic stack towers with cloistered spaces only for the gifted or the elite patron, and for individual pursuit of scholarship, is only now being changed by the construction of alternative library architectures, which see libraries as places for collaboration and connectivity, both personal and technological.

The research on mental models tells us that mental models may or may not be accurate reflections of the world. Developing new mental models that respond to the conditions of the present and future information environments is a major challenge for future staff development programs in libraries because of the persistence of old schemas, old "scripts", traditional routines, and familiar policies that provide a sense of safety. Cultivating new mental models is difficult without concrete examples in the library and information profession of alternative service delivery models, innovative instruction programs, and visionary library architectures. However, staff development programs will facilitate growth of new mental models through these critical thinking skills: evaluating hypothetical scenarios for alternative futures; considering unusual perspectives on service delivery; and questioning rigorously all assumptions about traditional practices.

These examples suggest just a few of the ways in which traditional staff development programs, focused on procedural thinking, group process facilitation, and humanistic development, may fail to produce the true learning organization. Another major management trend, Total Quality Management, has important conceptual linkages with the "learning organization" concept, especially in its emphasis on team learning. What is needed for a future staff training development model for libraries, however, is explicit identification of elements of critical thinking that make both the learning organization and Total Quality Management possible.

CRITICAL THINKING: THEORETICAL BACKGROUND

One of the most important theorists of critical thinking, Richard Paul, has written extensively of the need for all professionals and citizens to become much more disciplined in their thinking in order to manage the complexity of the contemporary world. His highly systematic approach to critical thinking and his insistence on escaping the bonds of narrow, egocentric thinking grow out of a lifetime of rigorous philosophical thought and practical work with educators and professionals. Paul's concept of critical thinking is definitely not simplistic, but a brief definition that captures much of his meaning follows:

Critical Thinking is a systematic way to form and shape one's thinking . . . It is thought that is disciplined, comprehensive, based on intellectual standards, and, as a result, well-reasoned.[3]

Paul's definition of critical thinking provides the essential cognitive underpinnings for Senge's concept of the "learning organization." The learning organization depends on the intellectual discipline of individuals and groups; on a comprehensive, systems-oriented approach to understanding the realities of organizations and their processes; and on criteria and standards for assessing the quality of thought of all managers and employees.

Paul's dimensions of critical thinking (intellectual

standards, traits of mind, elements of reasoning, intellectual abilities) form a network of cognitive and affective abilities that, understood properly, will help any library manager, team leader, coach, or facilitator develop staff development programs in libraries that transcend "training."[4] Paul's traits of mind, for example, include the following; an example of a needed application in library working relationships and staff development is shown in the parallel column.

Trait	Application
Intellectual independence	Responsibility in team problem-solving in designing a new instruction program
Fairmindedness	Looking beyond the needs of one's own unit or team toward the needs of the organization
Intellectual Perseverance	Working through a difficult automation project characterized by numerous delays, technical 'glitches', and misunderstandings by others in the organization

Likewise, Paul's intellectual standards provide much of the underpinning for the learning organization and for quality staff development programs. True group learning and worthwhile discussion of future scenarios for libraries can only occur if participants discipline their own minds by thought that is accurate, relevant, specific, clear, precise, logical, deep, broad, complete, significant, and fair, among other criteria for critical thinking.[5] Staff development and team learning are not possible without a shared understanding of what makes for quality thought; discussions of various options for delivering information services depend on critical thinking abilities of all the participants because of the never-ending changes and ambiguity in the information environment, in the client population, and in the library profession itself.

CRITICAL THINKING IN STAFF DEVELOPMENT PROGRAMS: A SUGGESTED MODEL

Staff development programs in future libraries must be serious, sustained continuing education rather than "one-shot" sessions that solve temporary problems. These programs must be an ongoing effort to raise the cognitive level of library managers and staffs in a systematic manner. Staff development programs must involve everyone, at all levels in a library organization, and must depend on a shared framework of critical thinking precepts so that everyone contributes to solving the problems of the organization. These critical thinking precepts are:

- Everyone can improve the quality of their own thinking.
- Cognitive diversity (various learning styles) should be encouraged and accommodated.
- Groups and teams must hold themselves to exacting standards for the quality of their decisions.
- Hasty decisions should be avoided.
- Mistakes resulting from good-faith experimentation should be seen as opportunities for intellectual growth rather than as failures deserving punishment.
- Ambiguous and uncertain situations should be seen as opportunities for creative solutions, rather than as impediments to action.

Curricular models and instructional design for future staff development programs must incorporate these principles. Some models and specific types of instructional design especially capable of inculcating critical thinking in a staff development program—and throughout an organization—include the following:

Future scenarios: hypothetical cases of what libraries will look like ten years from the present, with delineation of all the services and programs, and evaluation of pros and cons for the right "mix" of services.

Problems-of-the-present: Group analyses of an especially difficult or cogent problem facing a given library, such as how to provide a financially feasible solution to printing for the proliferating full-text resources available to patrons.

Role-playing: Placing oneself in the role of a staff member from another library unit or team; or placing oneself in the role of a regular library user.

Research-and-Development Center: A model emulating R & D groups in private industry, with rigorous scrutiny of the library's present practices, research studies of patron behavior, studies of the library's internal processes, and recommendations for new products and services. This model can be "scaled down" for a series of staff development workshops, or obviously be instituted on a permanent basis as part of the organization.

These are just a few devices that provide a challenging environment for critical thinking in a staff development program. The crucial aspects of these instructional models include: deliberate introduction of uncertainty and ambiguity; looking at a variety of different perspectives and seeing the needs of an entire organization rather than one's own particular unit or "turf"; experimenting with alternative futures for an organization; and bringing together research and daily professional practices for examination and review in a reflective setting.

In one way, staff development programs based on critical thinking can help turn libraries into nonpartisan "think tanks" that advocate only for the best quality services for users. "Think tanks" are places for research, discussion, reflection, and active testing of ideas. Libraries that value critical thinking will necessarily become like these research institutes and will see staff development as the essential tool for becoming centers for collaboration, connectivity, and intellectual rigor on their campuses, rather than as service centers warehousing books and other materials, or as "study halls" for students or as sacred mausoleums for esoteric research.

In 1946, Albert Einstein said, "The unleashed power of the atom has changed everything save our modes of thinking and we thus drift toward unparalleled catastrophe."[6] We in the library profession realize how much has changed in our profession within the past fifteen years, and how technological change in particular continues to hurtle down upon us. Although we may be not be drifting toward "unparalleled catastrophe," we can sense the unease in the profession caused by rapid technological and social change and an uncertain future. Libraries are venerable institutions, but we should not expect that they will remain so, especially if we do not change our thinking and insist on a higher cognitive dimension for the library profession. We may have given insufficient attention to static mental models in our profession, and to the quality of our thinking and decision-making overall. Staff development programs based on critical thinking principles will help make the "learning organization" a reality and will improve the quality of thinking of library managers and library staffs alike—with resulting benefits to organizational climate and culture and the people served by intellectually reinvigorated libraries.

ENDNOTES

1. Stephen R. Covey. *The Seven Habits of Highly Effective People: Restoring the Character Ethic.* (New York: Simon and Schuster, 1989), p. 40
2. Peter M. Senge. *The Fifth Discipline: the Art & Practice of the Learning Organization* (New York: Doubleday & Currency, 1990), p. 6–11.
3. Richard Paul. *Critical Thinking: How to Prepare Students for a Rapidly Changing World* (Santa Rosa, CA: Foundation for Critical Thinking, 1993), p. 20.
4. Paul, p. 20–22, 319.
5. Paul, p. 319.
6. Albert Einstein, Telegram Sent to Prominent Americans, *New York Times*, May 25, 1946.

Rethinking Organizational Structure: Academic Library as Network Organization

By Susan Jurow
Association of Research Libraries

INTRODUCTION

I recently received a flyer for a state-of-the-art, video conference workshop on the "fishnet organization," broadcast from Silicon Valley, California. This organization was defined as "an ad-hoc cooperative web, rather than a permanent competitive citadel."[1] One of the things I have found most interesting in my reading about network organizations is the use of metaphor to describe their shape and functioning. Because they are, for the most part, so unlike anything experienced in the past in organizations and, in many cases, exist only as theoretical constructs, metaphor seems to be one of the best ways to express their features and their potential.

Network organizations are alliances that permit a group of enterprises to do together what they would not be able to accomplish individually. Through use of a strategic center, they bring a focus to what an organization does best, allowing each one to add value to the work of the others. They are able to bring high quality goods and services to market quickly and less expensively, encouraging a high degree of flexibility and creativity.

This paper begins with some background on the evolution of the concept of organizational structure and the relationship between structure and strategy. The academic library is placed in a value chain with other industries and the role of core competencies is explored. The key components of a network organization are outlined with examples of how they might be applied to an academic library model. Some implications for the internal management of these organizations are offered. The conclusion focuses on the urgency of accelerating a change in the organizational strategy of academic libraries and their concomitant structures.

In this paper, I use the word "flexibility." The ability to react rapidly and effectively to predictable and unanticipated change, to be able to do things differently, and to do different things according to the requirements of a new or changing situation, and to recover and take advantage of the negative effects of change, these are at the heart of the organizational experiments discussed here.

While change has been a factor in the life of academic libraries for the past twenty years, over the next twenty years, the higher education environment in which they operate is likely to undergo unprecedented restructuring. If it is not possible to prepare for a specific change because it is unknown and unknowable, then the best preparation is the fluidity and flexibility to "morph" based on changing conditions. A network organization is one approach.

BACKGROUND

To accommodate the wide range of economic, technological, and demographic challenges they face, organizations in both the profit and not-for-profit sectors are experimenting with new organizational strategies and new organizational structures to support those strategies. The need to be focused, yet agile, customer-centered, yet efficient, and innovative, yet cost effective, are changing both the businesses they're in and the way they do business.

This link between what an organization is trying to accomplish and how it is structured is a critical one. In organizations as in architecture, form should follow function. Alfred Chandler, winner of the Pulitzer Prize in 1978 for history, offered the thesis in organizational terms. He stated "That different organizational forms result from different types of growth can be stated more precisely if the planning and carrying out of such growth is considered a strategy, and the organization devised to administer these enlarged activities and resources, a structure."[2]

Organizational structures are designed to control and coordinate activity and resources to achieve a purpose. It is time to rethink the structure when the purpose changes. While the fundamental purpose, the support of research and teaching, has not changed for academic libraries, the strategy by which this support is accomplished has changed. These libraries have expanded the scope of their programs and services beyond the development of local resources. They now act as gateways to global information resources. Many are looking for ways to add value to traditional forms of information about and within their collections, and to other available electronic resources. Most academic libraries are presently structured to do the work of the past, and some are organizing to do the work of the present; few are organized to do the work of the future.

For most of Western pre-industrial society, there was one structure, hierarchy, for the only large organizational bodies that existed—the government, the church, and the army. Hierarchy, an ordering or ranking of people where each layer is subordinate to the one above it, has existed with little variation since pre-Roman times. It is only in the Industrial Age with the addition of technological complexity that other dimensions, such as communication, problem solving and decision making, begin to affect the shape of organizations.

Organizational structure today is affected both by human and market factors. On the human side, organizational structures are deeply affected by mental models. Because hierarchy has been the enduring structure of our most basic social functions, it is deeply embedded in our mental model of organizations and how they should operate.

Mental models are the intellectual constructs, based on experience and theories, that each of us creates to understand and to predict behavior. In a recent study, Francis Fukuyama found that span of control as an aspect of organizational structure varies from one country to another based on cultural assumptions, or mental models, about trust.[3] Peter Senge considers shared mental models a key to the kind of constant, conscious organizational learning that will be required to operate effectively in the twenty-first century.[4]

In the 1970's, Miles et al. found some correlation between managerial assumptions and the organizational strategy of managers.[5] Those who professed traditional beliefs tended to focus their approach to administrative problem solving on efficiency and organizational stability. Managers whose expectations were shaped by the managerial assumptions of the Human Resources model were more interested in facilitating systems that create dynamism and flexibility.

To change our thinking about how resources are organized to produce goods and services requires an openness to different approaches to managing relationships within and across organizations. It requires a willingness to experiment, to try new approaches that may be less successful than hoped, and to build on the experiences of others. It means testing assumptions and rethinking the means by which results are achieved.

VALUE CHAIN AND CORE COMPETENCIES

Placing libraries within a value chain and the concept of core competencies are fundamental to the potential application of the network organization model to academic libraries.

To one degree or another, all enterprises form links in a chain that produces and distributes goods and services. Within a communication value chain, Paul Peters, Executive Director of the Coalition for Networked Information, places libraries as buyers somewhere between the creators (authors) and the users (readers) of intellectual works.[6] Other participants in this value chain are the sellers (publishers) and the intermediaries, such as book jobbers and other vendors who may emerge in the move to a more electronic environment.

Traditionally, the boundaries around each of these players have been rigid and impermeable. Each enterprise had its piece, and any change in relationship was seen as one gaining and another losing its portion. The concept of a network organization requires a different perspective. The value "chain" metaphor encourages enterprises to see themselves as "linked" to each other as collaborators in bringing the highest quality goods and services to the user or customer.

To do this, each enterprise must identify what it does best, or its core competencies. Core competencies are the skills, technologies, and work processes an organization develops that make the programs, products, and services it offers unique and valuable. In the communications value chain Peters outlines, functions include creation, production, distribution, protection, acquisition, organization, preservation, and utilization. Academic libraries assume that some of these functions are their core competencies, such as acquisition, organization, and preservation.

In a world of increasingly limited resources and a market broadening through electronic initiatives, the idea of a network organization offers academic libraries the opportunity to rethink what they do best, to decide where best to make a contribution, and to create a framework where choices can be made about which programs and services to support. Because they have different levels of funding, support different missions, and operate in different environments, there is no reason why academic libraries must arrive at a monolithic response to these questions. One would expect the core competencies of libraries to differ based on their individual circumstances.

To be successful, it is also necessary to increase the level of trust between organizations. This is particularly difficult in the value chain discussed here because it mixes for-profit enterprises, such as publishers, with not-for-profit, educational enterprises, such as libraries and universities.

NETWORK ORGANIZATION

Over the past ten years, a wide variety of organizational experiments have been undertaken, more often in the for-profit arena, to support and to take advantage of effective organizational behavior within the context of the current environment. With more effective means of direct communication between the strategic core of the organization and the front lines of service or production, organizations are removing layers of managers and widening the span of control of remaining managers. They are using self-managed and self-directed teams to undertake the traditional functions of managers. They are building external collaborative relationships to permit a sharper focus on the core competencies of the enterprise, to share risks in new ventures, and to provide greater flexibility.

"Constellation," "spherical," "federation," and "hollow" are all words used to characterize the network organization, more metaphors designed to conjure up a host of qualities and assumptions about relationships. Network organizations are being touted in the business community as a means of lowering costs, and increasing flexibility and efficiency.

In 1984, Miles and Snow suggested the name "dynamic network" to describe an emerging organizational structure capable of assembling and disassembling capabilities based on current conditions.[7] The characteristics of these organizations included vertical disaggregation, brokers, market activation, and full disclosure of market information.

Vertical disaggregation means that the ranges of functions traditionally done within an organization are provided by a group of independent organizations tied together by a network. In a for-profit company that might mean design, manufacturing, marketing, and sales for a particular product would each be offered by a different company. In a library it would mean functions such as cataloging, reference, collection management would be offered by independent organizations which could also offer their services to other libraries or companies.

Brokers are the organizations that locate and link together the team of service providers. They serve as a strategic core. The relationship may be one of a leader and subcontractors, or the partners may have equal status in the enterprise. Nike is recognized as one of the most successful network organizations currently in existence. It serves as the lead firm that provides research and development, and marketing for a network that also includes companies that design, manufacture, and distribute the products.

In a network organization configuration, a library could take one of two approaches; it could link externally or diversify within. A library could put together and coordinate companies to do the range of activities necessary to provide the services desired for that institution at that particular time. The library could also choose to maintain what it considers its core competency, such as collection development and management, or research services, and bring together other companies to add value to that activity.

The network organization is market activated. It creates, maintains, and decommissions itself based on market demands and results. In the for-profit arena, network organizations can be put together and dismantled based on demand. In a dynamic network, libraries would be able to stay at the leading edge, creating and offering new programs and services as soon as new technologies or products become available.

Unlike the traditional competitive situation, partners in a network organization make their information systems fully available to each other, so that all parties can have access to data needed to be successful, and contributions to the overall enterprise can be recognized. Information includes data and ideas on best practices, costs, trends, and performance. It is intriguing to think about libraries being part of a network organization where the full costs of providing information and educational services to users could be tracked and understood.

By 1992, Miles and Snow felt confident enough about the existence and characteristics of network organizations to describe variations, offer examples of varying approaches, and outline some of the pitfalls of these new structures.[8,9] Internal and stable networks were differentiated from the dynamic network that had been originally described. General Motors was used as an example of a company integrating the network into its internal structure. BMW was used as an example of a company that outsourced over half its operations to create a stable network.

Problems that arose in the early application of the network organization model tended to come from trying to push the structure beyond its capabilities and from making modifications that ran counter to the operating logic of the structure. The most successful network organizations recognized that their most valuable asset turned out to be the knowledge their human resources bring to their work.

CLOSING

On a certain level I am presenting the idea of academic libraries engaging with for-profit companies in a network organization as a strawman. I want to encourage my colleagues to explore their assumptions and mental models about libraries in a broader social context than academe. One has only to look at the Harvard Business Review for the past three years to experience the growing appreciation within the corporate world for the value-added potential of information. One of my concerns is whether academic and research libraries are moving operationally, organizationally, and psychologically far enough fast enough.

Because of their funding situation and traditional service approach, much of the current focus in academic libraries is on maximizing the ability to meet the needs of primary users efficiently. For long-term viability, these libraries must position themselves to meet challenges that will emerge as for-profit organizations develop expertise in the exploitation of information technologies. As I read the following words written in relation to the revitalization of corporate performance, I felt I could have been reading a warning to academic libraries, "Against such competitors, marginal adjustments to current orthodoxies are no more likely to produce competitive revitalization than are marginal improvements to operating efficiency."[10]

In his book, Images of the Organization, Gareth Morgan demonstrates how different metaphors lead to insights into the strengths and weaknesses of organizational structures.[11] He follows up this idea in a later work where he "shows how traditional concepts of organization can be radically transformed through imaginative processes whereby new images and metaphors are used to create evocative and energizing patterns of shared meaning."[12] I believe that new conceptual models, creative play such as metaphor, and the experimental application of new structural forms borrowed from other sectors offer the greatest opportunity for academic libraries to remain central to the educational and research processes.

Form may follow function, but it must be remembered that function is context-based. The world is changing around us, and we must find the tools to reinvent ourselves to match that new reality. To be successful, academic libraries must consider programs, services, structures, and processes strategically within the context of the potential of the future, a future with many more and different partners and competitors than the present or the past. It is imperative that they seek flexible structures that can accommodate complexity, take advantage of distinctive competencies, and make best use of human resources if they are to thrive in the 21st century.

ENDNOTES

1. "The Fishnet Organization: New Computing Tools and New Management Challenges." A National Live Interactive Videoconference produced by De Anza College Television in association with the community College Satellite Network, February 14, 1995.
2. Alfred Chandler, Jr. *Strategy and Structure:*

Chapters in the History of the American Industrial Enterprise. Cambridge, MA:MIT Press, 1962, p. 13.
3. Francis Fukuyama. *Trust: Social Virtues and the Creation of Prosperity.* New York: Macmillan, 1995.
4. Peter Senge. *The Fifth Discipline.* New York: Doubleday, 1990.
5. Raymond Miles, et al., "Organizational Strategy, Structure, and Process," *Academy of Management Review,* vol. 3, no. 3 (July 1978), pp. 546–62.
6. Paul Evan Peters, "Cost Centers and Measures in the Networked Value Chain" (paper presented at the Conference on Challenging Marketplace Solutions to the Problems in the Economics of Information, Washington, D.C., September, 1995).
7. Raymond Miles and Charles Snow, "Fit, Failure, and the Hall of Fame" *California Management Review,* v. 26, no. 3 (Spring 1984), pp. 10–28.
8. Charles Snow, Raymond Miles, and Henry Coleman, Jr., "Managing 21st Century Network Organizations," *Organizational Dynamics,* v.20, no. 3 (Winter 1992), pp. 5–20.
9. Raymond Miles and Charles Snow, "Causes of Failure in Network Organizations," *California Management Review,* v. 32, no. 4 (Summer 1992), pp. 53–72.
10. Gary Hamel, "Strategic Intent," *Harvard Business Review,* v. 67, no. 3 (May-June 1989), p. 63.
11. Gareth Morgan. *Images of the Organization.* Newbury Park, CA: Sage, 1986.
12. Gareth Morgan. *Imaginization.* Newbury Park, CA: Sage, 1993, p.283.

Team-Building, Collaboration, and the Reengineering of Library Services: A Two-Part Discussion

Part 1: Team-Building, Collaboration, and the Reengineering of Library Services

By Joan K. Lippincott
Coalition for Networked Information

THE NATURE OF COLLABORATION

Within many institutions, librarians and computing professionals, teaching faculty, and researchers are developing collaborative relationships. Many of these collaborative relationships have evolved in the context of networked information resources and services. What are the characteristics of successful collaborative relationships? This presentation will provide a framework by which to analyze partnership or collaborative relationships, based on the work of some writers in the management and organizational behavior field and then will categorize and discuss the range of existing collaborations in the networked information environment, focusing on examples from academic institutions.

The roles and job functions of librarians and information technologists have been changing over the past five to ten years, in part, in response to developments in automation and more recently in networked information. In some universities and colleges, this has resulted in administratively merged libraries and computing centers, in others it has resulted in increased collaboration by professionals in two administratively distinct units, and in some, it has led to the duplication of some functions by the libraries and computing centers.

In the development of local library automated systems, libraries often contracted with computing centers to run mainframe systems, make programming changes to the system software, and manage the reliability and integrity of the system. Sometimes the library system hardware was physically located in the computing center. In this kind of arrangement, the library was responsible for the conceptualization of the project and for the actual content of what was run on the computer system, for example, determining cataloging rules, format of acquisition and circulation records, etc. Parallel examples of the computing center contracting with the library for services have not generally been customary. However, as the information environment has become increasingly networked, information technologists and librarians have begun to form new patterns of relationships to implement resources and services for the institution.

These new relationships tend to be more egalitarian in terms of:

- conceptualization of the project
- authority
- contribution of resources

Some researchers characterize these new relationships as collaborations or partnerships (these two terms will be used interchangeably in this presentation). In Shared Minds, Michael Schrage (1990) defines collaboration as "the process of shared creation: two or more individuals with complementary skills interacting to create a shared understanding that none had previously possessed or could have come to on their own. Collaboration creates a shared meaning about a process, a product, or an event."

(p. 40) He feels that collaboration is a "different quality of interaction" from cooperation or other types of working together. (p. 31) In such collaborations "are people who realize that they can't do it all by themselves. They need insights, comments, questions, and ideas from others. They accept and respect the fact that other perspectives can add value to their own." (p. 40) Schrage's conceptualization of collaboration focuses on the characteristics of the process of interaction among the partners, with an emphasis on an intangible—shared meaning—and a quality of interaction among the partners that can best be described as mutual respect.

Schrage's view of collaboration, then, includes the following features:

- Shared creation
- Complementary skills of individuals involved
- Development of new, enriched, shared understandings
- Realization that the individuals need the insights and expertise of their partners

Kanter (1994) describes productive partnerships as those that evolve and continue to yield benefits, create new value together (which Kanter describes as collaboration), and work through interpersonal connections and internal infrastructures that enhance learning. She identifies eight characteristics of the best partnerships:

- each partner contributes something of value,
- the relationship addresses major strategic objectives of the partners,
- the partners need each other because they have complementary assets and skills,
- each partner makes an investment in the other,
- communication is reasonably open,
- the partners develop mechanisms to work together smoothly,
- each partner becomes both a teacher and a learner, and
- the relationship is characterized by integrity and trust.

In Kanter's conceptualization, collaborations have distinct differences from "exchange" relationships, which I refer to as contractual relationships. In collaborations, each partner contributes something of value and makes an investment in the other, unlike a contractual relationship in which one unit pays for the services of the other and neither makes a true investment in the other. The investment focuses on the building of the partnership relationship, in which partners must work to develop communication channels and working mechanisms, teach each other, and build trust. Kanter's characteristics of successful collaborations are similar to Schrage's in that they emphasize the mutual reliance of the partners, the need for each to contribute skills and/or knowledge, and the development of trust. She focuses more than Schrage on the mechanisms that enable collaborations, such as good communication patterns and each partner assuming the role of both teacher and learner.

Kanter adds a component, not explicitly stated by Schrage, that I believe to be the key to developing partnership relationships in institutions or organizations. That is the realization by both parties that their partnership addresses a common mission or strategic objective. The partners do not work together just out of an altruistic desire to help the other out, nor merely for a monetary incentive, nor because of a directive from upper levels of administration. They work together because they see that it is the best strategy for achieving their mission or strategic goals.

In the context of computer centers and libraries, there are reasons, prompted by the networked information environment, that encourage librarians and computing professionals to see that they have some communality of mission or strategic objectives. For example, ten years ago, it is likely that neither the library nor the computing center would have named building a campus-wide information service (CWIS) as one of their strategic goals. However, now many campuses expect that a campus-wide information service will be developed by some unit(s) on campus. Both the library and the computing center have reasons to see the development of a CWIS as part of their strategic objectives. By jointly contributing resources, pooling talents of professionals, and learning from each other, the two units can develop a collaborative project to enhance the information climate of their campus. The process of partnership or collaboration would then yield shared meaning, if the project proceeded successfully.

In a true collaboration, each unit considers the collaborative endeavor to be mission-critical. In a contractual relationship, only one party is involved in the relationship because the project is mission-critical; the other party is involved primarily because part of its mission is to provide support services, not because the project itself is critical to its mission. Another feature which distinguishes partnerships from other types of arrangements between parties is the shared risks and benefits feature. Each party accrues benefit to the achievement of its institutional mission if the project succeeds and each party loses ground in achieving its mission if the project fails. In a contractual relationship, all or most of the benefit accrues to the contracting party if the project succeeds, and if the project fails, the party providing services generally still retains its promised benefit (e.g. payment for staff time and equipment, etc.) while the contracting party loses ground.

COLLABORATIVE PROJECTS IN NETWORKED INFORMATION

Arthur Young states, "If we recognize the converging paths of information technology and libraries, and embrace the essential nature of collaboration, then the prospect brightens for a virtual information commons on our campuses." (1994, p. 6) In the context of academic institutions, the shared mission of many collaborative efforts between libraries and computing centers can be the development of a unified, seamless information infrastructure for the university community. While this may be an overall goal embodied in strategic planning efforts, it can be achieved through building the components in an incremental fashion. A number of practitioners suggest that focusing on particular projects is a useful mechanism for collaboration and Schrage emphasizes the project basis of most collaborations. (Young, 1994, McMillan and Anderson, 1994, Schrage, 1990)

Many collaborative projects focused on networked information resources and services and networking infrastructure are being developed across the U.S. and in many countries. The professional library and computing literature begins to yield articles on library and computing center convergence, partnership, or collaboration in 1985, starting with Pat Molholt's pacesetting "On Converging Paths: The Computing Center and the Library" and Raymond K. Neff's "Merging Libraries and Computer Centers: Manifest Destiny or Manifestly Deranged?"

Woodsworth (1988) suggests a number of areas in which libraries and computing centers can derive benefit from working together:

- institutional budget support
- development of user services
- development of information and network services
- vendor negotiation
- management of information technology units
- space and facility planning
- assessment of computing and information services

An increasing number of articles and conference presentations provide examples of collaborative projects. These include reports of merged service units or integrated services (Shapiro and Long, 1994; Flowers and Martin, 1994, Branin, D'Elia, and Lund, 1994), jointly created facilities for education (Creth, 1994; Lowry, 1994), instructional programs, including those focused on Internet training (Channing, 1994, Schiller, 1994), professional development programs (Hess and Bernbom, 1994), development of campus information policies (Graves, Jenkins, and Parker, 1995), creation of information resources (Gusack and Lynch, 1995), development of campus-wide information services (CWIS) (Koopman, 1995), and provision of an overall "information environment." (McMillan and Anderson, 1994) These projects demonstrate varying degrees of actual collaborative effort. Some projects are largely based on contractual relationships with a glimmer of collaboration while others demonstrate a more fully developed collaborative model. One article (Koopman, 1995) describes a project which began by using the "consumer/producer" or contractual model but evolved into a cross-unit team partnership.

Projects related to the development and delivery of information services are often targeted for collaboration between libraries and computing centers. This may be due to the perception of common mission of the library and computing center to provide information services to the campus community. Five years ago, the mission of providing information services to the campus community would have meant very different things to the library and to the computing center than it does today. Developments in the networked information environment, first through library catalogs available on the Internet, next the access to information via gopher, and now the increasing amount of information available through the WorldWide Web, have brought the operationalizations of the libraries' and computing centers' missions closer together. The professionals involved in networked information projects often state their complementary skills in the shorthand of "content vs. conduit," the notion that librarians are the content specialists and computing professionals are the conduit (or networking) specialists. While this compartmentalization of skills is becoming more blurred, it has served as a good starting point for many collaborations. The cultures and personality styles of information services professionals in computing centers and libraries may have some commonalities that would not exist with other subsets of the two professions, e.g. programmers and collection development specialists, and lead to easier working relationships and fewer clashes than among other cross-unit partnerships.

Collaboration on service projects that have concrete outcomes, for example the establishment of a teaching facility or the development of an Internet training program, may be a good starting point for an institution new to collaboration between the library and computing center. Such projects offer the opportunity for staff from the computing center and the library to begin to talk about common mission, can provide the mechanism for sharing skills, and can open up opportunities for mutual teaching and the development of shared meaning. Overall efforts to merge or revamp information services contain many more challenges to the parties involved and will not result in the quick demonstration of success that can be a boost to many efforts.

The development of campus information policies, seen by parties in both the library and computing center as a critical need and a timely issue, is another fruitful area for collaboration. Such a project would provide fertile ground for the exchange of conceptions of the mission of the library and computing center, would leverage the principles and practical experience of librarians and computing professionals, and would lead toward a development of shared meaning.

There are many other forward-looking, creative ways to leverage partnerships between librarians and information technologists. The most important thing is to begin the effort with an open mind and an attitude that each group has much to gain from the other.

DIFFICULTIES OF MAINTAINING COLLABORATIONS OR PARTNERSHIPS

At times, partnerships between librarians and information technologists are smooth and fruitful, resulting in new and innovative resources and services available to the campus community. In other instances, attempts at partnership result in turf wars, verbal stereotypes, unfinished projects, and a fragmented information resources infrastructure on campus.

While many articles report successful collaborative efforts, it is a more difficult task to document the problematic areas in collaboration between librarians and information technologists. Kanter (1994) suggests that one area of difficulty can be caused by the fact that the partnership may have been instigated and formalized solely by top administrators. Sometimes this results in staff at lower levels, who may not have the same vision or commitment as their administrators, charged with actually implementing the project. Other common pitfalls are that inadequate staff is dedicated to the partnership activities, operational and cultural differences emerge, and mistrust develops between employees at lower levels of the organizations. Kanter's point that operational and cultural differences can cause difficulties seems particularly applicable to collaborations between librarians and information technologists. In many undocumented conversations at professional meetings, team members report that differences in authority structures, reporting, and decision-making styles between the library and computing center have led to problems and tensions, and in some cases dissolution of partnerships.

Another factor inhibiting the development of collaborations on campuses is the desire for both the library and computing center to maintain its power and control over its traditional functions and to extend its reach in the networked environment. Billings (1993) captures some of the tension between librarians and information technologists in his statement, "Attempting to work cooperatively with computing and other technical staff who seemed ready to absorb libraries into rather frightening unlibrary-like campus agencies left librarians feeling defensive and even more contrary among themselves." (p. 35) Branin, D'Elia, and Lund (1994) describe the organizational challenges they faced when they tried an experimental service unit joining library and computing services for two schools at the University of Minnesota. They reported that while their attempt to create organizational integration of the library and computing centers at an organizational mid-level made sense for theoretical and practical reasons, it was not a comfortable experience. They write, "Conflicts and competition over access to end users and jurisdictional and resource allocation disputes were as much a part of the experience as were cooperation and collaboration." (p. 37) Schiller (1994) surveyed librarians and information technologists about their efforts in Internet training and reported that comments on the survey revealed that librarians were concerned about being "made obsolete" by the computing center and the computing professionals felt they were being "encroached upon" by the librarians. (p. 43)

Top administrators of libraries and computing centers have a critical role to play in the successful implementation of collaborative projects between their two units. First, the library and computing heads must share their vision of the project and the way in which it addresses the mission of their unit, with all staff involved. Second, they must demonstrate an attitude that discourages power struggles between the units. Finally, top administrators must demonstrate their mutual respect and help create a climate in which others in their unit can develop shared understandings.

CONCLUSION

While I have focused on collaborations between librarians and information technologists, librarians have also been involved in many successful collaborations with other professionals, including teaching faculty, publishers, media designers, and instructional specialists. Such projects are becoming increasingly common in the environment of the WorldWideWeb. There is a strategic advantage for today's librarians and libraries to seek out collaborative relationships within the academic environment or outside of it. No one individual or profession has all the skills that it takes to develop an information infrastructure for a community of users.

In conclusion, when establishing a collaborative relationship in the context of a project, each partner should have a stake in it that relates to its own mission. Developing a shared understanding of the way in which a project contributes to each unit's mission will have a beneficial impact on each team member. The individuals involved need to pay as much attention to the relationship among the partners as to the outcome of the project. They need to emphasize the process aspects of the partnership, particularly the complementary expertise that each member of the team brings, the need for open and easy communication, the opportunities for mutual teaching and learning, and the development of trust and respect. Working on the development of shared meaning among all the team members should be an explicit goal of the project. Finally, partners need to focus on the ultimate benefit of collaborative relationships—improved products and services for our community of users in an increasingly complex and sophisticated information environment.

REFERENCES

Billings, Harold. "Supping with the Devil: New Library Alliances in the Information Age." Wilson Library Bulletin 68 (October, 1993) 33–7.

Creth, Sheila D. "The Information Arcade: Playground for the Mind." Journal of Academic Librarianship 20 (March, 1994) 22–3.

Creth, Sheila D. and Anne G. Lipow, eds. Building Partnerships: Computing and Library Professionals. Berkeley: Library Solutions Press, 1995.

Flowers, Kay and Andrea Martin. "Enhancing User Services through Collaboration at Rice University." CAUSE/EFFECT 17 (Fall, 1994) 19–25.

Graves, William H., Carol G. Jenkins, and Anne S. Parker. "Development of an Electronic Information Policy Framework." CAUSE/EFFECT 18 (Summer, 1995) 15–23.

Gusack, Nancy and Clifford A. Lynch, eds. "Special Theme: The TULIP Project." Library Hi Tech 13 (No. 4, 1995) 7–74.

Hess, Charlotte and Gerald Bernbom. "INforum: A Library/IT Collaboration in Professional Development at Indiana University." CAUSE/EFFECT 17 (Fall, 1994) 13–18.

Kanter, Rosabeth Moss. "Collaborative Advantage: the Art of Alliances." Harvard Business Review 72 (July-August, 1994) 96–108.

Koopman, Ann. "Library Web Implementation: A Tale of Two Sites." CAUSE/EFFECT 18 (Winter, 1995) 15–21.

Lowry, Anita. "The Information Arcade at the University of Iowa." CAUSE/EFFECT 17 (Fall, 1994) 38–44.

McMillan, Marilyn and Gregory Anderson. "The Prototyping Tank at MIT: 'Come on in, the Water's Fine.'" CAUSE/EFFECT 17 (Fall, 1994) 51–2.

Molholt, Pat. "On Converging Paths: The Computing Center and the Library." Journal of Academic Librarianship 11 (November, 1985) 284–288.

Neff, Raymond K. "Merging Libraries and Computer Centers: Manifest Destiny or Manifestly Deranged?" EDUCOM Bulletin 20 (Winter, 1985) 8–12.

Schiller, Nancy. "Internet Training and Support: Academic Libraries and Computer Centers: Who's Doing What?" Internet Research 4 (Summer, 1994) 35–47.

Schrage, Michael. Shared Minds: The New Technologies of Collaboration. New York: Random House, 1990.

Shapiro, Beth J. and Kevin Brook Long. "Just Say Yes: Reengineering Library User Services for the 21st Century." Journal of Academic Librarianship 20 (November, 1994) 285–90.

Woodsworth, Anne. "Computing Centers and Libraries as Cohorts: Exploiting Mutual Strengths." Journal of Library Administration 9 (No. 4, 1988) 21–34.

Young, Arthur P. "Information Technology and Libraries: A Virtual Convergence." CAUSE/EFFECT 17 (Fall, 1994) 5–6.

Part 2:
Knowledge Management: A Case Approach to Team-Building and Collaboration[1]

By Avra Michelson and Kathleen Flynn
The MITRE Corporation

There is growing evidence that a capacity for team-building and collaboration represent key success factors in modernizing library services.[2] Richard Lucier, only a handful of years ago, termed the kind of team-building and collaboration needed as "knowledge management." According to Lucier, interdisciplinary teams that include librarians, technologists, and domain specialists represent the new paradigm for delivering information services.[3] In the ensuing years while the academic community has significantly strengthened the bonds between academic computing facilities and library staff, it has proved more difficult, on a broad operational level, to put teams of technologists, librarians, and domain specialists to work on delivering customized information services.

This paper presents a case study of a knowledge management program designed to deliver specialized information services across a large technical organization. It describes the pilot program begun at The MITRE Corporation in 1994 where team-building and collaboration resulted in the redefining of the role of librarians within this not-for-profit federally funded research and development center (FFRDC). Although many organizations have downsized library staff in recent years arguing that as a result of technology librarians are expendable, this paper documents one organization's efforts to expand the role of librarians in conjunction with the development of a new web-based enterprise-wide information infrastructure. The paper explores an alternate model for considering the relationship between technology and information services that led to an augmented role for librarians. The key elements of the model adopted by MITRE include defining the role of librarians as team members rather than as customer service providers within departments; as collaborators working at the front-end of the research process to identify information needs instead of simply responding to information requests; and as key builders of the emerging organization-wide information infrastructure, instead of those being displaced by it.

This paper will provide background on the MITRE information infrastructure and the set of services that constitute the changing role of librarians in conjunction with the new technical infrastructure particularly as they pertain to team-building and collaboration. It also will explore strategies that may be useful in gaining the acceptance of this model in other organizations. It will conclude by considering the relevance of the chief "lessons learned" from this initiative for the academic research library community.

BACKGROUND

The MITRE Corporation is a not-for-profit federally funded research and development center (FFRDC) that was chartered by Congress to operate in the public interest by providing objective technical support to government and the not-for-profit sectors. MITRE's regulatory environment explicitly forbids the organization from engaging in manufacturing, holding commercial investment in any product, or from competing with the commercial sector. These regulations were designed to create an organization capable of providing unbiased, technical consulting. MITRE's corporate culture is as unique as its role within industry with a core tenet being that we "live with the technology we recommend." This aspect of the corporate culture along with a strong commitment to leverage the full capabilities of the organization for any one customer's problem prompted

MITRE several years ago to develop a new web-based common information infrastructure that serves as the organization's corporate memory.

MITRE'S INFORMATION INFRASTRUCTURE

MITRE's Information Infrastructure (MII) integrates the enterprise's personal, project and organizational home pages with legacy databases (human resources, procurement, financial, etc.) and related information resources and services (corporate library, etc.). All of the information published on the MII is indexed and can be accessed by searching or browsing. The MII is akin to campus-wide information systems (CWIS) that rely on glue, extensions, scripts, and so forth to weave together a common enterprise-wide information infrastructure. The MII is in use across The MITRE Corporation's 150 geographically-dispersed sites by all levels of the organization, from security personnel who use the infrastructure to confirm the identity of staff who have forgotten their badges by accessing their photo ids, to technical staff who as a team publish and store their project documents, to senior managers who search the MII to identify who among the staff possess expertise in an obscure software needed by a sponsor. The knowledge management program at The MITRE Corporation was introduced to complement the new technological base.

KNOWLEDGE MANAGEMENT PROGRAM

MITRE's knowledge management program drew inspiration from the seminal work of Nina Matheson and Richard Lucier at Johns Hopkins' Welch Library where librarians were teamed with technologists and domain specialists to deliver customized services to select user populations. The development of a new technical infrastructure at MITRE prompted the organization to question the role of central library services. However, instead of reducing the role of librarians as a result of new delivery mechanisms MITRE's leadership recognized that while the roles and contexts were shifting the need for information specialists remained great. It should be noted that the knowledge management program was championed not by the corporate library staff but rather by a group of mid- and senior-level managers who assumed primary responsibility for the organization's Digital Libraries Department.[4] Indeed, the administrative placement of this program outside of the corporate library shaped the initiative. From the outset the program received enthusiastic support from MITRE's president and thus high visibility across the organization.

The new program piloted in the Digital Libraries Department from 1994–95 included elements that differentiated the work of the knowledge managers from the typical activities performed by corporate or academic librarians: 1) the knowledge managers were "owned" by the department, not by the library, and served as full team members on project teams, transforming encounters with "customers" into relationships with "team members"; 2) the positioning of knowledge managers as team members on projects enabled them to help staff articulate their information needs at the front-end instead of just responding to specific information requests, resulting in skyrocketing usage by the department of the corporate library; and 3) the knowledge manager, rather than being replaced by the new enterprise-wide information infrastructure, became one of its many builders and promoted its use by using it to deliver information services. The unique approach to team-building and collaboration adopted by MITRE and formalized in its knowledge management program represents a key success factor in the modernizing of information services and will be described in some detail below.

TEAM MEMBER COLLABORATION VS. CUSTOMER SERVICE PROVIDER

The placement of the knowledge manager as a team member administratively owned by a department proved critical to the knowledge manager's ability to deliver specialized information services and a key factor in the overall success of the program. This placement insured that the knowledge manager's priorities continually were aligned with the needs of a rapidly changing environment. Working side-by side with end-users on a daily basis provided the knowledge manager with a greater understanding of the users and insight into their work process and information needs. The insights gained through the teaming relationship enabled the knowledge manager to tailor responses, both in scope and format, to the individual and to incorporate them into the department's services and products.

Not only does the Digital Libraries Department specialize in work with rapidly changing technologies, but it doubled in size in the initial year of the knowledge management program. To be effective in this dynamic environment, the knowledge manager had to be capable of redirecting her work program in accord with the changes surrounding her. Rather than adopting a rigid position description, the responsibilities of the knowledge manager evolved, changing in conjunction with the demands of the environment. The ability of the knowledge manager to refocus her services in response to departmental priorities resulted in her assuming a broader range of responsibilities than are traditionally associated with information service providers. For example, when rapid growth made it difficult for managers to track the technical capabilities of its staff, the knowledge manager quickly compiled a survey and used it to develop a resource for capturing and updating staff capabilities. In other examples of customized service delivery, the knowledge manager was called on to beta test software, participate in the development of a user query language, and coordinate an effort to survey the usability of an internal network. The deep domain and technical insights attained from each of these efforts enhanced her ability to perform the more conventional activities associated with her position.

The placement of the knowledge manager as a team member within the department facilitated performance of the more commonly recognized tasks of filtering information to staff in anticipation of their needs along with responding to specific requests for resources. A large portion of the department's staff specialize in networked information discovery and retrieval (NIDR) technologies. These are new and rapidly evolving technologies. The best technical and background documentation about these tools is often available only on the Internet, in the form of web sites, listservs, and newsgroups. Services for this staff typically focused on exploiting these sources more often than the traditional technical journals. Delivering resources and services was accomplished by creating virtual information collections presented as web sites along with the electronic delivery of copyrighted work. Publishing the reference services conducted for any one project on web pages as part of the MII provided the organization with a means to leverage corporate memory across the enterprise. For the knowledge manager, the opportunity to create resources with NIDR technologies as well as monitor these technologies led to a greater understanding of the specific work of the department and the domain's vocabulary.

As a team member the knowledge manager was able to be involved in multiple departmental projects from their inception, which positioned her to apply the knowledge accumulated on one task simultaneously across many projects. This administrative placement increased the capacity of the department to leverage its own knowledge, contain costs and improve the caliber of customer support while tending to minimize duplication of efforts and maximize the speed with which "lessons learned" were transformed into institutionalized practices. For example, the concepts developed in conjunction with departmental research on metadata were integrated within weeks into the development of metadata requirements for the MII, significantly reducing the time spent in establishing those requirements. These requirements then informed the discussions surrounding the creation of search tools and interfaces for external customers. In each case the knowledge manager ensured that knowledge accumulated from previous efforts was applied across project teams.

Another benefit of teaming knowledge managers with their customers is the degree to which the process for requesting information can be facilitated. The Digital Libraries Department is in a separate building from the MITRE library and many of the staff had never visited the central library. The proximity of the knowledge manager to her "customer base" meant that information requests could be made as a result of hallway encounters, at project meetings, and in the course of routine office visits. This placement within the user community also allowed the knowledge manager to participate in informal information sharing, which has been identified as a crucial component in an information structure.[5] The needs and priorities of individuals and teams often were articulated in the course of casual conversation and the placement of the knowledge manager within this informal information structure provided "insider information" unmatched in the formal library structure. This placement offered the knowledge manager a greater understanding of the user community and therefore a greater ability to anticipate needs and to further customize products and services, both of which were important in establishing the knowledge manager as an effective member of the organization.

BUILDER OF ENTERPRISE INFORMATION INFRASTRUCTURE

Although in many organizations new technologies have been introduced with the intent to downsize the organization's information providers, at MITRE growth in the role of the knowledge manager has been intimately linked to the growth of MITRE's internal information networks. In fact, the knowledge manager has been a key participant on organizational teams devoted to building the new technical infrastructure, often serving as the sole non-technical person on the team. This involvement has insured that content (apart from conduit) issues get addressed as well as the information management concerns paramount in library science. In conjunction with the MII, the knowledge manager developed core digital libraries of content, evaluated new tools, and advised on the suitability of new capabilities for end-users. The process of defining end-user requirements and needs for the MII developers improved the design of profiling, searching and workspace tools capabilities implemented on the server and also increased the knowledge manager's understanding of the end-user community. A short term assignment included redesigning the top level pages of the MII to meet an early deployment goal. The knowledge manager was particularly well-suited for this task because of her unusual familiarity with the technical staff's research process that she had gained as a result of team-oriented work during the previous six months.

KNOWLEDGE MANAGEMENT PROGRAM AND THE CORPORATE LIBRARY

It is ironic, but not surprising, that a knowledge manager program conducted administratively apart from the corporate library resulted in a resounding increase in the use of the central library by department staff along with expanded appreciation by the organization for the expertise of librarians. Beyond striking increases in library usage, the collaboration between the knowledge manager and the central library created a venue for the department to provide valuable feedback to the library on its needs which has influenced collection development as well as service delivery. The frequent contact between library staff and the knowledge manager (both in casual and formal exchanges) gave the collection officers greater insight into which resources in which formats were most useful to their patrons. For example, the knowledge manager created a web site to respond to a request by a senior manager for information on electronic commerce. A broader range of resources was added by the knowledge manager as additional requests came in from managers in other departments within our division. When it became apparent that the topic generated interest beyond the departments that comprise our division, the library addressed the broad need by creating an online "mini-library" which features internal and external resources, recent articles, Internet sites, and analysis. This collection, now one of twelve mini-electronic-libraries on current topics of widespread interest, are updated regularly by the library and reside on the MII.

Each new employee in the Digital Libraries Department is introduced to library services by the knowledge manager as part of the modified bibliographic instruction program. The program, beyond providing an introduction to the MII, includes instruction on the library's holdings and services. This orientation provides the library with broad exposure to its customer base. When the library introduces new services or resources the knowledge manager disseminates this information to the staff and trains end-users on library systems. This type of personalized instruction which may be difficult for a small library staff to support is relatively easy for a knowledge manager responsible only to a single department.

An unanticipated result of the knowledge management program has been increased recognition for the library staff and an expansion of their roles beyond conventional library functions. During the past year, corporate librarians have been offered opportunities to augment their roles by assuming responsibility for construction of a specialized thesaurus in conjunction with network capabilities, development of customized internal news digests, and by serving on teams as consultants, developers and beta-testers.

NEW MODELS FOR INFORMATION SERVICES

MITRE's knowledge management program conceptually was built on a post-custodial model of information services. This model recognizes a shift in information services from a bounded, intermediary-driven environment that is centrally managed and supported, to a global, end-user-driven model that features distributed management and charging mechanisms. These high-level shifts involve changes in the performance of traditional library functions: 1) subscription-based selection and acquisition are giving way to the licensing and filtering of information; 2) description achieved through catalog representations and classification schemes is evolving in the new environment into networked navigation tools and browsing facilities; 3) access through borrowing or onsite use is accomplished in the new model through online, distributed networked availability of resources; and 4) preservation programs designed to support conversion to more permanent media (e.g., microfiche) are expanding into efforts to migrate data through generations of technology. Figure 1 details the key features of the traditional and post-custodial models of information services.

Within our organization the transition from a traditional to a post-custodial set of information services is expected to evolve unevenly and incrementally. As a significant segment of recorded memory continues to be available only in print, programmatic bridges are needed between print-based practices and the electronic services. Further, since the technologies that support resource discovery and retrieval in the networked environment are quite primitive, the full capabilities of the post-custodial model can be realized only as the NIDR tools mature. The evolution to the post-custodial model will rely on substantial human effort.

KNOWLEDGE MANAGER ROLES

As a complement to the development of the MII, the department-based knowledge manager originally was envisioned as the "tailor and profiler of information specific to the department domain." The role has evolved over the year to include a wider set of tasks and services:

- assist staff in defining information needs
- compile digital libraries of domain-relevant resources
- satisfy expressed information needs of staff
- anticipate staff needs and filter information to them
- deliver resources and services through networked access
- orient new employees to available information services
- provide collection development inputs to library
- select tools and technologies for growing the MII
- serve as appropriate in systems engineering capacity on project teams

A word about these roles. First, the reliance on the knowledge manager by the more than fifty staff in the department (many of whom had rarely used the corporate library before) has been so great that a second knowledge management position is being created. We are currently searching for an appropriate candidate. And second, demand for the knowledge manager involvement in projects in a systems engineering capacity grew far more rapidly than the department expected. It was assumed that by about year two of the program the knowledge manager would begin to perform systems engineering tasks on digital library projects appropriate with her formal education. In less than a year the demand for the knowledge manager as a team member in a systems engineering capacity on projects was so great that it has become difficult for her to continue performing the knowledge management portions of the job.[6]

STRATEGIC CONSIDERATIONS

Today's campuses are full of exemplary teaming relationships between libraries and computing staff.[7] The MITRE experience in team building and collaboration differed in one key respect from the experience typical in academia: the knowledge manager was "owned" by a department not the library. The administrative placement of the knowledge manager as a team member rather than as a customer service representative had substantive consequences. The knowledge manager was completely integrated into the work of the organization she served. Her work priorities were able to change dynamically in reaction to changes in the department's priorities. Her position as a staff person within the department served as a bridge to information services that had been underutilized in the past. The break with the past represented by her proactive use of technology and her role in building the new information infrastructure solidified her acceptance.

There is a message in the MITRE experience for academic environments. The natural outgrowth of distributed access to information resources may be the emergence of decentralized information services

	TRADITIONAL MODEL	**POST-CUSTODIAL MODEL**
Environment	• Bounded • Centrally managed • Central financial support • Intermediary-driven	• Unbounded • Distributed management • Distributed charging mechanisms • End-user driven
Selection of resources	• Subscription-based • Performed by subject specialists	• License-based selection • Augmented by subscription • Performed by domain specialists (e.g., knowledge managers)
Acquisition of resources	• Physical holdings • Augmented by ILL	• Site licenses • Filtering applications • Newsfeeds, listservs, etc. • Augmented by ILL
Description of resources	• Catalogs • Classification schemes	• Custom networked browsers • Automatic generation of metadata • Common command language to support searching
Access to resources	• Used at library or borrowed • Assistance provided by reference staff	• Online, distributed, print-on-demand • Augmented by borrowing • Assistance through filters, networked directories, knowledge managers
Preservation of resources	• Conversion to more permanent media	• Migration through generations of technology

Figure 1: Models of Information Services

that coordinate with but bureaucratically are separate from the central library. One of the best ways of achieving improved information services on campuses may be by promoting a department-based knowledge management program quite apart from the central library. The value an organization places on librarians traditionally has been measured by its investment in a central library. Our organization's experience suggests that the centralized delivery of services through the institution's library may no longer represent the most effective means of service delivery and that the way to expand the role of librarians and information services in an era of distributed, networked computing is by promoting non-library based alternatives.

ENDNOTES

1. The authors wish to thank Joan Lippincott for her contributions on team-building and collaboration as well as their colleagues at MITRE, Ray D'Amore and Marcia Kerchner, for their helpful suggestions in preparing this article.
2. See for instance the Final Report, Information Resources Division, Gettysburg College (December 1994); or Cornell University's Albert R. Mann Library : A Prototype for Today's Electronic Library, In Library Hi Tech , Issue 47, 12:3 (1994), pp. 31–88.
3. Richard Lucier, "Knowledge Management: Refining Roles in Scientific Communication," EDUCOM Review (Fall 1990), pp. 21–27.
4. The organization's visionary champions for the program included Michael Josephs, Geoff W. Lipsey, Jeffrey S. Rogers, and William A. Ruh.
5. Davenport, Thomas H, "Saving IT's Soul: Human Centered Information Management" Harvard Business Review (March/April 1994), pp. 119.
6. This is despite the fact that a sizable proportion of the department's staff have a background in library science.
7. To name just a few: Gettysburg College, Dartmouth College, and the University of Iowa.

The Human Side of Organizational Effectiveness: On Delegation in Libraries

By G. T. Mendina
University of Memphis

"No one develops as much as the [person] who is trying to help others to develop themselves." Peter Drucker, *Management*, 1976

"Truly involved people can do anything!" Tom Peters, *Thriving on Chaos*, 1987

INTRODUCTION

In the paper which follows I examine the managerial act of delegating authority and responsibility within the organizations known as libraries. I hope that the discussion has relevance for other types of organizations as well. I begin by affirming the importance of delegation, which of course implies that delegation—precisely because it is so terribly important—may be a problematic area for both management and employee. I consider the idealized view of delegation in organizations—at its most morally elevated, delegation is seen as a kind of "golden-rule" behavior in which the superordinate treats the subordinate as the superordinate would wish to be treated with beneficent results for both, as in the Drucker quotation above.

I refer to some of the situational realities and then move to a basic question: Are there features intrinsic to the organizations known as "libraries" which make delegation unusually problematic in those organizations? If so, what can be said of those features and their implications for delegation, managerial behavior, and employee motivation, performance, and job satisfaction?

Finally, I add a note on delegation in an era of downsizing and an appendix on "how to delegate." I should say that when I use the term "delegation" below I am most often talking about something broad, like "empowerment," or "involvement," as in Tom Peters' quotation above. Delegation or empowerment in my sense may be long-term—the creation of a new position in the organization for the right employee. Even if the assignment is not long-term, hopefully the effects on the employee and the organization would be. Or empowerment may be of briefer duration—a relatively brief project assignment, or even asking the employee to attend a series of meetings in my stead. Even a brief episode of empowerment can have dramatic effects.

In addition, I hope that what is said here about delegation and empowerment bears on "non-delegation" as well. What is "non-delegation"? Non-delegation, or "anti-empowerment," has occurred when a supervisor or manager usurps part or all of the role of the employee, and particularly so if the supervisor or manager does so with an obvious air of contempt and frustration. My sense is that this is not an uncommon occurrence in libraries. I will leave speculation on the reasons to the librarian-reader.

But this much can be said: it is not necessarily easy to empower employees; I don't mean to suggest that it is. It is work, the work of the savvy and responsible manager, work that requires several steps and considerations. (See my appendix on "How to Delegate.") The manager will almost always find it easier, at least in the short run, to give up on delegation and "do it her/himself," give up on the development of the employee precisely because it is a long-term job of work requiring reflection and planning.

A final introductory word: sentiments favoring humane management practice like employee development are at least as old as the Human Relations approach to management as developed by Elton

Mayo at Harvard in the 1930s. And there is considerable continuing interest in delegation—empowerment, involvement—in the 1990s, as I show below. Thus I claim no particular originality for this paper. As James Autry has said recently, "Some things are indeed worth saying, again and again. The point is *affirmation*, not information." (285, my emphasis) And while I am not quite prepared to advise library managers to "involve everyone in everything," as Peters (343 ff.) presumably would, I think that the spirit of his advice is appropriately disconcerting for those who never delegate, period.

DELEGATION ACCORDING TO THE "TEXTBOOKS"

One person is not an organization, at least not in the modern sense of "organization," derived from the social sciences. By nature, organizations combine and coordinate the efforts of a multiplicity of persons. The better the development and coordination of employee talent, the more productive the organization, other things being equal. Organizations exist, in fact, in order to take productive advantage of the coordinated contributions of many, or so theory has told us. As Tom Peters says, "delegation of responsibility has been a central topic in management texts through the ages." (544)

That early student of the division of labor in organizations, Adam Smith observed that "the division of labor . . . occasions . . . a proportionable increase of the productive powers of labor," (5) and held that the tendency to divide human labor was a function of a deep-going dimension of human nature. Max Weber, that prophet of the advent of the modern bureaucracy, extolled the efficiency and speed of the organization (bureaucracy), stating that "it is superior to any other form in precision, in stability, in the stringency of its discipline, and in its reliability." (337) Presciently enough, Weber emphasized the importance of technical knowledge as the source of the superiority of bureaucracy. Peter Blau, the well-known sociologist of modern organizations, states that "a work organization is simply an explicit system for organizing the work of many persons in a common enterprise." (164) Blau stresses the increasingly complex division of labor which modern organizations develop as they take on increasingly large tasks.

Delegation, the charging of staff with authority and responsibility for conducting ongoing operations or bringing specific projects to successful completion, is among those six or seven functions (e.g., planning, goal-setting, organizing, delegating, motivating) that are regarded as basic to the overall managerial task in organizations. Indeed, delegation is coextensive with the function referred to as "organizing," partitioning the total task of the organization for purposes of efficiency, effectiveness, and fairness, as I indicate below. While Peter Drucker, in his classic work on management, does not deal with delegation per se, it is probably because he views such an activity as so implicitly basic to the overall managerial task. The specific resource that the manager works with is man, Drucker says, and " 'working' the human being always means developing him." (402)

Organizations are hierarchies of authority (again, *vide* Max Weber), but the literature on managerial leadership is replete with warnings against authoritarianism as management style and predictions that the non-team-oriented manager will become a "bossasaurus." (Manz) Organizations are, most importantly, composed of human beings, creatures who entertain visions of self-worth and independence, and who are resistant to unreasoning domination. Such characteristics have been noticed by those concerned with delegation as it relates to empowerment (Keller), democratic leadership (Gastil), situational leadership (Irgens), the personality of the "real leader," (Brown), the role of values in organizations (Newland), team-building (Steckler), leadership for the new millennium (Lloyd), and other topical areas of organizational behavior. The overarching vision is that of delegation as a key to employee development, to an organization of tasks which promotes efficiency, to wise and humane leadership, and to overall organizational effectiveness through careful attention to the human dimension of the organization.

A scan of current references to delegation reveals no shortage of admonitions to delegate. Kroll advises that "a good manager has to delegate" and extols delegation as a means of lightening work loads, getting jobs done faster, and developing employees. Masak says, "Dare to delegate," to managers and sees delegation as a vital aspect of time management as well as a means of challenging staff. Gadson says straightforwardly to the manager (in the insurance industry), "You need help: delegate or die in the

1990s," a period when more head-office tasks are being passed down to the agency office. Johnson sees delegation as part of the Total Quality Management (TQM) movement and holds that empowerment leads to long-term commitment to quality.

Nor is there any shortage of advice on how to delegate. (An appendix to this paper tries to summarize the advice.) Morgan provides "guidelines for delegating effectively," while Ninemeier gives "tips for delegating tasks." Pollock reveals the "secrets of successful delegation." *Women in Business* assuages the anxiety of many managers by telling "how to delegate work and make sure it's done right."

Noel even indicates "what you say to your employees when you delegate." Ayres-Williams and Buscher see delegation as an "art," probably correctly. Straub answers the question, What should you do if delegation doesn't work? (Do not over-react; discuss the matter with the employee calmly, reviewing previously agreed-upon standards; determine what aspects of the task the employee can retain.) Bordeaux suggests that managers should be selective about the tasks delegated and should never delegate those which require executive decision-making. McConalogue, on the other hand, emphasizes trust in employees as well as the responsibility which managers bear to challenge and reward employees. McConalogue also emphasizes that managers should listen sensitively and communicate clearly. Gaedeke maintains that the problems associated with delegation can be minimized by carefully fitting the task to be delegated to the skills and interests of the employee by providing the employee full information about the delegation and the task, providing needed resources, authority, and freedom to the employee, and also providing feedback and recognition after the task is done.

Carter values delegation as an effective motivator, but advises that managers must be familiar with the tasks that they delegate in order to correctly match tasks and employees. Delegation might best begin with simple tasks. Like Gaedeke, Carter stresses that management's expectations should be made clear, and adequate authority should be extended to the employee. Scheduled progress reports as well as feedback and completion dates should be utilized. Johnson holds that delegation, an essential aspect of leadership and a means of empowering employees, involves three guiding elements: responsibility, authority, and accountability.

Chapter seven, "Delegation," of G. Edward Evans' venerable text on library management is in fact a discourse on organization. Rizzo states that "the major purpose of delegation is to allocate functions and decision-making prerogatives throughout a group of people," and suggests that the realization of that purpose brings about "some form of organization structure." (105) Delegation, of course, interacts with other managerial functions, motivation, for example. Indeed, Rizzo refers to delegation within the context of job enrichment and implies that delegation can be an important motivational tool when implemented properly. (167–168)

Townsend advises his reader of the importance of his chapter, "People," where he says, "Organizations work when they maximize the chance that each one, working with others, will get growth in his job." (170) In general, Townsend makes the point that employee growth is a result of skillful delegation of responsibility and authority by management. Every leader ought to look for a chance to give an employee "a whole job" simply because "people who are normally half-dead from boredom or frustration during office hours come alive when given a whole job...." (53) Tom Peters, in his best-selling *Thriving on Chaos,* indicates that delegation is "the sine qua non of empowerment," (689) that is, the essence of the managerial task of providing employees the independence, resources, prerogatives, and sense of "ownership" sufficient to get the job done in a maximal way. Among these, as Peters makes clear, the granting of true independence, or even autonomy, to employees is the most difficult aspect of "empowering" staff, so much so that many managers only "sorta let go" of these delegates. Not only must managers guard against "sorta" letting employees go, but they must heed other principles of successful delegation, such as the setting of high performance standards.

DELEGATION IN THE "REAL WORLD" OF LIBRARIES

Thus, the reader of the managerial lore on delegation might reasonably expect that most managers bend over backwards to "empower" employees through copious delegation of tasks and provision of authority necessary to get those tasks done. In those managers' organizations, highly independent employees confidently march forward to their tasks and projects under the benevolent glow of full managerial trust. Basking in the warmth of employee self-worth that "empowerment" has generated, management can be seen in the background smiling the smile of benevolent reason as one after another project is conquered by a fiercely-motivated workforce which takes enormous pride in its prerogatives and independence. After all, as Townsend affirms, it is management that will receive credit for the successes that come from shrewd delegation-motivation. (53)

The vision of employee empowerment through delegation is hardly an accurate one when measured against organizational reality, as many librarians (and others) could attest. In reality, delegation, or "empowerment," is subject to the vicissitudes of managerial inclination and attitude. Many managers who could delegate responsibility and authority are in fact more comfortable with their own work-overload crises than with delegating responsibility for some of that work to others. They miss appointments and deadlines, but who could level blame at someone who is so heroically engaged with work? Their staffs are frustrated and resentful at the lack of trust in them, but who is attentive to the feelings and aspirations of the staff? What is the impact of managerial heroics upon the organization? In many cases, if one were given access to the innards of the organization, one would observe staff whose most important duties had been usurped by a superior. Townsend notes that "many give lip service, but few delegate authority *in important matters*. And that means all they delegate is dog work." (50) Even the unimportant tasks tend to be usurped at times by a manager, or managers, who are already "busy" beyond any realistic expectation. There is never any hesitancy to "*dis*empower" employees when the "SuperLibrarian" feels motivated to take over the task or project or routine duty. As Dennis says, "Superman didn't delegate." What is left behind for the employee is, of course, the "dogwork."

For that reason, among others, the employee finds it impossible to suppress indignation towards the SuperLibrarian who usurps the roles of the librarians beneath her or him and who never delegates with trusting decisiveness. Such indignation tends to go unarticulated and to build as time passes. Make no mistake about this: this growing indignation is basically an experience of personal pain. But the present purpose is to suggest why that anti-delegating—and ultimately untrusting—behavior is at least explainable within the realities of the organizations known as libraries.

WHY DON'T LIBRARIANS DELEGATE?

The present section explores the reasons why non-delegation may be prevalent in libraries and why it is in fact the expectable course of action for many library managers.

Rizzo, in his classic work on library management, emphasizes the wisdom of pushing decision-making to the lowest effective level in the organization (106) but observes that "in many organizations, tasks and decisions are located at levels much higher than they need to be and managers cling to certain functions and refuse subordinates the right to act with more authority." (106) Rizzo gives reasons why this non-delegation may be the case: Sometimes superiors like to retain the work that could be delegated, oblivious to their employees' feelings and desires for new opportunities. Second, bosses may fear loss of power if they delegate work. Third, bosses may fear that subordinates are unable to do jobs adequately. ("If you want something done well, do it yourself.....") To be sure, non-delegation may occur as the result of employee attitudes and behavior, e.g., resentment of additional responsibility, fear of failure or of the boss's reaction to mistakes, or the feeling that more pay should accompany more responsibility.

Rizzo's reasons for non-delegation on the part of the "boss" inspire us to look for others. I wish to point to some additional reasons for non-delegation that may well be rooted in the very nature of the organization known as "the library" (although many of the reasons will relate to other organizations as well). As Rizzo emphasizes, libraries are public-service organizations with all the pitfalls and vulnerabilities that that status implies. Libraries do not generate profits, at least in dollars-and-cents terms, but rather depend largely upon public funds, levies, and the largesse of parent organizations. Often, libraries are not funded on the basis of performance, nor is performance tested in the marketplace. Thus, as Rizzo observes, "energies of the [service] organization are aimed at pleasing those who allocate resources," and "service organization activities or programs may exist in order not to alienate crucial support from a trustee, city manager, or university president." (64) The situation becomes more sensitive when librarians present budgets for approval that are not based upon planning or performance. Then, the library's susceptibility to criticism and the potential for ill feelings increase.

Rizzo also observes that "some libraries act as if their purpose is to provide housing for independent professionals," (67) and otherwise evince indifference to the needs and expectations of their clienteles and to the benefits of positive marketing techniques. Writing in 1980, he concluded that "according to some authors in the field, the library profession has a long way to go in . . . developing the service orientation." (68) (Are librarians much more service-oriented in 1996 than in 1980? I don't have a definitive answer.)

Shields, speaking within the context of federal legislation and libraries, echoes Rizzo when he observes that "the library as a social institution has never achieved a level of understanding and support sufficiently broad and fervent to insure adequate support from the taxpaying public." (3) Shields goes on to note that "in a nation long noted for its general antipathy to intellectualism, the library for many was and has been the symbol of scholarly pursuit and/or frivolous consumption of fiction." (3)

Rizzo's and Shields' observations tend to support the suggestion that is implicit in this paper: the status of libraries and of librarians is often tenuous, indeed even low, from the viewpoints of parent-organization administrators and sometimes of the library's public. The welfare of the library is often not a top priority in given societal and institutional environments. Part of the reason for the antipathy—where it exists—probably has to do with the difficulties, for both library and parent-organization managements, of measuring the positive effectiveness of libraries as organizations. (It is not particularly difficult to measure the number of complaints the library receives, but reacting to complaints may contribute insubstantially to the effectiveness of the library.) As a result, library managers may avoid or be oblivious to the need for delegation, and for a number of reasons related to the low status of libraries, as suggested below.

1. The boss does not delegate because she is disinclined to alter the lines of authority and definitions of roles in the organization.

Delegation is part and parcel of organizing the work group for effectiveness. Delegation goes hand in hand with the shape of the organization because it has impacts upon the amounts and quality of responsibility and authority that are conferred on staff within the organization. Delegation has impact upon roles and the interaction of organizational roles. Some bosses will avoid delegation by way of avoiding change or explicitness about the amounts and lines of responsibility and authority in the organization. This inexplicitness can be a function of a number of motivations, including uncertainty about the appropriate shape of the organization. In any case, inexplicit or non-existent delegation almost inevitably leads to a certain degree of disequilibrium in the organization.

Some bosses may rationalize this disequilibrium as advantageous—some might even view it as "creative," as contributing to a sort of spontaneity that has good effects upon the organization. ("Chaos," as Tom Peters calls it. . . .) Although the textbooks tell us that just the opposite is the desired state of things—that organizational roles and lines of responsibility and authority should be made as explicit as possible for maximum organizational effectiveness—in the real interpersonal and political world this explicitness is not always the goal.

Why might this avoidance of delegation be characteristic of libraries? The answer probably lies in part in the fact that librarians themselves often do not view libraries as organizations. Rather, libraries are seen as repositories for books, periodicals, microforms, other materials—that is, libraries are viewed as warehouses and the sites of offices for independent professionals, to use Rizzo's language. It may well be the case that the library's status in the community of its colleagues is a function of its collection size, in fact. The fact that libraries are organizations with contours and dynamics resembling those of most other organizations remains a matter of non-importance. The situation may be intensified by the indifference of parent-organization administrators to delegation within the library. The same case can be made, *mutatis mutandis*, if the library is seen by its public as an electronic-database center. Warehouse for books or maintainer of databases—in either case the library as organization is not the emphasis.

2. The boss does not delegate because he is apprehensive of new organizational shapes.

Textbooks tell us that a pattern of delegation which emerges over time may suggest new and more effective organizational contours in a way that complements planning per se. Nonetheless, to the boss who fears new organizational shapes—or tends to fear the future in general, with all of its ominous unknowns—delegation is anathema.

Why is this fear of newness to be found in abundance in libraries? Perhaps because "newness" is today so prevalent within the library and information fields, a newness that is often threatening to library director and staff as well. Will the accelerating impact of electronics make libraries obsolete within a matter of years or a decade? With such an overwhelming rate of change, what should the organizational shape of the library be anyway? If a decision about the organization of the library is made today, will that decision be obliterated by the configuration that has evolved in the larger organization under, say, a new Chief Information Officer who has distinct opinions about the shape and role of the library within the total information-provision wing of the parent organization?

Is this apprehension about "newness" unique to libraries? In all likelihood not. Such apprehension is fully warranted in any organization associated with the quickly-evolving phenomenon of information technology, at least. In a rapidly-shifting environment, managers of organizations may avoid actions that lead to organizational specialization (as Hannan and Freeman indicate), and explicit delegation might be one of those actions.

3. The boss does not delegate because higher management has told her to be beyond blame in this era of heightened accountability.

This particular apprehension, fear of losing control of accountability, is perhaps understandable in this period of heightened financial and organizational stress. The matter is only made worse if the library organization is not held in high esteem—or is essentially ignored unless there is a visible problem. Here is where the threat of "non-delegation," or "anti-empowerment," on the part of the "boss," or library manager or supervisor (as mentioned in my Introduction above), becomes very real indeed. Here is where the boss may be sorely tempted to "take over" for the employee—and "empowerment" be hanged!—when the employee has run afoul of some administrative rule or procedure and has brought the auditors down on the boss's head.

The greater the number of employees in the library who know sensitive information, the greater is the vulnerability of the organization to breaches of accountability—or so the parent-organization's management might reason. Top-level management might prefer that administrators of components of the large organization keep important information privy to themselves. Naturally, this preference will have an inhibiting effect upon the inspiration to delegate authority and responsibility even to deserving employees.

4. The boss does not delegate because his superior has told him not to, either explicitly or implicitly.

We must not forget that the boss is himself in a chain of command much like the one in which his staff find themselves. The boss's immediate organizational superior might well have the "Do it yourself and it'll be done right" attitude and transmit that attitude to your boss. The boss's superior does not want to see an underling on his doorstep when it is time to report on the results of an important assignment. The superior wants to see *the boss*, see, in essence, that the boss has accepted full responsibility for the important task and has followed through.

Why would the administrative superordinate to the head librarian indicate that he should not waste time with delegation? As suggested earlier, the answer probably lies in the non-awareness on the part of the administrator to the library-as-organization. Since the library is just a warehouse or database-center, why waste time creating functional work teams? Besides, the high-level administrator has never bothered to go "behind the scenes" of the library—or of any of her accountable units, for that matter—and meet staff at the middle levels of the organization. Why waste time getting to know mid-level staff who are being "developed" or "empowered" by the head librarian? Even less is the high-level administrator particularly concerned about reinforcing the kind of organization that the head librarian thinks is functional.

5. The boss does not delegate because she fears the acquisition of power by those receiving new authority or responsibility.

The fear of loss of power—or of the gain of power by others in the organization which might tend to diminish one's own power—as a result of imprudent delegation is a perennial one. Although support for employee "empowerment" is frequent in the management literature of today, would Machiavelli have given away the Prince's kingdom through copious delegation of power to ministers and other underlings? Hardly likely. (Actually, Machiavelli did advocate generous treatment by the Prince towards ministers in order to give them office, duties, and perquisites which would presumably make them beholden to the Prince and thus unrebellious.) There might be very valid reasons for hesitating to extend power to an employee who is otherwise deserving of new responsibility and authority.

But is this kind of apprehension endemic to libraries only? Of course it isn't. Why, then, would it be more pronounced in libraries than in other organizations—if indeed it is? Again, the answer would have to be a function of the low status of libraries—and of librarians, including the library director—within the total context of university, municipality, firm, etc. The anxiety caused by that tenuous status tends to produce a possessive attitude towards position and power and an unwillingness to elevate others into potentially threatening positions through delegation—regardless of the lip service paid to "empowerment" and "development" by the management of the larger organization.

6. The boss does not delegate because he has a low opinion of his own work performance and tends to generalize that opinion to others.

This important "reason" why managers do not delegate refers to the manager's psyche and to a poor self-image and low estimation of his own effectiveness as a manager. The low self-estimation is of course related to the estimation of the manager's organization as held by higher administrators. Why should the manager take a chance with delegation when she or he deeply—if perhaps unconsciously—believes that his or her decisions in any area are suspect or, more likely, totally ignored? A manager whose confidence has been profoundly shaken for whatever reason—valid or less than valid—is probably going to be hesitant to make the kinds of decisions that delegation requires, i. e., the kinds of decisions that have profound impact upon human beings and upon the organization into the foreseeable future. The risks are just too great for more failure, either self-perceived or perceived by superordinates.

But is this failure of confidence on the parts of highly-placed managers isolated to libraries? Of course it isn't. At the same time, one might argue that, in light of the low status of libraries in some contexts, the library manager's confidence may be challenged on a daily basis—his ability to run things, to make decisions, to handle difficult personnel matters, and so on.

"DOWNSIZING" AND ITS IMPACT ON DELEGATION

As long as "downsizing" is de rigueur—should I say fashionable?—as a means of creating a quick, positive profit picture for the organization, some members of the workforce may have conflicted reactions to the manager's attempts to empower. On the one hand, delegation can be seen as a vital dimension of "strategic downsizing" and an important element of the more flexible staffing strategies that corporations will need under current conditions. (Mathys and Burack) It would seem that an ethos of professionalism is replacing the old ethos of loyalty and that a vital element of "professionalism" is "life-long learning." (Noble) Delegation can be one of the keys to such life-long learning and one of the keys to the kind of adaptability that employees will need in the foreseeable future. Kirk refers to employees who have had to adapt to downsizing by cultivating "indispensable" skills which will be useful even if the ax falls. Tanikawa tells of Japanese executives who have productively engaged in job-switching.

On the other hand, we need to note that increased delegation to members of a downsized staff may work to exacerbate feelings of guilt and depression already affecting employees, who may view themselves as the "survivors" and fear that they may be the next to go—what Kirk calls the "Survivor Syndrome." There may be intense resentment at the prospect of increased production expectations in order to compensate for the work that was previously performed by those released from the organization. Such resentment may persist even though management claims that delegation represents employee development. Hearing that argument on the part of management, the employee may view delegation as preparation for separation and not as enhancement of transferable job skills. Or the employee may view delegation as "compensation" for higher productivity expectations on the part of management.

Thus, resistance to "development" or "empowerment" may be animated by insecurity, resentment, suspicion, and other feelings. Employees' reasons for hesitancy about delegation may resemble those of the manager contemplating acts of delegation: lack of trust between worker and management, lack of confidence in work performance, unwillingness to give up accustomed prerogatives, ambiguous signals from higher management, and so on.

Nonetheless, management in an era of downsizing should not abandon delegation as an effective approach to employee development and enhancement of organizational effectiveness. It is this author's position that Robert Reich is correct when he argues that downsizing is a "dubious path to profitability" (54) and recommends that management eschew "butchering" of the workforce and instead invest in employee training, profit-sharing, and frontline prerogative as a means of enhancing productivity in the long run.

Rougeau notes that "a culture that places little value on commitments between employers and employees will no doubt show similar disregard for commitments in other areas of social life," a disregard for commitment in relationships, Rougeau argues, that has issued in a plethora of social ills in the United States over the last thirty years. Instead of viewing the economic market as all-encompassing, shouldn't we see it as "just one part of a complex set of social relationships that make up our culture?"

"Downsizing" itself will, in all likelihood, come under scrutiny as its effects come to be fully felt (e.g., on organizational and community morale, on the family, on the benefits of accumulated job experience, on a consumption-driven economy, on productivity, on customer service, on the future staffing of the organization when the need for more employees becomes apparent). As Reich observes, "employees fearful of getting the ax are hardly likely to pursue labor-saving innovations." (54)

Autry reminds us that employees who witness massive lay-offs "stop spending and start preparing for their own possible unemployment." (96) There is at least some chance that labor unions will regain some clout, although they may take the form of groups like the recently-conceived Working Today, which attempts to provide networking, advice, and a national voice for workers (as Bob Herbert has reported). But, for the time being, it is likely that management will continue to take what Reich calls the "low road to competitive advantage." He points out that slashing payrolls generates at least short-term profit for the organization, profit which is reflected in the value of the stock held by so many of the organization's managers. (Translation for the not-for-profit sector: the salary increase which the manager enjoys after he "courageously" cuts costs by "rightsizing" the organization).

As long as the short-term motivations ring true for managers, acts of delegation and empowerment may be viewed with a certain skepticism by workers.

REFERENCES

Autry, James A. *Life and Work: A Manager's Search for Meaning*. New York: William Morrow and Company, Inc., 1994.

Ayres-Williams, Roz. "Mastering the Fine Art of Delegation." *Black Enterprise*, 22 (1992): 90–93.

Blau, Peter. "Interdependence and Hierarchy in Organizations," *Social Science Research*, vol. 1, pp. 1–24 (1972); reprinted in Oscar Grusky and George A. Miller, *The Sociology of Organizations*, 2nd ed., New York: The Free Press, 1981.

Bordeaux, Darlene B. "Dealing with the 90's Workforce." *Manage* 46 (1994): 6–8.

Brown, Tom. "Real Leaders Can Change Lives." *Industry Week* 243 (1994): 30.

Buscher, Jim. "Empowering Employees—the Forgotten Art of Delegation." *Pet Product News* 47 (1993): 12.

Carter, Jane Houser. "Minimizing the Risks from Delegation." *Supervisory Management* 38 (1993): 1.

Dennis, Michael C. "Only Superman Didn't Delegate." *Business Credit* 95 (1993): 41–42.

Drucker, Peter F. *Management: Tasks, Responsibilities, Practices*, New York: Harper and Row, 1976.

Evans, G. Edward. *Management Techniques for Librarians*, New York: Academic Press, 1976.

Gadson, Ron. "You Need Help: Delegate or Die in the 1990s." *Managers Magazine* 68 (1993): 15–17.

Gaedeke, Andrea R. "Ease Your Burden—Delegate." *Managers Magazine* 67 (1992): 30–31.

Gastil, John. "A Definition and Illustration of Democratic Leadership." *Human Relations* 47 (1994): 953–974.

Hannan, Michael T. and John Freeman. "The Population Ecology of Organizations." *American Journal of Sociology* 82 (1977): 929–940.

Herbert, Bob. "Strength in Numbers," *New York Times*, Nov. 3, 1995.

Irgens, O. M. "Situational Leadership: A Modification of Hersey and Blanchard's Model." *Leadership and Organization Development Journal* 16 (1995): 36–39.

Johnson, Richard S. "Leadership for the Quality Transformation." *Quality Progress* 26 (1993): 47–49.

Keller, Tiffany and Fred Dansereau, "Leadership and Empowerment: A Social Exchange Perspective." *Human Relations* 48 (1995):127–146.

Kirk, Margaret O. "When Surviving Just Isn't Enough." *New York Times*, June 25, 1995.

Kitchen, Patricia. "Coming to Grips with the Need to Loosen Reins." *American Banker* 158 (1993): 1.

Kroll, Barbara Nelson. "A Good Manager Has to Delegate." *RN* 56 (1993): 23–25.

Lloyd, Bruce. "Leadership for the New Millennium." *Leadership and Organizational Development Journal* 16 (1995): 24–26.

Machiavelli, Niccolo, *The Prince* and *The Discourses*. New York: International Collectors Library, 1940 [1532].

Manz, Charles C. "bossasaurus," *Financial Executive* 10 (1994): 65.

Masak, Ingrid. "Dare to Delegate," *Management Accounting Magazine* 66, (1992): 6.

Mathys, Nicholas J. and Elmer H. Burack. "Strategic Downsizing: Human Resource Planning Approaches," *Human Resource Planning* 16 (1993): 71–85.

McConalogue, Tom. "Real Delegation: The Art of Hanging On and Letting Go," *Management Decision* 31 (1993): 60–64.

Morgan, Rebecca L. "Guidelines for Delegating Effectively," *Supervision* 56 (1995): 20–21.

Newland, Chester L. "Marshall Dimock on Leadership: Keeping the Human Element Alive in Large Institutions," *International Journal of Public Administration* 17 (1994): 1979–2008.

Ninemeier, Jack D. "Ten Tips for Delegating Tasks," *Hotels* 29 (1995): 20.

Noble, Barbara Presley. "If Loyalty Is Out, Then What's In?," *New York Times*, Jan. 29, 1995.

Noel, Rita Thomas. "What You Say to Employees When You Delegate," *Supervisory Management* 38 (1993): 13.

Peters, Tom. *Thriving on Chaos: Handbook for a Management Revolution*, New York: Harper & Row, 1987.

Pollock, Ted. "Secrets of Successful Delegation," *Production* 106 (1994): 10–11.

Reich, Robert B. "Companies Are Cutting Their Hearts Out," *The New York Times Magazine*, Dec. 19, 1993.

Reich, Robert B. "Frayed-Collar Workers," *Memphis Commercial Appeal*, September 10, 1995.

Rizzo, John R. *Management for Librarians: Fundamentals and Issues*, Westport, CT: Greenwood Press, 1980.

Rougeau, Vincent D. "Society's Ill-Fated Trade-Off," *New York Times*, September 3, 1995.

Shields, Gerald R. "Federal Legislation and Libraries," in *Libraries in the Political Process*, ed., E. J. Josey, Phoenix: Oryx Press, 1980.

Smith, Adam. *An Inquiry into the Nature and Causes of the Wealth of Nations*, New York: The Modern Library, 1994.

Snyder, John R. "When Delegating Is Not the Answer," *Medical Laboratory Observer* 26 (1994): 7.

Steckler, Nicole and Nanette Fondas, "Building Team Leader Effectiveness: A Diagnostic Tool," *Organizational Dynamics* 23 (1995): 20–35.

Straub, Joseph T. "What Should You Do If Delegation Doesn't Work?," *Supervisory Management* 39 ( ): 3.

Tanikawa, Miki. "In Japan, Some Shun Lifetime Jobs to Chase Dreams," *New York Times*, June 25, 1995.

Townsend, Robert. *Further Up the Organization*, New York: Harper & Row, 1984.

Weber, Max. *The Theory of Social and Economic Organization*. New York: The Free Press, 1964.

"How to Delegate Work and Make Sure It's Done Right," *Women in Business* 46 (1994), 22–23.

APPENDIX

"How to Delegate" as Gleaned from the Experts

The following "how-to" points are ones that managers should consider and for the most part implement as they begin to contemplate the act of delegation. They are extracted from the writings listed in my References which give advice on delegating.

1. Know thyself.
Or at least, know thy job circumstance.

Employee development per se is rarely a totally adequate justification for delegation. Far more often, delegation must meet a need. What need in your own or your organization's work circumstance that might make you consider delegation of increased duties and responsibilities? What goal or objective are you trying to achieve as you contemplate turning over more authority to Staff Member X?

Do you have a special project that will need leadership, e.g., the computerization of one or more library processes? Do you need to build a Friends of the Library group? Do you need to take additional steps towards securing funds from private sources and elaborating your development efforts? Do you need to enhance your role in the extension-education efforts of your parent organization and work more closely with program principals? Do you need to conduct an ongoing inventory of your collections?

While it is often perfectly legitimate to assign menial duties to the appropriate staff member, the manager really ought to avoid unconscionable "dumping" of unattractive duties. Don't cumulate all of the "no-brain" work of the department or other organizational unit and dump it on one or two employees. The repercussions on morale will counteract any short-term efficiencies that are realized. The manager only creates martyrs and unsettled relationships between them and the other staff who fear that the same thing might happen to them.

2. Consider the means, consider the ends.

One of Tom Peters' emphases within the context of delegation is that the boss must have a clear vision of the objective or goal for which the delegation is done. Further, the boss must have "ridiculously high standards" which she or he has already actualized in her work life and which she transmits to the employee. Clear vision of the goal, high standards for the delegate and the outcome: these are necessities.

As for the means, you are going to give Employee X a good deal of authority and prerogative to achieve the goal, and so that the employee does not have to come running to you when she or he needs resources. But does your organization have the available resources for achieving the goal? Can you afford the means to the end? Will your promises of resources to Employee X be credible? Make certain that the resources are adequate and available.

Finally, the most important resource is the reward that you will give to the delegate for performance, although that reward may not be solely in terms of dollars. Have the reward money—or the non-monetary equivalent—ready, even if it's not a lot.

3. Get help . . . willingly.

Talk to yourself. Tell yourself that you need help, because you almost surely do. Remember, only Superman doesn't delegate. Peters says, no doubt correctly, that "nine of ten managers haven't delegated enough." (545) Your organization needs the full participation of all its employees if the total job is going to get done—if you are going for nothing less than excellence rather than mere adequacy. The organization needs to push work down to the level where it can best be accomplished.

You yourself are important and accomplished already. You will be even more so when it is known that you are a wise and benevolent developer of human beings. Your staff will idolize you. Your boss will refer to you in the right circles as her best employee. You will be recommended for promotion. You will gain an aura. Superperson does delegate!

Grant authority. Extend responsibility. Make resources available through your good offices. Bask in your largesse as manager. Go for It! Delegate! And don't just "let go": *Really* let go. . . . (Peters, 545)

4. Know and respect your staff members.

You have a goal. Do you have the woman or man to do the job? Do you have someone with talents and interests that are especially appropriate for the job at hand? Would that staff member be receptive to new challenges? Has she or he earned a chance at increased responsibilities and, hopefully, increased rewards? Is she acknowledged as a superior performer by the work group and organization? Or, do you have a person who, with appropriate training, would be ideal for a certain short-term project or long-term responsibility? Keep in mind Peters' belief that training is a corollary of involvement. (386) Once the employee is "let go," the delegator must place a very deep belief in the delegate and a genuine commitment to their development and achievement. Peters says that management should "only promote people whose greatest pleasure is bragging about the accomplishments of their front-line troops."

5. Communicate!

This old adage applies within the delegation context, also. Sit down with the delegate and share your vision of goals, objectives, and the route from "here" to "there." Tell the employee that you are considering asking her to be the point person on the project and heed his or her response. Interest? Dismay? Asks the right questions? Wants to get started yesterday, or "maybe next month"?

Be absolutely candid about the challenges of the new position. In almost every case increased responsibility brings increased pressure, scrutiny, and longer hours. If the move is into a supervisorial role then the employee's world will have changed drastically, as she or he begins to be accountable for the actions and attitudes of others. Discuss all of the "thorns" fully and honestly. Don't be in hurry. Discuss the goals, objectives, methods, resources, problems, etc. as fully as the employee wishes. You might want to encourage the employee to "sleep on it" for a night or two before making the decision to accept the new role.

Communication in one form or another permeates these hints on delegation. Keep in mind that the manager must open up full communication with the employee identified for fuller responsibilities, but also with the work group as a whole. In many cases the wise manager has been "testing the waters" with carefully selected staff members prior to the action of delegation. In other cases it may be appropriate to introduce the "new employee," i. e., the old employee with a new role, at a staff meeting or in some other collective context.

It is impossible here to prescribe the exact terms in which, and on which, the manager must communicate with her particular work group in a particular circumstance. The general principle is: Full communication is always better than sparse, or cryptic, communication. It may well be that the Art of Management is in fact the Art of Communication.

6. Assure support and follow through.

Assure the employee that you will supply all the authority, funding, advice, team members, support staff, office space, contacts, computers and printers, etc. that the employee will need to get the job done—and then follow through on those offers. You are making a contract, in effect, with your employee and you need to hold up your end of that contract. Don't make promises that you can't keep (see point 2 above). Know what's available to you, at least in general terms, before you discuss the project or responsibility with the employee.

Keep in mind that "support" often means little more than a good word, a "pat on the back," a thumbs-up at the right time. Given those encouragements, good employees often find their own ways through to the successful completion of a project even if the resources run short.

7. Negotiate duties and goals.

You have a clear vision of the outcomes and results you would like to see from this project or assignment. Communicate these to the employee, but also get feedback. If the employee is good enough to give additional responsibility, then that employee is good enough to have opinions on the assignment that you will listen to. Communicate to the employee the benefits (to customers or patrons, for example) that you believe will result from the successful completion of the project or assignment.

8. Together, plan your strategy.

Be explicit about your strategy, your time frame, your milestones, your completion date, the context of the project or assignment. If desired, make a PERT chart or the equivalent. Use computer resources for planning and monitoring and producing periodic reports. Go into excruciating detail. Agree upon progress reports or updates on achievements, their format, their due dates, their contents. Decide on the organization, including staffing, that will be needed. Be explicit about needed resources. Get everything down in writing, leave nothing unsaid and unwritten. Sign and copy the plan. Tell your staff member that the plan is the guiding light for both of you. If there are significant changes in strategies, then there need to be joint changes in plan. Then plan your next meeting.

9. Take the holistic view.

The manager who has delegated needs to monitor, not only the performance and productivity of the individual with increased responsibilities, but also the reactions of surrounding staff members. As Blau, among a legion of others, points out, the relatively small, interlocking subgroups within the organization are the sites of employee socialization, not only into the subgroups, but into the larger organization as well. Are interrelationships in a group in which an employee with new responsibilities and authority is situated going smoothly? Does the group as a whole accept the new arrangement? Is there resentment or jealousy? Will this pass, or will it result in a climate of conspiracy against the employee?

More generally, is the overall performance and output of the department or organizational unit (or organization as a whole) improved as a result of the act of delegation? Is there the feel that things have settled into the place where they should have been all along, or is there some other less comfortable feeling?

10. Just one of those things?

Despite the best intentions, planning, and communication, the delegation may not work. The employee may turn out to be uncomfortable or ineffective with more responsibility and authority. Supervision may not be her cup of tea at all. The new role may be too complex in its detail and ramifications. Maybe the employee cannot leave worries related to the new role and its demands at work, thus complicating family life to an unacceptable degree. Some other worrisome aspect of the new role might have gone uncontemplated, despite the intention of covering all of the bases in advance.

The manager must not overreact when the act of delegation seems to be threatened with failure. If the employee was good enough to receive heightened responsibility and authority, then the employee is good enough to have her or his morale and level of responsibility in the organization preserved. The first step after performance has turned down noticeably is to communicate, to discuss the situation with the employee in a forthright, candid way. The manager must, of course, have documentation at hand.

Hopefully, the delegation will not be totally reversed, returning the employee ingloriously to the old role. (We are assuming that the employee does not want a return to the old role, although some employees ask for precisely that.) Rather, it may be possible to preserve at least a portion of the new role to the benefit of all involved. The primary thing is to find a middle ground that is mutually agreeable and productive for the organization—no small task, but a characteristic managerial challenge.

Staff Training and Development in an Era of Rapid Change: A Model Program

By Elizabeth Bentley Menna and William D. Hollands
The New York Public Library

INTRODUCTION

The New York Public Library is one of the world's great research libraries. For a century it has taken a leadership role. At the conclusion of its Centennial year, the Library will celebrate the opening of its fourth research center, the new Science, Industry and Business Library (SIBL). A one hundred million dollar project, SIBL is the nation's largest public information center devoted solely to science and business. It will provide access to 1.5 million volumes, over 10,000 current periodical titles, and more than one hundred databases.

The Science, Industry and Business Library (SIBL) opens on May 2, 1996. As planning for this new facility commenced and evolved the Library naturally focused on its physical facilities and technology infrastructure. At the same time its staff and services came under scrutiny. It became apparent that to prepare SIBL's staff and management for a new information center with a service orientation and a strong technology base, an ambitious staff training and development project needed to be undertaken. Indeed, a change in institutional culture was required. A grant from the W.K. Kellogg Foundation in 1994 enabled the Library to embark on such a project. The project encompasses three principal areas of training: technology competencies, service excellence, and professional development. Today we would like to relate to you our experience, as a practical example of staff reengineering in a real library setting.

TECHNOLOGY

Four principal objectives were initially identified for the technology training piece of this project: 1) To insure a minimum level of technology competency and a standardized foundation of knowledge and skills; 2) To give all public service staff a working knowledge of the major vendors' retrieval software systems and CD-ROM search software especially in the subject areas of science and business; 3) To develop competencies in the use of networked resources, especially those available via the Internet; and 4) To develop, execute, and evaluate a training curriculum which will enable staff to gain the competencies necessary to participate in a digital library environment. As the first two years of this three-year project come to a close, it will be fruitful to examine the extent to which these objectives have been fulfilled, or in some cases modified.

First it is necessary to provide some background on the staff and the working environment. Traditionally, The New York Public Library's focus as a research library with extensive print collections—often considered the "library of record"—influenced staff in its thinking about its mission: they tended to see themselves as caretakers of archival print collections. SIBL's new mission would be to change this archival orientation to one that incorporates service and technology. In addition, the professional staff of SIBL has tended to be experienced librarians with many years in the field—often having worked their way up through NYPL's system. Many did not have experience with external models and were not quickly or deeply exposed to technological changes—exposure which might happen at library school or other institutions.

Much of the work of reengineering the staff to embrace technology has occurred by changing the work environment—namely, exposing them to technology which previously had not been part of their working existence. When the project began, few professional staff had PC's on their desktops, and those computers that did exist were non-networked and outdated. In addition, while many staff had e-mail accounts, it was an awkward system, and e-mail was far from a ubiquitous form of communication.

Finally, no training facilities were readily available to staff. The Library has invested much to change this infrastructure, and has used Kellogg money to leverage funding to acquire networked PC's for everyone on his or her desktop.

One thing we have learned is that for staff to adopt a certain technology, this technology has to be immediately accessible. Currently, each librarian and many support staff have a fully networked Pentium PC or Macintosh with a full suite of office software, as well as Internet access and e-mail. All staff have been given an e-mail account and the Library has switched to a more user-friendly and robust e-mail package. Finally, a training lab with networked PC's was set up for internal training sessions.

This infrastructure has made the success of the technology training possible because not only has it facilitated individual exploration, it has also allowed staff members to practice and utilize the skills and knowledge they have acquired. In terms of the first objective—ensuring a minimum level of competency and a standardized foundation of knowledge and skills—much progress has been made. A core list of competencies was developed that all professional staff were expected to have, and this gave us a way to set performance standards and provided a base line upon which all future assumptions and activities could be based. These were very specific and included knowledge of listed tasks for particular software applications, including word processing, spreadsheets, electronic mail, and various operating systems. As we went through the grant period, the environment changed so quickly that the core list of competencies and expectations had to be modified and enriched. For instance, World Wide Web navigation and hypertext markup language (HTML) became required competencies for all staff.

An initial self-assessment of skill-levels was performed, in which staff members were asked to rate themselves as to proficiency in these various areas. This method of assessment was chosen because it was felt to be the least threatening and it was important that staff "buy in" to the program. After the assessment, most training was conducted by external, professional trainers to fill in the gaps. This has been for the most part quite successful. It has created an environment where everyone—both staff and public—can expect that all staff will have a certain technology skill set, across the board.

Most of the work on the second objective—training on various electronic databases—has been conducted in-house in what is called the "Adopt-a-CD" program. In this program, each staff member takes responsibility for a certain number of the databases in SIBL and is charged with training the rest of the staff in a number of small group sessions. A different database is done each week. In addition, as part of their responsibility, staff must produce a user guide for each of their databases. This program 1) ensured that every staff member had training in the 100 databases to be offered in SIBL; and 2) gave staff members teaching experience, which will be important when they begin to conduct group training sessions in SIBL's Electronic Training Center. This teaching experience has also strengthened their work with individual users.

This program has been important for "mainstreaming" electronic resources in the services of SIBL. In the past, there was a separate Electronic Information desk, which was staffed by only a select few staff members who had knowledge of the products. This meant that the librarians who only worked at the traditional reference desk were not as aware of the information that was available on the databases and could not integrate that into the larger "information picture." However, now the "Adopt-a-CD" program has coincided with the rotation of all librarians onto the Electronic Information Center desk, as well as the traditional reference desk. This has resulted in a better understanding of the entire information environment, especially as it relates to business, science, and government information.

Much of the technology training has focused on the third and fourth objectives, the Internet and other aspects of the digital library. Initially, Internet training emphasized Gopher and the then fairly new Mosaic browsing software for the World Wide Web, and coincided with the introduction of Internet-accessible PC's for the public in SIBL's divisions. This training was related to collection development and emphasized business, science, and government information on the Internet.

As the World Wide Web gained prominence, we initially trained a core group of staff members in

HTML. However, very quickly the rest of the staff demanded to be included, and this is when we knew we were starting to change the culture within the Library. Every librarian in SIBL has been trained in HTML, and this training has been tied to the development of specific projects for SIBL's portion of The New York Public Library's Web site. Finally, the program has expanded to include training for a core group of staff in the Standard Generalized Markup Language (SGML).

We feel that the technology training portion of this project has had a profound impact on the staff and the operations of SIBL. There is now a standard level of technological knowledge that all staff possesses, both in terms of "back office" operations and public service. In addition, staff at SIBL are looked upon as leaders in this area. As the project has developed, in addition to training existing staff, SIBL has added new staff who have come in "technology ready". We feel that all SIBL staff members are now prepared to provide service in the new setting with a vastly enlarged Electronic Information Center and a new Electronic Training Center. They also have the foundation and confidence to adapt and acquire new skills as information technology continues to evolve.

SERVICE EXCELLENCE

The overall goal of service excellence is to create a process of continuous improvement in all areas of operations and management. Objectives include:

- To develop a shared mission and vision so that all staff have a common purpose and a sense of ownership in the goals of the organization.
- To provide specific customer service skills that will enable staff to achieve customer satisfaction in a combined print and electronic information environment.
- To enable staff to communicate effectively within the SIBL organization to emerge as outreach agents and to serve as ambassadors for SIBL.
- To develop the skills to achieve shared management responsibility through team work.

To achieve these goals, we have done fairly extensive preparatory work with a consultant. Exercises include Myers-Briggs testing, team building, time management, and shared visioning. All staff who work with the public went through an intensive two day customer services training program, Wilson Learning's "Signature Service: The Key to Customer Satisfaction." A core group also went through Wilson's "Train the Trainer" sessions. Hourly paid student assistants who retrieve, deliver, and reshelve materials were offered an in-house customer service program. A mission statement, a vision statement, and a management philosophy statement have also been developed.

Working with consultants, a team structure has been developed and is being implemented. Teams relate both to programmatic goals and to vision statement goals. For instance, there is a Small Business Team related to our targeted services goal and a Service Definition Task Force related to our vision goal of creating and maintaining a user-focused service program that begins by defining levels of service and establishing service standards and guidelines.

PROFESSIONAL DEVELOPMENT

To realize SIBL's public service mission, it is necessary for all staff to increase their knowledge and expertise as information professionals and paraprofessionals in an age of electronic information. Two primary areas of opportunity are being offered: To understand the evolution of the library business into the information business by learning about new products, services, philosophies, and technologies that will affect SIBL's role in the information age. To gain organizational skills necessary to service excellence, setting priorities, time management, and dealing with difficult customers. To achieve these goals, we are bringing to NYPL speakers who can inform and update our staff on such things as what new products are being developed, new or different service scenarios, interesting uses of technology, etc. The Internet training provided to all staff plays a role here, too. Additionally, senior managers have attended American Management Association courses aimed at honing their management and team building skills. Also, previously mentioned customer service training is appropriate to these goals.

SUCCESS

We think that for the most part the program has been quite successful. An assessment of technology training needs done at the start as measured against the training staff received shows a large growth in technological competencies. Customer service is harder to measure, but we see a difference in attitudes, language, and approaches to dealing with the public. As we worked with our consultants on mission, vision, management philosophy, and team building, periodic surveys of staff were done to assess progress. These indicated a growing attitude among staff that we would achieve success. Professional development also has grown. We have gone from a rather insular environment to one actively engaged with the global community.

The program allowed us to bring together technology and services in a meaningful way. It afforded the staff the opportunity to experience a realistic preview of what the new work environment will be like and allowed each to make a personal decision. Some staff were, in fact, unable or unwilling to buy in and we did experience some retirements. We also have many staff who have accepted the challenge and made real commitments. Our management structure has evolved into a self-motivated one. Our team structure has changed. The SIBL Advisory Council is now composed of staff from all levels. A learning organization environment in which we constantly evaluate, solicit feedback from users, and search for ways to improve services has developed. We have achieved much greater flexibility in our staff.

NEXT STEPS

We have learned the value of an organized formal training program and its beneficial effects. The program serves as a model for The Research Libraries as we create the Center for the Humanities. Here, too, collections and services will be rethought and change effected to create a team-based, learning organization environment. We have won the enthusiastic support of our Trustees and senior administrators, who have bought into the model created by SIBL.

As we open our electronic library, we have made a strong commitment to technology. We have, however, also made a strong commitment to our staff. If we give them the proper tools and competencies, they will be our strength in making our venture a success.

Restructuring Academic Libraries: Organizational Development in the Wake of Technological Change

By Charles Schwartz
University of Massachusetts Boston

The general theme of my talk can be summed up in a short theorem: A primary problem for academic libraries is the lag in their organizational development behind rapid technological change. Until now, the literature on technology in libraries has focused not on organizational development but on a different, narrower process called social adaptation. Let's begin, then, by distinguishing between these two processes of change.

Social adaptation to new information technologies occurs mainly at the level of the individual. It involves what are by now familiar, practical staff concerns about "keeping current with technology," "using electronic communications effectively," "assisting faculty and students with information resources," and so forth. All those concerns were listed at the top of a 1993 ACRL survey on what librarians found to be their most pressing challenges.[1]

Our profession will shift its attention in the next few years to the more fundamental problem of organizational development. This shift does not, of course, depend on our having somehow resolved the problem of social adaptation to new information technologies; we may never fully adjust to the speed of change. Still, the more interesting conferences, books and articles will take the ongoing process of social adaptation as a given (as a ground-assumption of the way we go about our work) and focus instead on the variety of ways that our institutional structures and interlibrary arrangements are adapting to new technologies. So far, that kind of research and analysis has only begun to attract serious attention.

In the brief time we have, I will talk about two broad, prospective patterns of organizational development. The first involves various emerging and far-reaching concepts of access. The other is campus-wide strategic planning to integrate new technologies in research and curricular programs.

These are not generally recognized as big concerns in 1996. Our profession is preoccupied with a reconfiguration of reference services or technical services. Actually, the kind of access I have in mind has been developed at fewer than ten libraries, and the kind of strategic planning at even fewer institutions.

At any rate, since the broad patterns of restructuring—far-reaching access and campus-wide strategic planning—will evolve in different ways from institution to institution, I decided to put together a book in which twenty writers looked at the theorem I mentioned: the lag of organizational development behind social adaptation and technological change. The book will be published by the Association of College & Research Libraries this summer.

EMPHASIS ON VARIOUS CONCEPTS OF "ACCESS"

"Access" generally refers to the collection development decision model we know as "access versus ownership." However, not long ago, access-versus-ownership was just an abstract slogan for what would be done, at some point in the indefinite future, about the "serials crisis." In 1990, for example, ACRL published "Guidelines for the Preparation of Policies on Library Access."[2] It is an excellent, though apparently little-known document that discusses the word "access" in a framework that hardly alludes to collection development or document delivery. Instead, access is said to carry "policy concerns about library users' rights . . . to enter and use a library's holdings without limitations in the form of:

—architectural barriers;
—sociological or economic factors;
—ideologically biased selection practices;
—usage or circulation restrictions;
—hidden (or unpublicized) services;
—unqualified staff;
—fees for the use of any materials or services."

Access became synonymous with the access-versus-ownership decision model a few years later, once the technology of document delivery by fax machine had improved enough that we could expect consistently legible transmissions. At that point, 1993 or so, two contrasting models of collection development began to dominate discussions.

The traditional ownership, or "just-in-case," model is one in which academic libraries function as warehouses of large research collections. The classic expression of this model appeared a half-century ago:

> Research materials are in a sense the building blocks of civilization; and the storage element in the function of the research library [is] just the sheer holding of books and periodical materials, not for any immediate use at all, but for some possible, and possibly very remote, future use.[3]

(The author of that statement, Freemont Rider, estimated that academic libraries were doubling in size every 16 years. Writing in 1944, he looked to microfilm as the solution to the space problem. Back then, the "cost problem" was not perceived to be in the acquisition of research materials but rather in the provision of a microfilm reader for every home!)

In the other model, called "just-in-time" or access, libraries have quite different functions: (a) to define and maintain an economically viable serials collection, and (b) to develop ways of delivering research materials that are both low in use and high in cost-per-use.

In recent years, a small number of libraries (nine, I believe) have begun to develop the access model on a comprehensive level by taking three initiatives:

—canceling the majority of low use, high cost-per-use journals (basically the bottom quarter or third of the collection that is gathering dust);
—reinvesting about 20–25% the monies saved in new access services, mainly a completely subsidized document delivery service (by which patrons get whatever they want that is not in the collection at no charge); and
—reinvesting the rest of the savings in new serial titles.

At my institution, for example, we found that science titles generally cost $65 per use, whereas low use, high cost-per-use science titles have an eight-fold average of $537. The 296 serials we identified for cancellation had been used last year a total of 303 times. If we assume, for the sake of argument, that each use resulted in an article request through a commercial document delivery service, the overall charge would have been merely 6% of the total subscription cost for all those titles. By canceling most of them, we save $200K—20% of that is enough to allow our patrons to order whatever they need through UNCOVER at no charge, and the remaining 80% will fund about 100 new subscriptions for our collection. (The other institutions doing this, by the way, are Louisiana State University, the University of Kansas, Washington University (in St. Louis), the New Jersey Institute of Technology, Colorado State University, the University of Cincinnati, the University of North Texas, and Oakland University.)

Why have so few libraries taken this approach? Why has this particular lag in organizational development occurred, especially in view of our technological opportunity and the sheer economic realities? We know from Internet surveys that, although scores of libraries have done cost-per-use analyses, their sole purpose has been to cut budgets—rather than to take proactive measures to reinvest monies in new titles and access services.

It is conceivable that our profession has a strong tendency to associate cost analysis with serial cuts, and that our profession has thereby developed a groupthink mentality—a superstition—against cost analysis because of perceptions of unpleasant campus politics.

If that is true, what a shame! All we have heard since the late 1980s is "serials crisis!" The implicit message is that we are helpless victims of greedy publishers and not particularly accountable for our own financial situation.

One of the things that makes collection development such an interesting area is how the nature of a problem is altered, the choices and constraints change, when we shift from one level of analysis to another level. At the top level is the scholarly communication system as a whole, comprised of all the libraries, publishers, learned societies, vendors, interlibrary consortia, and the scholars themselves. At that perspective, there is a "serials crisis." If we shift down to the level of a particular library that is using cost analysis to make informed access-versus-ownership decisions, the whole picture changes: now we can afford new titles and offer free access services!

Shift the level of analysis again—from the individual library part way up to a state or regional consortium—and the picture is altered again. Now, a completely different consideration arises: how to maintain historical archives of journals. We tend to trust only our own profession to do that—not document delivery companies.

While maintaining archives is an important concern, it is not necessarily a big problem provided that consortia assume greater responsibilities and certain new roles:

—to devise a division of labor among member-libraries for the preservation of paper archives;
—to achieve cost-economies through the sharing of database licenses and document delivery contracts; and
—to do more cooperative collection development of book-based literatures.

Earlier I quoted a 1944 expression of the "just-in-case," or ownership, model of collection development, in which research materials were described as "building blocks of civilization."

A few weeks ago, I encountered the same expression, for the same concern of preservation, in an e-mail note from Sue Medina, who is director of the Network of Alabama Academic Libraries: "Can we count on the vendors [to keep archives] for 100 years? The profession needs to focus attention on reclaiming our responsibility as repositories of the world's cultural heritage—perhaps not needed by today's researcher, but there 'just in case.'"

I agree with this position but do not consider it as an argument against our making periodical collections cost-effective at the level of an individual institutional. The only resolution is for consortia to take the necessary initiatives to make interlibrary arrangements balance commercially-based access services.

CAMPUS-WIDE STRATEGIC PLANNING TO INTEGRATE NEW INFORMATION TECHNOLOGIES INTO RESEARCH AND CURRICULAR PROGRAMS

This is a key process in shaping the prospective leadership role of academic libraries on campus. Strategic planning for new information technologies campus-wide is what policy analysts call an "ill-structured problem." It is a process characterized by:

—ambiguous, open-ended goals;
—problematic choices;
—hazy technology for decision-making;
—occasional "paradigm conflicts" among academic departments over electronic versus print-age library resources;
—drifting participation of different groups in the decision arena over time; and
—the lack of any general cost-benefit analysis to indicate how investments in information technology relate to gains in campus productivity.

In our profession, the literature in this area has a number of less-than-helpful or unrealistic characteristics. The literature tends to focus on strategic planning within the library itself, without looking at higher, campus-wide levels of analysis. It dwells on organizational charts, with boxes and arrows showing how one thing is supposed to lead to another. And many writers have used the popular metaphor of a soccer team to emphasize how libraries should have flexibility and interdependency. The actual process of strategic planning, of course, is broader than the library and more complex than flowcharts or teamwork.

From the perspective of the planning process having open-ended goals, problematic choices, and drifting participation of various groups, the academic library as a "soccer team" finds itself in campus politics playing on a very irregular field:

Picture a round, multi-goal soccer field of varying slopes. Many people can join or leave the game at different times. Some people throw balls into the game, others remove them. Individuals while in the game try to kick balls in the direction of the goals they like and away from the goals they wish to avoid.[4]

Game balls are technology choices or policy initiatives. The different goals range over a diversity of traditional or emergent library functions that compete in terms of limited budgets. Players represent various constituencies on campus.

A slope in the field reflects either a technological opportunity or some group's ground-assumptions about the role of the library. Together, the slopes in the field produce a series of biases in how the balls (opportunities or initiatives) roll. Predicting which goals are eventually reached is not easy because players tend to wander in and out of the decision arena. Thus, the attention paid to strategic planning for new technologies can be unstable and remarkably independent of the importance of a given goal.

The library's prospective role may be to instill and maintain collaborative problem-solving strategies among the different constituencies—scholars in the sciences, in the social sciences, and in arts and the humanities; the librarians themselves; the computing center staff; and university administrators. Each group has its own view and sphere of influence in the decentralized academic environment.

Actually, this scenario of the library's prospective position in such an "organized anarchy" might be somewhat idealistic, for whether librarians are afforded an integral role in the decision process is an important question for consideration.

In conclusion, here are some challenges for the latter half of the decade:

—in the short run, to develop cost-effective periodical collections within our own institutions so that we can get past the "serials crisis";
—to organize historical archives of journal literatures within our consortia;
—and, in the longer run, to provide leadership in the campus-wide process of integrating Internet resources into research and curricular programs.

The last challenge goes way beyond something fairly technical and practical like developing Web homepages; it suggests a much closer collaboration with faculty and administration than we have previously enjoyed. It might even lead to a restructuring of the library's presence in the university.

ENDNOTES

1. Althea H. Jenkins, "Members Shape ACRL's Future," College & Research Libraries News 55 (June 1994):368–72.
2. Kathleen Gunning, "ACRL Guidelines for the Preparation of Policies on Library Access," College & Research Libraries News 51 (June 1990):548–56.
3. Freemont Rider, The Scholar and the Future of the Research Library (New York: Hadham Pr., 1944), p. 21.
4. Adapted from James G. March and Pierre Romelaer, "Position and Presence in the Drift of Decisions," in James G. March and Johan P. Olsen (eds.) Ambiguity and Choice in Organizations (Bergen, Norway: Unversitetsforlaget, 1976), p. 276.

Appendix: Demonstrated Papers for the Finding Common Ground Conference

Their highly-visual format does not allow us to publish them in these proceedings, but we wish to acknowledge the excellence of the demonstrated conference papers and thank the authors for their work in contributing to the quality and success of the conference. The following demonstrated papers were presented at a special no-conflict conference session on Sunday, March 31, 1996:

Beland, Judith P., Laurie Rudnicki, and John Carper, Harvard University. "Developing an Information Desk at the Countway Library of Medicine."

Bosseau, Don L., San Diego State University. "A Virtual First in Electronic Libraries: Experience Gained and Lessons Learned."

Bridges, Anne E. and Russell Clement, University of Tennessee at Knoxville. "On the Threshold of Rocket Mail."

Budd, John M. and Lynn Silipigni Connaway, University of Missouri-Columbia / University of Denver. "Effects of Information Networking on the Communication and Collaboration of Scholars."

Burkhardt, Joanna, University of Rhode Island. "Many Roads Lead to Rome: A Range of Options for URI/CCE Library Users."

Clack, Mary Beth, Harvard University. "Creativity in the Workplace."

Daniels, Esther, University of Washington Bothell. "Developing a Library Instruction Program to Reflect Differing Academic Program Needs."

deBruijn, Deborah, Anita Cocchia, and Sheila Comeau, Electronic Library Network of British Columbia. "Leveraging Our Investments: British Columbia's Electronic Library Network as a Fulcrum and Agent of Change."

Driscoll, Tim, Harvard University. "Documenting for the Public Interest: The Role of Manuscripts Libraries in Managing Archives Programs for Unaffiliated Institutions."

Gross, Ben, University of Illinois at Urbana-Champaign. "Preserving the Electronic Record."

Jafari, May M. and Randi L. Stocker, Indiana University / Purdue University, Indianapolis. "The Electronic Term Paper: A Metaphor for Changing Academic Environments."

Keeran, Peggy and Lorraine Evans, University of Denver. "Educating for Research Diversity: Electronic, Print, and People."

Lucas, Kari, University of California at San Diego. "Studio in a Box: Computer Animation Comes to Library Instruction."

Mandel, Debra, Northeastern University. "High-Speed Connections: Building Alliances Between Media Centers and Other Library Departments and Instructional Support Services."

McCarthy, James and Kathleen Brown, DeAnza College. "Creating Libraries of the Future: Using Client Surveys as a Decision-Making Tool."

Myatt, Angela and Karen Marsh, University of Cincinnati. "The Ohio Valley Community Health Information Network."

Paietta, Ann, New York Academy of Medicine. "Grateful MED: Serving the Medical and Health Sciences Information Needs of Diverse Populations."

Ragains, Patrick, Montana State University at Bozeman. "Access to U.S. Census Data in Traditional and Electronic Formats: Chaos or Boon to Users?"

Shedlock, James, Northwestern University. "Library Buildings Facing Technological Change: The Galter Library's Renovation Experience."

Williams, Helene, University of Washington. "Beyond the Basics: The Uwired Partnerships in Upper-Division Courses."

A Pragmatist's Index

Note: This index is not meant to be exhaustive; an exhaustive index for a proceedings of this size could not reasonably be accommodated in the space available. Thus, although some terms (such as HTML) appear in many papers, we have only indexed the term in those papers for which it was a major theme.

AACR2 (Anglo-American Cataloging Rules 2) 168, 340, 399–400
Abbott, Andrew 107
access vs. ownership 204
acquisitions 363
acquisitions units 363
active learning 156
adult learners 156, 158
Agyeman, Yaw 134
Ahronheim, Judith 333
Albert Einstein College of Medicine 306
alternatives to ownership 310
America Online 30
Americans with Disabilities Act (ADA) 47
Anderson, Chris 84
Anderson, Gary ix
architectural design metaphors 58
architectural metaphors 60
architecture 58
archiving 375
Arp, Lori 114, 225
Art Humanities Image Reserve Collection 243
artifact 213
artificial intelligence 164
assessing customer satisfaction 415
assessing staff training needs 416
Association of Research Libraries (ARL) 209, 210, 409, 429
Atkinson, Ross 376
Auburn University 294
Austin, Willard 103

Baish, Mary Alice 290
Baker, Betsy 99

Baker, Nicholson 48, 75
Barnum, George 275
Bartelstein, Andrea 86
Bartoo, Gillian ix
Baruch College 225
Basile, Abbie 111
Beacom, Matthew 358–359
Bechtel, Joan 106
Becker, Sarah ix
Begg, Amy 27
Beland, Judith 466
Benedikt, Michael 59
Benson, Larry 232, 236
Bentley, Stella ix, 294
Bettelheim, Bruno 247
bibliographic access 209
bibliographic description 381
Bibliographic Description of Rare Books (BDRB) 381
bibliographic expertise 197
bibliographic instruction SEE library instruction
bibliographic product 197
bibliographic record 127
bibliographic resources 168
bibliographic specialists 196
bibliographic systems 333
bibliographical metadata 398
Bibliotheca Universalis 326
Billings, Harold xiii
Billington, James 269
Birkets, Sven 75
Blainey, Geoffrey 326
Blake, Michael ix
Blau, Peter 448

Blier, Suzanne ix
Bloom's Taxonomy 144
Bobay, Julie 405
Bohn, Roger 164
Bosch, Allan 424
Bosseau, Don 466
boundary-crossing research 254
Bourneuf, Joe ix
Bowers, Fredson 382
Bowling Green State University 193
Bridges, Anne 466
Bridges, William 74
Bristow, Ann 116, 124
Brookes, Kim 37
Brown University 47, 48, 50, 51
Brown, Kathleen 467
browsing the stacks 215
Bryan, Jane 124
Budd, John 375, 466
Burden, Cheryl 290
Burg, Barbara ix
Burkhardt, Joanna 466
Burley, Cheryl 345
Bush, Vannevar 60, 203
Butterfield, Kevin 333
Byrum, John 369

Calhoun, John C. 77
Calvin and Hobbes 78
Cameron, Heather ix
Campbell, James 42
Campbell, Jerry 101, 231
Cannon, Tyrone ix
card catalog 20, 21, 48, 75 SEE ALSO electronic
    catalog, library catalog, OPAC
Cargill, Jean Boise 37
CARL 30
Carpenter, Ken ix
Carper, John 466
Carroll, John 83–84
Case Western Reserve University 275
catalog librarian 359
cataloging 337, 388
Centenary College of Louisiana 161
centralized decentralization 346
Chappell, Virginia 81
Cherepon, Lois 229
Cheverie, Joan 290
Churbuck, David 392
CIESIN 345–346, 348–350

CitaDel 30, 32
Ciuffetti, Peter 337
Clack, Mary Beth ix, 466
Clement, Gail 394
Clement, Russell 466
Cleveland, Harlan 226, 227
client-server cataloging code 398
Coalition for Networked Information (CNI) 1, 434
Coccaro, Cynthia 298
Cocchia, Anita 467
Cohen, Ellen ix
collaboration(s) 93, 333, 434, 437, 440–441
collaborative environment 335
collaborative projects 334
collaboratory 87
collection decisionmaking 42
collection development 8, 15, 306
collection management 14
College of William and Mary 168
College of Wooster 275
Columbia University 194, 240, 313
Comeau, Sheila 467
community standards 3
computer classroom 91
computer conference system 140
computer-assisted instruction 112, 226
conference classes 141
Constantine, Paul 121
container technologies 8
controlled vocabulary 393
convergence 17, 22
cooperative agreements 310
cooperative collection development 209
copyright 13, 14, 129
copyright infringement 8
core competencies 161, 163, 430
core technological capabilities 162
Cornell University 121, 357, 363
Cornish, Edward 227
cost and benefits 233
cost benefit analysis 234, 236
Covey, Stephen 425
Coyle, Karen 328
Crawford, Walt 16
Creating a Financial Plan 232
Crist, Margo 131
critical thinking 80, 148, 233, 424, 426
cross-cultural communication 413
cross-disciplinarity 263
cryptography 4

cultural differences 257
Cummins, Thompson 234
CUNY 229
curriculum 86, 87, 251
customer education 311
customer service 214, 416, 441
cybernetic creationism 203
cyberspace 58, 63–64

Dana, John Cotton 100, 103
Daniels Esther 467
Daniels, Mary 37
Davis, Christopher 345
Davis, Murray S. 105
DeAnza College 467
deBruijn, Deboral 467
DeCandido, GraceAnne 232
DeDonato, Ree 240
DeGennaro, Richard ix, xiii, 1
delegation 447–454
DeLorenzo, David 37
demographics 205
Denison University 275
Dewey, Melville 106
Diaz, Bob 408
Digital Age 209, 373, 375 SEE ALSO Information Age
digital artifacts 338
digital content 14
digital finding aids 41
digital image(s) 128, 211, 213
digital information 15, 44
digital initiatives 210
digital library 8, 12, 42, 74, 77, 78, 220, 241, 334, 337, 357, 359, 360,
digital media 211
digital objects 12, 354
digital priorities 210
digitization projects 210
Dillon, Andrew 322
disciplinary boundaries 253
disenchantment 75, 76
disengagement 75
disidentification 75, 76
disinformation 5
disintegration 77
disorientation 77
distance education 153, 227
distributed digital documents 353
diversity awareness 413

Dixon, Lana 112
document delivery 307–308, 310
document-like objects 12
Dowler, Larry ix
Dowling, Thomas 394
Down, Nancy 193
downsizing 453
Driscoll, Tim 467
Drucker, Peter 448
Dublin Core 341, 401
Dunkin, Paul Shaner 382
dynamics of inquiry 205
Dysart, Jane 231

Eagan, Ann 394
electronic catalog 172 SEE ALSO card catalog, library catalog, OPAC
electronic collections 367
electronic document delivery 298, 304
electronic environment 42
electronic instruction 111, 154
electronic library 58, 77, 182–183, 189, 357, 363 SEE ALSO digital library, virtual library
Electronic Library Network of British Columbia 467
electronic publications 364
electronic reference 50, 375
electronic resources 184, 189, 309, 405
electronic scholarship 219, 220, 225, 229, 240
Electronic Text (E-text) Center 388
electronic texts 193, 388
electronically-challenged 136
Eliade, Mircea 247
Elliott, Clark 196
Emory University 74
End of Education 99
engineering Internet resources 392
envelope technology 9
Evans, Lorraine 467
every book its user 105
expert systems 164

fair use 8
Farber, Evan 103
Fark, Ronald 47
Farmington Plan 209
Farwell, Laura ix
Feary, Ginger 134
Federal Depository Library Program 275–290
feeling types 78

Ferriero, David ix
Finckel, Matt 291
finding aids 37, 39
Finding Common Ground xi, xii, xiii, 1, 99, 121, 212
FirstSearch 30, 32
Fister, Barbara 82
Fitzgerald, Michael ix, 37
Five Laws of Library Science 104, 105, 106 SEE ALSO Ranganathan
flexibility 429
Flynn, Kathleen 440
Fordham University 219
Freides, Thelma 101
funding decreases 309
future libraries SEE library of the future
Future Libraries: Dreams, Madness, & Reality 16

G7 Electronic Libraries Project 326
G7 Information Society Program 326
Garson, Deb ix
Gateway project 114
gateways 262
generalists 120, 256, 258
Generation X digital catalog librarians 361
Genocide and the Politics of Memory 174, 178–179
geographic information 211
geographical boundaries 3
geographical community 5
George Mason University 424
George, Lee Anne ix
Gibson, Craig 424
Gifford, Anne 33
Gilbert, Steven 81
Gilmore, Fred 134
global electronic library 326
global information system 345
global university 228
Goins, Rod ix
Gorman, Michael 16, 232, 369, 400
Government Printing Office (GPO) 275–290
Grassian, Esther 136
Green, Samuel Swett 100
Greene, Richard Tabor 163
Griffiths, Jose-Marie 233
Gross, Ben 467
Gustafson, Sonia ix
Gutierrez, Carolyn 140
Gwinn, Nancy 27

Halporn, Barbara ix
Hamel, Gary 161
handle resolution 355
handle system 354
Handlin, Oscar 102
Harloe, Bart 375
Harmon, Charles ix
Hartman, Ann ix
Harvard Digital Finding Aids Project 37
Harvard University 37, 196, 201, 381, 466–467
Hazen, Dan ix, 201
Heaney, Michael 400
help desk software 137
Hinding, Andrea 378
Hirsch, Herbert 174
historical scholarship 198
Hoffmann, Gretchen McCord 111, 113, 114, 144
holistic library 42
Hollands, Williams 459
HOLLIS 37, 39, 384
Hooper, Kristina 64
Hopper, Michael ix
Horrell, Jeffrey ix
How to Catalog a Rare Book 382
HTML (hypertext markup language) 43, 70–71, 92, 153, 164, 211, 383
Hubbard, Taylor 82
humanities 211
hybridization 263
HYPERMARC 400
HyTime 41

imagination 80
indexing languages 393–394
indexing principles 392
Indiana University 116, 194, 405, 467
individual personal assistance 117
information access 5
Information Age 19, 78, 149 SEE ALSO Digital Age
information agility 369
Information for a New Age: Redefining the Librarian 225
information infrastructure 441
information literacy 15, 144, 149
information marketplace 12
information navigation skills 88
information overload 10
information services 443
information space 59

information specialists 200
information technology 2, 3, 5, 6, 161, 465
instruction librarians 265, 266
instructional methods 189
instructor training 148
intellectual property 8, 13
intellectual warrant 394
intelligent filtering agents / software 136, 137
interactive learning software 187
InterCat SEE OCLC InterCat
interdisciplinarity 263, 294
interdisciplinary collaborations 213, 294, 297
interdisciplinary inquiry 295
interdisciplinary research 255, 258
interdisciplinary science, scientists 253, 255
interlibrary loan 306, 308, 327
International Standard Bibliographic Description for Older Books (Antiquarian) 381
Internet Branch 60
Internet training program 240
interpersonal communication 414
Introduction to Reference Work 101
intuitive types 78
Iowa State University 398
Itami, Hirayuki 164

Jacobson, Trudi 182
Jafari, May 467
Johns Hopkins University 152, 153
Joint Electronic Document Delivery Software (JEDDS) 327
Jones, Rebecca 231
JOSIAH 49
JSTOR 286
Jurow, Susan 408, 429
just in case 306
just in time 306

Kalfatovic, Martin 27, 29
Kameny, Fred 129
Kanter, Rosabeth Moss 93
Kara, Bill 358, 363
Katz, William 101
Kautzman, Amy ix
Keeran, Peggy 467
Kent State University 392
Kent, Carrie ix
Keyes, Alison 236
King, Donald 233
Kirk, Elizabeth 152

knowledge creation 106
knowledge engineering 164
knowledge management 164, 170, 440, 441, 443, 444
Kuhn, Thomas 207
Kupersmith, John 58

Laden, Bernice 86
LaGuardia, Cheryl ix, 1, 128, 147
Lancaster, F. W. 236
Langstaff, Eleanor 225
Lasher, Rebecca 353
Layers of Learning 221, 223
learning 80
learning organization 424–425
Learning to Teach 112
learning with computers 83
Leazer, Gregory 400
Lee, Susan ix
Lehman report 8
Lester, Linda 211
Levy, David 357
Lewis, David 116, 127
library's instructional role 217
library catalog 169, 338 SEE ALSO card catalog, electronic catalog, OPAC
Library Cost Benefit Analysis 233
library instruction 81, 83, 87, 101–102, 140, 143–147, 157, 216, 225–228
Library of Congress 269
Library of Congress Information System (LOCIS) 30, 32
Library of Congress Subject Headings 173
library of the future xi, 6, 7, 275, 424
library of the past xi
library services 434
Libutti, Patricia O'Brien 219
lifetime learning 228
Lin, Serena 63
Linfield College 80
Lippincott, Joan 434
literary texts 193
living edge 49
local content 4
local research priorities 208
Logan, Susan 68
logical research 202
Lucas, Kari 467
Lucker, Jay 76
Lyman, Peter 80
Lynch, Clifford 1

Machiavelli 453
machine-based retrieval systems 80
Malamud, Judie 306
Management by Planning 412
Mandel, Debra 467
Mann, Thomas 171
manuscript repositories 212
MARC format 168, 169, 173, 340–341, 399–400
MARC III 400
Marcum, James 161
Marko, Lynn 333
markup 38
Marnon, Dennis ix
Marsh, Karen 467
Marshall, Karen Kates 211
Martin, James 162
Matthews, Nancy 29, 33
Maxymuk, John 394
McCarthy, James 467
McCarthy, Maryellen ix
McClure, Charles 101
McCombs, Gillian 358, 369
McCormick, Mona 82
McCue, Janet 357, 359
McGarr, Sheila 291
McHugh, William 99
McKinzie, Steve ix, 251
McLuhan, Marshall 63
McManus, Jean 375
Memex 60, 203
Mendina, G.T. 447
Menna, Elizabeth Bentley 459
mental models 426
metadata 327, 337, 339–340, 342, 347, 359, 398, 400
metadata specialist 361, 373
Metcalfe, Bob 137
Michelson, Avra 440
microforms 212
Milton's Web 152, 154–159
Minsky, Marvin 83
misinformation 5
MIT (Massachusetts Institute of Technology) 76, 196
Mitchell, Barbara ix
Mitchell, William 59
Mitre Corporation 440
Mitroff, Ian 164
model of transition 78
Montana State University at Bozeman 467

MOO (multi-user object oriented environment) 61, 125
Moore's Law 16, 17
Moore, Gordon 16
Morris, Leslie 37
Mudrock, Theresa 86
multidisciplinarity 263
Myatt, Angela 467
Myers-Briggs Personality Inventory (MBTI) 77, 410, 461
mythbreaking 16
Myths, Dreams and Mysteries 247

National Archives and Records Administration (NARA) 281, 286–288
National Digital Library Federation 328
National Endowment for the Humanities (NEH) 200
National Library of Australia 326
National Museum of American History branch (NMAH) 29
needs' assessment 311
NetFirst 173
NETMA-L ("Nobody Ever Tells Me Anything") 76
network organization 429, 431
neutral zone 76
new breed catalog librarians 360
New York Academy of Medicine 467
New York Public Library 459
Nielsen, Brian 118
Nolan, Anne Cerstvik 47
Nonaka, Ikujiro 164
Norman, Donald 63
Northeastern University 467
Northwestern University 99, 467
Novak, Marcos 63
novice researchers 152
numeric imagery 12

O'Hanlon, Nancy 68, 72
Oberman, Cerise 146, 226
OCLC 174
OCLC InterCat 168, 169, 170, 340
OCLC Internet Cataloging Project 373
OCLC metadata 327
off-site closed stacks 216
Office of Management Services (OMS) 410
Ohio State University 68
OhioLINK 298–304
OhioLINK 70, 71

Oka, Christine ix
On Learning to Read 247
Once Upon a Campus 175, 180–181
online books 313, 319, 321–322
Online Books Evaluation Project 242, 313
online catalog searching 187
online communities 137
online database searching 187
online instruction 111
OPAC 170–172 SEE ALSO card catalog, electronic catalog, library catalog
Oregon State University 80
organizational communication 413
organizational culture 370
organizational development 463
organizational disidentification 74
organizational effectiveness 447
organizational learning 162
organizational model 405
organizational reengineering 162
organizational structure 76, 429
organizational transitions 74
organizing information 13, 372
organizing metaphor 62
ORION 138
Ouderkirk, Jane ix
outreach 111–112
outsourcing 77–78
Oxford Text Archive 193–194

Paietta, Ann 467
Palmer, Carole 253
Parmer, Colleen 291
partnerships 311, 437
Paul, Richard 426
pay-per-use electronic files 204
Pelster, Natalie 99
Penniman, W. David 61
Perseus 46
personal computers 10
personal mastery 425
personal systems 11
perspective drawings 61
Peters, Tom 164, 448
Petrof, Barbara 104
Phipps, Shelley ix, 408
physical book 213
physical library 62, 211, 215
Pierian Press 169–172
Pintozzi, Chestalene 309

Plain Vanilla ASCII 193
podular 87
Pollard, Russell Owen 381
polyspeciality 263
Postman, Neil 99, 104, 107
Powell, David 291
Powell, Margaret 275
PowerPages 301–304
Prahalad, C. K. 161
preservation 9, 14
primary sources 212
print 212
problem-solving skills 80
Project Access 27, 29, 32, 33
Project Bartleby 194
Project Gutenberg 193–194
Prophet, Mary Webb 275
providing the answer 101
psychological transition 78
public domain 13
public policy 14
public service librarians 127–129
publishing industry 19
Purdue University, Indianapolis 467

quality control 14
quality dialogues 414

Radcliffe College 37
Ragains, Patrick 467
Ranganathan 104, 232
rare book cataloging 384
Reddick, Mary 262
reengineering 163, 434
reference 99, 121, 116, 124, 213–214, 298, 300–301, 304
reference books 322, 376
reference librarians 100, 213
reference mission 99
Reis, Tovah 47
relocating reference service 214
remote access 182–183, 185, 215
remote sensing data 12
remote services 111
remote users 115
Rensselaer Polytechnic Institute 111
reorganization 75
research agendas 201
research experience 197
research instruction 252

research libraries 2, 116, 118, 121, 122
Research Libraries Group, Inc. (RLG) 16
research strategies 140, 196, 211, 252–253,
research workers 117
resource services librarian(s) 155, 159
restructuring 408, 463
retention 376
Rettig, James 81–82, 100, 104, 145, 149, 168, 375
Richard Stockton College of New Jersey 140
Rielly, Loretta 80
Rockman, Ilene ix
Roecker, Fred 68, 70–72
Rosenberg, Jane 200
Rosenblum, Joseph 100
Rothstein, Samuel 100–116
Rubens, Donna 81
Rudnicki, Laurie 466
Runciman, Lex 84

Saarinen, Eliel 63
San Diego State University 466
Sarkodie-Mensah, Kwasi ix
Saunders, Virginia 291
Sayers, W.C. Berwirk 106
Schankman, Larry 284
Schenck, William 269
scholar's workstation 20
scholarly access, usage 196, 394
scholarly communication 201–204, 210
scholarly literature 199, 202
scholars 200, 219, 269, 320
Schreibstein, Florence 306
Schuman, Patricia Glass ix
Schwartz, Charles 463
Schwartz, Roberta ix
Science, Technology, Mathematics (STM) journals 22
Sears, Mary ix
Second Self: Computers and the Human Spirit 81
self-publishing 22
sensing types 78
serial costs 309–310
serials cancellation project 310
serials crisis 201
service excellence 461
Seymour, Daniel 175
SGML (standard generalized markup language) 38, 39, 41, 43, 44, 169
Shedlock, James 467
Shieber, Stuart ix

Shieh, Jackie 388
Shores, Louis 106
Short Course Series in Electronic Information 217
Silicon Snake Oil xi
Silipigni Connaway, Lynn 392, 466
SilverPlatter Information, Inc. 337
Simon, Heidi ix
Sittig, William 269
smart machine 359
Smith, Adam 448
Smith, Barbara 29
Smith, Mackenzie 37
Smithsonian Institution 27
Smithsonian Institution Libraries (SIL) 30, 32
Smithsonian Institution Research Information Service (SIRIS) 29, 32
Snow Crash 12, 136
social science data 211
social science research 262, 265
sociology of innovation 203
Solomon, Alan 127
spatial orientation 58
specialist librarian 120
Sreebny, Oren 86
St. John's University 229
staff development programs 424
staff training 459
Stam, Julian ix
Stamps, Hazel ix
Stanford University 353
Stephenson, Neal 12
Stewart, Tom 164
Stocker, Randi 467
Stoll, Cliff 20
strategic planning 465
strategic value streams 162–163
Straw, Joseph 298
Strohm, Kyle 291
Structure of Scientific Revolution 207
subscription maintenance 364
Sullivan, Maureen ix, 410
Summerfield, Mary 242, 313
Superintendent of Documents (SOD) 280–281
Svenningsen, Karen 229

Tallent, Ed ix
team leader training 411
teambuilding 76, 408, 417, 434, 440, 461
Tebbetts, Diane 236
technical services 357–358, 369–370

technological change 463
technological determinism 203
technological discontinuities 162
Technopoly 107
technostress 58, 425
telemetry 12, 13
telephone reference 156, 215
Tenopir, Carol 236
thinking types 77
Tiefel, Virginia 68, 71, 72
Tillett, Barbara 400
time management 461
TQM (total quality management) 163
traditional libraries 62, 74, 76–77, 211, 334
Trail, Mary Ann 140
training programs 424
training the trainers 416, 461
trans-disciplinarity 263
trans-specialty 263
transition 75, 77, 144
transitional library model (TLM) 231
Treadwell, Jane 74
Tufts University 375
Turkle, Sherry 81
Turrock, Betty 232
Tyckoson, David 182

U.S. government information 275
UnCover (CARL UnCover) 30
Uniform Resource Names (URNs) 353–355
unique permanent identifiers 353
universal service 13
University at Albany, State University of New York 182, 369
University of Arizona 309, 408
University of California at Los Angeles (UCLA) 136
University of California at San Diego 467
University of California at Santa Barbara 294
University of Cincinnati 467
University of Denver 392, 466–467
University of Houston 144
University of Illinois at Urbana-Champaign 253, 467
University of Massachusetts Amherst 131
University of Massachusetts Boston 463
University of Memphis 447
University of Michigan 131, 333
University of Missouri-Columbia 466
University of Pennsylvania 124

University of Rhode Island 466
University of Tennessee at Knoxville 466
University of Texas at Austin 59, 194
University of Utah 262
University of Virginia 211, 388
University of Virginia 42
University of Washington 86
University of Washington Bothell 467
unpublished materials 5
user behavior 168, 182, 185
user education 216
user interfaces 42
user study 131
UWired 86, 87, 89, 92, 93

value chain 430
value-added education 15
Van der Rohe, Mies 64
van Herwijnen, Eric 38
Vasi, John ix
Vavrek, Bernard 106
Victorian Women Writers Project 194
VIRGO 217
virtual building 59, 63
virtual desktop 59, 127
virtual library xi, 60–64, 157, 211, 215–216, 358
virtual office 63
virtual reality 59, 61
virtual services 124
virtual space 60
virtual stacks 61
virtual terminal 61
Von Salis, Susan 37

Wagers, Robert 100
Waite, Ellen 171, 373
Wallace, Danny 392
Wallace, Julia 291
Wallace, Patricia 81
Washoe County (Nevada) Library 58, 60
Watson-Boone, Rebecca 317
Watterson, Bill 78
way-finding 58
Webb, Kerry 326
Weber, Max 448
Weibel, Stuart 12
Weick, Carl 58
Weiner, Jan ix, 1
Welch, Patricia 134
Westbrook, Lynn 131, 134

Whyte, Susan Barnes 80
Williams, Helene 467
Wolff, Ralph 233
Woodruff, Eleanor 105
Wool, Gregory James 398
worldwide library 339
Wunderlich, Cliff ix
Wurman, Richard Saul 64
WWW Freshman Survival Guide 89
WWW Gateway to Information 68

Wyer, James 100

Yale University 127, 359
Young, Peter 229

Z39.50 43, 58, 342, 401
Zald, Anne 86
Ziff, Larzer 247
Zuboff, Soshana 164

DATE DUE

MAY 27 2000			
JAN 04 2001			
FEB 0 2 2003			
APR 2 8 2003			

Demco, Inc. 38-293